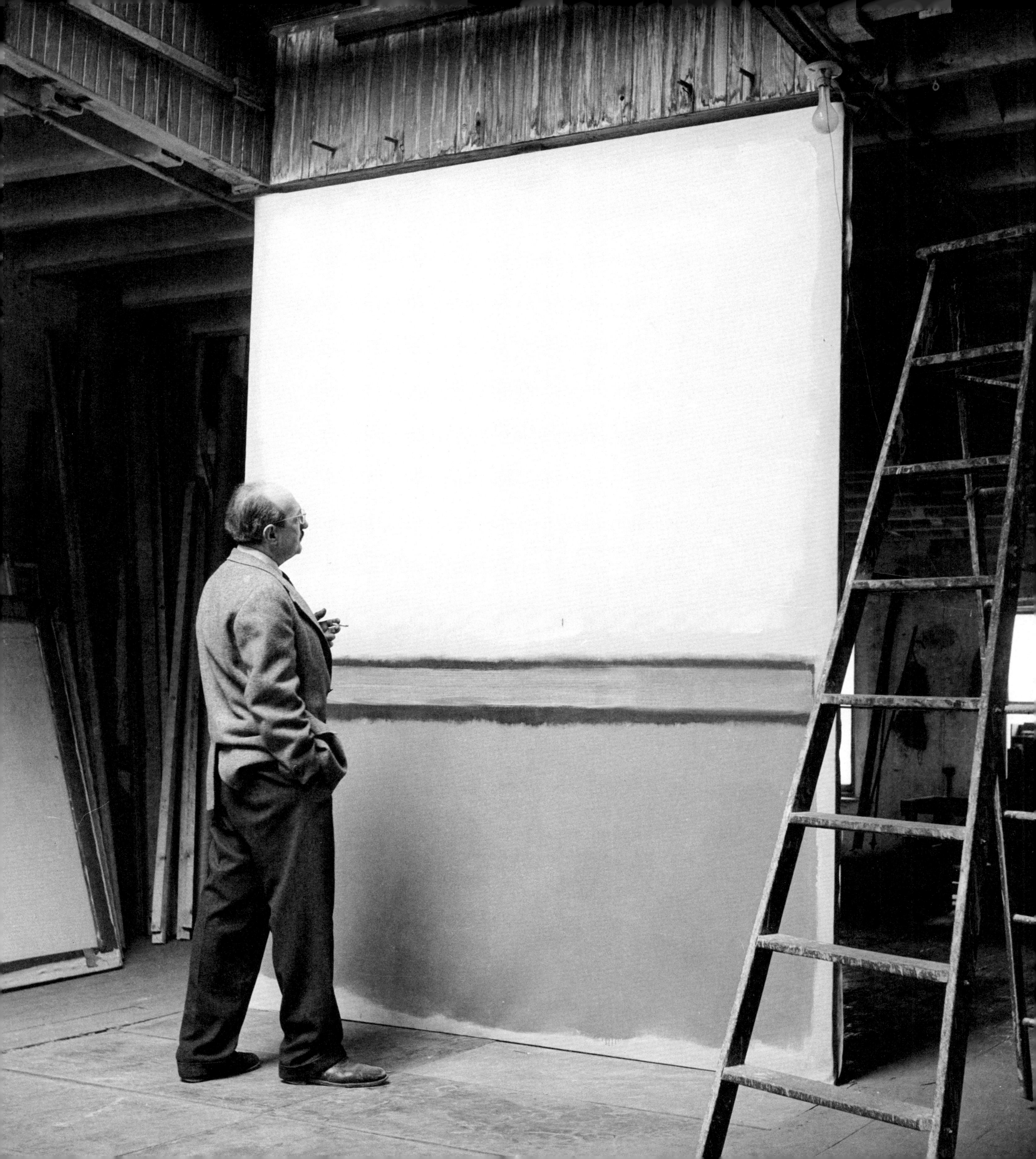

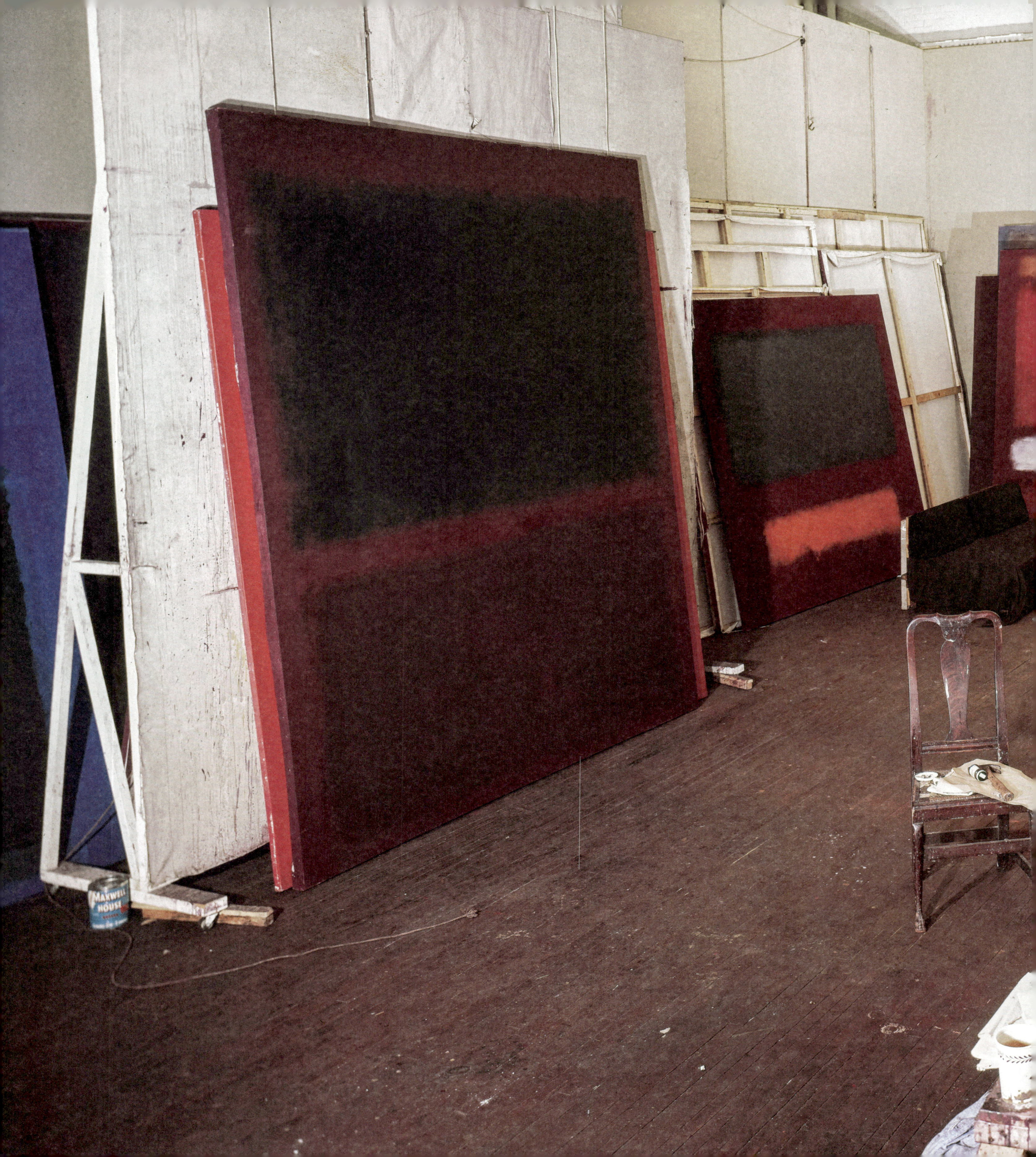
MAXWELL
HOUSE

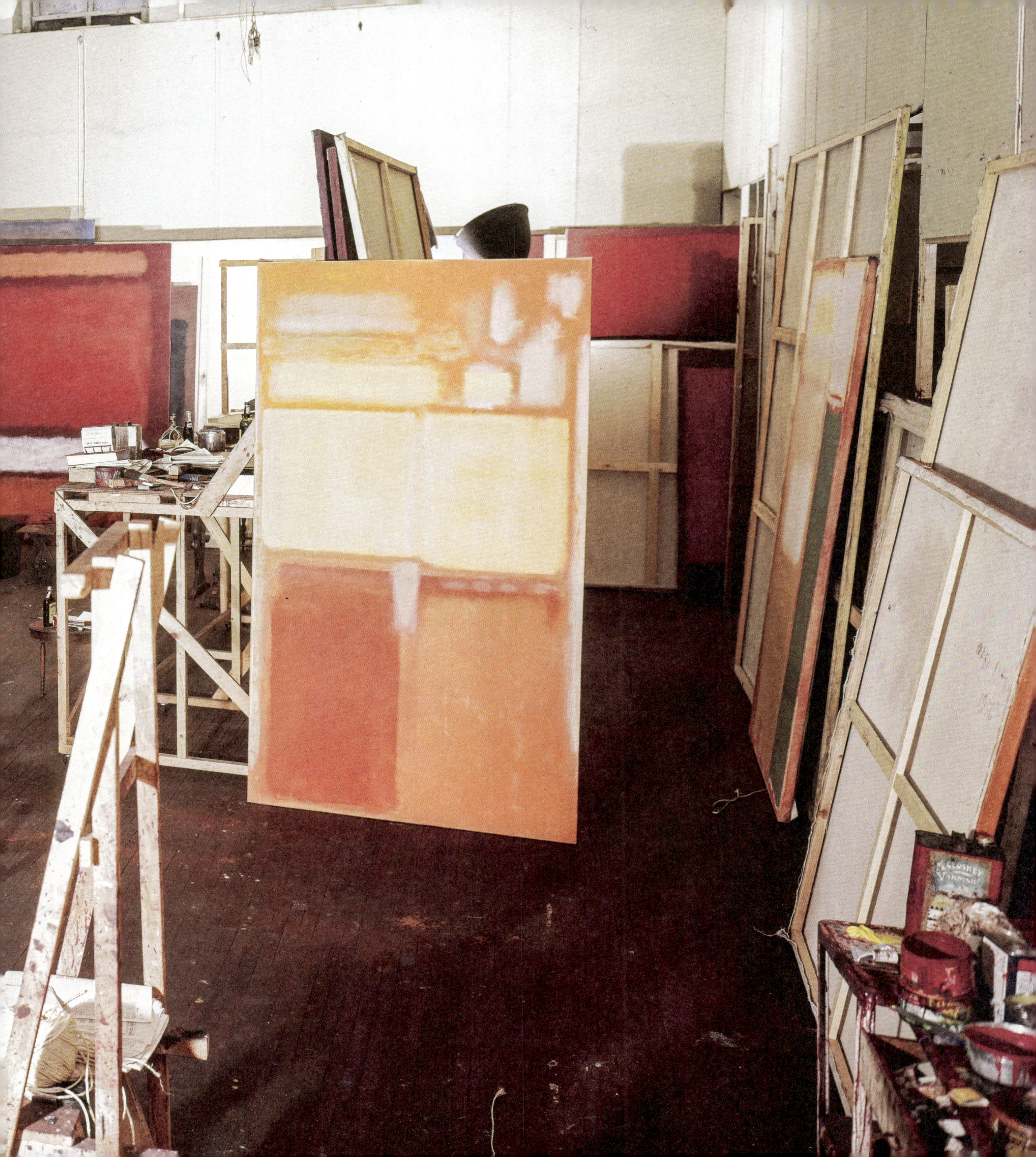

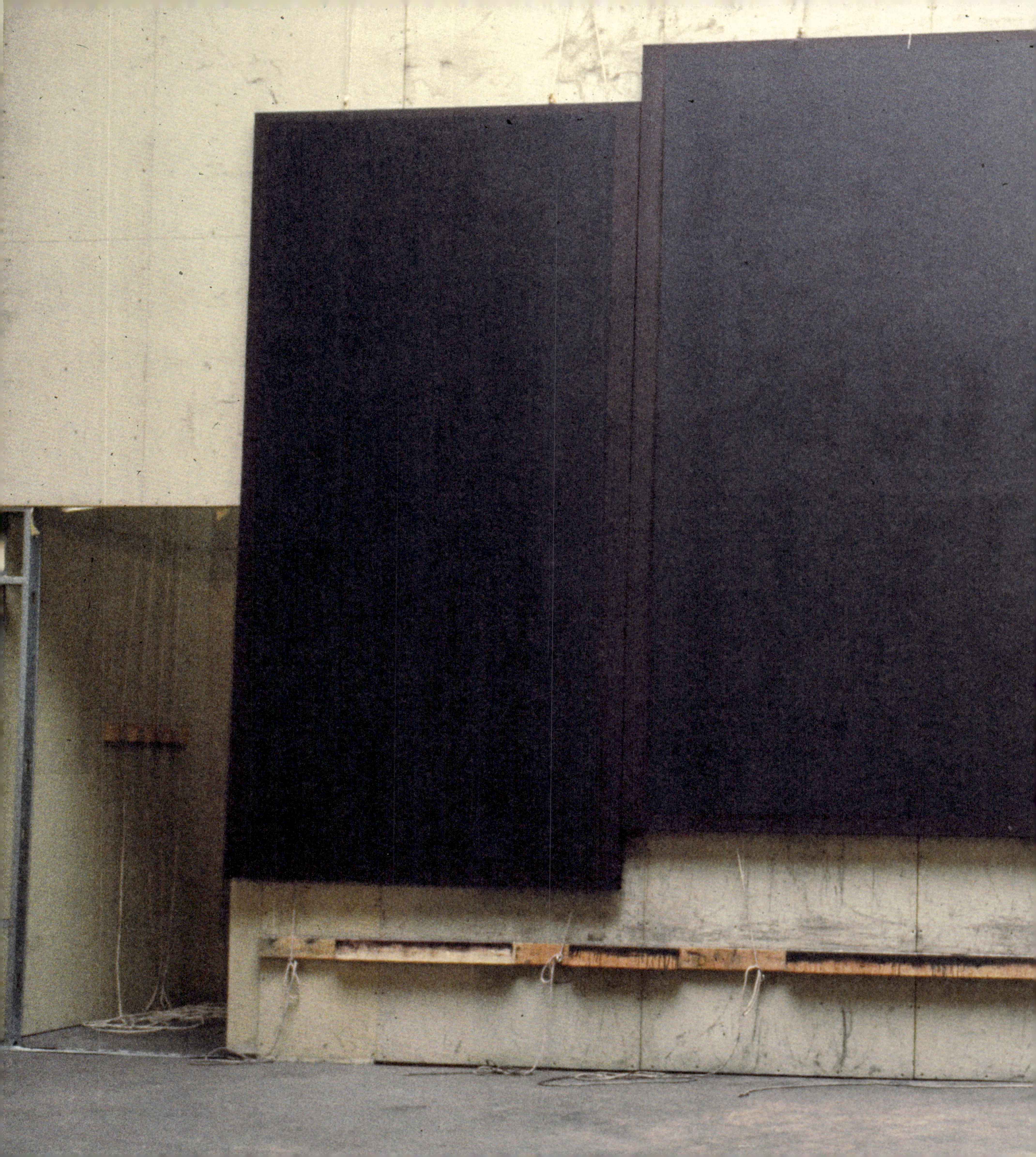

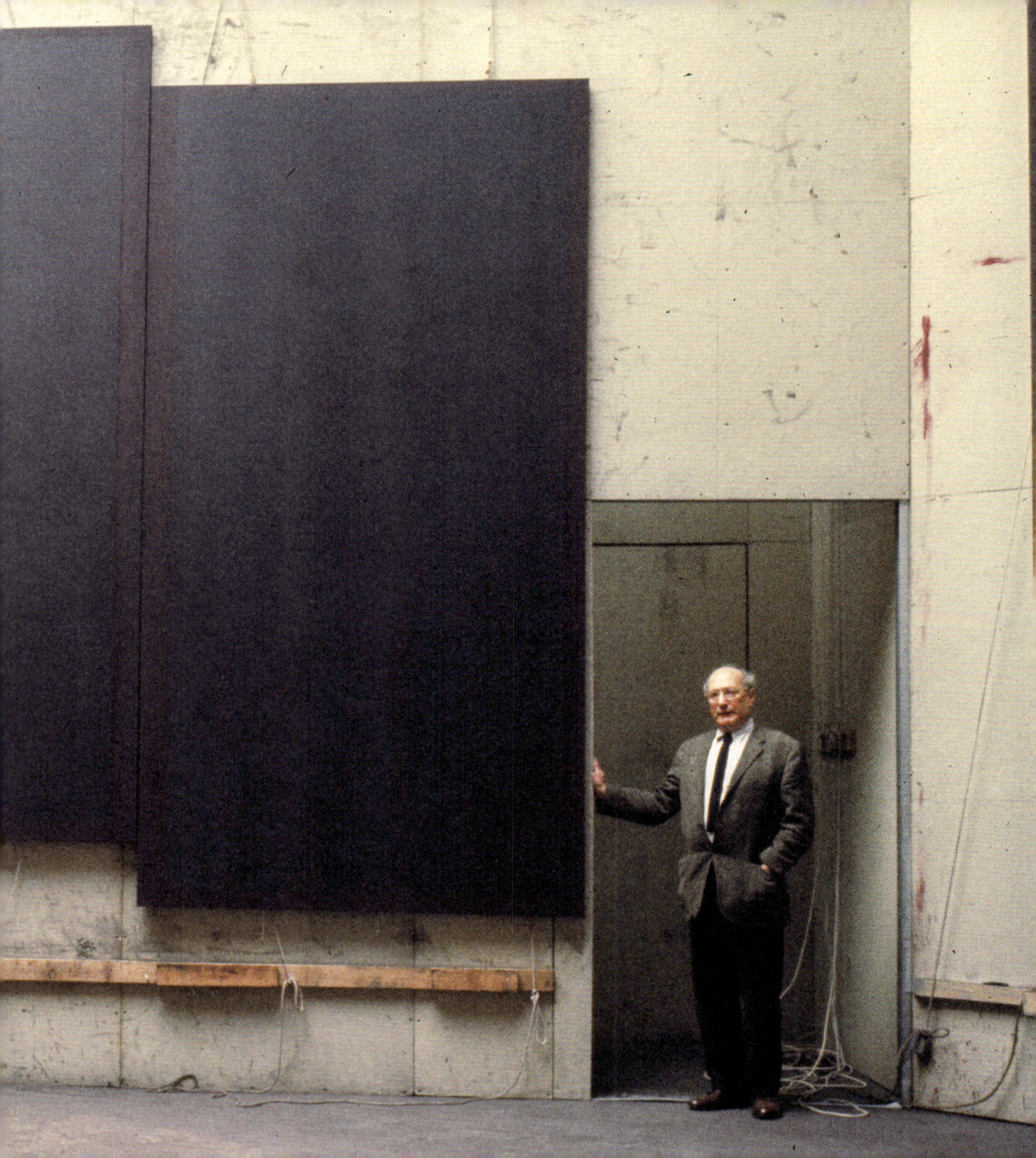

Front cover
No. 14, 1960, oil on canvas, 114 ½ × 105 ⅝ in., San Francisco Museum of Modern Art (CR 679)

Back cover
Hans Namuth, Mark Rothko, 1964, National Portrait Gallery, Smithsonian Institution, Washington, D.C.

Previous pages
Kay Bell Reynal, Rothko gazing at *No. 25,* 1951
Herbert Matter, Rothko's studio, 222 Bowery, New York, 1960, The Rothko Family Archive
Alexander Liberman, Rothko in his New York studio with the completed triptych for one of the side walls of the chapel in Houston, May 1967, Getty Research Institute, Los Angeles

Facing and following page
Hans Namuth, Mark Rothko, 1964, National Portrait Gallery, Smithsonian Institution, Washington, D.C.
Hans Namuth, Rothko in his studio, New York, 69th Street in with the unfinished painting for the entrance wall of the chapel in Houston, 1964, Collection Center for Creative Photography, The University of Arizona, Tucson

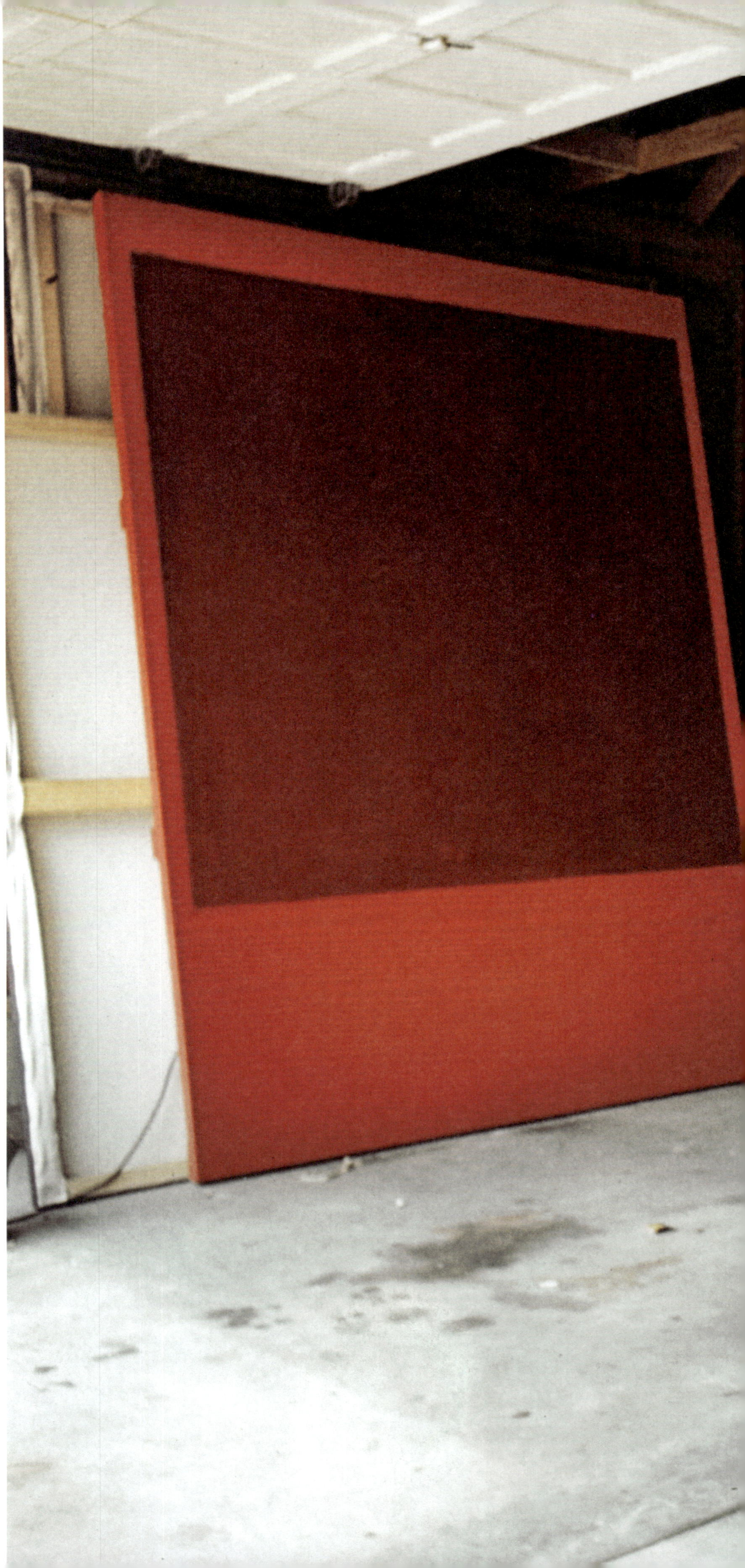

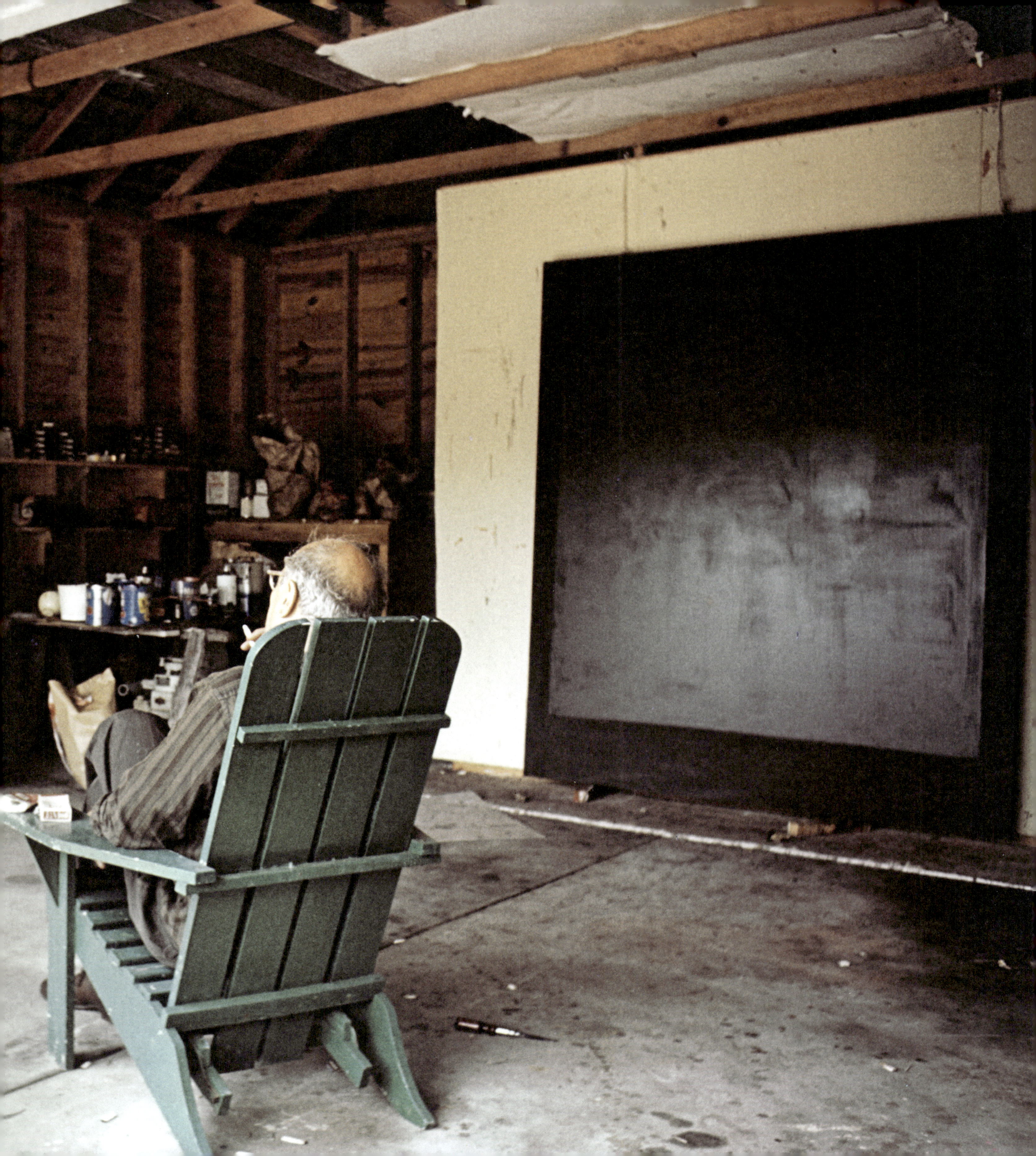

Mark Rothko

CITADELLES
& MAZENOD

FONDATION LOUIS VUITTON

Acknowledgements

Our heartfelt thanks go first of all to Christopher Rothko and Kate Rothko Prizel for their decisive support and loans.

Lenders

This event could not have happened without the generosity of the collectors, museums, and other institutions who agreed to lend us major works. We are extremely grateful to all of them.

Museums and institutions
We are notably indebted to: the National Gallery of Art, Washington, D.C., and its Director, Kaywin Feldman; Tate, London, and Maria Balshaw, its director, as well as Frances Morris, then Director of Tate Modern and Karin Hindsbo; the Phillips Collection, Washington, D.C., in particular Dorothy Kosinsky its former Director and Dr. Jonathan P. Binstock, Mary W. and Donald R. Clark Director.

In the United States and Canada provided key loans: The Art Gallery of Ontario, Toronto (Stephan Jost, Michael and Sonja Koerner, Director and CEO); the Berkeley Art Museum & Pacific Film Archive (Julie Rodrigues Widholm, Executive Director); the Chrysler Museum of Art, Norfolk (Erik Neil, the Macon and Joan Brock Director); Governor Nelson A. Rockefeller Empire State Plaza Collection, New York (Joseph Madeira, Director); the Frederick R. Weisman Art Foundation, Los Angeles (Billie Milam Weisman, Director); Glenstone Museum, Potomac, Maryland (Emily and Mitchell Rales); the Hirshhorn Museum and Sculpture Garden, Smithsonian Institution, Washington, D.C. (Melissa Chiu, Director); The Houston Museum of Fine Arts (Gary Tinterow, Director and Margaret Alkek Williams Chair); the Menil Collection, Houston (Rebecca Rabinow, Director); MOCA, Los Angeles (Johanna Burton, The Maurice Marciano Director); the Modern Art Museum of Fort Worth (Dr. Marla Price, Director); MoMA, New York (Glenn D. Lowry, the David Rockefeller Director); the Munson Museum, Utica (Anna Tobin D'Ambrosio, President and CEO); SFMOMA (Christopher Bedford, Helen and Charles Schwab Director); the Sheldon Museum of Art, University of Nebraska–Lincoln (Wally Mason, Director and Chief Curator); the Harry W. and Mary Margaret Anderson Collection, Stanford University (Jason Linetzky, Director); the Art Institute of Chicago (James Rondeau, President and Eloise W. Martin Director); the Fogg Museum, Harvard University Art Museums, Cambridge, Massachusetts (Martha Tedeschi, Elizabeth and John Moors Cabot Director); the Metropolitan Museum of Art, New York (Max Hollein, Marina Kellen French Director); the Toledo Art Museum (Adam M. Levine, Edward Drummond and Florence Scott Libbey Director); the University of Arizona Museum of Art, Tucson, Arizona (Jill McCleary, Deputy Director and Acting Head); the Walker Art Center, Minneapolis (Mary Ceruti, Executive Director); the Whitney Museum of American Art (Adam D. Weinberg, Alice Pratt Brown Director); and The Katharine Ordway Collection, Yale University Art Gallery (Stephanie Wiles, Henry J. Heinz II Director).

In Europe and Asia
Our thanks also go to the Fondation Beyeler, Basel (Sam Keller, Director); the Louisiana Museum of Modern Art, Humlebæk (Kirsten Degel, Curator and Head of Collections); the Centre Pompidou, Paris (Laurent Le Bon, President, and Xavier Rey, Director of the Musée National d'Art Moderne); the Fondation Marguerite et Aimé Maeght (Adrien Maeght, President, and Isabelle Maeght), Staatsgalerie Stuttgart (Prof. Dr. Christiane Lange) and the Yageo Foundation, Taiwan (Pierre Chen and Jasmine Chen).

Private collections
We are particularly grateful to all the collectors who agreed to part temporarily with precious artworks: Nahmad Collection; Elie and Sarah Hirschfeld; and Adriana and Robert Mnuchin, not forgetting all those who wish to remain anonymous.

Fondation Louis Vuitton

The tireless efforts of the entire team at the Fondation Louis Vuitton were crucial. Warm thanks go in particular to: Sophie Durrleman (Executive Director), Vincent Villepelet (Administrative and Financial Director), Élodie Berthelot (Cultural Production Director), Raphaël Chamak (Publications Director), Pascale Hérivaux (Legal Director), Joachim Monégier du Sorbier (Public services and mediation Director), Sébastien Bizet (Director of Communication), and their teams.

We would also like to acknowledge the help provided by numerous professionals and persons, first of all to Catherine Grenier, as well as Lynne Addison, Noëlle Albert-Loisel, Putter Anderson Pence, David Anfam, Audrey Antoni, Donna Austria, Rebecca Barresse, Barbara A. Bertucio, Raphaëlle Bianchi, Amy Black, Annette Blattmacher, David Breslin, Jeffrey N. Brown, Patricia Brunerie, Tom Callas, Ariel Carusso, Alban Chain, Françoise Cohen, Patrice Contensin, Cathy Cordova, Claudia Corrales, Marie-Monique Couvergnes, Michele De Shazo, Sophie Eloy, Elizabeth Estabrook, Annie Farrar, Emily Foss, Eliza Frecon, Chloé Geary, Arne and Marc Glimcher, Lily Goldberg, Meredith Gray, Laura Graziano, Marine Guyé, Stephanie Harris Akin, Sandy Heller, Margaret K. Hofer, Jessica Hong, Shaz Hussain, Olivia Jacquinot, Andrea Jain, Marion Kahan, Ashley Kane, Nicole Linderman, Di Luo, Jean MacDougall, Lisa MacDougall, Henry Mandell, Noemie Monetti, Rania Moussa-Morin, Melanie Neil, Eyal and Marilyn Ofer, Kelly Parady, Romy Peires, Mark Ramirez, Marta Ramirez, Kacie Rice, Alyson Rolington, Almudena Ros, Mark Schlemmer, Shannon N. Schuler, Kirsten Schmidt, Nina Schmitz, Sabina Schumpf, Jenna Shaw, Susan Slepka Anderson, Michael Somple, Barbi Spieler, Jacqueline Stevens, Ann Temkin, Martina Vacziova, Inés Vallejo, Kova Walker-Lečić, Stacey Walsh, Katy Wan, Jeannine Zimmer, and Annie Pérez for her contribution to the catalogue.

Finally, we must pay tribute to our late colleague, Achim Borchardt-Hume, who was present at the very start of this adventure.

S. P.

Exhibition organized by the Fondation Louis Vuitton, Paris
from October 18, 2023 to April 2, 2024

Exhibition

Chief curators
Suzanne Pagé and Christopher Rothko
with
François Michaud
and
Ludovic Delalande, Claudia Buizza,
Magdalena Gemra, Cordélia de Brosses

Production
Élodie Berthelot
Cultural production director
Matthieu Blanchard
Head of museographic management
Marie Grenier
Production and coordination assistant
Marine Martineau
Head of artworks and exhibition management

Restoration and conservation of works
Benoît Dagron, conservation register,
Fondation Louis Vuitton
Émilie Lormée, restorer

Administration and finance
Vincent Villepelet
Administrative and financial director

Legal
Pascale Hérivaux
Legal director
assisted by Yuliya Garreau,
Assistant to the executive director

Exhibition design
Agence Bodin & Associés
Jean-François Bodin, Head architect
Assited by Hélène Roncerel, Architect

Agence Arter
Renaud Sabari
Director
with Coralie Goyard, Manon Darphin

Signage
Yan Stive

Lighting
Laurent Escaffre, Ingélux

Transportation
Lp ART Transport d'œuvres d'art
Jean-Michel Floret, President
Marie-Cécile Roques, Manager
Mathilde Simmonot, Sales manager

Installation
Cadre en Seine

Press and communication
Sébastien Bizet, Director of communication
Nicolas Alpach, Head of digital communication
Caroline Cadinot
Head of press and public relations
Elodie Leroux, Head of on-line project

Capece Consulting:
Isabella Capece Galeota,
Adviser for communication

Joonam Partners:
Roya Nasser, Director,
with Alix Roché

Catalogue

Chief editors
Suzanne Pagé and Christopher Rothko

Coordination
Ludovic Delalande

Éditions de la Fondation Louis Vuitton
Raphaël Chamak
Publications director
Gaëlle Perroteau
Media manager and picture researcher
Olivia Jacquinot
Documentation

Graphic design
Studio Marie Lusa

Translation from the French
Deke Dusinberre for the texts of
Bernard Arnault, François Michaud,
Cordélia de Brosses, Claudia Buizza
and Magdalena Gemra
Charles Penwarden for the texts of
Suzanne Pagé, Ludovic Delalande
and Annie Cohen-Solal
Annie Perez for the artists' comments

Éditions Citadelles & Mazenod
Geneviève Rudolf
Chief editor
Ingrid Bœringer
Production
Bernard Wooding
Copy-editing
Salomé Perrineau
Picture researcher

Legal deposit: December 2023
ISBN: 978 2 85088 950 9

Lithography
Les Artisans du Regard, Paris
Printed in Italy
by EBS, San Giovanni Lupatoto

The Black and The White, 1956, oil on canvas, 94 × 53 ¾ in., Harvard Art Museum, Fogg Museum, Cambridge (CR 572; pl. 73)

Foreword
Bernard Arnault
President of the Fondation Louis Vuitton

Exhibiting such a broad, thorough, and representative set of works by Mark Rothko at the Fondation Louis Vuitton in the autumn of 2023 is the fulfillment of a long-standing personal wish. Rothko is one of my favorite artists. Yet he is still too poorly known and acknowledged in France and Europe. I therefore wanted the Fondation to redress this injustice, to fill an unfortunate gap largely explained by his under-representation in museums and collections here.

I would like to express my gratitude to all those who helped to bring this complex and ambitious show to fruition. The spectacular results—now before your eyes—contribute to our knowledge as well as our acknowledgment of an intensely rich oeuvre in which artistic and existential issues confront mystical ones.

I know that Rothko, despite the apparent simplicity of the shapes he arranged on canvas, was extremely exacting and precise in conception and invention. Although the shapes themselves may seem straightforward—to the point where we see only rectangles or stripes—the colors are elaborated with extraordinary skill. And yet color seems to have been less important to Rothko than the harmonies generated by the chosen hues: he had a true sense of music.

Whenever a given color in one of Rothko's abstract paintings, lacking any figurative allusion, reminds us of some other work by him, I've noticed that merely bringing them together in the same room shows us how different they actually are. Each work is absolutely unique. For Rothko, each one represented an entirely new experience, every time. They all follow and interact with one another in a constant drive for creativity, in the urgency and intensity of a moment, one matched only by the experience familiar to great composers and performers (to return to the sphere of music).

Going to museums in the United States and, less commonly, in Europe, will give an idea of Rothko's painting, but rarely will it reveal the oeuvre as a whole. Whether in New York, Washington, D.C., or many other cities in North America, or in London or Basel, people who have seen Rothko's works where they now hang have been able to experience impressions and feelings that long remain in the memory. But only a retrospective makes it possible to follow the artist step by step, to see how his works interact, how they come together and sing in chorus as Rothko's unique music resounds.

Rothko realized that his paintings would create their own space. He needed an architecture that suited him. So shouldn't a building conceived by Frank Gehry for the Fondation Louis Vuitton have to face up, sooner or later, to Rothko's oeuvre in its entirety? On several occasions during his lifetime, Rothko had to imagine the future of his paintings in buildings designed by the greatest twentieth-century architects: Ludwig Mies van der Rohe and Philip Johnson for the Seagram building, and Johnson again for the chapel in Houston devised by John and Dominique de Menil.

The recently restored Rothko Chapel now enjoys the patronage and commitment of LVMH—to our great pride. Beyond this show at the Fondation Louis Vuitton, we intend to prove our deep and lasting attachment to Rothko's oeuvre as well as to the mission being carried out by his son Christopher Rothko, and by all those people working to preserve the Rothko Chapel and to develop the artistic and scholarly activities associated with it.

The Fondation Louis Vuitton had to call on the skills and energy of everyone on its team in order to pull off a public retrospective of this sort. The exhibition required a personal experience of Rothko's work and the way it should be displayed. The Fondation's artistic director, Suzanne Pagé, brought Rothko's paintings to the Musée d'Art Moderne de la Ville de Paris back in 1999 when she was director there—an exhibition that Christopher Rothko has openly acknowledged as a crucial experience for him. Furthermore, the plans for our retrospective would never have come to fruition without our good relations with the heads of major international museums. I would also like to thank Christopher Rothko for the intensity and enthusiasm of his commitment—so essential to the dazzling success of our show—and to the entire exhibition team, constituted over the four years of preparation, united by the same belief in an undertaking for which there are few precedents, bringing together all the paintings required to reveal to everyone the scope and diversity of a highly particular oeuvre. Today these paintings are being displayed thanks to the generosity of lenders who can never be adequately thanked. Several have now become the Fondation's regular partners, such as the Museum of Modern Art in New York and Tate Modern in London—who lent us the entire set of *Seagram Murals*—as well as the Philips Collection in Washington, D.C., which agreed to provide the Fondation with three works from the group that Duncan Philips originally assembled. Finally, we are proud to be able to present to the public the many paintings lent to us by the National Gallery of Art in Washington, D.C., and by Kate Rothko Prizel and Christopher Rothko.

Bernard Arnault

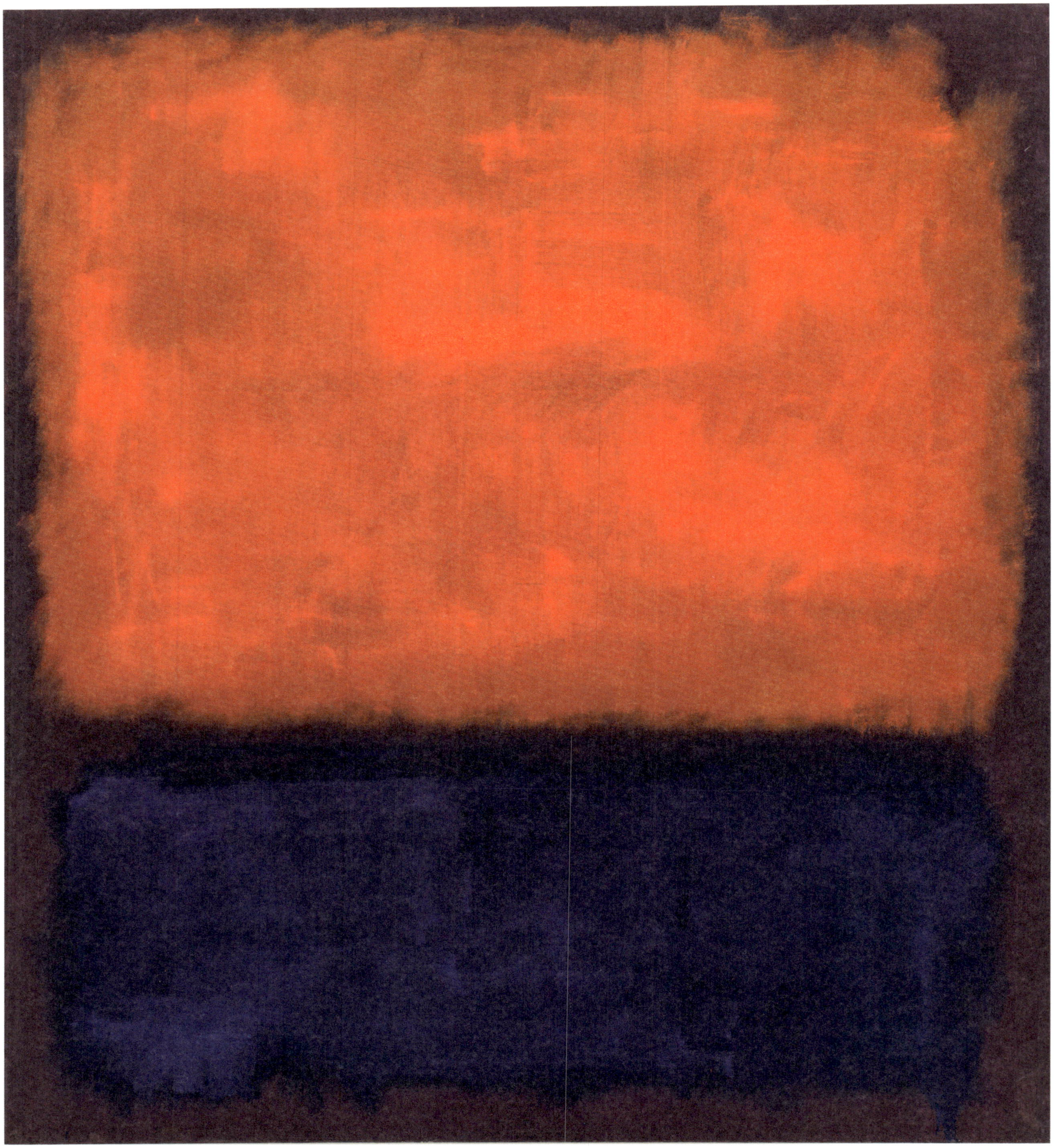

No. 14, 1960, oil on canvas, 114 ½ × 105 ⅝ in., San Francisco Museum of Modern Art (CR 679; pl. 88)

Preface
Suzanne Pagé

How to say what cannot be said and yet is felt so intensely?

How can words be used to introduce work that brought pictoriality, a language irreducible to any other, to its incandescence?

What are these viewers seeking, captivated by what speaks so powerfully to their eyes, to their heart, to their whole being?

What is the artist himself so relentlessly seeking? Rare photos show him in the studio, tirelessly scanning the color fields to which he has gradually reduced his canvases.

Why, even today, does this work seem so necessary in the timeless urgency with which it evokes the *human condition*, that *poignancy*[1] buried deep within each one of us, just as Rothko wanted it to be at the heart of his work, and as it figures constantly in his notebooks?

From the mid-1940s onwards, Robert Motherwell maintained an ongoing dialogue with the brooding, moody Rothko, based on a shared and *acute metaphysical angst*. After his friend's death, he said that "his real genius was that he had created a language of feeling", and he described his work as having "a luminescent glow from within, not the light of the world." Thus, abstract art was able to draw on an unsuspected dimension in order to express for Rothko *fundamental human emotions*.

This is the very reason why this exhibition is being held today.

The first presentation of Rothko's work in Paris in 1962, a travelling exhibition from MoMA shown in the basement of the MAM, was a disaster, and a painful experience for the artist. Dora Vallier bore witness to this, visiting the closed rooms alone, where the frost had taken its toll. In 1999, in the same museum, the work received a triumphant welcome and visitors seemed hypnotized, coming back time and time again to the paintings. What were they looking for? What did they find?

1 Words and sentences in italics are Rothko's own words.

Our exhibition opens in Gallery 1 with the artist's only self-portrait, dating from 1936. This dense, imposing figure exudes gravitas, his gaze hidden behind dark glasses. Impenetrable, he seems focused on an inner vision that reveals nothing of the man or the painter.

The sequence ends in Gallery 10 with a black and gray "Cathedral," marked out by sculptures by Giacometti, an artist with whom he shared, in a state of constant, nagging doubt, both humanism and a mastery of space.

At the heart of the exhibition are abstract works from the so-called "Classic" period—from the late 1940s onwards—in which a unique colorist asserts himself in the radiant, mysterious brilliance of color raised to incandescence. This, his best-known period, will be particularly well represented here—Galleries 4 to 11—by some seventy works, including two exceptional ensembles, one from the Phillips Collection in Washington, D.C., and the *Seagram Murals* from Tate.

More broadly, this retrospective aims to present the full extent of his work, from the initial figurative paintings onwards, and to reach beyond its formal ruptures to the permanence and depth of that same quest, that same questioning.

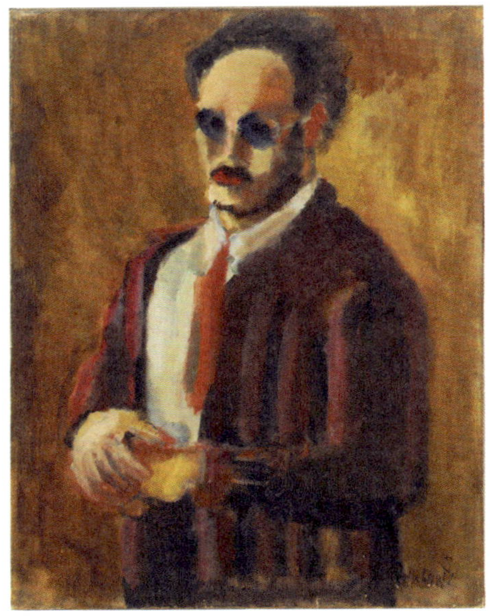

Self-Portrait, 1936, oil on canvas, 32 ¼ × 25 ¾ in., Collection of Christopher Rothko (CR 82; pl. 4)

Born Marcus Rotkovitch*, and having left his native Russia at the age of ten after a stint at Talmudic school, the artist was forever enriching his approach to painting with readings and reflections on art and philosophy. After leaving Yale, where he had studied a broad range of subjects—mathematics, economics, biology, physics, philosophy, psychology, languages—and driven by a permanent sense of social engagement linked to a constant desire to share his concerns, witness the newspaper he co-founded; it was in the school of life that he next tested himself. He was briefly tempted by the theater before the chance discovery of painting at the Art Students League in 1923 inspired him to study there, notably with Max Weber and become a member—he taught there, then left in 1930. He became a naturalized American citizen in 1938, and took the name Mark Rothko two years later.

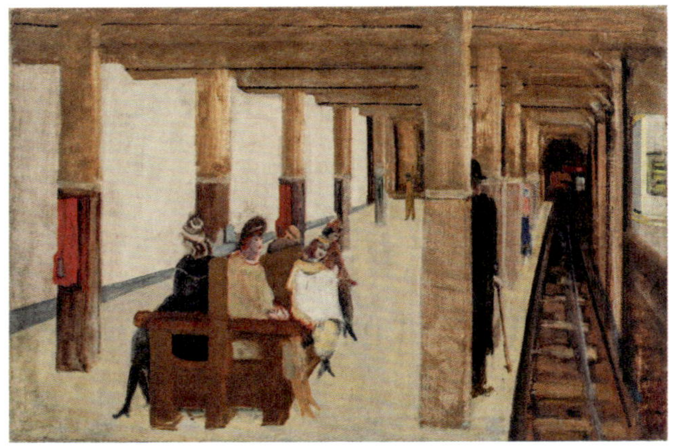

Untitled (The Subway), 1937, oil on canvas, 24 × 36 in., Collection of Elie and Sarah Hirschfeld (CR 104; pl. 5)

Our broadly chronological exhibition begins in these years, after a few attempts at landscape and the pivotal encounter with Milton Avery in 1928.

The crisis atmosphere prevailing in New York at the time is perceptible in a series of figurative canvases in muted colors, centered on a few nudes, interiors, and urban scenes, notably the subway, where enclosed, coercive spaces encircle anonymous, solitary figures, stretched and trapped in architectural space, as if held back. While he acknowledged the impossibility of expressing what he was trying to say through the human figure *without mutilating it*, Rothko's questing spirit drove him *to find another mode of expression*. He started to develop his ideas by writing a manuscript that he left unfinished and that remained unpublished during his lifetime, *The Artist's Reality*. This text attests to his constant concern to elucidate, for himself and others, the purpose of art as the language of the spirit.

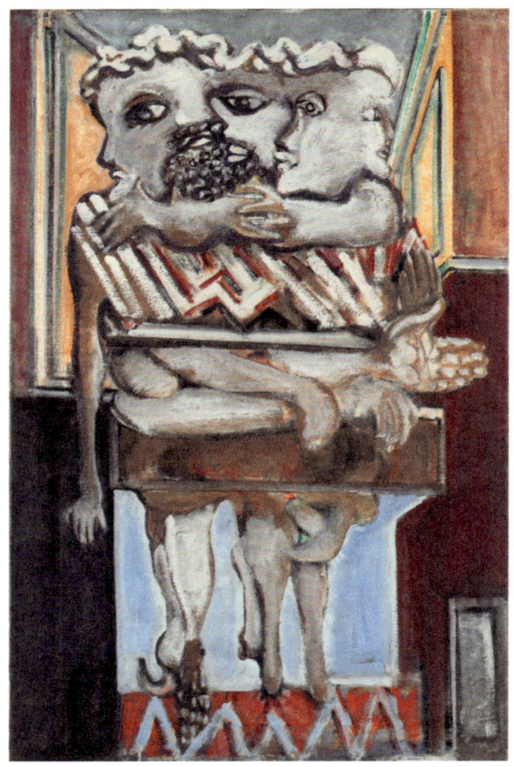

Untitled, 1941–42, oil on canvas, 35 13/16 × 23 7/8 in. (91 × 60.6 cm), National Gallery of Art, Washington, D.C. (CR 192; pl. 20)

In the 1940s, amidst dire international circumstances, his work evolved significantly. Along with others, the artist raised the crucial question of the "subject" of painting and of its *tragic and timeless* dimension, through unifying myths seen as universal. He was a great reader of Nietzsche—*The Birth*

* There are several possible transliterations of Rothko's Russian name; we have decided to mostly use the following one: Marcus Rotkovitch.

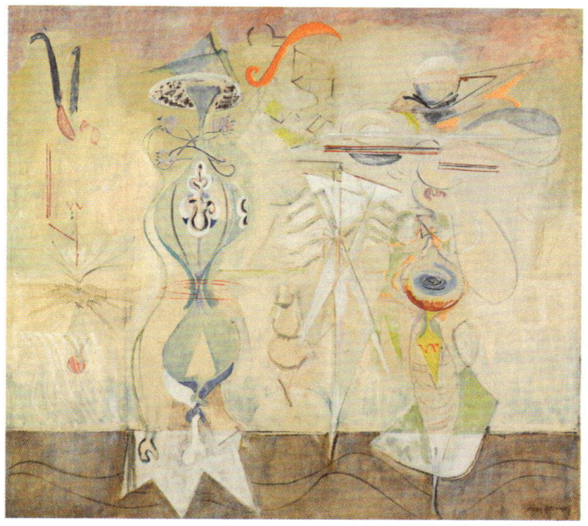

Slow Swirl at the Edge of the Sea, 1944, oil on canvas, 75 ¼ × 85 in., Museum of Modern Art, New York (CR 248; pl. 32)

of Tragedy—and of the theater of Aeschylus, which offered him a repertoire with mythological resonance. He reflected back the distorted image of archaic heroes as monsters with hybrid, split, dismembered, shredded bodies. For Rothko, this echoed intimately with unspoken memories of the pogroms of his childhood, and was soon intensified by spreading information about the Shoah. The animality in the human self and the element of fantasy expressed in these works also drew on Surrealist influences, perceived through the intellectuals and European artists who arrived in New York and the works presented at a landmark exhibition at MoMA in 1936—including Ernst, Chirico, and Miró, etc. Some of them also frequented Peggy Guggenheim. Rothko's paintings of this period were characterized by greater fluidity of space and vegetal and animal forms, in which plants and birds, totems and "organisms" drift through subaquatic spaces whose subdivision into differentiated zones would become a constant. The titles, which would later disappear, explained contents whose evolution was driven by the urge *toward clarity; toward the elimination of all obstacles between the painter and the idea, and between the idea and the observer.*

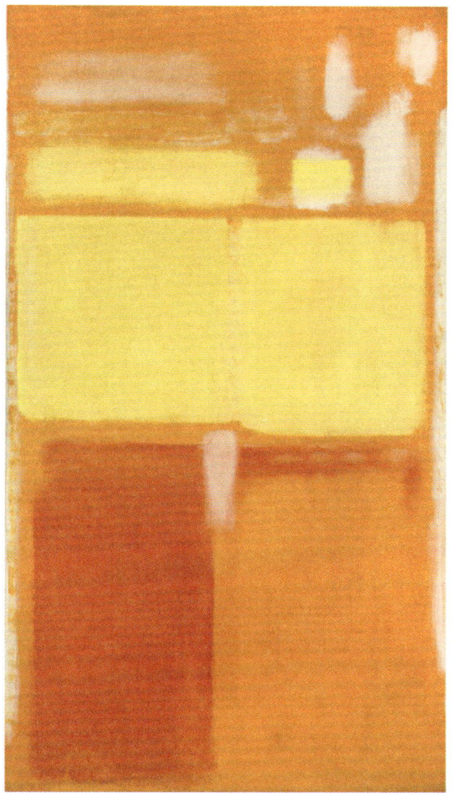

No. 21 (Untitled), 1949, oil and mixed media on canvas, 94 × 53 ⅜ in., The Menil Collection, Houston (CR 407; pl. 44)

The years 1945 to 1949 saw a decisive shift toward abstraction, with paintings freed from the easel and classified as "Multiforms." Undefined chromatic fields were invaded by biomorphic elements, with thin layers of color everywhere replacing drawing in floating, transparent spaces.

In the late 1940s and early 1950s came the so-called Classic works, icons that later became Rothko's signature works. In a falsely monochromatic or highly contrasted chromatic field, rectangular shapes of radiant color with undefined edges are arranged, usually vertically, in a binary or ternary rhythm. Here, through multiple translucent strata—between dilation and concentration, opacity and reflection, surface and depth—infinite variants of tones, values, chords, and dissonances are played out, constantly pulsating or skillfully resolved into a flamboyant, chromatic apogee.

Mysterious and magical, an atmospheric touch suffuses the entire space. And emotion happens. Beyond simply looking at it, the viewer sinks into the work all the more delightfully as the scale becomes more and more monumental and immersive. *I paint large pictures because I want to create a state of intimacy. A large picture is an immediate transaction; it takes you into it.* This was partly the result of the fascination he, like Avery, felt with Matisse's *The Red Studio,* recently acquired by MoMA, in which a space populated by objects is unified by monochrome color and flattened along the picture plane, to the point that *you became that color.*

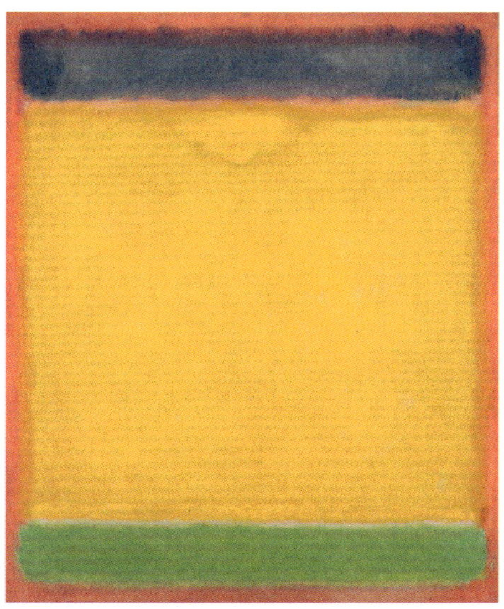

Untitled (Blue, Yellow, Green on Red), 1954, oil on canvas, 77 ¾ × 65 ½ in., Whitney Museum of American Art, New York (CR 514; pl. 60)

This is also what Rothko was looking for in the mid-1950s (1954–57), when he told Duncan Phillips of his wish to present his paintings as a separate ensemble in his museum, in a dedicated space saturated with the ochre and red mixed with gray of the paintings, giving his collector the sensation of being absorbed in a "contentment suddenly darkened by a cloud" (Gallery 7).

Fearing that his works would be perceived as decorative, Rothko even refused to be described as a "colorist" and insisted instead on the importance of light. Yet he knew that his art *lives and breathes*, and Rothko was aware of the sensual power of his works, which he accepted *as a relationship of pleasure with what exists*. Likewise, he acknowledged their emotional grip, but makes a point of clarifying its nature: *I would like to say to those who think of my pictures as serene, whether in friendship or mere observation, that I have imprisoned the most utter violence in every inch of their surface.*

So what is it that really compels the visitor, a captive of the irresistible aura of these works whose reflexive effects help to trap them, even as the artist speaks of *wrenching*, or even *cataclysm*?

For this indeed is the depth at which Rothko touches us. It can be seen at work in the *Seagram Murals* (1958–59), whose meditative interiority is served by a darker range of colors. A response to a commission, this ensemble was intended to satisfy Rothko's desire to create a *place* with his works alone, in a space and set-up of which he was in full control.

The set of nine works presented here—the entire "Rothko Room" at the Tate, and in the artist's intended configuration—was originally commissioned for a dining room designed by Philip Johnson in a building by Mies van der Rohe. Rothko eventually abandoned the commission, realizing that the context was decidedly at odds with his aim of recapturing the quality of the space/enclosure of the Laurentian Library in Florence, which he had once visited.

Punctuating the immersive field, the rectangle disappears in favor of a more or less open sign that some have read as a portal, others as a threshold or a ring. Color takes on a new gravity here. A range of reds and browns takes precedence, with a muted intensity, while the relationship with architecture is accentuated, creating a contemplative hold on the viewer.

These two parameters attain their transcendental finality in the Houston chapel. Those who commissioned his work there, John and Dominique de Menil, were initially attracted by the interiority evoked by the *Seagram Murals*. In the end, they agreed with Rothko's proposal to create a specific, global space that would engage the architecture itself, by creating an octagonal plan with filtered natural light. On completing this project, which occupied him fully for some three years, from 1964 to 1967, when he worked in a huge studio, the artist declared that *it is teaching me to extend myself beyond what I thought possible for me.* For anyone who has experienced it this is unforgettable. Breaking away from the secular space, they are initially gripped by darkness, the colors—plum, black, purples—gradually emerging without revealing anything other than what the visitor gradually discovers within themselves—as if in a rapture—in this encounter of great intensity.

In this same, decidedly much more austere order, the black and gray canvases of Gallery 10, punctuated by Giacometti sculptures, are shown as Rothko had thought of presenting them as part of a commission for the new UNESCO building in Paris, accompanied by Giacometti's *Walking Man.*

The overall scale is reduced, with the surfaces delimited by a white border establishing a certain distance that makes us feel less like immersing ourselves in them and more like looking at them. These paintings with their turbulent touches are clearly structured in two contrasting zones of black, brown, and blue-gray tones, separated by a continuous line.

Orange and Red on Red, 1957, oil on canvas, 68 7/8 × 66 3/8 in., The Phillips Collection, Washington, D.C. (CR 599; pl. 70)

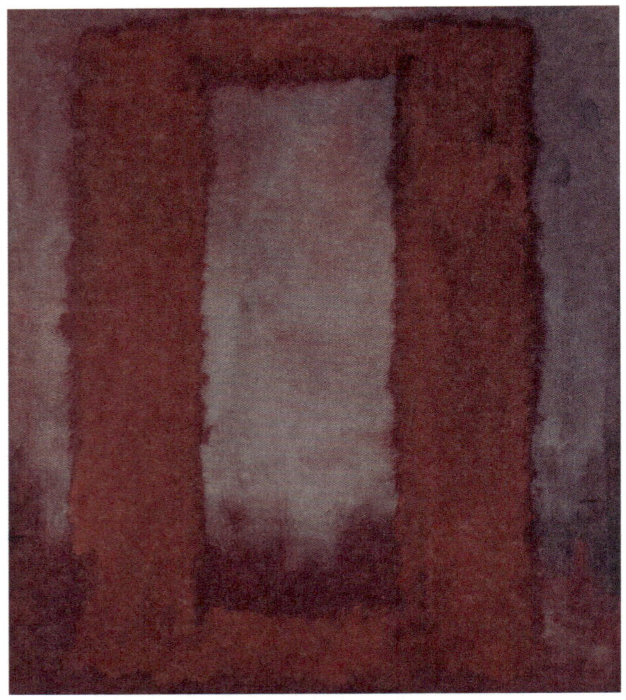

Red on Maroon, 1959, oil paint, acrylic paint, glue tempera and pigments on canvas, 105 × 94 in., Tate Modern, London (CR 660; pl. 82)

Blue and Gray, 1962, oil on canvas, 79 1/4 × 69 in., Beyeler Fondation, Riehen / Basel (CR 723; pl. 91)

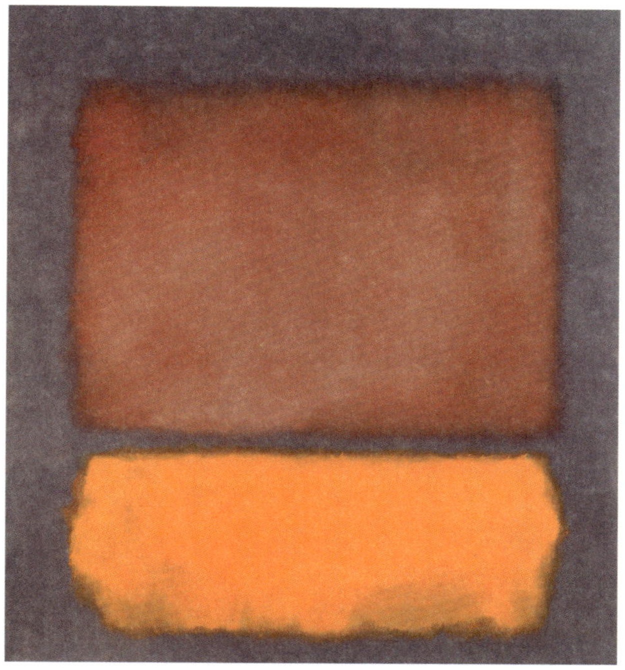

Untitled, 1962, oil on canvas, 85¼×76 in., Staatsgalerie Stuttgart (CR 720; pl. 92)

Untitled (Black and Gray), 1969/1970, acrylic on canvas, 68×60¼ in., The Museum of Contemporary Art, Los Angeles (CR 829; pl. 111)

No. 3 (Untitled/Orange), 1967, oil on canvas, 81×75 15/16 in., Yale University Art Gallery, New Haven (CR 810; pl. 115)

The restraint and apparent uniformity of these works, constituting a series, initially met with incomprehension. Reconsidering them again today, the somewhat sketchy biographical interpretations based on the painter's health and depressive state now seem outdated. Here, in resonance with Giacometti's sculptures, they bestow a taut density and solemnity in which the *poignancy* sought by Rothko recurs with a new kind of resonance.

A number of contemporary artists have expressed a preference for these late works, speaking of their esthetic advance, one that, for them, opened up the radical paths of a minimal art that broke with Abstract Expressionism.

In contrast, the works in Gallery 11, next door, retrieving the bright colors of his Classic paintings. Right up to the last unfinished work, a symphony in red and pink, these oil and acrylic canvases (1967–70) argue against any attempt to equate Rothko's colors with his psychological state.

Such contrasting and always intense interpretations are at the heart of the visitor's personal experience of this exhibition. What was he looking for? What has he found?

For the artist yesterday, as for today's visitor, what kind of exile does this art betoken? What kind of quest sealed deep within each one of us?

The state of hypersensitivity exuded on the surface of the paintings and developed through the works—as if by an excess of beauty—arouses and sharpens both plenitude and incompleteness. At the same time as sensory rapture blooms so a sense of expectation deepens, followed by questions about the kind of transcendence that these works seem to give access to. Everyone will find their own words, whether seraphic or tragic. Between bliss and the nothingness relating to *the obsession of being mortal* Rothko does not choose. *If people want sacred experiences they will find them here; if they want profane experiences, they'll find them too.*

* * *

Aware of the responsibility involved in staging a Rothko exhibition today, and of the difficulty of bringing together rare and extremely fragile works by such an essential artist, I was keen to involve Christopher Rothko, the artist's son and guardian of the Rothko legacy, who expressed particular satisfaction when he visited the MAM exhibition.[2] This collaboration has enabled us both to fulfil our respective missions.

A great deal of thought went into the hanging, taking into account the artist's repeatedly expressed wishes and interpreting them in the space, with the architects and collaborators striving to satisfy Rothko's desire to give space *the greatest possible eloquence and poignancy*.

This exhibition of an artist for whom music—Mozart, Schubert—was vital, and who wanted to raise painting to *the same pitch of intensity as music and poetry*, will be marked by an exceptional creation from composer Max Richter, inspired by Rothko's work.

2 Where I was director and curator at the time.

A retrospective of a major figure of the twentieth century, this exhibition will satisfy the expectations of a wide public that has not had the chance to see these works in Paris for some twenty-five years. Bernard Arnault, Chairman of the Fondation, personally wished to create this opportunity, as he has a particular feeling for this artist. His advisor Jean-Paul Claverie actively followed every stage of the project, and offered his unfailing support.

Essential and decisive, our close collaboration with Christopher Rothko was marked by constant exchanges—months of emails and texts crisscrossing the ether—constantly underpinned by rigor and mutual understanding. I would like to acknowledge the attentive presence at his side of his sister Kate Rothko Prizel. Both were also generous lenders.

At the Fondation, I would like to express my gratitude to all those who worked with me whose commitment and motivation made the exhibition possible, first and foremost François Michaud, curator at the Fondation Louis Vuitton, and Ludovic Delalande, who coordinated the catalogue. Claudia Buizza and Cordélia de Brosses assisted us closely and carried out remarkable research work, with Magdalena Gemra in charge of follow-up. Claire Staebler was especially involved in the project at the initial stage.

This exhibition has provided the opportunity for a fresh interpretation of Rothko's work thanks to contributions to the catalogue by various authors: Christopher Rothko and Riccardo Venturi wrote the introductory essays, while Harry Cooper, Ludovic Delalande, François Michaud, Nancy Spector and Jeffrey Weiss each analyze and explore in depth one of the periods in the artist's work. Annie Cohen-Solal has provided an essential insight into Rothko's life. Claudia Buizza, Cordélia de Brosses, and Magdalena Gemra have documented specific points relating to Rothko's biography and the commissions he received. I warmly thank them all.

The hanging of the works, particularly delicate in the case of Rothko, was devised with his usual talent by Jean-François Bodin, together with Hélène Roncerel, to whom we are most grateful.

The constant collaboration of the Fondation's teams was decisive. Special thanks are due to Sophie Durrleman, executive director, Vincent Villepelet, administrative and financial director, Élodie Berthelot, cultural production director, Raphaël Chamak, publications director, Pascale Hérivaux, legal director, Joachim Monégier du Sorbier, public services and mediation director, Sébastien Bizet, director of communication, and their teams.

Bringing together one hundred and seventeen works, the exhibition showcases exceptional ensembles from all periods. We are deeply indebted to the lenders without whose generosity this project would not have been possible, above all Christopher Rothko, Kate Rothko Prizel and Ilya Prizel. We are also grateful to the public and private museums and institutions, and to the individual collectors listed on page 11 above. Their indispensable contributions give this retrospective its full scope. In particular: the National Gallery of Art, Washington, D.C., and its director Kaywin Feldman; Tate Modern, London, and its then director Frances Morris; the Phillips Collection, Washington, D.C., and Dorothy Kosinsky, as well as Dr. Jonathan P. Binstock; SFMOMA and its director Christopher Bedford.

Suzanne Pagé

Following double-spread page
Aaron Siskind, Mark Rothko at the Betty Parsons Gallery, New York, 1949,
The Rothko Family Archive

As I discuss at length in my catalogue essay, if you see a void when you look at a Rothko painting, it is necessary to look again. In the case of the Rothkos in this exhibition, one of the things you will "see" are the many people responsible for getting these works on the wall of the Fondation Louis Vuitton and into the catalogue. I thank all of you, and if I do not call you out in print, please know that I will see you and thank you every time I look at this catalogue.

There are many works from private collections in the exhibition, and I want to give special thanks to those who loaned or helped secure loans of works I never thought I would see in Paris, or perhaps anywhere: Elie and Sarah Hirschfeld, Pierre Chen and Jasmine Chen, Manuel Fontán del Junco, Adriana and Robert Mnuchin, Nahmad Collection. North American museums have been extremely generous in loaning some of the finest (and largest) paintings my father ever painted. I deeply appreciate your trust and commitment to the arts, sending these works thousands of kilometers away (and patiently enduring our persistent requests): The Phillips Collection, The Los Angeles Museum of Contemporary Art, The Menil Collection, The Anderson Collection at Stanford University, The Munson Museum, MoMA, The Whitney Museum and The Metropolitan Museum of Art have all loaned at least two works. I would also like to thank our British neighbors at Tate for lending us the Seagram Murals.

I also wish to express special thanks to all lenders, public or private, listed on p. 11.

As has been true for nearly forty years, The National Gallery of Art in Washington has been an extraordinary partner. They have created a living legacy from the works given to them by the Mark Rothko Foundation, fostering research and supporting Rothko exhibitions around the globe, as well as creating their own. They, individually and corporally, are beyond category.

My sister Kate Rothko Prizel is my collaborator, my counsel and my corrector in all things Rothko. She has, as ever, been so in the case of this exhibition, and loaned extremely generously from her collection. Our long-time Collection Manager, Marion Kahan, and Project Manager, Henry Mandell, have done the work of twelve and ensured that exhibition and catalogue have miraculously come together.

Architects Jean-François Bodin and Hélène Roncerel have been fabulous design partners—they know the Fondation Louis Vuitton better than anyone save Frank Gehry himself. The team I have worked with at Fondation Louis Vuitton extends farther than I know, but I must particularly thank my curatorial colleagues, François Michaud, Ludovic Delalande, Claudia Buizza, the indefatigable researcher, Cordélia de Brosses, and Magdalena Gemra, who has somehow kept all the pieces together.

And it has been a renewed delight meeting up again with my co-curator, Suzanne Pagé. She is tireless in the pursuit of excellence and it shows in all her work.

To present a Rothko exhibition with this scale and impact approaches the impossible today, so my tremendous gratitude goes to Bernard Arnault. First because he had the vision to build this remarkable museum and second, for giving us carte blanche to pursue our most ambitious vision for Rothko in Paris.

My sincere thanks extend to Jean-Paul Claverie, advisor to the president, for his continuous support.

Christopher Rothko

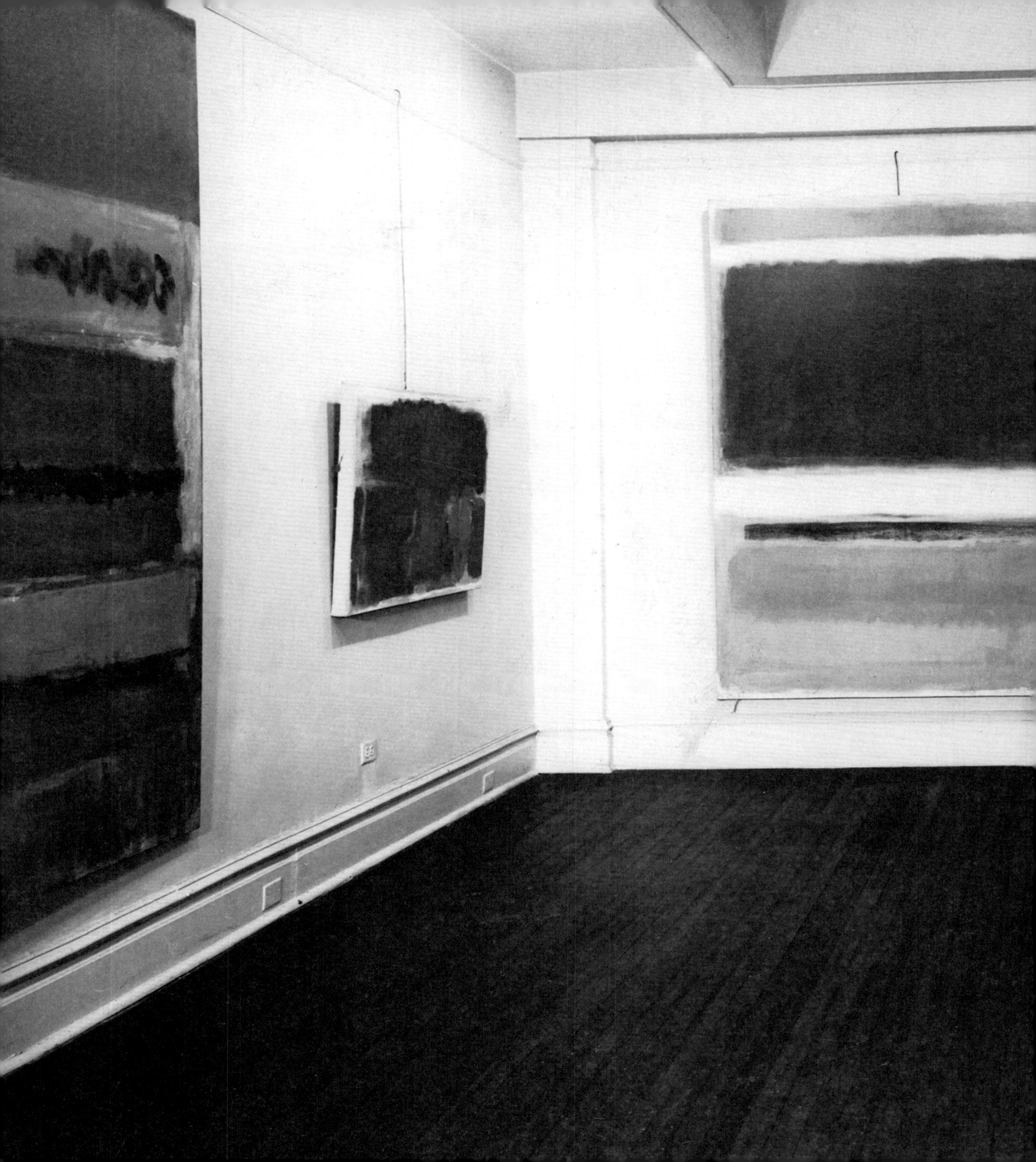

Prelude: Tabula Rasa

Tabula rasa. A clean slate, a fresh start, a new beginning. Slough off the old to better observe the new; unfettered, unencumbered, unbiased, unbeholden to what came before. We think of such an image when we think of Mark Rothko's classic, color-field abstractions of the 1950s and 1960s: broad, unblemished, undifferentiated expanses of near formless color, free of readily observable figures, distinct marks and distractions. And of content? But this is not necessarily what Rothko thought of.

Tabula rasa. This was certainly the effect when the New York school finally won notice with their striking new abstractions of 1947–50. These artists were a fresh wind that blew through the New York art world, and Mark Rothko was amongst those at the center of the turbulence. Paintbrushes in one hand and philosophical manifestos in the other, the color field painters—Gottlieb, Motherwell, Newman, Rothko, Still and many others—produced work that immediately challenged the relevance of figurative painting and anything that smacked of the academic or sentimental. Their large, often muscular, forms pushed away the cluttered pictorial space of the previous generations and boldly announced their arrival. There was no going back, only forward.

Tabula rasa. We think of such an image when we imagine the effect these painters had on the art scene around them, and more broadly on the history of art. Their bold (non-)gestures resounded through the art establishment, demanding attention and a defense of artwork that lacked their works' pioneering modernism. Their new aesthetic essentially deleted figuration from the discussion. Abstraction became not simply topical but de rigueur. In the 1930s, when his works still actively featured the figure, Rothko emphasized the abstraction in his paintings.[1] By the same token, when his paintings had become demonstrably abstract in the 1950s, he claimed that he was not an abstract painter.[2] The *tabula rasa* was not necessarily what Rothko thought of.

1 Mark Rothko, *The Artist's Reality*, ed. Christopher Rothko (New Haven: Yale University Press, 2004), p. 28.
2 Notes from a conversation with Selden Rodman in 1956, in Mark Rothko, *Writings on Art*, ed. Miguel López-Remiro (New Haven: Yale University Press, 2006), p. 119.

What, then, was on Rothko's slate? First, let us remember that we are not speaking of a blank slate. *Tabula rasa* means an *erased* slate. In a world where, as my father would be the first to remind his viewer, there is nothing new, the difference between these two understandings is enormous. History is on some level indelible, in art as much so, if not more, than in other fields. That history consists not only of marks, but also of the action of making those marks, as well as the memory of marking and of seeing those marks. No matter how vigorous the erasing, the remnants remain, both obscurely on the slate and with varying amounts of clarity in memory: personal memory and cultural memory. Whether the process involves the archeological, the anthropological, or the psychoanalytical, those previous actions and thoughts can always be retrieved—fragmentary, distorted, and transformed, no doubt, but with lingering resonance. Those archived and exhumed memories endure on the societal level but also within the individual. That chalky residue is at once the Jungian collective unconscious and the personal unconscious, both of which these artists mined in their work, and experienced as fully present That residue cannot be divorced from our understanding of the world. Ask the artist who has drawn the figure for twenty years to make an abstract drawing. Inevitably, her hand will be influenced—in some way—by what it has drawn before. It cannot be unlearned.

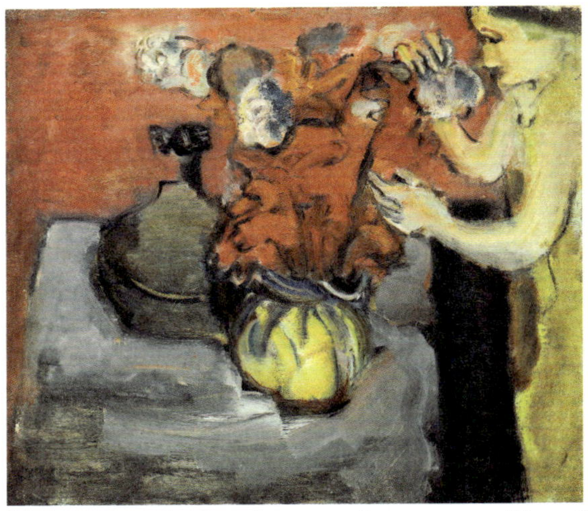

Untitled (Woman arranging flowers), c. 1935, oil on canvas, 22 13/16 × 26 11/16 in., National Gallery of Art, Washington, D.C. (CR 76)

Why have I persisted with *tabula rasa* and engaged in what is arguably no more than an exercise in semantics? Not least because Rothko's work is frequently misunderstood as empty, and his iconic image mistaken for a void.[3] I will spend many of the pages that follow helping the reader fill in that void, but as I have suggested above, that apparent emptiness is already filled with murmurs and shadows of what came before and what might be percolating just beneath the surface.

Similarly, that blank slate which that New York school apparently created with a single gesture at mid-century would have been unfamiliar to Rothko. My father saw no need to destroy, no need to erase art history (as the Pop generation was determined to do, but a decade later). He swept many superficial items away, but he certainly did not wipe his slate clean. His process was additive, involving an active conversation with the art of his predecessors. He consumed it whole and birthed something newly conceived but saturated with both the spirit and much of the substance of what came before.

Most importantly, I evoke the notion of the erased tablet because, with its lingering streaks and stains, echoes and suggestions, it is filled with the recombinant DNA of a Rothko painting. It is the material we must draw upon, from within ourselves and within the painting, to actively populate his work and make it personally present. Newly made and always was. Surprising, yet inevitable. Ultimately, to find the material in these "voids" involves a journey; a journey to the familiar by means of the strange and unfamiliar. By equal measure, ours is a journey to the unknown by means of what we know most intimately.

Untitled (Plum and Brown), 1964, oil on canvas, 81 × 69 1/8 in., private collection (CR 769; pl. 99)

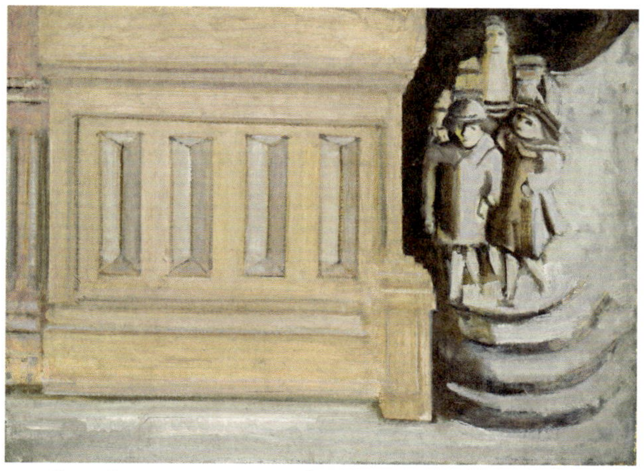

Street Scene, c. 1936 / 1937, oil on canvas, 28 15⁄16 × 39 15⁄16 in., National Gallery of Art, Washington, D.C. (CR 113; pl. 13)

Content and Form

Rothko spoke on more than one occasion of endeavoring to express the human condition—the human *drama*—in his work.[4] This focus on our common experience is a constant touchstone in his output, whether a canvas depicting recognizable persons undertaking recognizable actions (CR 76), or the most minimal of color field abstractions (CR 769). His ideas may be broadly applicable and universal in intent, but their roots are concrete and derived from human experience. He is translating aspects of his own consciousness for the viewer—not so much a personal, subjective experience—but his understandings of the world, as a fellow human, derived from that experience. Whatever means he employed and whatever additional subject matter that he may have introduced in any given painting, elements of our shared humanity form the essential content of my father's painting.

In the first two decades of Rothko's career, this human element was often filtered through socio-political ideas centered on the dehumanizing effect of modern Western culture and economic structure. Single figures look lost, characters in a group setting seem disengaged or distant from one another, and the predominantly urban settings feel stifling. Works such as the two *Street Scene*s (pl. 11 and 13) in the exhibition evoke this sense of bewilderment and isolation in the urban environment. We also see this in his many works depicting the New York subway, where the figures look utterly disconnected from one another, rendered irrelevant by the architecture and generally oppressed by the dark, faceless environment (pl. 5 and 8). Rothko the socialist decries the system, but Rothko the artist of deep sensibilities looks not so much at the masses, but instead at the individual suffocated and muted by the circumstances of modern life.

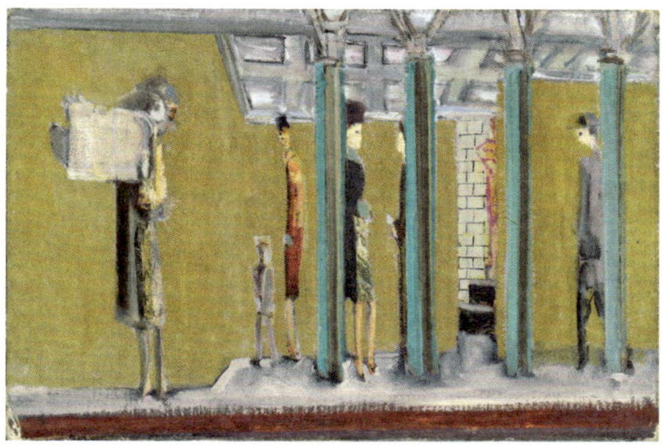

Untitled (Subway), 1937, oil on canvas, 20 1⁄8 × 30 in., National Gallery of Art, Washington, D.C. (CR 108; pl. 8)

My father discusses the ideas that underpin this representation of humankind in his book of philosophical writings, *The Artist's Reality*.[5] His argument is lengthy and tangled (and incomplete), but at core he bemoans modern society's lack of a unifying "myth." For him, the myth is the encapsulation of a commonly held philosophical / theological / scientific understanding of how the universe is ordered and functions. Lacking this, we have lost essential common footing for how each of us experience the world and engage with our fellow beings. The Enlightenment brought us a new individuation and greater sense of personal agency, but in so doing, it undermined our essential connectedness. He was quite clear that the industrialized, commercialized world in which he found himself had not provided any viable surrogates.

Recognizing the basic existential problem of finding and expressing shared meaning, Rothko turned explicitly to mythic subjects in the early 1940s. The figures become less distinctly human but they are imbued with the weight of mythic reference and subject matter (pl. 20 to 25). By evoking specific myths, he hoped to address more universal themes and communicate large portions of commonly understood material that would touch his viewers at an elemental level. The myths would be familiar to educated Westerners and, given the recurrence of mythic themes across cultures, would readily translate to other viewers. It is not clear how directly my father was embracing notions of Jungian archetypes and our shared

3 Indeed, Robert Rosenblum, one of Rothko's most dedicated champions describes them affectionately as "luminous voids." Robert Rosenblum, *Modern Painting and the Northern Romantic Tradition: Friedrich to Rothko* (New York: Harper & Row, 1975), p. 199.

4 Mark Rothko, Address to Pratt Institute, November 1958 in *Mark Rothko, Writings on Art*, ed. Miguel López-Remiro (New Haven: Yale University Press, 2006), p. 126.

5 Mark Rothko, *The Artist's Reality*, ed. Christopher Rothko (New Haven: Yale University Press, 2004), p. 83.

unconscious understanding of our world, but he was undoubtedly drawing from this well as he looked to communicate broadly with his viewers on a nearly instinctive level.

Rothko's work became increasingly abstract in the mid 1940s, as he sought an artistic vehicle with greater potential to speak universally than either the figure or ancient myth (pl. 23 to 32). Often still drawing on mythic subjects and embracing many of the pictorial elements of Surrealism, he remained committed to the human, experiential content of his work. With these works he tried to engage his viewer on a much more primitive plane, touching raw emotion, unconscious and pre-conscious thought. In this regard, these neo-surreal works address the viewer in much the same way that the classic abstractions do. Rothko is seeking a conversation, a meeting of minds about common human experience, but he begins that conversation on an elemental level, where our reactions are involuntary and propelled by feeling.

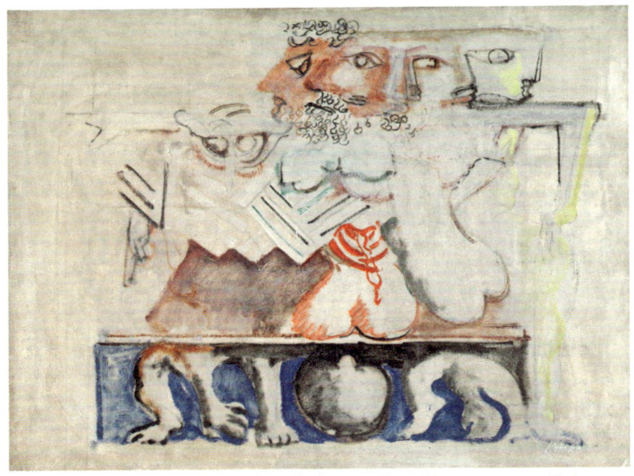

Antigone, 1939 / 1940, oil and charcoal on linen, 34 × 45¾ in., National Gallery of Art, Washington, D.C. (CR 178; pl. 23)

As he moves into the full abstraction of his "multiforms" in 1946–47 (pl. 35 to 45), and his classic works, beginning in 1949 (pl. 46 to 102), Rothko has entirely relinquished the figure as a catalyst in his expression of the essentially human. Figures, even highly abstracted, were too particular. Myths, however, universal in content, were still rooted in language, place, and theistic system. By instead engaging emotion and psyche through saturated color and drama-charged space, he could speak a more immediate and profoundly human language. That apparently minimalist classic format with typically two or three rectangles floated in a field of color could appear, at first glance, to be empty or void of content. Such a first impression would certainly be misleading, however, for Rothko infused his new paintings, more actively than ever before, with his still partially digested understanding of the world around him, an understanding that exceeded, or rather, defied, graphic pictorial representation.

Nor should we read the turn to abstraction as a sign of resignation or of pessimism about the potential to find real meaning through interaction with artwork. Quite the contrary. The more he reduces the phenotypic content of his work (as occurred in a steady progression into the later part of his career, largely through the vehicle of public commissions), the more he trusts his viewer to participate actively in creating new and personally relevant meaning; meaning drawn from the innards of the painter's image and mixed alchemically with the substance of their own. Let us look more closely at some of the means through which Rothko continually reasserts the real and present substance of his paintings.

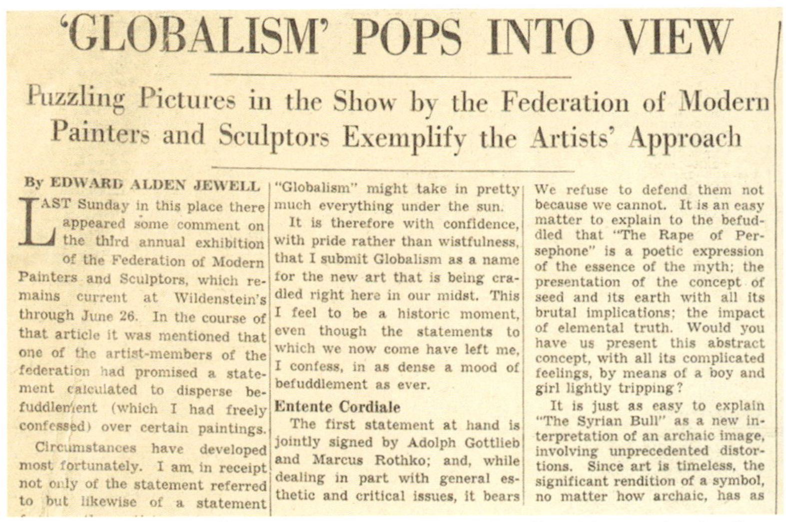

'GLOBALISM' POPS INTO VIEW

Puzzling Pictures in the Show by the Federation of Modern Painters and Sculptors Exemplify the Artists' Approach

By EDWARD ALDEN JEWELL

LAST Sunday in this place there appeared some comment on the third annual exhibition of the Federation of Modern Painters and Sculptors, which remains current at Wildenstein's through June 26. In the course of that article it was mentioned that one of the artist-members of the federation had promised a statement calculated to disperse befuddlement (which I had freely confessed) over certain paintings.

Circumstances have developed most fortunately. I am in receipt not only of the statement referred to but likewise of a statement

"Globalism" might take in pretty much everything under the sun.

It is therefore with confidence, with pride rather than wistfulness, that I submit Globalism as a name for the new art that is being cradled right here in our midst. This I feel to be a historic moment, even though the statements to which we now come have left me, I confess, in as dense a mood of befuddlement as ever.

Entente Cordiale

The first statement at hand is jointly signed by Adolph Gottlieb and Marcus Rothko; and, while dealing in part with general esthetic and critical issues, it bears

We refuse to defend them not because we cannot. It is an easy matter to explain to the befuddled that "The Rape of Persephone" is a poetic expression of the essence of the myth; the presentation of the concept of seed and its earth with all its brutal implications; the impact of elemental truth. Would you have us present this abstract concept, with all its complicated feelings, by means of a boy and girl lightly tripping?

It is just as easy to explain "The Syrian Bull" as a new interpretation of an archaic image, involving unprecedented distortions. Since art is timeless, the significant rendition of a symbol, no matter how archaic, has as

Edward Alden Jewell, "Globalism pops into View; Puzzling Pictures in. the Show by the Federation of Modern Painters and Sculptors Exemplify the Artists' Approach," in the *New York Times*, June 13, 1943, The Adolph and Esther Gottlieb Foundation, New York

Substance and Materiality: "there is no such thing as good painting about nothing"[6]

In 1943, Mark Rothko and Adolf Gottlieb, virtual unknowns outside their small circle of New York artists, had the audacity not only to rebut their critic, Edward Jewell of the *New York Times*, but to do so in the public forums of the *Times* itself and of New York arts radio WNYC. Jewell had published a dismissive review of their recent exhibition, expressing, as much as

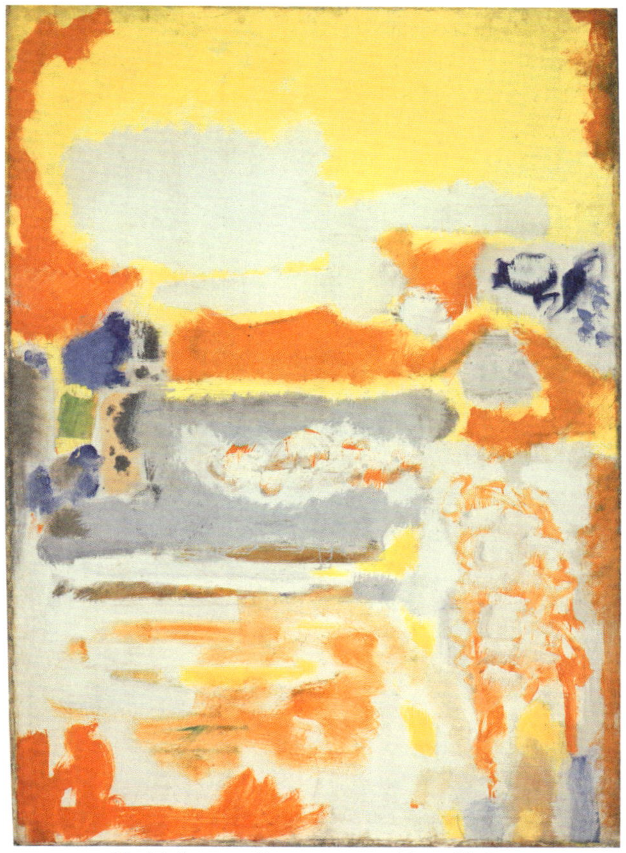

Untitled, 1947, oil on canvas, 53 ½ × 39 9/16 in,
Collection of Christopher Rothko (CR 362)

anything else, his bewilderment at what he saw on the gallery walls, and his inability to find real, communicative content in their work. Gottlieb and Rothko were quick to provide some help.

While the exhibition featured Rothko works in a mythological vein, his comments from the radio broadcast apply equally to his later abstractions. In fact, more so. As I discovered consistently when editing his manuscript of philosophical writings (published in 2004 as *The Artist's Reality*), Rothko's ideas about art, often expounded early in his career, are indicative of an *ideal*, one he did not yet know how to fully express pictorially. A chronological examination of his career is, in fact, to witness a progression to more thorough, more fluent, and ultimately more impactful expression of those ideas in his painted subjects.

In their letter to the *New York Times*, the two artists were emphatic, not only about the centrality of subject matter in their artwork, but also the high seriousness of that subject matter: "Subject is crucial and only that subject matter is valid which is tragic and timeless."[7] Their painting directed the viewer to those themes common to all human existence, the ideas most central to our beings but frequently only on the edge of consciousness. For Gottlieb and Rothko, it was the role of the artist to bring these existential questions into direct focus, to redirect us from the trivial and help us confront the real. Thus not only was their work not *nothing*, it was quite emphatically *something*, something of the greatest urgency.

For Rothko, that somethingness was not only the subject of his work, but it was also central to his artistic practice, a critical element in making a painting *believable*, a work that not only warranted, but demanded, engagement. He emphasized that his paintings were real, tangible objects—not a depiction or reference to something else—but substantial items in their own right. Rothko employed several mechanisms to reinforce the immediacy of his work but one of the most striking occurred in 1946, the dawn of his abstract, multiform works: he dispensed with the frame. While at first this appears merely an esthetic maneuver, for Rothko it transformed the viewer's interaction with the painting. By eliminating the frame, he undercut the sense that we were peering into another place from outside. By dispensing with the (gilded) border, he removed the aura of presentation, of decoration, or of something to be studied, and instead made his paintings tangible elements on the wall that we confronted directly. The "as if" was struck from the painting-viewer interaction so that we immediately encountered Rothko's piece of reality, not a semblance of what might be, once was, or could be imagined.

"A painting is not a picture of an experience. It is an Experience"[8]

My father's well-known statement makes explicit not only the actuality of his work, but the central role of the viewer in the work's purpose. Art is not something being told, a story related to us about someone else. Art is a process in which the viewer is engaged in the first person. Art has to be lived, an object/ event that, through the viewing process, we make about

6 Rothko and Gottlieb's letter to the editor, 1943, in Mark Rothko, *Writings on Art*, ed. Miguel López-Remiro (New Haven: Yale University Press, 2006), p. 36.
7 Ibid., p. 36.
8 Mark Rothko, quoted in Dorothy Seiberling, "Mark Rothko," in *LIFE magazine* (November 16, 1959), p. 82.

ourselves. Not ourselves as the *object* of the art; ourselves as the *subject* of the art, actively finding those common, most human elements through the conversation with (a) Rothko.

To maximize these experiential factors, Rothko made his paintings as direct and genuine as possible. As he details in *The Artist's Reality*, he will not use illusory techniques such as linear perspective and foreshortening to create imaginary spaces that seem large or deep or impressive. He will not, like Michelangelo, paint figures that give the visual impression of mass, intuited through their muscular build, while neglecting to illustrate convincing "tactile" elements of weight and substance.[9] Rothko insists on creating real spaces that speak to our sense of touch—our first-developed and most fundamental sense that assures us most readily of the reality of things. This preoccupation was already apparent in his figurative work at the time of his writing. Here the flat perspective of the painting and the color maintained intensity throughout the expanse of the canvas, and the palpable presence of the figures, whether in the "foreground" or "background," were all in the service of the communicative power of the piece, not manipulated to create an illusory scene or fictive place.

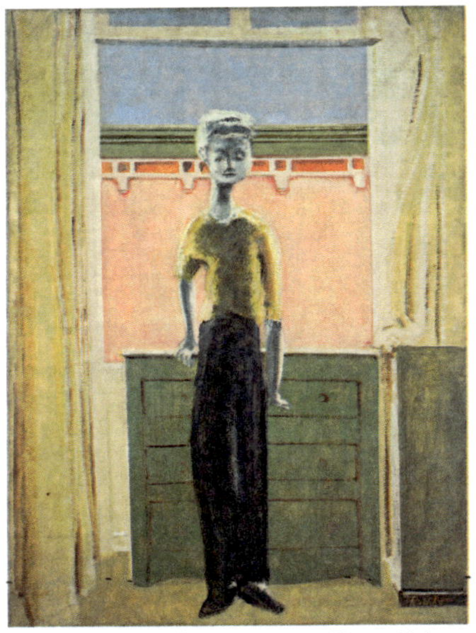

Portrait, 1939, oil on canvas, 39 ⅞ × 30 ¼ in., Collection of Christopher Rothko (CR 164; pl. 15)

Rothko's abstractions are built from the same material. He creates a pictorial space that, for all its mysteriousness, is direct and palpable (pl. 61), with color intensity that is maintained throughout and no sense that the painting is referring to something else (thus to see a Rothko as a "landscape" or a "window" is to violate its basic function, except insofar as those serve as metaphoric points of entry into an internal space). A Rothko painting is an object and it represents its own reality. Indeed, the seemingly miraculous leap to the Classic work of 1949 is certainly not the consequence of a new embrace of color, and only tangentially related to his simplification of form. The impact of the fully realized Classic image results from my father's newfound ability to speak boldly, honestly, unequivocally, in a manner that became almost impossible to ignore. It is a revolution of communication, powered by his palpable sincerity.

The viewer can be forgiven if Rothko's reality is not immediately perceived (pl. 66). The materiality is clearly there—he makes no attempt to disguise his media, or to suggest that we are looking at anything other than a painting. But if he is telling us about the world we live in, there may be some adjustment required. One key is to stop looking *at* the painting. One must look *through* the painting, Rothko having created in his classic format essentially a series of portals to foster that process. The horizontal fields stem from our fields of vision, the artist creating the most natural possible framework for looking. Starting in the late 1950s, my father made increasing use of reflective surfaces, in part to distinguish like-colored areas of the painting, but also to alter the relationship with his viewer. Yes, these canvases remain works to look through, and yet they are also mirrors, painted environments in which we can see ourselves. By the time we reach the Rothko Chapel (a project completed in 1967 but not built until 1971, a year after the artist's death, see pp. 275–83), the artist leaves only a hint of himself, inviting us to journey largely alone.

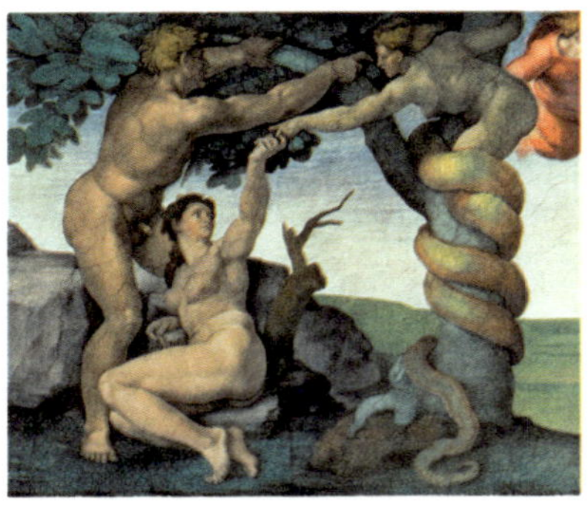

Michelangelo, *Adam and Eve* (detail from Sistine Chapel, Vatican), 1508–1512, fresco

To find environs we recognize in a Rothko painting, we must also stop grasping for the familiar. The world of the painting is indeed *our* world, "ours" meaning the viewer's and Rothko's. We are seeing his distillation of the world around us. It is his job to render the familiar as unfamiliar so that we can look at it anew and recognize elements we may previously have missed. This is not done willfully or perversely. Instead, he is showing us, for example, the nearby things we do not see because our focus is consistently distal. A Rothko painting works to distract us from what we see, so we can entertain an alternate view. Most importantly, it interrupts our thoughts so we can find what has been there from the first.

My father spends some time in *The Artist's Reality* praising "Modern Art" (c. 1930–40) for its honesty:[10] it does not pretend to be something other than what it is. Its techniques and mechanisms are fully on display. Nothing is hidden. It is perhaps ironic that Rothko would single out these aspects of modern art for praise, as he himself was accused, later in his career, of being secretive and guarding his studio methods jealously.[11] It is true that my father created his own paints from dried pigments, using a variety of binders and additives that in some cases remain obscure. This is hardly unique. He also did not like people watching while he painted, no doubt creating a persona to some people of reclusiveness and guardedness. And there is no question that the rapid rise of the young Pop generation, so shortly after the hard-won, late-life recognition for the Abstract Expressionists, made him resentful and not especially welcoming to other artists in his studio.

Untitled (Red, Black, White on Yellow), 1955, oil on canvas, 105 ½ × 93 in., National Gallery of Art, Washington, D.C. (CR 535; pl. 61)

However warranted his reputation for secretiveness may have been, I believe there was a much stronger motivation for Rothko's reluctance to speak of his technique. Materials, methods, even titles were a distraction from our experiential absorption in his art. He just wanted you to look, to *be* with his artwork. If he were here today, he would urge you to stop reading this essay, stop reading the wall label, stop wondering about where he bought his paints, whether or not he wore his glasses while he painted, or the lighting in his studio. Look at the painting. Look *into* the painting. My father does not want you to be preoccupied with how he made it, he wants you to experience what he experienced when he was making it.[12] He does not want a student and he does not want an observer—he wants, he *needs*, a co-creator.

The Ethereal and the Mystical: Approaching the Void

Rothko may have advocated for directness and openness, but there is undeniably a sense of mystery about his classic paintings,[13] works whose subject matter and forms often hover just out of reach. Indeed, despite his insistence on the centrality of materiality and tactility, many of the classic works appear to shimmer from another plane, their rectangles afloat by unknown means. There is the strong suggestion of magic at work here, of physical laws suspended and an internal energy with no visible source. What is this world we have been invited into? Is it real? Is this the "here and now"[14] that Rothko insists is inherently the source for, and material of, an artist's painting?

9 Rothko, *The Artist's Reality*, p. 53.
10 Ibid., p. 110.
11 Unpublished text by Robert Motherwell, on Rothko, Shakespeare, and related subjects, 1970, p. 3. Courtesy Dedalus Foundation.
12 Notes from a conversation with Selden Rodman in 1956, in Mark Rothko, *Writings on Art*, ed. Miguel López-Remiro (New Haven: Yale University Press, 2006), pp. 119–20.
13 Many writers have commented on this quality but Brian O'Doherty summarizes it perhaps best: "too positive to be a void, too negative to be a substance. We can call it a mystery or an enigma." Brian O'Doherty, *The Voice and the Myth: American Masters* (New York: Universe Books, 1988), p. 154.
14 Rothko, *The Artist's Reality*, p. 112.

There is unquestionably an element of the seductive in Rothko's classic format, a Siren's call coded in color. The paintings lure us inside them with an intriguingly palpable nothingness. Their many layers of paint invite us to peel away in search of an answer, our own perspectives guiding whether we see those layers as historical, anthropological, emotional, or some other type of content. At the same time, our experience of a Rothko work is governed by an undeniable gestalt effect, an emotional summation that contains the raison d'être of the composition. For all their elusiveness, for all their implied mysticism, Rothko's paintings create a *believable* space, one that touches us in a place we know. He may draw upon the *sfumato* of previous eras, but it hardly necessary: there is a tangible quality to the emptiness he paints.

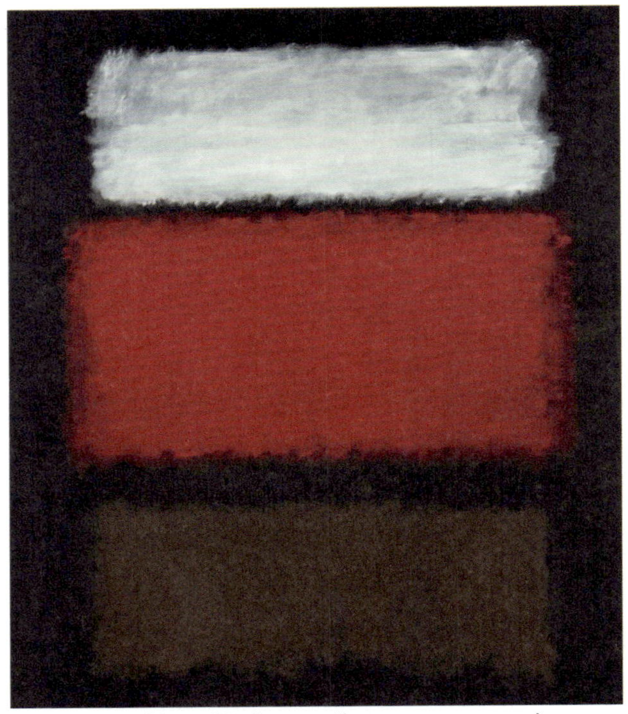

No. 1 (White and Red), 1962, oil on canvas, 102 × 90 in., Art Gallery of Ontario, Toronto (CR 717; pl. 93)

Rothko was aware of the questions raised by his abstract format several years before he began to paint in his classic style, its most absolute manifestation: "I adhere to the material reality of the world and the substance of the things. I merely enlarge the extent of this reality … Art to me is an anecdote of the spirit, and the only means of making concrete the purpose of its varied quickness and stillness."[15] Thus Rothko makes clear that, despite mystical appearances, his work is tied concretely to the world, and to our experience of that world.

How then to make sense of the space of a Rothko painting? How to understand what he means when he declares space "the most comprehensive statement of the artist's attitude toward reality … the key to the meaning of the picture"?[16] Part of the difficulty originates in the duality Rothko establishes. He wants you *inside* the picture, in direct emotional engagement with the content he has introduced into the painting. Rothko's paintings are also famously expansive, however, inviting movement well beyond their frameless borders. They appear to escape their physical bounds and bring us along into that "enlarge(d)" reality of the spirit he describes above. Is the content thus inside the painting or beyond? Are the paintings concrete objects with which to wrestle or gateways to another emotional level?

If we answer these questions with option B (although, I believe firmly that the correct answer to this either / or choice is: both), do we move away from art and more strongly to the religious and the mystical? The movement inward or outward, the progression beyond the borders—for the objects of the painting but more importantly for the viewer—all these smack strongly of a spiritual quest. Is this ultimately the journey Rothko wishes us to pursue through his artwork? He is once again equivocal. He speaks of the viewer who cries in front of his paintings as having "the same religious experience (he) had when painting them."[17] Rothko also dreamed of installing small "wayside chapels" with a single painting, where the traveler could find nourishment for the soul.[18] And yet he is at other points, entirely dismissive of religion and its practice.[19]

Standing in front of the three imposing temples at Paestum in 1959, Rothko remarked, "I have been painting Greek temples all my life without knowing it."[20] In this statement we encounter both a confessed religious intent and its denial. For Rothko acknowledges that he has been constructing means for seeking and speaking to the gods, and yet he would have us believe that this was by happenstance, that the creation of his art was not a religious quest but instead the fortuitous product of a spiritual soul. We should also note that the religious culture he has embraced is one with a strictly historical presence, not one that continues to inspire active practice.

Certainly, Rothko's art is not religious in any formal sense. He walked away from organized religion (Judaism) as a boy and never renewed contact. His artwork has no explicitly religious content, save for a handful of 1940s works with crucifixion references. We should remember, however, that the paintings from this moment in his career draw heavily on mythological subjects, and that his writings in *The Artist's Reality* speak repeatedly of the Christian myth (this is Rothko speaking to the function of Christian lore, not their validity). It is clear that he exploits this material for its mythic quality (God become man, the son sacrificed by his father, etc.) rather than for any specifically religious message. His one painting on a Jewish (that is, pre-Christian) theme is *Rites of Lilith* (pl. 26), which boldly captures the elemental fury of Adam's first wife. Again we should note that the subject is outside the canon, drawn from the apocryphal writings, not the books of law or acknowledged prophets.

And yet there is a beyond-the-self search for deeper meaning and explanations that pervades Rothko's oeuvre from the earliest figuration to the most abstract. Regardless of style, format, or media, he manages to make our insistent, timeless need to understand our origins and our fate palpably present. Is this necessarily a religious undertaking, however, or is religion simply the system most commonly used for addressing the questions inherently raised by human existence? Perhaps we miscast Rothko's journey as a religious one, when it is in fact a manifestation of his existential preoccupations. Indeed, Noreen Khawaja, whose recent book, *The Religion of Existence*, explores the human struggle *with* religion, notes that the writing of even so-called atheistic existentialist philosophers (such as Sartre and Heidegger) *feels* religious to its readers.[21] The search for the meaning of existence is common to all religion, and likewise, it is particularly central for the existentialist thinkers, who must posit a source of meaning in a godless universe. And for Rothko?

As with all things Rothko, evidence is fragmentary and contradictory, but there is certainly reason to believe that Rothko engaged with his existentially infused artistic undertaking in active dialogue with existentialist thought. For a variety of reasons, the library left to us by my father is merely a remnant, and certainly not reflective of the breadth and depth of his reading. It is worth noting, however, that among the surviving texts are Sartre's *Nausea* and the ever-so-aptly-named *La Condition Humaine* by Andre Malraux. We can know with some confidence, therefore, that he was pursuing questions of existence and the human condition not only in religious terms but in philosophical ones as well. Rothko is on record as having embraced the work of two other notable philosophers as well: Kierkegaard and Nietzsche. Kierkegaard, while certainly a Christian thinker, is also regarded as a prime progenitor of existentialism,[22] particularly with regard to his emphasis on "authenticity" (to self, as defined by experience).

Rothko cited Nietzsche extensively early in his own career, and specifically *The Birth of Tragedy*, also an early work of Nietzsche's. Reading

15 Personal Statement, 1945.
16 Ibid., p. 60.
17 Notes from a conversation with Selden Rodman in 1956, in Rothko, *Mark Rothko, Writings on Art*, pp. 119–20.
18 Interview between Rothko and Ethel Schwabacher from May 30, 1954. Ethel Schwabacher Papers, Archives of American Art.
19 "My wife once told him that she thought he must be a mystic, because his paintings conveyed, to her at least, a sense of magic and ritual, verging on the religious. He denied it. 'Not a mystic. A prophet perhaps—but I don't prophesy woes to come. I just paint the woes already here,'" "The Easy Chair: Portrait of the Artist as an Angry Man," in op. cit., *Writings on Art*, p. 135. David Anfam, author of the catalogue raisonné of Rothko's works on canvas, notes: "In some seven years of research on the Rothko catalogue raisonné, I have never encountered a colleague, friend or acquaintance of the artist who was prepared to describe him as even remotely religious," in "Dark Illumination: The Context of the Rothko Chapel," in *The Chapel Commission* (Houston: The Menil Collection, 1996), p. 14, note 8.
20 Ibid., p. 137.
21 Noreen Khawaja, *The Religion of Existence: Asceticism in Philosophy from Kierkegaard to Sartre* (Chicago: University of Chicago Press, 2016), p. 16.
22 William McDonald, "Søren Kierkegaard," *The Stanford Encyclopedia of Philosophy* (winter 2017 edition), Edward N. Zalta (ed.), https://plato.stanford.edu/archives/win2017/entries/kierkegaard/.

The Birth of Tragedy in the late 1930s or early 1940s helped fire Rothko's preoccupation with the mythic, focusing his eye upon myth's ability to capture essential, universal, non-transient aspects of the human condition. In other words, myth would become for Rothko, first and last, a vehicle for addressing central existential concerns (*Tiresias*, pl. 28). And lest we think that the artist's existential focus was merely a consequence of his interest in the myth, superseded by other ideas once he left explicitly mythic work behind, we must remember that this is the artist who stated that "the progression of a painter's work … will be toward clarity."[23] Rothko's subsequent espousal of abstraction was not a change in direction but instead a better means of addressing the "human condition" more forthrightly and with concomitant emotional impact on the viewer. He continues to confront many of the human-focused questions he engaged with during his mythic period but with a different, and he believed more universal, artistic language.

Black on Maroon, 1958, oil paint, acrylic paint, glue tempera and pigment on canvas, 105 × 155 in., Tate Modern, London (CR 642; pl. 81)

We can look at Rothko's paintings, therefore, not as quasi-religious totems or as portals to a type of modernist religious experience. Instead, we can see them as essential tools in an existential quest for meaning and purpose; tools to speak with his viewer and meet them on common ground as fellow beings in a process of exploration. To engage with a Rothko painting is thus to put our other concerns aside and wrestle with our understanding of the universe—which may include religion—and which for Rothko was a means of finding grounding in a world that did not inherently provide much. That was my father's practice: creating artwork constructed on ideas embodying "a communication about the world to someone else."[24] When we look at a Rothko painting, therefore, we must not focus only on *his* "communication"; we must also focus on the "someone else."

Despite Rothko's deep involvement in the communicative process, he cannot tell you what it means to be you. Only you can find that meaning. As Sartre declared in his lecture "Existentialism Is a Humanism,"[25] "existence precedes essence." He reminds us that it is pointless to speak of essences, or forms, because there are no generalized truths about what it means to be human. That meaning can only be personal, derived from the experience of one's own existence. This inherently phenomenological approach, of meaning that only comes to into being through personal experience, is central to how Rothko's work operates. The substance of a Rothko painting can be actual only for the individual viewer and only in that moment. It is born in the act of viewing, and will necessarily be different for other viewers, and likely for the same viewer at a different time.

Black on Maroon, 1959, oil paint, acrylic paint, glue tempera and pigment on canvas, 105 × 155 in., Tate Modern, London (CR 647; pl. 78)

If personal meaning is the only source of truth, however, is not a Rothko painting inherently *unheimlich*, Heidegger's notion of the *other*; something that not only is foreign to the self, but in fact reinforces our sense of alienation?[26] It would be easy to see Rothko's increasingly dark, minimal, and less overtly sensual paintings of the mid 1960s as reflecting a sense of that alienation, an inability to communicate meaning, and the inherent emptiness of all things outside the self. Existentialism and nihilism[27] are close cousins, and it is easy to tip into despair if facing a godless universe, where life has no inherent meaning, where universal values are societally generated and collapse under close scrutiny by the individual.

Rothko himself, as early as the 1930s, was pining for the "unity" of antiquity, when religion, philosophy, and science were all one, their truths derived from a common understanding of the order of the universe.[28]

We must ask then if Rothko's paintings are essentially representations of the void, of an inherently empty universe. These could be material representations, in that they show nothing recognizable and suggest a lack of identifiable content. Or, these paintings could be representations of our interaction with the void as a process, in that their blankness engages us in a Sisyphean exercise to fill them; an attempt to create meaning and substance in a world where there can be none. It is a lonely place, indeed. While I will shortly argue against this position, there are viewers, and indeed scholars[29] who see Rothko, in his late works, pushing us to the edge and daring us to look over the precipice, asking if we have the courage to gaze into the abyss. Can we endure the realization that there is nothing beyond the self? If we accept this understanding of Rothko's work, we could well ask that, if there is nothing, why bother painting it? His art when seen in this guise would simply become a "communication about the world," an understanding that he feels incumbent upon himself to share with his fellow humans, no matter how bleak the view.

The act of making art—even depictions of the void or works devoid of content—inherently involves a belief in the power and consequence of communication—a belief that we have sufficiently shared meaning systems and mindsets to make the act of speaking our truths about these matters relevant to others. And to paint such ideas is an act of tremendous faith (or perhaps folly) that what one says / shows can touch another being in a manner both comprehensible and inspiring. I think that many who see my father's dark works as despairing or a depiction of nothingness are not sure themselves how they feel about that precipice, and may have conflated my father's biography with his art. For to paint one's ideas, indeed to paint one's ideas about the most difficult existential topics, is an act of considerable optimism. It involves an inherent belief that what one does matters, that one can create meaning, and that that meaning can ultimately be meaningful for others. And despite many physical and emotional obstacles, my father did that more times in the last two years of his life than at any other. Perhaps the desperate acts of a man who knew time was short, but one still eager to engage his fellow beings and able to trust that it could be worthwhile.

Postlude: Tableau Vivant

A review of the foregoing arguments makes clear that communication between artist and viewer is absolutely central to finding and actualizing content in a Rothko. We have considered, however, two essentially opposing positions:

Universally shared. We looked earlier at Rothko's quest for a universal language through which he could speak to all. This began with figurative representations of the human condition as he lived it, moved through mythological stories as carriers of essential human truths, and

23 "The progression of a painter's work, as it travels in time from point to point, will be toward clarity: toward the elimination of all obstacles between the painter and the idea, and between the idea and the observer. As examples of such obstacles, I give (among others) memory, history or geometry, which are swamps of generalization from [which] one might pull out parodies of ideas [which are ghosts] but never an idea in itself. To achieve this clarity is, inevitably, to be understood." "Statement on His Attitude in Painting," 1949, in op. cit., *Writings on Art*, p. 65.
24 Ibid., Pratt lecture, november 1958.
25 1946 (2001). "Existentialism is a Humanism," B. Frechtman (trans.), in eds. Charles Guignon and Derk Pereboom, *Existentialism: Basic Writings* (Indianapolis: Hackett Press).
26 Katherine Withy, *Heidegger on Being Uncanny*, (Harvard: Harvard University Press, 2015).
27 Nietzsche, Rothko's go-to philosopher early in his painting career is closely associated with the birth of this philosophical concept. See Richard Schacht "Nietzsche and Nihilism," in *Journal of the History of Philosophy*, Johns Hopkins University Press, vol. 11, no. 1, January 1973, pp. 65–90. We do not have any evidence, however, that Rothko read Nietzsche's writings on this topic.
28 Rothko, *The Artist's Reality*, p. 26.

ultimately embraced abstraction as the most distilled embodiment of those truths. Indeed, Rothko's abstract canvases do not negate his earlier work (none of which he destroyed) or render them obsolete. They are his *tabulae rasae* – his *erased* slates. If myths contain the whispers of time immemorial, so are Rothko's apparently blank canvases filled with the echoes of those myths, the shards of collective memory, the stray marks from his drawings of the human body, etc. They are fragments of song, outlines of ideas, repositories of gestures, both his own and those passed down to him through shared history.

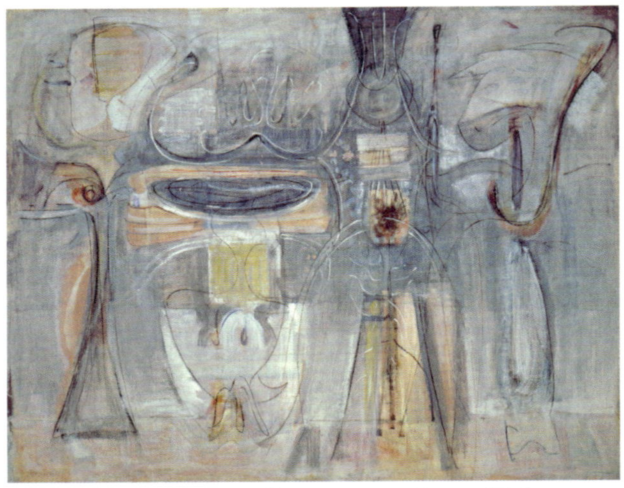

Rites of Lilith, 1945, oil on canvas, 80 ⅞ × 106 39/64 in., private collection (CR 266; pl. 26)

Phenomenologically derived. At the same time, we have spoken of the highly personalized meaning found in these paintings, of meaning that can only be garnered through personal experience. If one viewer gleans a certain truth from an abstract canvas, and another its contrapositive, wherein does the truth lie? Can it reside in the painting? Are we not tempted to conclude that Rothko's paintings are indeed voids, *tabulae rasa* on to which we project our own thoughts? Can such paintings do anything save to underscore the emptiness of a world that has no inherent meaning outside the self? And if meaning can only exist on a personal level, what, in fact, does Rothko offer his viewer?

The distinction I have drawn may apply to, and derive from, a Rothko painting, but it recapitulates, in condensed, highly simplified fashion, long-standing philosophical dichotomies. As an artist, however, Rothko need not toe the line of any particular orthodoxy. He can embrace both of these arguments and demonstrate their points of intersection through the example—that is the method, function, and effect—of his paintings.

Rothko works actively with the phenomenological, with understanding rooted in our personal experience. Each person's concept of a Rothko painting has the potential to be unique and valid. Yet while specific meaning comes into being only for the individual, this does not mean work is devoid of content. Rothko has filled the painting with his "communication about the world," his understanding derived from his experience. That content is constant but the interaction with that content will be different for each individual. He makes art in order to have a conversation with the viewer, and from that conversation new content will be born. This is communication as a creative act, one that helps complete (repeatedly) the potential of the painting.

West Triptych, Rothko Chapel, Houston, 1964–67, oil paint, acrylic paint, glue tempera and pigment on canvas, 134 ⅗ × 245 ¾, photo Paul Hester, Courtesy of The Menil Collection, Houston (CR 801–803)

Rothko's embrace of communication, his creation of a directly communicative art, is an inherently optimistic act. He may see us as isolated beings in a fragmented society, but through our quest for meaning, we are bound together in shared human experience—bound together with Rothko in a moment of "consummation[30] between painting and viewer" and bound together as a species with a common purpose. Ultimately, we cannot know to what degree Rothko endorsed Jungian notions of the collective experience that permeates our psyches, or how fully he accepted existentialist notions of complete solitude. What we can know is that his paintings put into practice a worldview in which there can be commonly held truths about our humanity, and that these form the basis for our interactions—with Rothko and with each other. We may be alone in the universe, but we are alone together—each of us absorbed in the same processes, even if the

29 Rosenblum (op. cit., *Modern Painting and the Northern Romantic Tradition*) suggests that the Rothko Chapel murals "pose an ultimate choice between everything and nothing," p. 218. Natalie Kosoi ponders this topic throughout her deeply considered article, "Rothko and Void—Nothingness Made Visible: The Case of Rothko's Paintings," in *Art Journal*, summer 2005, 64, 2.

30 Rothko and Gottlieb's letter to the editor, 1943, in op. cit., *Writings on Art*, p. 36.

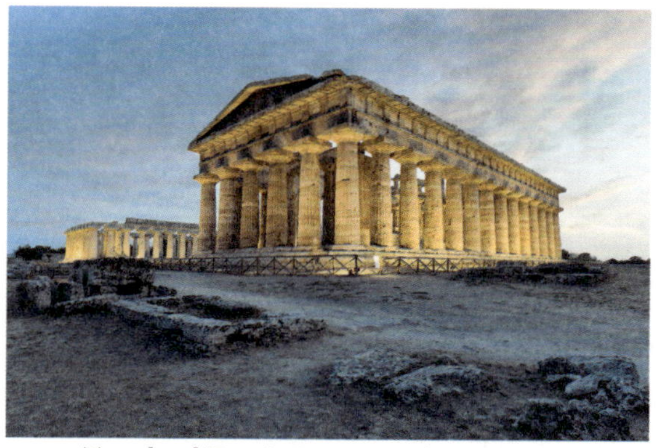

Temple of Hera in Paestum, 6th century BC

truths we derive are personal. The Rothko Chapel, seen by many as one the world's great sites for meditation / contemplation, is Rothko's ultimate realization of this understanding of the world. There may be several people sitting in the room, in conversation with the art and with the space. They are absolutely alone, and profoundly joined, in solitary journeys.

Unquestionably, as we progress through the 1960s, Rothko's outreach to the viewer, his passionate extension of self into the work, becomes more reduced. He provides less overt content and demands more of the viewer, a demand that that they give more of themselves in the conversation with the painting. It would, again, be tempting to see this shift in Rothko's stance as a withdrawal, as a reflection that he has suspended some of his belief in the process of communication between art and public. And yet we can also see an inherent optimism in this change; that by giving less of himself he expresses even more faith in his viewer to complete the exchange.

For Rothko, answers are potentials—they come into being through the asking of the question. The artist who engages in making the painting and the viewer who engages in "speaking" with the painting are involved in a positive, hopeful act. Their interaction will create truths that are personal and concrete, and did not exist as such until that moment. Creativity is not, therefore, simply what the artist imagines. It is what artist and viewer imagine and understand together. It is a 360 degree process.

Tabula rasa? Hardly. Certainly not as traditionally understood. Rothko's works are *tableaux vivants*! It is art inhabited by the viewer, animated and continually reanimated by the living.

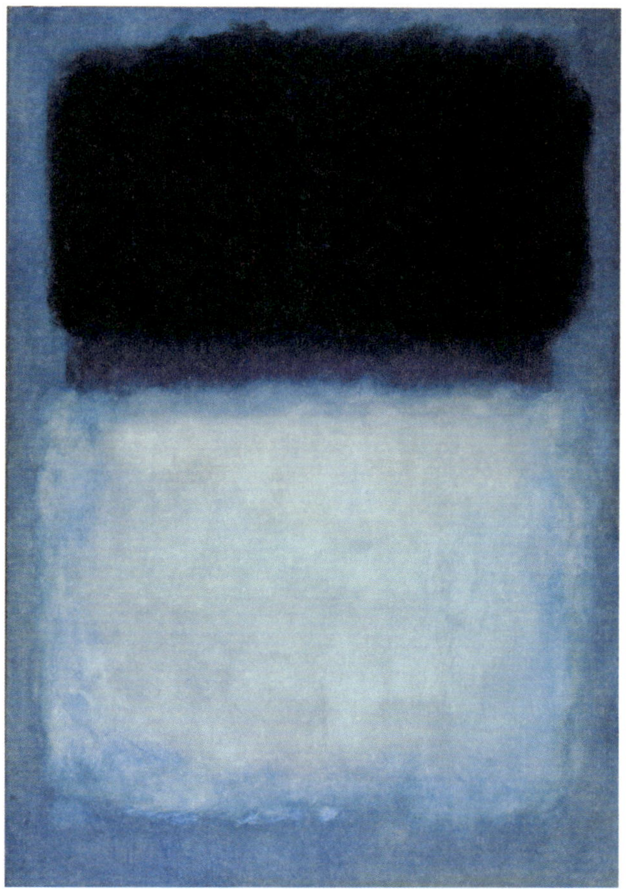

Green on Blue (Earth-Green and White), 1956, oil on canvas, 91 ¼ × 64 ⅜ in., The University of Arizona Museum of Art, Tucson (CR 543; pl. 66)

Untitled, 1970, acrylic on canvas, 60 × 57 ⅛ cm, National Gallery of Art, Washington, D.C. (CR 834)

"It Lives and Breathes": Depicting Human Drama

Riccardo Venturi

"Mark the first page of the book with a red marker. For, in the beginning, the wound is invisible." Reb Alcé
Edmond Jabès, *The Book of Questions*[1]

I. *Invading human affairs*

In the beginning was a memory that links the childhood of Marcus Rotkovitch (1903–1970) to his painting, although it is hard to say how accurate it was. His friend, artist Alfred Jensen, recounted Rothko's recollection as follows: "The Cossacks took the Jews from the village to the woods and made them dig a large grave. Rothko said he pictured that square grave in the woods so vividly that he wasn't sure the massacre hadn't happened in his lifetime. He said he'd always been haunted by the image of that grave, and that in some profound way it was locked into his painting."[2]

In a lecture given at the Pratt Institute in 1958, Rothko ironically listed all the ingredients required to make a good painting, including "a clear preoccupation with death—intimations of immortality."[3] The centrality of this preoccupation was confirmed by Rothko's reply to actor and director John Huston, who asked him—during the Houston chapel period—what he was painting. "The infinity of death," he said, and then specified, "the infinite eternity of death."[4]

While there was no lack of sagacious critics who saw, as early as the 1950s, what Herbert Crehan called a "wall of light"[5] and a sense of serenity in every Rothko painting, Rothko was resolutely seeking the opposite, leaving no doubt about the fact that his painting was not decorative.[6] As early as the 1930s Rothko spoke of violence in an essay on Nietzsche's *Birth of Tragedy*; and during his so-called Classic years, he told Dore Ashton that he "was creating the most violent painting in America."[7] To people who sought or found serenity in his paintings, he commented, "I would like to say that they have found endurable for human life the extreme violence that pervades every inch of their surface."[8] A note in a sketchbook from 1954 reads, "The manger of my

1 Edmond Jabès, *The Book of Questions*, vol. 1, trans. Rosmarie Waldrop (Hanover, N.H.: Wesleyan University Press, 1991).
2 Mark Rothko to Alfred Jensen, quoted in Budd Hopkins, *Art in America* 61 (summer 1973), pp. 92–93. Jensen told this story to Ulfert Wilfe (*Diary*, October 12, 1962), who repeated it to Rothko himself, who then confirmed it (*Diary*, March 6, 1963). See also James E. B. Breslin, *Mark Rothko: A Biography* (Chicago and London: University of Chicago Press, 1993), pp. 17, 326, and 567–68 (note 40).
3 Mark Rothko, *Writings on Art 1934–1969*, ed. Miguel López-Remiro (New Haven and London: Yale University Press, 2006), p. 125.
4 Sheldon Nodelman, *The Rothko Chapel Paintings: Origins, Structure, Meaning* (Austin: University of Texas Press, 1997), p. 306.
5 Herbert Crehan, "Rothko's Wall of Light," *Arts Digest* 29, 3 (November 1, 1954), pp. 5 and 19.
6 See, however, Éric de Chassey, *La Violence décorative: Matisse dans l'art américain* (Paris: Éditions Jacqueline Chambon, 1998).
7 Dore Ashton, *About Rothko* (New York: Da Capo Press, 1996), p. 38.
8 Thomas Crow, "The Marginal Difference in Rothko's Abstraction," in eds. Glenn Phillips and Thomas Crow, *Seeing Rothko* (Los Angeles: Getty Research Institute, 2005), p. 35.

pictures is violence—and the only balance admissible is the precarious before the instant of disaster.... I am (therefore) always surprised to hear that my pictures are peaceful. They are a tear. They are born in violence."[9]

Rothko was here referring to his painting's penultimate quality, as though he had halted just before the disaster, subdued and filtered by bands of color. This is suggested by a statement made in 1959 in which he went straight to the point: "Look again. I am the most violent of all the New Americans. Behind the color lies the cataclysm."[10]

Rothko's positions were mockingly repeated and distorted by two former friends, the Abstract Expressionist artists Barnett Newman and Clyfford Still. When Rothko's solo show at the Sidney Janis Gallery was announced in April 1955, Newman explained his refusal to attend the opening to Janis: "It was Rothko who in 1950 said to me that he could not look at his work because it reminded him of death. Am I to disagree with him? Why should I look at his death image? I am involved in life, in the joy of the spirit."[11] (On the other hand, Newman would paint a cycle on *The Stations of the Cross: Lema Sabachtani* from 1958 to 1966.) Meanwhile, Still, a key observer, criticized Rothko by warning Janis that his friend produced morbid, tyrannical, nihilistic art, resulting from frustration, resentment, and aggressiveness. To find an attitude closer to Rothko's own sensibility we have to turn to Elaine de Kooning, the artist friend with whom he conversed at the time; it was she who grasped the aggressive quality of his paintings. In one of the few critical essays discussed with Rothko paragraph by paragraph, she argued that his pictures do not sit quietly on the wall like easel paintings, but are "threatening" because "they invade human affairs."[12]

Where do this effect and these more or less disinterested reactions come from? Let us re-examine and reformulate these passages: Rothko did not claim that a childhood memory was the inspiration behind his paintings. More subtly, he was haunted by a memory even as he pointed out that he wasn't certain he actually witnessed the dreadful event; and this story, whether actually experienced or reconstructed later, invaded his surfaces of abstract color. What Rothko wanted to depict and convey to others—what truly interested him, as man and artist (if the two can be separated)—was human tragedy. That preoccupation, which remains hard to put into words, ran through his entire oeuvre, expressed through a painterly approach freed from easel painting and, from the late 1940s onward, through abstraction alone.

Given this ambitious artistic project, at a historical moment and in a part of the Western world where painterly abstraction reached its zenith, the question of its execution remained open. Using the resources of non-representational painting, was it possible to convey the most violent aspects of the human drama, its most traumatizing events, whether experienced or invented as a screen memory?

The challenge was clearly formulated not so much by critics as by abstract artist Brice Marden, impressed by Rothko's "new way" of painting: "It was kind of 'Now you see it, now you don't....' He was one of the last painterly painters, really into the act of painting." Marden went on: "With Rothko there is a belief that touch and paint are about emotion, whereas for the others paint is simply about paint. You can really empathize with Rothko's works.... His touch affects the whole feel of the painting: it's an empathetic, emotional

9 Mark Rothko, unpublished sketchbook, "The Property of (A. Selzer & Co., Inc.)," 1954, pp. 34–35, quoted in Oliver Wick, "'Do they Negate Each Other, Modern and Classical?' Mark Rothko, Italy and the Yearning for Tradition," in ed. Oliver Wick, *Rothko*, exh. cat., Palazzo delle Esposizioni, Rome, 2007 (Milan: Skira, 2007), p. 9.

10 Rothko to Brian Corney, 1959, quoted in Chris Stephens, *Mark Rothko in Cornwall* (Tate St. Ives, 1996), p. 10.

11 Letter from Barnett Newman to Sidney Janis, April 1955, printed in Barnett Newman, *Selected Writings and Interviews*, ed. John P. O'Neill (Berkeley: University of California Press, 1992), p. 121.

12 Elaine de Kooning, "Kline and Rothko: Two Americans in Action," *Art News Annual* XXVII (1958), pp. 86–97, 174–79.

13 Brice Marden, interview by Mark Rosenthal, September 19, 1997, in ed. Jeffrey Weiss, *Mark Rothko* (New Haven and London: Yale University Press, 1998), p. 360.

14 Rothko, *Writings on Art*, pp. 119–20.

15 "The Wild Ones," *Time Magazine*, February 20, 1956, p. 75, quoted by David Anfam, "Dark Illumination: The Context of the Rothko Chapel," in eds. David Anfam and Carol Mancusi-Ungaro, *Mark Rothko: The Chapel Commission*, exh. cat. (Houston: The Menil Collection, 1996), p. 6.

16 Although biographer James Breslin expressed his doubts (see Breslin, *Mark Rothko*, pp. 55–56), the incident was recently confirmed by Kate Rothko Prizel. "[H]e starred in a summer theater production in Portland in which Clark Gable had been his understudy. This story, once thought to be apocryphal, was recently borne out when a playbill from the production surfaced." Kate Rothko Prizel, "Mark Rothko: A Daughter's Sketch," in eds. Christopher Rothko et al., *Mark Rothko* (New York: Rizzoli Electa, 2022), p. 34.

17 Mark Rothko, *The Artist's Reality: Philosophies on Art*, ed. Christopher Rothko (New Haven and London: Yale University Press, 2004), p. 47.

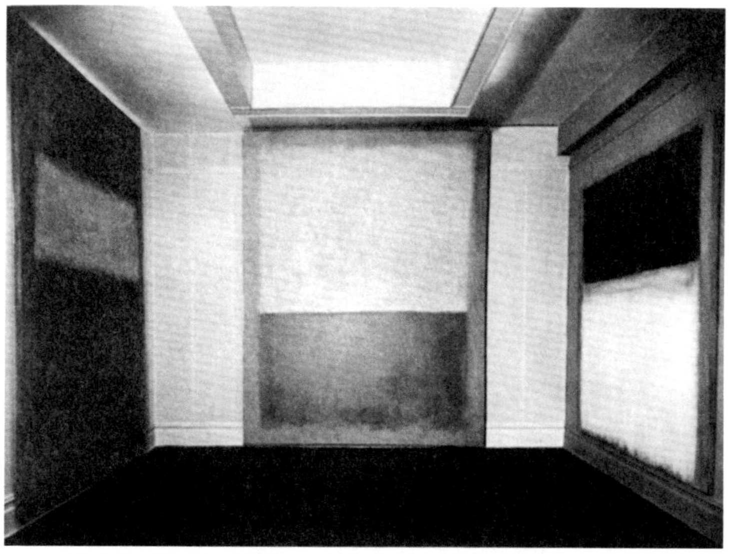

Mark Rothko's Exhibition, Sidney Janis Gallery, New York, 1955

response that I have.... [His] touch was much more integrated [than Willem de Kooning's], and less of a separated or isolated act."[13]

Such was the watershed traced by Rothko's work: either you recognize his paintings' ability to convey formless emotions, bringing them to life in Rothko's own way, in accord with the overall atmosphere evoked by Marden; or else you view them as the product—however brilliant it may be—of an obstinate, fulgurating conviction, to be analyzed with the historical tools of postwar American art.

Marden had no doubt: it is important to ask how Rothko managed to create chromatic atmospheres through the simple juxtaposition of bands of color, all the while remaining careful not to lose the essential thing, namely the human drama imbuing the picture and the visual experience it triggers. It is this clutch of human feelings that make Rothko, at least in this respect, an "Abstract Expressionist" (a label that remains, in other respects, too brief). It is no coincidence that Rothko highly valued strong if indefinite emotional reactions to his paintings, which sometimes moved people to tears, as numerous accounts attest.

"I'm interested only in expressing basic human emotions—tragedy, ecstasy, doom and so on.... And if you, as you say, are moved only by their color relationships, then you miss the point!"[14] Color is generally the first, and sometimes the only, feature associated with Rothko's art, even though he stated: "I'm not interested in color. It's light I'm after."[15] Compared to color, this light is simultaneously within and outside the canvases, involving the space in which we perceive them. How did Rothko conceive his pictures, how did he orchestrate their vision, so that the human drama—that visual memory niched in his paintings—could emerge and be transmitted?

II. An urban stage

The theater, not painting, was Rothko's first love. In 1924, when still roughly twenty years old, he acted in Josephine Dillon's theatrical troupe in Portland, Oregon, which included Clark Gable. Rothko bragged that Gable had once been his understudy (originally thought to be an exaggeration, this incident has recently been confirmed).[16] Leaving Portland for New York the following year, he applied for a scholarship to the American Laboratory Theater—we might wonder what turn his life and work would have taken had he been granted the scholarship.

Indeed, right from the 1930s, when he decided to paint, he habitually used theatrical images to describe painting, to the point where a picture became a voyage taken by the beholder. In *The Artist's Reality* (1940–41), a manuscript Rothko ultimately decided not to publish, he wrote: "Actually, the artist invites the spectator to take a journey within the realm of the canvas. The spectator must move with the artist's shapes in and out, under and above, diagonally and horizontally... at varying and related intervals." And he concluded, "Without taking the journey, the spectator has really missed the essential experience of the picture."[17]

A book crucial to Rothko's early years was Nietzsche's *Birth of Tragedy,* which Nietzsche himself described as "a book perhaps for artists." Meanwhile, theatrical references—Greek tragedy, Shakespeare's irony, Beckett's absurdity—

dot Rothko's entire career. While that career can be divided into artistic periods or, less convincingly, into two halves—one representational, the other abstract—it will be viewed here as a coherent whole.

Greek tragedy served as a central hub for Rothko's ideas and work. On the one hand, he never took an interest in Zen or other Asian philosophies due to their lack of a tragic sense, constantly present in his mind. Although "Zen followers and priests had singled him out as their significant artist," Rothko stressed the fact that he "never had use for Zen since they had no sense or didn't recognize tragedy, which brings [me] closer to the Greeks."[18] From the visual angle, Greek tragedy provided a wonderful range of deformations, hybridizations, and dismemberings of the human body (as in Dionysiac rituals). Starting with Aeschylus, mythological and archaic subjects invaded Rothko's paintings from the 1930s, with their thematic repertoire of crime and punishment, threat and war, and sacrifice and destruction, not to mention familial, societal, and political breakdown, the fragmentation of individuals doomed to an ungraspable, unredeemable fate.

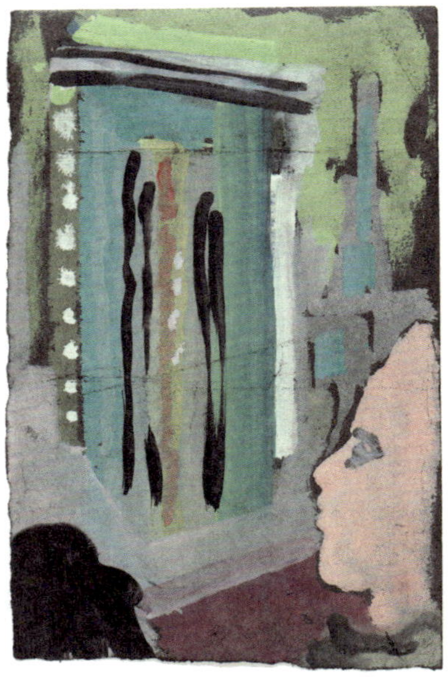

Untitled (Interior with figure), 1936 / 1937, watercolor on construction paper, 9⅜ × 6⅛ in., National Gallery of Art, Washington, D.C.

On the other hand, tragedy led to a visual output from which Rothko soon adopted a distance. As he put it in the Pratt Institute lecture cited above, "I belong to a generation that was preoccupied with the human figure." And yet "whoever used it, mutilated it," something Rothko wanted to avoid at all cost.[19] Thus the permanent elimination of figures from his pictures—the adoption of a single-minded path with no hesitation or turn-around—should not be seen as a simple progression from representational to abstract but rather as a kind of safeguard.

Now, as determining as the influence of Greek tragedy may have been, Rothko knew he was not living in fifth-century BC Greece, nor in the Renaissance (from which most of the artistic references in *The Artist's Reality* are drawn). Nor in the Romantic period, if we entertain Robert Rosenblum's argument that Rothko was heir to the landscapes of Caspar David Friedrich—although Rothko always denied depicting landscapes. "Absolutely not. There is no landscape in my work."[20] At the height of modernism, Rothko was living in Manhattan and would never live anywhere else once he left Portland, to the point where Donald Blinken could consider him "the quintessential New York artist."[21]

During an interview in 1952, cutting short certain overly idealized interpretations of his work, Rothko told William Seitz, "One can be a Seventh-day Adventist, etc. [i.e. separate self from world]. Not true of me. I live on Sixth Avenue, paint on 63rd street, am affected by the television, etc. etc. [i.e., diverse particularity of life]. My paintings are part of that life."[22]

Rothko undoubtedly immersed himself in the metropolis of New York, with its movie theaters, museum collections, and architectural skyline. Italian director Michelangelo Antonioni was not far off when, in a letter to Rothko noting the affinities between a painter and a filmmaker interested in the void and nothingness, he described *No. 19* (1958) as follows: "There is all the steel of New York in the color of the upper square, so isolated from the dark ground: it gives you a feeling of panic, cosmic panic. It is angst depicted."[23]

Two scenes of urban life replaced the stage for the young Rothko—movie theaters and subway stations. While he would later be internationally associated with color-field painting, Rothko's cinematic and metropolitan

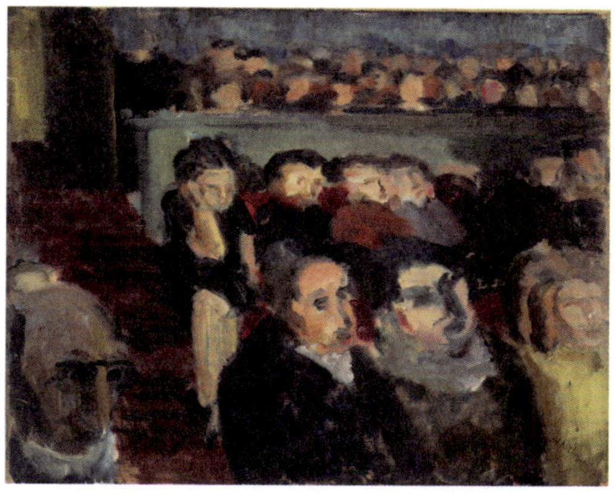

Movie Palace, 1934 / 1935, oil on canvas, 24 × 31½ in., private collection (CR 64; pl. 1)

views stem from a different genealogy, one that would interest Mike Kelley for his 1985 performance piece *Plato's Cave, Rothko's Chapel, Lincoln's Profile.*

While training as an artist in New York, Rothko not only read books on art history that guided his thinking on the visual arts, as developed later in *The Artist's Reality.* At that same time, Rothko met Milton Avery, the American painter who probably exerted the greatest influence over him. Together, they would not only discuss the color in Matisse's paintings or the future of painting in general, they would also go to see films, as Sally Avery, Milton's wife, recalled. "He [Avery] and Rothko would spend most of their days in the movies. They loved the movies."[24]

What could be more popular and modern in the twentieth century than seeing a film? It served as the subject of many early, little-known yet crucial works, such as *Movie Palace* (1934–35), which reveal his relationship to visual culture. Rothko did not focus on the movie itself, but on the audience's reactions, plunged into darkness and absorbed by the screen (even if some people allow themselves to snooze). The first two rows are depicted in detail, while the faces of those behind have no expressions, becoming mere spots of color that contribute to the depth of the scene. As in the photos taken in his studio, the stress is placed on the spectator, to the point where, in depicting the movies (the protagonist of the picture, as the title indicates), Rothko turns his gaze away from the moving pictures. Their presence is suggested not by the screen, which remains out-of-frame (or off-screen), but only by the reflected light on the faces of the audience, notably the people in the front rows, literally bathed in light.

This expedient would recur decades later in one of Jeff Wall's early series of photographs, *Movie Audience* (1979), as well in a film by Iranian director Abbas Kiarostami, *Shirin* (2008).

Going back into the past, we are not far from comments on the movies made by Kafka, an author Rothko had read. Kafka said he could not bear "dancing pictures" because he felt he was "too Optical". And "the cinema disturbs one's vision. The speed of the movements and the rapid change of images force men to look continually from one to another. Sight does not master the pictures, it is the pictures which master one's sight. They flood one's consciousness. The cinema involves putting the eye into uniform, when before it was naked."[25]

Beyond *The Trial* and the parable of "Before the Law"—to which Rothko's large abstract paintings might serve as a visual pendant—Kafka and Rothko here converge. The "Cinema of the Blind" as described by Kafka ("Every cinema should be called that!") could be said of the work of Rothko's classic period as a whole. And *Movie Palace* is a painting about the spectatorship specific to the movies (rather than the moving pictures themselves), as though Rothko wanted "to stress an inward, psychologized side to the act of looking. The seers rather than the seen are its subject."[26]

Right from his first sketchbooks Rothko was attracted to the most alienating—as opposed to frantic—aspects of metropolitan life. This attraction led to the combination of two inextricably linked features: a human presence, depicted in its singularity or in small groups, and the presence of architecture. Over a good twenty-year period, the development of Rothko's art entailed a constant back-and-forth between these two elements, human and

18 Notes by Ulfert Wilke dated January 21, 1968, reported by Breslin in James E. B. Breslin Research Archive on Mark Rothko, 1940–93 (hereafter JBRA), Getty Research Institute Research Library, box 9, folder 27.
19 Rothko, *Writings on Art*, p. 126.
20 Quoted by Eliza Rathbone, "Mark Rothko: The Brown and Gray Paintings," in eds. E. A. Carmean, Jr., Eliza Rathbone, and Thomas B. Hess, *American Art at Mid-Century: The Subjects of the Artist* (Washington, D.C.: National Gallery of Art, 1978), p. 269.
21 Quoted in ed. Diane Waldman, *Mark Rothko in New York*, exh. cat. (New York: Solomon R. Guggenheim Museum, 1994), p. 5.
22 Rothko, *Writings on Art*, p. 76.
23 Letter from Michelangelo Antonioni to Mark Rothko, May 27, 1963. JBRA, box 1, folder 12. Quoted in Wick, *Rothko*, p. 55.
24 Sally Avery, Interview with Louis Sheaffer, quoted in David Anfam, *Mark Rothko: The Works on Canvas—Catalogue Raisonné* (New Haven and London: Yale University Press, 1998), p. 69 (note 188).
25 Gustav Janouch, *Conversations with Kafka*, trans. Goronwy Rees (New York: New Directions, 2012), p. 160.
26 Anfam, *Mark Rothko: The Works on Canvas*, p. 22 (note 16).

architectural. Although he experimented with heterogeneous relationships, he never managed to find the right balance, and the architectonic tended to dominate the human.

Such was the case with the scenes that take place in the subway, where the platform serves as a narrow, artificially lit stage—empty, anonymous, with few features, yet overwhelming. Through osmosis, these scenes intensify the urban alienation and psychological solitude of the characters populating them. Rothko turned them into actors caught in the pose of waiting, in a collective loneliness, in interaction with the subterranean architecture. He observed their bodies, the way they held themselves and protected themselves from the presence of others and from an environment dotted with the names of stations.

These considerations matured in the 1950s when the vestibule of Michelangelo's Laurentian Library in Florence became Rothko's spatial model of a way to impart feelings. It was an empty space, filled with the presence of the void removed from the clutter of things, one in which we sense a feeling of claustrophobia. According to Rothko, Michelangelo "achieved just the kind of feeling I'm after—he makes the viewers feel that they are trapped in a room where all the doors and windows are bricked up, so that all they can do is butt their heads forever against the wall."[27]

The vestibule showed how to suggest strong physical sensation and pressure on the body solely through the arrangement of certain architectural features. Rothko drew inspiration from those blind, walled-up windows that took the breath away in a perfectly controlled context. Perhaps the theater had become, in the period between the 1930s and 1950s, a space with no horizon?

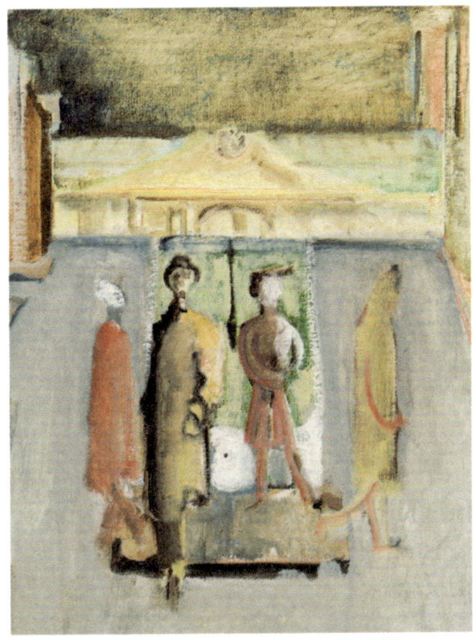

Untitled (Four Figures in a Plaza), 1935 / 1939, oil on linen, 24 × 18 1/16 in., National Gallery of Art, Washington, D.C. (CR 114)

III. A theater of abstract events

In the late 1940s Rothko plunged into an unknown, resolutely non-representational, world. The theatrical model did not disappear, as might have been expected. Instead, it was reactivated in an original way, as explained in his most accomplished article, "The Romantics were Prompted," written in 1947 when he was working on his *Multiforms.* "I think of my pictures as dramas; the shapes in the pictures are the performers. They have been created from the need for a group of actors who are able to move dramatically without embarrassment and execute gestures without shame."[28]

In this crucial passage, Rothko effects a series of transformations: the painting becomes a stage, painted shapes become actors, and the illusion of movement—that voyage he described in *The Artist's Reality*—becomes drama. His pictures thereby acquired a performative quality that radically reinvented the theatrical mechanism, extending it beyond anthropomorphism.

What do these new, non-human "actors"—the bands of color—do on the "stage" constituted by the canvas? Whoever has seen a classic Rothko knows the answer, and also knows that the answer is never unequivocal. Sometimes these rectangular fields push against the edges, disperse, and thin out, sometimes they contract, cluster, and thicken. The paintings conduct countless permutations and variations on these minimal actions, through coats of color

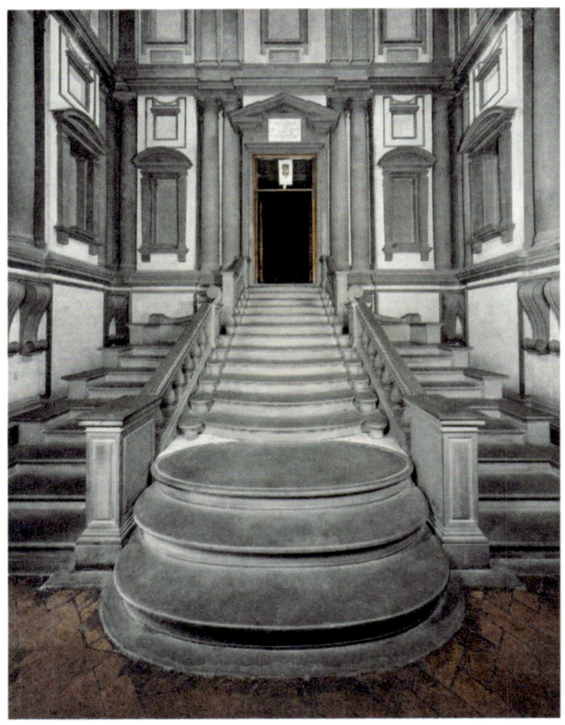

Michelangelo, Laurentian Library vestibule, 1525 / 1571, Florence

applied in transparent layers that generate shapes with ragged outlines, and that liberate the surface and edges of the canvas from the frame.

This process began with his Surrealist paintings, whose forms Rothko described as "organisms with volition and a passion for self-assertion."[29] In a spatially vague, indeterminate setting, dominated by a watery element whose presence and consistency distinctly differ from the invisibility of ether, the urban claustrophobia dissolved and the actors became organisms.

This increased fluidity became more pronounced with the *Multiforms,* an extraordinarily uneven series—perhaps the most ambiguous within the Rothko corpus. Rather than being a straightforward anticipation of his classic style, they represented one of his most fertile creative periods. Stripped of all associations and all narrative, of any preparatory drawing or composition, the paintings proceeded to dissolve all references to the outside world. "The familiar identity of things," wrote Rothko in "The Romantics were Prompted," "has to be pulverized in order to destroy the finite associations with which our society increasingly enshrouds every aspect of our environment."[30]

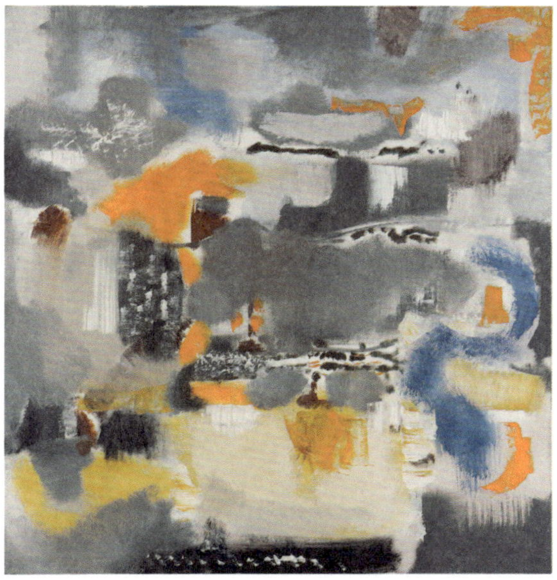

Untitled: Abstraction Number 11, 1947, oil on canvas, 39 ½ × 38 ½ in., Munson Museum, Utica, NY (CR 334; pl. 36)

In 1949, that *annus mirabilis,* Rothko began to articulate his signature style, the classic approach he would follow for the twenty subsequent years. All human figures and representational elements, which had already decomposed into the colored phantoms of the *Multiforms*, vanished forever. The figures retreated and the ground advanced—or, to remain in the theatrical sphere, there was no longer any distinction between actors and backdrop. What dominated was a symmetrical, frontal composition of a limited number of fuzzy-edged bands of color arrayed vertically, setting off a chromatic explosion that seemed to evolve over time, without equivalent in the history of modern painting. In 1953, Rothko told Alfred Jensen, "Maybe you have noticed two characteristics exist in my paintings; either their surfaces are expansive and push outward in all directions, or their surfaces contract and rush inward in all directions. Between these two poles you can find everything I want to say."[31]

And we know that what Rothko "wanted to say" was precisely the whole human drama. The polarity existed only in the beholder's gaze and body, yet it was staged by the artist. The drama played out on fields of color as well as the gaps between fields, on the interrelationship between two fields that advanced and receded within themselves or to the edges of the picture. This series of events was quite different from Hans Hoffman's straightforward perceptual gambit (which heavily influenced the Abstract Expressionists), in which alternating colors—cool versus warm, light versus dark—generated a "push and pull" effect, a mechanical movement of the pictorial surface through dilations and contractions. This post-Cubist give-and-take created an illusion of depth that remained too mechanical for Rothko.

In fact, the floating effect of the *Multiforms* and later works did not possess the rhythmic beat that, art historically speaking, dated back to Marcel Duchamp's *Anémic Cinéma* (1925) and *Rotoreliefs* (1934). It was more a vague pulsation of varying intensity, devoid of deliberate balance or composition; it was a dance, almost a light show, that extended beyond the boundaries of the picture. In short, it was more like breathing.

Rothko "often talked about breathing paint on canvas; he would like it to be just like a breath of air with no brush stroke," recalled his friend, the artist Regina Bogat Jensen.[32] Rather than glazes of diaphanous colors, he

27 Rothko, *Writings on Art*, p. 131.
28 Rothko, *Writings on Art,* p. 58.
29 Rothko, *Writings on Art*, p. 59.
30 Rothko, *Writings on Art*, p. 59.
31 Mark Rothko to Alfred Jensen, 1953, in Alfred Jensen, "Conversations with Rothko," JBRA, box 4, folder 5, p. 103. See also the Italian edition: Alfred Jensen, *Conversazioni con Mark Rothko*, ed. Riccardo Venturi (Rome: Donzelli, 2008).
32 Regina Bogat Jensen, Interview, February 5, 1986. JBRA, box 2, folder 2.

sought vibrant surfaces, breathing membranes, epidermal textures that he conceived as "skins that are shed and hung on a wall."[33] He thereby imparted an unexpected materiality to paintings that many people hastily took for ethereal, for little more than vapory colors or bodiless images, as though Rothko were a Bonnard who had incinerated all residue of representation.

That is how Rothko gave materiality to paintings that he did not think were abstract. When Sophie Tracy, standing in front of one of his paintings, asked, "Is this abstract art?" Rothko firmly replied, "My art is not abstract, it lives and breathes."[34] In an almost sententious way, he repeated this idea in an undated letter to Clyfford Still: "From my point of view, there can be no abstractions. Any shape or area which has not the pulsating concreteness of real flesh and bones, its vulnerability to pleasure or pain, is nothing at all."[35]

His pictures bristle at being limited to the boundaries of the canvas, they overflow and fill the entire sphere of exhibition and, by extension, experience. Exhibition and experience tend to coincide, modeling themselves on one another. The painting thus saturates our field of vision, invades our realm of life, becoming itself a field of vision. In conceiving the picture as drama, Rothko takes from the theatrical system not its scenic construction but rather the dramatic experience, which must be entirely resolved through painting, with the means and limitations specific to that medium. Given the absence of anthropomorphic figures, script, or theatrical architecture, all that remains is the action or maybe even—given the absence of any narrative—just an "act" characterized solely by the two-phase rhythm of breathing. Rothko thereby invented a theater that transcended things human. It was a theater of abstract, apparently simple, events, whose orchestration required four decades of work.

That work is evident not only in the large paintings but also in five small, very rare drawings (*Untitled*, 1961). Although they may go unnoticed, these drawings represent the epitome of his graphic philosophy. There are no chromatic markings, color is merely suggested through the variable density of washes and pen marks. In some instances, the picture consists of multiple series of vertical lines or concentric rectangles, drawn upon a ground of watery ink. In other cases, the rectangles remain empty, blank, and the graphic impact focuses on the demarcations between two zones and the borders, enclosing the entire image with a dense perimeter of ink.

These drawings are not simple preparatory sketches in black and white, but rather an attempt to suggest the overall, enveloping, and immersive effect of the paintings, a graphic re-creation of their pulsating effect. They are drawings of the experience of vision that project a perceptual effect and mental state, although the question that animates them is still human drama. They are a development of the light from a movie screen projected onto the faces of the audience in the theater plunged into the darkness of the 1930s.

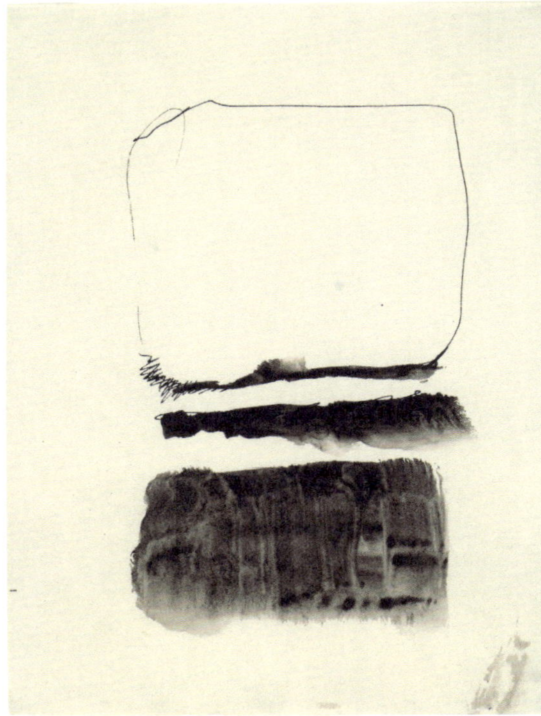

Untitled, pen and ink and graphite on wove paper, 11 1/16 × 8 9/16 in., National Gallery of Art, Washington, D.C.

IV. Beyond the bounds of the picture

"The painting looks easy. It looks as if it just happened."[36] Abstract artist Robert Ryman, upon seeing Rothko's paintings (displayed by dominant color rather than chronologically when he was working at MoMA from 1953 to 1961), perceived them as a spontaneous event. They seemed to have just been painted,

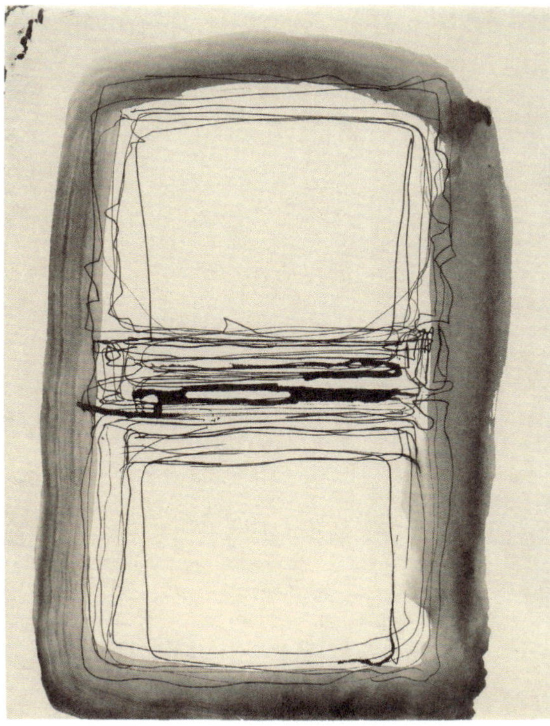

Untitled, pen and ink and wash on wove paper, 11 × 8 ½ in., National Gallery of Art, Washington, D.C.

completed just before we see them, as though not offering the beholder something to see, but staging—theatrically—an event. They reflected an activity that went beyond a mere picture conceived as a closed, autonomous, separate entity with a message to be encoded. Yet this opening up could be an impediment because, as Rothko realized in the 1950s, the visual experience they generate is hard to contain in a single picture.

Thrusting beyond the bounds of the picture—a necessary stage in the orchestration of the visual experience and the human drama—is to be understood in two ways. First, the edges of the painting teem with life. As Carolyn Carlson, the dancer and choreographer, put it in a poetic way when confronted with Rothko's work: "A corner of infinity burns."[37] It is impossible to contain Rothko's color fields within a picture's standard mechanisms: we are confronted with images of a fire that burns before our eyes—and even threatens to burn us.

For that matter, in the 1950s some people saw the halo of nuclear explosions in his paintings—ongoing explosions, as though the picture constantly generated more painting. After all, didn't Rothko himself scribble in a notebook, "Radiance is the afterglow of the explosive"?[38] The light on the audience's faces has thus turned cataclysmic.

Second, the bounds of the picture were breached in a series of paintings that Rothko carefully arranged in order to enhance the visual experience and to make the beholder "turn in space," as Katherine Kuh observed.[39] The painting spurred viewers not to magnetically attach themselves to one surface but to grasp the global effect, what that painting does to space. It was a living space, brought to life in Rothko's manner: wherever the gaze turned, it encountered one of his paintings, or rather an atmosphere steeped in Rothko's vision. The theatrical idea henceforth pushed the setting beyond script, beyond stage, beyond the fourth wall—an effect obtained through a development of painting.

Consequently, size increased. In November 1958, answering questions from the audience during a lecture, Rothko said, "Since I am involved with the human element, I want to create a state of intimacy—an immediate transaction. Large pictures take you into them. Scale is of tremendous importance to me—human scale."[40]

Whereas his figures were originally disproportionate in relation to the settings—whether urban or domestic—which were smothering and restrictive of those figures' movement, the large size of Rothko's abstract paintings created a sense of space that enveloped the beholder.

This represented another extension of the power of painting: images create space, and they do so with a carefully controlled poverty of means. Through these paintings, increasingly conceived as sets of canvases arranged in space rather than as individual entities, Rothko felt he was "controlling the situation."[41] Yet that was not all, if we think of his famous comment about the *Seagram Murals*: "I have made a place."[42] Whether it concerned his studio, a gallery, a museum, a restaurant, a refectory, or a chapel, Rothko strived to create a closed space conducive to immersion. The idea was hardly new, going back at least as far as the frescoes from Pompeii that Rothko admired at the Metropolitan Museum in New York before travelling to see them in situ in the summer of 1959.

33 Quoted in Breslin, *Rothko: A Biography*, p. 306.
34 Sophie Tracy, "Modern Art & Civilization," College of New Rochelle, *Homage to Mark Rothko*, July 1976. JBRA, box 9, folder 13.
35 Undated draft of a letter to Clyfford Still, published in Clifford Ross, *Abstract Expressionism: Creators and Critics* (New York: Harry N. Abrams, 1990), p. 170, and quoted by David Anfam, "Interrupted Stories: Reflections on Abstract Expressionism and Narrative," in ed. David Thistlewood, *American Abstract Expressionism* (Liverpool: Liverpool University Press, 1993), p. 29.
36 Robert Ryman, interview by Jeffrey Weiss, May 8, 1997, in Weiss, *Mark Rothko*, p. 367.
37 Carolyn Carlson, *Au bord de l'infini, suivi de Dialogue avec Rothko*, bilingual edition, French translation by Jean-Pierre Siméon (Paris: Le Passeur Éditeur, 2011), p. 158.
38 Rothko, 102 W. 54th notebook, quoted in Anfam, *The Works on Canvas*, p. 78.
39 Katherine Kuh, quoted in Weiss, *Mark Rothko*, p. 320.
40 Rothko, *Writings on Art*, p. 128.
41 Ashton, *About Rothko*, p. 147. See also Dore Ashton, "Rothko's Passion," *Art International* 22, 9 (February 1979), pp. 6–13.
42 Ashton, *About Rothko*, p. 155.

With his wall paintings, Rothko adopted the habit of hanging the largest canvases in the smallest spaces, as at the Sidney Janis Gallery in 1955. The impact on the beholder justified this counter-intuitive approach. During the Rothko retrospective at MoMA in 1961, critic Robert Goldwater commented on the small room holding three *Seagram Murals*. "It is significant that at the entrance to this room one pauses, hesitating to enter. Its space seems both occupied and empty."[43]

In a major museum like MoMA, you pause on the threshold.

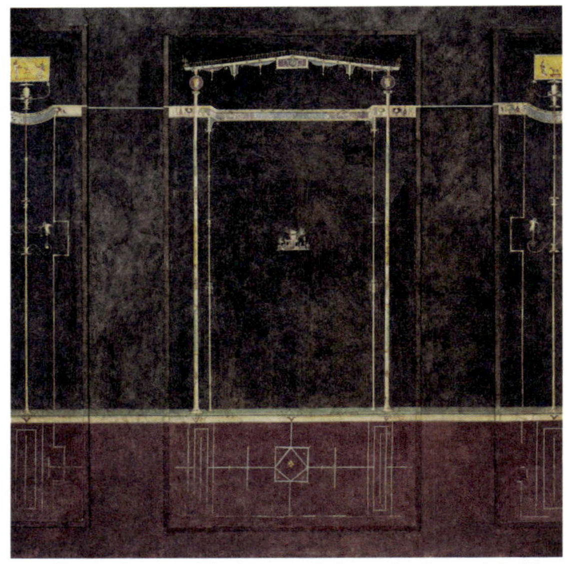

Wall paintings on black ground: from the imperial villa at Boscotrecase, last decade of the 1st century BC., 91 ¾ × 45 in., The Metropolitan Museum of Art, New York

V. Toward silence?

Although Rothko never attended the installation and opening of the Rothko Chapel, he was involved in the project from 1962 onward, while working on the murals for Harvard's Holyoke Center. Painter and writer Ethel Schwabacher visited his studio during that period, and on seeing the series she exclaimed, "They ought to build you a museum!" To which the artist replied, "No, a chapel."[44] Rothko was therefore already thinking of a place of worship as an exhibition venue prior to the commission of 1967–68. He wavered between two irreconcilable places: an upscale restaurant in the nerve center of Manhattan (the *Seagram Murals*) and an ecumenical chapel in Texas.

The idea of finding an alternative to both the restaurant and the "white cube" of galleries and museums emerged clearly in the 1950s. "I feel it would be good if little places could be set up all over the country, like a little chapel, where the traveler, or wanderer, could come for an hour to meditate on a single painting, hung in a small room, and by itself."[45]

In August 1959 he visited an unused chapel in Lelant, Cornwall, with the idea of turning it into a personal museum for the *Seagram Murals*.[46] The theater was turning into an intimate space, with a single work and a fixed temporal framework. Indeed, when the artist's conditions and instructions were respected in terms of hanging, lighting, and spacing, they created the experience of a slow unfolding of time. Thus Brice Marden, after visiting the Rothko Chapel several days in a row under different lighting conditions, was favorably impressed by the way the pictures changed over time and by "that almost touchy-feely thing about [the] painting."[47]

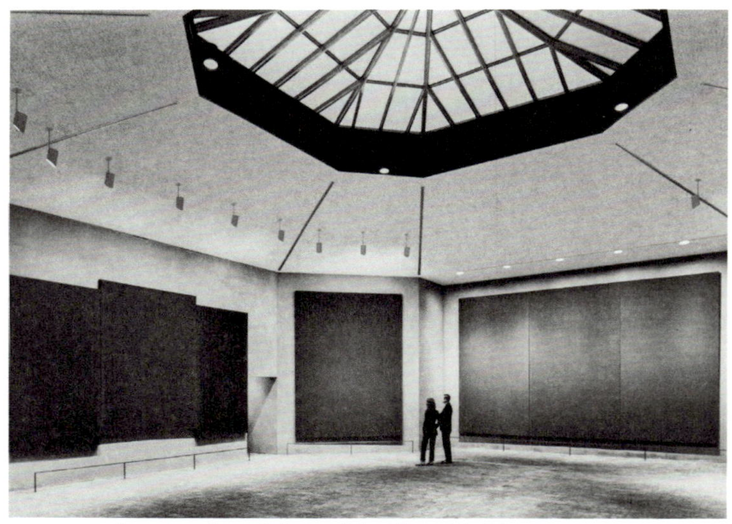

Interior view of the Rothko Chapel in Houston, 1971

How much theatricality survives in the Rothko Chapel (ideally located near the Menil Collection, a small Cy Twombly museum, and—from 1997 to 2012—a Byzantine fresco chapel)? It survives in the act of watching something, or maybe simply watching, watching nothing in particular. But even this aspect is apparently overlooked by people who go to the chapel several days in a row to sit before a triptych with eyes closed: physical presence is transfigured into a feeling that frees itself from vision. We begin to resemble the artist, who in 1936 depicted himself wearing dark glasses that hid his gaze (*Self-Portrait*).

"You would… not only see his paintings, you would breathe them," said Stanley Kunitz.[48] Such is the paradox: people who go to the chapel don't even look at the paintings, they feel them. Feel the pictures by closing their eyes, in a deeper gaze that includes listening. That was the pose adopted by Rothko in his studio, where his armchair was the most important piece of furniture: he became absorbed, far from the fray made by Pollock on entering the artistic arena. It is no coincidence that the finest commentary on the Rothko Chapel is a musical score by Morton Feldman (*The Rothko Chapel*, 1971), a composer attuned to abstract painting.

For that matter, Rothko claimed that he wanted to paint "pictures you wouldn't want to look at."[49] That is exactly what happened in the chapel, which is actually a place of blindness, of darkness, of the obliteration of painting. It is a saturnine place: "Often, towards nightfall, there's a feeling in the air of mystery, threat, frustration—all of these at once. I want my painting to have the quality of such moments."[50] Perception takes the form of expectation. If we choose to overlook the religious context of the ecumenical chapel for which these paintings were made, this expectation might be understood in a secular, degree-zero manner: we expect something to become visible, expect something to show itself. "It's not a question of watching in the darkness in order to see something, but of really watching the darkness."[51] We wait, and we notice certain details (the relationships of one painting with another, with the architectural space, with the light filtered from above, with our movements), but despite all our efforts no epiphany occurs. The expectation is not met, the revelation doesn't come, and in the last resort we fall back upon ourselves.

Untitled, 1969, acrylic on canvas, 81 1/8 × 76 1/4 in.,
National Gallery of Art., Washington, D.C. (CR 820; pl. 108)

We remain silent. All that remains is silence. Yet we mustn't forget that, for Rothko, silence had a double meaning. Although "silence is so accurate,"[52] rarely do we recall "the Daemonic and terrible nature of silence."[53] Rothko attributed this same double nature to light, in an Apollonian sense: "In the burst of splendor not only is all illumined but as it gains in intensity all is also wiped out."[54]

The Houston paintings are marked by an absence of pictorial events that exasperate people familiar with the lively effects of Rothko's Classic works. Here we sense a desire to display undifferentiation, to dilute the vibratory quality characteristic of his painting, to minimize chromatic and compositional gaps, both pictorial and architectural. This would come to fruition with the *Black on Gray* paintings, where Rothko's brilliant variations on monotony merely perpetuated his quest for human drama. As Barnett Newman said to Thomas Hess in 1996, "When Picasso does *Guernica,* he cannot do it in color, he does it in black and white and gray. I couldn't make a green Passion or a red one. You wouldn't have me make a purple Jesus or something like that."[55]

In the last years of his life, Rothko found black and gray to be the right colors to express the human drama he was still seeking. But they would only be his next-to-final word.

VI. Sensing presence

Rothko, like other artists of the New York school such as Newman and Adolph Gottlieb, had no direct experience of the battlefield or the ravages of war. In the 1930s, in order to appropriate events with which he was unfamiliar, he turned to mythology and archaism, understood as a visual repertoire uncontaminated by the surrounding socio-political reality.

43 Robert Goldwater, "Reflections on the Rothko Exhibition," *Arts Magazine* 35: 6 (March 1961), reprinted in *Mark Rothko: A Retrospective Exhibition, Paintings 1945–1960*, exh. cat. (London: Whitechapel Art Gallery, 1961), pp. 21–25, and *Mark Rothko 1903–1970*, exh. cat. (London: Tate Gallery, 1996), pp. 32–35.
44 Nodelman, *The Rothko Chapel Paintings*, p. 40.
45 Ethel Schwabacher, *Essays on Mark Rothko* [1954]. JBRA, box 7, folder 33, 1960, also quoted in Breslin, *Rothko*, pp. 375–76.
46 See Thomas Kellein, *Mark Rothko: Kaaba in New York*, exh. cat. (Basel: Kunsthalle Basel, 1989), p. 17.
47 Marden, interview by Rosenthal, in Weiss, *Mark Rothko,* p. 359.
48 Stanley Kunitz, interview, February 7, 1986. JBRA, box 4, folder 21.
49 Quoted in Nodelman, *The Rothko Chapel Paintings,* p. 342.
50 David Sylvester, "The Ugly Duckling", in ed. Michael Auping, *Abstract Expressionism: The Critical Developments* (London and New York: Thames and Hudson, 1987), p. 140. See also David Anfam, "To See, or Not To See," in eds. K. C. Eynatten, Kate Hutchins and Don Quaintance, *Image of the Not-Seen: Search for Understanding,* The Rothko Chapel Art Series (Houston: A Rothko Chapel Book, 2007), p. 73.
51 Alessandro Carrera, *Il colore del buio* (Bologna: Il Mulino, 2019), p. 98.
52 De Kooning, "Kline and Rothko," p. 174.
53 Mark Rothko, Denmark Notebook [1954], unpublished sketchbook, p. 26. quoted in Wick, "Do They Negate Each Other?" p. 22.
54 Rothko, *Writings on Art*, p. 144.
55 Barnett Newman, *Selected Writings and Interviews*, ed. John P. O'Neill (Berkeley: University of California Press, 1992), p. 277.

"During World War II it became nonsensical to get involved in painting men playing violins, or cellos, or flowers."[56] This attitude, expressed by Newman, was probably shared by Rothko, who admitted to John Fisher that he was "not a mystic. A prophet perhaps—but I don't prophesy woes to come. I just paint the woes already here."[57] Or the ones he thought he experienced in childhood, to return to the story of the Cossacks cited at the outset of this article, which leads us naturally to its conclusion.

Untitled (1970) is an unfinished, bright red canvas. It was sitting on the easel in his studio on the morning of February 25, 1970, the day Rothko took his own life. His earthly parabola ended in monochrome red. According to one of many anecdotes, in the 1960s a rich collector came to his studio on 69th Street, where Rothko, as usual, had set up several works, which were often black. The disconcerted lady said she was looking for "a pink and red and yellow and orange painting, a joyous painting." The artist retorted, "Pink, red, orange and yellow—aren't those the colors of an inferno?"

Compared to the darkened hues of his last series, almost the entire surface of *Untitled* (1970) is infused in bright red—the colors of the inferno never left him. While seeing this red as the blood shed by the Cossacks has to remain an inference, here we clearly fall back upon the tragic tonality that Rothko orchestrated throughout his artistic life.

It may seem surprising, but even an artist we might never associate with Rothko's world, such as performance artist Marina Abramović, has commented sensitively on his painting:

> "When you see a Rothko painting, you may not even know what colors it's made of, but as soon as you stand in front of it, it acts in a way that you cannot define rationally. A good work of art should make you turn around when you're not looking at it, the same way you can feel somebody looking at you when you're sitting in a restaurant. You're not sure, but you turn round and there is really somebody there. That energy is really beyond cultures."[58]

Abramović has grasped the main effect Rothko sought to convey: poignancy. Which can also be sensed from behind. Perception becomes a broader feeling that invades and overwhelms the human sensorium. "Rothko said he wanted a presence, so when you turned your back to the painting you would feel that presence the way you feel the sun on your back."[59]

Abramović went to Rothko and Pollock shows in New York in 1999. What struck her was the simultaneous view of a whole group of paintings by Rothko. "I found him to be a complete artist. From the beginning he explored different states of consciousness. It was so luminous. It was such a spiritual experience to see the progression of this work until its culmination in blackness. It was a kind of fulfillment. You see how the end of life comes and all that he went through. As an artist, you have to know how to live, how to die, and when to stop working."[60]

How to live, how to die. Beyond sensibilities, the visual arts sometimes manage to picture the drama of human existence. Rothko's work might be compared to Shakespeare's *Tempest,* not in relation to a particular character but in terms of what philosopher Richard Wollheim called "a form of suffering and of sorrow, and somehow barely or fragilely contained," which subtends the play.[61] T. J. Clark's attempt to sum up Rothko's oeuvre in a single

56 Newman, *Selected Writings*, p. 274.

57 Rothko, *Writings on Art*, p. 135.

58 Interview by Bernard Goy in the *Journal of Contemporary Art* 3: 2 (Fall / Winter 1990), p. 51, quoted by Bojana Pejić, "Being-in-the-Body: On the Spiritual in Marina Abramović's Art," in ed. Friedrich Meschede, *Marina Abramović* (Berlin: Neue Nationalgalerie / Cantz, 1993), p. 36.

59 Murray Israel, quoted in Breslin, *Mark Rothko,* p. 275.

60 Janet A. Kaplan, "Deeper and Deeper: Interview with Marina Abramovic [December 3, 1998]," *Art Journal* 58, 2 (summer 1999), p. 16.

61 Richard Wollheim, "The Work of Art as Object," *Studio International* 180: 928 (December 1970), reprinted in eds. Charles Harrison and Fred Orton, *Modernism, Criticism, Realism* (New York: Harper & Row, 1984), p. 16, and eds. Charles Harrison and Paul J. Wood, *Art in Theory 1900–2000: An Introduction of Changing Ideas* (Malden: Blackwell Publishing, 1992, 2003), p. 809.

62 T. J. Clark, "In Defense of Abstract Expressionism," *October* 69 (Summer 1994), reprinted in T. J. Clark, *Farewell to an Idea: Episodes from a History of Modernism* (New Haven and London: Yale University Press, 1999), p. 387.

quip—"*The Birth of Tragedy* redone by Renoir"[62]—is misleading. There is only one way to recognize Clark's mistake, the way desired by Rothko throughout his career and his life: to experience his painting directly. Only then can we grasp the human drama, can we realize that, yes, we may be standing in front of the *Birth of Tragedy*—but as painted by Rothko. He alone, and no one else, could have painted it thus.

Catalogue

1. *Movie Palace*, 1934 / 1935, oil on canvas, 24 × 31 ½ in. (64.8 × 82.2 cm), private collection (CR 64)

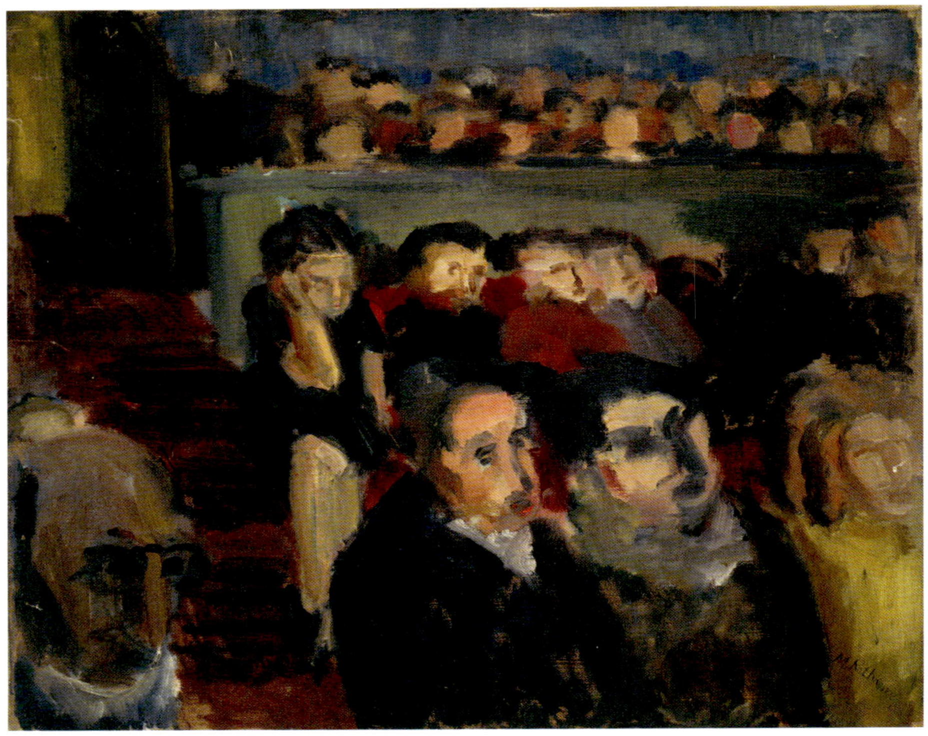

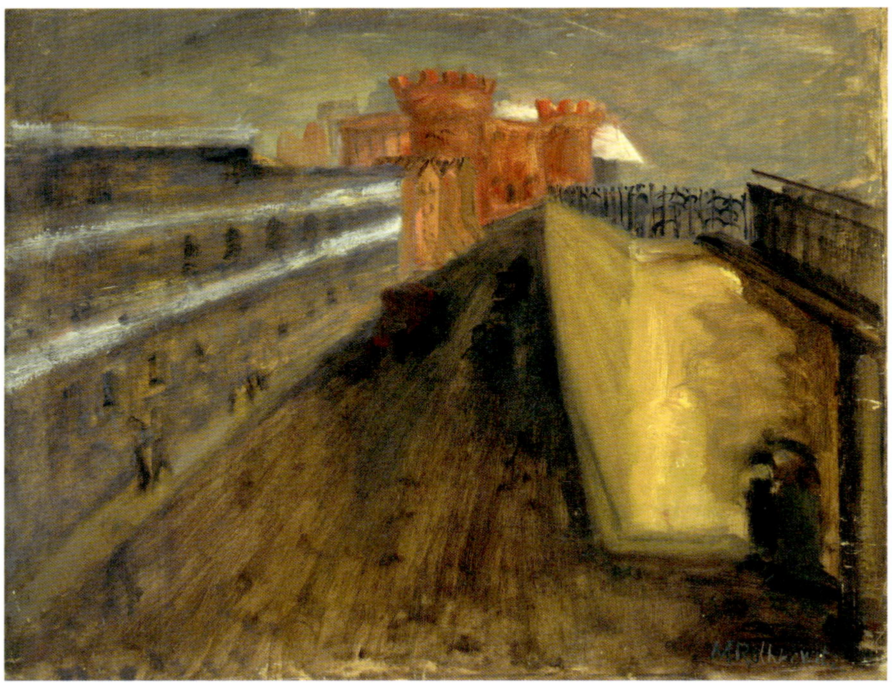

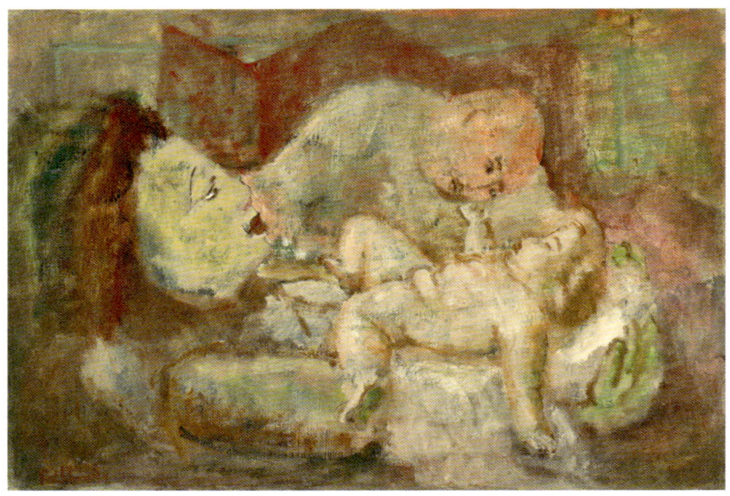

2. *The Road*, 1932 / 1933, oil on canvas, 24 × 31 ½ in. (61 × 80 cm), private collection (CR 26)
3. *Family*, c. 1936, oil on canvas, 20 ¼ × 30 ⅛ in. (51.4 × 76.5 cm), National Gallery of Art, Washington, D.C. (CR 89)

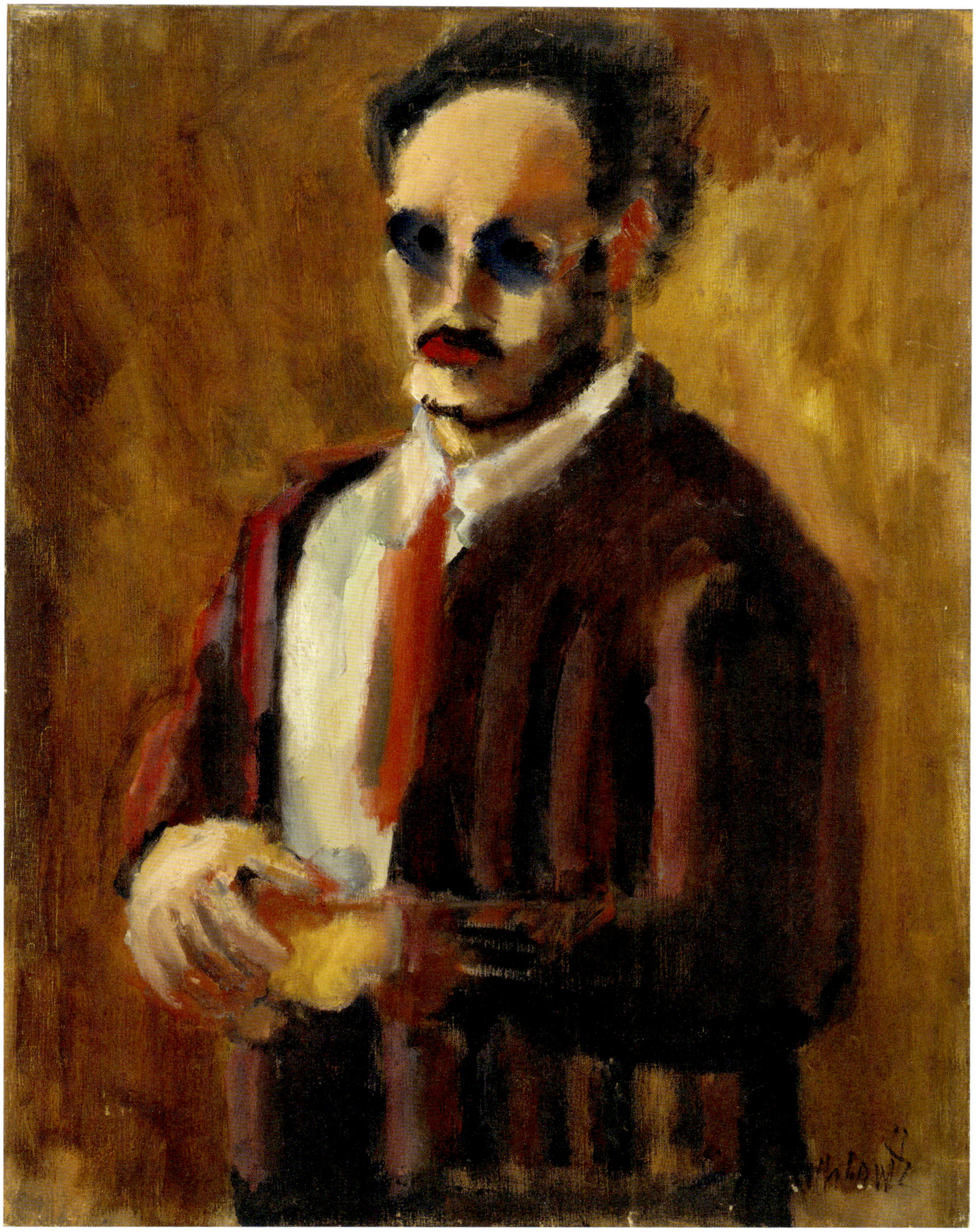

4. *Self-Portrait*, 1936, oil on canvas, 32 1/4 × 25 3/4 in. (81.9 × 65.4 cm), Collection of Christopher Rothko (CR 82)

5. *Untitled (The Subway)*, 1937, oil on canvas, 24 × 36 in. (61 × 91.4 cm), Collection of Elie and Sarah Hirschfeld (CR 104)

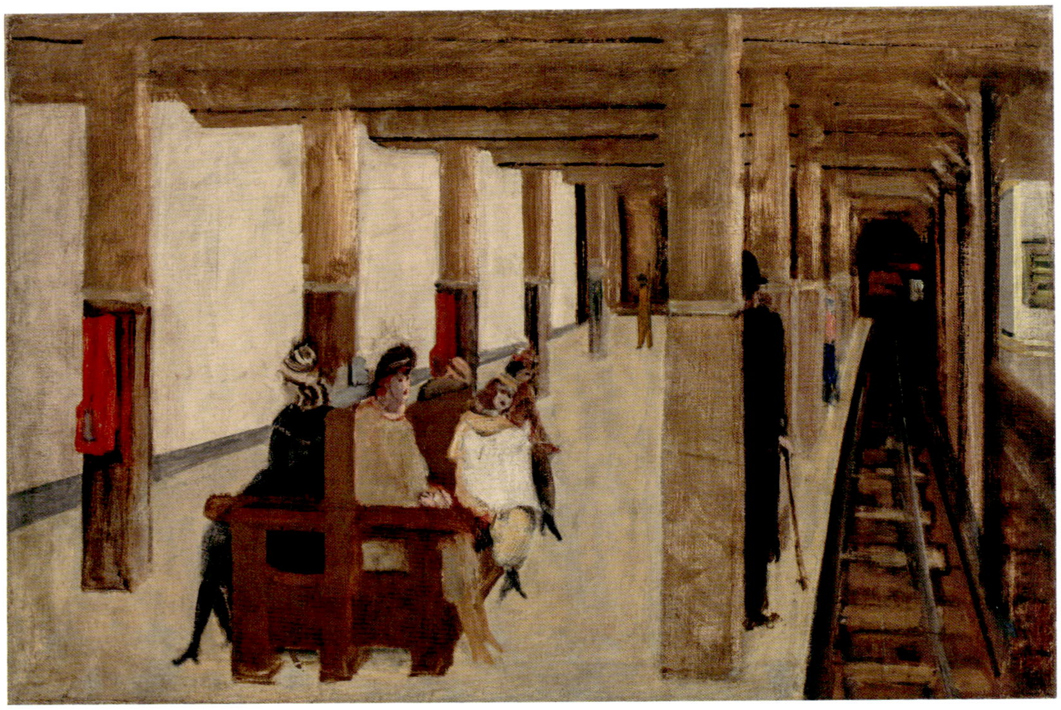

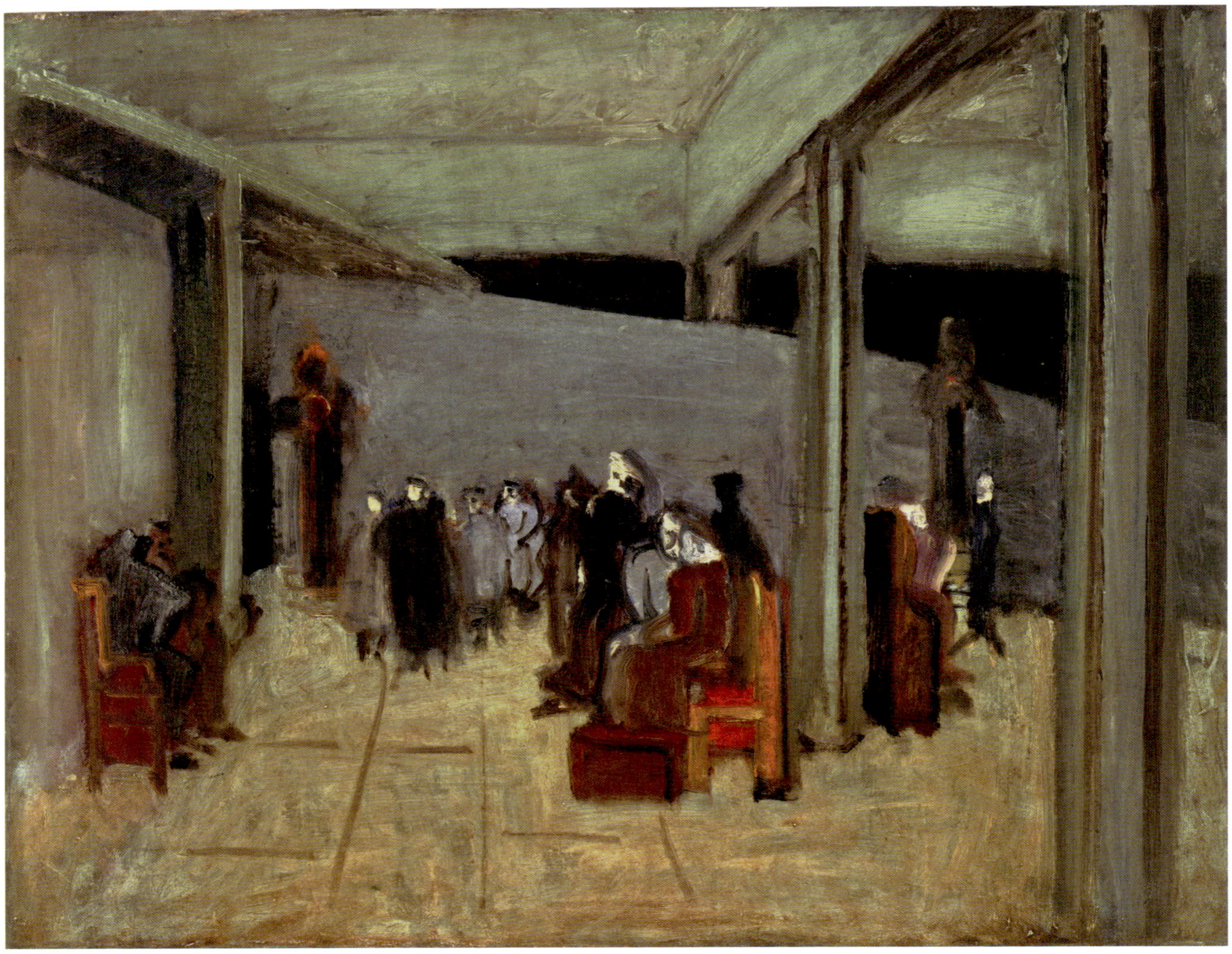

6. *Untitled*, 1935, oil on canvas, 32 3/8 × 42 in. (81.3 × 106.7 cm), Collection of Kate Rothko Prizel and Ilya Prizel (CR 70)

7. *Entrance to Subway*, 1938, oil on canvas, 34 × 46 ¼ in. (86.4 × 117.5 cm), Collection of Kate Rothko Prizel and Ilya Prizel (CR 135)

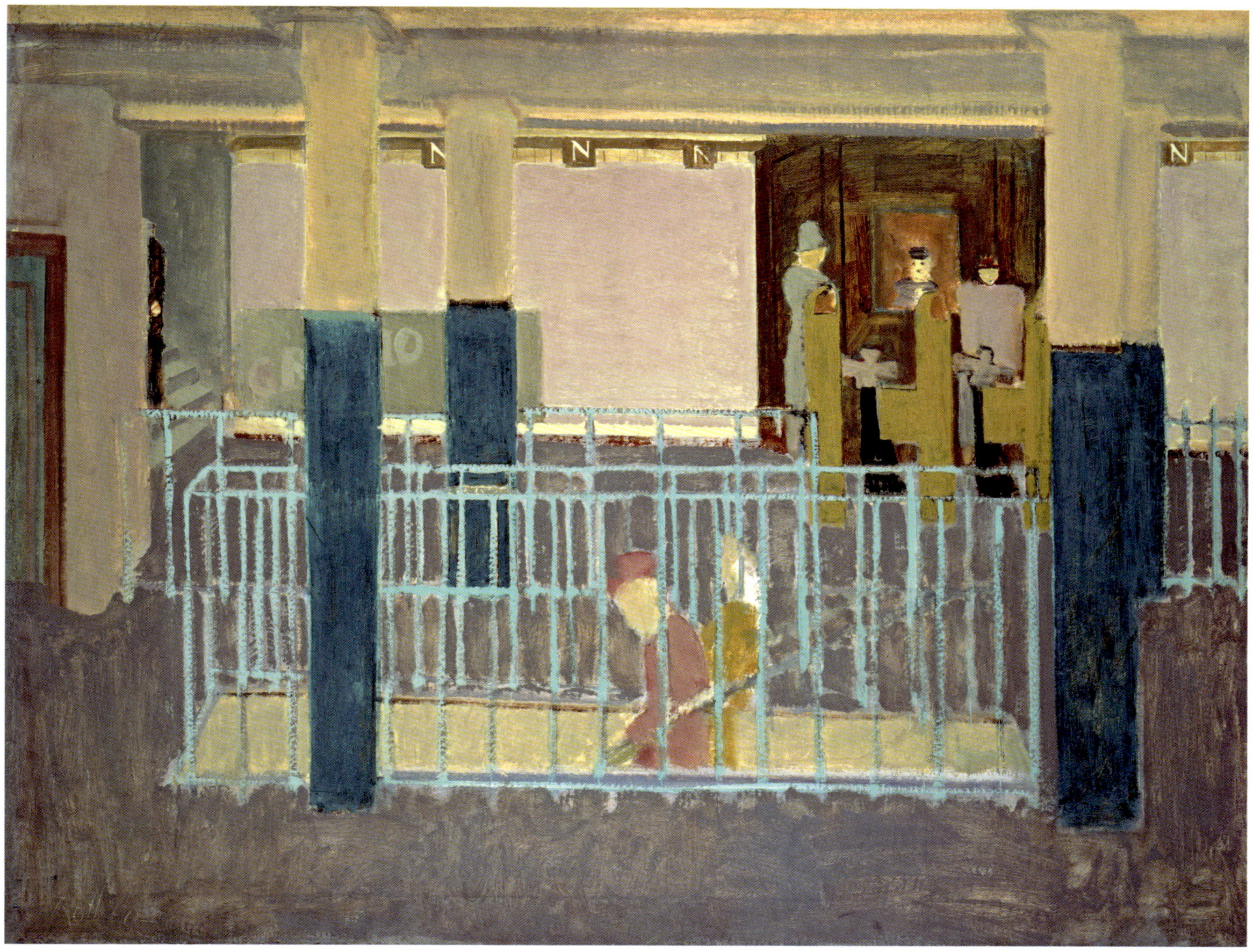

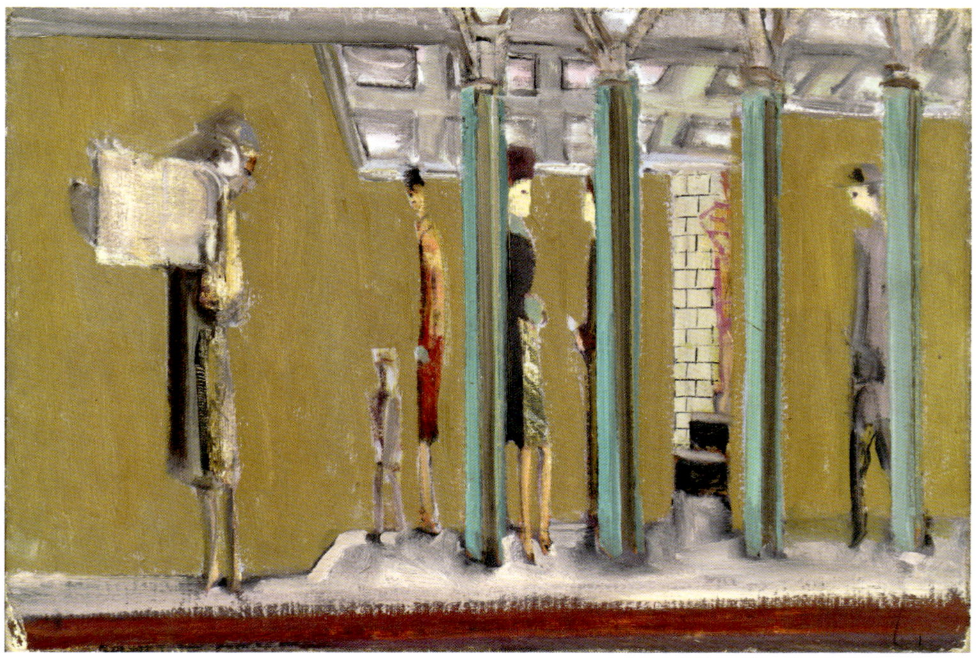

8. *Untitled (subway)*, 1937, oil on canvas, 20 ⅛ × 30 in. (51.1 × 76.2 cm), National Gallery of Art, Washington, D.C. (CR 108)

9. *Interior*, 1936, oil on hardboard, 23 7/8 × 18 1/4 in. (60.6 × 46.4 cm), National Gallery of Art, Washington, D.C. (CR 79). Not exhibited

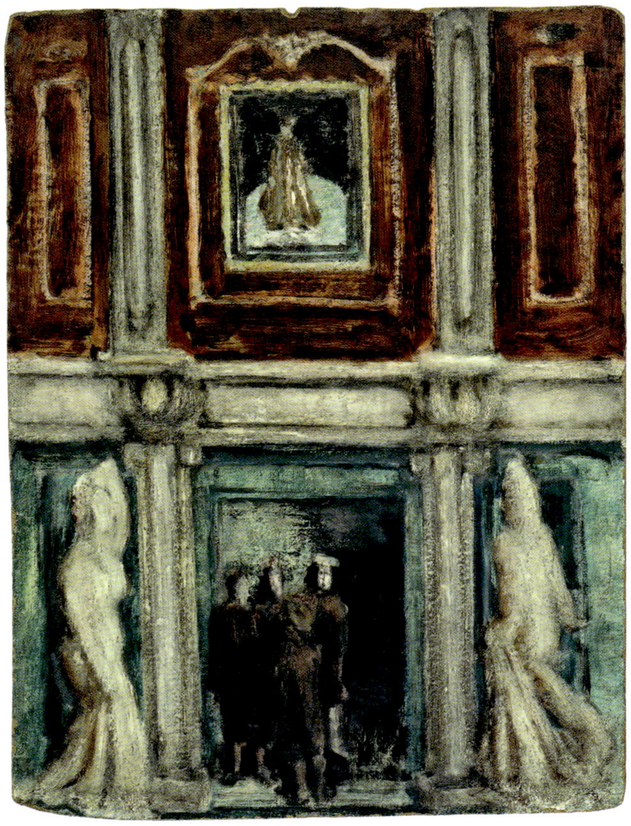

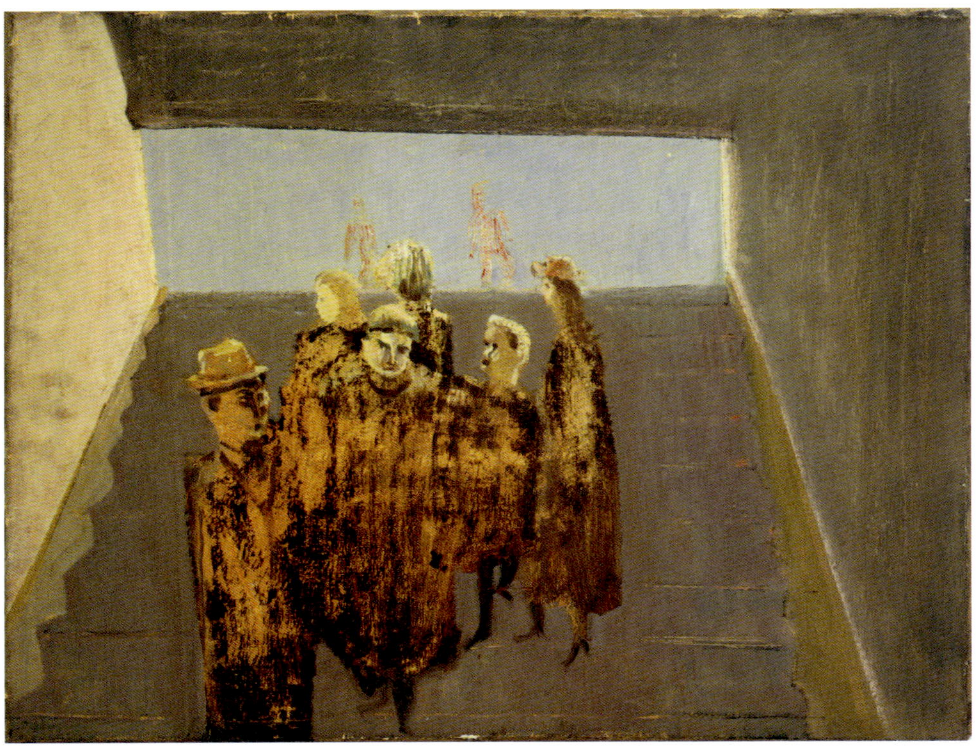

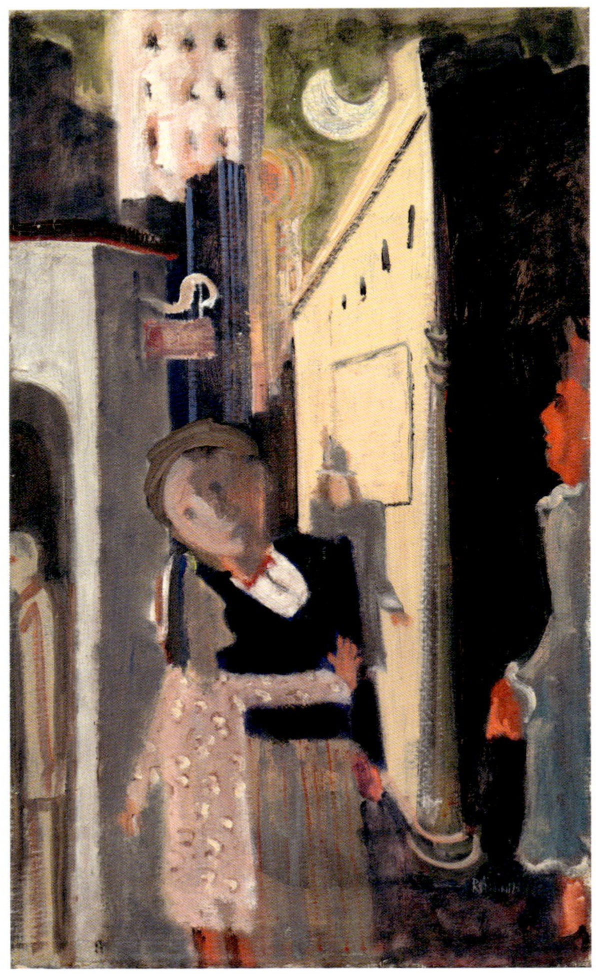

10. *Untitled*, 1939, oil on canvas, 24 × 32 in. (61 × 81.3 cm), Collection of Kate Rothko Prizel and Ilya Prizel (CR 167)
11. *Street Scene*, 1936 / 1937, oil on canvas, 36 × 21 15/16 in. (91.5 × 55.8 cm), National Gallery of Art, Washington, D.C. (CR 96)

12. *Underground Fantasy*, c. 1940, oil on canvas, 34 3/8 × 46 9/16 in. (87.3 × 118.2 cm), National Gallery of Art, Washington, D.C. (CR 174)

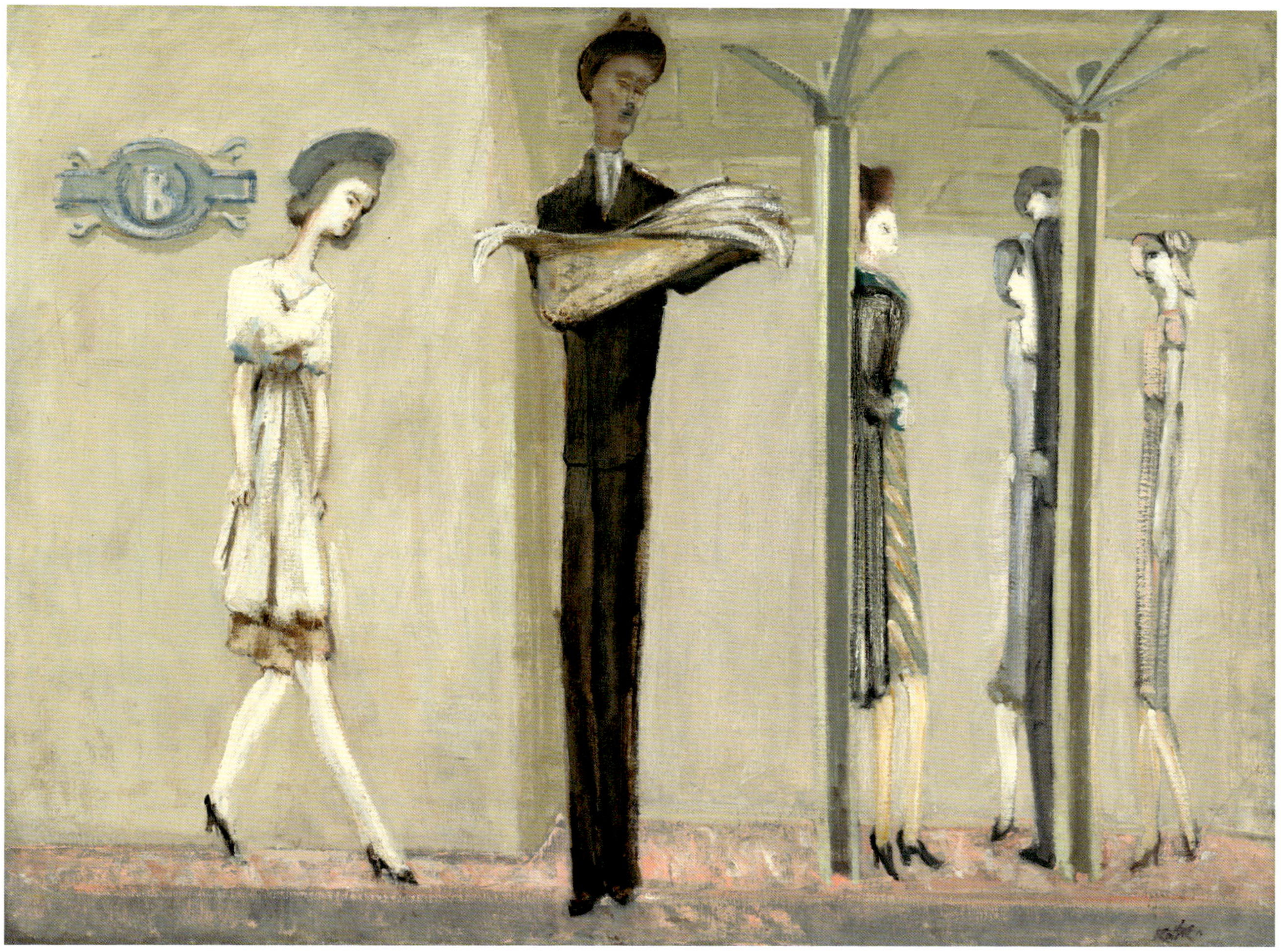

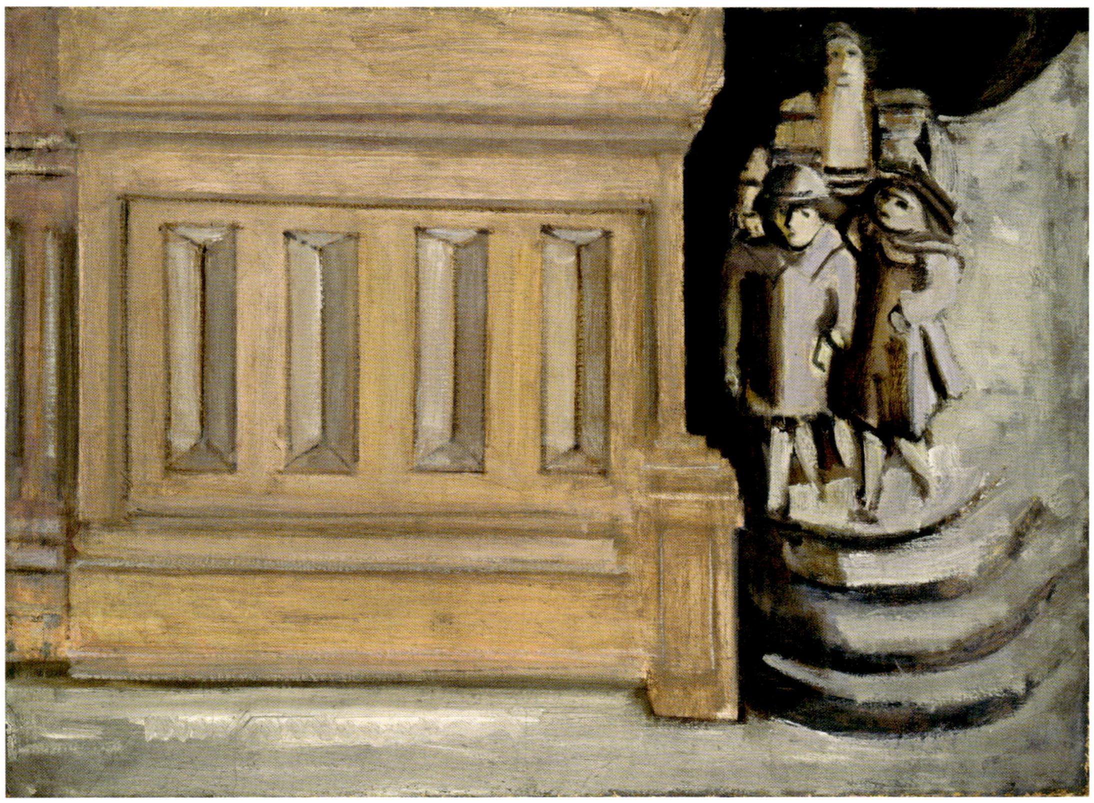

13. *Street Scene*, c. 1937, oil on canvas, 28 15/16 × 39 15/16 in. (73.5 × 101.4 cm), National Gallery of Art, Washington, D.C. (CR 113)

14. *Untitled*, 1938 / 1939, oil on canvas, 40 × 30 in. (101.6 × 76.2 cm), Collection of Christopher Rothko (CR 163)
15. *Portrait*, 1939, oil on canvas, 39 7⁄8 × 30 1⁄4 in. (101.6 × 76.5 cm), Collection of Christopher Rothko (CR 164)

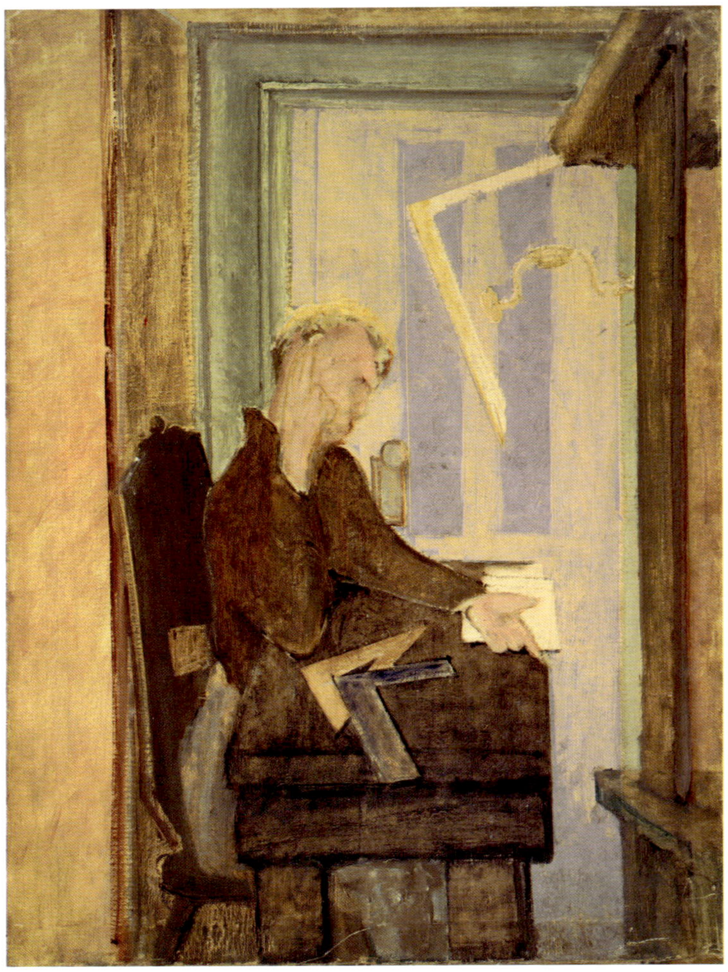

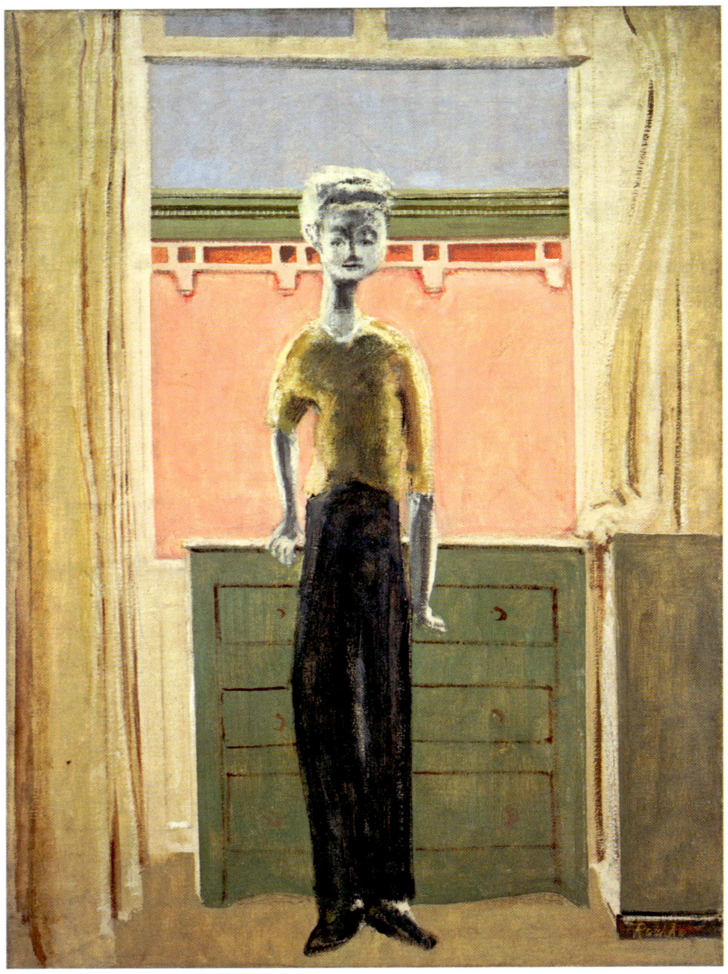

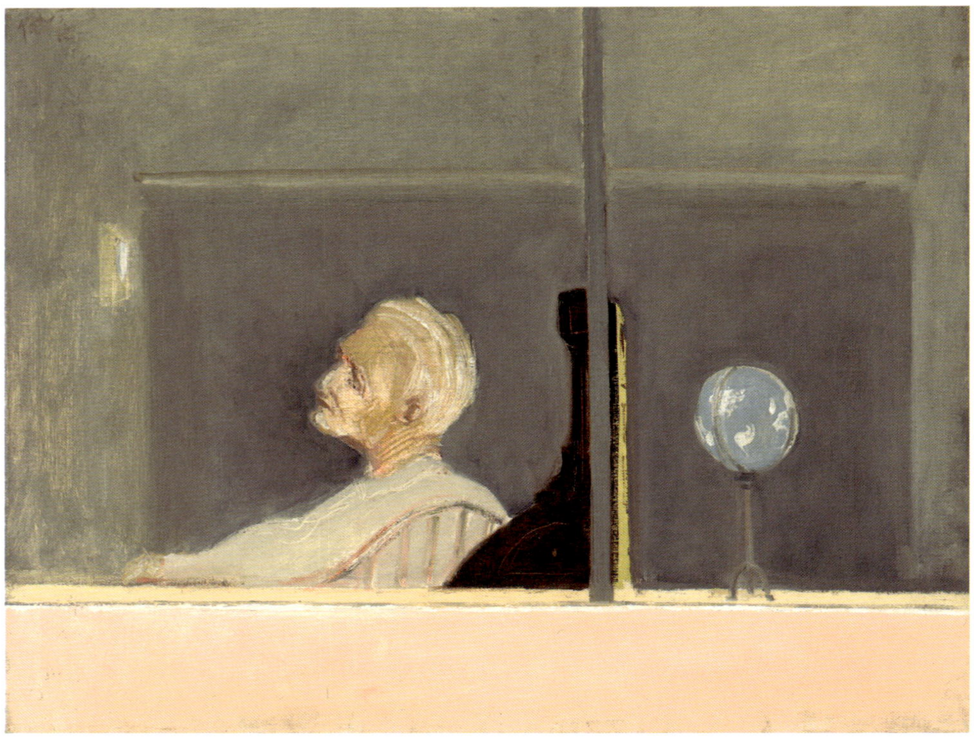

16. *Contemplation*, 1937 / 1938, oil on canvas, 24 1⁄8 × 32 in. (61.4 × 81.3 cm), National Gallery of Art, Washington, D.C. (CR 116)

17. *Untitled*, 1938, oil on canvas, 50 × 37 in. (127 × 94 cm), private collection (CR 144)
18. *Nude*, 1938–1939, oil on canvas, 36 × 24 in. (91.4 × 61 cm), private collection (CR 161)

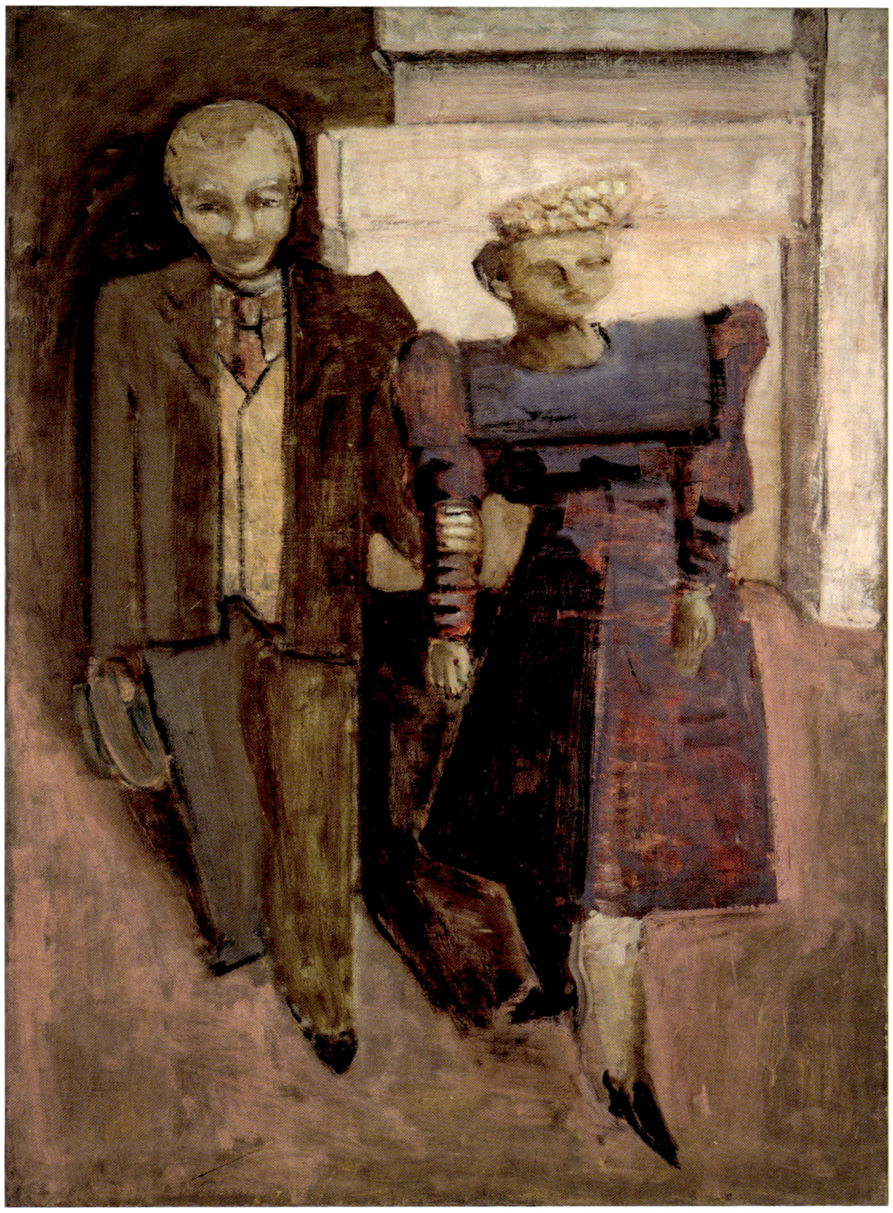

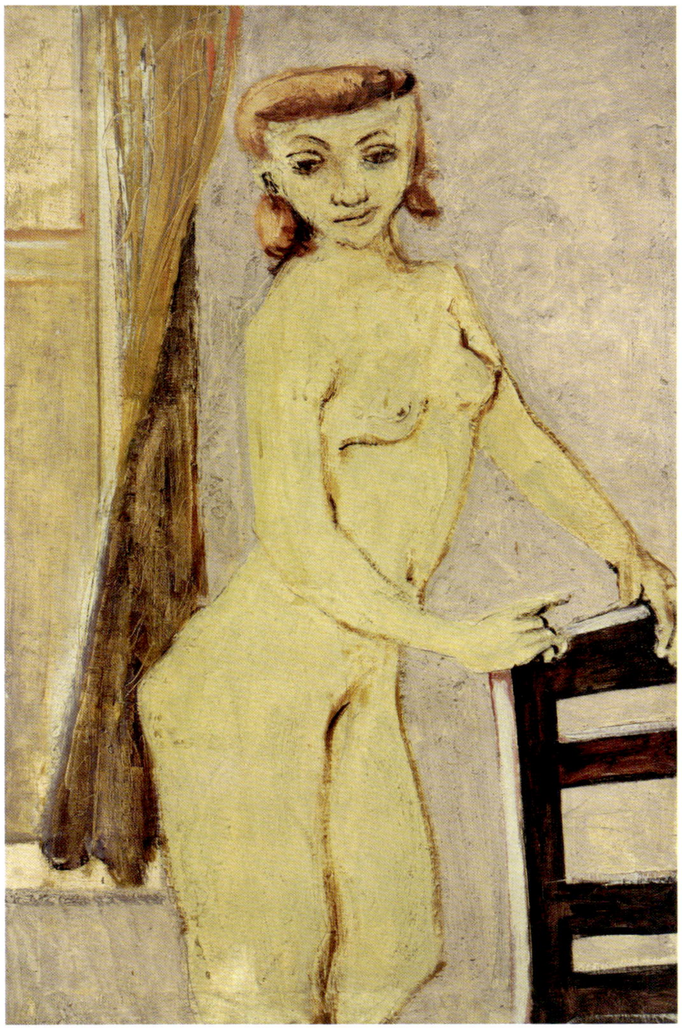

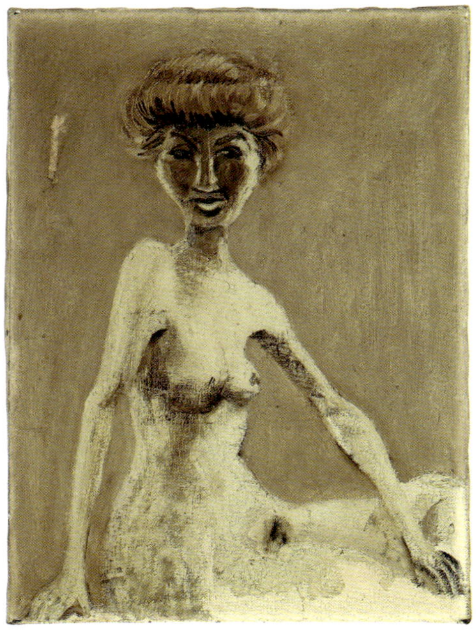

19. *Untitled*, 1939, oil on canvas, 23 5/8 × 18 in. (60.6 × 46 cm), private collection (CR 171)

20. *Untitled*, 1941–42, oil on canvas, 35 13/16 × 23 7/8 in. (91 × 60.6 cm), National Gallery of Art, Washington, D.C. (CR 192)
21. *Untitled*, 1940–41, oil on canvas, 36 1/16 × 28 1/16 in (91.6 × 71.3 cm), National Gallery of Art, Washington, D.C. (CR 181)

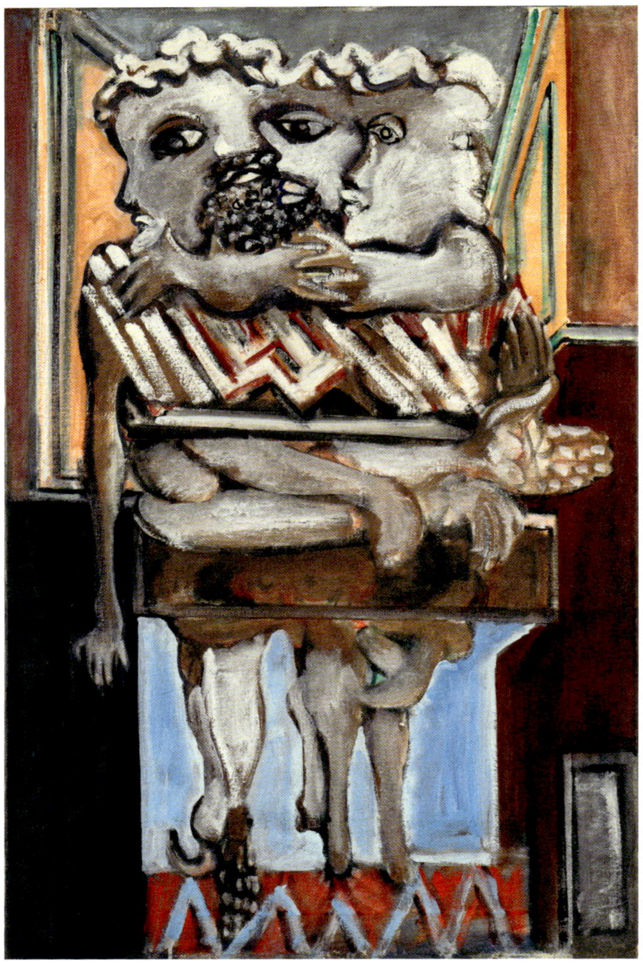

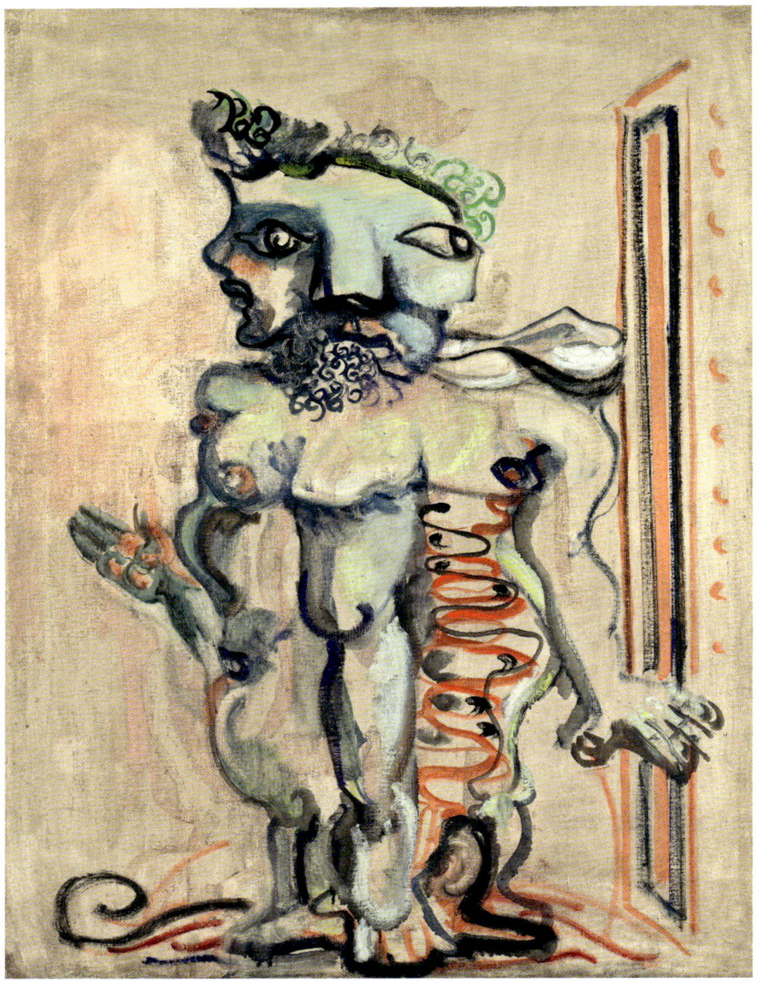

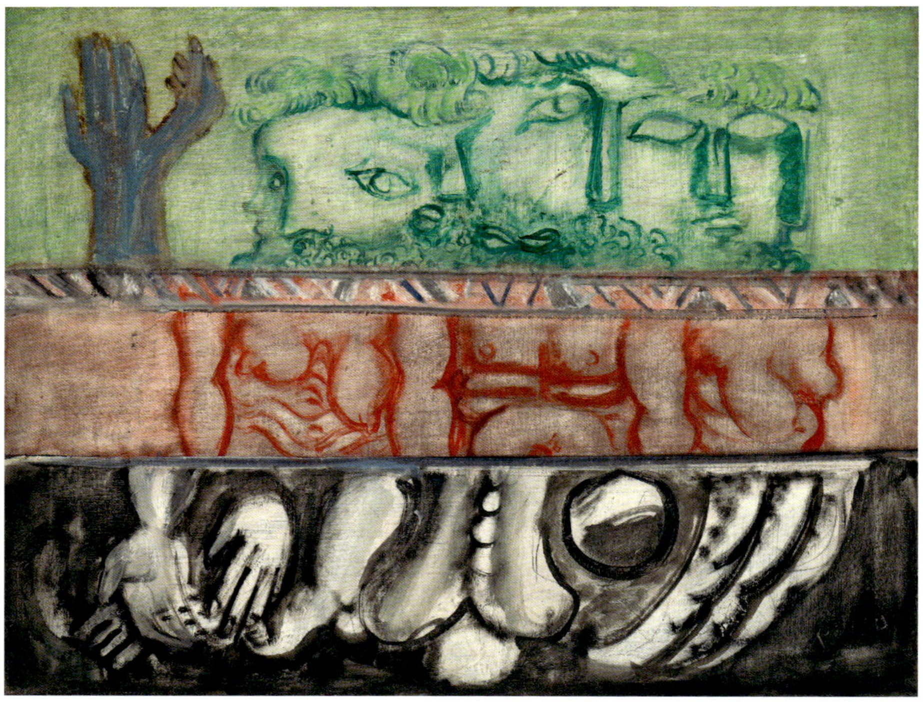

22. *Untitled*, 1941–42, oil on canvas, 24 × 31 7/8 in. (61 × 81 cm), National Gallery of Art, Washington, D.C. (CR 189)

23. *Antigone*, 1939–40, oil and charcoal on canvas, 34 × 45 ¾ in. (86.4 × 116.2 cm), National Gallery of Art, Washington, D.C. (CR 178)

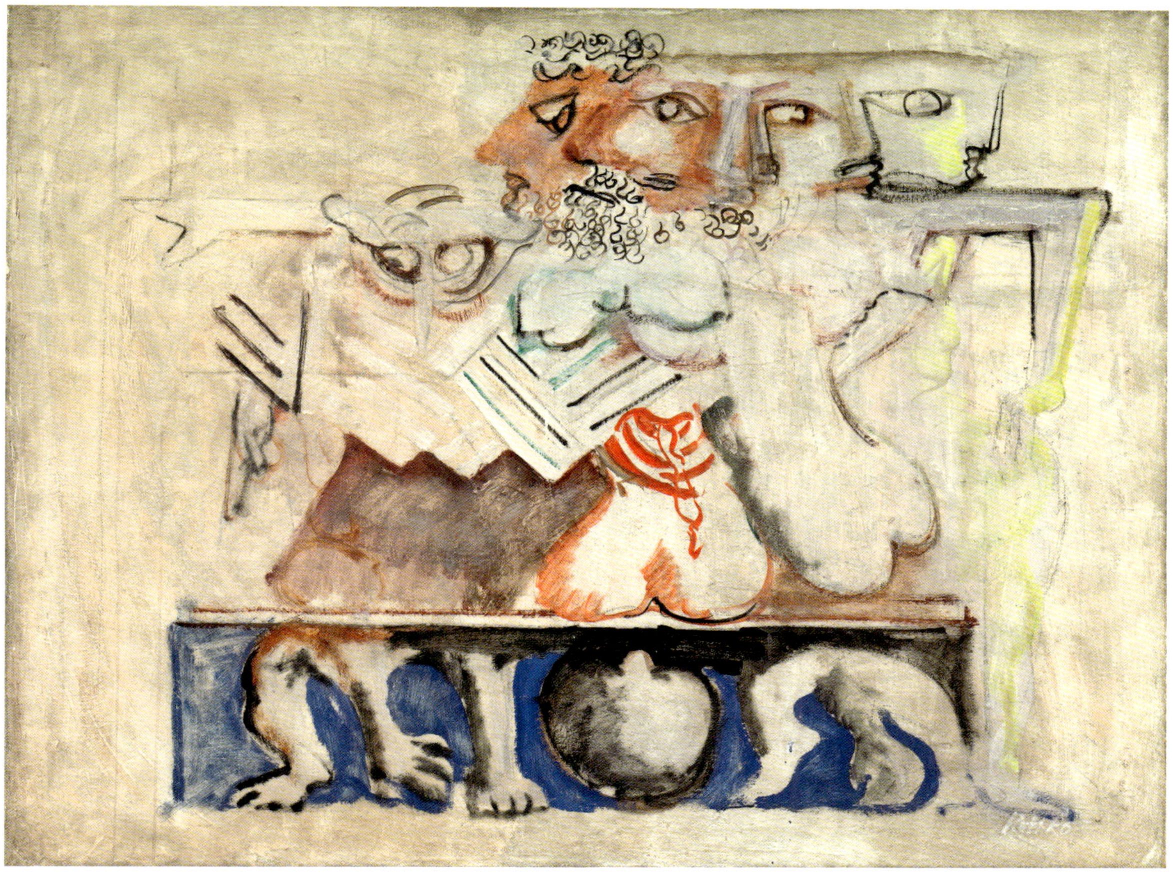

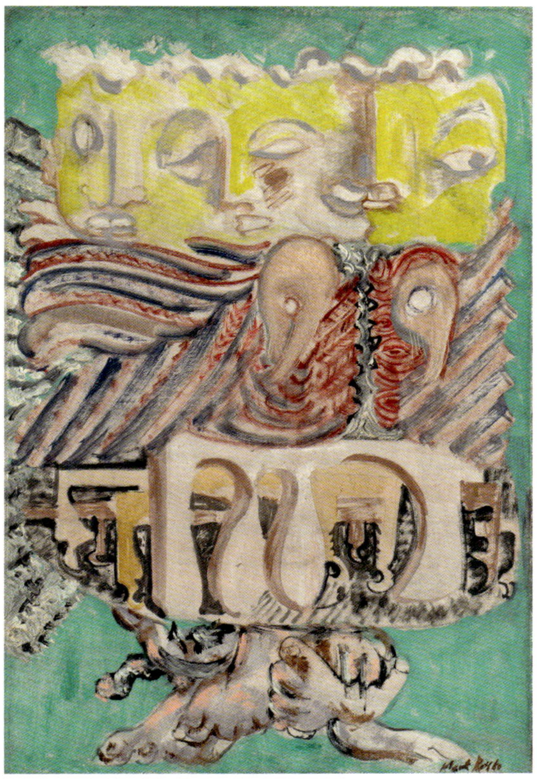

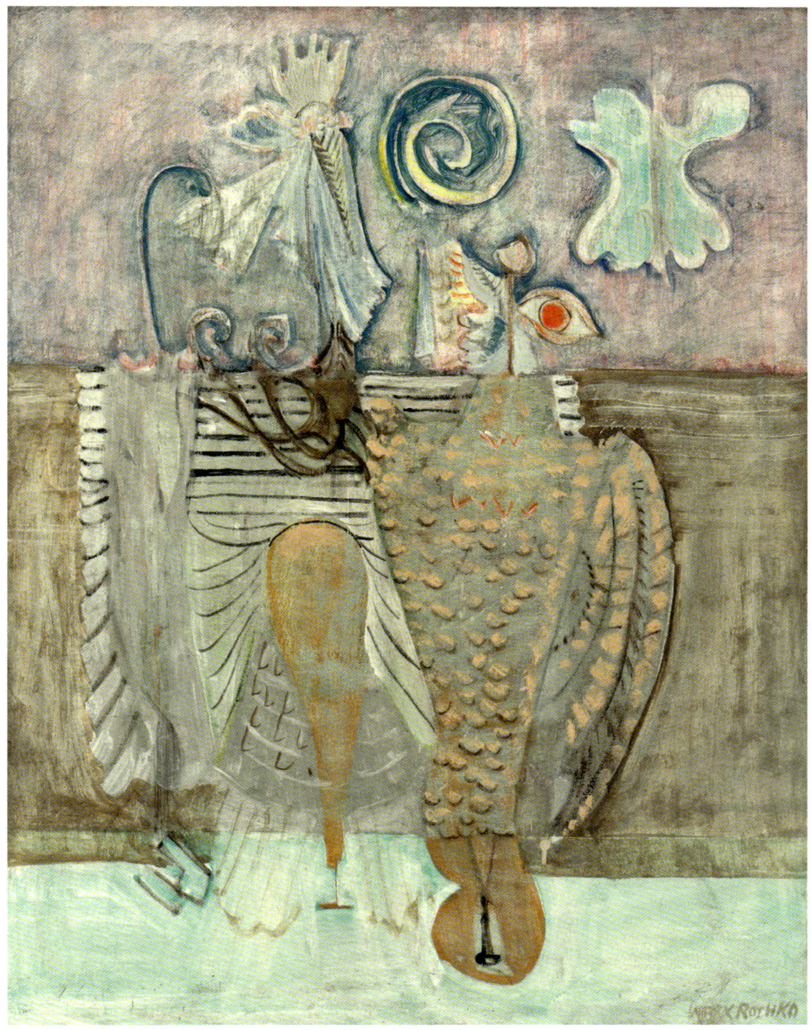

24. *The Omen of the Eagle*, 1942, oil and graphite on canvas, 25 ¾ × 17 ¾ in. (65.4 × 45.1 cm), National Gallery of Art, Washington, D.C. (CR 206)
25. *Hierarchical Birds*, 1944, oil on canvas, 39 ⅝ × 31 ¹¹⁄₁₆ in. (100.7 × 80.5 cm), National Gallery of Art, Washington, D.C. (CR 239)

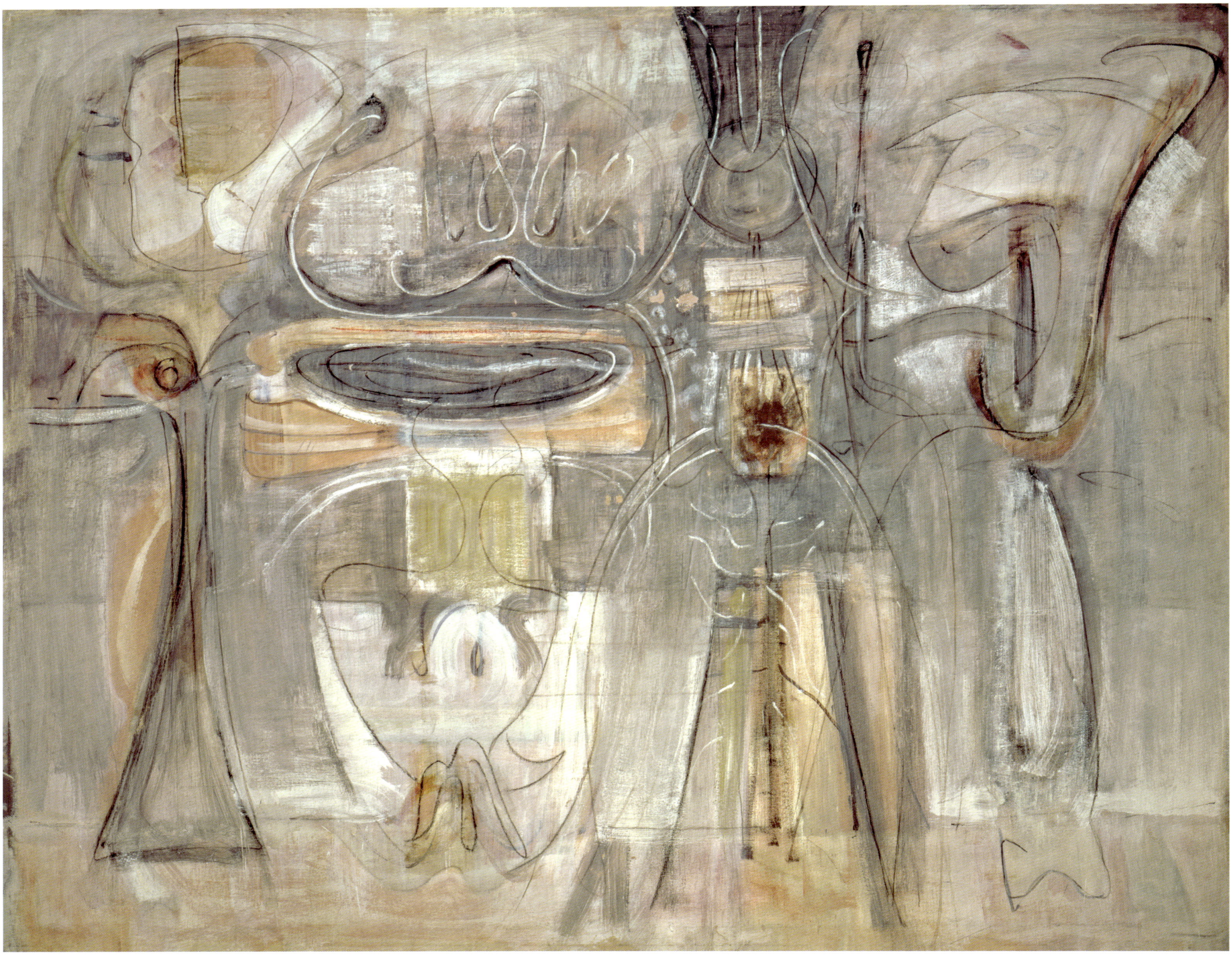

26. *Rites of Lilith*, 1945, oil on canvas, 82 × 106 ⅝ in. (208.3 × 20.8 cm), private collection (CR 266)

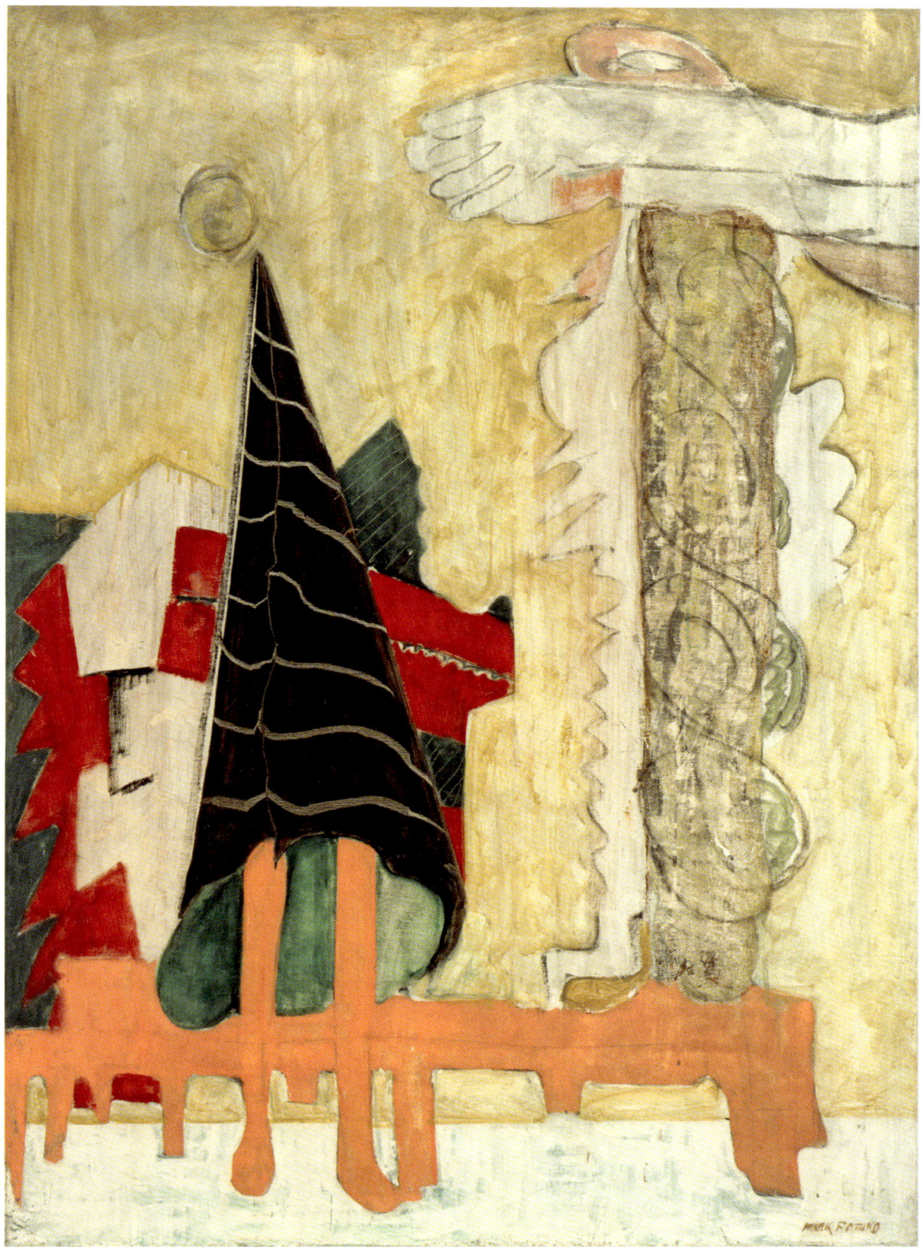

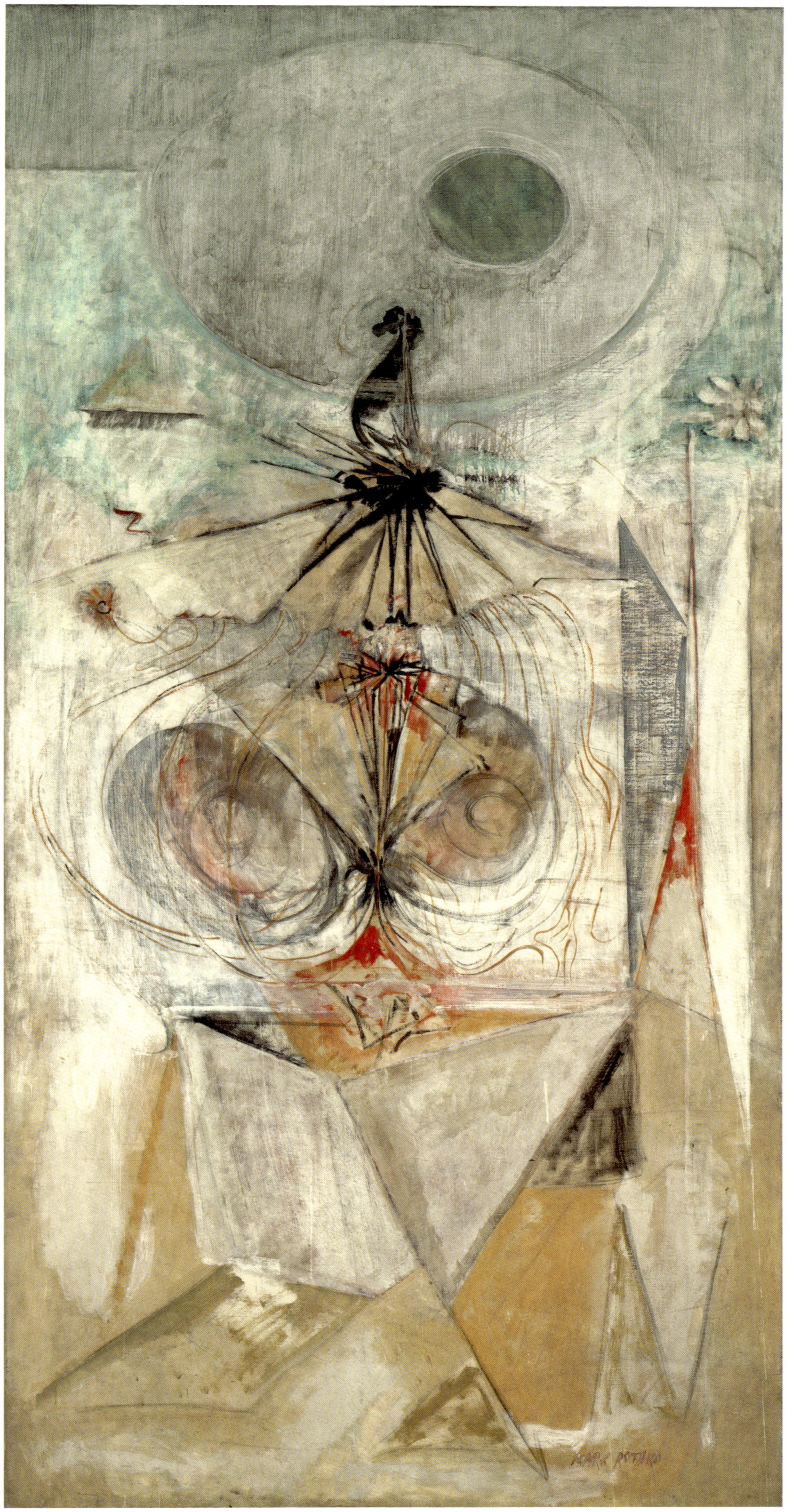

27. *Sacrifice of Iphigenia*, 1942, oil and graphite on canvas, 50 × 36 ⅞ in. (127 × 93.7 cm), private collection (CR 210)
28. *Tiresias*, 1944, oil on canvas, 79 ⅞ × 39 ⅞ in. (202.6 × 101.3 cm), Collection of Christopher Rothko (CR 247)

29. *Gethsemane*, 1944, oil and charcoal on canvas, 54 3/5 × 35 1/2 in. (138.1 × 90.2 cm), Collection of Kate Rothko Prizel and Ilya Prizel (CR 244)
30. *Sea Fantasy*, 1946, oil on canvas, 44 × 36 1/8 in. (111.8 × 91.8 cm), National Gallery of Art, Washington, D.C. (CR 298)

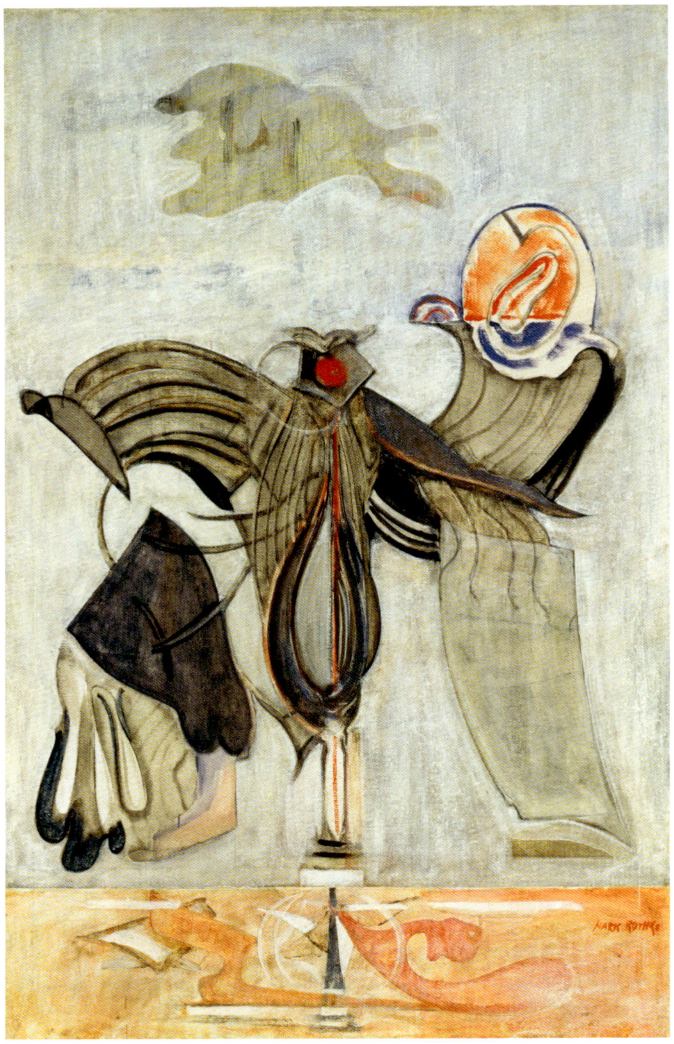

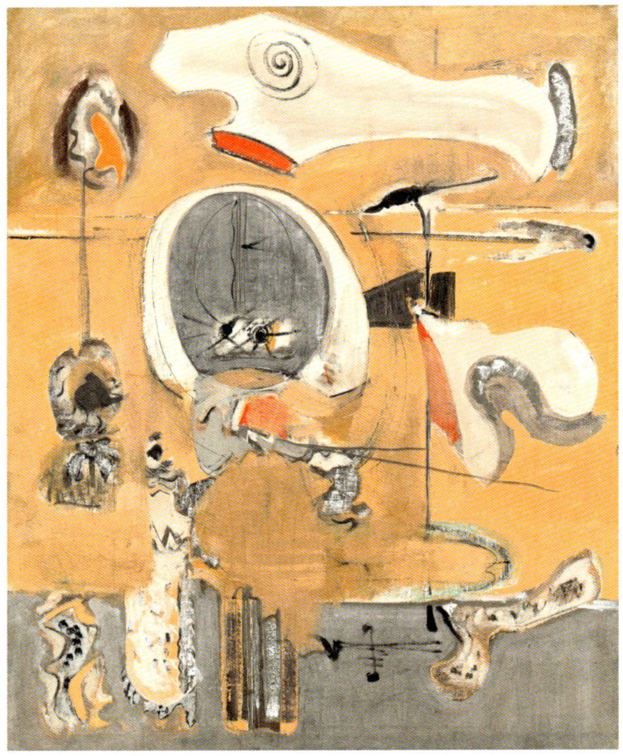

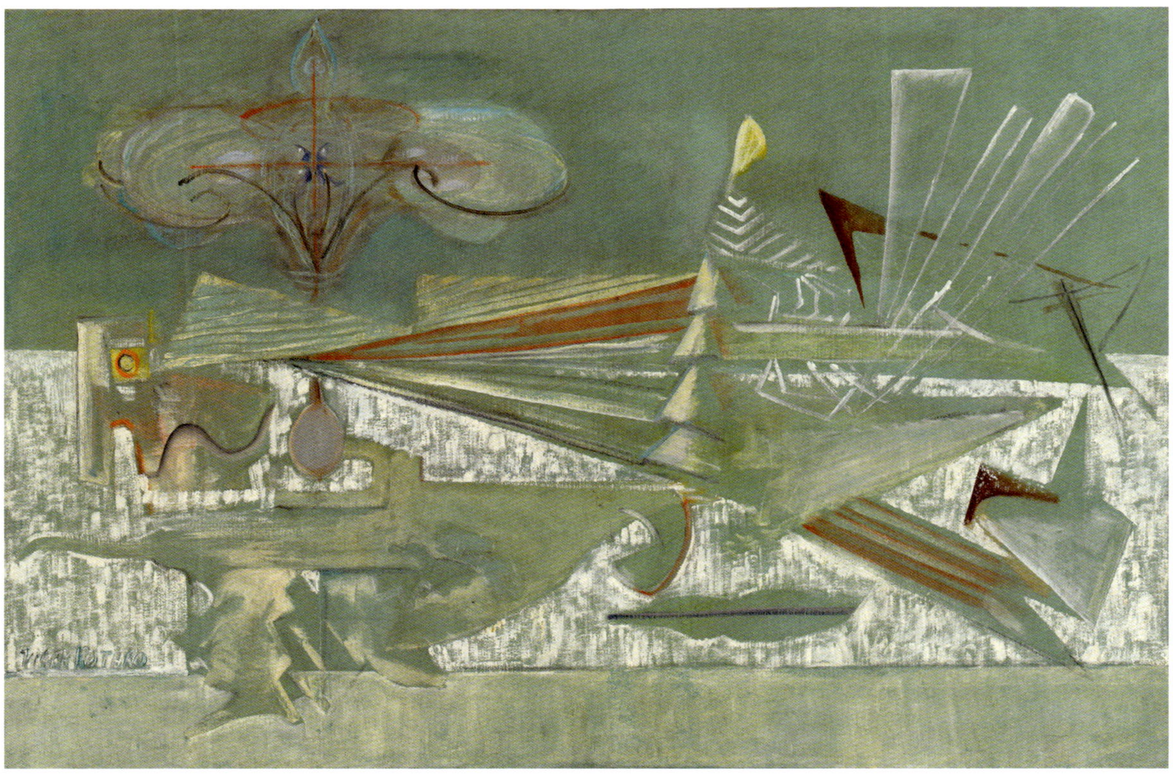

31. *Agitation of the Archaic*, 1944, oil on canvas, 35 5/16 × 54 1/4 in. (89.9 × 137.8 cm), Whitney Museum of Art, New York (CR 240)

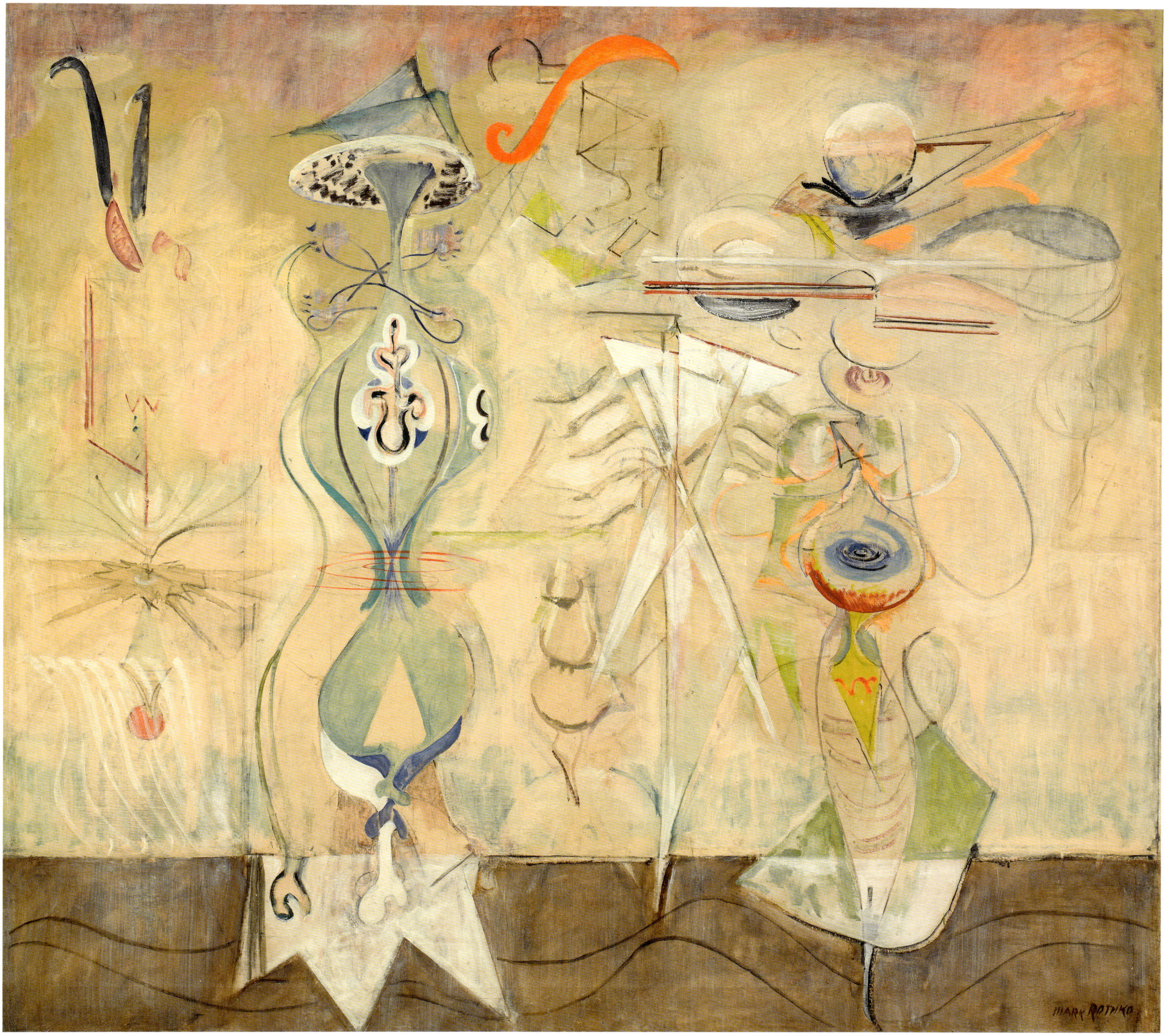

32. *Slow Swirl at the Edge of the Sea*, 1944, oil on canvas, 75 ¼ × 85 in. (191.1 × 215.9 cm), Museum of Modern Art, New York (CR 248)

33. *Untitled*, 1946, oil on canvas, 54 ⅛ × 27 ⅖ in. (137.5 × 69.5 cm), Collection of Kate Rothko Prizel and Ilya Prizel (CR 317)

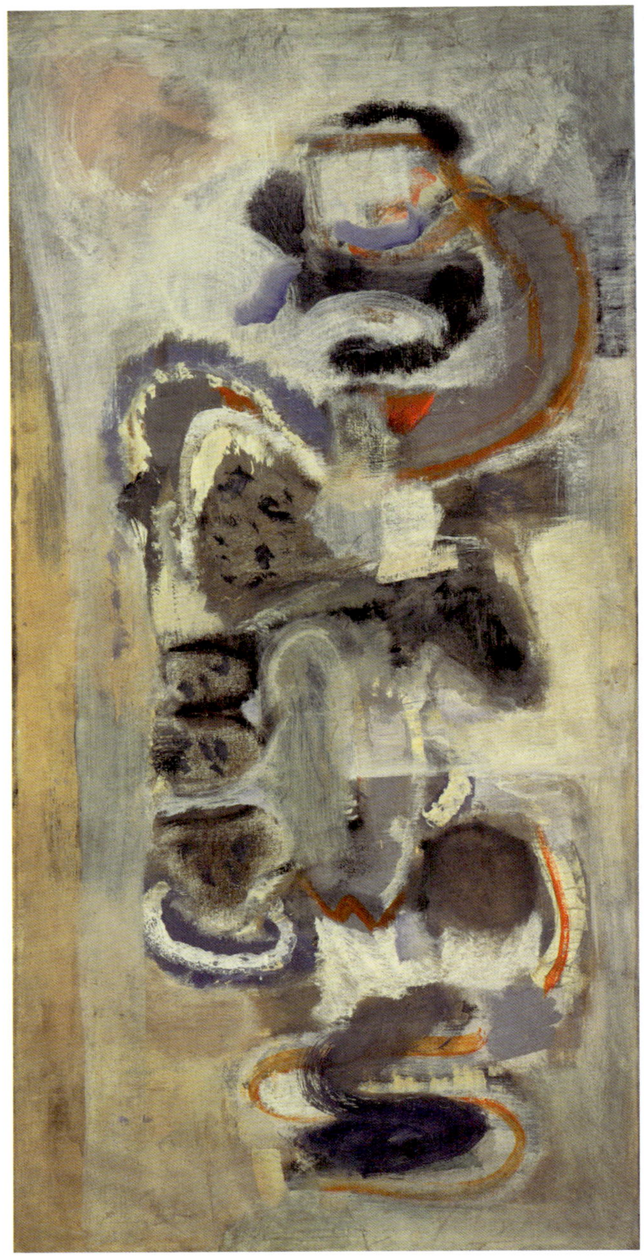

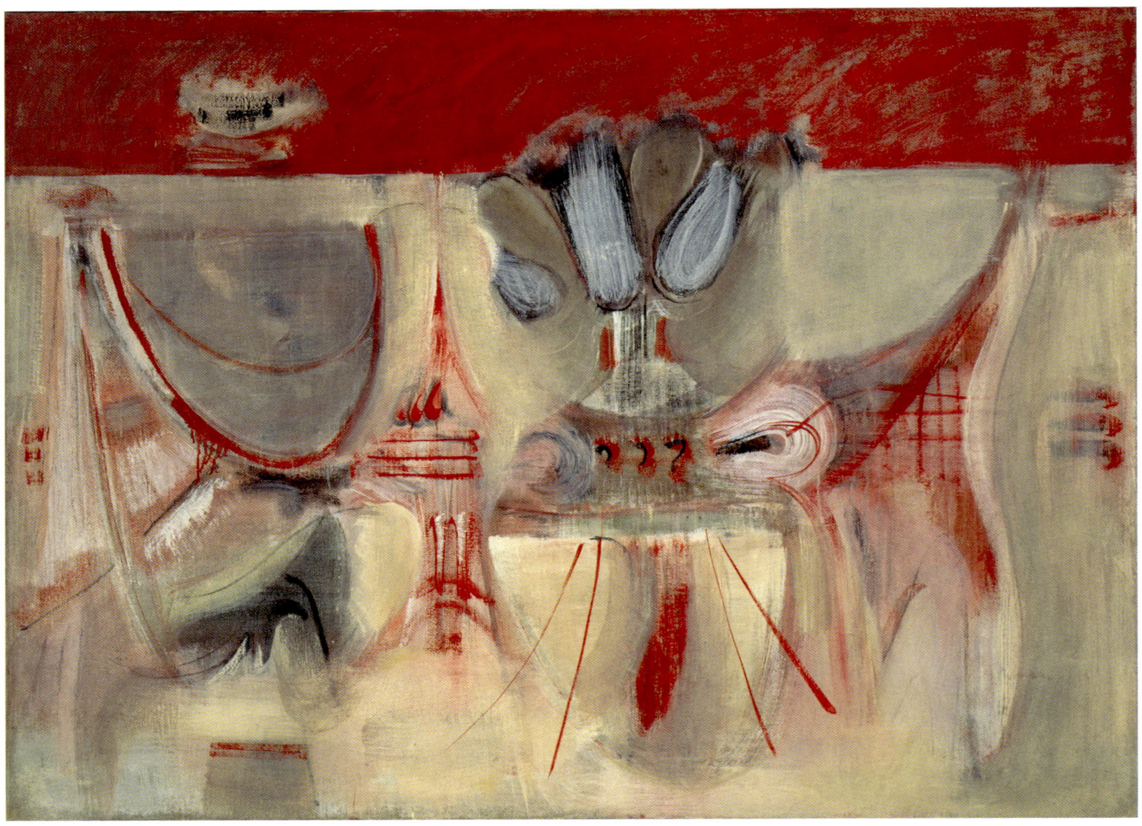

34. *Aeolian Harp / No. 7*, 1946, oil on canvas, 38 ½ × 54 ⅜ in. (98.4 × 138.1 cm), Collection of Christopher Rothko (CR 308)

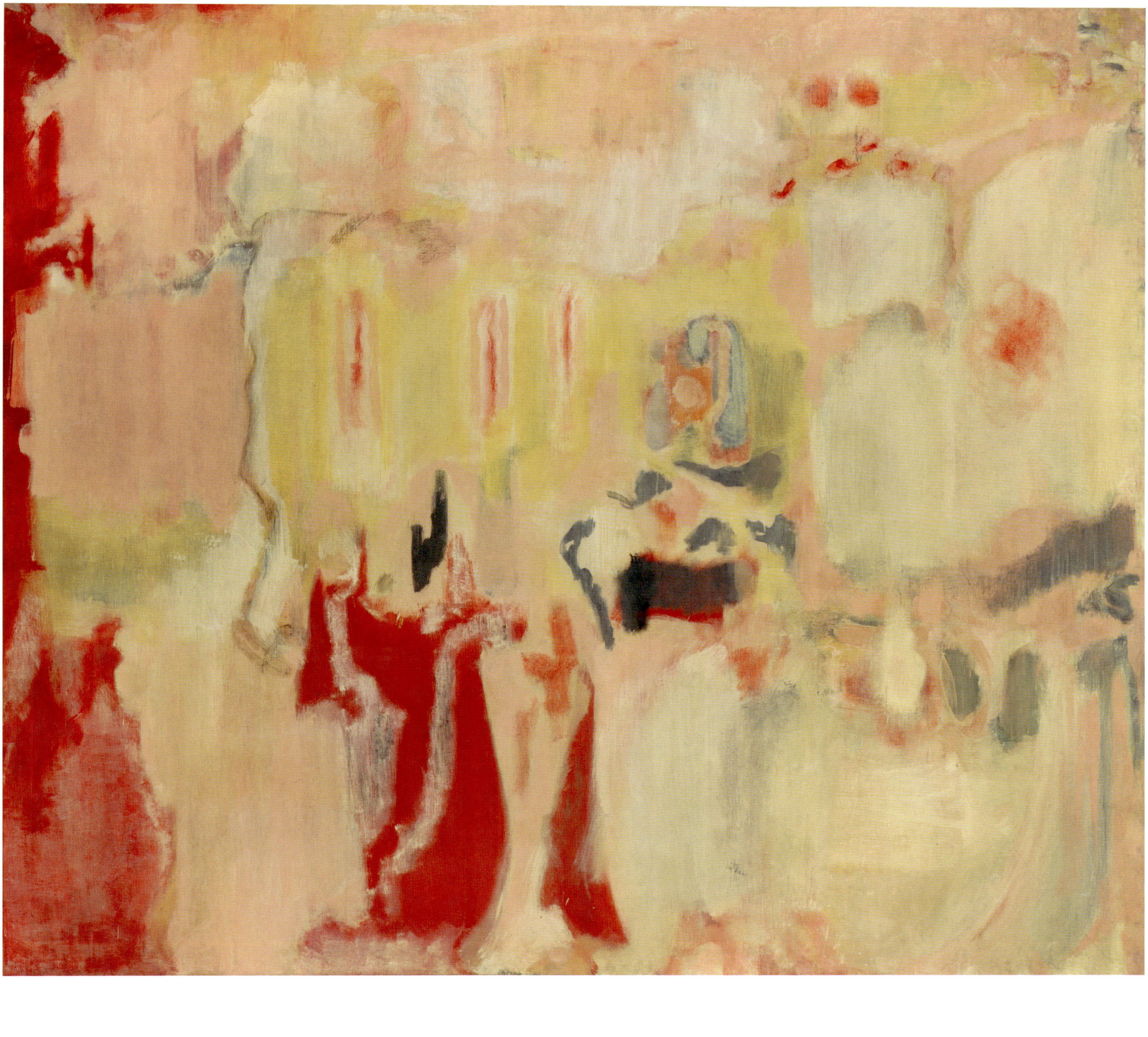

35. *Untitled*, 1946, oil on canvas, 89 ½ × 105 ⅞ in. (228 × 268.6 cm), private collection (CR 323)

36. *Untitled: Abstraction Number 11*, 1947, oil on canvas, 39 ½ × 38 ½ in. (100.3 × 98.1 cm), Munson Museum, Utica, NY (CR 334)

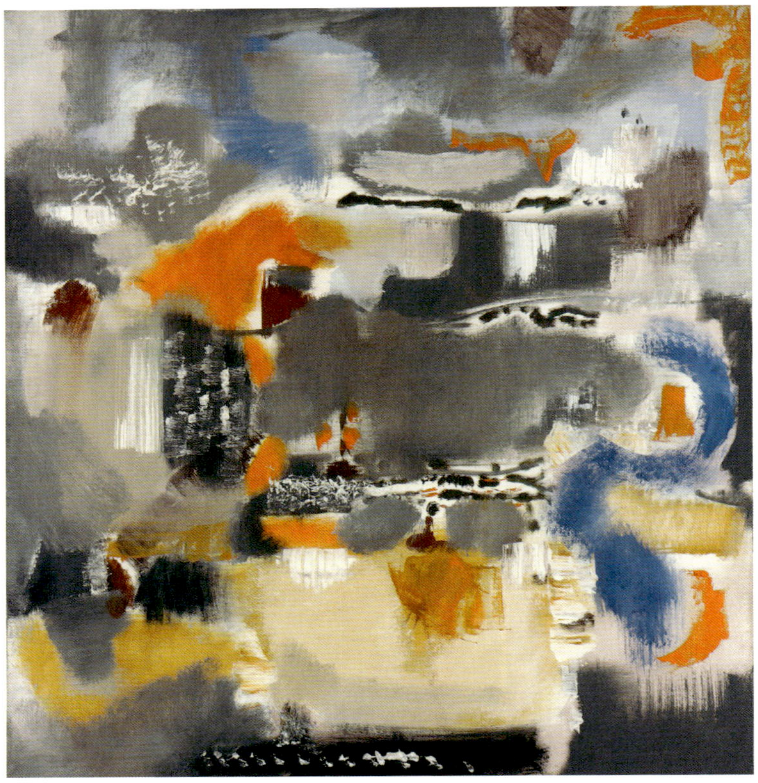

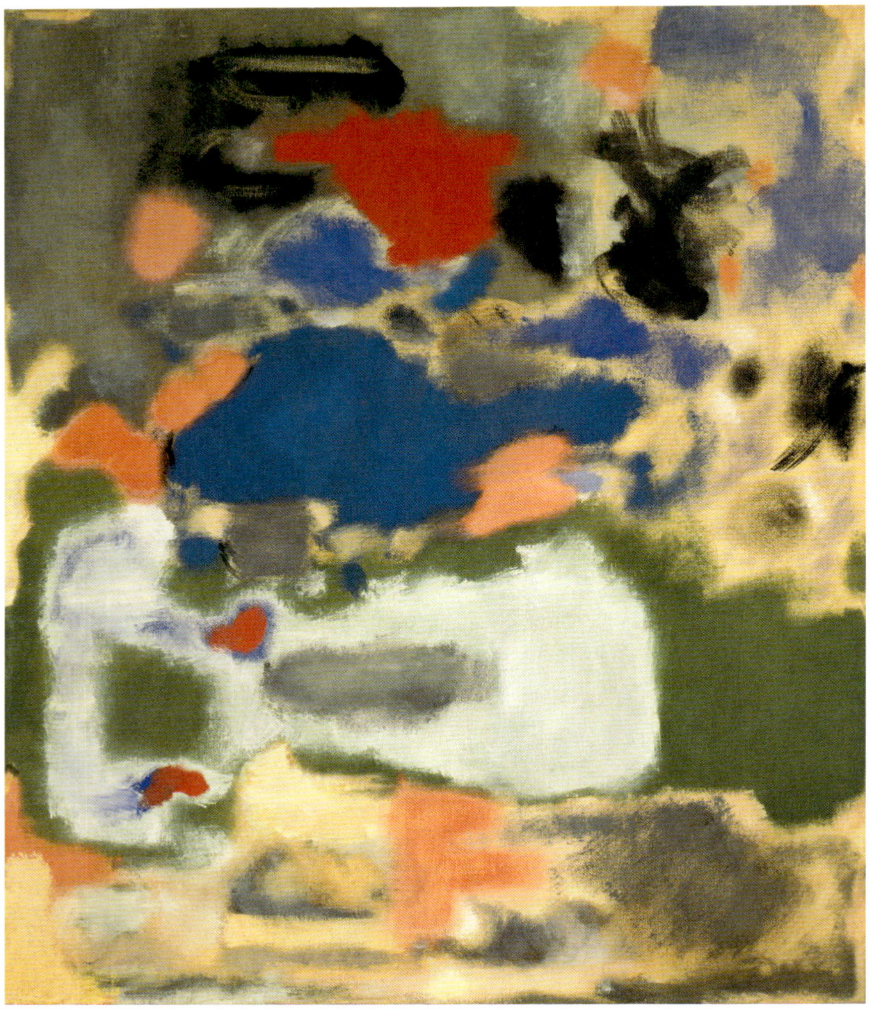

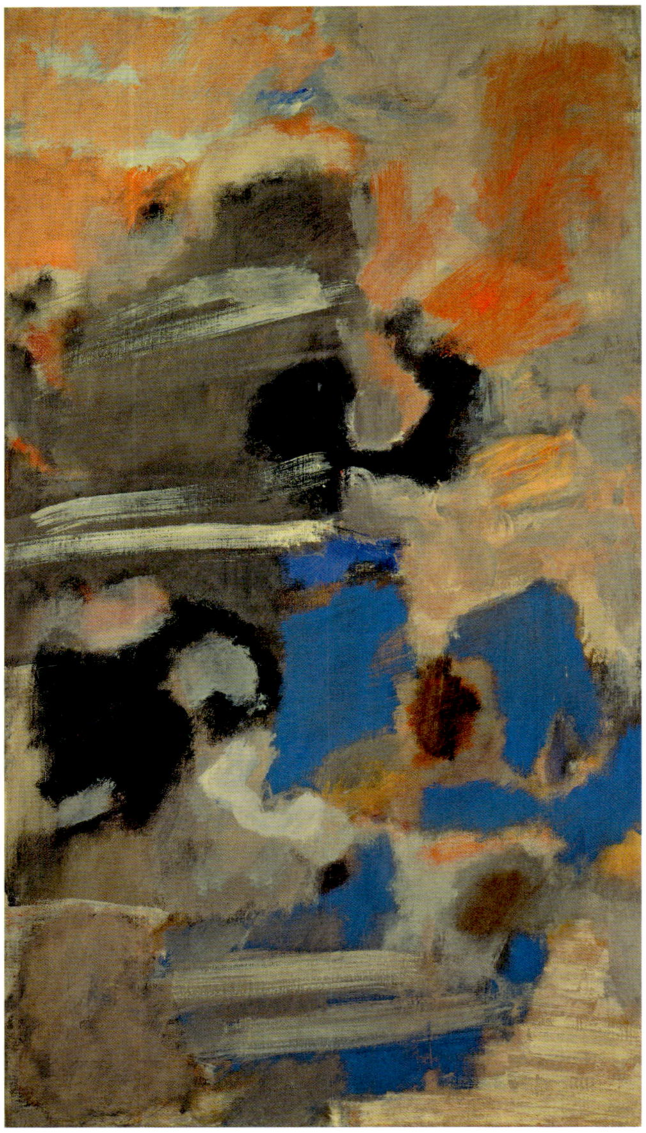

37. *Untitled*, 1948, oil on canvas, 50 ¼ × 43 ¼ in. (127.6 × 109.9 cm), Collection of Kate Rothko Prizel and Ilya Prizel (CR 370)
38. *Untitled*, 1948, oil on canvas, 53 ⅞ × 30 ⅞ in. (136.8 × 78.4 cm), private collection (CR 374)

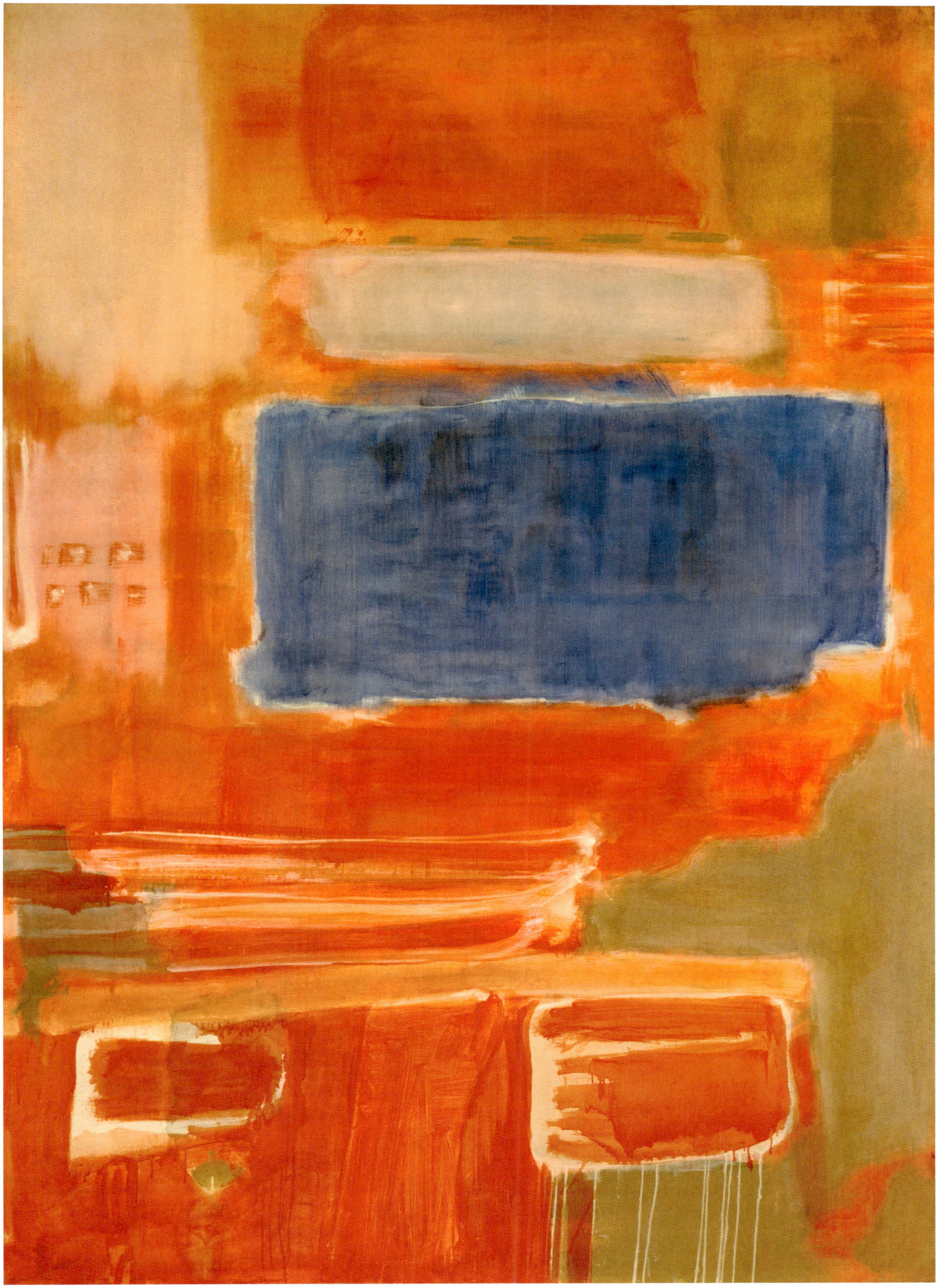

39. *Untitled (Multiform)*, 1948, oil on canvas, 89 × 65 in. (226.1 × 165.1 cm), Collection of Kate Rothko Prizel and Ilya Prizel (CR 391)

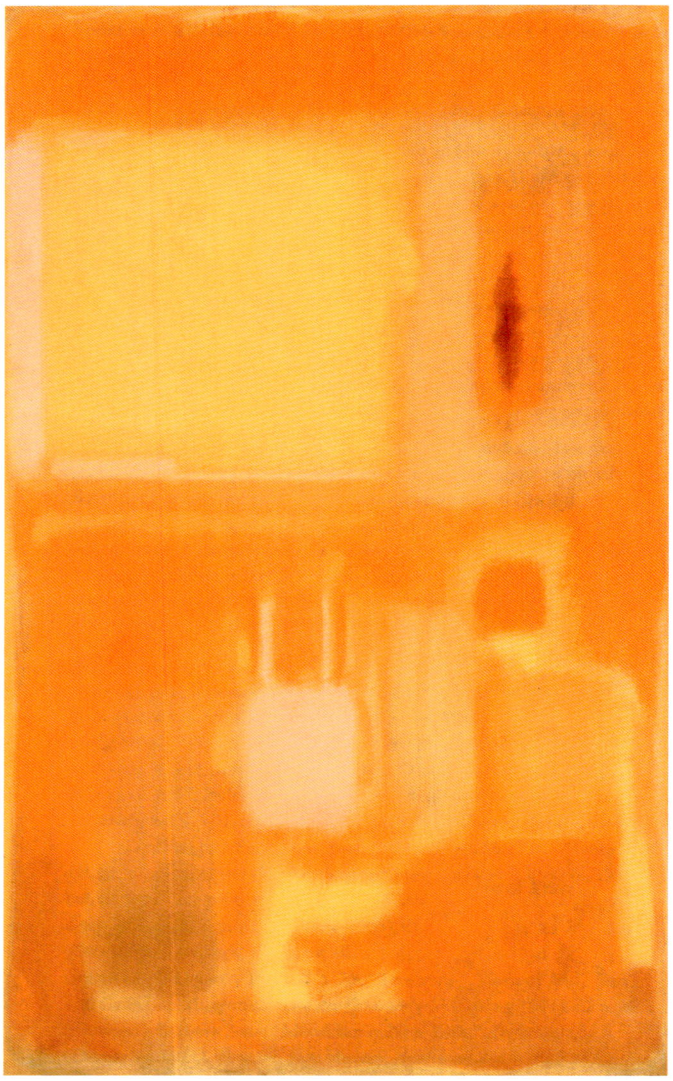

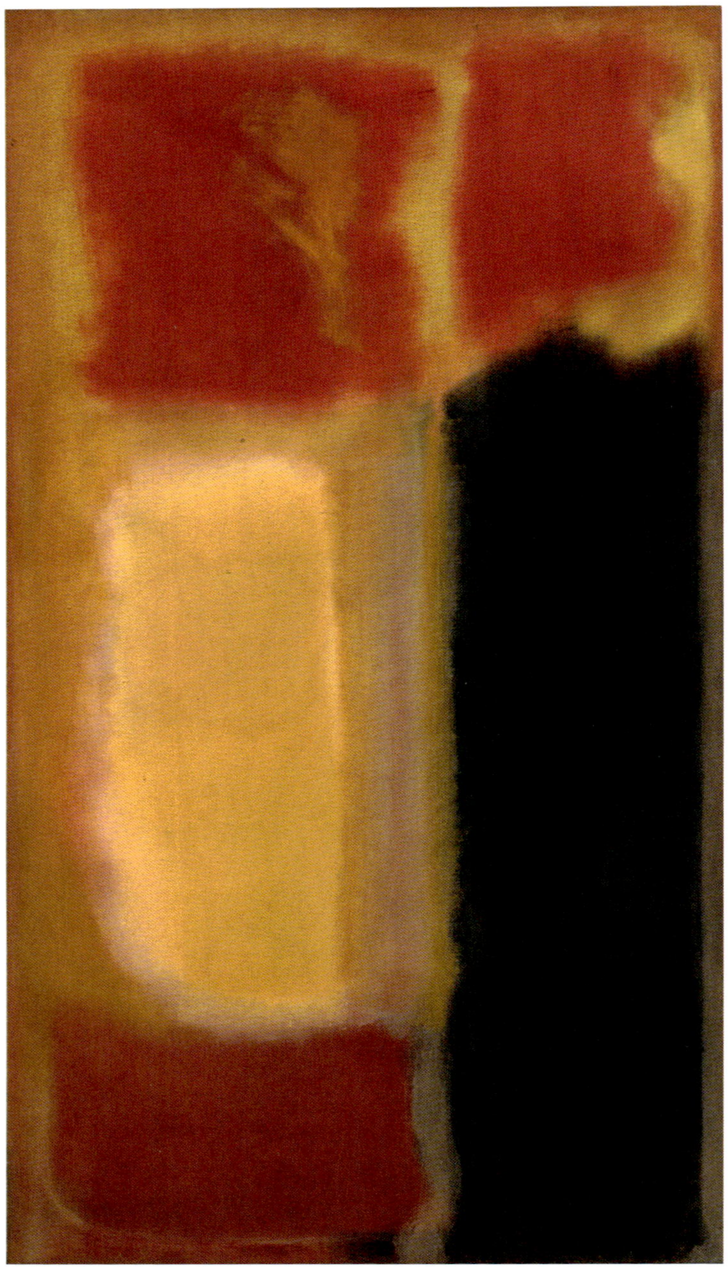

40. *No. 17/No. 15*, 1949, oil on canvas, 51 ⅞ × 29 ⅛ in. (131.8 × 74 cm), National Gallery of Art, Washington, D.C. (CR 401)
41. *No. 14 (Golden Composition)*, 1949, oil on canvas, 66 × 41 ⅛ in. (167.6 × 104.5 cm), Private Collection, Torino (CR 398)

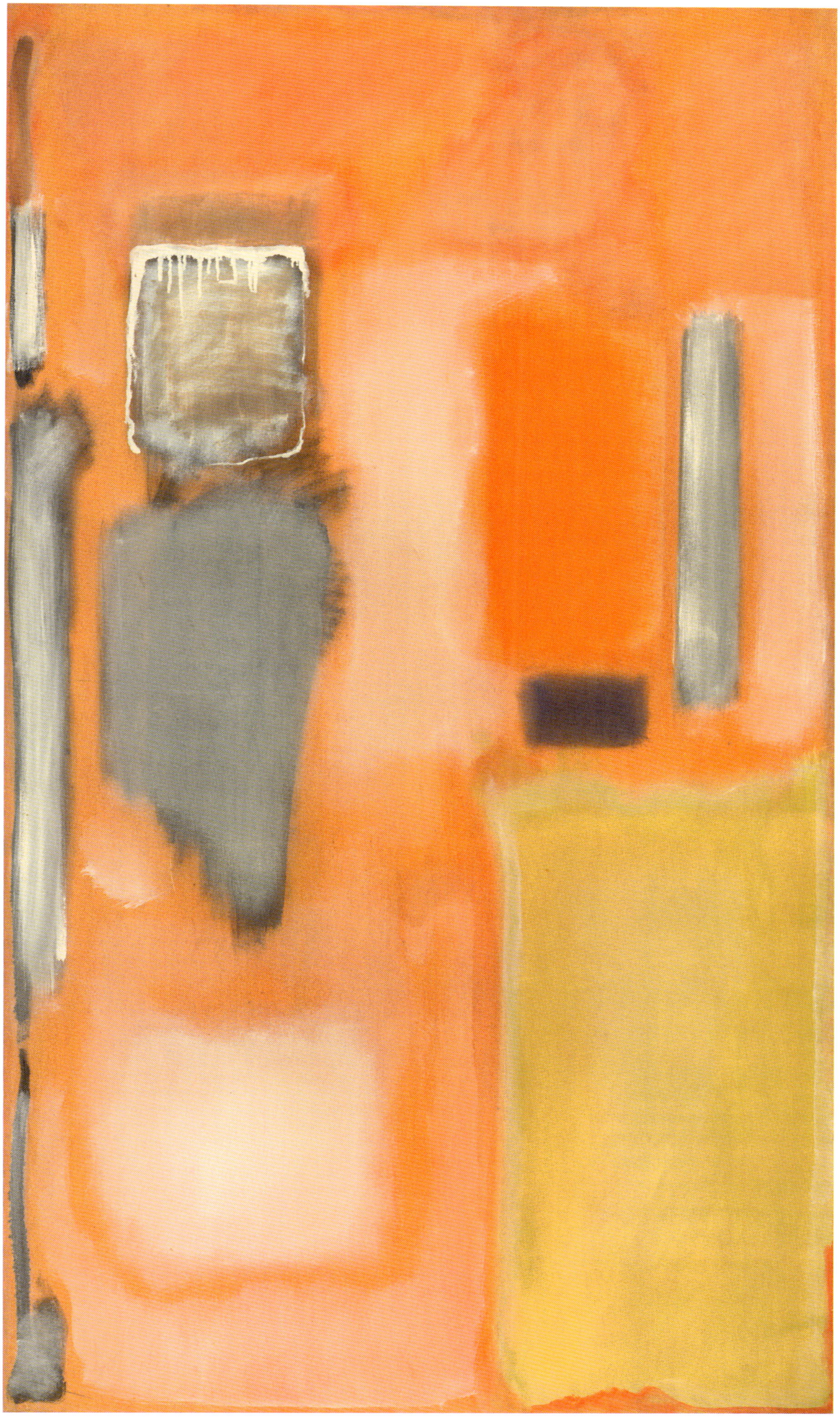

42. *Number 19*, 1949, oil on canvas, 68 × 40 ⅛ in. (172.1 × 106.4 cm), The Art Institute of Chicago (CR 403)

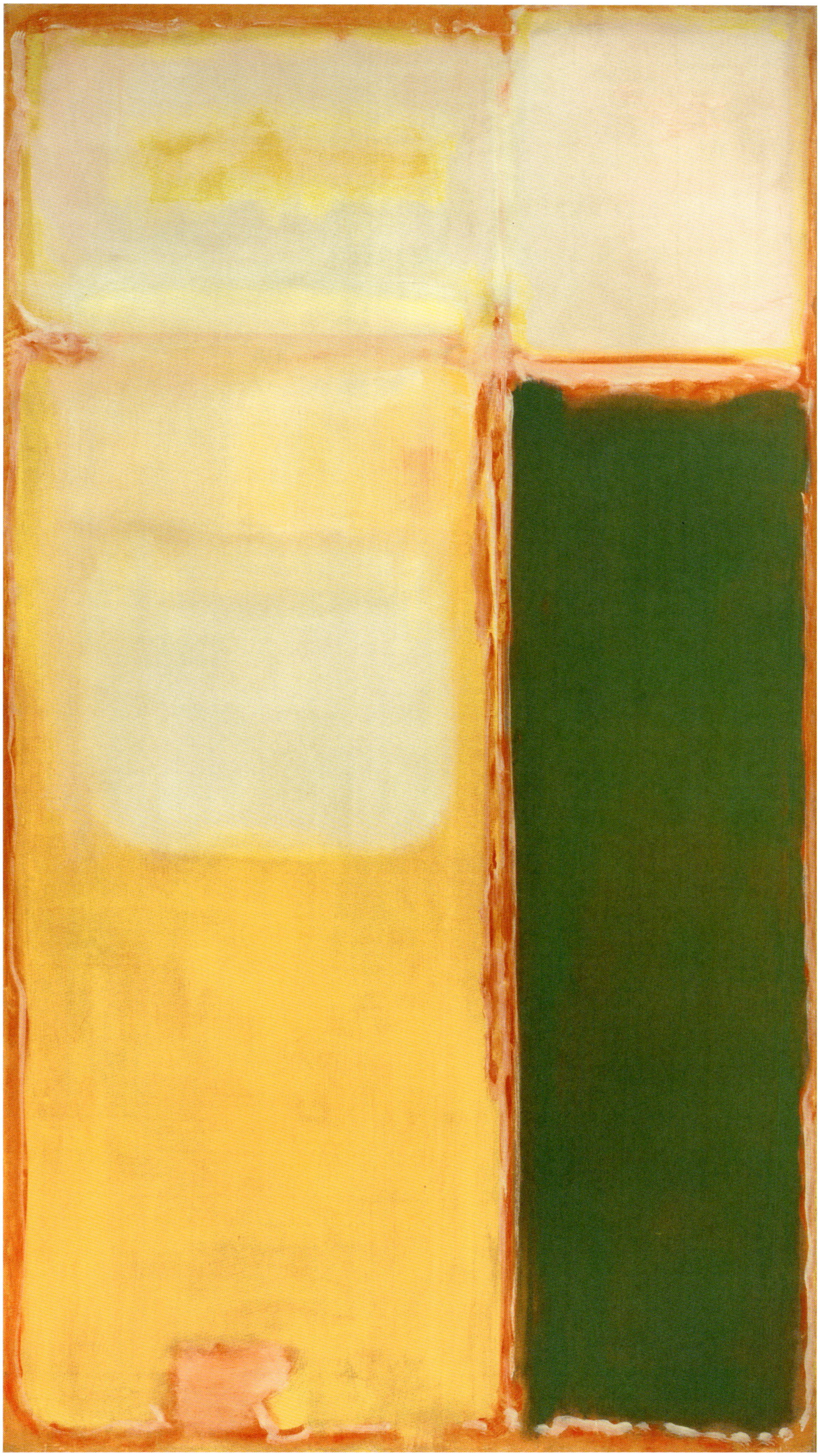

43. *No. 11/No. 20*, 1949, oil on canvas, 93 ¾ × 53 in. (238.1 × 134.6 cm), Collection of Christopher Rothko (CR 419)

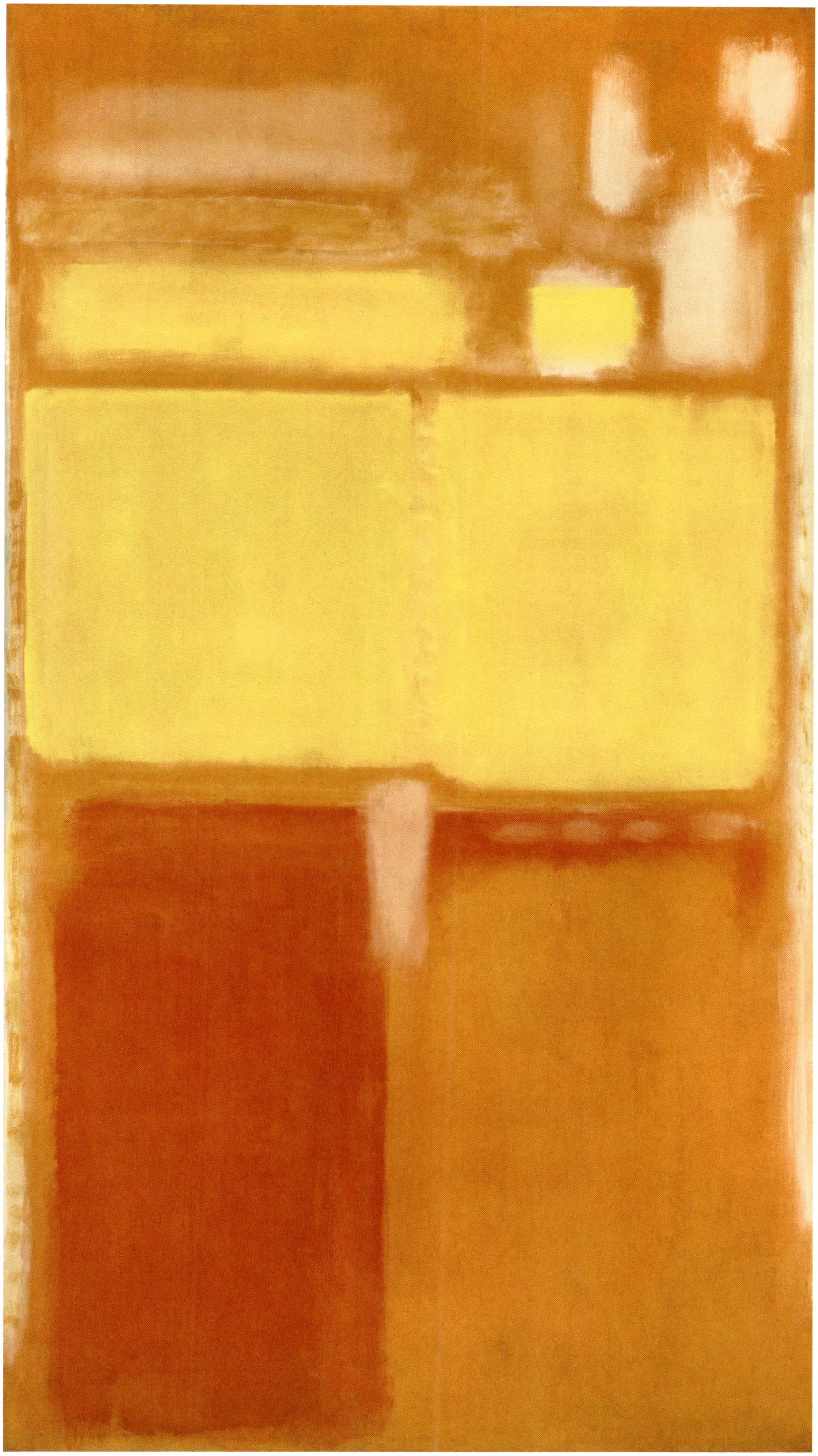

44. *No. 21 (Untitled)*, 1949, oil and mixed media on canvas, 94 × 53 ⅜ in. (238.8 × 135.6 cm), The Menil Collection, Houston (CR 407)

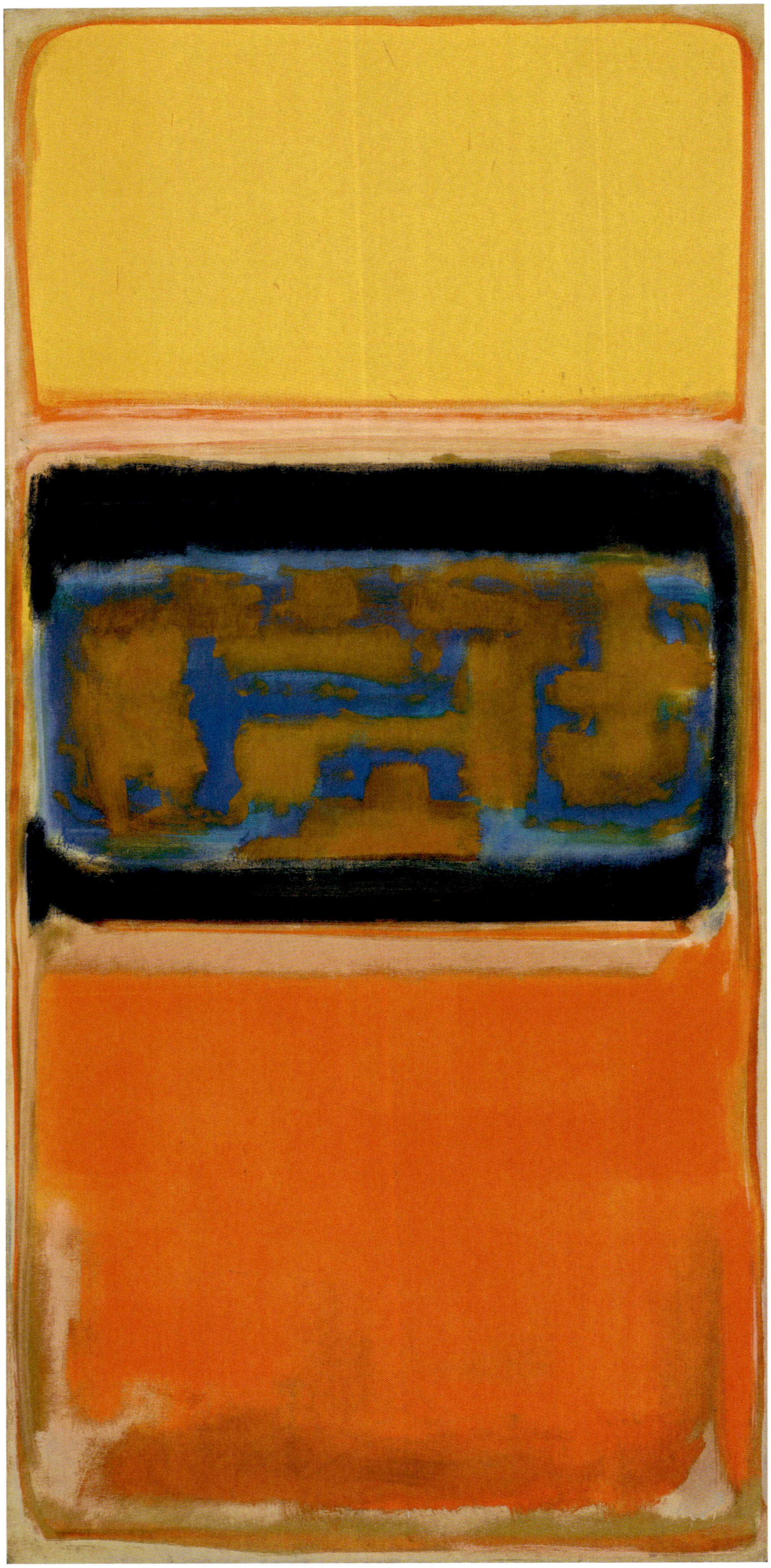

45. *No. 1*, 1949, oil on canvas, 78 × 38 ¾ in. (198.8 × 98.4 cm), private collection (CR 408)

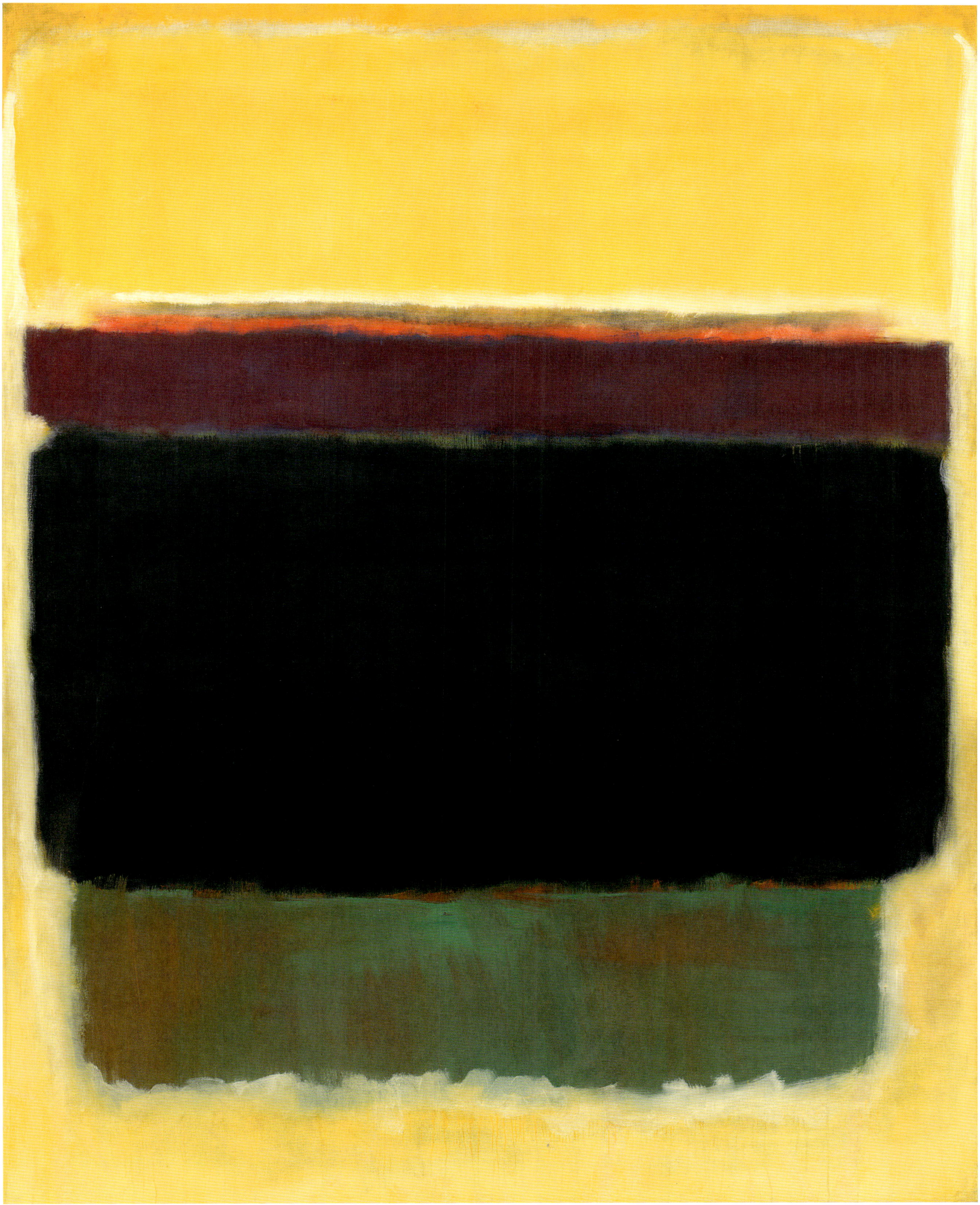

46. *Untitled*, 1949, pigmented hide glue and oil on canvas, 80 ⅜ × 66 ⅜ in. (206.7 × 168.6 cm), National Gallery of Art, Washington, D.C. (CR 425)

47. *Untitled*, 1949, oil and acrylic with powder pigments on canvas, 56 ⅛ × 33 in. (142.6 × 83.8 cm), The Metropolitan Museum of Art, New York (CR 421)

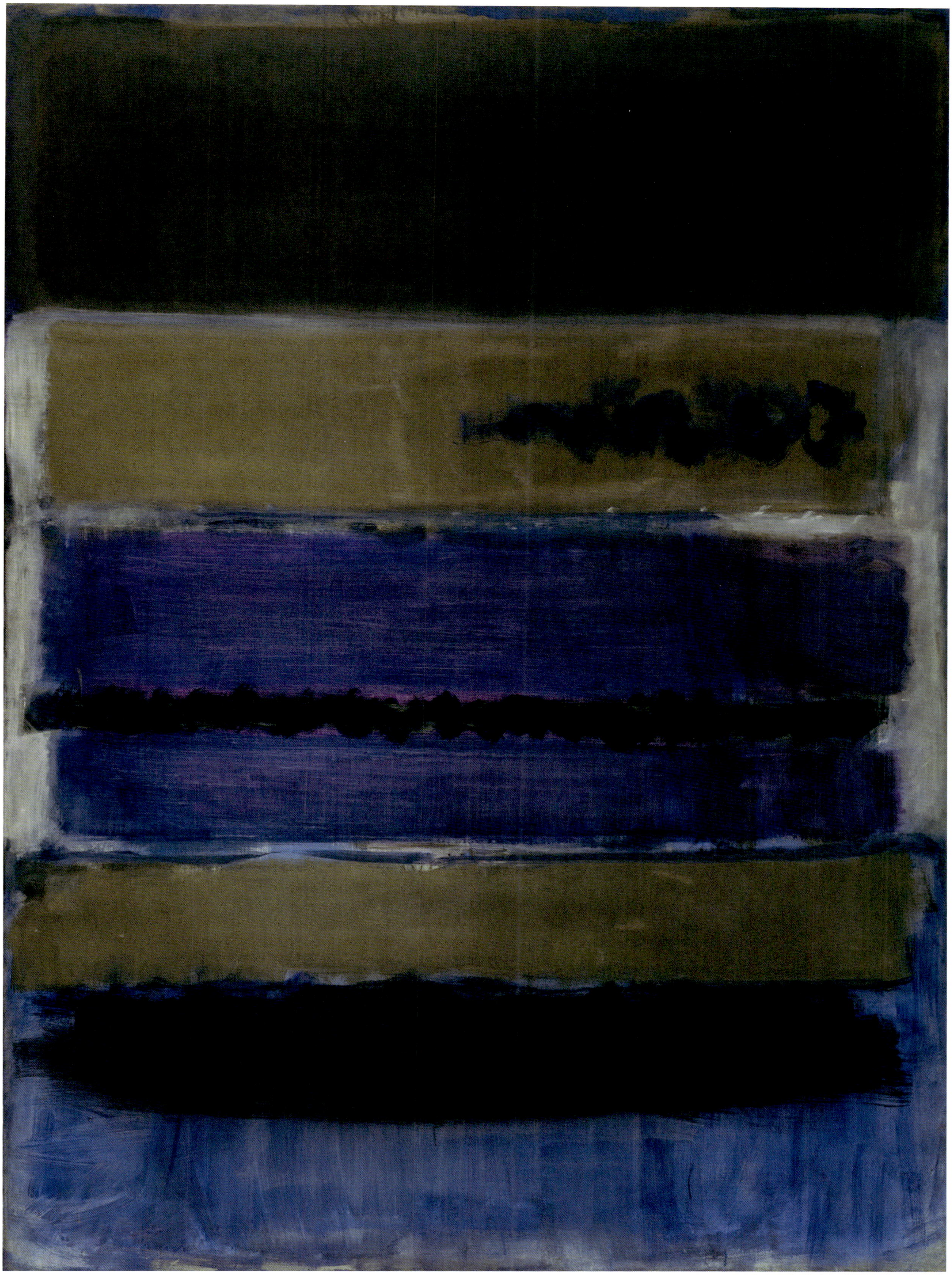

48. *No. 5*, 1949, oil on canvas, 85 × 63 in. (215.9 × 160 cm), Chrysler Museum of Art, Norfolk (CR 412)

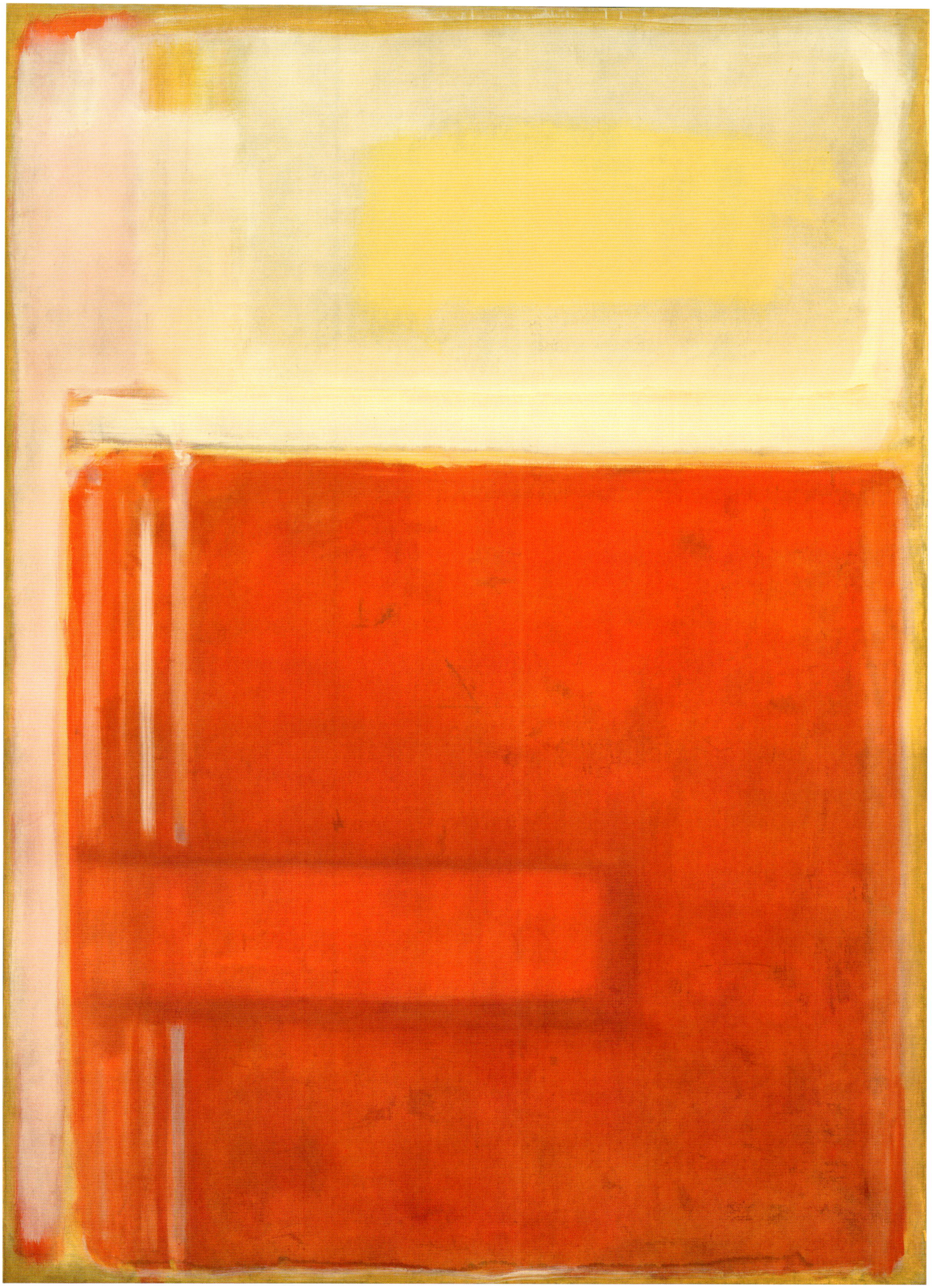

49. *No. 8*, 1949, oil and mixed media on canvas, 89 ⅞ × 65 ⅞ in. (228.3 × 167.3 cm), National Gallery of Art, Washington, D.C. (CR 415)

50. *No. 5/No. 22*, 1950, oil on canvas, 117 × 107 in. (297.2 × 272.1 cm), Museum of Modern Art, New York (CR 442)

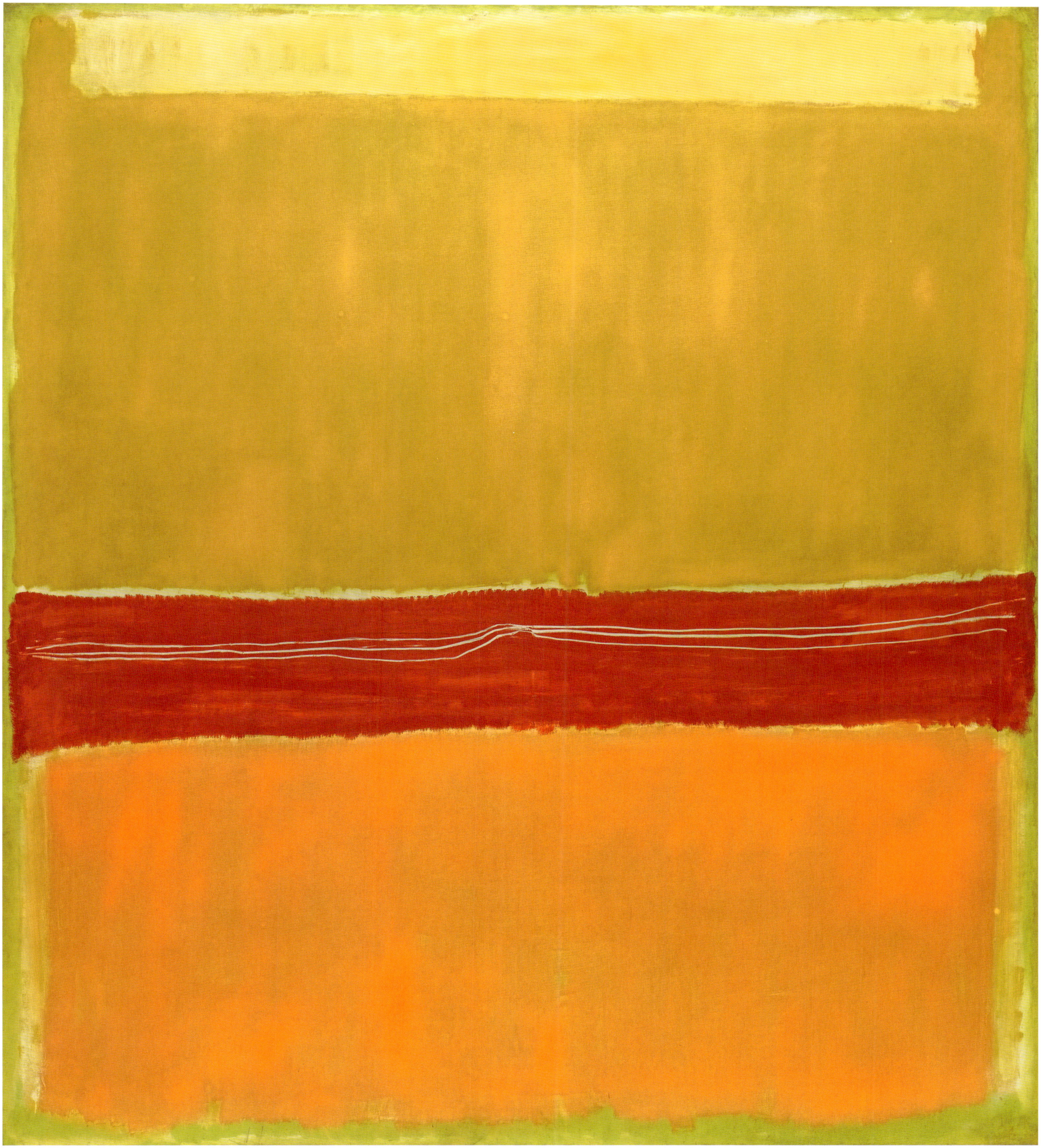

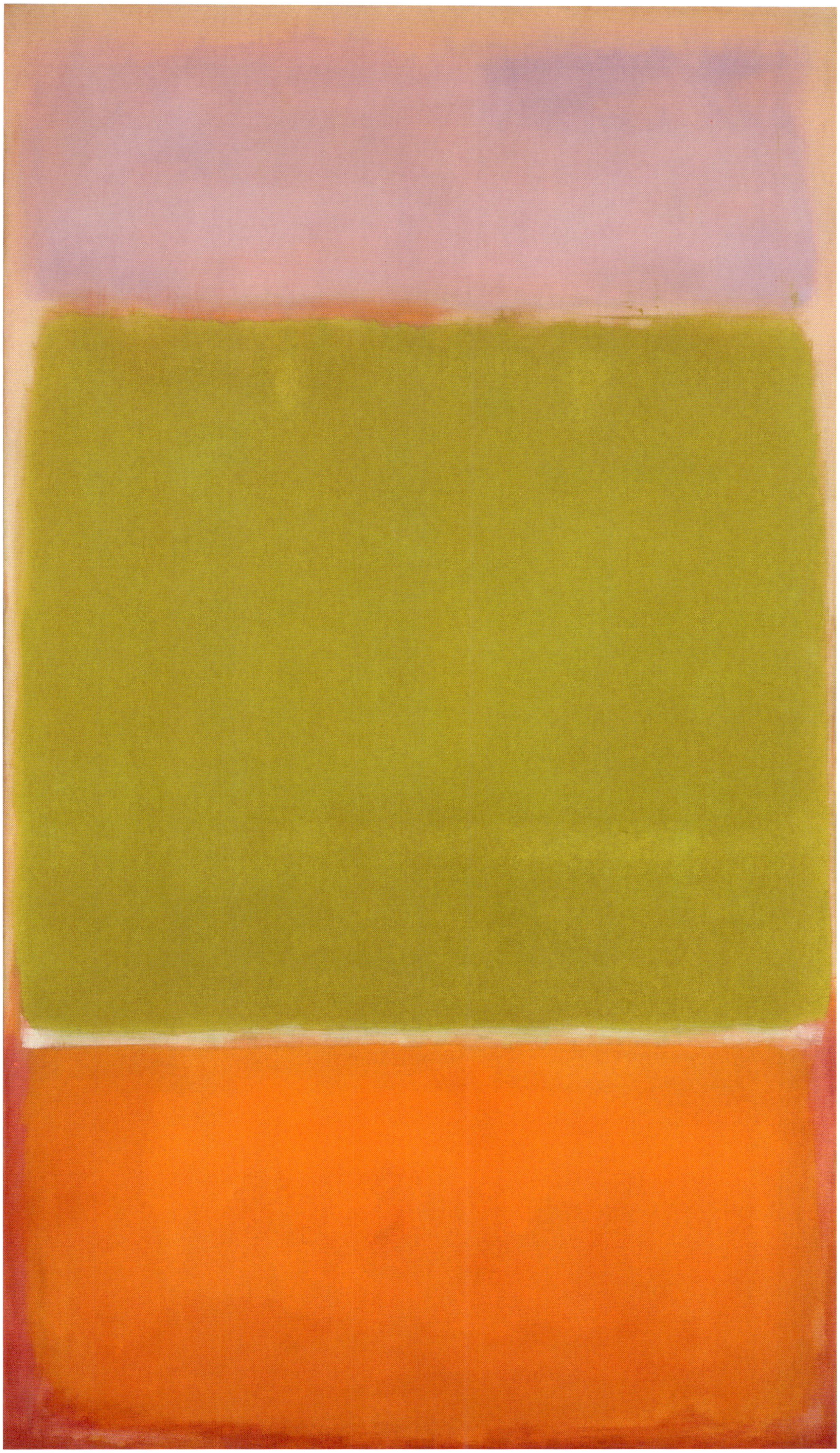

51. *No. 7*, 1951, oil on canvas, 94 ¾ × 54 ⅝ in. (240.7 × 138.7 cm), Yageo Foundation, Taiwan (CR 455)

52. *No. 16*, 1951, oil on canvas, 67 5/8 × 44 5/8 in. (171.8 × 113.4 cm), Collection of Christopher Rothko (CR 462)

53. *No. 7 (Dark over Light)*, 1954, oil on canvas, 90 ⅛ × 58 ⅝ in. (228.8 × 148.8 cm), Nahmad Collection (CR 506)

54. *No. 9/No. 5/No. 18*, 1952, oil on canvas, 116 × 91 ½ in. (294.6 × 232.4 cm), private collection (CR 477)

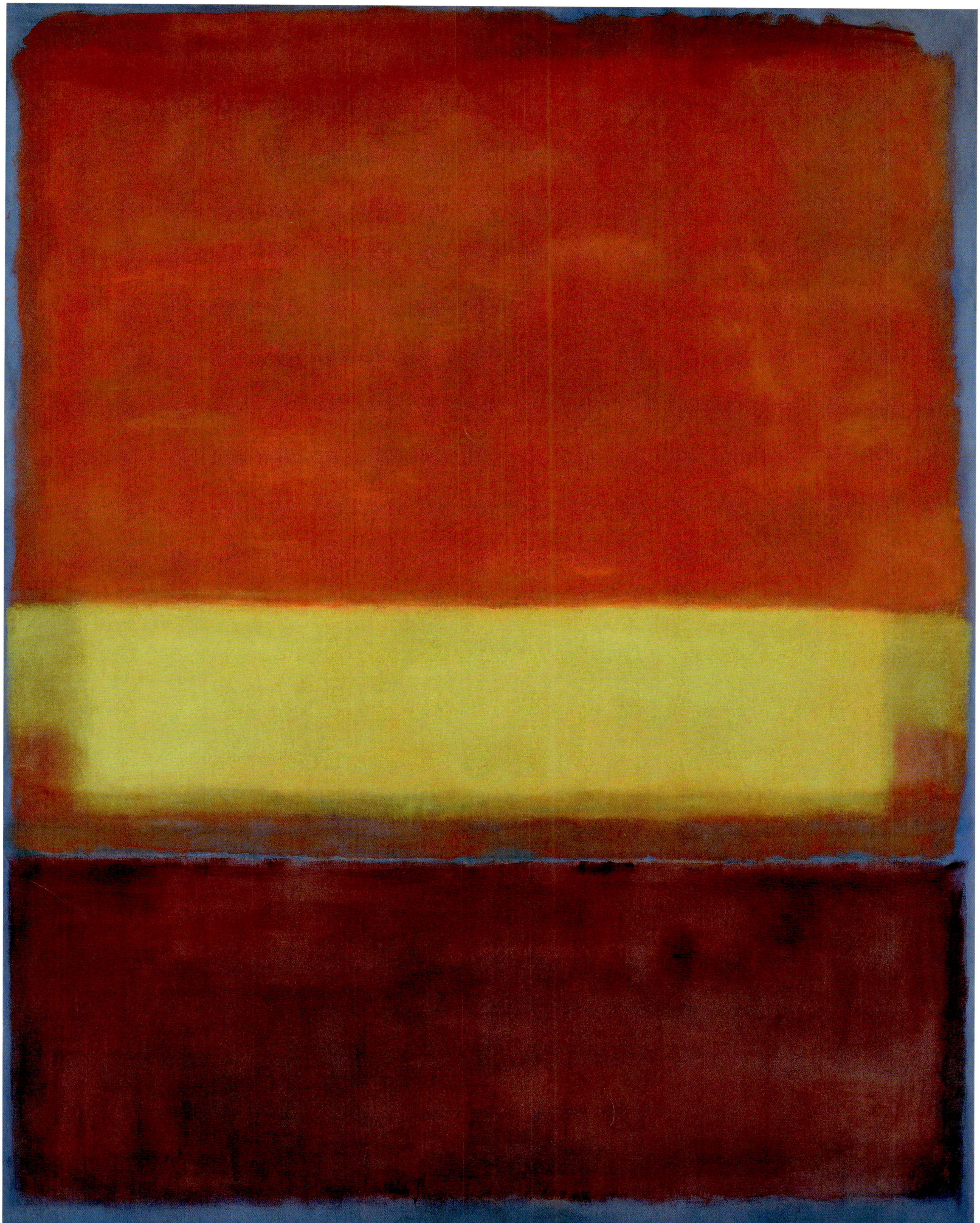

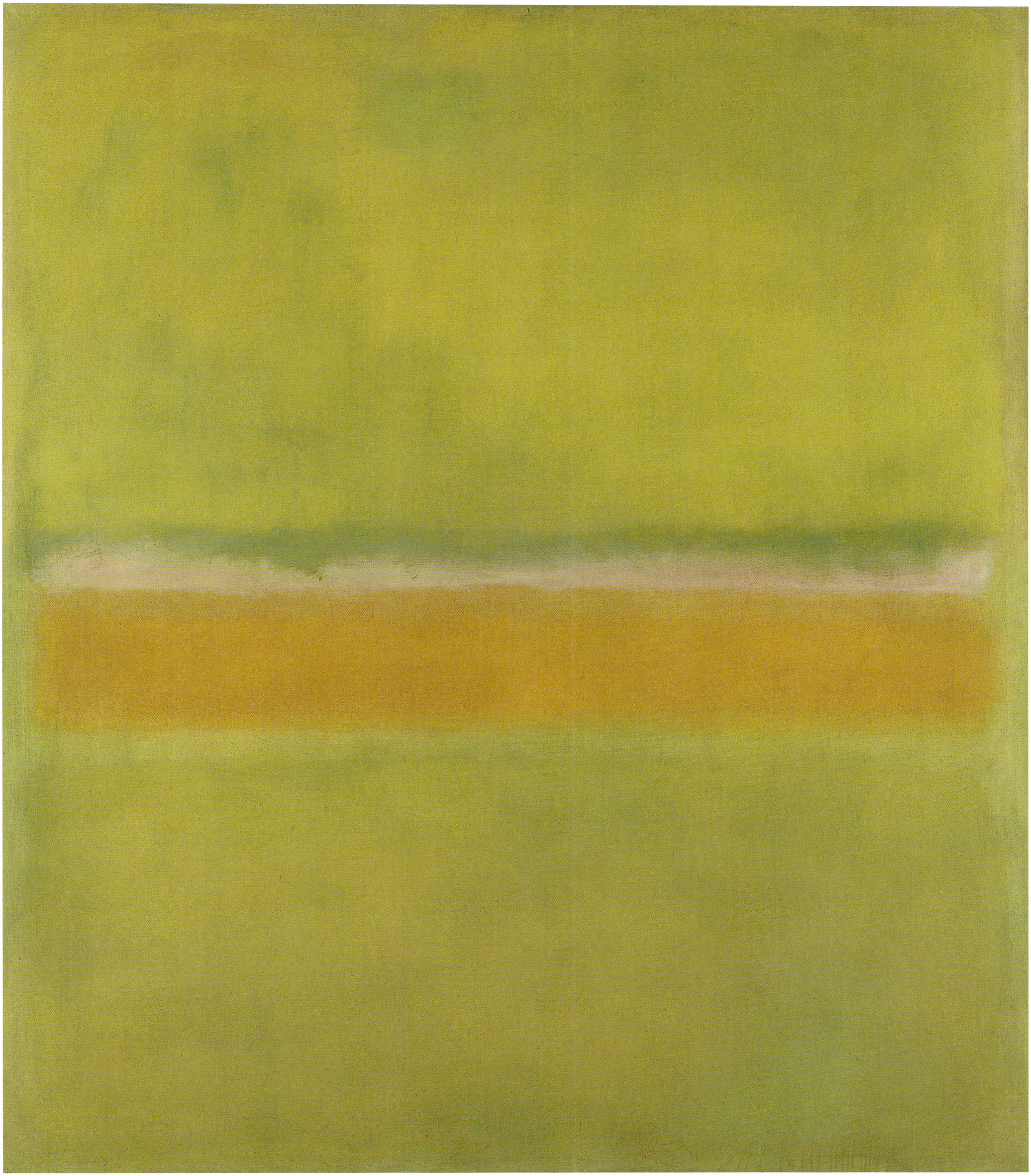

55. *No. 14 / No. 10 (Yellow Greens)*, 1953, oil on canvas, 77 × 67 ¾ in. (195 × 172.1 cm), Frederick R. Weisman Art Foundation, Los Angeles (CR 499)

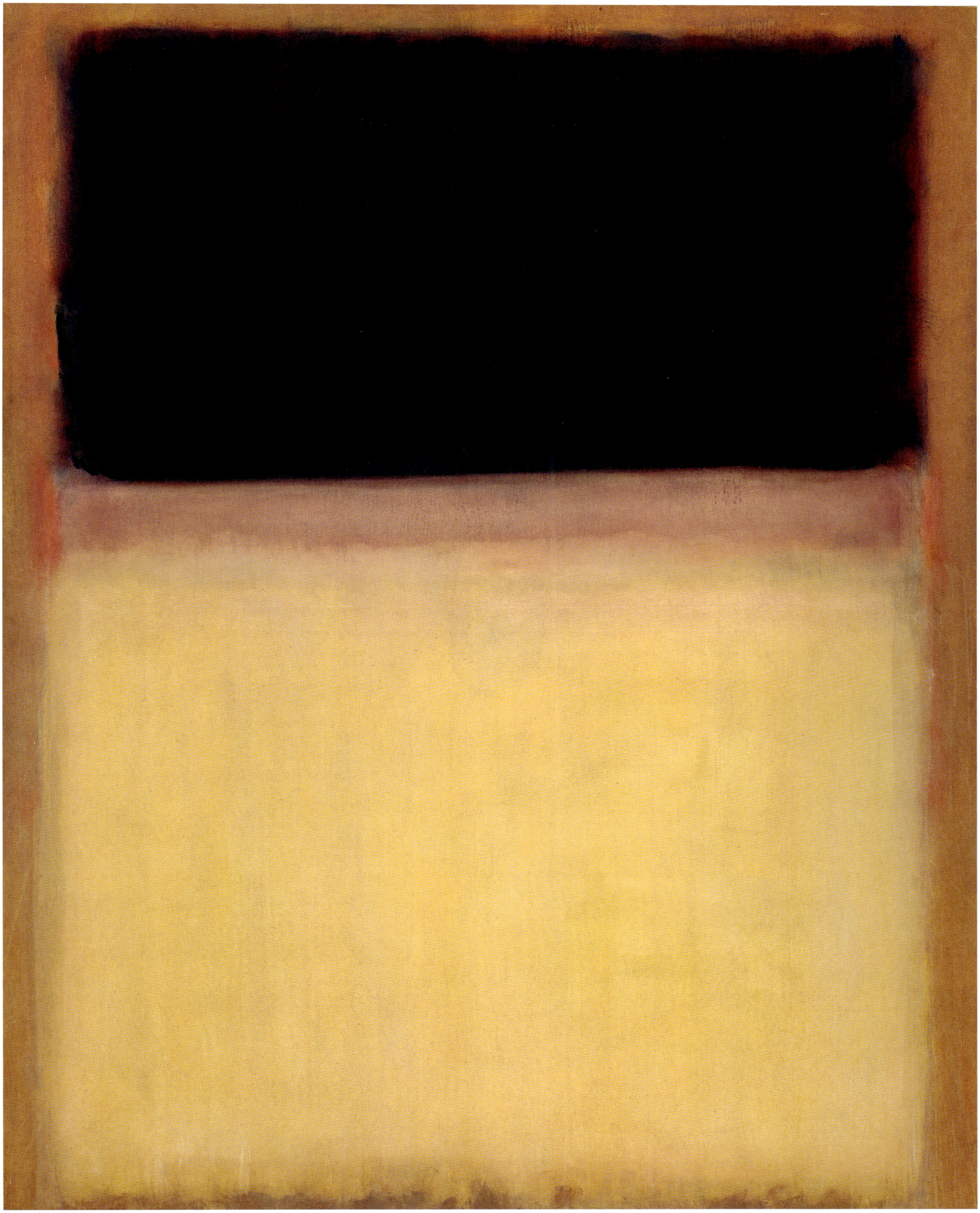

56. *No. 9 (Dark over Light Earth/Violet and Yellow in Rose)*, 1954, oil on canvas, 83 ¼ × 68 in. (212.1 × 172.1 cm), The Museum of Contemporary Art, Los Angeles (CR 508)

57. *Untitled*, 1955, oil on canvas, 91 3/5 × 69 in. (232.7 × 175.3 cm), Yageo Foundation, Taiwan (CR 523)

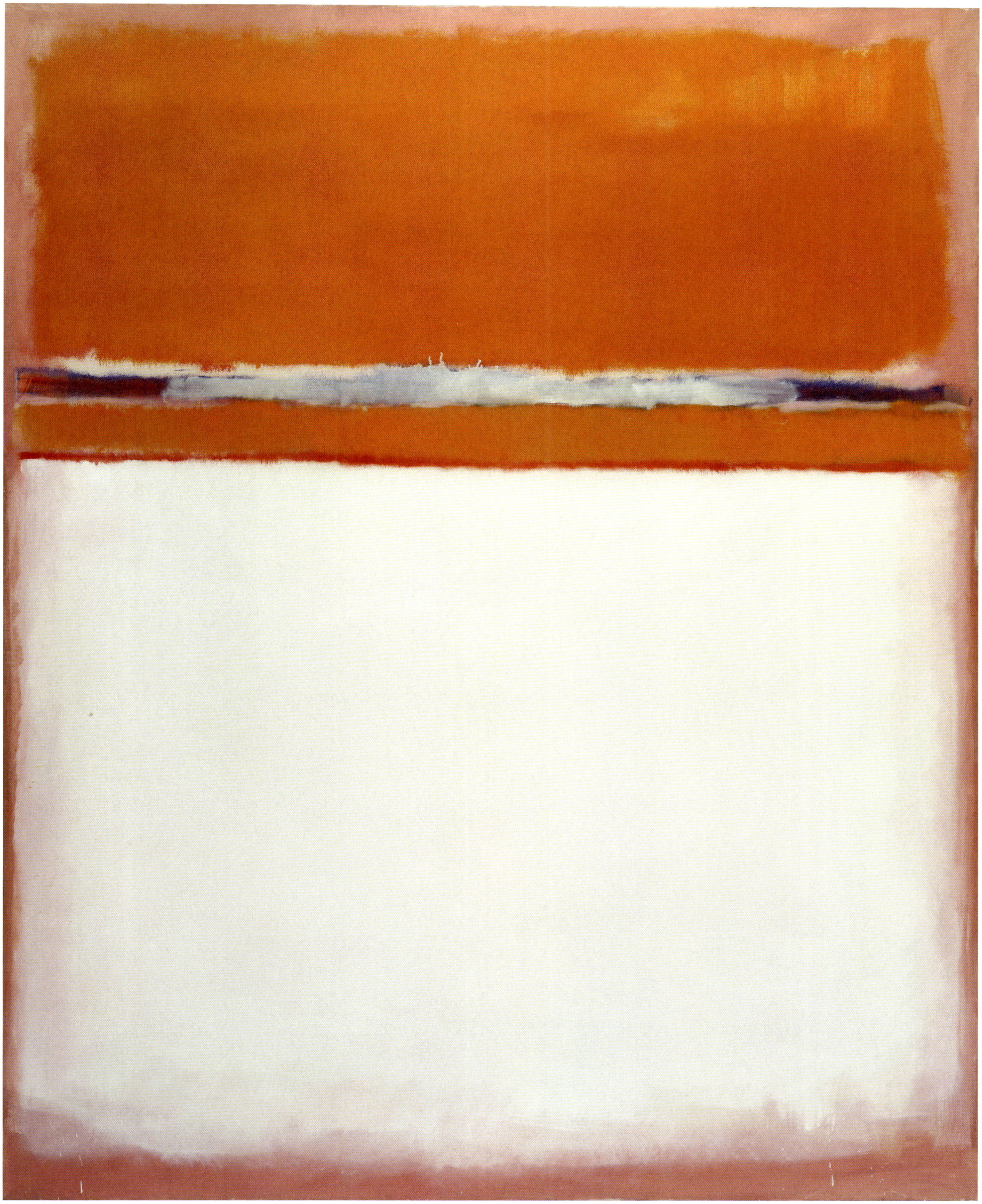

58. *No. 18*, 1951, oil on canvas, 81 ½ × 69 ⅞ in. (207 × 170.5 cm), Munson Museum, Utica, NY (CR 464)

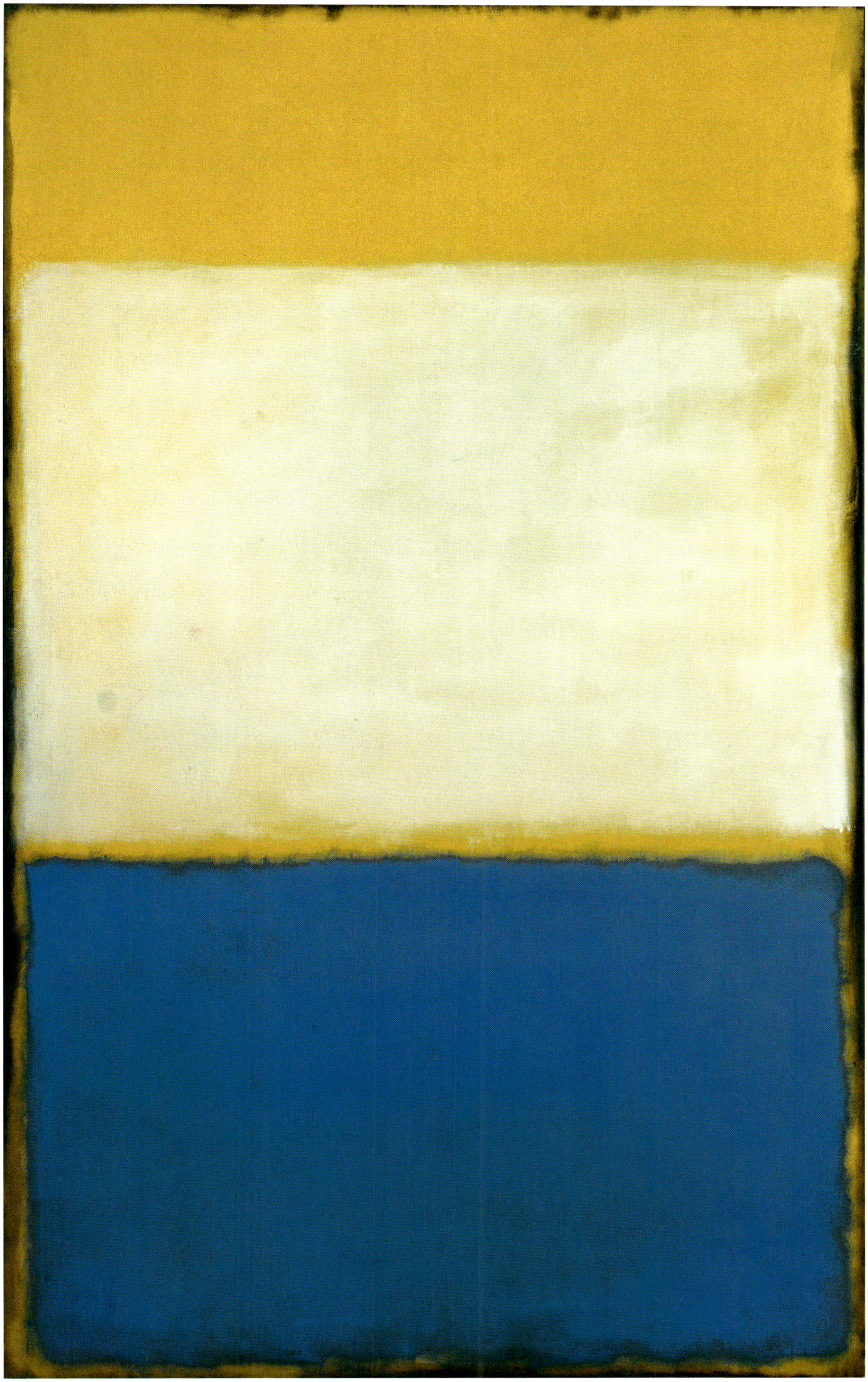

59. *No. 6 (Yellow, White, Blue over Yellow on Gray)*, 1954, oil on canvas, 94 ½ × 59 ¾ in (240 × 151.8 cm), private collection (CR 505)

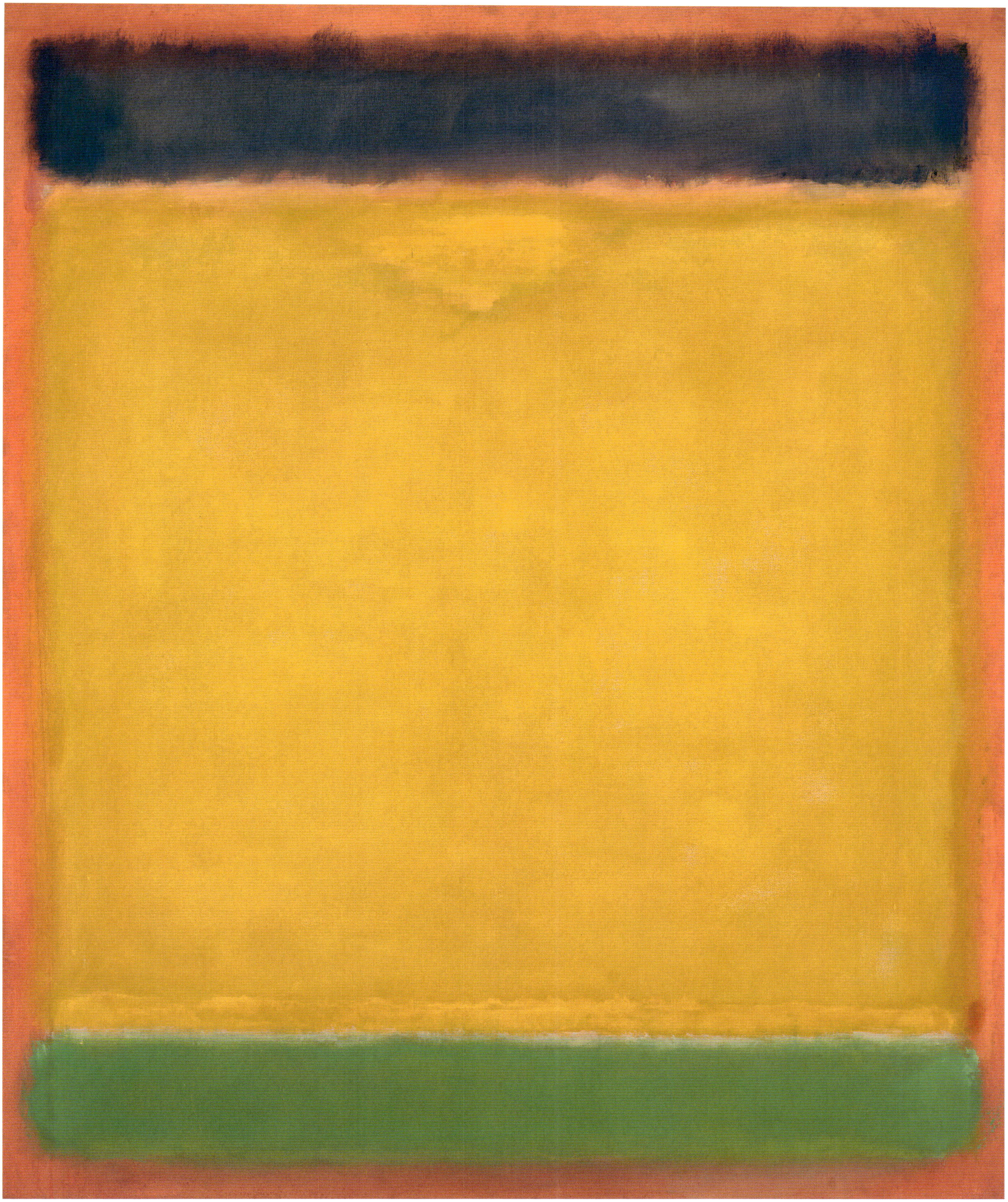

60. *Untitled (Blue, Yellow, Green on Red)*, 1954, oil on canvas, 77 ¾ × 65 ½ in. (195.7 × 166.4 cm), Whitney Museum of American Art, New York (CR 514)

61. *Untitled (Red, Black, White on Yellow)*, 1955, oil on canvas, 105 × 93 in. (266.7 × 236.2 cm), National Gallery of Art, Washington, D.C. (CR 535)

62. *Untitled*, 1955, oil on canvas, 81 ½ × 59 ⅝ in. (207 × 151.4 cm), private collection (CR 542)

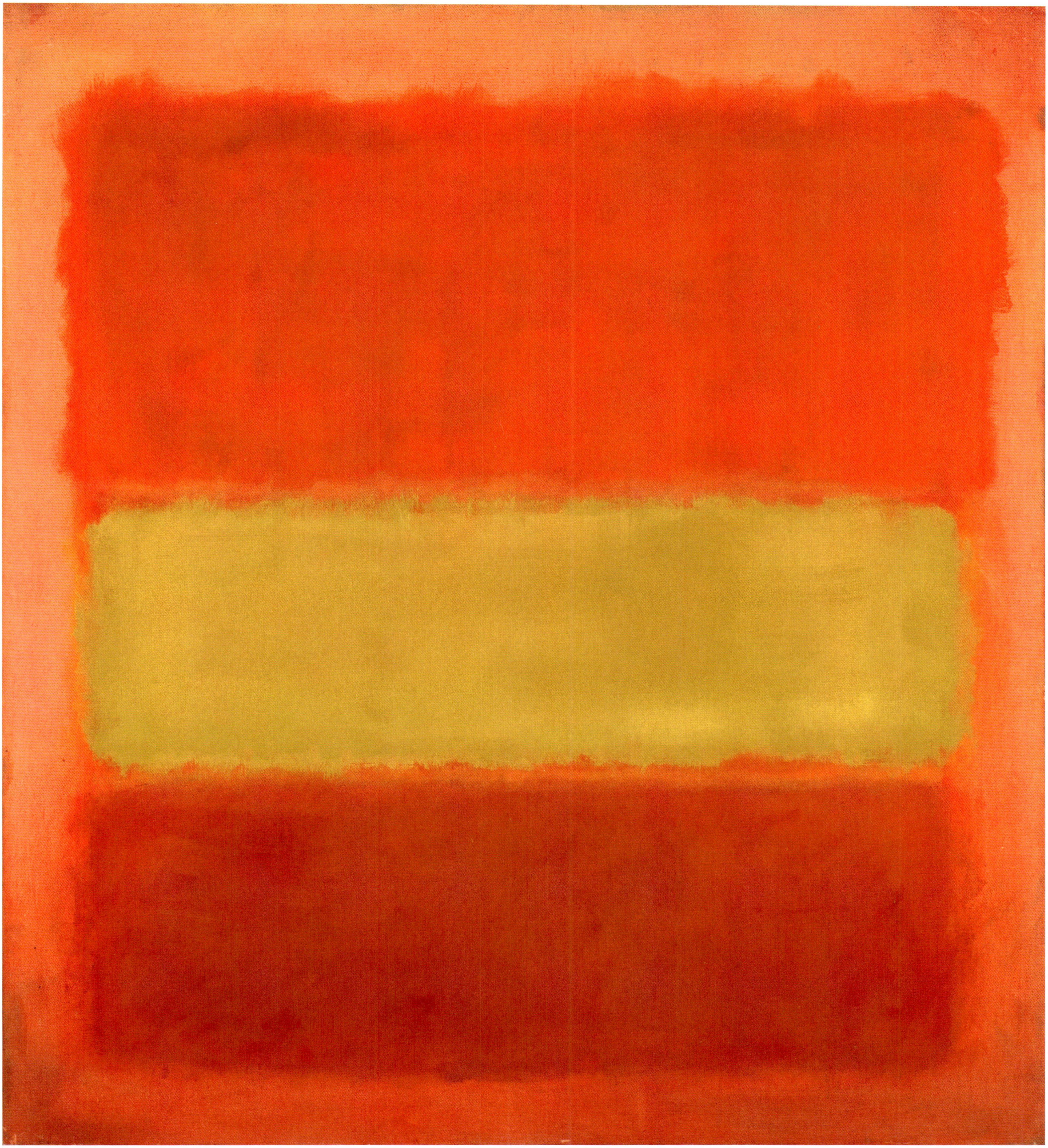

63. *Yellow Band*, 1956, oil on canvas, 86 × 79 ½ in. (218.8 × 201.9 cm), Sheldon Museum of Art, University of Nebraska-Lincoln (CR 555)

64. *No. 10*, 1957, oil and mixed media on canvas, 69 ¼ × 61 ½ in. (175.9 × 156.2 cm), The Menil Collection, Houston (CR 585)

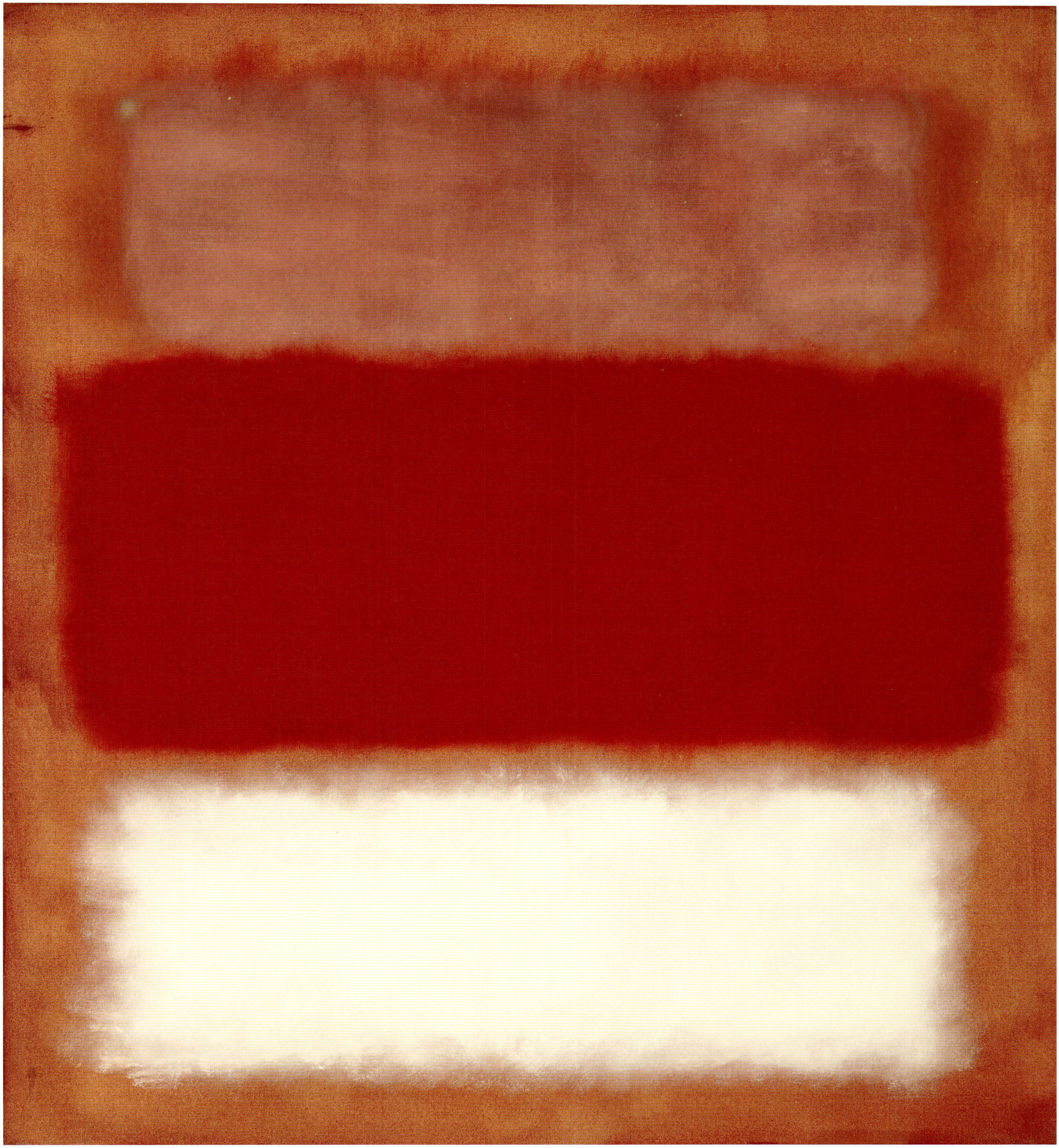

65. *Light Cloud, Dark Cloud*, 1957, oil on canvas, 66 × 61 ¾ in. (167.64 × 156.85 cm), Modern Art Museum of Fort Worth (CR 574)

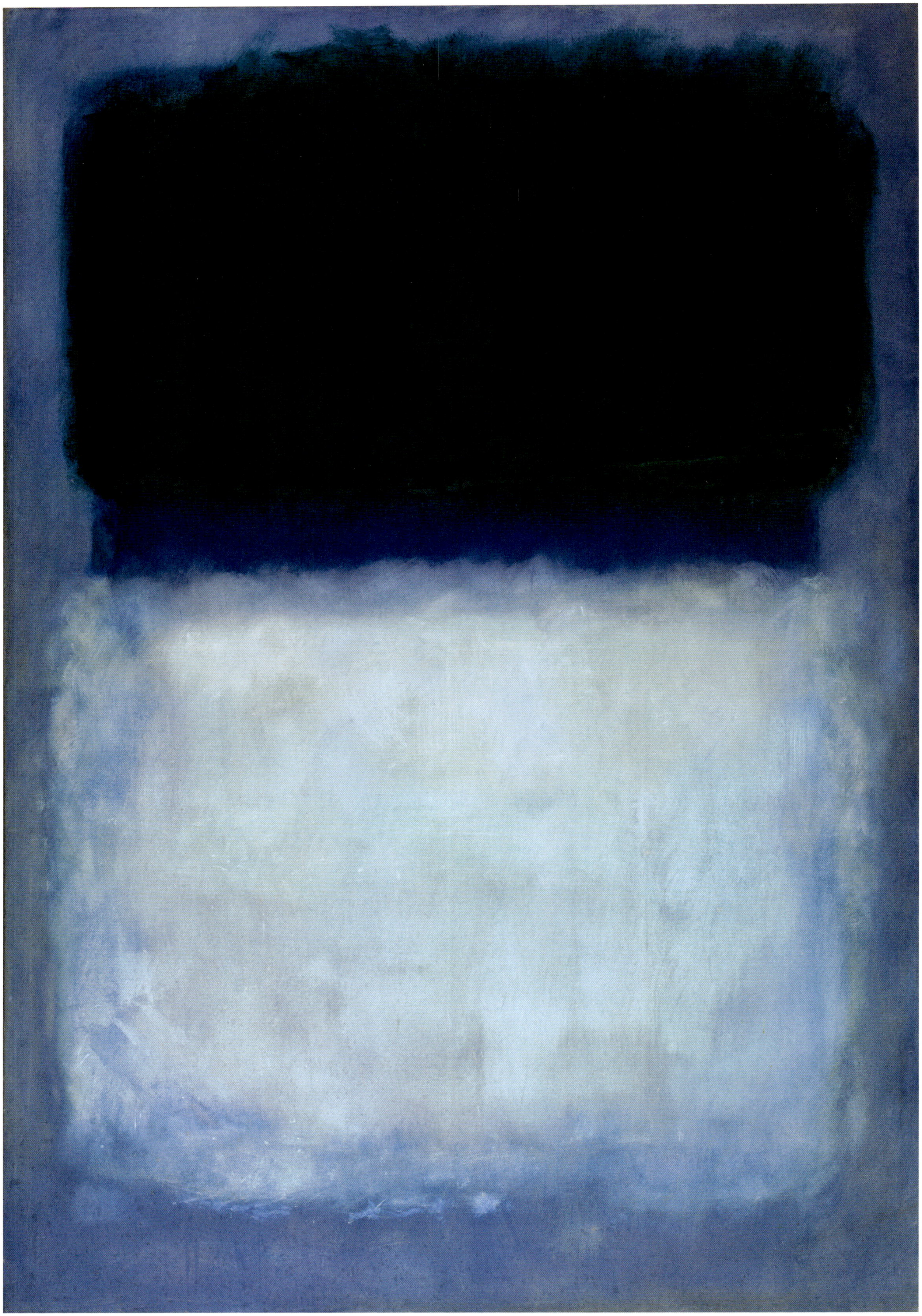

66. *Green on Blue (Earth-Green and White)*, 1956, oil on canvas, 91 ¼ × 64 ⅜ in. (228.6 × 161.3 cm), The University of Arizona Museum of Art, Tucson (CR 543)

67. *No. 3*, 1957, oil on canvas, 79 ½ × 69 ½ in. (201.9 × 176.5 cm), private collection (CR 581)

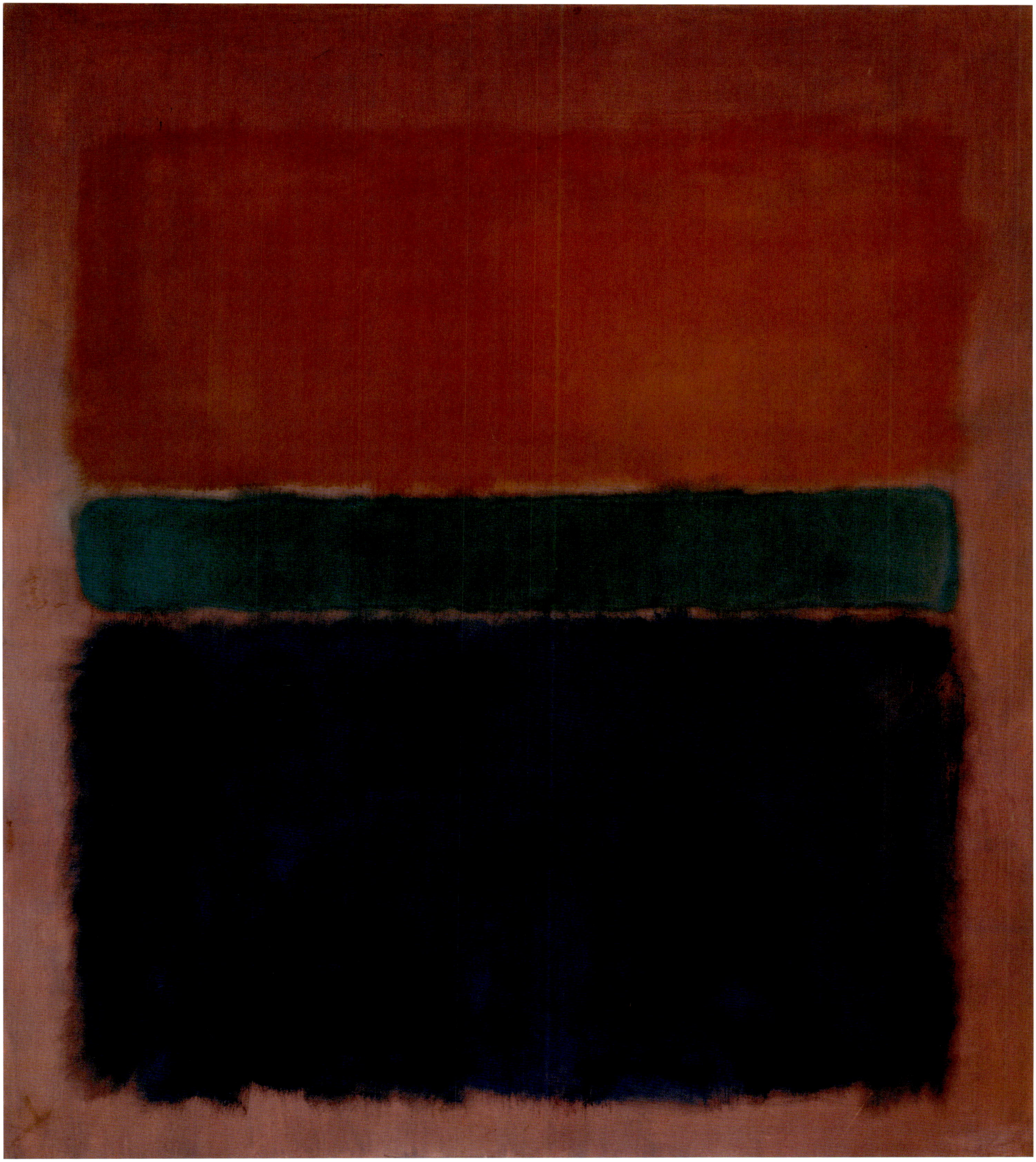

68. *No. 15*, 1958, oil on canvas, 92 ¾ × 83 ⅜ in. (235.6 × 211.8 cm), private collection (CR 622)

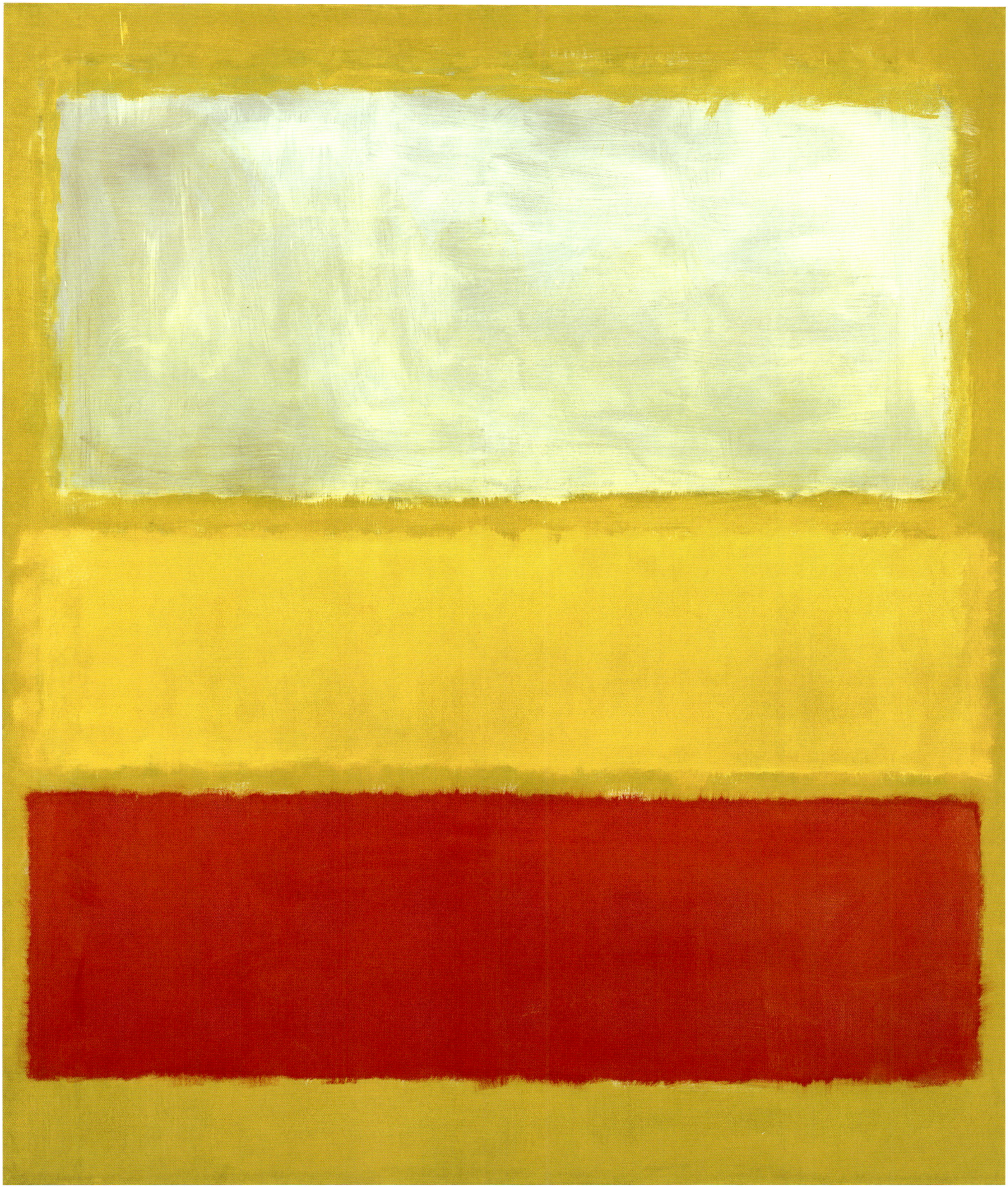

69. *No. 13 (White, Red on Yellow)*, 1958, oil and acrylic with powdered pigments on canvas, 95 ¼ × 81 ⅖ in. (241.9 × 206.7 cm), The Metropolitan Museum of Art, New York (CR 620)

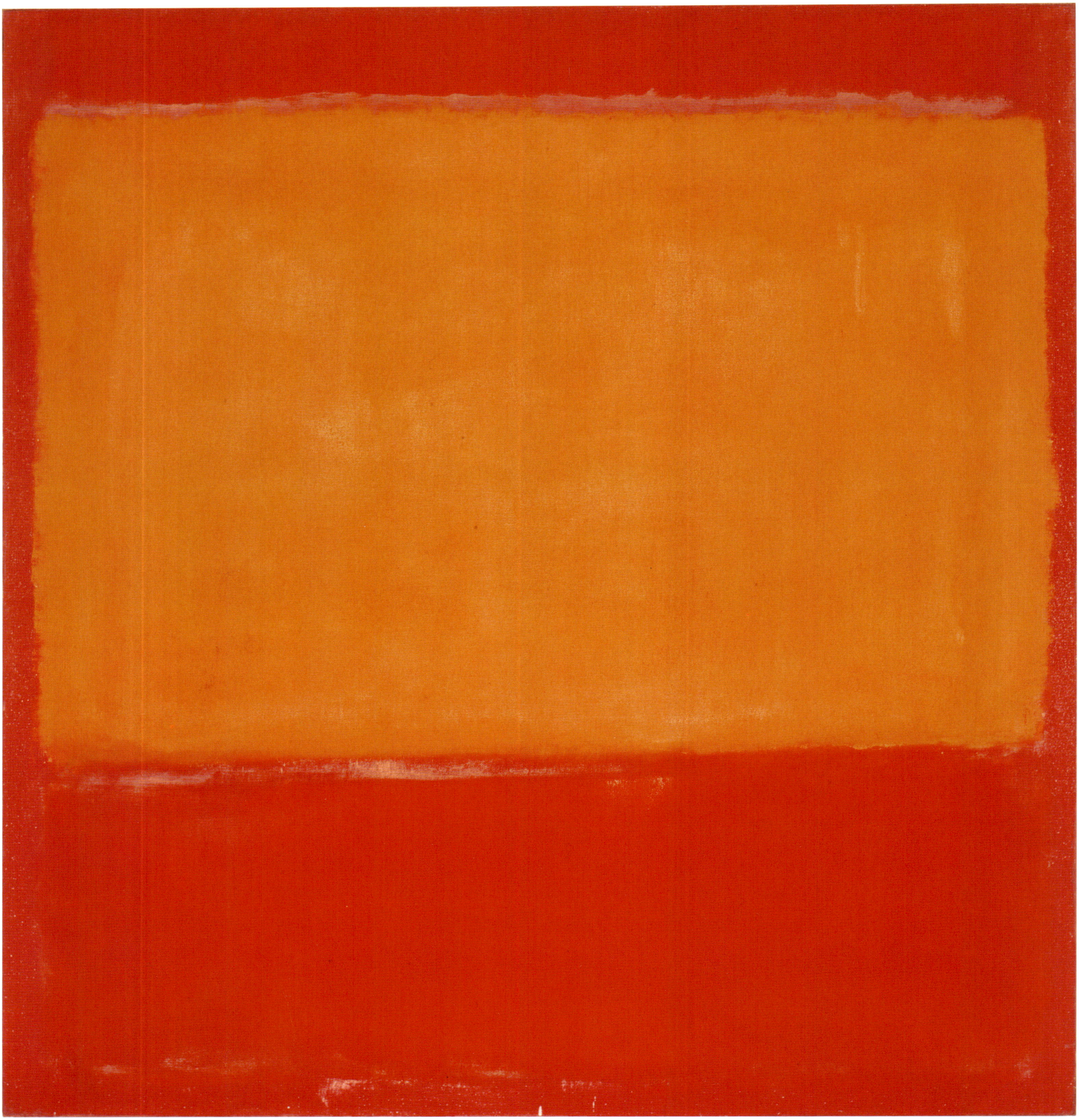

70. *Orange, Red on Red*, 1957, oil on canvas, 68 7/8 × 66 3/8 in. (172.4 × 168.5 cm), The Phillips Collection, Washington, D.C. (CR 599)
Following pages: The "Rothko Room" in the new wing of the Phillips Collection, 1989, The Phillips Collection, Washington, D.C.

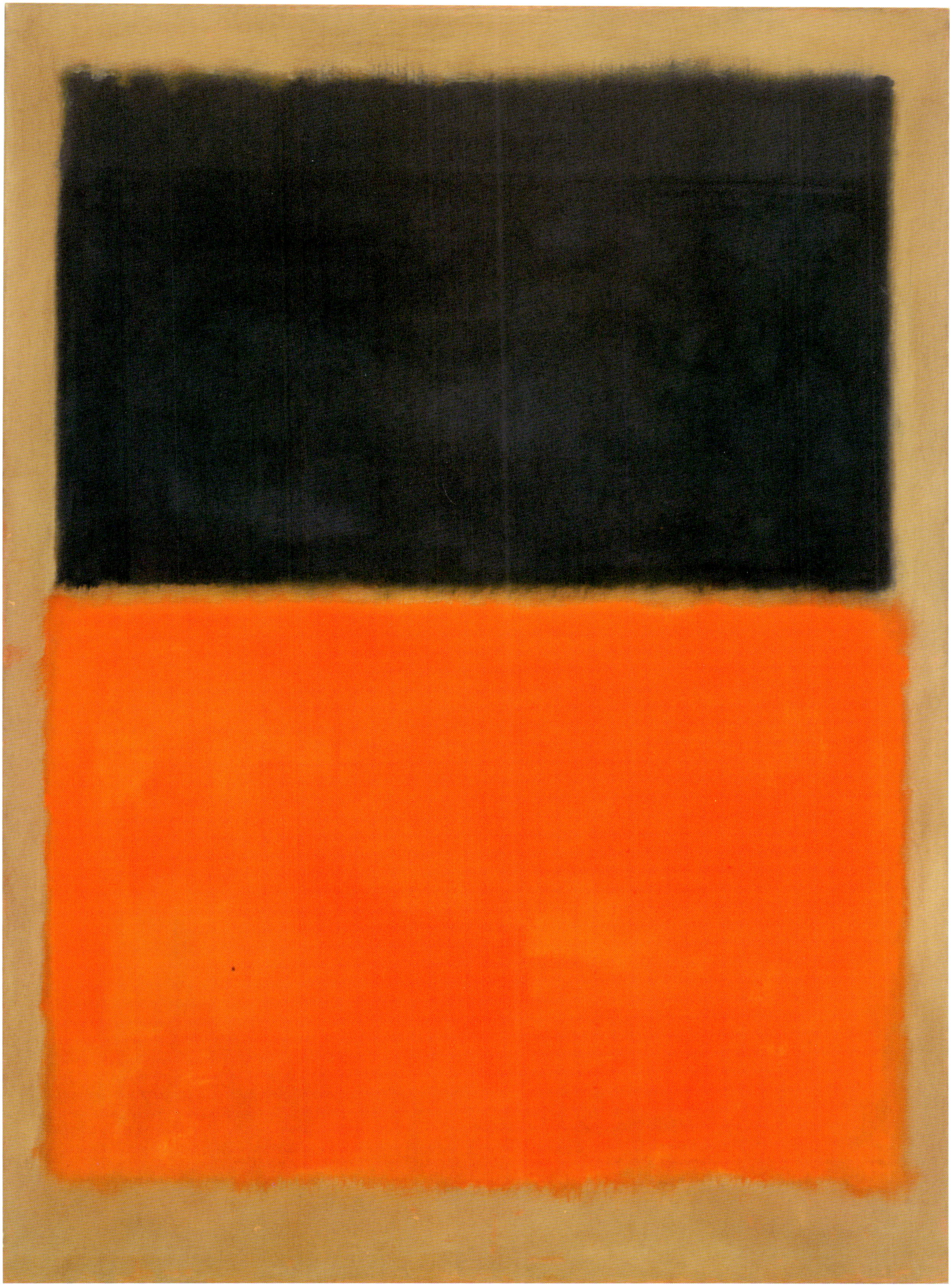

71. *Green and Tangerine on Red*, 1956, oil on canvas, 93 ⅝ × 69 ¼ in. (237.9 × 175.9 cm), The Phillips Collection, Washington, D.C. (CR 562)

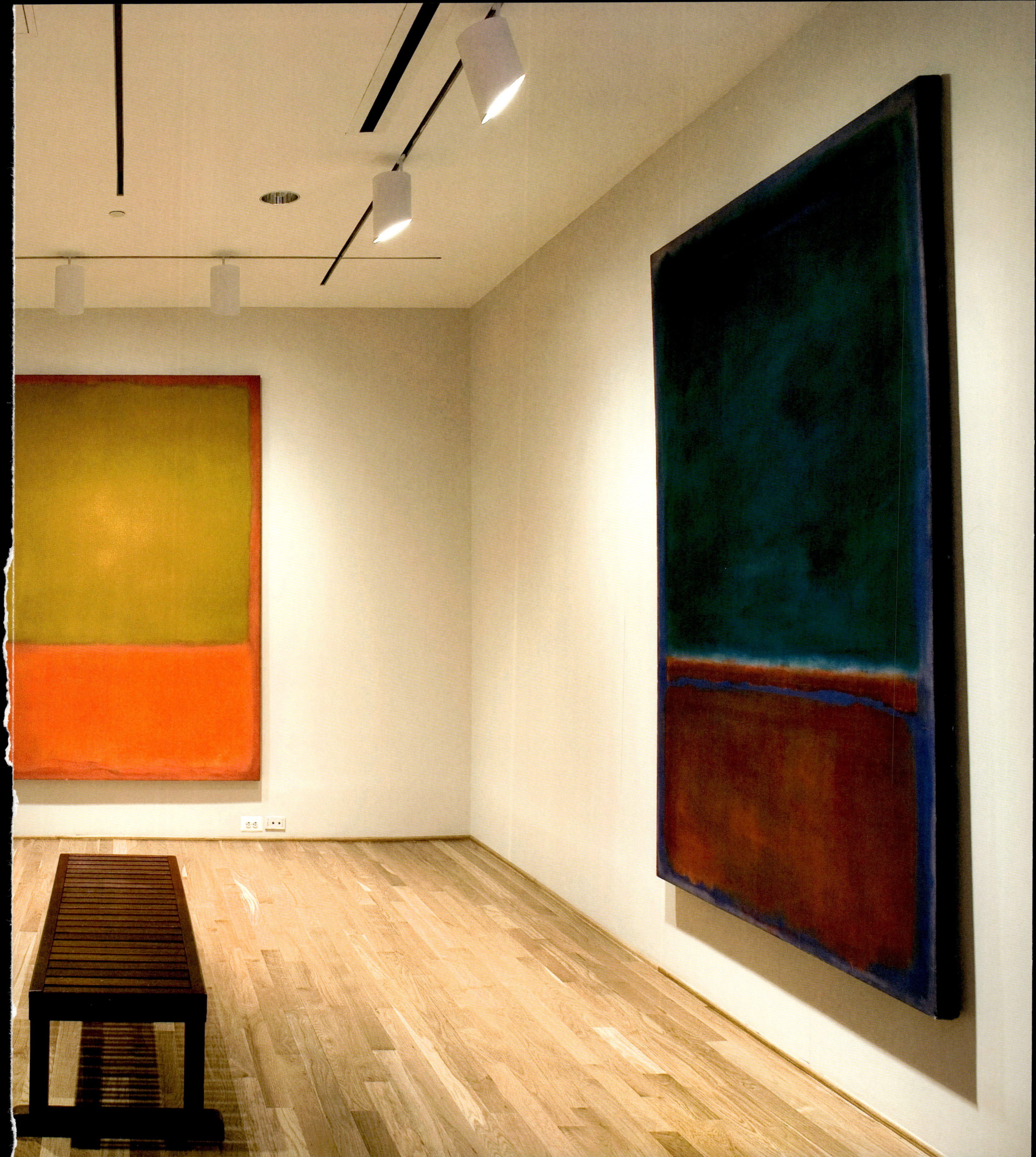

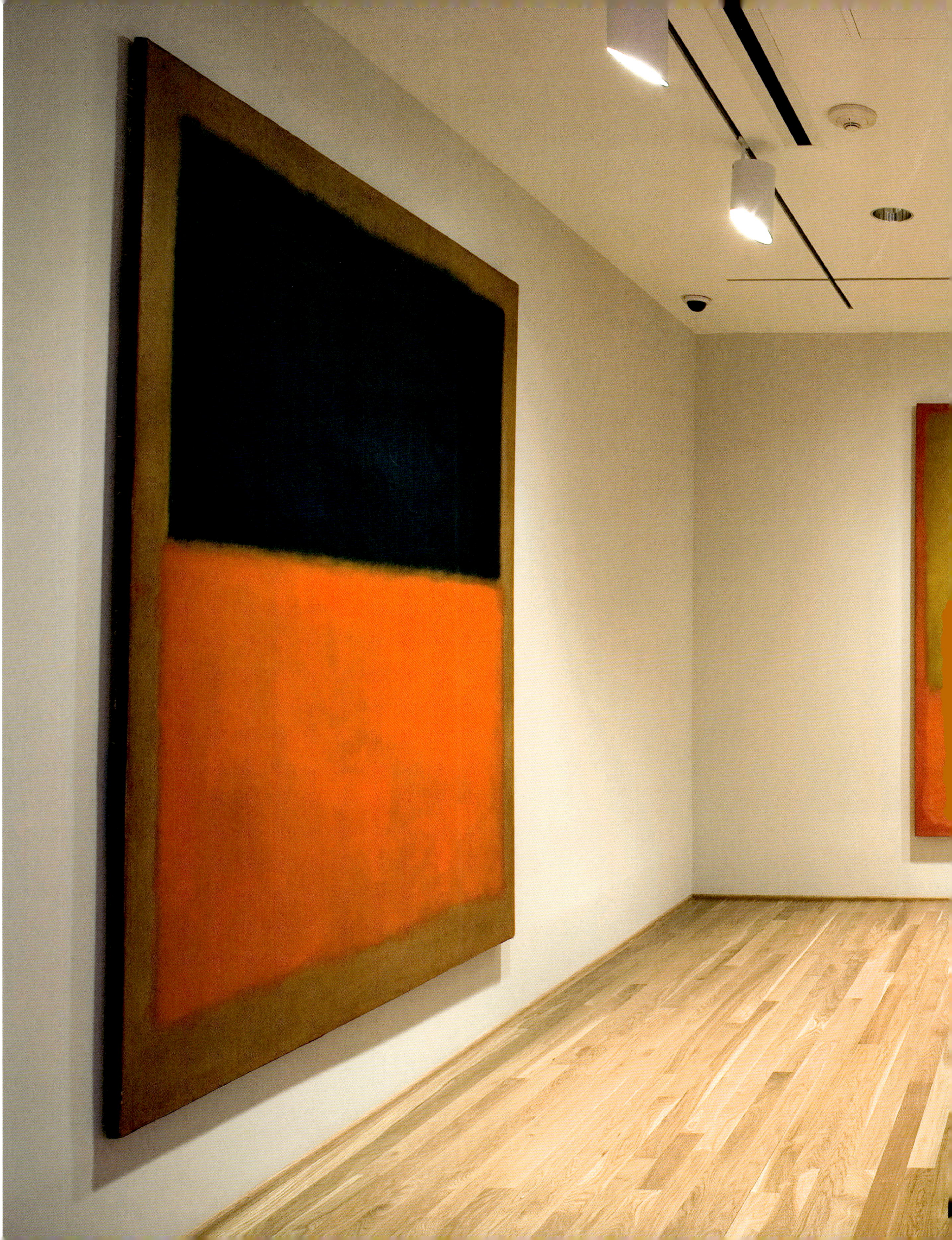

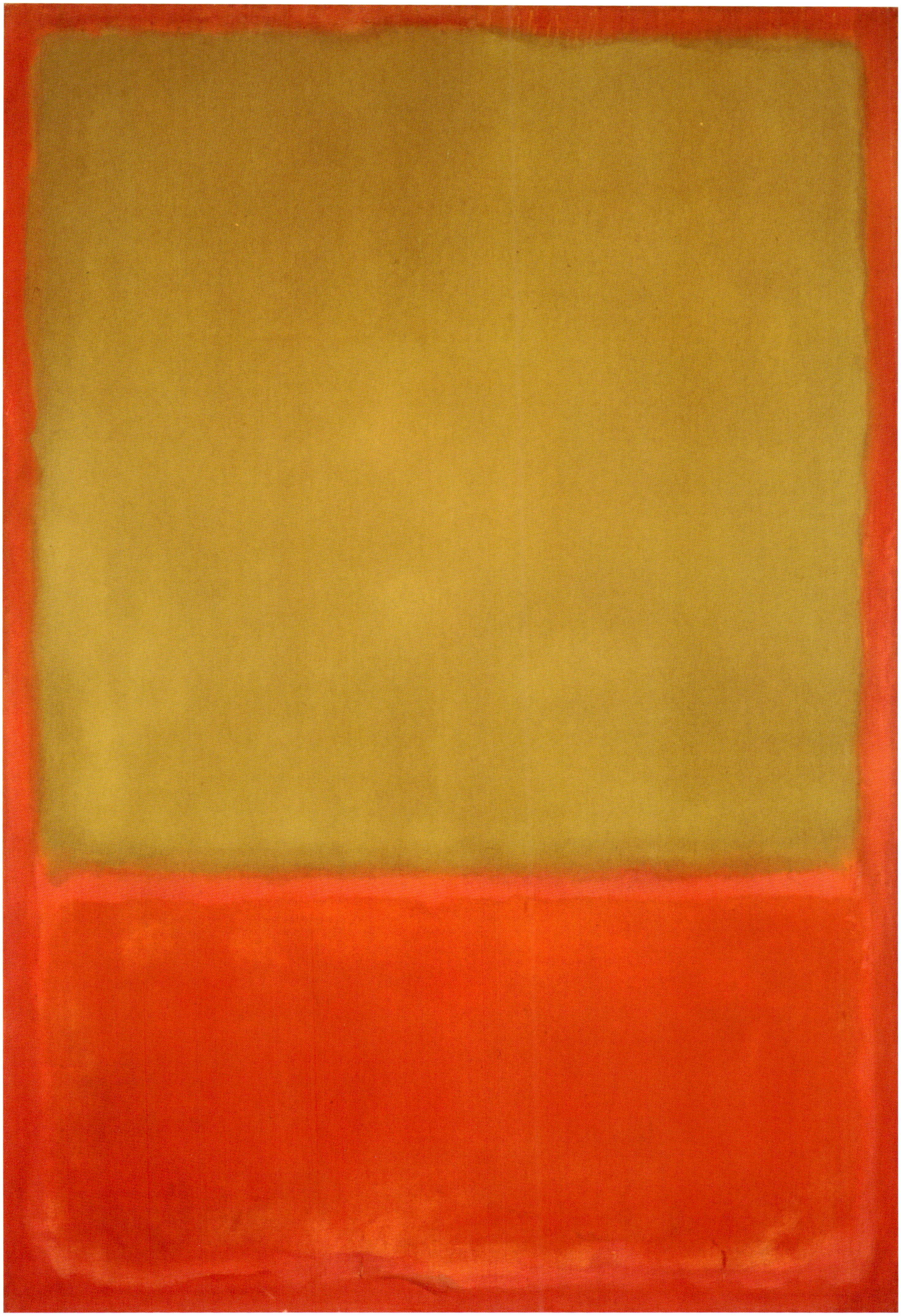

72. *Ochre, Red on Red*, 1954, oil on canvas, 92 5/8 × 63 3/4 in. (235.3 × 161.9 cm), The Phillips Collection, Washington, D.C. (CR 517)

73. *No. 15*, 1957, oil on canvas, 103 × 116 ½ in. (261.6 × 259.9 cm), private collection (CR 589)

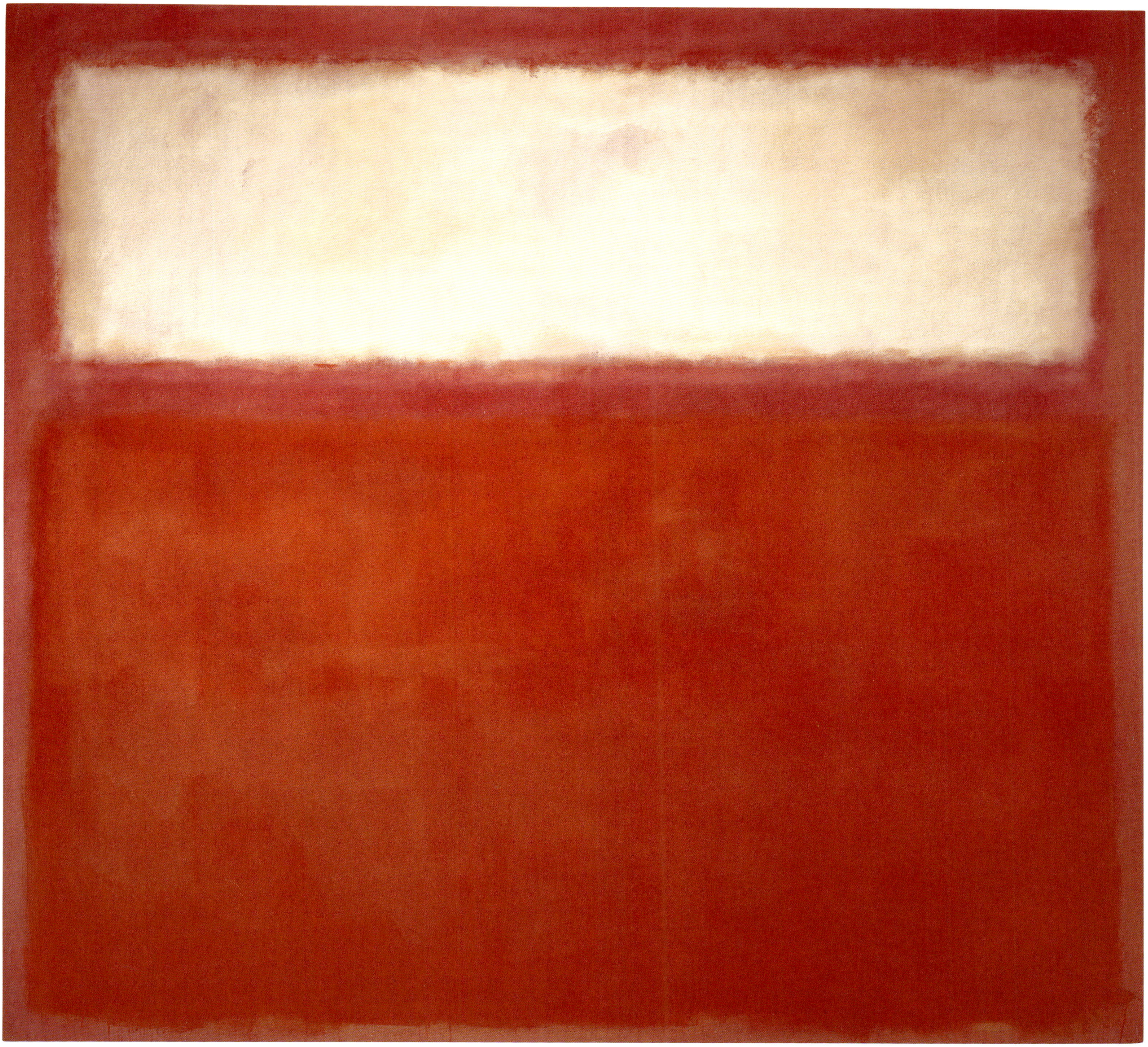

74. *Pink and White over Red*, 1957, oil on canvas, 105 × 116 in. (266.7 × 294.6 cm), Anderson Collection at Stanford University (CR 577)

75. *The Black and the White*, 1956, oil on canvas, 94 × 53 ¾ in. (238.8 × 136.5 cm), Harvard Art Museums, Fogg Museum, Cambridge (CR 572)

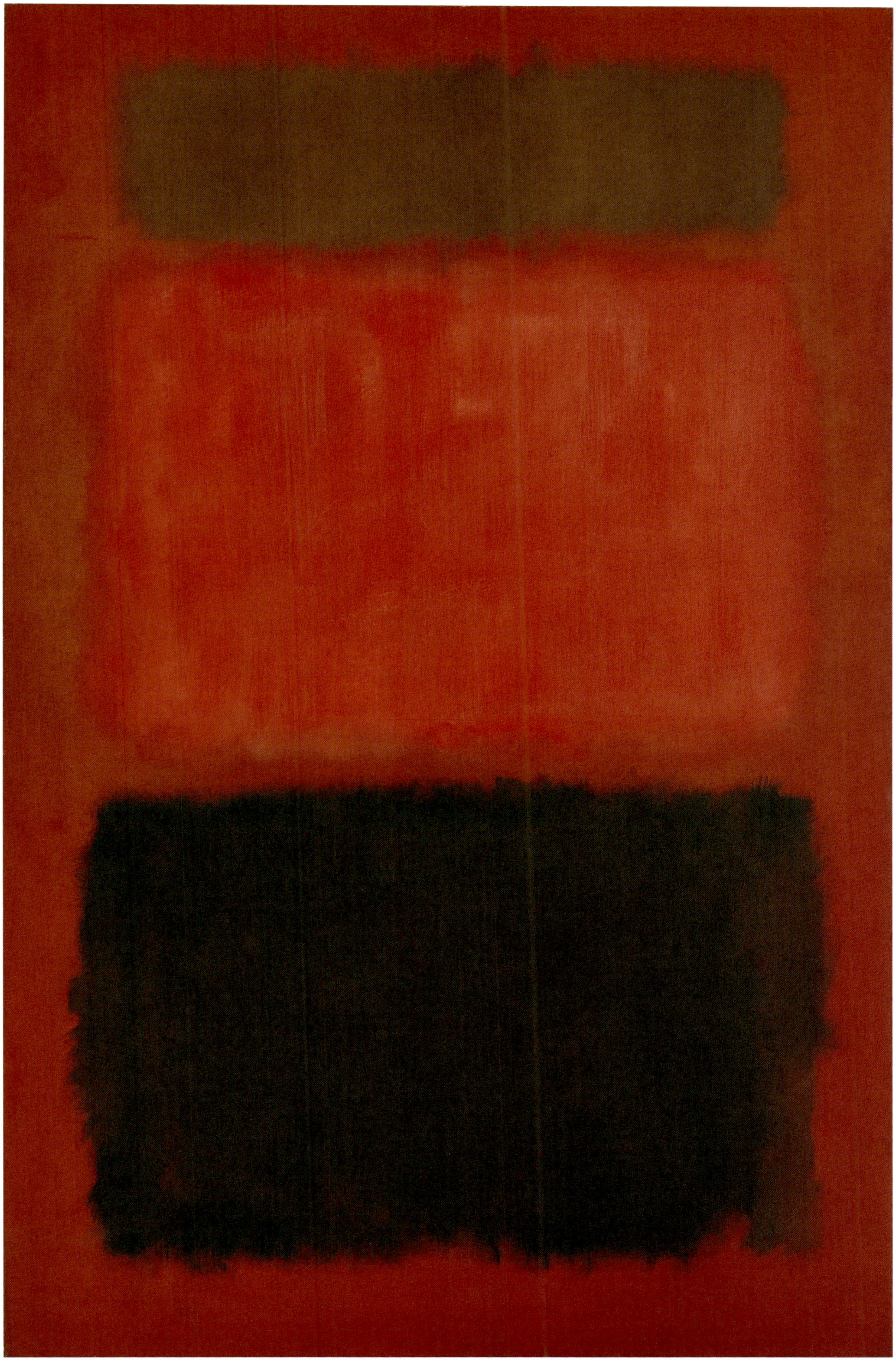

76. *Brown and Black in Reds*, 1957, oil on canvas, 91 × 60 in. (231.1 × 152.4 cm), Collection of Adriana and Robert Mnuchin (CR 602)

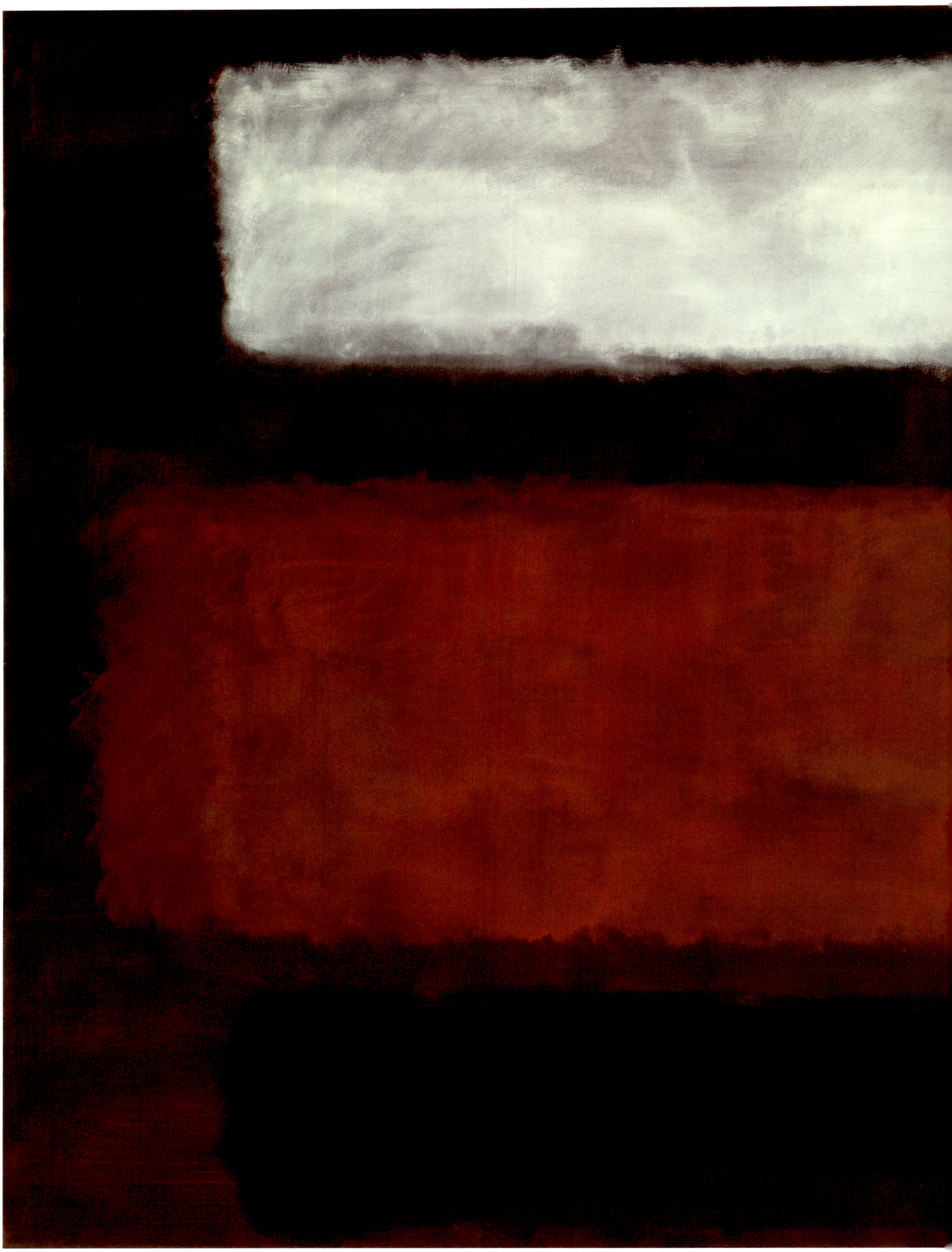

77. *No. 9 (White and Black on Wine)*, 1958, oil on canvas, 105 × 168 ¾ in. (266.7 × 428.7 cm), Glenstone Museum, Potomac, Maryland (CR 616)

78. *Black on Maroon*, 1959, oil and acrylic with powdered pigments on canvas, 105 × 90 in. (266.7 × 228.6 cm)
Tate: Presented by the artist through the American Federation of Arts 1969 (CR 647)

79. *Black on Maroon*, 1958, oil paint, acrylic paint, glue tempera and pigment on canvas, 90 × 81 ½ in. (228.6 × 207 cm)
Tate: Presented by the artist through the American Federation of Arts 1969 (CR 636)

80. *Black on Maroon*, 1958, oil paint, acrylic paint, glue tempera and pigment on canvas, 105 × 95 in. (266.7 × 241.3 cm)
Tate: Presented by the artist through the American Federation of Arts 1969 (CR 644)
Following pages: *Seagram Murals* display at Tate Modern, c. 2008

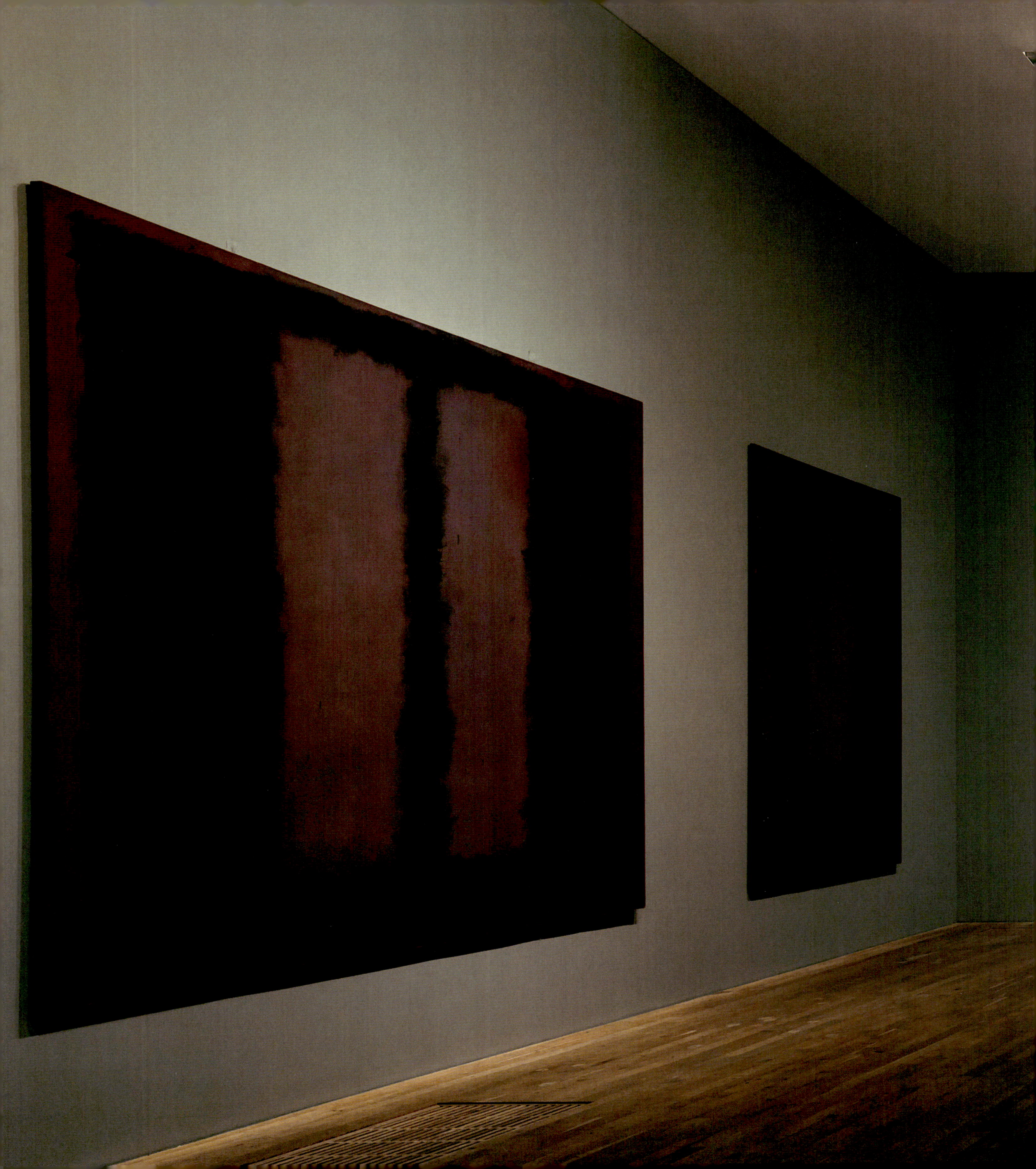

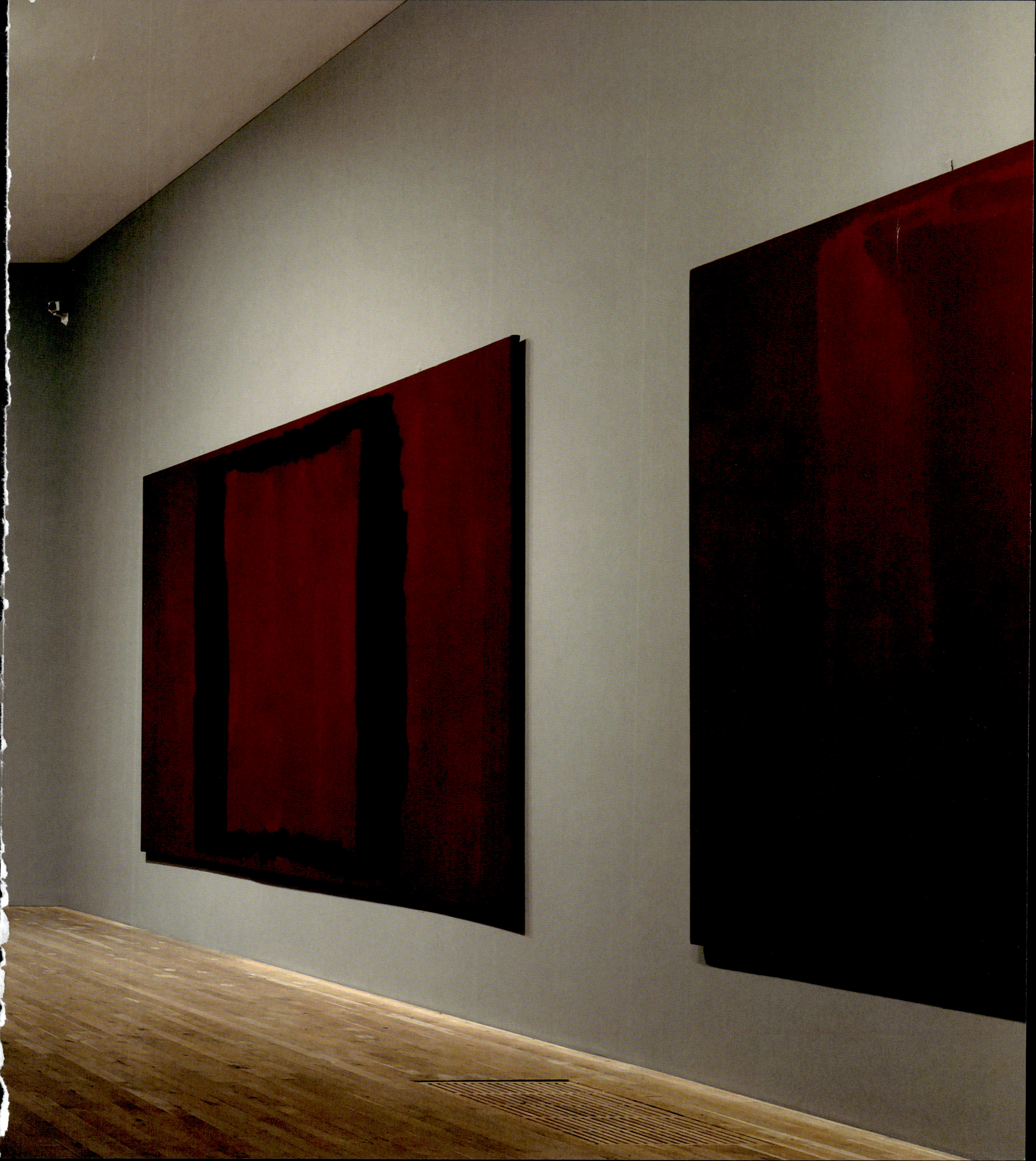

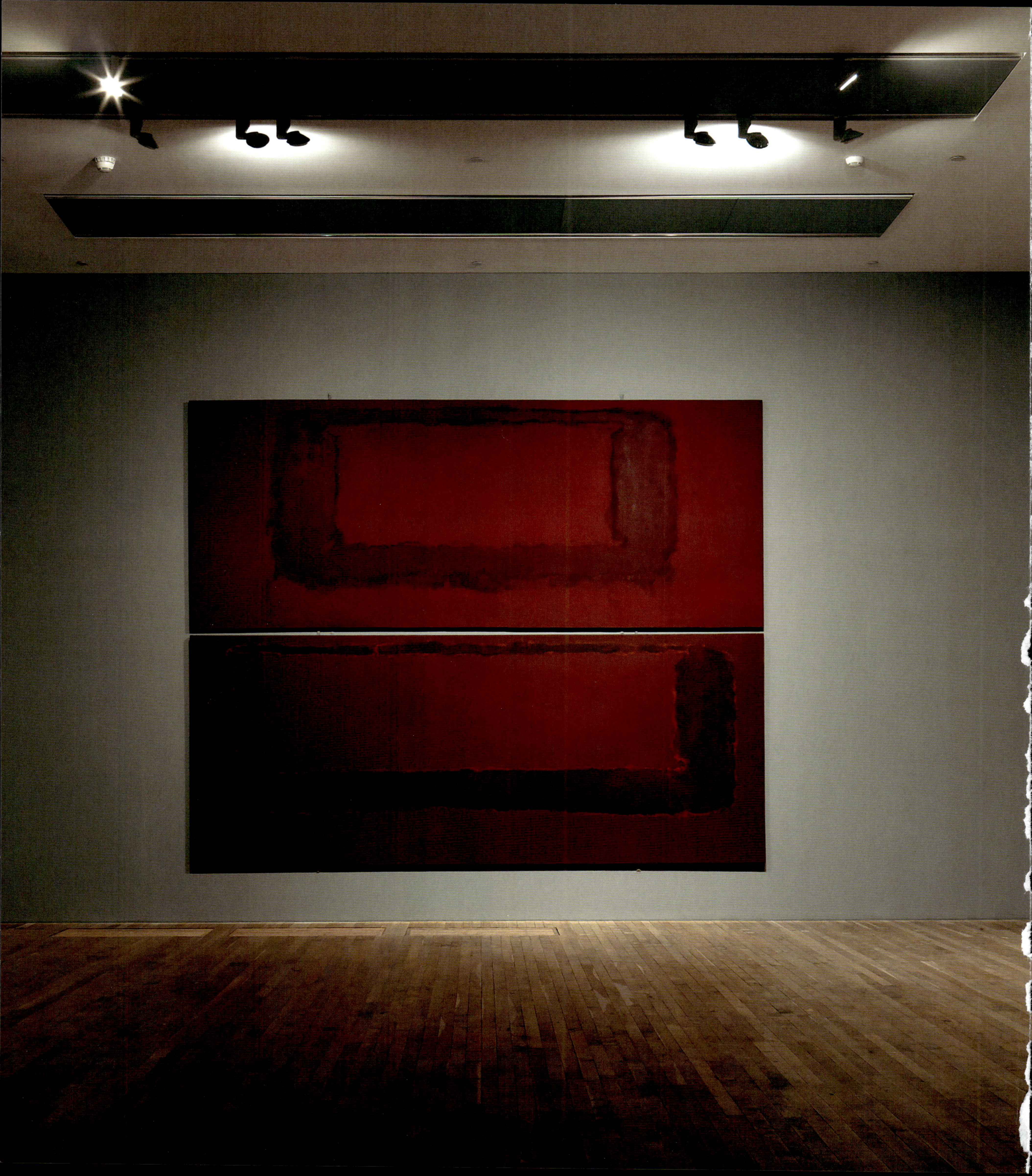

81. *Black on Maroon*, 1958, oil paint, acrylic paint, glue tempera and pigment on canvas, 105 × 144 in. (266.7 × 381.2 cm)
Tate: Presented by the artist through the American Federation of Arts 1968 (CR 642)

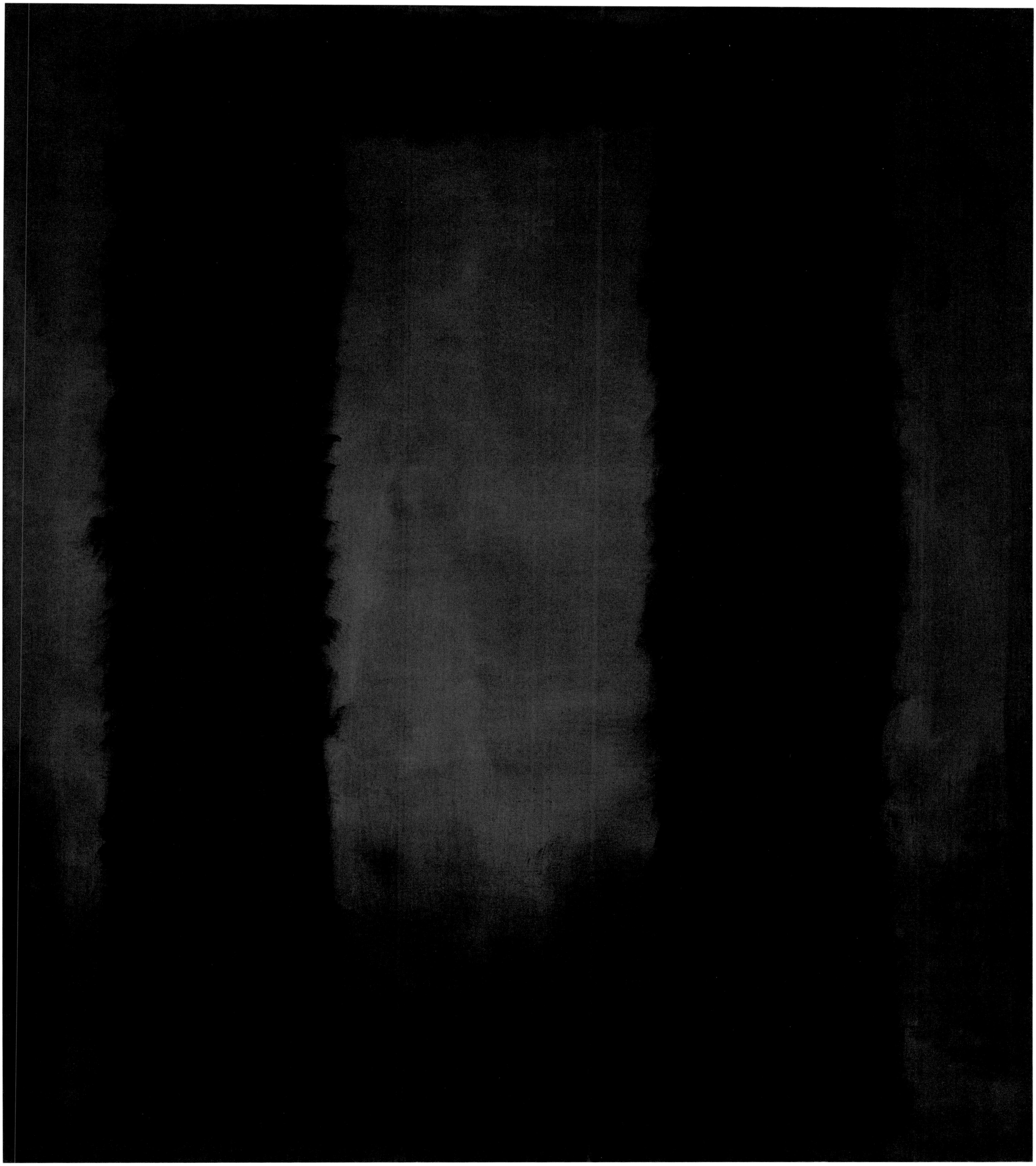

82. *Red on Maroon*, 1959, oil paint, acrylic paint, glue tempera and pigment on canvas, 105 × 94 in. (266.7 × 238.8 cm)
Tate: Presented by the artist through the American Federation of Arts 1969 (CR 660)

83. *Red on Maroon*, 1959, oil paint, acrylic paint, glue tempera and pigment on canvas, 72 × 180 in. (182.9 × 457.2 cm)
Tate: Presented by the artist through the American Federation of Arts 1969 (CR 663)

84. *Red on Maroon*, 1959, oil paint, acrylic paint, glue tempera and pigment on canvas, 72 × 180 in. (182.9 × 457.2 cm)
Tate: Presented by the artist through the American Federation of Arts 1969 (CR 661)

85. *Black on Maroon*, 1959, oil paint, acrylic paint, glue tempera and pigment on canvas, 105 × 180 in. (266.7 × 457.2 cm)
Tate: Presented by the artist through the American Federation of Arts 1969 (CR 658)

86. *Red on Maroon*, 1959, oil on canvas, 105 × 180 in. (266.7 × 457.2 cm)
Tate: Presented by the artist through the American Federation of Arts 1969 (CR 657)

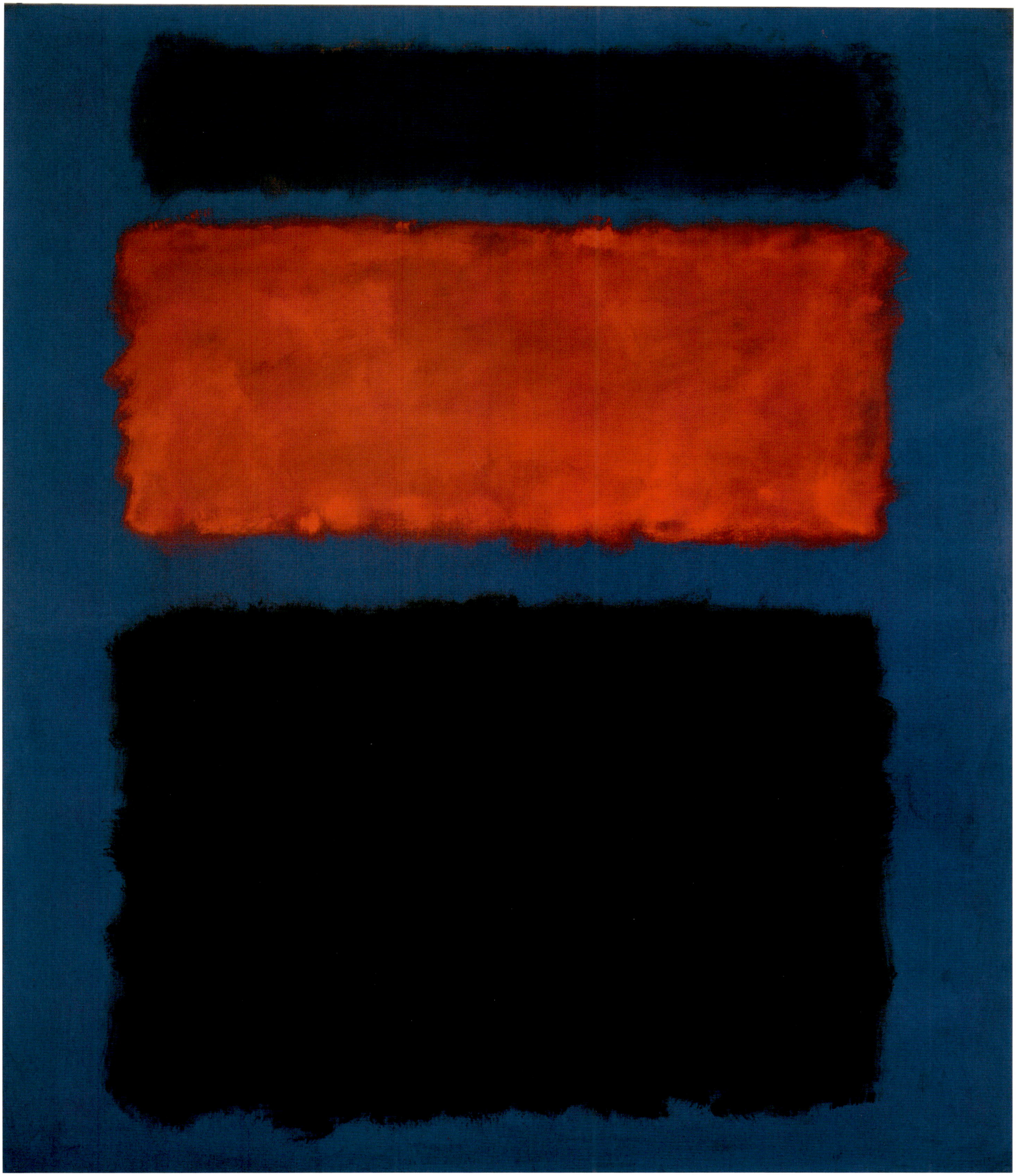

87. *Untitled*, 1960, mixed media on canvas, 92 ⅞ × 81 in. (235.9 × 205.7 cm), The Toledo Art Museum (CR 670)

88. *No. 14*, 1960, oil on canvas, 114 ½ × 105 ⅝ in. (290.8 × 268.3 cm), San Francisco Museum of Modern Art (CR 679)

89. *Number 207 (Red over Dark Blue on Dark Gray)*, 1961, oil on canvas, 92 ¾ × 81 ⅛ in. (235.6 × 206.1 cm), University of California, Berkeley Art Museum and Pacific Film Archive (CR 707)

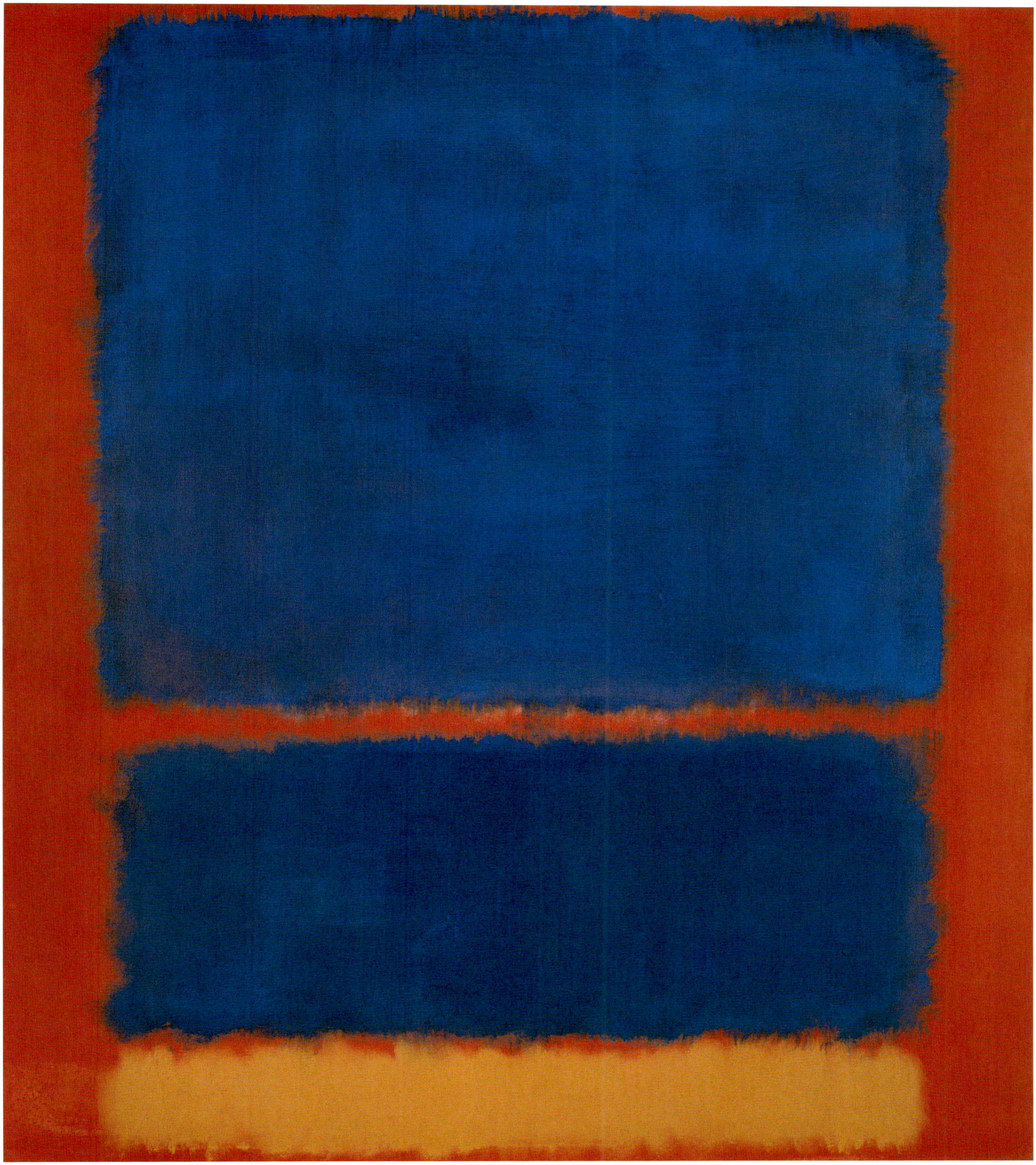

90. *Blue, Orange, Red*, 1961, oil on canvas, 90 ¼ × 81 ¹⁄₁₆ in. (229.3 × 205.9 cm), Hirshhorn Museum and Sculpture Garden, Smithsonian Institution, Washington, D.C. (CR 700)

91. *Blue and Gray*, 1962, oil on canvas, 79 ¼ × 69 in. (193 × 175 cm), Beyeler Foundation, Riehen / Basel, Beyeler Collection (CR 723)

92. *Untitled*, 1962, oil on canvas, 85 ¼ × 76 in. (206.5 × 193.5 cm), Staatsgalerie Stuttgart (CR 720)

93. *No. 1 (White and Red)*, 1962, oil on canvas, 102 × 90 in. (259.1 × 228.6 cm), Art Gallery of Ontario, Toronto (CR 717)

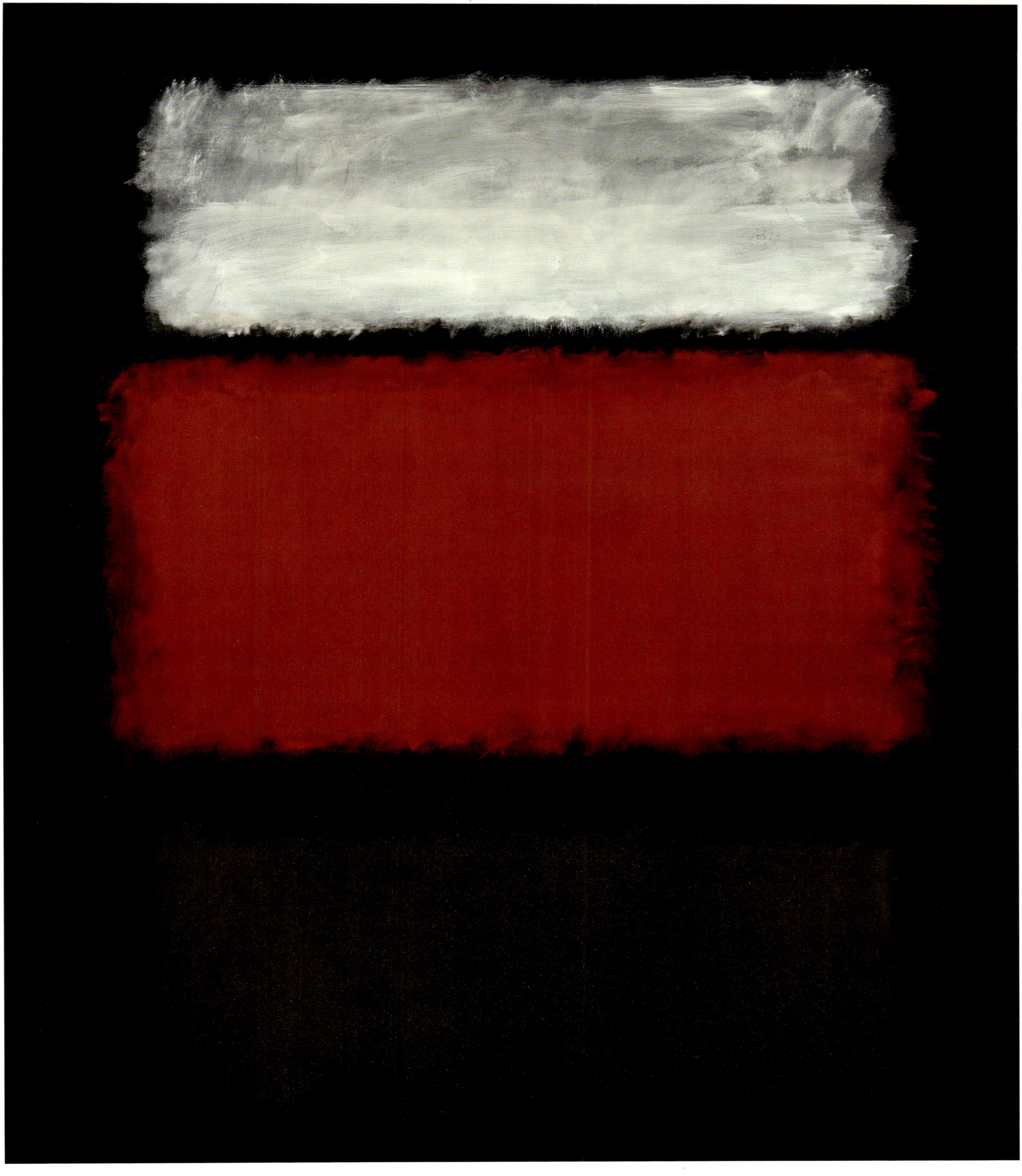

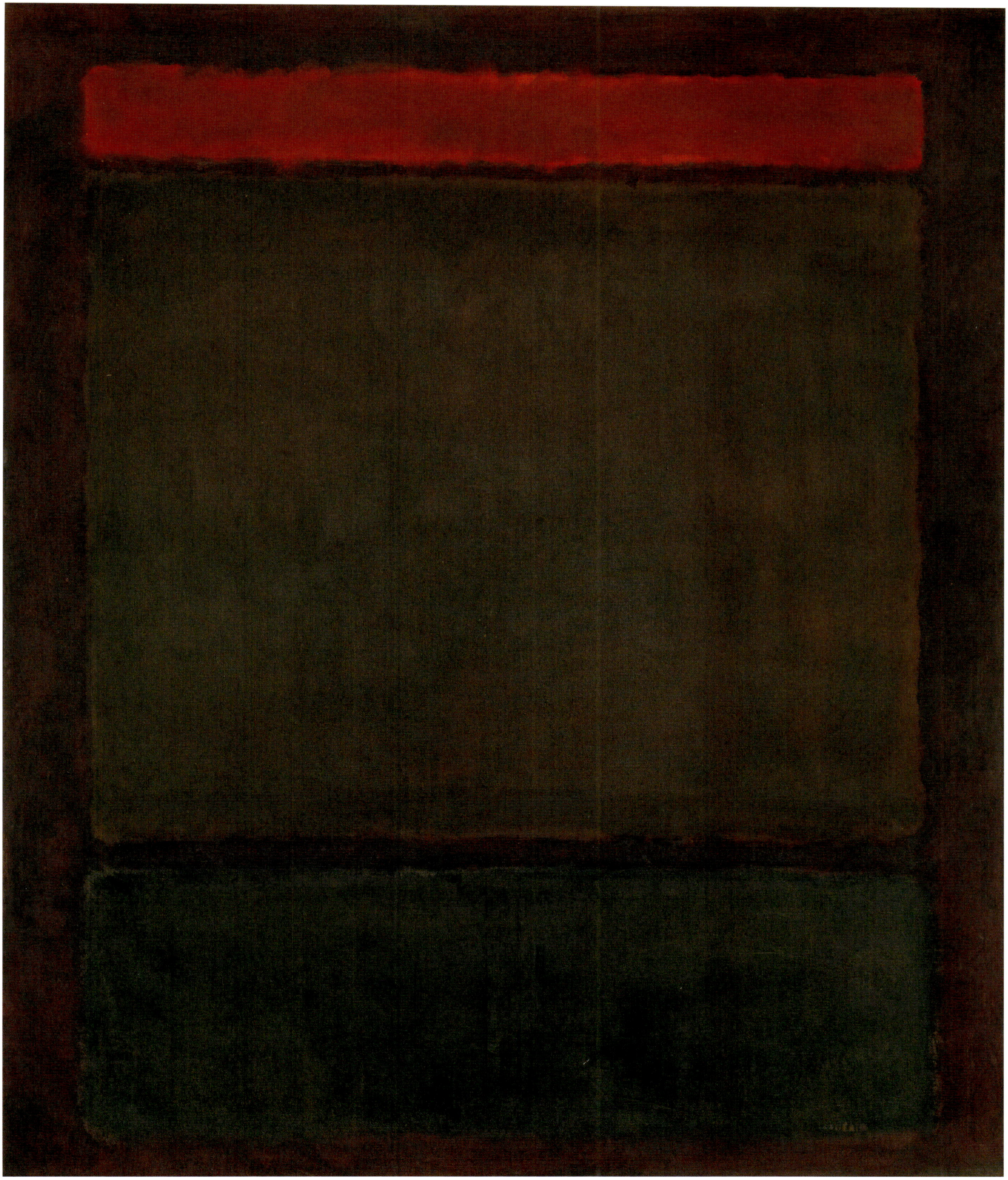

94. *No. 14*, 1961, oil on canvas, 92 7/8 × 80 in. (235.9 × 203.2 cm), Museum of Fine Arts, Houston (CR 701)

95. *No. 5*, 1963, oil on canvas, 90 × 69 in. (228.6 × 175.3 cm), private collection (CR 746)

96. *No. 2*, 1963, oil, acrylic, glue on canvas, 80 ¼ × 69 ⅛ in. (203.8 × 175.6 cm), Walker Art Center, Minneapolis (CR 744)

97. *Untitled (Black, Red over Black on Red)*, 1964, oil on canvas, 80 ¾ × 76 in. (205 × 193 cm), Centre Pompidou – Musée National d'Art Moderne, Paris (CR 764)

98. *No. 8*, 1964, oil, acrylic and mixed media on canvas, 105 ¼ × 80 ¼ in. (266.7 × 203.2 cm), National Gallery of Art, Washington, D.C. (CR 781)

99. *Untitled (Plum and Brown)*, 1964, oil on canvas, 81 × 69 1/8 in. (205.7 × 175.6 cm), private collection (CR 769)

100. *Untitled*, 1964, oil and acrylic paint on canvas, 69 ⅛ × 66 ⅗ in. (176 × 168.5 cm), Louisiana Museum of Modern Art, Humlebaek (CR 767)

101. *No. 3*, 1967, oil on canvas, 66 ⅛ × 68 ⅛ in. (168 × 173 cm), private collection (CR 807)

102. *Untitled*, 1967, oil on canvas, 80 × 69 in. (203.2 × 175.3 cm), The Governor Nelson A. Rockefeller Empire State Plaza Art Collection, New York (CR 806)

103. *Untitled*, 1969, acrylic on canvas, 92 × 78⅞ in. (233.7 × 200.3 cm), Collection of Christopher Rothko (CR 814)

104. *Untitled*, 1969, acrylic on canvas, 54 ¼ × 68 ¼ in. (137.8 × 173.4 cm), National Gallery of Art, Washington, D.C. (CR 823)

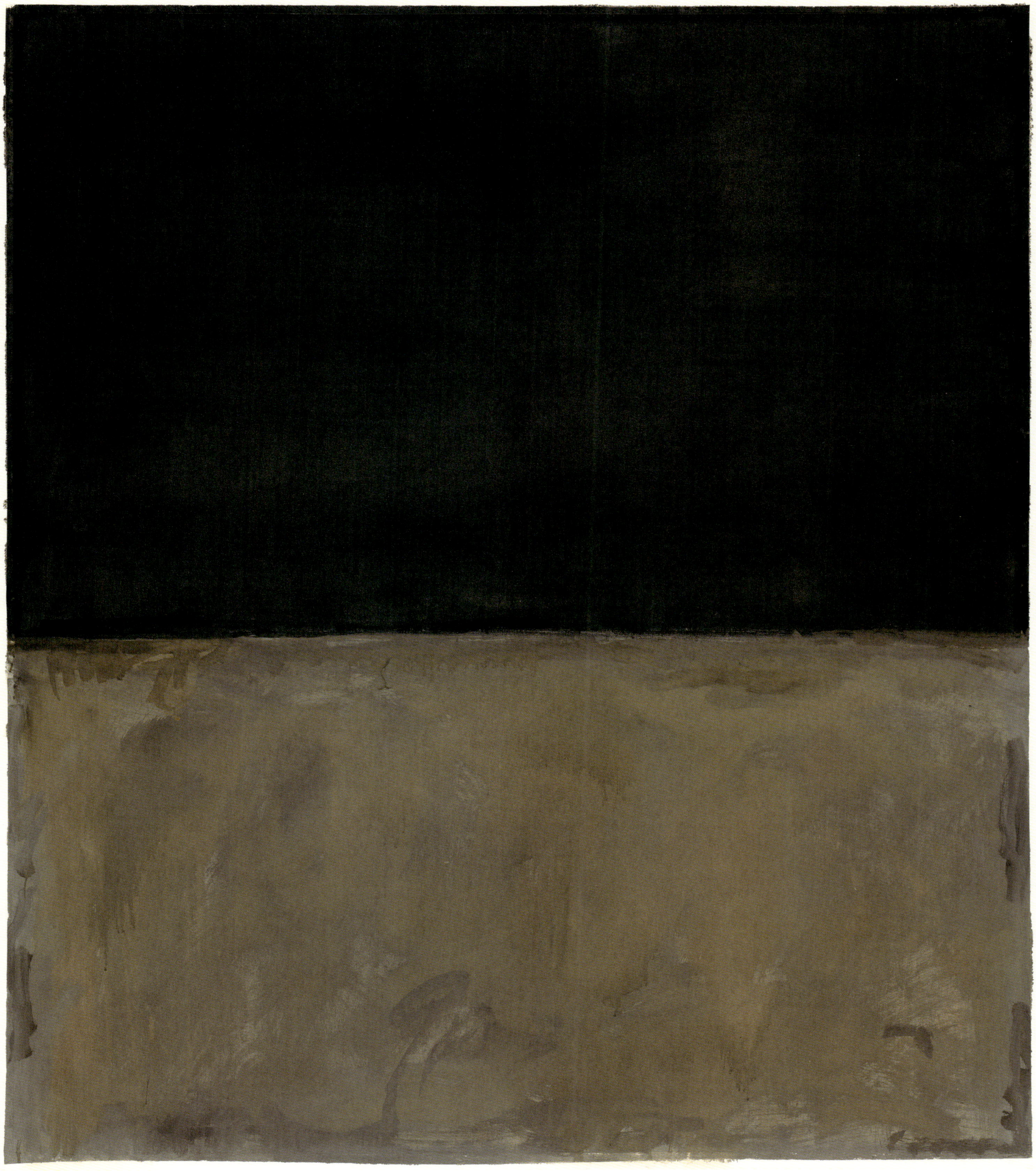

105. *Untitled*, 1969, acrylic on canvas, 69 ⅝ × 62 ⅛ in. (176.8 × 157.8 cm), National Gallery of Art, Washington, D.C. (CR 817)

106. *Untitled*, 1969/1970, acrylic on canvas, 68 × 64 in. (172.7 × 162.5 cm), private collection (CR 831)

107. *Untitled,* 1969, acrylic on canvas, 100 ⅛ × 79 ⅞ in. (254.3 × 202.9 cm), private collection (CR 816). Not exhibited

108. *Untitled*, 1969, acrylic on canvas, 81 ⅛ × 76 ¼ in. (206.1 × 193.7 cm), National Gallery of Art, Washington, D.C. (CR 820)
Following double page: simulation of an installation at the *Mark Rothko* exhibition, Paris, Fondation Louis Vuitton, Gallery 10, level 2

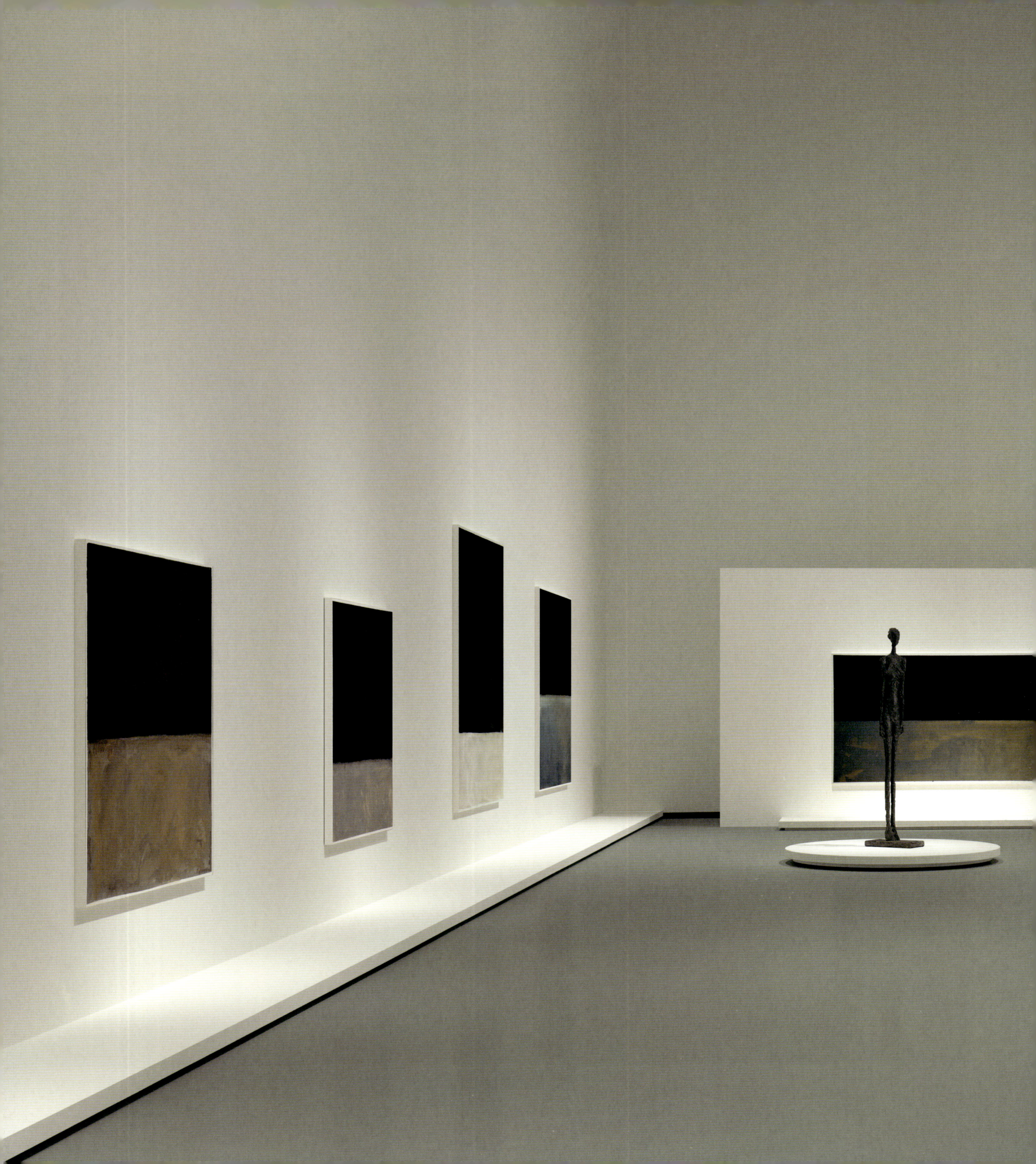

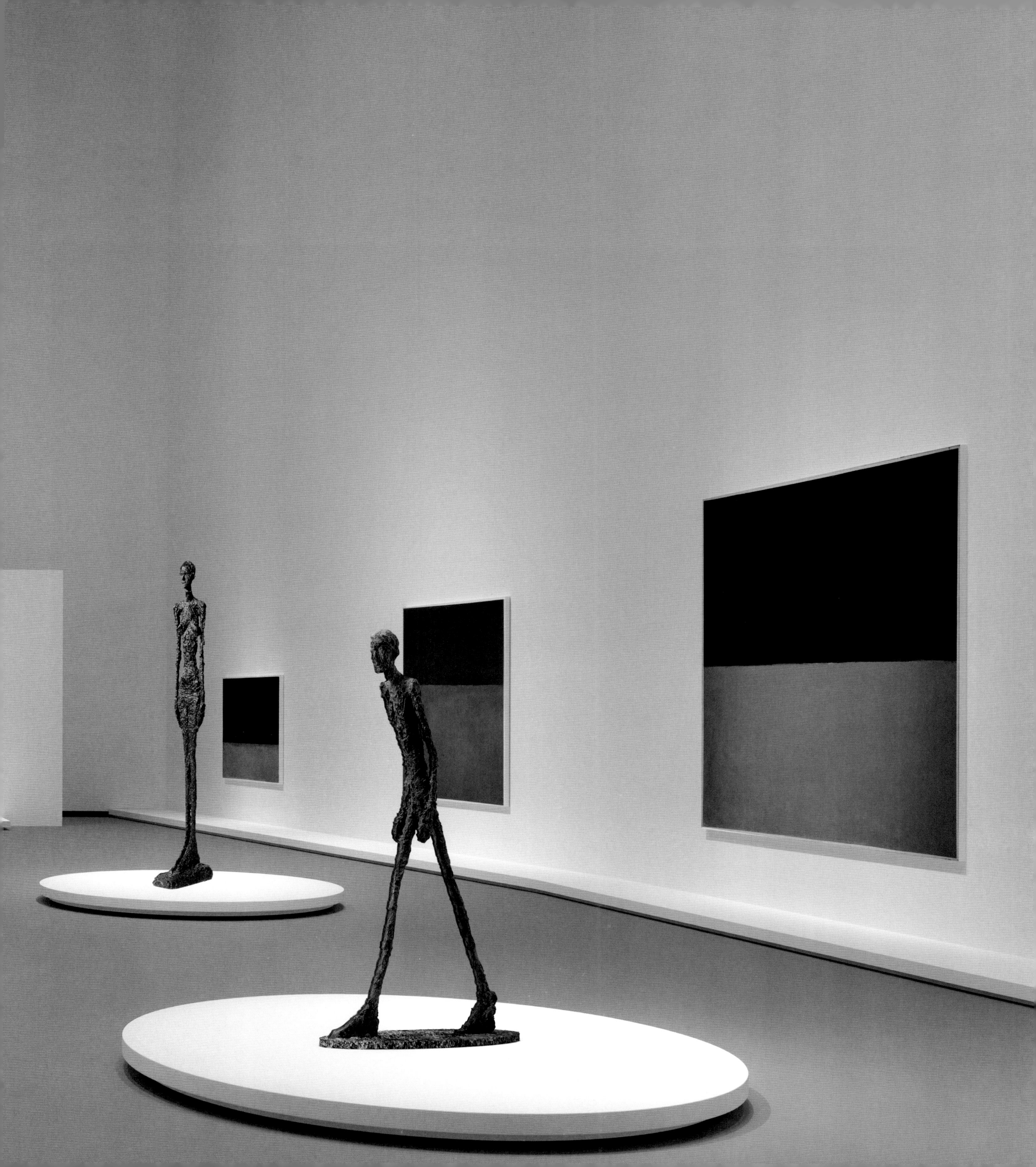

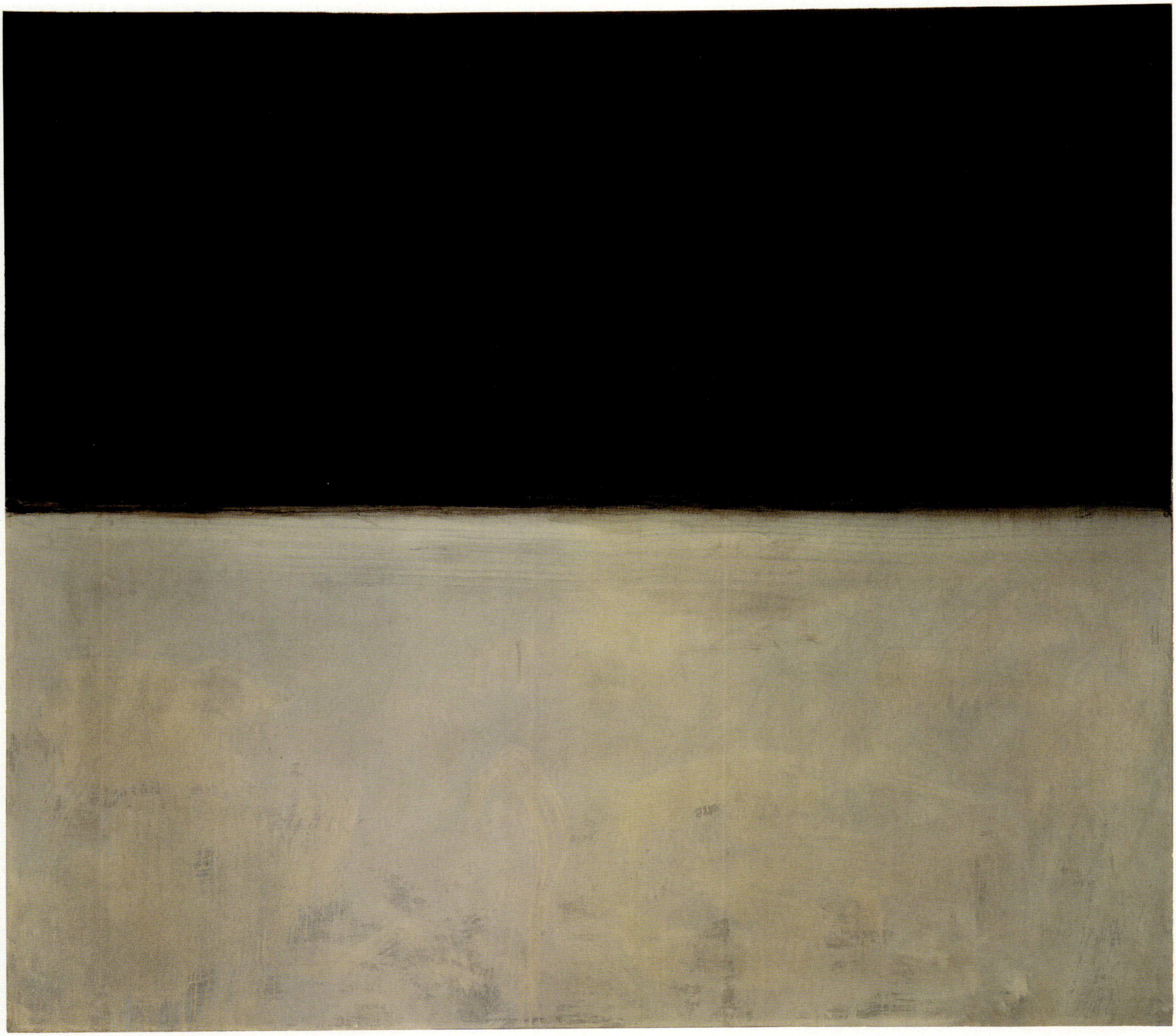

109. *Untitled,* 1969, acrylic on canvas, 81 ¼ × 93 in. (206.4 × 236.2 cm), private collection (CR 825)

110. *Untitled*, 1969, acrylic on canvas, 105 × 114 in. (266.1 × 289.6 cm), private collection (CR 824)

111. *Untitled (Black and Gray)*, 1969 / 1970, acrylic on canvas, 68 × 60 ¼ in. (172.7 × 152.4 cm), The Museum of Contemporary Art, Los Angeles (CR 829)

112. *Untitled*, 1969, acrylic on canvas, 69 ¾ × 117 in. (177.2 × 297.2 cm), private collection (CR 826)

113. *Untitled (Black and Gray)*, 1969, acrylic on canvas, 93 × 76 ⅛ in. (236.2 × 193.4 cm), Anderson Collection at Stanford University (CR 822)

114. *Untitled*, 1967, oil on canvas, 68 × 60 ¼ in. (172.7 × 153 cm), private collection (CR 808)

115. *No. 3 (Untitled/Orange)*, 1967, oil on canvas, 81 × 75 15/16 in. (205.7 × 196.6 cm), Yale University Art Gallery, New Haven, Katharine Ordway Collection (CR 810)

"I became a painter because I wanted to raise painting to the level of poignancy of music and poetry."

"the real essence of the great portraiture of all time is the artist's eternal interest in the human figure, character and emotion—in a short in the human drama."

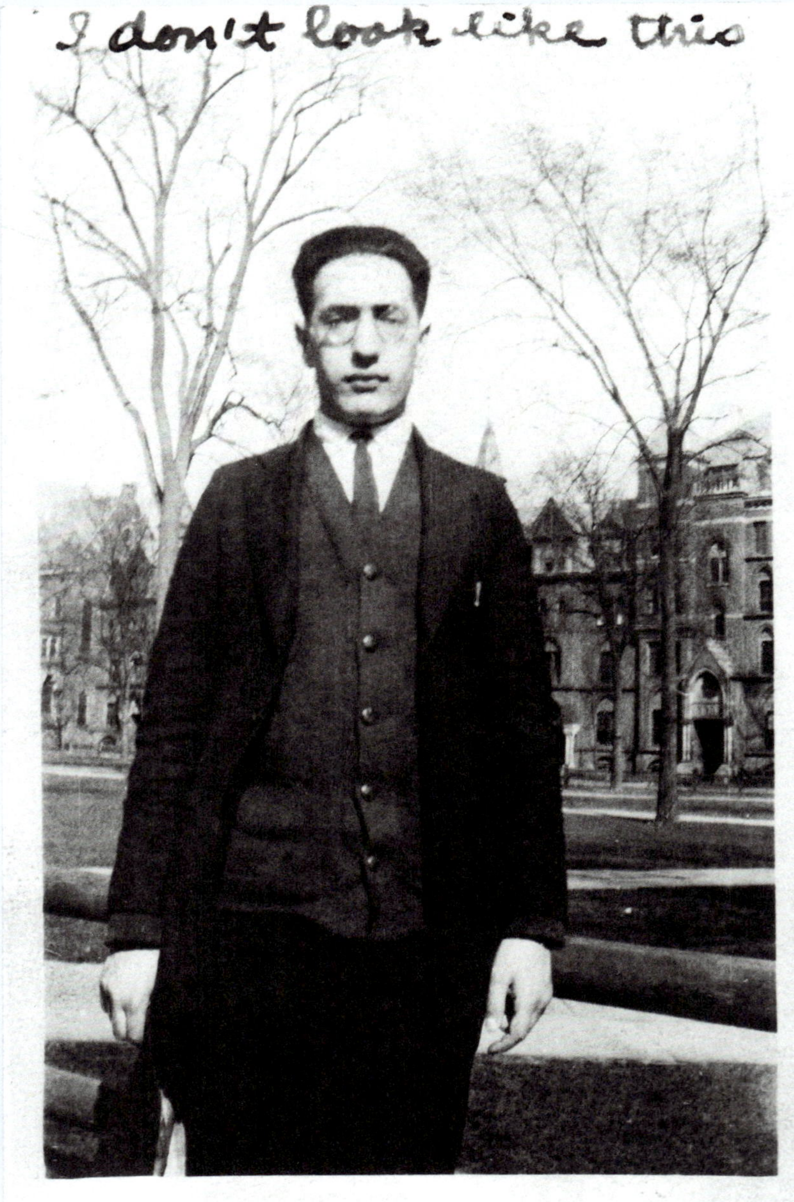

Portrait of Marcus Rotkovitch, student at Yale University, with a personal handwritten annotation, c. 1923, The Rothko Family Archive

Ludovic Delalande

Rothko before Rothko: early works

During the first fifteen years of his career, between 1925 and 1940, well before he became a symbol of postwar American abstraction, Mark Rothko was a figurative painter. This aspect of his work is less well known, less exhibited and less theorized than his abstract work. His figurative period began with his earliest works and is key to understanding the artist's trajectory, the evolution of his formal visual vocabulary and the theoretical foundations that govern it.

When he arrived in New York for the second time,[1] in 1923, two years before he made it his permanent home, Marcus Rotkovitch[2] had just abandoned his studies at prestigious Yale University, which would have opened up a career as a lawyer or engineer, and was about to make a major change of direction. No particular predisposition—no conspicuous gift or education—cut him out for a career in the arts, until that day when a friend took him to the Art Students League, an increasingly popular art school founded in 1875. His sense of vocation was immediate: "Then one day I happened to wander into an art class, to meet a friend who was taking the course. All the students were sketching this nude-model and right away I decided that was the life for me."[3] Having decided, after this fortuitous but decisive event, to became a painter, the young novice began with a few months training at the Art Students League with George Bridgman, who took life classes, and Max Weber, who taught still life, and at the New School of Design with Arshile Gorky. But he soon turned away from this type of academic training and chose to proceed as an autodidact. This marked the start of a period of learning, experimentation, and research, during which, while regularly producing works on canvas and paper, he also read art history books, visited galleries and museums, familiarized himself with the art of his time and with classical painting, and met and exchanged with his peers on the New York art scene, forming several fruitful and inspiring relationships. It was not in the solitude of the studio that his work took shape, but in his heightened awareness of the world around him. As he began to show his work in group exhibitions[4] and solo shows[5] across the U.S., he also began teaching,[6] even though he himself was still only starting out, as well as writing,[7] all of which constantly nourished his understanding of the pictorial medium. In fact, Rothko the practitioner was also someone who thought about and theorized painting, and this constant dialectic would mark his entire oeuvre, with the artist continually writing and publishing about art from 1934 to 1969. It was against this backdrop of artistic and intellectual emulation that the 177 works[8] of his figurative phase emerged, a heterogeneous corpus united by a concern with the human figure, a favored theme for this artist driven by the inner need to express himself about the world, the very need that, unconsciously or not, had decided his destiny. For Rothko, "the real essence of the great portraiture of all time is the artist's eternal interest in the human figure, character and emotions—in a short in the human drama."[9] To depict the human drama, or the human condition: this is the artistic and existential quest that runs through and animates the whole of his work, the quest to which Rothko devoted his entire life. According to Annie Cohen-Solal, he became an artist for social and political reasons, because "as an artist, you have something to say about the world."[10]

Apart from a small number of landscapes, still lifes, and urban views, Rothko painted mainly portraits, nudes, interiors, and exteriors featuring male and female figures, alone or in groups. With the exception of the occasional name given in the title, these figures are anonymous: Rothko was not trying to render the character or emotions of any particular individual. As he argued, "the artist's real model is an ideal, which embraces all of human drama rather than the appearance of a particular individual."[11] From the outset, his work had a universal dimension.

While immersing himself in the paintings of artists who inspired him—Milton Avery and Adolph Gottlieb among his American peers, Matisse and Cézanne for the European moderns, and Vermeer, Rembrandt, Fra Angelico, Filippo Lippi, and Botticelli of the Old Masters—Rothko was seeking his own language. From his earliest works, his vocabulary was expressionistic, drawing on the avant-garde movement of European origin that was increasingly echoed by American artists looking for an alternative to the objective representation and transcription of the world. Working with great freedom, he explored all the density and complexity of the pictorial medium, constantly renewing his approach as he pushed back the limits of representation and tested the plasticity of figures, developing a style that moved ever more toward the stylization, simplification, and reduction of forms. He would often repeat a motif and composition from one work to another, subjecting it to different formal and chromatic solutions. Rothko was constantly experimenting and innovating. Over the years, as work followed work, his style evolved. Rather than divide his production into series, he would work simultaneously and over an extended period of time on several subjects that fed off each other. For Rothko, nothing was ever fixed; he was always searching.

A major part of this production is devoted to the female nude, a classic pictorial theme that Rothko tackled from his earliest works, and to which he would return again and again. In two late examples, *Nude* (1938–39; pl. 18) and *Untitled* (1939; fig. 1), the female figures, represented respectively full-length and at bust height, emerge from a monochrome background with which they share, almost to the point of merging with it, the same muted hues. The color palette is limited. With little in the way of features, the interiors are left bare so as to highlight the tightly-framed figure. But if the bodies are stylized and elementary, the faces are clearly drawn and their expressions emphasized—a contrast made all the more striking by the fact that the outline of the woman with the bun in *Untitled (Nude)* is almost disappearing into her own body mass.

Another classic theme that the artist enjoyed reinventing was the genre scene, to which he devoted a very large number of canvases, including *Untitled* (1938–39; fig. 2) and *Portrait* (1939; pl. 15). The handling of these figure is similar, one seated and in profile, the other standing, facing us. Typically of Rothko's images at this time, these figures are doing nothing in particular and seem to have been captured in an ordinary, calm, silent moment. The expressions on their elliptical or even non-existent features are impossible to read. The same is true of the shape of their bodies—or at least that which still makes them identifiable as such; their boundaries seem to be defined only by the color of their clothing. Particular attention is paid to the choice of colors, whose application in zones, along with the formal simplification, evokes the importance of the influence exerted by the work of Milton Avery, an American painter almost twenty years his senior whom Rothko considered a master.[12] From the moment they met in 1928,[13] the two painters forged a profound friendship and artistic relationship. Rothko became a regular at the weekly drawing sessions organized by Milton and Sally Avery, whose home was a great place for meeting and talking about art. Together, they exchanged thoughts on the work of Henri Matisse, to whom Rothko had been introduced by Avery and whose fundamental influence can indeed be felt in the aforementioned compositions, which are indirectly derived from his work. The use of pale, opaque, even dull colors—a palette that Rothko also borrowed from Avery—contrasts with the strange luminosity that emanates from these two interior scenes. The sun streams in through the windows, indicated by flat areas of blue sky that open up the canvas and extend it outwards. The figures are backlit, which no doubt explains the haziness of their faces. The surface around them expands, making way for elements of furniture (chest of drawers, curtain, chair, table) and architecture (wall, window, ceiling). From this point onwards, it is not just a question of dealing with the figure, but of placing it within a space, and this dimension opens the way to new perspectives that the artist continues to explore in the so-called urban scenes.

This shift from private to public space led Rothko to consider the figure in a new context: its interaction with the city. Over time, the architecture with which the figures cohabit becomes dominant, starting to come across as the main subject. In *Street Scene* (c. 1937; pl. 13) and *Interior* (1936; fig. 3), the building facades are so massive that they dominate the entire surface of the canvas, and therefore the figures, which seem to be relegated to the background. Pushed into the right-hand side of the picture, the couple in *Street Scene* seem packed and frozen, ready to slip away into the ground whose gray tones they share. This sense of being crushed is reinforced by a frontal view whose tight framing blocks any perspective, but also by a treatment akin to collage, in which all the elements are brought together on the same plane. This is even more apparent in *Interior*, where the characters, grouped in a mass with shapeless contours, disappear into the architecture that engulfs them, with colors and shapes mingling until they merge.

Following on from these reflections, in the mid-1930s Rothko began a series of works emblematic of his figurative phase using the New York subway as a backdrop. Known under the generic title of *Subway Paintings* (pl. 5 to 8),[14] the fifteen or so canvases he executed between 1935 and 1940 mark a new stage in the representation of the human figure, with more complex, even more accomplished compositions that undoubtedly testify to a better mastery of the pictorial medium and its tools. After a few attempts at multiple figures, as evidenced by the small group in *Untitled (Waiting Room)* (1935), the first work in this new ensemble, Rothko reduced the number of figures. In subsequent paintings, the scene being played out—or the drama, if we refer to Rothko's interest in Greek tragedy and Shakespeare—is identical. Men and women, rarely children, in profile, sometimes frontal, stand at a distance from each other. There's no interaction; they don't even seem to see each other. Each person is absorbed in themself. They are rarely in motion, but rather static, their gestures mute. Time seems suspended. There is no gathering of waiting figures, no train, no advertisement, no sign or signage to characterize this place. Rothko does not seek to render or recreate the atmosphere of the subway and its urban vitality, or even to praise speed in the post-industrial era. What he brings out in the space are its architectural qualities: the platform, the ceiling, the columns, the handrail, like so many geometric warps and wefts, vertical and horizontal lines out of which Rothko builds compositions in which the figure seems to be no more than a pretext. As Christopher Rothko states, "Geometric patterns are not simply the principles of organization, but the pictorial elements that interest him most."[15] The figures are reduced to the bare essentials, blurred outlines and absent or lightly sketched faces. They are more like apparitions, evocations whose presence wavers in frail, fragile shadows, with "a spectral, bloodless, ephemeral existence, each like Giacometti's absorbed in his own world,"[16] notes Seitz, as if "these figures had been wrung and stretched by the pressure of the surrounding atmosphere." In *Untitled (Subway)* (1937, pl. 8) and *Underground Fantasy* (c. 1940; fig. 5), their deformed silhouettes no longer respect anatomical proportions, but stretch out, elongated, between floor and ceiling, into the height of the space and the canvas, along the columns with which they tend to merge in a fusion with the architecture, which now dominates. This impression is reinforced by constructions that annul the

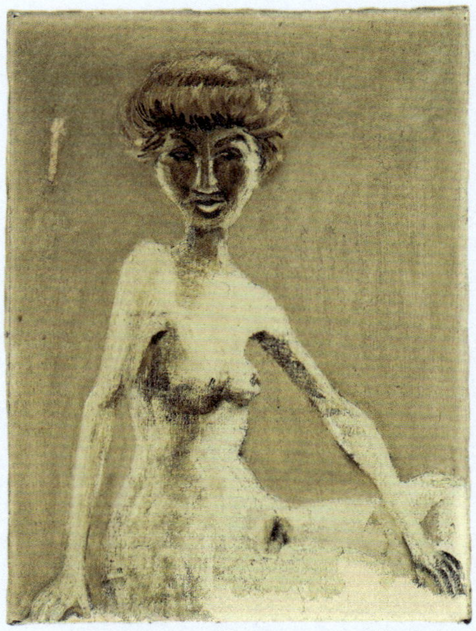

fig. 1 *Untitled*, 1939, oil on canvas, 23 ⅝ × 18 in., private collection (CR 171; pl. 19)

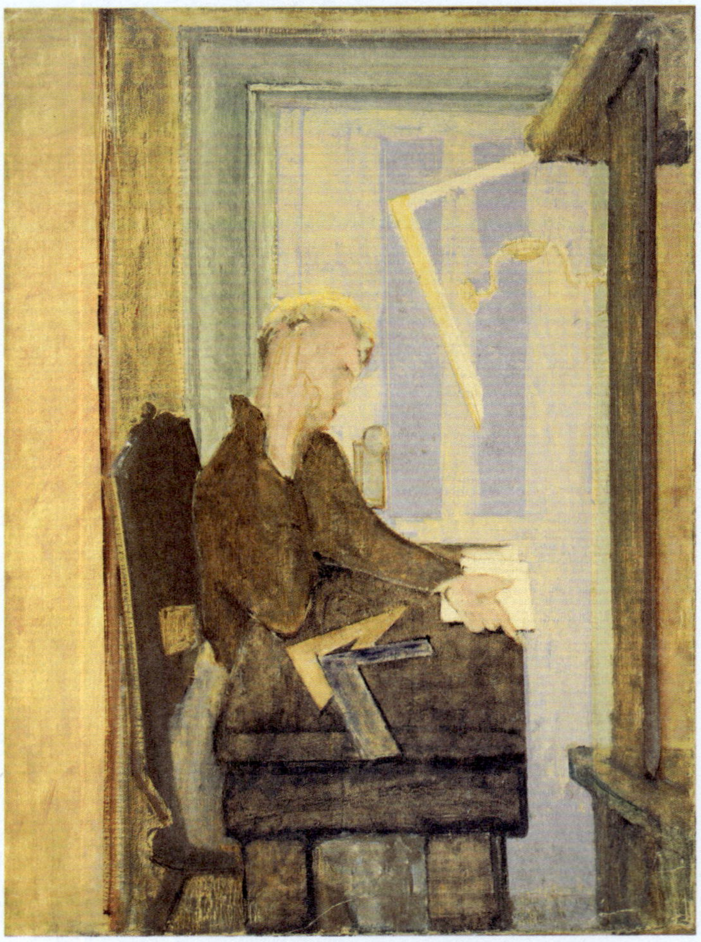

fig. 2 *Untitled*, 1938 / 1939, oil on canvas, 40 × 30 in., Collection of Christopher Rothko (CR 163; pl. 14)

distance between foreground and background, as if the surface were compressed into a single plane, blocking all lines of escape. The space appears even more constrained and limited by the handling of the colors, which contributes to this effect, with predominantly cool hues that spread out in flat tints invading the surface or underlining the presence of architectural elements. As Riccardo Venturi observes, "however much the artist experiments with heterogeneous relationships, he never manages to find a balance, and the architectonic tends to prevail over the human."[17] A sense of anguish pervades these enclosed, dark, underground spaces, in which the anonymous, confined and encircled city dwellers seem on the verge of disappearing, diluted into shapes and colors. Without doubt, these *Subway Paintings* echo the context of the time and the morosity caused by the recent stock market crash of 1929, which had plunged the country into a terrible, deep depression. They reveal Rothko's interest in social issues.

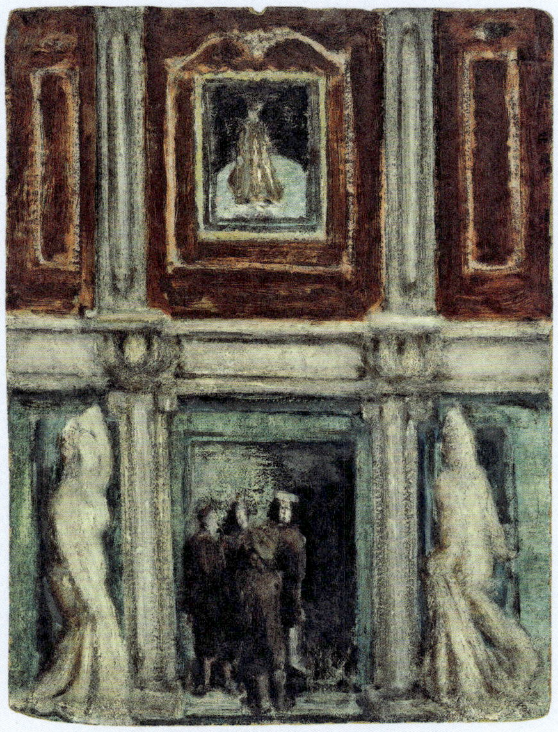

fig. 3 *Interior*, 1936, oil on hardboard, 23⅞ × 18¼ in., National Gallery of Art, Washington, D.C. (CR 79)

In 1936, when Rothko painted his self-portrait, the only one in all his oeuvre, he was a recognized painter playing an active role on the New York art scene; in particular, he had just joined the Artist Union and helped found the group The Ten.[18] In this self-portrait, the artist is shown at bust height in three-quarter face, hands clasped, shaggy hair and deep-red lips. He wears a dark suit set off by a white shirt and red tie. His dark lenses nevertheless allow us to see the two black dots of the pupils. No expression can be read or guessed on his face. His gaze is lost; out of the frame. There is no setting: his stylized silhouette fills most of the pictorial surface and stands out against a brown background, a monochrome plane worked in expressive strokes. Notable for its great economy of means, this composition was freely inspired by Rembrandt, for whom Rothko had a profound admiration (he spent hours observing his self-portraits at the Metropolitan Museum of Art). Likewise, as is often the case with the Dutch master, none of the painter's attributes are to be seen here. Furthermore, as Rothko's biographer James Breslin points out, the two tools necessary for painting—hands and eyes—appear damaged.[19] He presents himself both as a seer of the dark and implicitly as a possessor of an inner sight. But shouldn't this simulated blindness also be taken to denote the thwarted ruminations of an artist unable to find what he's looking for? Could we go so far as to see here the anticipated admission of his forthcoming failure—namely, in the use of figuration to express himself? Is the artist in the same frame of mind here as when he was about to leave Yale University, in 1923? A photograph taken at that time strangely prefigures the self-portrait.

In early 1940, Mark Rothko was on the verge of another fundamental change. Despite all his repeated and relentless attempts to create a language capable of depicting the human condition in accordance with his personal vision, the artist became aware of the limits of representation. Faced with this realization of failure, he decided to abandon figurative painting, never to return to it again. By his own admission, "I belong to a generation that was preoccupied with the human figure, and I studied it. It was with the most reluctance that I found that it did not meet my needs. Whoever used it mutilated it.... I refuse to mutilate, and had to find another way of expression."[20] For the time being, however, and before he entered the second phase of his career, Rothko had reached an impasse and saw no other way out than to put down his brushes. As he recalled, "The last phase of this direction in my work was exhibited by J. B. Neuman in his galleries in 1939. Shortly thereafter, I became convinced of the limitations of that tendency for the expression of my whole equipment and predilections. I stopped painting and spent nearly a year developing both in writing and studies my ideas concerning the Myth and anecdote which are the basis of my present work."[21] During this short hiatus, which in fact lasted no more than a few months, Rothko devoted himself to writing a text, the manuscript of which only came to light posthumously and was published in 2004 under the title *The Artist's Reality*,[22] a theoretical book which bears witness to this intense period of reflection during which Rothko continued to ponder painting and no doubt to conceive, consciously or unconsciously, its future development.

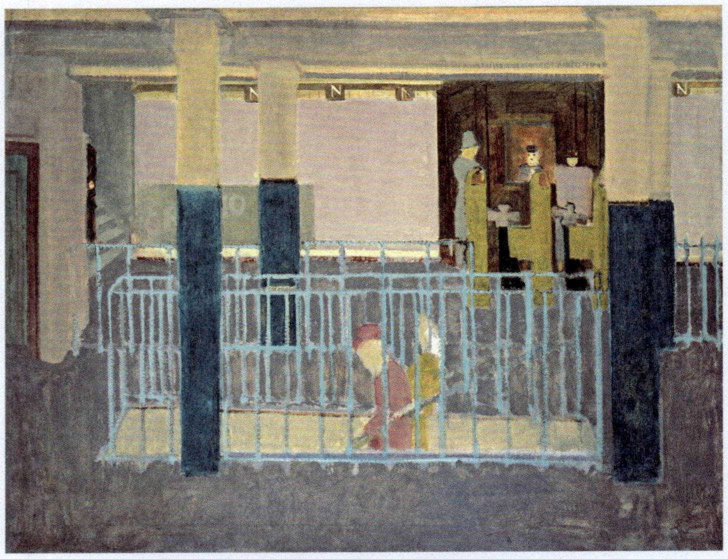

fig. 4 *Entrance to Subway*, 1938, oil on canvas, 34 × 46 ¼ in., Collection of Kate Rothko Prizel and Ilya Prizel (CR 135, pl. 7)

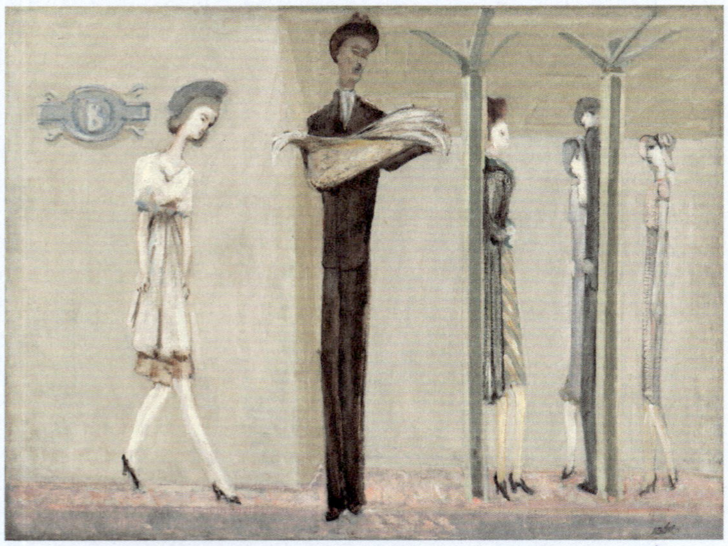

fig. 5 *Underground Fantasy,* c. 1940, oil on canvas 34 ⅜ × 46 $^{9}/_{16}$ in., National Gallery of Art, Washington, D.C. (CR 174; pl. 12)

1 Mark Rothko came ashore in New York for the first time in 1913, having crossed the Atlantic from his native Europe.

2 Born Marcus Rotkovitch, he changed his name to Mark Rothko in 1940, in response to the rise of Nazism and anti-Semitism.

3 Mark Rothko, in James E. B. Breslin, *Mark Rothko: A Biography* (Chicago and London: University of Chicago Press, 1998), p. 54.

4 Rothko's first public exhibition was a group show organized in 1928 by Bernard Karfiol at Opportunity Gallery in New York.

5 He had his first solo exhibition at the Portland Museum of Modern Art in 1933.

6 From 1929 to 1949, Rothko taught painting and drawing to children at the Brooklyn Jewish Academy in New York, a seminal and richly instructive experience which stimulated his reflection on his own painting.

7 Mark Rothko wrote about art from 1934 to 1969, publishing his texts in magazines, newspapers, and exhibition catalogues. To this corpus can be added transcriptions of notebooks, lectures and interviews, as well as extensive correspondence with fellow artists on the New York scene, historians, galleries, and museum curators.

8 According to the catalogue raisonné of Mark Rothko's work, edited by David Anfam, 177 works on canvas were recorded between 1924–25 and 1940.

9 Mark Rothko, *Writings on Art, 1934–1969*, ed. Miguel López-Remiro (New Haven and London: Yale University Press, 2006), p. 38.

10 Annie Cohen-Solal, in *Mark Rothko, Toute une vie*, radio broadcast, France Culture, March 22, 2014.

11 Rothko, *Writings on Art*, p. 38.

12 In his tribute to Milton Avery, Rothko wrote: "This conviction of greatness, the feeling that one was in the presence of great events, was immediate on encountering his work. It was true for many of us who were younger, questioning and looking for an anchor. This conviction has never faltered. It has persisted, and has been reinforced thru the passing decades and the passing fashions." "Tribute to Milton Avery," handwritten document, Smithsonian Archives of American Art: https://www.aaa.si.edu/collections/items/detail/tribute-to-milton-avery-13579

13 Rothko and Avery met in 1928 at Opportunity Gallery in New York, where they were both showing in the exhibition *Artists Selected by Bernard Karfiol.*

14 Christopher Rothko in *Rothko*, Rizzoli Electa, 2022, Hong Kong Rizzoli Electa, 2022, p. 13.

15 William Seitz in Riccardo Venturi, "Plasticité et espace dans l'oeuvre de Mark Rothko", *Ligeia*, no. 73–76, 2007–1, pp. 160–188 [p. 185].

16 Ibid.

17 Riccardo Venturi, "Plasticité et espace dans l'œuvre de Mark Rothko," pp. 160–88.

18 "The Ten" is the name of a group of New York artists that formed in reaction to the highly conservative approach of the Whitney Museum of Art. Its members included Adolf Gottlieb and Mark Rothko. They exhibited together from 1935 to 1939.

19 Breslin, *Mark Rothko, a Biography* (Chicago and London: University of Chicago Press, 1998).

20 Rothko, *Writings on Art*, p. 126.

21 Ibid., p. 42.

22 Mark Rothko, *The Artist's Reality*, ed. Christopher Rothko (New Haven: Yale University Press, 2004).

"To us art is an adventure into an unknown world, which can be explored only by those willing to take the risks."

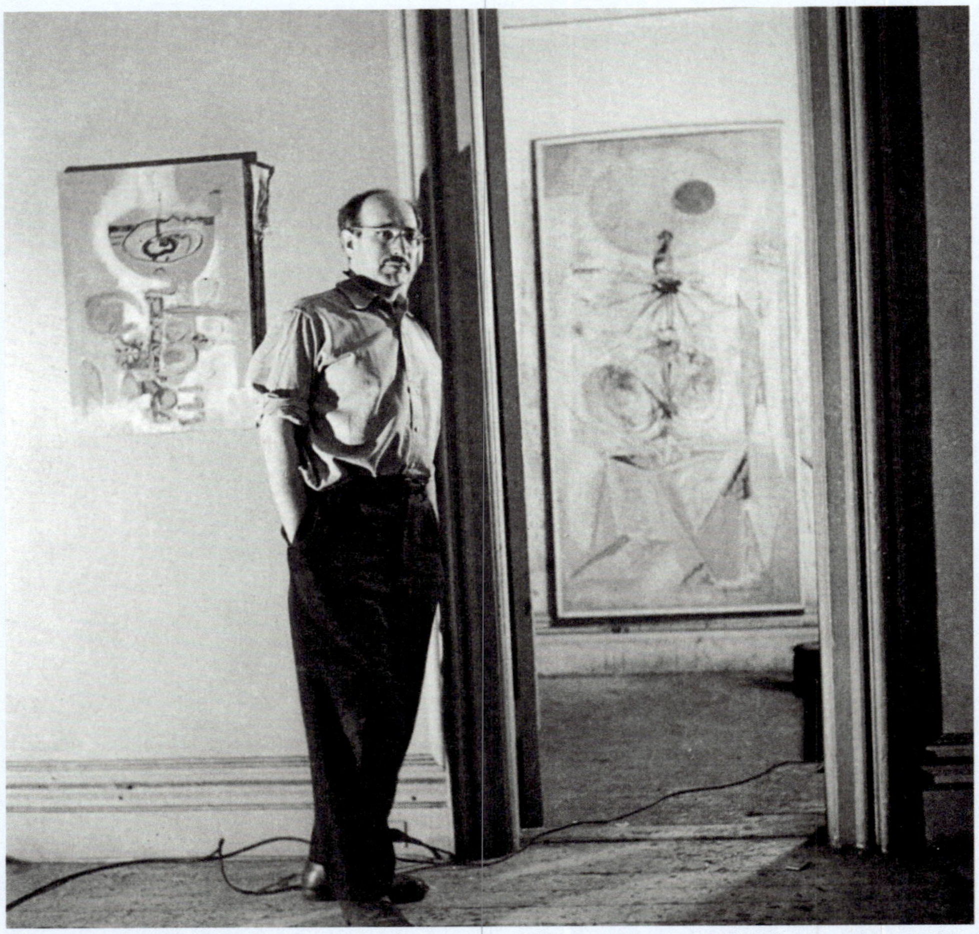

Mark Rothko in his studio, West 52nd Street, ca. 1945, in front of *Untitled*, 1945 (CR 285) and *Tiresias* (fig. 3), The Rothko Family Archive

François Michaud

A Saffron-Hued Robe: Mythology and Surrealism

The Surrealists tended to hypostatize the unconscious and to regard even highly contrived, fastidiously worked and finished images as somehow having issued from their unconscious minds. The New York School artists remained more faithful to an abstract notion of the unconscious as a fluid mental space and to the ideal of a process of working which engaged that space.[1]

The Resurgence of Tragedy

When the United States entered the war in 1941, Rothko moved away from realism, introducing strange deformations and references to ancient sources into his work. His paintings became populated with figures derived from Antiquity, which he then deformed: a nude, sculptural figure with a double face halfway between Janus and Picasso [pl. 21]; heads merged in a frieze-like way, with features typical of Greek art (curly hair and beards, elongated eyes, classical torsos) yet whose lower limbs were replaced by less identifiable, fragmentary components that might be skeletal or animal-like [pl. 20 to 24]. While the images might startle, the often-explicit titles invoked one consistent register—*Antigone*, *Iphigenia* and *Tiresias* expressed Rothko's debt to Greek theater and the world of Homer and Hesiod. At that time, these allusions to classical culture constituted a source common to the three lands with which Rothko identified—Russia, America, and Europe—yet during the war they also took on a specific meaning. Although nothing could offset the stupefaction produced by the scope of the conflict and by the violence unleashed against the Jews a decade earlier, the Trojan War served as a unifying myth and a repertoire conducive to a timeless expression of the unbearable harshness of the present.

Rothko's preoccupation with a primal archaism that could combine all mythologies and, along with them, highly varied forms of artistic expression, was present in his work from the early 1940s, just as it was in the work of Adolph Gottlieb and Barnett Newman, to whom he was particularly close. Before them there henceforth stretched not only an inexhaustible number of subjects and a method suited to theoretical elaboration, but an entire world to be explored.[2]

In 1943 an unexpected incident offered them the possibility of stating their ideas in a kind of manifesto. Rothko and Gottlieb, having been slammed by critic Edward A. Jewel after their show at the Federation of Modern Painters and Sculptors, fired off a riposte. They used their right of reply to the newspaper to explain the principles underlying their art: "We assert that the subject is crucial and only that subject matter is valid which is tragic and timeless."[3] Their letter appeared in the *New York Times* on June 13, 1943, reaching a far larger audience than the exhibition, which would otherwise have remained a quiet affair.

Rothko had begun to read Nietzsche much earlier, probably when a student at Yale, and he later acknowledged the importance to him of *The Birth of Tragedy*,[4] as well as the tragedies themselves, including the *Oresteia*. He thus referred to the first play of Aeschylus's trilogy, *Agamemnon*, when commenting on one of the works which the text of 1943 relates to: *The Omen of the Eagle* (fig. 1). That painting was reproduced the following year in Sidney Janis's book *Abstract and Surrealist Art in America*, with a caption supplied by Rothko: "The theme here is derived from the Agamemnon Trilogy of Aeschylus. The picture deals not with the particular anecdote, but rather with the Spirit of Myth, which is generic to all myths at all times. It involves a pantheism in which man, bird, beast, and tree—the known as well as the knowable—merge into a single tragic idea."[5] Rothko stressed the "subject" of a work as though he wanted to counter, in advance, any accusation of meaninglessness, but he immediately challenged an overly literal interpretation. What was at stake was not the anecdote, but the "spirit of myth." What he called the "anecdote" was the omen mentioned at the outset of the play, which served as the title of his painting—two eagles appeared in the sky, then dived upon a pregnant hare, prefiguring the war against Troy launched by the two sons of Atreus, Agamemnon and Menelaus. Clytemnestra, mother of Iphigenia and wife of Agamemnon, reveals that the latter had sacrificed their daughter in order to ensure the fair winds that enabled the Greeks to take to the sea. This child-killing, once known, justifies the murder that Clytemnestra is about to commit. The play ends with the death of King Agamemnon, triggering the ongoing cycle of Orestes's revenge against his murderous mother.

Ancient theater offered this universal foundation to which everyone could refer in seeking to understand not only the real tragedy into which the world had suddenly fallen, but also the universal nature of a human condition marked by a fate that absorbs and transcends it.[6] Sartre did that very thing when, during the German occupation of France, he turned the Orestes legend into a modern play, *The Flies*, which was performed at the Théâtre de la Cité in Paris in June 1943, just when Rothko and Gottlieb were countering the *New York Times* critic.[7]

Rothko felt that the war and the persecution of Jews[8]—to which his childhood experiences made him particularly sensitive[9]—certainly constituted the two faces of a Janus terrible to behold. In a way, his painting constituted a portrait of this frightful, multifaceted deity. Rothko's obsession with depicting assemblages of human heads in his early "mythological" works was perhaps related to this. Beings are multiple—the theory of primal goodness is challenged, at the very least. Such duplicity or multiplicity prohibits the depiction of a single subject or individual, since the subject of art must be, above all, "tragic and timeless." If we truly look at the pictures themselves, however, what emerges most immediately is the idea of "masks," those entities who agitate, who sometimes inveigh against an absent protagonist (*Antigone* [pl. 23]), reminding us once again of Greek tragedy and the role played by the protean character of the Chorus. After 1943, Rothko would abandon this vestige of human presence in his more abstract works, which contemporary commentators like Sidney Janis labeled "surrealist." He nevertheless continued to compare his paintings to theater up to the late 1940s. "I think of my pictures as dramas."[10]

The Spirit of Myth

Ancient myth soon seemed too restrictive to Rothko, and since the idea of communicating directly with the beholder—without the use of words—was already present in his thinking at that time,[11] he had to draw on a broader register if he wanted to achieve his goal. Indeed, awareness of art's social role, which he shared with most artists of the New York School, could not be based solely on European foundations which, in the twentieth century, were far less broadly accessible than they had been to the Greeks and Romans. Although this repertoire of figures and forms might embody positive universal values and a humanism that opposed Nazism, allusions meaningful to a university-educated elite could not speak to everyone. Now, if artists, like the tragic poets of yore, wanted to address the widest audience—and Rothko wanted to do so all the more, since he conceived this message along the lines of poetry and music: thought without language, an idiom without words[12]—then they had to draw on other repertoires and, especially, they had to take the great leap of venturing into unknown lands from which all recognizable figures had vanished. This *terra incognita* was the "new New World" sought by Rothko and his friends when exercising their right of reply to the *New York Times* and thereby employing one of the best media of the day to defend what they felt was much more than a new formal style. "To us art is an adventure into an unknown world, which can be explored only by those willing to take the risks."[13] In *Mark Rothko: Subjects in Abstraction,* Anna Chave noted the kinship between that comment and one by André Breton in his "Prolegomena to a Third Manifesto of Surrealism or Else": "In art there is no great expedition which is not undertaken at the risk of one's life ... each artist must set out on his own search for the Golden Fleece."[14] Artists can take up ancient legends as their own—and thereby become myth-makers in turn. Breton's article was read all the more for being published in English in the first issue of *VVV*, the poetic and political voice of the Surrealist group in exile; furthermore, 1942 was the year of the *First Papers of Surrealism* exhibition and the opening of Peggy Guggenheim's Art of this Century gallery. In his article, Breton criticized the copying and repeating of historic Surrealist works, announcing that Matta himself would one day be copied in turn.[15] Not only was there no mimicry of earlier works in Rothko's painting, but his adoption of ancient mythological sources was soon accompanied by abstract shapes, combined with other, more identifiable ones. Such was the case with *Tiresias*, painted in 1944, from which emerges what may be an eye—presumably the soothsayer's, although it makes him seem more like a cyclops—as well as two disks that might be the breasts of the androgynous protagonist (fig. 3). As to the *Sacrifice of Iphigenia,* done two years earlier (fig. 2), remotely anthropomorphic elements are presented as uniform patches of color in which only a threatening hand alludes to the story of the heinous crime. Finally, the bird in *Hierarchical Birds* (1944) (pl. 25) could be viewed as a Surrealist "quotation"—of Max Ernst in particular—aimed at the crowd associated with Peggy Guggenheim, who exhibited this painting the following year; but a bird is a symbol that belongs to all myths and is present on every continent.[16] It also has an ancestral, even autochthonous, resonance, and is a symbol Rothko employed earlier in the Aeschylus-inspired *The Omen of the Eagle* (fig. 1).[17] In that same year of 1944 Rothko painted *Agitation of the Archaic,* now in the Whitney Museum, which seems to acknowledge another debt, namely one toward Jungian thought or at least the idea of a heritage transmitted from the remote past to literate societies.[18] The title appears generic, citing no name, and the work itself is more abstract than earlier ones. The only thing apparently expressed here is the principle of a formation—an almost crystalline growth—upon some invisible substrate, although the ground itself is clearly defined, as in the series of mid-1930s works that Ernst titled *Garden Airplane-Trap*. In contrast, Rothko's *Rites of Lilith* (pl. 26), painted the following year, seems to describe the agitation and primal whirlwind prior to the formation of being. The work is composed of swift, looping lines in which Chave perceives traces of the automatic drawing Rothko practiced most especially on his works on paper, pencil and watercolor being swifter of execution.[19] The title of the painting alludes to Hebraic sources and to a parallel tradition of Genesis that makes Lilith the first partner of Adam; she is a primitive, wild Eve who continued to exist as a shape-shifting she-demon,[20] one liable to become an evanescent figure like the *Grands Transparents* heralded by Breton, to which Matta sought to give form.[21] An artist, like a poet, is a demiurge who creates form, and even if language or art pre-exists the artist, it is the artist who speaks and gives life to a *logos.*

"Agitation of the Archaic"

Painters are also oracles; and, if heard and understood, will not waste their breath the way Cassandra does at the start of *Agamemnon*. Rothko said he profoundly loved Aeschylus, later preferring Shakespeare and King Lear, who also offered a glimpse of the possibility of madness and its opposite: a total clear-sightedness that others cannot comprehend.

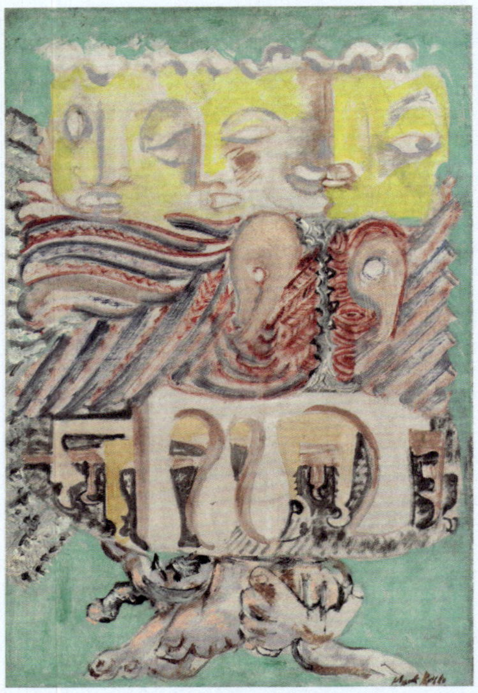

fig. 1 *The Omen of the Eagle*, 1942, oil and graphite on canvas, 25 ¾ × 17 ¾ in., National Gallery of Art, Washington, D.C. (CR 206; pl. 24)

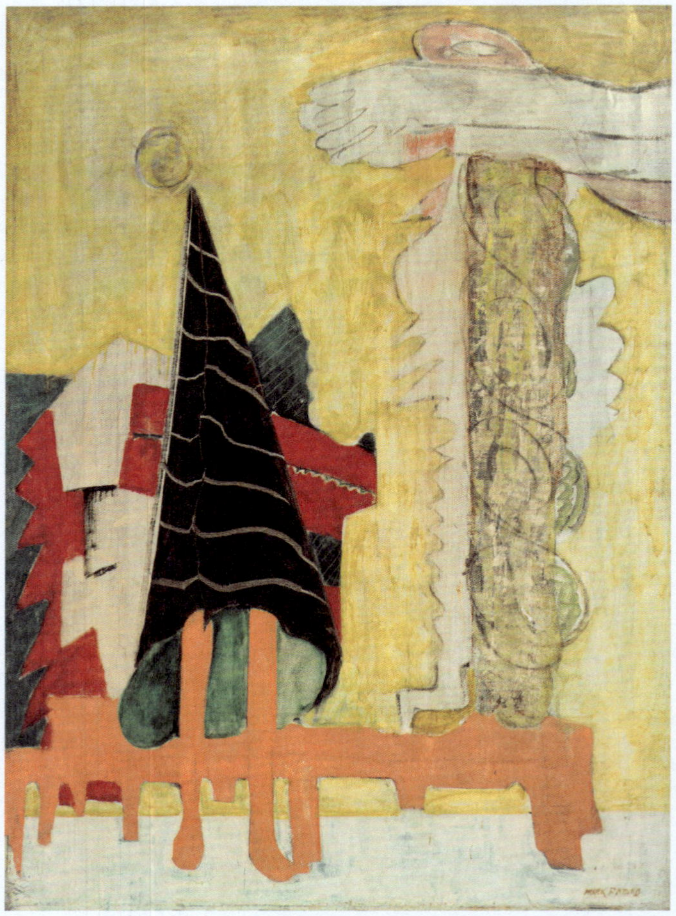

fig. 2 *Sacrifice of Iphigenia*, 1942, oil and graphite on canvas, 50 × 36 ⅞ in., private collection (CR 210; pl. 27)

Thus people who incarnate a madman are condemned to wander in a world that remains deaf to them indefinitely. Was that not one of Rothko's lasting fears? Rita Reinhardt explicitly said so,[22] and while she knew him after the period under discussion, this feeling of possible incomprehension seems to have troubled the artist long before his definitive adoption of abstraction. A hint of it can be found in the manifesto-letter of 1943, and again when Rothko repeated those ideas in a radio broadcast with Gottlieb in October 1943,[23] and finally in a text of his own that appeared in 1947 in *Possibilities*, the magazine published by his friend Robert Motherwell.[24] He tried each time to explain his ideas by reformulating them and introducing comparisons that would make him better understood. The transcription of the broadcast thus includes this passage: "There is, however, a profound reason for the persistence of the word 'portrait' because the real essence of the great portraiture of all time is the artist's eternal interest in the human figure, character, and emotions—in short, in the human drama. That Rembrandt expressed it by posing a sitter is irrelevant. We do not know the sitter but we are intensely aware of the drama. The Archaic Greeks, on the other hand, used as their models the inner visions which they had of their gods. And in our day, our visions are the fulfillment of our own needs."[25]

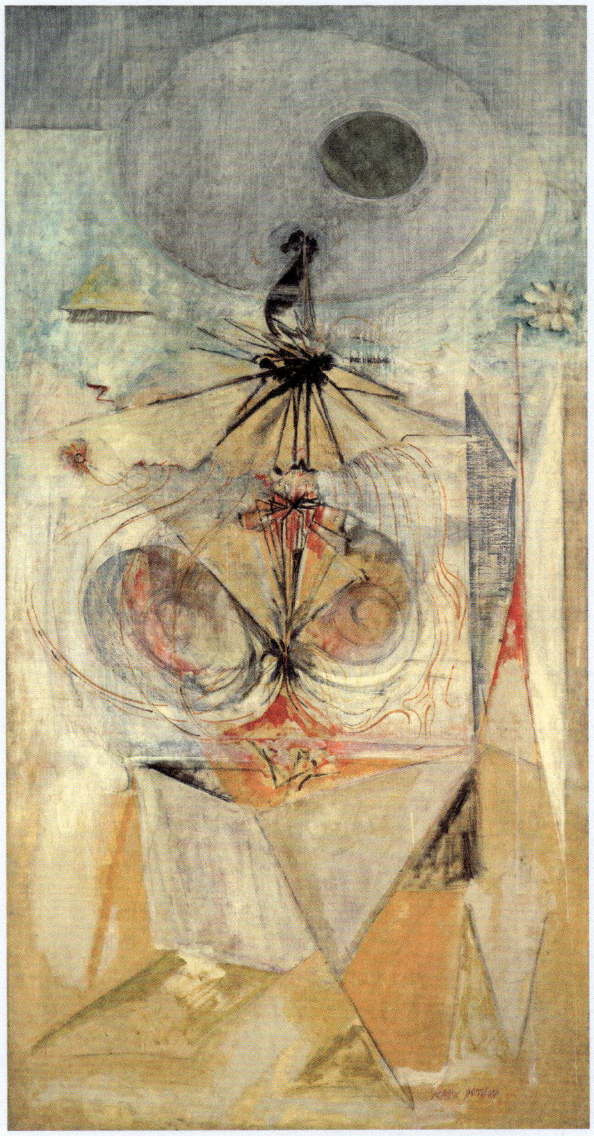

fig. 3 *Tiresias*, 1944, oil on canvas, 79 ⅞ × 39 ⅞ in., Collection of Christopher Rothko (CR 247; pl. 28)

When Rothko depicted Iphigenia, he had the "inner model" in mind. Thus all deformations were allowed, occulting characters and leaving only a trace of them (like the yellow color that invades the canvas) or else condensing the expression of tragedy through morphological alterations (*Guernica* was in everyone's mind at the time, along with Picasso's expressive depiction of the destruction of the martyred city and, via that destruction, the stifling of the hopes born of the young Spanish Republic). While the characters of the drama are evoked, they are the abstract ones Rothko mentioned in 1947 when comparing the canvas to a stage,[26] rather than the figures summoned up by Aeschylus's play. What remains, however, is a large yellow surface with clear-cut outlines. And Aeschylus's text precisely states that just when the sacrifice is to occur, the king's daughter appears in her saffron-hued gown, her young girl's garb. Her life ends before it had barely begun. References to color are rare in Greek, and this one was liable to attract a painter's eye.

The *Sacrifice of Iphigenia* demonstrates that titles were of crucial importance to Rothko, and that color sometimes underscored the title, even when its symbolic meaning escapes the beholder. *Rites of Lilith*, suffused in bluish gray, evoked the chaos or tension between poles—and perhaps, literally, the vision described in *The Alphabet of Ben Sira* of Lilith's flight across the seas, completing the transformation of the first woman into a demon.[27] A 1944 painting now in New York's Museum of Modern Art, *Slow Swirl at the Edge of the Sea* (pl. 32), provides a strong contrast with the previous ones. Rothko decided to show it with *Sacrifice* at the Guggenheim gallery in 1945. Perhaps *Slow Swirl* should be heard as much as seen: the calm, peaceful sound of potential stability. Botticelli's *Birth of Venus* has been invoked in describing this canvas,[28] but while Botticelli was one of the artists Rothko blithely mentioned in his early writings, this picture should perhaps be seen as more than just the recollection of a painting exhibited at MoMA in 1940, one that all painters knew—one of those images that, like a tunic, Rothko's oeuvre was slowly discarding.

Whereas *Slow Swirl* appears more balanced, testifying to the artist's development, the expressive power of *Iphigenia* is carried by just a few colors: red, green, and orange, all dominated by yellow. Shapes fade and blur, but color remains, to the extent of taking up all the space. Space that it would soon occupy completely, even if—as Rothko said—color was not the subject. "I am not interested in colors. I am interested in the image which is created."[29]

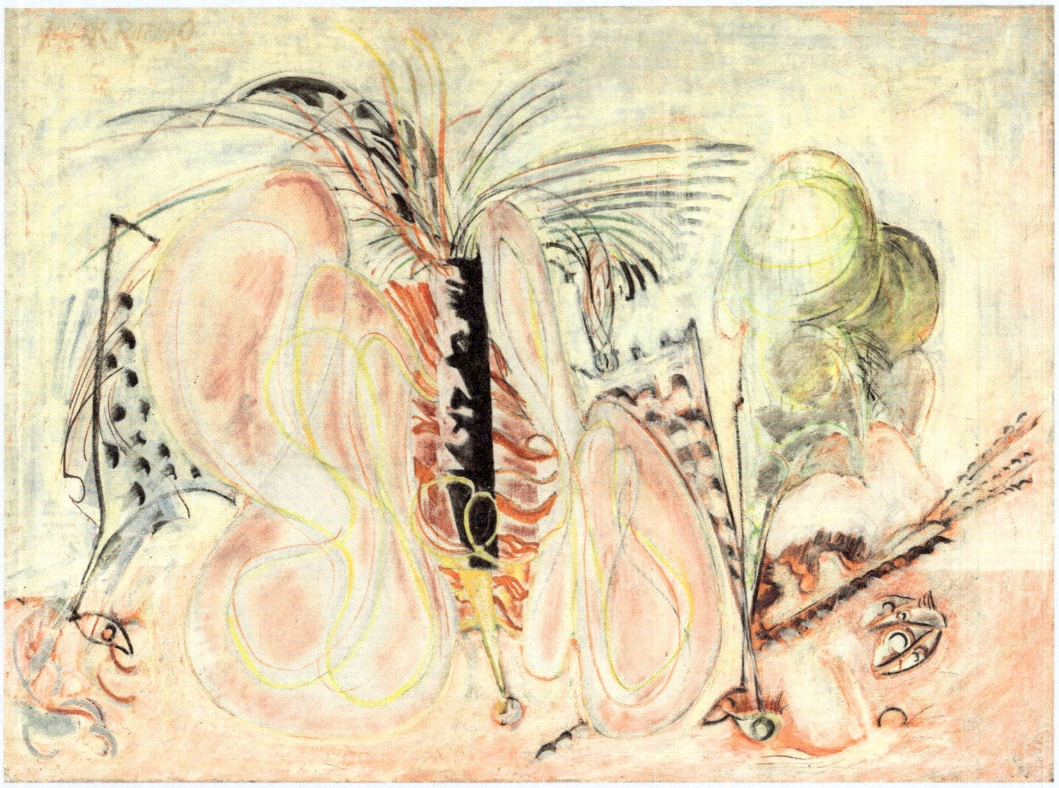

fig. 4 *Birth of Cephalopods,* 1944, oil and graphite on canvas, 39 ½ × 53 ½ in., National Gallery of Art, Washington, D.C. (CR 231)

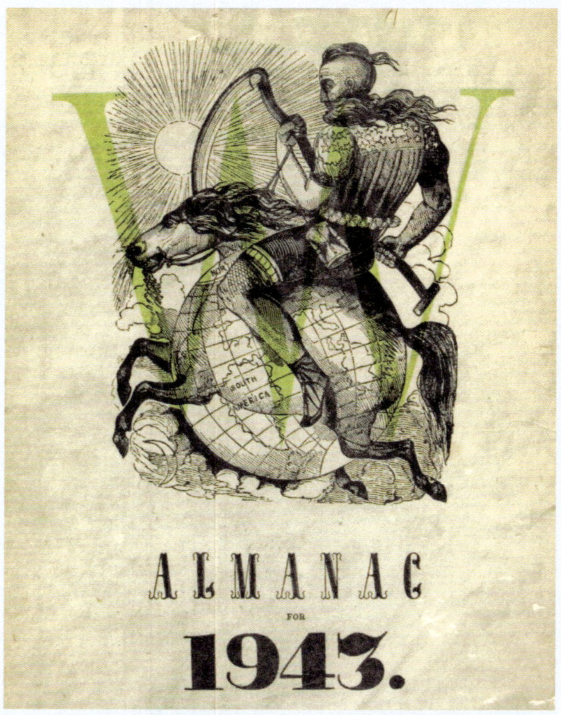

fig. 5 Marcel Duchamp, Cover of *VVV* magazine, Almanach for 1943, no. 2–3, New York, March 1943, Philadelphia Museum of Art

1 Anna C. Chave, *Mark Rothko, Subjects in Abstraction* (New Haven and London: Yale University Press, 1989), p. 68.

2 Michael Leja explained the functioning of this fusion of "antiquity" with "archaic" and "primitive" via the influence of James Harvey Robinson's *The Mind in the Making*, published shortly after World War I, which examined the persistence of an ancient mode of thought in modern mentalities. "While Robinson was scrupulous about distinguishing between two categories—the primitive and the ancient—many of those who adopted his genetic format were not. In the broad terms and sweeping scope of this literature, the comparison was often between the conditions of modern life and those of 'human antiquity'—a composite of the primitive and archaic categories." See the chapter on "Mythmakers" in Michael Leja, *Reframing Abstract Expressionism: Subjectivity and Painting in the 1940s* (New Haven and London: Yale University Press, 1993), p. 58. This was the point of departure for artists who, like Rothko, sought to forge myths without however needing direct recourse to Jungian thought.

3 *New York Times*, June 13, 1943, reprinted as "Rothko and Gottlieb's Letter to the Editor," in Mark Rothko, *Writings on Art*, ed. Miguel Lopez-Remiro (New Haven and London: Yale University Press, 2006), p. 36. Barnett Newman helped to write the reply but was not one of the signatories; see James E. B. Breslin, *Rothko: A Biography* (Chicago and London: University of Chicago Press, 1998), pp. 195–96.

4 Breslin, *Rothko*, p. 174, n. 86; Chave, *Mark Rothko*, p. 79, n. 30. Nietzsche was mentioned in *The Yale Saturday Evening Pest*, the student magazine that Rothko started with his friends at Yale.

5 Sidney Janis, *Abstract and Surrealist Art in America* (New York: Reynal & Hitchcock, 1944), p. 118.

6 The *Oresteia* certainly took on a personal dimension for Rothko, even though it would be risky to interpret it in terms of the artist's own story, since he never openly discussed the meaning it might hold for him.

7 This simultaneity did not escape Annie Cohen-Salal, who also noted other literary and philosophical connections of the day. See Annie Cohen-Salal, *Mark Rothko* (Arles: Actes Sud, 2013), p. 94. For Sartre, the tragic situation gives the protagonist the possibility of taking his fate in his own hands, even if it is initially perceived as overwhelming—which, above all, is the ancient moral. The moral drawn by the myth-making painters was related to both positions, since artists must venture into unknown territory and be ready to take all kinds of risk.

8 Although information on the deportations and exterminations arrived in a fragmentary, delayed manner during the war, anti-Semitic measures and their concrete effects were well known from 1933 onward, regularly fueled in the U.S. by people who managed to emigrate or by sustained contact, whenever possible, with those who had not managed. Anne Frank's diary, now known in its entirety, shows how such information reached people who sought it, despite the barriers.

9 Breslin, *Rothko*, pp. 17–19; Cohen-Salal, *Mark Rothko*, pp. 21 sff.

10 Mark Rothko, "The Romantics Were Prompted," *Possibilities* 1 (1947–48), reprinted in Rothko, *Writings on Art*, pp. 58–59. Discussed by Nancy Spector in this catalogue, p. 233 ff.

11 Mark Rothko, *The Artist's Reality: Philosophies of Art*, ed. Christopher Rothko (New Haven and London: Yale University Press, 2004), pp. 65–66 and 223–24.

12 "I became a painter because I wanted to raise painting to the level of poignancy of music and poetry," quoted in Brian O'Doherty, *American Masters: The Voice and the Myth* (New York: Random House, 1973), p. 153.

13 Rothko, *Writings on Art*, p. 36.

14 Chave, *Mark Rothko*, p. 80, quoting and commenting on André Breton, "Prolegomena to a Third Manifesto of Surrealism or Else," *VVV* 1 (June 1942), p. 22. Here is reproduced the cover of double issue 2–3 (fig. 5).

15 Breton, "Prolegomena…," p. 11.

16 When Franz Werfel began writing his last novel, *Star of the Unborn*, in California in 1943, he envisaged a world in which all birds had disappeared. The troubling strangeness of the novel is heralded by their absence.

17 It is possible that Rothko painted *Hierarchical Birds* as an "updated" version of the same subject in the new Surrealist idiom that he had just adopted. The painting was shown in the Art of this Century gallery in 1945 alongside *Slow Swirl at the Edge of the Sea* and *Sacrifice of Iphigenia*.

18 As Christopher Rothko points out in this catalogue (p. 31), we don't know how aware of Jung's writing Rothko was, but many popularizations—mingling various sources—were accessible at the time (see Leja, *Reframing Abstract Expressionism*, *cf. supra*, n. 2.

19 Chave, *Mark Rothko*, p. 67. See notably her discussion of his 1944 work, *Birth of Cephalopods* (National Gallery of Art, Washington, fig. 4). It was Matta and Gorky—not forgetting the role played by Masson—who passed on the practice of automatic drawing to their friends in New York.

20 See "Histoire de Lilith selon les sources bibliques, post-bibliques, talmudiques et cabalistiques," *Idixa*, https://www.idixa.net/Pixa/pagixa-1607092237.html, accessed May 2023.

21 See the chapter on "Matta et *Les Grands transparents*" in Fabrice Flahutez, *Nouveau monde et nouveau mythe: Mutations du surréalisme de l'exil américain à l'"Écart absolu," 1941–1965* (Dijon: Les Presses du Réel, 2007), pp. 127 ff. Flahutez stresses the importance of the intellectual exchanges between Matta and Breton once they had met in Paris in the late 1930s, conducive to the emergence of this theme in Breton's thinking, subsequently passed on to the New York artists.

22 Rita Reinhardt Bedford interviewed by Dominique de Menil and Susan Barnes, September 13, 1980, Menil Archives.

23 *The Portrait and the Modern Artist*, radio broadcast by Mark Rothko and Adolph Gottlieb, WYNC radio station, October 13, 1943. Reprinted in Rothko, *Writings on Art*, pp. 37–40.

24 Rothko, "The Romantic Were Prompted", *cf. supra*, n. 10.

25 Rothko, *Writings on Art*, p. 38.

26 Rothko, "The Romantics Were Prompted."

27 "The angels left God and pursued Lilith, whom they overtook in the middle of the seas, in the mighty waters where the Egyptians were destined to drown." See "Histoire de Lilith selon les sources bibliques…", https://www.idixa.net/Pixa/pagixa-1607092237.html.

28 Breslin, *Rothko*, p. 215; Bradford R. Collins, "Beyond Pessimism: Rothko's Nietzschean Quest, 1940–1949," in Collins (ed.), *Mark Rothko: The Decisive Decade, 1940–1950* (New York: Skira Rizzoli, 2012), p. 52 and n. 34.

29 "Notes from an interview by William Seitz, March 25, 1953," in Rothko, *Writings on Art*, p. 85.

"I do not believe that there was ever a question of being abstract or representational. It is really a matter of ending this silence and solitude, of breathing and stretching one's arms again."

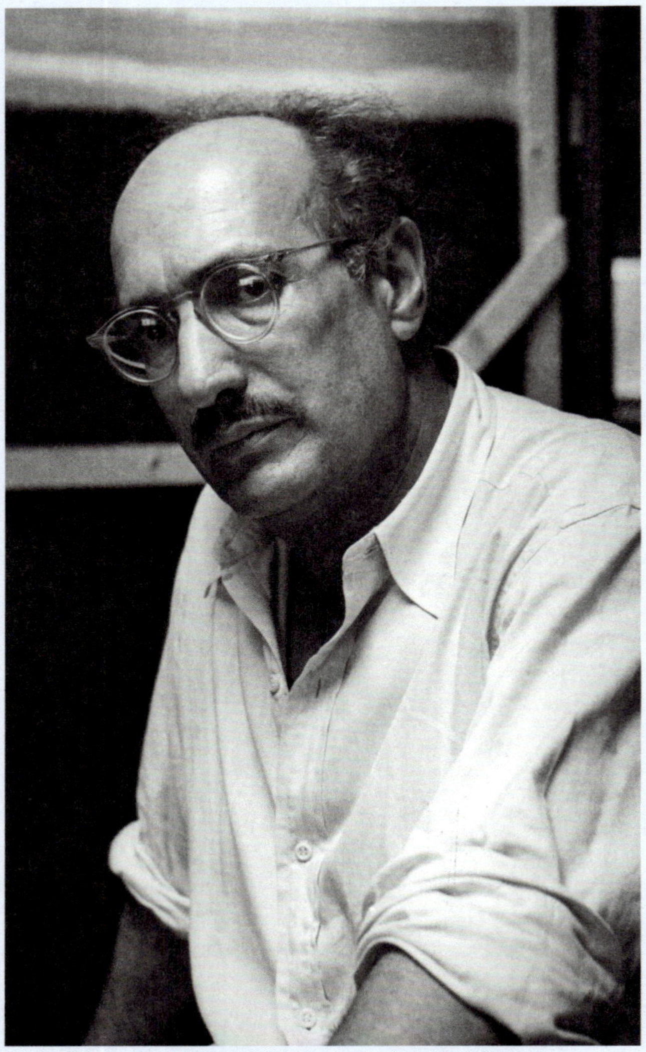

Henry Elkan, Mark Rothko in his studio, 53th Rue, New York, c. 1953, The Rothko Family Archive

Harry Cooper

Rothko's Multiforms

In a "profuse, almost frenetic output" of some one hundred paintings and a handful of related works on paper between late 1946 and sometime in 1949, Rothko stepped from a kind of biomorphic Surrealism into near-total abstraction.[1] These works, the multiforms, have been called "pieces of a puzzle poised to come together" because they paved the way for the much simpler, more unified compositions of rectangles that Rothko unveiled at the Betty Parsons Gallery in January 1950 and pursued until his suicide in 1970.[2] Exactly how they paved the way is not obvious and will be the subject of this essay.

This kind of reading is, of course, highly teleological, and indeed the term "multiform" has teleology written into it, for there is nothing especially multiple about their compositions compared to Rothko's preceding work; they only appear so retrospectively, in contrast to the works that came after. David Anfam notes that "the actual term [multiform] does not appear to have been used by the artist himself," and Dore Ashton reports that she "never heard Rothko refer to them that way."[3] The individual works in the group are either untitled or merely numbered.[4] However, an inventory of Rothko's studio conducted under loose supervision by his assistant Dan Rice in 1968–69 lists over fifty works as "multi-form" or "multi-form surreal style," suggesting that Rothko was aware of the designation, however and whenever it might have been invented.[5] Perhaps he coined the term himself, in his own act of retrospection.

Let us begin with the multiform at the Harvard Art Museum, *Untitled*, 1947 (CR 342, fig. 1). The formal elements of this painting are typical of the group: a mass of fairly evenly distributed forms swirling in a kind of primordial soup held and loosely shaped by the rectangular frame; a limited palette, sharply divided into darks (black and maroon in this case) and more predominant lights (mainly white, light blue, pale yellow) with little middle ground;[6] thin, matte paint, often applied in layers but still revealing the texture of canvas beneath; a haloing of one color by another, with small margins of separation and soft edges between them; and a confusion of figure and ground, due in this case partly to the way shapes interlock, at once framing and framed by one another.

This description leaves out one crucial element: two drips of white paint near the middle of the painting, silhouetted against black and running dramatically upward. These testify not only to Rothko's willingness to leave an accident in place but, more importantly, to his turning the canvas 180 degrees from the way in which he had painted at least part of it.[7] These drips powerfully weaken the sense of "up" or "down" in the work, contributing to a feeling that, in looking at the painting on the wall one is nonetheless looking down *onto* a horizontal scene of interactions, as with an aerial view, rather than *into* a vertical plane, as with most paintings (including those that preceded the multiforms, the banded backgrounds of which suggests strata or horizons).[8] And this in turn makes it more difficult to see the picture as one of forms in space or of figures on a ground, despite the presence of figurative suggestions in many of the works. In short, Rothko was moving here toward a radically nonfigurative painting, one that would resist the pull of illusionism and declare itself as paint on canvas. What was brewing was abstraction.

From this forward-looking kind of account, one can take an equal step in the opposite direction and find vestiges of figuration in the multiforms, as Anna Chave does when she sees in them a motif that Rothko favored in the 1930s: two figures, light and dark, cleaving together, just like the rhyming black and white forms (partly separated by maroon) in the lower half of the Harvard painting.[9] Anfam too notes a fleeting reappearance of earlier figurative elements in the first multiforms, which he calls the "late 1946 transitionals." As for the more mature multiforms, he points out that *No. 18*, 1946 (CR 319) reprises a compositional type of large spheroid "head" on herm-like "body" going back to *Tiresias*, 1944 (CR 247; pl. 28). He even finds trails leading back to both the portrait heads and the landscapes of the 1930s. For Anfam, all this suggests that Rothko, in a strategy of *reculer pour mieux sauter*, retrieved such elements precisely in order to cancel them, to "pulverize ... the familiar identity of things," as Rothko declared in 1947. Writes Anfam, "The past was summoned to be annulled."[10]

What distinguishes Anfam's from Chave's tracing of the multiforms' figurative lineage is that his reading points forward, not back: rather than reducing abstraction to hidden, subconscious figuration, he sees a conscious, proleptic attack on the figure. What the two readings have in common is that they both read *through* the multiforms, defining them in terms of what came before or after, making of them (as they were even called by a critic at the time) an "art of transitions."[11] And yet the multiforms are more than just Rothko's bridge between Surrealism and abstraction. If they look forward and backward in a "both / and" movement, they are also very much a pause, a suspension, an interregnum with their own materiality and thematics. Neither / nor.

* * *

Allow me to return to a phrase from my earlier description, no doubt prompted by something disorganized and almost random in the composition: *primordial soup*.[12] This phrase suggests a long history of speculation about the origin of life from inorganic matter, or abiogenesis. The modern theory that a primordial or primeval soup served as the matrix for life can be traced to Charles Darwin, who speculated that the first organism might have been born "in a warm little pond, with all sorts of ammonia and phosphoric salts, lights, heat, electricity, etc. present, so that a protein compound was chemically formed ready to undergo still more complex changes."[13] This hypothesis, further developed in the 1920s by Alexander Oparin and J.B.S. Haldane, and still alive today, might well have been familiar to someone of Rothko's education.[14] Intriguing evidence is provided by the fact that in his theoretical writings he described the spatial structure of "tactile" painting (a tradition in which he included his own work, as opposed to "illusory" painting) as "a plate of jelly."[15] Hardly a commonplace of studio talk, this phrase suggests the basic laboratory technique, invented in the 1880s, of using agar in a Petri dish as a growth medium for microorganisms.[16] While Rothko's explicit purpose in using the metaphor was to convey a thick, shallow, palpable space in which (as he wrote) "a series of objects are impressed at various depths," he might well have intended the association with the study of basic life forms.

Let us recall that Barnett Newman, one of Rothko's closest friends and colleagues in the 1940s, not only studied botany at the time but made a number of works suggesting organisms seen under magnification. One of his earliest extant drawings, *The Blessing*, 1944, features a "germinated seed shape."[17] William Baziotes, another New York school artist, "spent long hours in The Museum of Natural History.... *The Flesh Eaters* [1952], for instance, contains floating ribbons that could be jungle plants or protoplasm."[18] Rothko's own works of that time, especially his drawings, may "have their origins in a microscopic world that serves as an analogue to man's inner realm; some forms call to mind ciliated protozoa, others flowing protoplasmic entities with pseudopods, and still others flagella."[19]

With this in mind, we can begin to see the multiforms as taking a shared set of mid-1940s, Surrealist-inspired interests in organic biology and biomorphism to a higher level of abstraction—to see them as scenes of emerging definition in which simple forms take shape and organize themselves before, or below, our eyes. The way that the drips of the Harvard painting both invade the black area and get swallowed by it presents a microcosm of the amoeba-like interactions of figure and ground, swallowing and swallowed, throughout the work. And the dramatic silhouette of the drips, a moment of hypnotic sharpness in an otherwise blurry scene, provides an animating visual spark analogous perhaps to the lightning bolt that, in "soup theory," catalyzes the formation of organic molecules. By preserving this dramatic accident and turning it upside down, Rothko converted the least willful moment in the painting, the place where gravity claimed the liquid nature of the medium, into a figure of assertion and organic emergence.

(Here the reader might well ask if I am not hanging too much on a mistake, a mere drip. But the multiforms abound in drips: four of them include white drips on black grounds, suggesting that that element in the Harvard work was not just a preserved accident but rather a solicited effect. Even more revealing of intentionality are Rothko's occasional imitation drips. In one of the last multiforms, *No. 9*, 1948 [CR 394], he takes a hint from six of the seven white drips at upper right and extends them down the canvas as brushstrokes.[20])

Rothko and several of his colleagues were thinking and writing at the time about painting as an organism, indeed the first organism. The idea that works of art, in their aesthetic autonomy, might seem to have their own lives is common in modernist thinking. Picasso said of Cubism: "When a form is realized it is there to live its own life."[21] This theme was dear to Rothko in the period of the multiforms. In "The Romantics Were Prompted," his 1947 statement for Robert Motherwell's short-lived journal *Possibilities*, he referred to pictorial shapes as "organisms with volition and a passion for self-assertion" that "move with internal freedom, and without need to conform with or to violate what is probable in the familiar world."[22] (Think of the uphill drips.) And in his catalogue essay for Clyfford Still's debut exhibition in February 1946 at Peggy Guggenheim's Art of This Century gallery, Rothko wrote: "Every shape becomes an organic entity, inviting the multiplicity of associations inherent in all living things. To me they form a theogony of the most elementary consciousness, hardly aware of itself beyond the will to live—a profound and moving experience."[23] But unlike Newman, who named a 1947 painting *Genetic Moment*, Rothko hesitated to enshrine such grand ideas in titles, and he soon regretted revealing as much as he did in the *Possibilities* piece.[24] The ideas were in the paintings themselves. What I have been suggesting, in short, is that the multiforms are not so much transitional works as works that take transition—the primary transition of birth or emergence—as their very subject.

* * *

When I wrote at the outset that Rothko "unveiled" his mature abstractions at the Betty Parsons Gallery, I was using a word that defines these works on the level both of meaning and technique. Around 1954, in a fragment on "space in painting," Rothko wrote beautifully of his "desire for the frontal, for the unveiled, for the experienced surface."[25] The path to that *unveiling*, with all its philosophical import for him, from Plato to Nietzsche, lay in a technique that allowed one color area to be seen through another: in a word, translucency, or what painters call transparency (as in the prized "transparent shadows" of academic practice). And it is transparency that most of the multiforms lack, even as they reveal a certain striving for it. The thinness of the paint Rothko used would seem well adapted to achieve it, and yet more often than not one layer covers another completely and opaquely—whether because all the layers soaked too quickly into

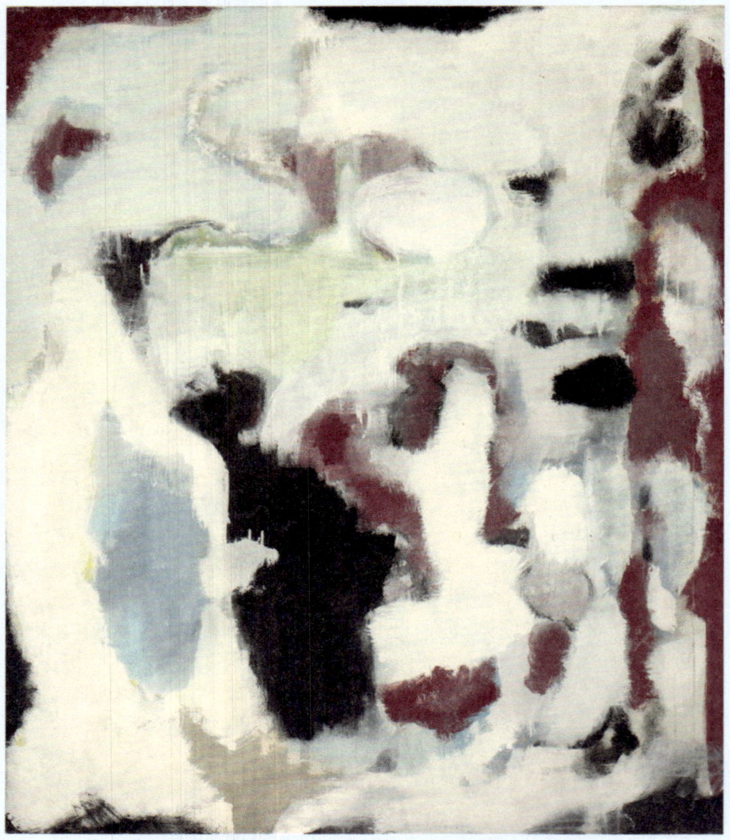

fig. 1 *Untitled*, 1947, oil on canvas, 41 ¾ × 36 ¾ in.,
Harvard Art Museums / Fogg Museum, Cambridge (CR 342)

the thin ground; or because the paint was so matte, thus lacking in luminosity;[26] or because Rothko used a lot of white, which tends to be opaque; or because his teacher, Milton Avery, was not the painter to transmit the lesson of transparency. (Avery's colors do show through one another, but most often because the top layer is loosely brushed or scratched through, not because of the paint itself.) All of Rothko's doing and undoing, feathering and scraping, dripping and scratching in the multiforms could be seen as an attempt to open up the painting, to show its depths without denying its "experienced surface," to achieve an equivalent of transparency through other means.

In the later multiforms, transparency comes to the fore.[27] Take *Untitled*, 1948 (CR 389, fig. 2). Two color patches centered in the lower third of the composition, one on top of the other, offer an object lesson in how one color can loom through another, whether it is blue coming through cream (in the patch above) or green coming through gray (below). And at lower left, in another quasi-rectangular patch of color, blue looms subtly through violet, in a passage that comes close to Rothko's mature manner. (The painting is a veritable set of test patches for Rothko's new tool of transparency.) And yet in the very center of the painting, as if impatient with such subtleties, Rothko brushes orange loosely and boldly over a white ground, creating a rough optical equivalent of transparency by means of intermittency, i.e., by leaving gaps in an upper layer so that a lower layer can show through.

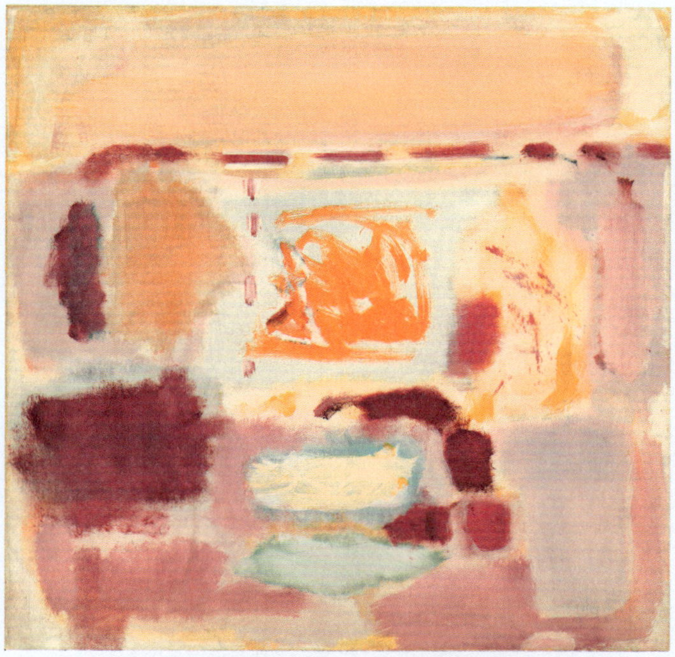

fig. 2 *Untitled*, 1948, oil on canvas, 42 ⅝ × 43 ⅞ in., National Gallery of Art, Washington, D.C. (CR 389)

Rothko seems to achieve transparencies truly and reliably just as the compositions of the multiforms begin to settle into the rectangular structures that anticipate the classic works: witness not only the "test-patch" work just cited but also *No. 9*, 1948. No doubt the calming of compositional energies allowed Rothko to focus on coloristic effects, but equally important must have been the two exhibitions of Pierre Bonnard's work in New York in 1948, for Bonnard (unlike Avery) was a master of veiling and unveiling.[28]

The work that seems to stand sentinel at Rothko's breakthrough is *No. 10*, 1948 (CR 385, fig. 3). Here, as in *Untitled*, 1946 (CR 321), Rothko takes a long step backward, to his early 1930s portraits (CR 17 and 18). Perhaps the solid Cézannian architecture of these busts helped Rothko rediscover the rectangle in paintings like *No. 10*, but this format also brought him back, via the figure, that ultimate marker of verticality, to a conception of the canvas as a vertical *plane* rather than a horizontal *plate*. However important the tipping-back had been for Rothko's push into abstraction in the multiforms, his mature work would require a re-erection of the picture plane, for unveiling is a matter of seeing *through*, not down. And this in turn helps to explain what is even more remarkable about *No. 10* than its last-minute figurative recourse, and what distinguishes it so starkly from Rothko's previous work on canvas (the watercolors are another, important matter), namely its deft use of translucent layering, whether to knock back the dark gray of the lower rectangle with a scumble of lighter gray on top, or to enliven the top rectangle of dark gray with a brick-colored layer underneath. The whole painting is a subtle study in transparencies. The "figure" is shot through—permeated, destroyed—with light, or is it with darkness? But in any case, the figure has reemerged for an instant, just long enough to bring Rothko back to verticality without endangering the gains he had made in abstraction with the multiforms. One step back, two steps forward. The result is a new clarity. Rothko had stopped stirring the soup.

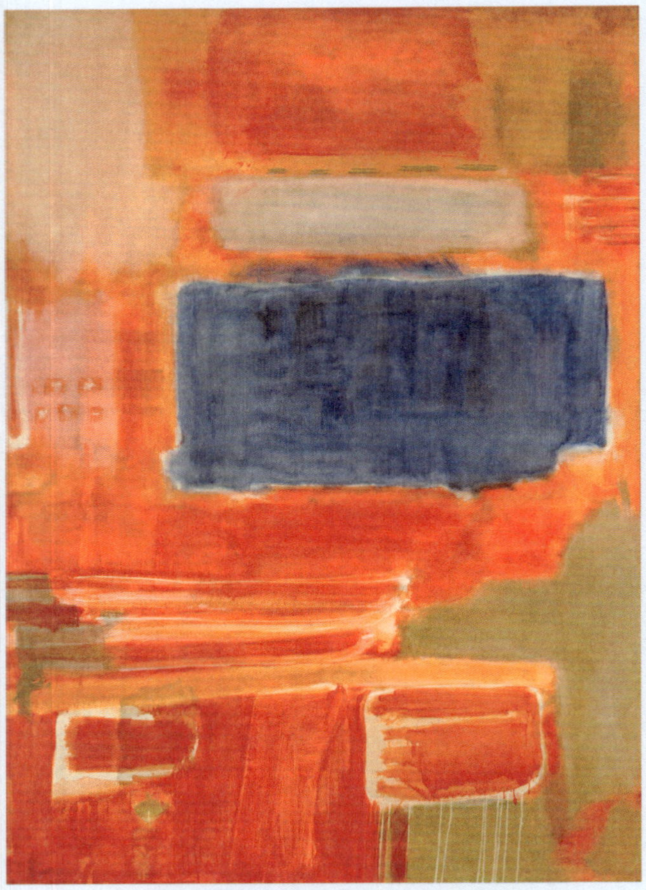

fig. 4 *Untitled (Multiform)*, 1948, oil on canvas, 89 × 65 in., Collection Kate Rothko Prizel and Ilya Prizel (CR 391; pl. 39)

fig. 3 *No. 10*, 1948, oil on canvas, 64 ⅝ × 42 ½ in., National Gallery of Art, Washington, D.C. (CR 385)

1 David Anfam, "The Paintings of Mark Rothko—A Complex Simplicity," in Anfam, *Mark Rothko, The Works on Canvas: Catalogue Raisonné* (New Haven and London: Yale University Press; Washington: National Gallery of Art, 1988), p. 69 n. 186. This will be referred to hereafter as *The Works on Canvas* and paintings will be identified by Anfam number. I have relied on Anfam's research and insights throughout.

2 Mark Stevens, "Mark Rothko," in *Mark Rothko*, exh. cat. (Pace Gallery, New York, 1990), p. 6.

3 David Anfam, "Rothko's Multiforms: The Moment of Transition and Transformation," in *Mark Rothko "Multiforms": Bilder von 1947–1949*, exh. cat. (Galerie Daniel Blau, Munich, 1993), p. 25. Dore Ashton, "Rothko's Passion," *Art International* 22:9 (February 1979), p. 8.

4 While Rothko had rejected titles since the fall of 1947, a typed checklist dated just before the opening of Rothko's March 1948 exhibition at Betty Parsons gallery includes a number of descriptive titles (Phalanx of the Mind, Beginnings, Sacred Vessel, etc.) that Rothko must have abandoned at the last minute in favor of numbers. Anfam, *The Works on Canvas*, p. 57.

5 Email to the author from Janet Blyberg, Rothko Online Resources Department, National Gallery of Art, August 15, 2011.

6 "Rothko may have noticed some of Bonnard's most characteristic color juxtapositions, deep blue purple with brown, often with a touch of alizarin crimson, for the deepest areas of a picture, the darkest object, as well as his juxtaposition of related brights." Bernice Rose, "Color and Light," in *Bonnard/Rothko: Color and Light*, exh. cat. (PaceWildenstein, New York, 1997), p. 12.

7 Determining proper orientation is not easy since few multiforms are signed or dated on the front and few were photographed or published during the artist's lifetime. Most have verso inscriptions of the year and the artist's name but these were done during the 1968–69 inventory and Anfam regards them as unreliable, ignoring them in some cases. The Harvard painting has no inscriptions but it has always been oriented with the drips going up. The very concept of orientation seems to have been a labile one for Rothko at this time. A "recurrent strategy during 1948," Anfam notes, was to turn paintings on their side to suppress "vestiges of a representational scheme." Anfam, *The Works on Canvas*, p. 69 n. 179. Taking the variously directed drips as evidence of canvas rotation and inversion, Jeffrey Weiss argues that the resulting "destabilization and disorientation were chief forms of experience in Rothko's work." Jeffrey Weiss, "Dis-Orientation: Rothko's Inverted Canvases," in Glenn Phillips and Thomas Crow, eds., *Seeing Rothko* (Los Angeles: Getty Research Institute, 2005), pp. 139, 146.

8 This tipping-forward of the line of vision or (to think of it the other way) tipping-up of the plane of imagery has a long history in modern art, from Paul Cézanne's still lifes to Pablo Picasso's and George Braque's Cubism to Piet Mondrian's Neo-Plasticism to Jackson Pollock's poured paintings.

9 Chave traces the juxtaposition of light and dark vertical rectangles in *No. 17/No. 15*, 1949 (CR 401) to the juxtaposition of light and dark figures in *Untitled [Two Seated Women]*, c. 1934 (CR 56), and *Nude [Untitled]*, 1933 (CR 38). Anna C. Chave, *Mark Rothko: Subjects in Abstraction* (New York and London: Yale University Press, 1989), pp. 111–13, cited in Clearwater, *The Rothko Book*, p. 90.

10 Anfam, *The Works on Canvas*, p. 59.

11 The phrase is from a review of the time and refers to the lack of definition between forms, but it uncannily captures the subsequent critical fate of the series. "The effort to avoid arresting the raw life in the pigment or the flow of its movement by any kind of definition leads to an impasse of empty formlessness, an art solely of transitions without beginning, middle or end." Sam Hunter, "Diverse Modernism," *New York Times*, March 14, 1948, section 2, p. 8.

12 At least one commentator has had the same association: Clearwater writes of *No. 18*, 1946 that "amorphous shapes seem to advance and recede in a primordial ooze." Ibid., p. 86. Anfam finds metaphorical suggestions both of mental / perceptual "blurring" and of the "mists of time." Anfam, *The Works on Canvas*, p. 60.

13 Darwin, letter to Joseph Dalton Hooker, February 1, 1871, in ed. Francis Darwin, *The Life and Letters of Charles Darwin, Including an Autobiographical Chapter* (London: John Murray, vol. 3), p. 18.

14 Rothko took a general biology course as a Yale University sophomore, and in high school his "College Preparatory Course" included science. Breslin, *Mark Rothko*, pp. 50, 35.

15 Rothko, *The Artist's Reality*, p. 56; cited in Clearwater, *The Rothko Book*, p. 77. Clearwater assumes that Rothko was describing the space of the multiforms, but Christopher Rothko argues in his introduction to *The Artist's Reality* (XVII–XVIII) that it is likely although not certain that the manuscript was written in the early 1940s.

16 The technique, known as agar plate, is the one of the few contexts in American English where one speaks of a gelatinous substance on a plate rather than in a pot or jar. There is a children's song popular in Britain, where Jell-o is more properly and generically called jelly, titled "Jelly on a Plate."

17 Thomas B. Hess, *Barnett Newman* (New York: Museum of Modern Art, 1971), p. 45; cited in Jeremy Strick, "Enacting Origins," in *The Sublime Is Now: The Early Work of Barnett Newman, Paintings and Drawings 1944–1949*, exh. cat. (PaceWildenstein, New York, 1994), p. 11. "Between 1939 and 1941, he [Newman] took courses at the Brooklyn Botanical Garden, vacationed at the Audubon Nature Camp in Maine, and attended summer classes in botany and ornithology at Cornell University." Lisa Mintz Messinger, "Barnett Newman," in *Abstract Expressionism: Works on Paper*, exh. cat. (Metropolitan Museum of Art, New York, 1992), p. 80.

18 Kay Larson, "Primal Dreams," *New York Magazine* (March 26, 1984), p. 77.

19 Robert C. Hobbs, "Mark Rothko," in *Abstract Expressionism: The Formative Years*, exh. cat. (Herbert F. Johnson Museum of Art, Cornell University, Ithaca, New York; Ithaca: Cornell University Press, 1978), p. 116.

20 For white drips on black grounds, see CR 344, 345, 346, and 348. Anfam notes the "mimic drips" in Anfam 348.

21 "Picasso Speaks" [interview with Marius de Zayas], in *The Arts*, May 1923, 315–26. Picasso linked this point to an assertion of the autonomy of Cubism itself. "Arts of transition do not exist.... Many think that cubism is an art of transition, an experiment which is to bring ulterior results. Those who think that way have not understood it. Cubism is not either a seed or a foetus, but an art dealing primarily with forms, and when a form is realized it is there to live its own life." Anfam points to the same constellation of ideas, citing Jackson Pollock's declaration that his poured paintings had "a life of their own." Anfam, "Rothko's Multiforms," p. 26.

22 Mark Rothko, "The Romantics Were Prompted," *Possibilities* 1 (winter 1947 / 48), p. 84.

23 Cited in Clearwater, *The Rothko Book*, pp. 71–72.

24 Rothko wrote to Newman in August 1950: "I am heartily ashamed of the things I have written.... My error in the case of Bob [Motherwell] is a thing of the past, but at least I must learn not to repeat it except by desire and conviction." Mark Rothko, *Writings on Art*, ed. Miguel López-Remiro (New Haven and London: Yale University Press, 2006), pp. 72–73. In my review of this book, I argue that Rothko's conception of painting as speech (rather than merely language, a more generic modernist idea) means that the more his art developed, the less willing he became to make or publish statements about it. Harry Cooper, "Painted Word," *Bookforum* 13:3 (September–November 2006), p. 25.

25 Rothko, *Writings on Art*, p. 112.

26 "He began to compose nonobjective paintings, conventionally known as 'multiforms' or 'transitional.' Simultaneously, Rothko abandoned traditional preparation of his canvas supports. He began to 'stain' the cotton canvas duck with an initial glue size mixed with powdered pigments.... The paintings of the late 1940s with amorphous forms floating on a glowing field are the result of layers of dry-brushed areas of synthetic or oil paint. The predominantly pastel-colored surfaces of these works are extremely porous and dry, almost frescolike in appearance." Dana Cranmer, "Painting Materials and Techniques of Mark Rothko: Consequences of an Unorthodox Approach," in *Mark Rothko: 1903–1970* (New York: Stewart, Tabori, and Chang, 1996), p. 191.

27 Anfam notes that Rothko's elimination of figurative presences in 1948 "goes hand in hand with a burgeoning, subtle interest in the reflectance or visual *éclat* of the paint surfaces, anticipated in the 'thin' to 'fat' pigment variations of the still dun but layered *No. 24* (CR 358)." Anfam, *The Works on Canvas*, 60. This parallels what I have been describing as Rothko's discovery of transparency; indeed, his manipulation of reflectivity and transparency would come to define his treatment of surface and light in the mature works.

28 Here I differ somewhat with Hilton Kramer, who writes of 1948: "Rothko's encounter with Bonnard at that crucial moment in his development gave him the means of making significant use of what he had learned about color from Avery without relapsing into imitations of Avery himself." Hilton Kramer, "Rothko's Surreal Killer May Have Been Greenberg," *The New York Observer*, June 15, 1998. While I agree with the suggestion that Bonnard allowed Rothko renewed access to Avery (a looming father figure he had to work hard to reject), I also believe that Rothko learned a lesson from Bonnard about transparency that Avery's work did not provide.

"Maybe you have notice two characteristics exist in my paintings; either their surfaces are expansive and push you toward in all directions, or their surfaces contract and rush inward in all directions. Between these two poles you can find everything I want to say."

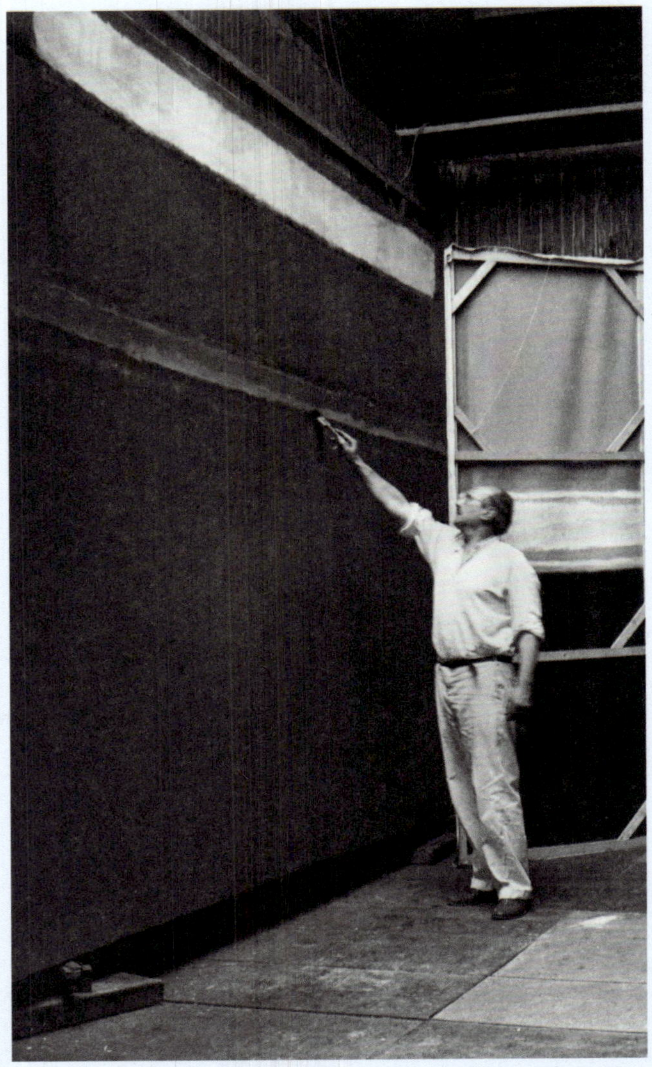

Mark Rothko painting in his studio, 53th Street, New York, 1953, photo Henry Elkan, The Rothko Family Archive

Nancy Spector

Mark Rothko's Classic Paintings: Theaters of the Mind

Famously reticent to explain the intentions behind his art—believing that words only detracted from the experience of his paintings—Mark Rothko nevertheless provided a blueprint for what has become known as the "classic period" of his oeuvre three years before it commenced.[1] In a 1947 text, "The Romantics Were Prompted," he asserted "I think of my pictures as dramas; the shapes in the pictures are the performers."[2] These dramas were to be enacted as "unknown adventures in an unknown space;" their performers (or compositional components) "move with internal freedom, and without need to conform with or violate what is probable in the visible world. They have no direct association with any particular visible experience, but in them one recognizes the principle and passion of organisms."[3] Rothko's allusion to drama here implies an understanding of his canvases as charged sites in which tensions play out in a narrative that unfolds over time. Written during a transitional moment in his practice, when the Surrealist-inflected, semi-abstract forms of his paintings from the early to mid 1940s were giving way to the free-floating, pulsating shapes in his *Multiforms* of 1947–49, this brief statement evinces the artist's imminent embrace of a pure, visual abstraction infused with "principle and passion"—defining elements of the human psyche, plot points of a classic drama, be it theatrical or operatic.[4]

By 1950, Rothko had achieved an inherent structural clarity in his painting by distilling his vocabulary to a soft-edged geometry delineated through oscillating chromatic contrasts and analogous color harmonies. Color, rhythm, and form became one. What emerged at the precipice of the classic period was a signature style comprising two or three stacked rectangular shapes hovering or even quivering on the surface of the canvas, its edges alternately framing or compressing the assembled components, providing just enough implied pressure to keep them from floating, metaphorically, into the ether. We see the last gasp of an abstracted vs. an essentially abstract presentation in Rothko's majestic painting *No. 5/No. 22* (1950; fig. 2), which he included in his fifth and final exhibition at the Betty Parsons Gallery in 1951 as a portal into the body of work that would consume him for the next fifteen or so years. A horizontal red bar bisects the canvas, barely missing the outer borders of the stretcher. It separates a deep orange quadrangle from a lighter yellow one on top—the entire assemblage seemingly suspended over a more subdued yellow background, the tint of which seeps into the grayish bar that fills an indentation on the upper register of the highest rectangle. The distinguishing element of the painting, however—and that which positions it as a provisional work—is the striation of three tenuous white lines that traverse the center of the picture. Hardly descriptive, they nevertheless introduce a reference to reality, an allusion, perhaps, to a horizon line or more allegorically to the bare threads of consciousness.[5] The commanding, vertical canvas *No. 10* (1950; fig. 1), also included in the Parsons exhibition, evinces Rothko's increasing mastery of his new pictorial strategy. While exploiting the bold contrast between primary colors, the deceptively simple configuration of stacked boxes offers, on close examination, an undulating experience of surface vs. depth and opacity vs. translucence. The background appears to be a deep cerulean blue, as it is visible on the top under a thinly brushed gray bar, along the sides and at the bottom of the central, densely painted yellow rectangle and the lower, diaphanous whitish-gray one. But the blue also transforms into its own geometry, compressed as it is between the topmost and middle forms. A layer of brownish pigment emerges ever so slightly from behind the plane of yellow and white / gray to further complicate this play of optical dimensionality. Trickles of yellow paint drip onto the misty, cloud-like patch at the bottom, anchoring it in place, confirming its solidity.[6]

Throughout the 1950s, Rothko immersed himself in the production of these exceedingly ambiguous, yet stunningly captivating paintings, the ambitions of which mystified his detractors and supporters alike. The canvases were, for instance, described alternatively at the time as unyielding "facades" by Elaine de Kooning, in that they tried to "hide behind" themselves,[7] or porous entities by Katherine Kuh, who wrote, "One tends to enter into his canvases not merely to look at them. A kind of atmospheric involvement takes place where physical boundaries are ignored."[8] As Jeffrey Weiss has astutely demonstrated, Rothko's emphatic embrace of a formal non-objectivity occasioned a flurry of discursive responses that tended to interpret the artist's canvases in spatial terms, seeing evocations of architecture or landscape, the latter securely positioned within the tradition of the Romantic sublime.[9] Additionally, the artist's unprecedented palette, amplified by a range of contrasting painterly effects distinguished by their degrees of translucency, brightness, saturation, and texture (with separate instances of each manifest on a single canvas), led many critics to describe Rothko as a colorist.[10] Duncan Phillips, an ardent collector, responded in 1960 to the emotive qualities of the artist's chromatic vision by acquiring three paintings that shared different hues of orange and red. He installed them, with the artist's blessings, in a specially designed room that is now a part of the Phillips Collection (see pp. 274–75). Their arrangement reflects upon Rothko's intense desire to create choreographed groupings of his canvases to underscore their relational nature and intensify the durational experience of each work.[11] But, as with all defining labels, the painter rejected being characterized by his mastery of color, which, in the critical discourse around Abstract Expressionism at the time, would have pitted him against Jackson Pollock, renowned for his signature "line." Robert Goldwater, Rothko's favored interlocutor, dismissed the designation, claiming that the painter had no interest in the "enjoyment of color for its own sake," and added that the chromatic harmonies and contrasts unique to the work "represent nothing and lead nowhere."[12] However, Dore Ashton, an early Rothko biographer, countered what she perceived to be Goldwater's mere parroting of the artist's contrived elusiveness, arguing that the artist "never abandoned the will to portray," and shared that in private he maintained that the paintings were "'portraits' of states of the soul."[13] In interviews and statements, Rothko himself vacillated between explanation and obfuscation, but always privileged meaning over pure formal analysis. In discussions during 1952 with then Ph.D. candidate William Seitz, who was researching key protagonists in Abstract Expressionism, the artist clarified that the figures (and their symbolic valences) that populated his earlier paintings had not disappeared from their striated backgrounds, but rather dissolved into the floating shapes that delineated his contemporaneous work.[14] While never articulating his "subject," Rothko consistently indicated there was one, claiming, for instance, that instead of color relationships or spatial analysis he was "interested in only expressing basic human emotions—tragedy, ecstasy, doom."[15]

Rhetorically, it is impossible to describe Rothko's "classic period" paintings without reverting to a discussion about their chromatic sensibilities, despite his own frequent eschewal of the subject. As with the paintings of his peers Barnett Newman and Ad Reinhardt, whose largely monochromatic, abstract canvases are categorized by the intensity of their specific pigments (even though they are deeply symbolic), Rothko's compositions *are* essentially their color. Over the years, their titles have vacillated from a somewhat ad hoc numbering system to the literal recitation of the particular colors dominating the respective pictures—descriptive titles which were mostly ascribed posthumously.[16] *Red, Black, White on Yellow* (1955; pl. 61), for example, is exactly that: a potent, vertical ocher canvas on which an amorphous rectangle of cardinal red hovers over a black horizonal belt separating it from the haze of white below. And *Blue, Orange, Red* (1961; pl. 90) is a stack of three quadrangular forms, increasing in scale from the lower to upper registers, on a cadmium red background. The bottom orange bar "supports" two differently rendered blue shapes, one indigo and the other cobalt. While *No. 14* (1960; pl. 88) does not benefit from an explanatory subtitle, one could easily call it "Orange and Blue over Purple," with its fiery field of orange vapor atop a denser arena of navy blue, both forms semi-obscuring the aubergine surface beneath them. But such prosaic accounts cannot approach the astonishing play of chromatic variation perceivable through the delicate and interlaced layers of pigment that comprise the paintings in the "classic period." Every hue on a Rothko canvas from the mid 1950s appears, after close study, to harbor another. Though exceedingly flat, the paintings are built from strata of pigments that seep into adjacent or anterior chromatic zones, assuring that each chromatic field is never just one color. Even the paintings that appear almost monochromatic comprise a range of hues, however subtle the shifts among them might be. Such is the case with the exceptionally yellow *No. 10* (1957; pl. 64), with its two supple rectangles—one canary, one saffron—cleaved by a feathery white band on a mustard ground. And the expansive *Pink and White over Red* (1957; pl. 77) radiates with an underlying golden glow that enhances the overall blush of the crimson painting. We know that Rothko was deeply inspired by two master painters, Rembrandt and Matisse, who used color to vastly different ends. From the former, he understood the meticulous buildup of oil glazes to create the illusion of radiance, despite the humbleness of much of the subject matter. The latter gave him permission, as it were, to delve deeply into color as a form of expression, completely independent from any means of mimetic representation. Rothko venerated Matisse's all-over interior composition *The Red Studio* (1911; fig. 5) and recalled spending "hours and hours" at the Museum of Modern Art once the radically monochromatic canvas was installed in their permanent collection galleries in 1949. "When you look at that painting," he explained, "you became that color, you become totally saturated with it."[17]

Rothko's vivid, polychromatic compositions darkened toward the end of the decade in anticipation of the paintings produced for his somber *Seagram Murals* commission in 1958—with their preponderance of burnt sienna, burgundy, orange, and black tones—and the transcendent yet elegiac canvases of undulant purple and black pigment (see pp. 277–81 and pl. 70 and 71) that comprise the Rothko Chapel installation (dedicated in Houston in 1971; see pp. 285–95). At one end of the "emotional" spectrum, the quieter canvases could, perhaps, invoke a sense of peaceful resolve. In *No. 3* (1957; pl. 67), the richly saturated blue, green, and purple-black hues, seem to bleed into and permeate one another, while still maintaining the structural integrity of their respective forms. This perceptual fluctuation between solidity and mutability—as one analogous color slips into another—is harmonious in its subtlety. Other, darker paintings from the early 1960s impact through intense chromatic contrasts, and could be interpreted as more readily substantiating Rothko's often cryptic commentary on the archetypal tensions in the paintings (though the full range of his creative output during this period must be understood holistically). In these canvases, deep brown to inky black quadrilaterals yield to high-keyed flashes of brilliant orange and red forms. The "drama" that Rothko described as inherent to his art in the 1947 statement intensifies with the muting of his overall palette and the simultaneous sharpening of its complementary color distinctions. However, the paintings—conceived as allegorical theaters of human emotion or states of being—can never

fig. 1 *No. 10*, 1950, oil on canvas, 76 3/8 × 57 1/8 inch., Museum of Modern Art, New York (CR 449)

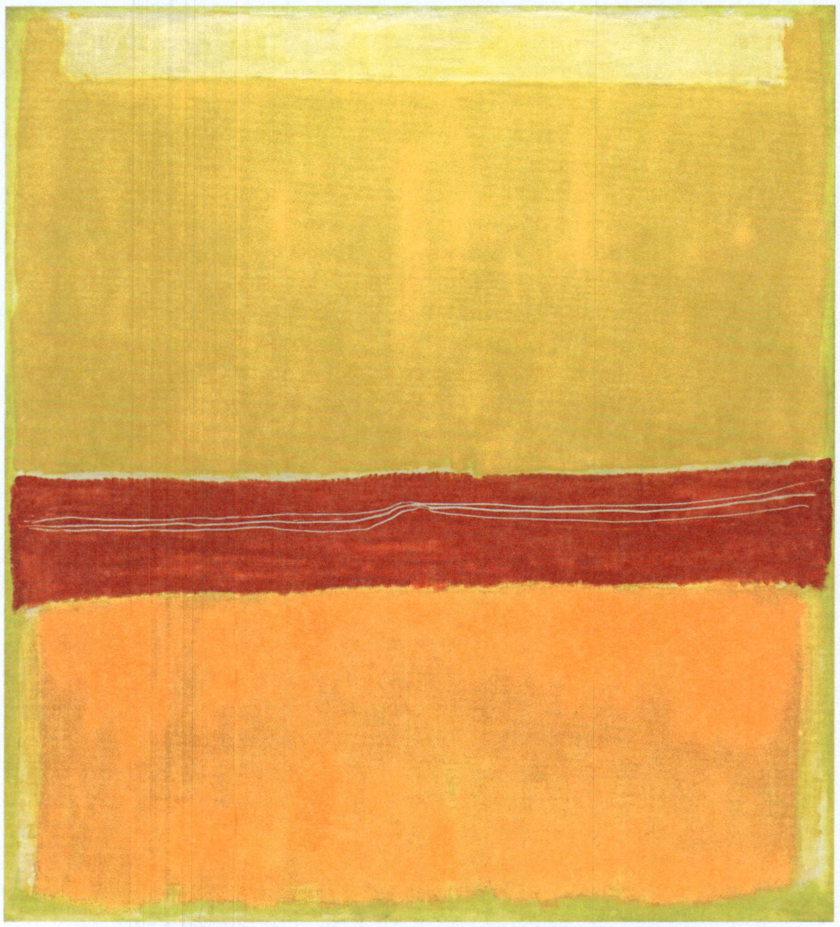

fig. 2 *No. 5/No. 22*, 1950, oil on canvas, 117 × 107 in., Museum of Modern Art, New York (CR 442; pl. 50)

be reduced to specific affects, despite the feelings they may elicit in a viewer.[18]

Rothko's oft-cited association between the catalytic impulses behind his art and drama was rooted not in thespian studies, but rather philosophy, specifically Friedrich Nietzsche's treatise *The Birth of Tragedy out of the Spirit of Music* (1872). This was a formative text for the artist and he attributed much to its influence, writing, "I found in this fable the poetic reinforcement for what I inevitably knew was my inevitable course."[19] The book discusses the dialectic between two opposing yet inextricably linked forces personified in Greek myth by the deities Apollo and Dionysius, who represented, respectively, order and chaos, rationality and the undifferentiated abyss. Nietzsche compared these two realms to the dream state and utter intoxication, the former embodying the Apollonian creative process, which he likened to a dream state, and the latter, the Dionysian siren call of an all-consuming "primordial unity." In dreams, one can fully invent but always remain aware of the artificiality of the construct, so for Nietzsche art (or technē) was thus an illusion of an illusion hiding the threat of self-dissolution looming within the void. Ancient Greek tragedy, with its interwoven choral (Dionysian) and spoken (Apollonian) segments, was believed by the philosopher to offer a "metaphysical solace" to this unfathomable paradox, not by erasing it but by aestheticizing and performing on that razor's edge between the will to live and the urge for self-destruction. For Rothko, art had the possibility of recuperating this blinding truth for the modern age by translating elemental human conflict into visible form, which for him eventually required "pulverizing" the "familiar identity of things" and embracing pure non-objectivity.[20] He wrote that it was the role of the artist in ancient times to risk the wrath of the gods by unveiling the true precariousness of reality through a kind of trickery—and, like "a stolen jewel of great value," this truth must be "exhibited only under certain disguises and conditions."[21] Rothko acknowledged that the perceived "serenity" of his paintings, which was the attribute that most attracted the "friendly" viewer, was intentionally "deceptive." The ethereal beauty of his canvases, a union in his mind of the Apollonian and Dionysian, gave cover for Rothko to "achieve the greatest intensity of the tragic, [the] irreconcilability of the basic violence which lies at the bottom of human existence and the daily life which must deal with it."

Rothko thought deeply about how his paintings should be encountered in an exhibition context in order to encourage a visceral, life-altering experience of them. Unframed and immense in scale—with some canvases from the 1950s and 1960s standing nearly ten feet high—the paintings were intended to envelop the viewer, providing for a profound sense of embodiment. For his 1955 exhibition at the Sidney Janis Gallery, the paintings including *No. 61 (Rust and Blue) [Brown, Blue, Brown on Blue]* (1953; CR 492), and *No. 1 (Royal Red and Blue) [Untitled]* (1954; fig. 4) were quite literally wedged into the space from ceiling to floor, "defeating" the walls and offering visitors a sentient confrontation with the "intimate and intense" pictorial revelations on view.[22] He persuaded exhibition curators that his paintings should be dimly lit in order to allow the richly saturated hues to resonate and what he described as the "inner light" of the paintings to materialize.[23] Additionally, he was highly skeptical about the adjacency of his works to those by other artists, often insisting that his paintings be installed together in designated rooms, hence his favorable reception to the mural commissions that occupied him in his later years. With the size of the canvases—being both large and private—Rothko created symbolic, painterly expanses that bridge what Weiss has called "the gap between imaginary and real space."[24] It is in this liminal territory that a viewer might sense the dramatic mise-en-scène in which the tragic narratives veiled behind the serene surfaces were metaphorically enacted. This is not the painterly domain described by critic Harold Rosenberg in 1952 as "an arena in which to act" in his characterization of contemporaneous American abstraction as the cumulation of a painter's gestures, a recording of process, in a demonstration of his (or her) rugged individualism.[25] Given Rothko's profound identification with Nietzsche's metaphysics and his affinity for the architecture of the ancient Greco-Roman world (as encountered in visits to Paestum and Pompeii), the symbolic space suggested in his paintings demarcates theaters of the mind, sites for a kind of cathartic exchange between artist and viewer.[26]

The sense of archaic tragedy conjured by Rothko's otherworldly paintings—to the extent it was ever understood by his public—needed not refer to the originary dialectic at the core of human fragility. It could, instead, have found its source in the shattered realities of postwar society, despite the trumped up optimism of the new liberalism in the U.S. and what was being promoted in tandem as the ascendency of American art. Whether theorized at the time as heroic self-expression (Rosenberg) or formalist self-reflexivity (Clement Greenberg), American postwar abstraction can only be understood in connection with the cataclysmic impact of World War II on an inconceivably global scale. Rothko's erasure of figuration, which he forecast in 1947, occurred just a few years after the 1945 bombing of Hiroshima and Nagasaki by the U.S. military. How could anyone ignore the horrific aftermath of nuclear annihilation and the unfathomable scale of genocide executed during the Holocaust (especially as a Jew of Eastern European descent)? Serge Guilbaut suggests that the fierce abstraction practiced by many artists associated with the New York School emerged as a "kind of unwriting, an art of effacement" in reaction to the existential crisis facing humanity at mid-century.[27] This turn from didacticism was less the result of avoidance than it was the impossibility of expression in the face of abject evil and total destruction. Such was the intellectual position of French philosopher Maurice Blanchot, who believed that the Holocaust defied all efforts at conceptualization, likening it to what he termed, the "disaster ... [which] ... is the unknown name for that in thought itself which dissuades us from thinking of it, leaving us, but its proximity alone."[28]

The fourteen meditative canvases that Rothko created for his chapel in Houston, in response to a commission by John and Dominique de Menil in 1965, can be interpreted as a further eradication of his formal vocabulary, an intense reduction in color contrast that may have been motivated in part by the inspirational nature of the assignment or the radically changing times or the artist's own deteriorating emotional state. Their sonorous, nearly monochromatic black and maroon surfaces are at once somber and mesmeric. Most accounts of Rothko's career follow a teleological thru-line from the chapel's solemn, all-encompassing environment to his late sepulchral black paintings as an indicator of the artist's encroaching suicide. But that chronicle omits the spasm of prismatic color found in a suite of four canvases from 1967 and the series of acrylic on paper works from 1969 that share the delicate chromatic trembling of the "classic" paintings. In *Untitled* (fig. 3) and *No. 3 (Untitled/Orange*; pl. 115) (both 1967), vibrant rectangular swaths of orange, magenta, and red coincide on large canvases, their edges barely touching, as if separated by thin bands of light or mere breaths of pigment. In *Untitled*, a grayish brown quadrangle hovers at the base of the composition, contrasting with the red shape above, alternately receding into a shadowy depth or remaining flat and sustaining the surface tension. The artist's last painting, *Untitled*, 1970, is a study of red in its most soulful and passionate state. It harks back to Rothko's infatuation with Matisse's *The Red Studio* and the concept of ecstatic, self-surrender to an experience of color. These late, exuberant paintings refute the notion that Rothko's palette and compositional complexity diminished exponentially and uninterrupted through the 1960s as a harbinger of his demise. They are not his "requiem"[29], rather than exclusively executing the dramatically paired down studies in grey and black, for which his later period is best known, Rothko continued and amplified his rigorous yet romantic deployment of prismatic color. That *Untitled*,—with its brilliant, all-over red tonality—is the artist's final work gives lie to the notion that his depressive state ditacted his artistic output. It is useful, therefore, to see both the dark canvases and the coeval, full color pictures as part of the essential Apollonian / Dionysian dialectic that informed the metaphysics of Rothko's lifelong approach to art and infused every element of his painting practice.

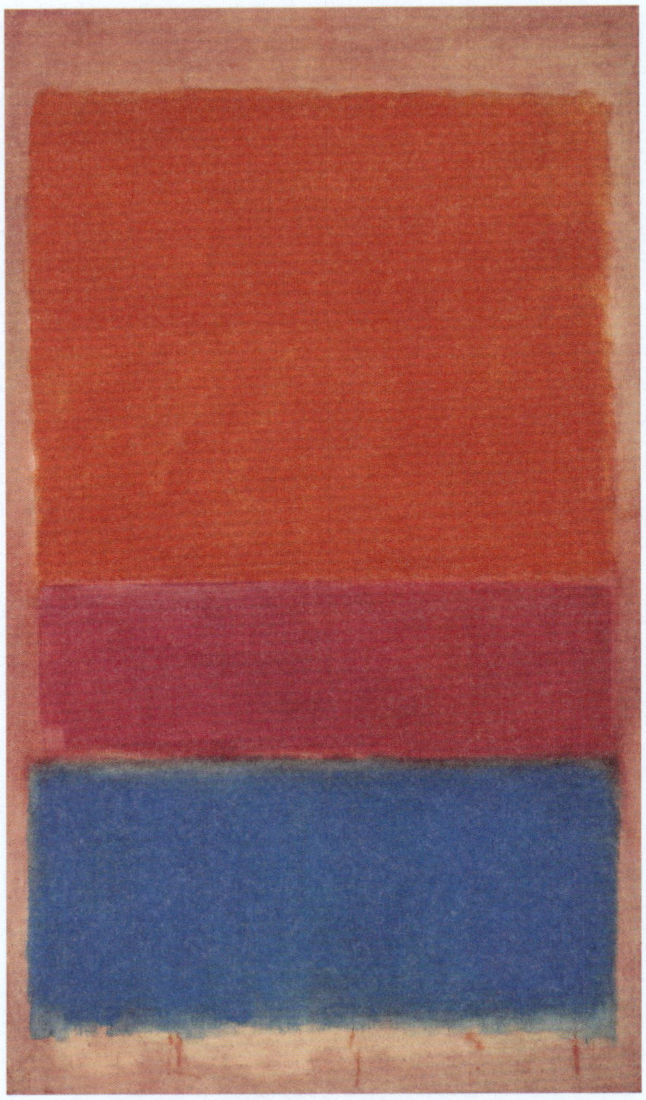

fig. 4 *No. 1 (Royal Red and Blue)*, 1954, oil on canvas, 113 ¾ in × 67 ½ in., private collection (CR 503)

fig. 3 *Untitled*, 1967, oil on canvas, 80 × 69 in., private collection (CR 808; pl. 114)

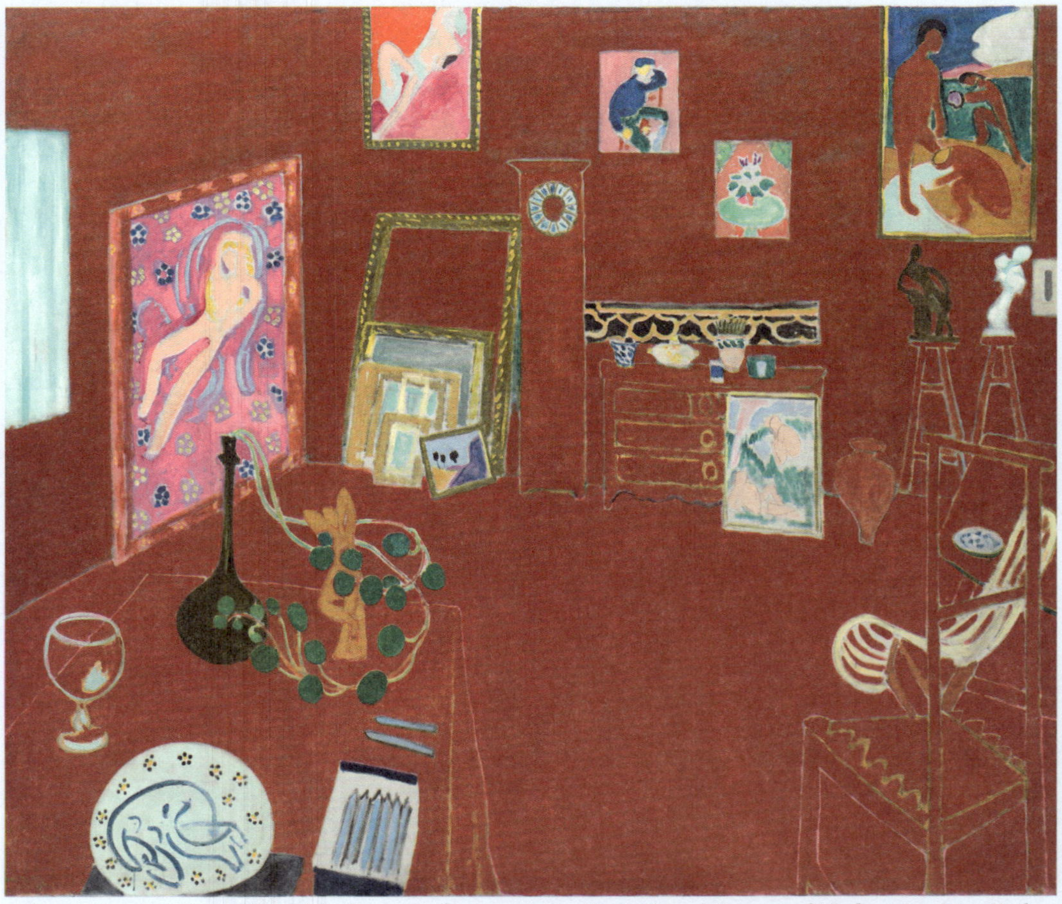

fig. 5 Henri Matisse, *The Red Studio*, 1911, oil on canvas, 71 ¼ × 86 ¼ in., Museum of Modern Art, New York

1 In the catalogue raisonné of paintings, *Mark Rothko: Works on Canvas*, author David Anfam assembles works created between 1951 and 1970 under the nomenclature, "The Classic Years" (New Haven and London: Yale University Press, 1998), p. 70.

2 Published in *Possibilities 1* (1947–48), p. 84. This issue, the first and only one published, was interdisciplinary in spirit. The editorial group comprised Pierre Chareau (architecture), John Cage (music), Robert Motherwell (art), and Harold Rosenberg (literature), reflecting the journal's mission to be the definitive word on avant-garde American culture in all its manifestations. The masthead alone indicates an equivalency of mediums and a desire for the cross-pollination among them. Reprinted in Miguel López-Remiro, *Mark Rothko: Writings on Art* (New Haven and London: Yale University Press, 2006), pp. 58–59. Citations are from this source.

3 Ibid., p. 59.

4 According to Anfam, Rothko likened his canvases to the different voices in an opera when configuring the ideal installation plans for the display of his paintings, Anfam, *Mark Rothko: Works on Canvas*, p. 71. Rothko's frequent reference to theater reflects his own grounding engagement with the discipline. As a young adult he enrolled in drama classes taught by Josephine Dillon in Portland, Oregon (where he had returned to his parent's home in 1924 after a stint in New York City). One year later, upon return to New York, he auditioned for a scholarship at the American Laboratory Theatre, which was founded on the Stanislavski system. His rejection occasioned his enrollment in the New York School of Design.

5 Rothko gifted this painting to The Museum of Modern Art in 1969, eight years after his solo exhibition there. His donation of this transitional work to such a significant cultural institution, one which served as an arbiter of the New York school of painting, signaled its importance to the artist.

6 For a detailed description of *No. 10* (1950) as emblematic of Rothko's new style, see James E. Breslin, *Mark Rothko: A Biography* (Chicago and London: University of Chicago Press, 1998), pp. 276–79. There is a recording of Christopher Rothko speaking about the painting, which is in the collection of The Museum of Modern Art, on their website, https://www.moma.org/collection/works/78594?, accessed February 19, 2023.

7 The term was used by Elaine de Kooning in her article "Americans in Action: Franz Kline & Mark Rothko," *Art News Annual XXVII*, 1958, pp. 86–97, 174–79. But when questioned about her meaning in an interview with Phyllis Tuchman twenty-three years later, de Kooning clarified she was speaking in psychological / emotive and not formal terms. https://www.aaa.si.edu/collections/interviews/oral-history-interview-elaine-de-kooning-11999, accessed February 19, 2023.

8 Quoted from Katherine Kuh, typed draft text for the *Art Institute of Chicago Quarterly*, written to accompany Rothko's solo exhibition at the Art Institute (October 18–December 31, 1954). Archives of the Art Institute of Chicago.

9 See Jeffrey Weiss, "Rothko's Unknown Space," in *Mark Rothko*, exh. cat. (Washington, D.C.: National Gallery of Art, 1998), pp. 303–29, for a detailed discussion of the changing understanding of the artist's formal and philosophical approach to pictorial depth in his paintings. Robert Rosenblum in particular discussed Rothko in the tradition of Caspar David Friedrich and J.M.W. Turner, likening his paintings to vistas onto a "sunset or moonlit night." See his "The Abstract Sublime," *Art News* (February 1961), vol. 59, no. 10, p. 56.

10 John Gage's essay, "Rothko: Color as Subject," in *Mark Rothko*, exh. cat., 1998, pp. 247–81, provides an excellent analysis of the artist's chromatic practice and the critical responses to it.

11 Duncan Phillips once asked Rothko, "Am I right that in your approach to your work, color means *more* to you than any other element," to which the painter replied, "No, not color but *measures*," in Breslin, *Mark Rothko: A Biography*, p. 469.

12 Originally published as a review of Rothko's one-person exhibition at The Museum of Modern Art in 1961 in *Arts Magazine*, vol. 35, no. 6 (March 1961), the article was so well-liked by the artist that he requested it be reprinted in the catalogue for his show at the Whitechapel Art Gallery in London, a subsequent venue of the MoMA exhibition tour. Quoted from its reprint in *Mark Rothko 1903–1970*, exh. cat. (London: Tate Gallery, 1987), pp. 32–33.

13 Dore Ashton, *About Rothko* (New York and Oxford: Oxford University Press, Inc., 1983). Quoted here from the unabridged republication (Cambridge, MA: Da Capo Press, 1993), pp. 165–67.

14 See Bonnie Clearwater, "Selected Statements by Mark Rothko," in *Mark Rothko 1903–1970*, exh. cat., 1987, p. 73.

15 Ibid., p. 73. Cited from a statement made by Rothko to Selden Rodman in 1957.

16 See James Breslin, *Mark Rothko: A Biography* (Chicago: University of Chicago Press, 1998), pp. 492–93 for an account of Rothko's attempt to inventory his work toward the end of his life. The titling of Rothko's paintings is dealt with in detail by Anfam in the 1998 catalogue raisonnné, pp. 17–21.

17 Quoted in Breslin, *Mark Rothko: A Biography*, p. 283. Breslin also cites Rothko's fascination with Rembrandt. See also Gage, "Rothko: Color as Subject," pp. 248–89 for more on Rembrandt in relation to Rothko's engagement with color.

18 In his recorded lecture at Pratt Institute in 1958, Rothko closed by saying that his "current pictures are involved with the *scale* of human feelings [sic] the human drama, as much of it as I can express," López-Remiro, *Mark Rothko: Writings on Art*, p. 126.

19 Otherwise unattributed comments by Rothko in this paragraph are from a series of unpublished, undated notes by the artist on the relationship between *The Birth of Tragedy* and his painting. Thanks go to Marian Kahan for locating this document in the Mark Rothko Archive. See Breslin, *Mark Rothko: A Biography*, pp. 174–76, for an account about when Rothko may have first encountered the book and how generative it was for his ideas about art and metaphysics. In a text fragment, possibly intended to be sent to Katherine Kuh at the Art Institute of Chicago as part of their pre-exhibition correspondence, Rothko shares how Nietzsche's treatise "left an indelible impression on my mind and forever colored the syntax of my own reflections in the questions of art," ed. López-Remiro, *Mark Rothko: Writings on Art*, p. 109.

20 Ibid., p. 59.

21 Ibid., p. 119.

22 These terms are quoted from Rothko's explanation to Katherine Kuh about his display preferences for his work. Ibid., p. 99.

23 Correspondence between Rothko and Bryan Robertson of the Whitechapel Art Gallery on the occasion of his exhibition there in 1961, cited in Michael Compton, "Mark Rothko: the Subjects of the Artists," in *Mark Rothko 1903–1970*, exh. cat., 1987, p. 59. "The light, whether natural or artificial should not be too strong: the pictures have their own inner light and if there is too much light the color in the picture is washed out and a distortion of the look occurs."

24 Op. cit., Weiss, "Rothko's Unknown Space," p. 325.

25 See Breslin, *Mark Rothko: A Biography*, pp. 385–89, for an account of Rothko's particular disdain for Rosenberg's theory and Elaine de Kooning's adoption of it in the essay she penned on his art in 1958.

26 For an account of Rothko's revelatory experience seeing the temple ruins in Italy and Greece, see Ashton, *About Rothko*, p. 147. Ashton also maintains that, for Rothko, the reciprocation between artist and viewer (an idea inherited from the Romantics) was paramount. See p. 78.

27 See Serge Guilbaut, "The New Adventures of the Avant-Garde in America," originally published in *October* 15, winter 1980, pp. 61–78. Quoted here from the reprint in Francis Frascina, *Pollock and After: The Critical Debate* (New York: Harper & Row, Publishers, 1985), p. 160.

28 Maurice Blanchot, *The Writing of the Disaster,* trans. Ann Smock (Lincoln: University of Nebraska Press, 1986), p. 5. In her biography of the artist, Ashton claims that Rothko's work should be read through the existentialist and phenomenological work of the French theorists, writing, "If there is a context within which Rothko's work may be considered as part of the modern history of thought, it would be found in the peopled silences invoked by a host of French writers from 1945 on—not only philosophers but poets, playwrights, and critics.… It would be found in the resurrection of Nietzsche, especially in France where Gide had first invoked him to support his fin de siècle rebellion against rationalism, and where Sartre and Blanchot would later find important matter for their definition of the modern spirit." Ashton, *About Rothko*, p. 119.

29 Quoted from Brian O'Doherty, "The Last Paintings," in ed. Arne Glimcher, *Mark Rothko: The Exhibitions at Pace* (New York: Calloway, 2019), p. 91.

"A picture lives by companionship, expanding and quickening in the eyes of the sensitive observer. It dies by the same token. It is therefore a risky and un-feeling act to send it out into the world."

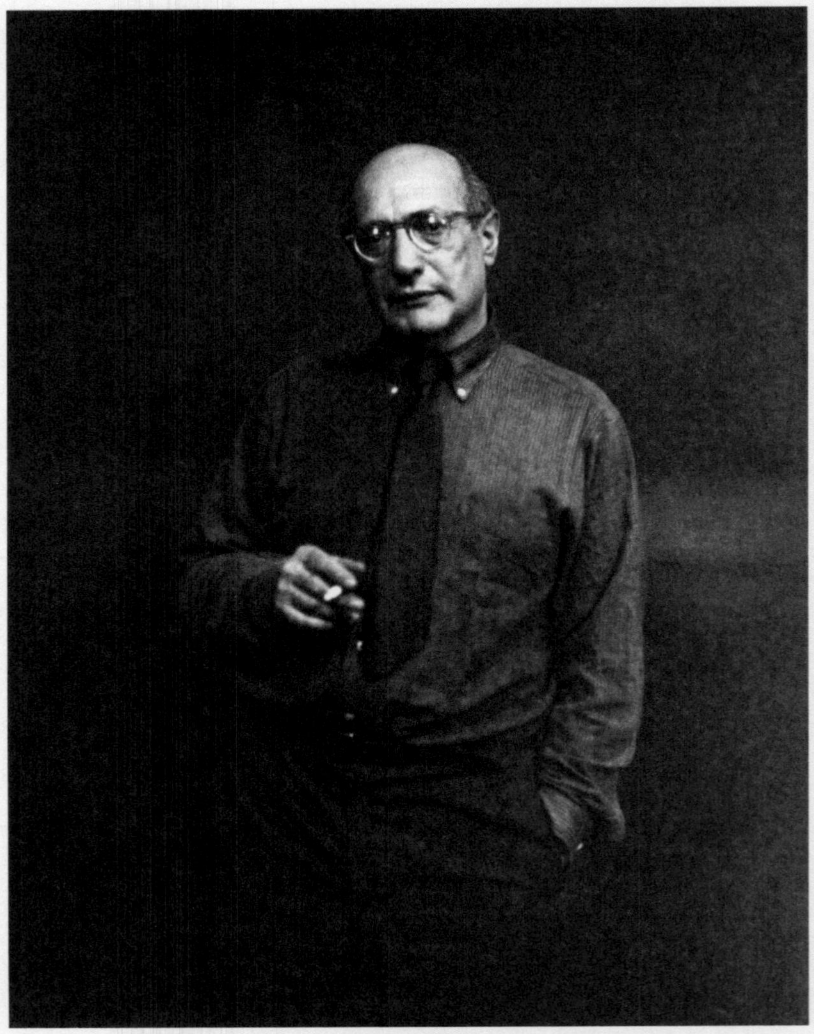

Rudy Burckhardt, Mark Rothko in front of *No. 7*, 1960

Jeffrey Weiss

Weights and Measures

A new form will always seem more or less an absence of any form at all, since it is unconsciously judged by reference to the consecrated forms.
Alain Robbe-Grillet

The so-called black-and-gray paintings produced by Mark Rothko in 1969–70, during the final months of his life, display a severity that sets them apart from the artist's work of the previous two decades. This distinction is unrelated to the fact that they are drained of luminous color. By this time, Rothko had made many paintings that are restricted to a dark palette, including the "black-form" paintings for the Houston Chapel commission of 1964. Rather, the paintings of 1969 are distinguished by their division into firmly defined upper and lower zones. This strict division is underscored in three ways. First, the stark opposition of black over gray is repeated from work to work, lending not just focus but relentlessness to the group. Secondly, the separation of top and bottom is represented by a continuous, unruled but even demarcation across the full width of the canvas; gone is the arrangement of rectangular forms that evenly lie within the margins, which typifies the work since 1950. Finally, a number of black-and-gray paintings possess an unprecedented framing edge in the form of a narrow white band. Formerly, Rothko had painted the entire surface as well as the tacking margins of his stretched canvas, which opened the works visually to the space of the wall and the room. Instead, with the white margin, the areas of black and gray—more fields than forms—are constricted, locked to the plane and held tight on all four sides.

The severity of the black-and-gray paintings implicates a self-conscious shift, which Rothko's early observers often associated with the artist's state of mind. Indeed, given what we know about his compromised health at that time and, above all, his suicide, the urge to ascribe the lowering light and constriction of form to a troubled psyche was almost inevitable. Rothko's interpreters have long since complicated this narrative, addressing his recourse to darkness in conceptual and thematic rather than personal terms. But consequently, such works, including the black-and-gray paintings, are now characterized by an ever-growing list of metaphorical allusions. The severity of the final paintings does conjure restraint, even renunciation, a sensation that implicates symbolic freight. But with recourse to the metaphorical, the slow labor of studio practice is bracketed out. Are new challenges of a pictorial kind at stake independent of psyche and the apparatus of allegory? Put differently, do making and meaning need to be kept apart?

* * *

"The more experience I acquire in my art, the more tormenting that art becomes. The trouble is, imagination remains stationary while taste matures." I take this remark by Gustave Flaubert, from a letter of 1857, to reflect on the limitations that condition any serious esthetic practice over time, in which invention and originality of means come early while growing discrimination and self-criticality can inhibit the production of later work. It is in this context, rather than a metaphysics of disconsolation, that I mean to position the shift represented by the black-and-gray paintings and anything like a crisis of doubt that it might reflect with respect to the ongoing production of work.

Several factors stand out in addition to the limitations of the palette, which consists almost solely of brown, ocher, black, and blue-gray, applied with the visible strokes of a wide brush. First, it is important to acknowledge that the black-and-gray paintings include works on both canvas and paper.[1] The works on paper are less studies than variants. Many are as large as those on canvas, measuring in height up to seven feet. But the paintings on paper tend to be thinner in paint application (one or two diluted layers), which makes the brushwork—down to the bristles—even more visibly pronounced, a sensation heightened by the fact that Rothko left the white sheet partly exposed through the paint surface. The white border probably originated with the works on paper, for which the sheets were cut from rolls and taped down onto hard flat surfaces to be worked. (Some were subsequently mounted on canvas for display.) In a related change of method, Rothko primed the black-and-gray canvases with a bright white ground, a notable departure from the pigmented ground he had used before.

A second significant characteristic of the black-and-gray paintings is their production as a sequence or group. The catalogue raisonné of Rothko's works on canvas records eighteen paintings of varying sizes, both vertical and horizontal in format. They measure from between 54 × 68 to 104 × 114 inches, dimensions that fall comfortably within the range of earlier work.[2] Six of these canvases appear together in a photograph of Rothko's studio on East 69th Street in New York City, which was probably shot just after his death by Morton Levine (fig. 6). In the photo the paintings stand on the floor; they may have been laid out that way by Rothko, but it is impossible to know. Nonetheless, as informal as it looks, the arrangement demonstrates two things. The first is the sameness, from work to work, of the top-bottom configuration of dark and light. Further, while the upper and lower fields occupy varying degrees of pictorial space, the photo shows the division between them forming an almost continuous line across the row of canvases. The continuity is partly accidental, since the paintings, which differ in height, stand together on the floor, where their bottom edges are aligned in a way they would not be when they are hung on the wall. But the coincidence of continuity in the photo is an artifact of the paintings' structural regularity. One would have to work hard to create the same impression using works of the 1950s.

Rothko probably intended multiple black-and-gray paintings to be shown together. In March or April 1969, he was contacted about a commission to produce work for the new Paris headquarters of UNESCO, a government agency that facilitated international collaboration on cultural heritage projects (see pp. 282–83). The commission was for one painting, which was to be installed on the large wall of a restaurant and bar and visible from three floors. The work would be accompanied by a large sculpture, a *Grande Femme* by Alberto Giacometti. According to artist Robert Motherwell, in notes from a conversation with Rothko in April 1969, Rothko planned to propose a group of paintings instead. In so doing, Motherwell reports, he was referring to the black-and-gray paintings, which he characterized as belonging to "a different world from myself."[3]

Motherwell remarked on the palette that the two artists shared, with reference to Giacometti's portrait paintings beginning in 1946. He was speaking not only of the blacks or browns and grays of Rothko's paintings of 1969, but of a handful of other muted hues—blue, yellow, pink—that can be found in a group of works on paper produced that same year.[4] But Rothko's interest in Giacometti, his contemporary, was deeper still. On another occasion, I have described this interest as possibly pertaining to the relation of actual to esthetic space: a duality of emptiness and fullness conjured by the perceptual ambiguities of open space, as theorized (in writings on Giacometti) by philosopher Jean-Paul Sartre.[5] In this regard, and given the UNESCO context, we should also consider the logistics of display.

Rothko may have believed that the severity of the black-and-gray paintings was sympathetic to the close physical proximity of Giacometti's sculpture to his work. As it turned out, the UNESCO committee had planned to install Giacometti's tall bronze figure in an outdoor patio space separated from the interior by glass. But at first, Rothko believed otherwise, and if he was at all motivated by the UNESCO commission, then he was envisioning a shared space. In that context, the relatively strict horizontal separation of the two fields of the black-and-gray paintings would have offset the vertical attenuation of Giacometti's figures, a contrast heightened by Rothko's evacuation of luminosity and color, such that the paintings match the dark timbre of the sculptor's medium, patinated bronze. Of relevance is the fact that the history of monochromatic painting, or *grisaille*, since the fifteenth century is closely associated with the practical and theoretical comparison—or *paragone*—of painting to sculpture.[6]

It is worth noting that during the sixties Giacometti's work appeared with some frequency in the international art press. There, philosophical and practical considerations of space and display constitute a running theme. Many published photographs of Giacometti's studio in Montparnasse show sculptures, mostly plaster and clay, in various states of finish, positioned within deep shadows and against crumbling walls. The images represent an intensive material reciprocity between sculpture and place. Some, taken by photographer Ernest Scheidegger, appeared in a monograph on Giacometti in 1963, where they accompany a lengthy, searching text (first published in 1958) by Jean Genet. Genet writes primarily about the apprehension of space in relation to the object, which inhabits a state of isolation—what he refers to as *the solitude of objects*. For example, to place a single figure of Giacometti's in an empty room is, he remarks, to transform that room into a temple. Genet also emphasizes distance: a figure by Giacometti can, he observes, be said to appear as if from far away, which intensifies a sensation of reverence. "The statues come to you as though from a great distance, from the cusp of an extremely remote horizon." Moreover, "regardless of where you find yourself in relation to them, they work to make it so that you, who look at them, are below them. They are, very much at a remote horizon, up on high ground, and you are at the foot of the mound."[7] With the undeniable allusion to Golgotha, Genet deliberately summons sacred awe.

Claims on behalf of Rothko's appeal to this aspect of Giacometti's work must remain speculative. Genet's text was available only in French at the time, and, if known, was probably not closely read by Rothko. But the essay is an intensive example of the mythos of physical and perceptual encounter commonly invoked by writers on Giacometti and by the artist himself, one that implicates the space in which the work is shown as well as the space that, in a manner of speaking, the work is thought to produce or carve out for itself. One key device for Genet, in the context of the black-and-gray paintings, is that of the *horizon*.

With respect to Rothko, "horizon" invokes landscape, a vexed metaphor in the popular and critical reception of his work in general. After the mid-1940s, Rothko was, of course, an exclusively abstract painter, yet allusions to landscape were often made by observers of his work, particularly regarding the horizontal division of forms, which was sometimes compared to landscape painting, with its cropped separation of earth or sea and sky. The comparison was not the artist's own, and, as a convenient allusion, it fails to account in any meaningful way for the work's attention to pictorial form. But, as attested to by the responses of contemporaries who saw them in the studio in 1969 or 1970, with the black-and-gray paintings (fig. 4; pl. 103 to 113) the uninterrupted divide of top and bottom seemed to justify the horizon as a reflexive allusion.

fig. 1 Mark Rothko, *Untitled*, 1969, acrylic on wove paper, 75⅞ × 48 in., Collection Kate Rothko Prizel et Ilya Prizel

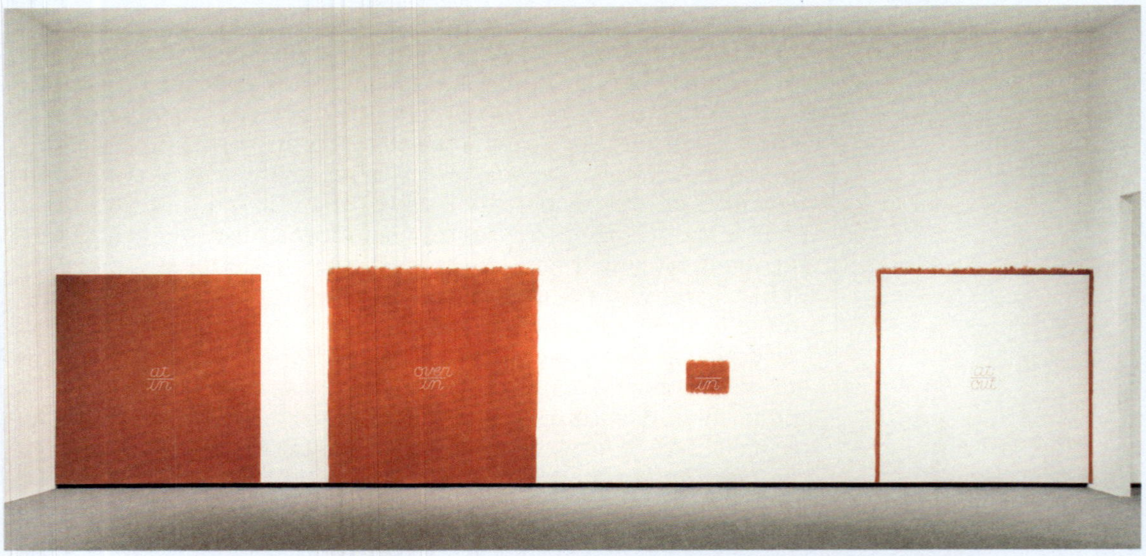

fig. 2 Mel Bochner, *Theory of Boundaries*, 1969 / 1970, chalk over pigments on a wall, variable dimensions, National Gallery of Art, Washington, D.C.

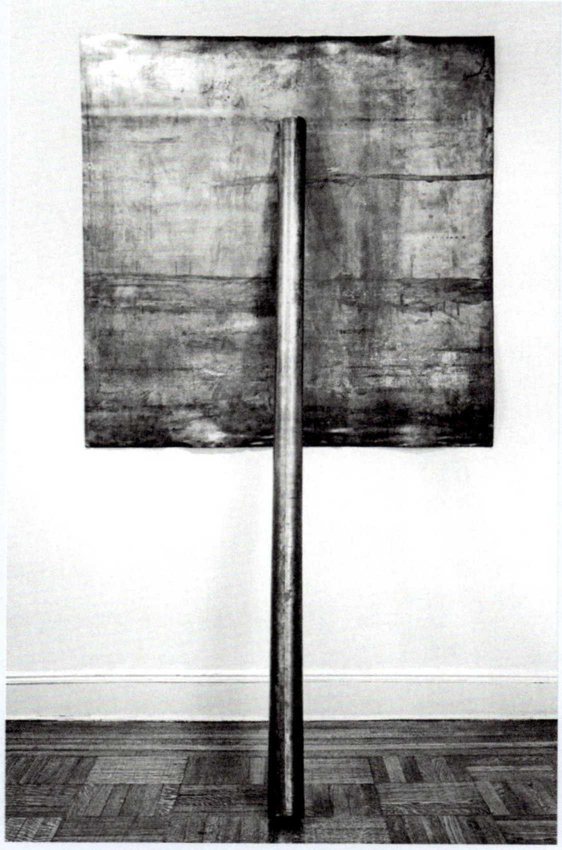

fig. 3 Richard Serra, *Prop*, 1968, lead, plate 60 × 60 × ⅛ in.; pole: 96 in. long, Whitney Museum of American Art, New York

Must the presence of something like a horizon line imply representation? Art historian Briony Fer refers to this division in the black-and-gray paintings as a "join" or "hinge," which serves an extrapolated purpose: it "hovers just a little below the level of our own eyes, corresponding with our line of sight, as if whatever we might think of as a horizon is not something out in a landscape so much as inside our eyes. It is what holds a picture together because it is what conjoins it with us, like a spirit-level that registers not only our presence but also our precarious equilibrium in front of the paintings."[8] Indeed, specific qualities of spatial orientation have long been thought intrinsic to Rothko's painted work. In 1970, in a text commemorating Rothko's death, critic Brian O'Doherty described the act of beholding in such terms. "Before a Pollock," he remarked, "people wander to and fro. Before a Rothko, each finds a spot appropriate to his own size and tends to stay there, or leave and return. It is uncanny to watch this. The picture eventually locates the spectator at a particular distance."[9] We note that Rothko himself said that the large canvas is not monumental but *intimate*, implicating a one-to-one relation to the body, and that he therefore preferred his work to be seen from close up. Perhaps O'Doherty's account is exaggerated, but the effort at physical orientation it depicts is striking in that it establishes a correspondence between the vertical disposition of pictorial form and the actuality of beholding. In the late works, then, the "horizon" both figures and actuates the relation of the painting to the situated observer in the space of the room. In turn, these factors serve the presumed correlation of those paintings to the "solitary" figures of Giacometti, works that were likewise often said to engage perception as a function of physical distance and time. The relation of painting to sculpture is that of horizon to plumbline.

* * *

Rothko ultimately pulled away from the UNESCO commission, probably due to flagging health. (The wall was ultimately installed with a single painting by Ellsworth Kelly.) But the opportunity seems to have instigated the chief qualities of the late paintings. In addition to the severity of the palette and the strict division of black and gray, the paintings also largely eliminate any contrast of figure and ground, which—no matter how closely the two were made to merge—had governed Rothko's work for twenty years. This new direction was supported by Rothko's active production of works on paper *apart* from those in black and gray, a body of work historians often ignore. There, with sheets often five or six feet high, the artist used a palette of brown, gray, blue, purple, and green, all extremely muted and / or dark (fig. 1). Most of the works are monochromatic—each being restricted to one of these hues. In some, the edges of the upper and lower fields—here roughly brushed rather than taped—are pushed very close to the outer margins of the support. Similarly, the separation of top and bottom is like a fissure—as narrow as possible without losing its function of demarcation altogether. In these late works on paper, we might say that a conventional opposition of figure to ground is replaced by the convergence of what art historian David Young Kim, writing of renaissance painting, characterizes as the three semantic fields referenced by *ground* as a pictorial term: "ground as material support; ground as terrain or platform; and ground as background."[10]

fig. 4 *Untitled*, 1969, acrylic on canvas, 105 × 114 in., private colletion (CR 824; pl. 110)

It can be tempting to see the black-and-gray paintings as works that are not just late but conclusive. What the works on paper reveal is that, in his studio practice of 1969, Rothko was less engaged in summation than in ongoing research, asking us to make room for an artist whose concerns were as much related to spatial and material challenges as to grand metaphysical themes. Even the opportunity to show with Giacometti can be understood in this way. The existentialist humanism the two artists shared marks the generation to which they belong. Yet they also shared a reinvention of means, pictorial and material changes that reflect on factors of both seeing and making: perception, distance, scale, gravity, spatial parameters, the opposition of figure to ground, and the material activation of a given medium—that of bronze or paint. With this in mind, we can turn to the work of younger artists for an expanded sense of the nature of Rothko's last works.

Advanced artmaking in New York during the 1960s—speaking of the work of Jasper Johns and Robert Rauschenberg, for example, and, subsequently, the studio and post-studio production of artists associated with Minimalist and Postminimalist art—had shifted decisively against the esthetic values of Rothko's generation. Yet these artists also both absorbed and transformed the spatial and material lessons of Rothko and his contemporaries, especially Jackson Pollock and Barnett Newman. In turn, this transformation reflects back on Abstract Expressionism. A painting by Rothko can be apprehended in a way that departs from his rhetoric of symbolic expression and affect yet is authentic to the direct urgency of making that the painting also reflects. In other words, new art can motivate us to re-see work that belongs to the historical past and identify qualities that reside, so to speak, in that work's pictorial or sculptural unconscious. Despite their sustained faith in transcendent themes, painters of the New York School stripped painting of most iconographical baggage and pushed abstraction to an expansive form of physical and pictorial breadth. Ambitious claims to myth and psyche aside, their works privileged process and scale in the service of a new, almost confrontational form of esthetic encounter. In turn, this aspect of their work bore implications for what artist Robert Morris called "the perceiving body"—for esthetic beholding in relation to the body of the beholder and the actual space of the room.[11]

It is in this context that Rothko's late work can be repositioned as an experimental turn. For all their exposed brushwork, the severity of the black-and-gray paintings supplants the nuances of spatial ambiguity in Rothko's previous work, with its intimations of a shallow pictorial depth within which forms appear to advance or recede and expand or contract. That ambiguity, along with the internal luminosity of the work, was directly associated with the potential for extra-esthetic meaning; the new method afforded greater presence to the activation of the materials and methods of painting. In an interview of 2008, painter Brice Marden spoke of his early debt to Rothko, despite their differences. But he also addresses the black-and-gray paintings in retrospect, paintings he did not know (as few did) that Rothko was making in 1969: "I think his late paintings are the best ones. They are incredible. I believe he had allowed himself to go to some sort of extreme."[12] Marden is tacitly applying criteria drawn from his practice, so deeply immersed in the extremism of the absolute monochrome, to his respect for Rothko, a forebear, for choosing to exceed the limits of his own work.

For the relevance of new art to an assessment of Rothko's late practice, we need look no further than the very moment when the black-and-gray paintings were made. A "prop" of 1968 by Richard Serra is a sculptural exercise in suspended animation, a balancing act in which several interdependent but unattached lead elements hold each other up through weight and mass—through gravity—alone (fig. 3). Certainly, a painting by Rothko cannot achieve the here-and-now literalism of a prop, nor would the artist have sought to accomplish such a thing. But the austere value relation of black to gray is the pictorial equivalent of a top-heavy configuration. While this equivalency remains a painterly, and therefore a metaphorical, conceit, it brings Rothko's new paintings closer than before to the expression of an elemental manifestation of orientation, load, and scale.

Indeed, while painting as a conventional medium was abandoned by Serra and many of his contemporaries, the pictorial advances of Rothko and his generation deeply informed their work, which more commonly takes the form of installations that fill or engage the space of the room. And from the elements of Mel Bochner's *Theory of Boundaries*, conceived in 1969 and first shown in 1970, we can extrapolate an intrinsic engagement with painting *per se* (fig. 2). The work consists of dry reddish-brown pigment applied with a sponge to a single long wall in four discreet rectangular areas. Each area is inscribed—using white chalk—in cursive script with prepositional "fractions" that articulate the relation of a paint surface to the borders, or *boundaries*, that delimit or contain it: AT / IN; AT / OVER; / IN; and OUT / AT.

For Bochner, a pioneer of Conceptual art, *Theory of Boundaries* is, in part, *about* painting, which he has called a "missing referent" in his work of the period.[13] In that regard, the prepositional fraction is an ingenious invention, since it allows the preposition, which signifies relations between things, to both identify and—through the slash—*enact* the physical limit conditions of painting. Recourse to language as a kind of device was common during this period. Compare Bochner's prepositions, for example, to Serra's celebrated list of transitive verbs that represent the process-oriented nature of his work of the late sixties. The list concerns itself, in an elemental way, with actions taken against a resistant medium: to roll, to fold, to tear, to sever, to drop, to flow, and so on. The list also contains prepositional phrases that itemize the work's larger stakes: of tension, of gravity, of mapping, of time.[14] Taken together, Serra and Bochner identify the artwork as a function of material process and / or a mapped orientation in space, including, it should be said, multiple references in their work to the horizon. These qualities are irreducible and, for that reason, existential. Held in abeyance is the conventional status of the work as a self-sufficient esthetic object—a noun.

Yet between process and mapping lie the means and measure of the large abstract painting, without which the art of the new generation would have been impossible. Rothko's late paintings may well have confounded his contemporaries, which partly accounts for the rhetoric of disquiet to which some turned. But when the artist referred to them as a "different world from myself," he reminds us that he was, esthetically speaking, acutely self-aware, and suggests that, far from pulling back to a place of safety or withdrawal, he was following the internal logic of his own work to bring his painting to what Marden described as a new formal extreme.

The evidence of the work matters most. In the black-and-gray paintings, severity activates a series of binaries. The gravity of dark over light does not prevent a remarkable range of difference in palette from work to work. The continuous division, or "horizon," pushes up against a visibly vigorous application of the brush. Given the white ground, the paintings' vaunted darkness does not preclude a certain degree of material transparency (as *opposed* to inner light)—something the works on paper condition us to see when we look at the paintings on canvas. Even the factor of repetition, which is a key aspect of the black-and-gray paintings as a group, amplifies the function of the series in two seemingly opposed ways: it focuses attention—the artist's and our own—on the deliberately restricted range of palette and form; and it establishes a deployment of those things as, in both spatial and temporal terms, an expansive field. The white framing edge may close off the paint surface, but in relation to a paint surface that goes all the way around the tacking margins, it represents, as Marden said, "a careful consideration about where the painting stopped in relation to the world"[15]—an investigation of the role of mediation that margins and borders, or *boundaries*, serve in establishing a painting's orientation to the envelope of the room.

Bochner relates a useful story in this context. In the summer of 1966, the two artists happened to attend the same social event, a birthday party for the painter Jack Tworkov. Sometime during the evening, Bochner found himself on the receiving end of harsh criticism for a review he had recently written for *Arts Magazine*, an essay in support of the exhibition *Primary Structures*, which had appeared at the Jewish Museum that spring. The show was a defining event in the history of Minimalist art. (Artists included Carl Andre, Donald Judd, and Dan Flavin.) Bochner's attackers were members of the older generation—contemporaries of Tworkov's and Rothko's. As Bochner tells it, a couple of them became quite agitated and at a certain point Rothko jumped in. "I read that piece and I liked it,' he said. "You know you can't dictate to young artists what they should or shouldn't be doing. You guys have become nothing but a bunch of conservative *alte kockers*!" Of course, as he further explains, Bochner had no idea that Rothko was at that very moment producing the enormous "black" monochrome paintings for Houston.[16]

What would Rothko have found in Bochner's text? A theorization of Minimalism as an irreversible shift away from, on the one hand, the utopian promise of modernist abstraction and, on the other, the "humanistic stammering of Abstract Expressionism." In the work, craftsmanship is superseded by standardized materials and forms. In sum, the new art represents nothing less than "the probable end of all Renaissance values."[17] To be sure, in contrast to his aging critics, Bochner, in his review, shows the presumptuousness of youth. Nonetheless, while dispensing with tradition would have been anathema to Rothko, that did not keep him from paying heed to the critical articulation of a serious break.

"There is nothing behind these surfaces, no inside, no secret, no hidden motive."[18] This citation, from Alain Robbe-Grillet's writing about the future of the novel, is Bochner's epigram and our cue. Finally, Rothko may well subscribe to what Robbe-Grillet called "suspect interiority" and "the old myths of 'depth'." Yet, in that they instantiate a pictorial form, the black-and-gray paintings begin by establishing plainer functions of apprehension: "measuring, locating, limiting [and] defining,"[19] to draw from Robbe-Grillet's account of new imperatives—first principles for beholding the world.

fig. 5 *Untitled*, 1969, acrylic on wove paper, 60 ⅛ x 48 ⅛ in., National Gallery of Art, Washington, D.C.

1 Once believed to have been produced beginning in 1968, the black-and-gray paintings on paper and canvas are now thought to have been made in a single campaign in 1969. My sincerest thanks to Adam Greenhalgh, author of the forthcoming catalogue raisonné of works on paper, for generously sharing information on this topic and various others pertaining to his new systematic inventory of Rothko's works in this medium. For the only consideration of works on paper prior to the new catalogue raisonné, see Bonnie Clearwater, *Mark Rothko: Works on Paper* (New York: Hudson Hills Press, 1984): pp. 51–55.

2 David Anfam, *Mark Rothko: The Works on Canvas. Catalogue Raisonné* (Washington, D.C: National Gallery of Art; London and New Haven: Yale University Press, 1998): cat. nos. 814–31.

3 For details of the commission, see Claudia Buizza, "Rothko, Giacometti et la commande UNESCO", pp. 282–83.

4 Motherwell, "Motherwell Muses," 1969, Archive, Dedalus Foundation, 1998.

5 Jeffrey Weiss, "Rothko's Unknown Space," in ed. Jeffrey Weiss, *Mark Rothko*, exh. cat. (Washington, D.C.: National Gallery of Art, 1998): pp. 324–29.

6 See Rudolf Preimesberger, "On Van Eyck's Diptych in the Thyssen-Bornemisza Collection," in *Paragons and Paragone* (Los Angeles: The Getty Research Institute, 2011): pp. 23–52.

7 Jean Genet, "The Studio of Alberto Giacometti" (1958, 1963), trans. Phil King (London: Grey Tiger Books, 2013): n.p.

8 Briony Fer, "Seeing in the Dark," in ed. Achim-Borchardt Hume, *Rothko: The Late Series*, exh. cat. (London: Tate Modern, 2008): pp. 42–43.

9 Brian O'Doherty, "Rothko," *Art International* 14, no. 8 (1970): p. 37.

10 David Young Kim, *Groundwork: A History of the Renaissance Picture* (Princeton and Oxford: Princeton University Press, 2022): p. 15.

11 Robert Morris, "Some Notes on the Phenomenology of Making: The Search for the Motivated" (1970), reprinted in *Continuous Project Altered Daily: The Writings of Robert Morris* (London and Cambridge, Mass.: The MIT Press, 1993), p. 90.

12 Brice Marden, interview with Simon Grant, "Landscapes of the Mind: Mark Rothko II," *Tate Etc.*, No. 14 (autumn 2008), n.p.

13 Bochner would later refer to the plane of the wall, which is so important to his early installation work, as "the space of painting." See Mel Bochner, "How Can You Defend Making Paintings Now?" a conversation with James Meyer (1993), first published in *As Painting: Division and Displacement*, exh. cat. (Columbus, Ohio: Wexner Center for the Arts, 2001); reprinted in Bochner, *Solar Systems & Rest Rooms: Writings and Interviews 1965–2007* (Cambridge, Mass. and London: The MIT Press, 2008): pp. 158–59. Recently, Bochner has remarked that, while the color of the pigment for *Theory of Boundaries* was, in 1969, chiefly associated for him with prehistoric cave painting, its correspondence to Rothko's palette was deliberate, as well. Bochner, conversation with the author, March 23, 2023.

14 Serra, *Verb List* (1967–68), in *Richard Serra: Writings and Interviews* (Chicago and London: The University of Chicago Press, 1994): pp. 3–4.

15 Marden, interview with Simon Grant, n.p.

16 Bochner, email correspondence with the author, April 6, 2023.

17 Mel Bochner, "Primary Structures," *Arts Magazine* (June 1966). Reprinted in Bochner, *Solar Systems & Rest Rooms*, pp. 8–11.

18 Bochner, "Primary Structures," p. 8.

19 Alain Robbe-Grillet, "A Future for the Novel" (1956), reprinted in Robbe-Grillet, *For a New Novel: Essays on Fiction*, trans. Richard Howard (Evanston: Northwestern University Press, 1989): pp. 21, 23, 24.

Following double-spread page
fig. 6 Morton Levine, Mark Rothko's studio, 69th Street, New York, early March 1970, Dedalus Foundation, New York

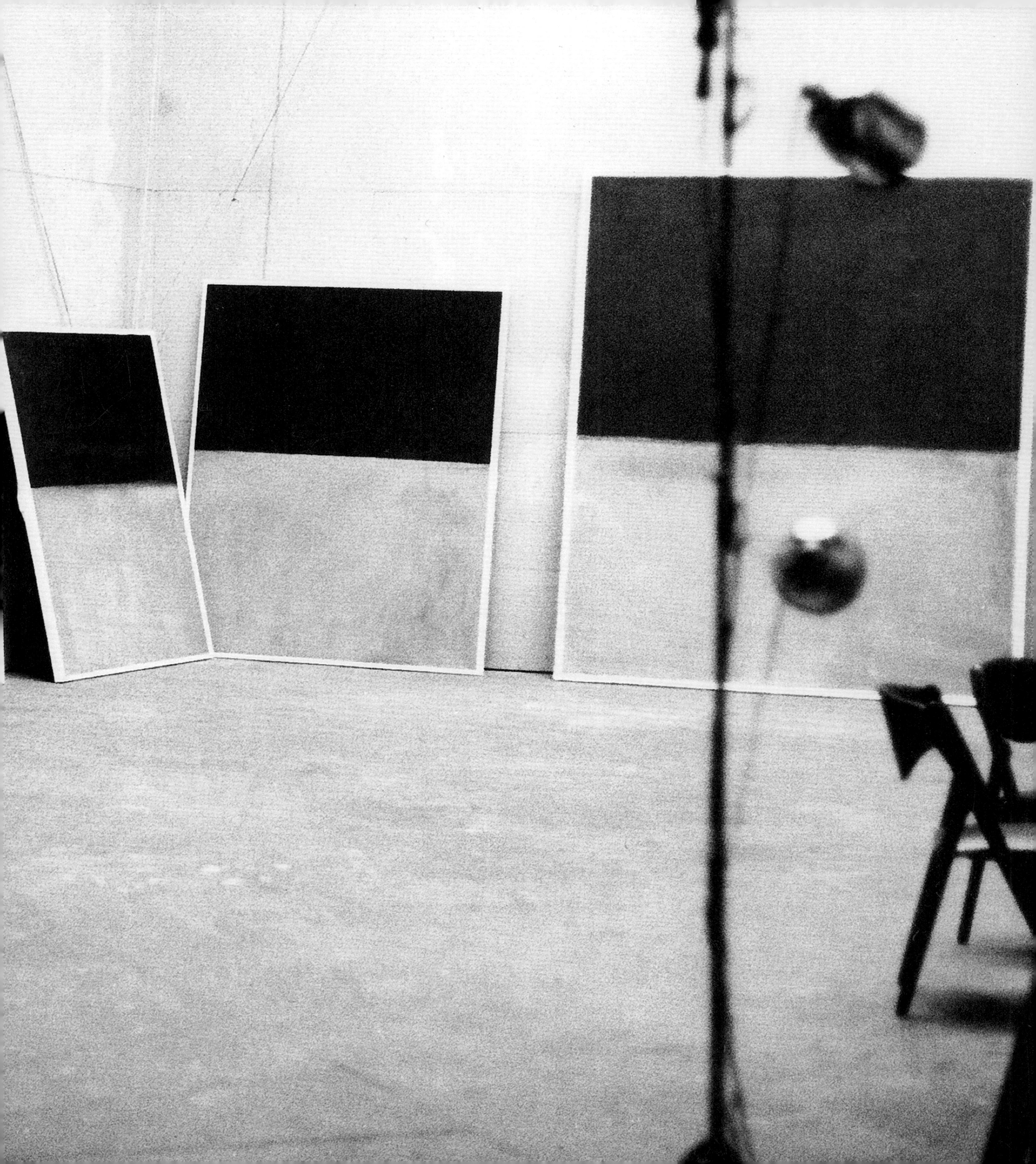

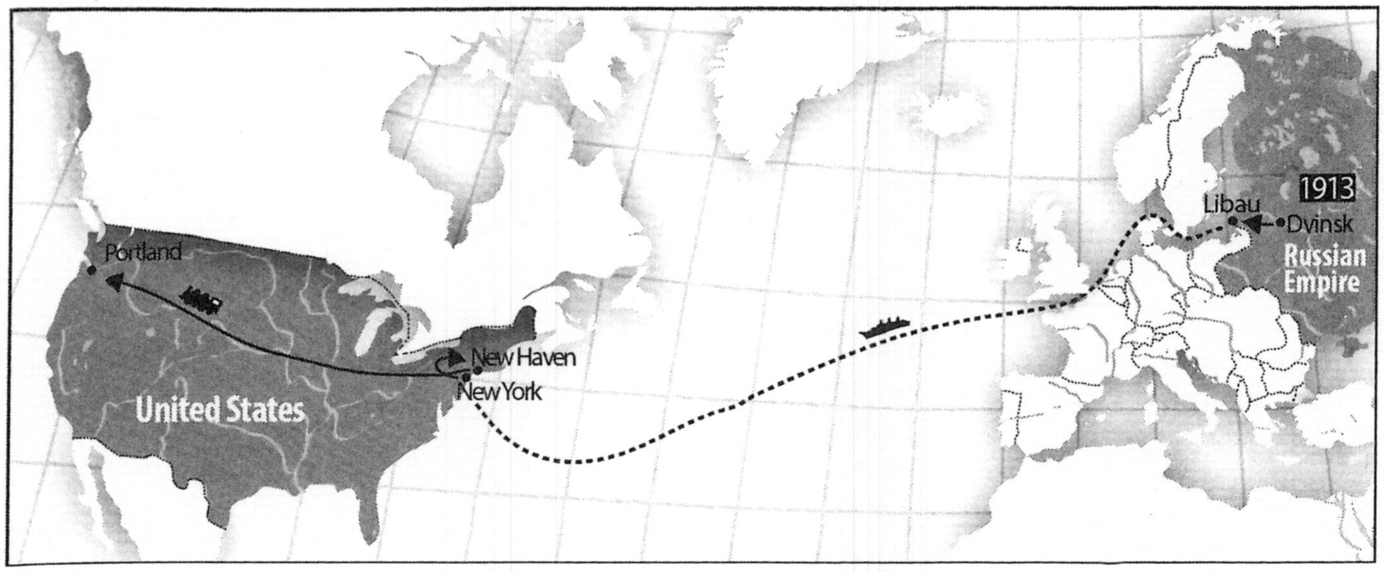

fig. 1 Journey of Marcus Rotkovitch in 1913 from Dvinsk to New York, then to Portland.

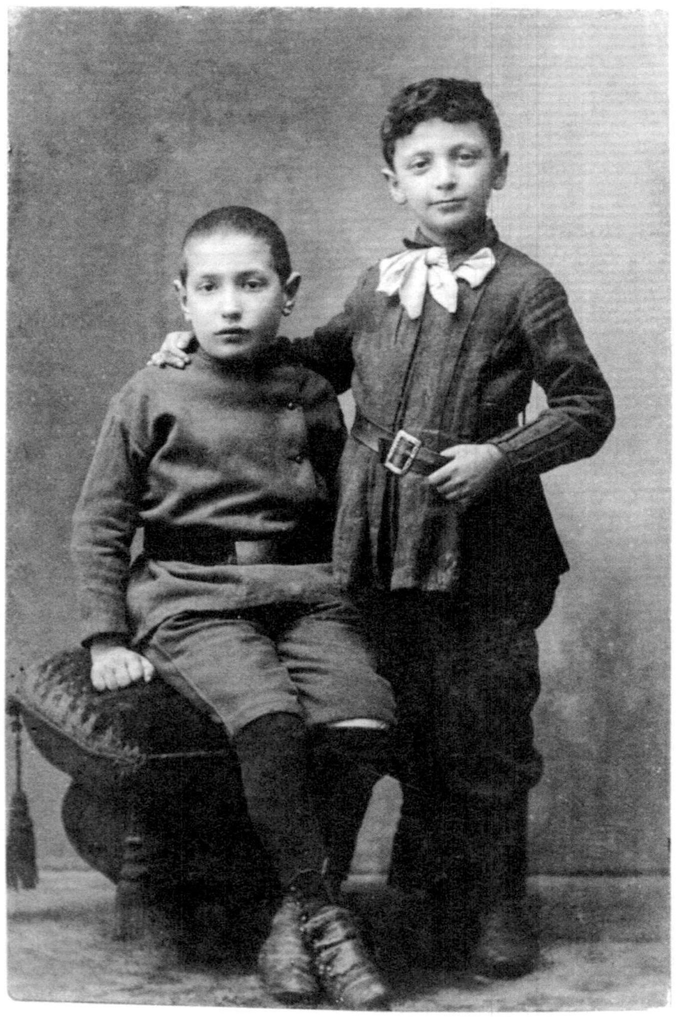

fig. 2 Marcus Rotkovitch aged four years (seated left) with a cousin, Dvinsk, 1907, The Rothko Family Archive

With Immigration in Common: The Odyssey of an Immigrant who Revolutionized the Language of Painting

Annie Cohen-Solal

In September 1913, a ten-year-old boy boarded a train to Portland (Oregon), on the west coast of the United States, the final stop in an odyssey that began several months earlier in Dvinsk, in the Russian empire. Marcus Rotkovitch wore the traditional black garb of his country's Talmudic schools and a label round his neck that read: "I don't speak English." Later, in a conversation with Robert Motherwell, the painter Mark Rothko would refer to wearing this shameful sign as one of the most traumatic experiences of his life. In leaving Russia, he had escaped the terror of savage pogroms and the risks of forced conscription into the imperial army, but the uprooting that he was to experience in the United States would prove far more unsettling than he had imagined.

In 1942, the Viennese sociologist Alfred Schütz gave a lecture at the New School for Social Research, where he had joined other European scholars in exile: "The stranger ... does not consider the cultural pattern [offered to him] as a protecting shelter at all," he explained, "but as a labyrinth in which he has lost all sense of his bearings."[1] Fifteen years after his arrival in the United States, Marcus Rotkovitch emerged from the labyrinth with the decision to turn into an artist. It took him twenty-five years to become a citizen of the United States and to Americanize his name to Mark Rothko; thirty-seven years to invent his own aesthetic, with floating, superposed rectangles of color; and forty-five to create a revolution in viewing with the Rothko Chapel. On its inauguration in 1971, it was described as a "sacred place, open to all, every day."[2] But this does not mean that Rothko conformed, integrated or identified with the culture of his host country. On the contrary, throughout his life he remained an outsider, a "social stammerer" who "stutters in the face of reality," remains "isolated from his original knowledge, always on the edge of the map, at the limit of the territory it covers."[3]

He arrived in the United States as part of one of the largest waves of migration from Eastern Europe: from 1880 to 1920, nearly two and a half million Jews landed on Ellis Island, prompting Congress to pass highly restrictive laws. Hence it was in this inhospitable context that the teenager with strong intellectual traditions and expectations was admitted to Yale at the age of seventeen. But although he was certainly *admitted to* this elite institution, he was not *integrated* and thus experienced a de facto quota system, a situation revealed in the correspondence of the Yale officials, who lamented the increasing number of "Hebrews enrolled in the science departments" or of students from "the chosen race," prompting the dean of the college to alert the president: "I think we shall have to change our view, in regard to the Jewish element.... A few years ago, every single scholarship of any value was won by a Jew ... We must put a ban on the Jews."[4] Two years later, disgusted with this elite institution, which he described as a "house of the dead," Rotkovitch dropped out of university.

He spent three years navigating between New Haven, Portland, and New York before entering the art world by chance. Thanks to the Ariadne's thread provided by the painters Max Weber and Milton Avery, he managed to find his way in life. The American artists he joined in the early 1920s were an isolated group, often ostracized by a society of pioneers and entrepreneurs.[5] It was in this marginal situation that Rotkovitch set about forming The Ten, "the first group of expressionists in the United States," an association of nine painters,

1 Alfred Schütz, "The Stranger: An Essay in Social Psychology," in *The American Journal of Sociology*, vol. 49, no. 6 (May 1944), p. 507.

2 Dominique de Menil, "A Statement" (1991), in *Ead, The Rothko Chapel. Writings on Art and the Threshold of the Divine* (New Haven: Yale University Press, 2010,) pp. 18–19.

3 Alfred Schütz, *On Phenomenology and Social Relations*, Chicago and London, The University of Chicago Press, 1970, p. 94.

4 Frederick S. Jones, Dean of Yale College, to President Angell, May 1918. See Dan A. Oren, *Joining the Club: A History of Jews and Yale* (New Haven, Yale University Press, 2000), p. 44.

5 For an analysis of the influence of the Protestant religion on the social situation of American artists, see the work of Neil Harris, *The Artist in American Society: The Formative Years* (Chicago and London: The University of Chicago Press, 1982).

linked by a social project more than by aesthetic affiliations and who "had in a way the mark of the damned on them and were homeless in the art arena."[6] All of them were men, Eastern European immigrants (first or second generation), politically engaged, involved in teaching or publishing activities. In his works of the time, it is this desperate isolation of the individual confronted with the rejection of the city and the swarming underground that Rotkovitch represents.

In 1940, however, the man who would henceforth call himself Mark Rothko made a radical decision: he put down his brushes. For a year, faithful to the intellectual paradigm that had shaped him from the beginning, he worked, read, and wrote a book, *The Artist's Reality*.[7] In it, he projected himself far back in time, into Egyptian and Greek antiquity and then into the European past, in order to construct his personal genealogy in the history of art and to anchor himself in it. After this undertaking, in the course of what was a crucial decade, the 1940s, the aesthetics of Rothko's paintings underwent successive shifts, by turns figurative, mythological, surrealist, and multiform. It was in the company of European artists in exile in New York, on the one hand, and thanks to his friendship with Clyfford Still, on the other, that Rothko moved toward abstraction. Finally, captivated by *The Red Studio* (a Matisse painting that had just been acquired by MoMA), he reached his signature style of superposed, floating colored rectangles. What he was seeking, just as blindly as Mallarmé once sought the absolute, was the means to represent transcendence.

Together with his acolytes Barnett Newman, Adolph Gottlieb, and Ad Reinhardt, as part of the Federation of Modern Painters, Rothko went on fighting the local, the regional, "the isolationist art [that] still dominates the American scene."[8] Then, in 1950, with the group The Irascibles, he organized a true insurrection against the Metropolitan Museum of Art, considered a fortress of conservatism for having rejected contemporary art from its own country. "American Painting Today," described as a "monster national exhibition" hostile to "advanced art," was then furiously attacked. "We draw to the attention of these gentlemen," wrote The Irascibles, "the historical fact that, for roughly a hundred years, only advanced art has made any consequential contribution to civilization."[9] It was thus a very narrow interstitial space—and for good reason—that Rothko then occupied in the American art world. "If Rothko and the others were against museums, against this or that," commented William Rubin, "it was not only because they doubted the institutions, but also because they were rejected."[10]

The next decade would prove very successful and, thanks to his new dealer Sidney Janis and his new aesthetic, Rothko was recognized as a "pioneer who is adding to the formal vocabulary of painting."[11] He had a string of successful exhibitions in galleries and museums. However, nine years later, the artist made a new break. Paradoxically, this was the time when American artists, supported by skillful critics such as Clement Greenberg—as well as enterprising gallery owners such as Leo Castelli—began to make a name for themselves on the international scene: in 1964, Robert Rauschenberg was awarded the Golden Lion at the Venice Biennale. A decade later, in 1974, contemporary American artists finally started to sell at auction. Then, at the very moment when the American art market was preparing for a period of exponential development, Rothko decided to move sideways once again. He broke off the contract for a fresco project for the Four Seasons Building, which he considered to be complicit in capitalist logic, and left his dealer Sidney Janis as a sign of his disagreement with the latter's choice to exhibit the young American generation,[12] thereby reiterating his antagonism toward the New York art scene.

In 1960, as in 1940, thanks to new experiments in decentering—in Great Britain and Italy—Rothko continued his research. He developed his educational concerns, which expressed his permanent rebellion against the consumerist culture of an all-powerful capitalism. He was now moving toward a revolution in viewing in order to offer the public not isolated paintings, but a whole environment; not a passing moment, but a genuine revelation; not a one-off visit but a real *experience*. In 1965, approached by the French collectors and philanthropists John and Dominique de Menil, Rothko accepted their commission for a chapel in Houston. Like Rothko, the de Menils had immigrated to the United States in 1941 and felt out of place in Texas; like Rothko, they had received a religious education; like Rothko, they were outsiders who struggled to identify

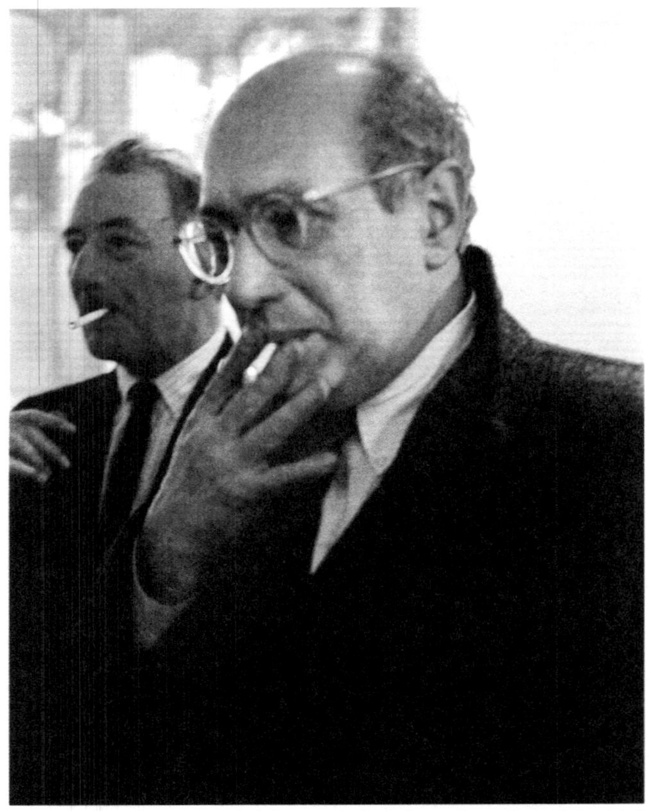

fig. 3. Fred McDarrah, Adolph Gottlieb (left) and Mark Rothko (right) at an unknown art opening, March 6, 1961, The Adolph and Esther Gottlieb Foundation, New York

with American institutions; like Rothko, they fought against the racist order that surrounded them, playing the open against the closed, the liberation movements of the black minorities against local political powers. Their understanding was nourished by several types of solidarity between minorities[13] and allowed them to sketch out the idea of a new space at the crossroads of art, politics, and the sacred, in which the transcendental dimension would be accessible to all. Rothko produced fourteen panels and organized their layout. More specifically, he installed two panels axially, "one in the entrance and one in the apse, as dialectically opposed as the mosaics in Torcello's church, the Last Judgment and the celestial vision of the Madonna and Child, in order to provoke, inside the chapel, a tension between condemnation and promise, between tragedy and hope."[14]

On the esplanade leading to the Rothko Chapel, as a silent challenge, the de Menils had installed *Broken Obelisk*, the Barnett Newman statue they dedicated to Martin Luther King, assassinated in 1968. A year after Mark Rothko's suicide, Dominique de Ménil inaugurated the chapel. "The magnitude ... of the task in which you have involved me," the artist had confessed to his patrons, "exceeds all of my preconceptions. And it is teaching me to extend myself beyond what I thought possible for me. And, for this, I thank you."[15] The abyssal fracture constituted by the experience of uprooting, the intertwined stigmas between which the painter had to navigate in order to make a place for himself in his host country, by means of art, played as both the constraints and the motors of the aesthetic subversion that Rothko effected on the very material of representation. By countering the identity prejudices that preside over national cultural references, by a series of geographical decenterings, by forging creative alliances with artists, patrons, and partners who had immigration in common, Rothko plowed a cosmopolitan furrow that became the crucible of his artistic research. Struggling with his alienated self, Rothko developed his work as a transnational strategist and underminer of borders. He belongs to that line of uprooted artists who transformed the uncertainty of geographical displacement into a veritable probe to detect the precarious zones of social imagination and forge the sensitive forms of our globalized world.[16]

Following double pages
From top to bottom, left to right
Henry Elkan, Mark Rothko holding a painting in his studio, 53rd Street, New York, 1953, The Rothko Family Archive
Rudy Burckhardt, Mark Rothko with *No. 7*, New York, 1960
William Heick, California School of Fine Arts, 1949–1950, The Rothko Family Archive
Alexander Liberman, Rothko in his studio, 69th Street, 1964
Kay Bell Reynal, Mark Rothko in his studio, 53rd Street, 1962
Regina Bogat (?), Mark Rothko in front of *No. 7*, 1960, The Rothko Family Archive

6 Joseph Solman, "The Easel Division of the WPA Federal Art Project," in ed. Francis Valentine O'Connor, *The New Deal Art Projects: An Anthology of Memoirs* (Washington, D.C.: Smithsonian Institution Press, 1972), p. 122.

7 Which was not published until half a century after his death: Mark Rothko, *The Artist's Reality*, ed. Christopher Rothko (New Haven and London, Yale University Press, 2004).

8 Foreword by Barnett Newman in "American Modern Artists (AMA)," exh. cat., Riverside Museum, January–February, 1943.

9 *New York Times*, 22 May 1950.

10 Marcelin Pleynet and William Rubin, *Paris-New York. Situation de l'art* (Paris: Éditions du Chêne, 1978), p. 19.

11 Stuart Preston, "Chiefly Abstract," *New York Times*, April 8, 1951.

12 Annie Cohen-Solal, *Mark Rothko: Towards the Light in the Chapel*, New Haven: Yale University Press, Jewish Lives series, 2015, p. 182.

13 Patrick Cabanel, *Juifs et protestants en France, les affinités électives xvie-xxie siècle*, Paris: Fayard, 2004. Although she converted to Catholicism at the time of her marriage, we can consider that Dominique de Menil, née Schlumberger, remained strongly influenced by her family genealogy throughout her life.

14 Dominique de Menil, *The Rothko Chapel*, op. cit., p. 15.

15 Mark Rothko to John and Dominique de Menil, January 1, 1966, http://www.rothko-chapel.org

16 A more developed version of this text provided the material for a lecture given at the Collège de France in October 2016, on the occasion of the symposium "Migrations, réfugiés, exil," organized by Patrick Boucheron (see Paris: Éditions Odile Jacob, 2017).

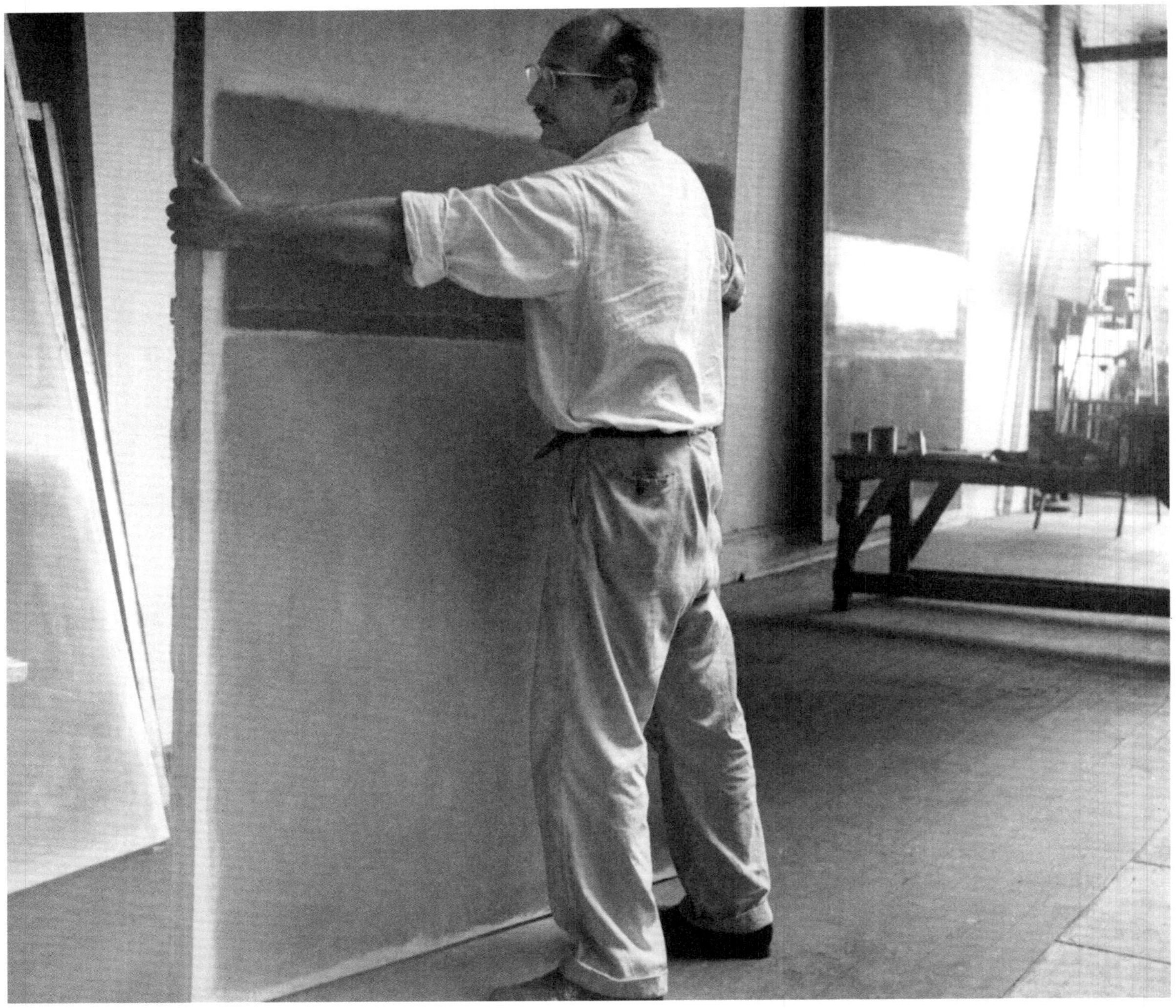

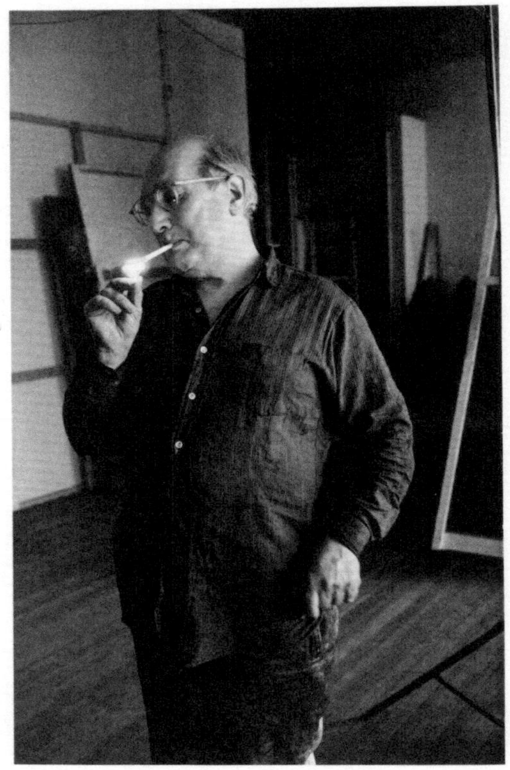

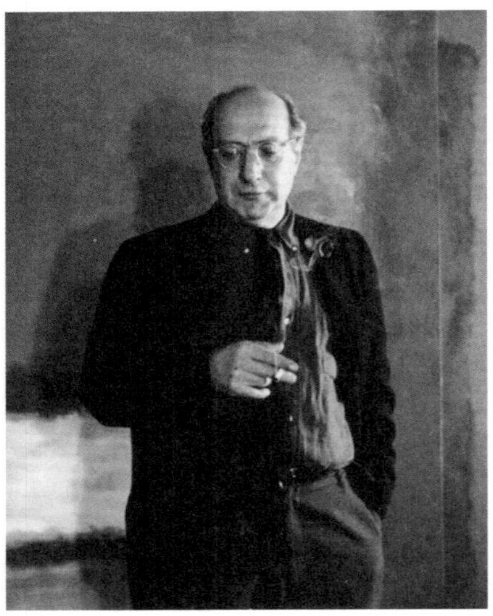

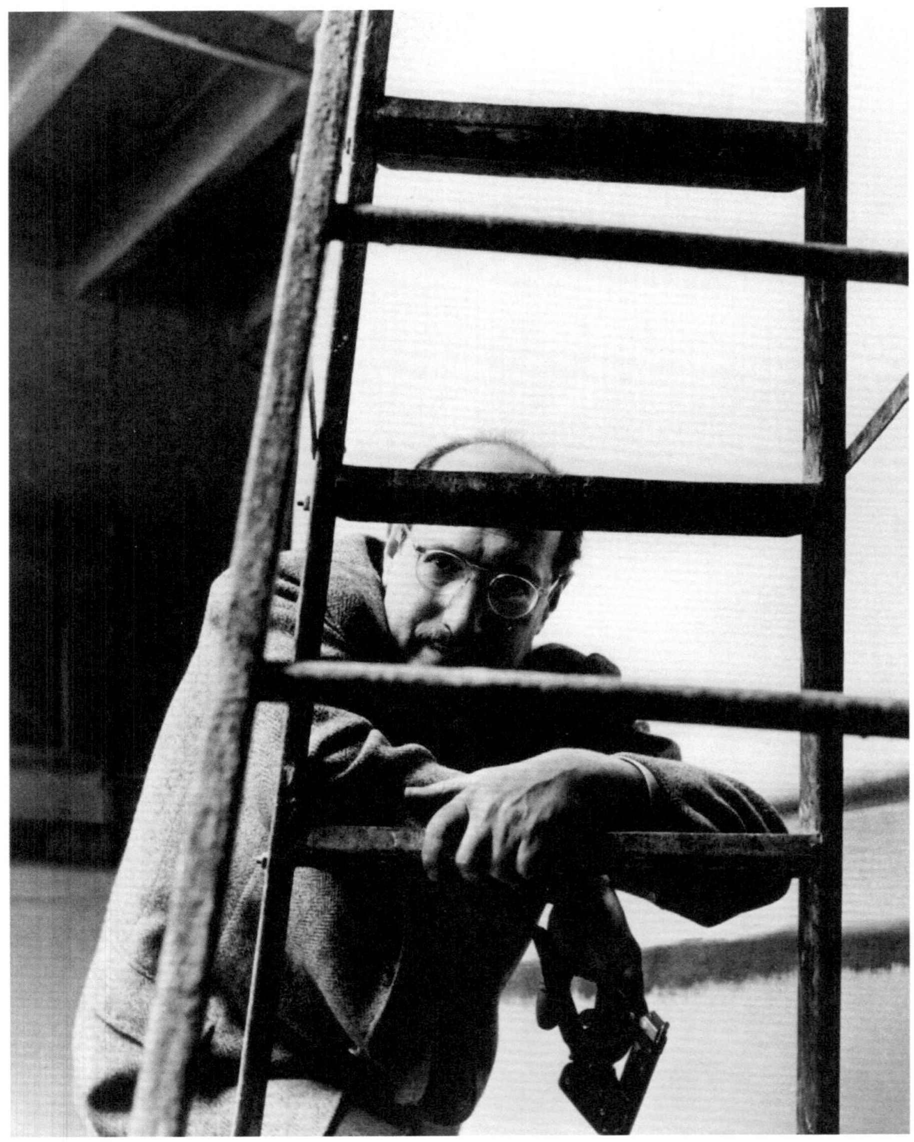

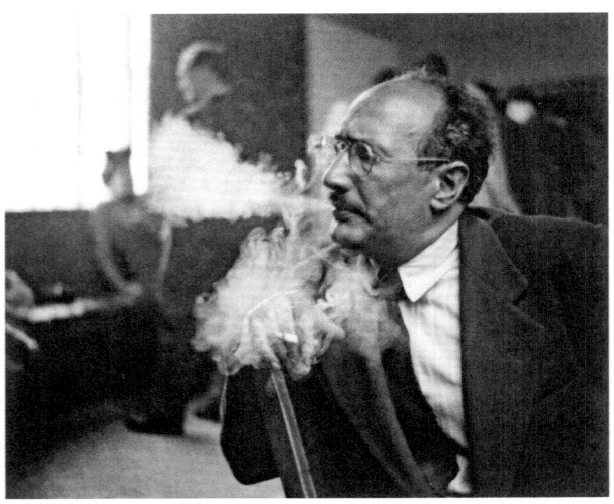

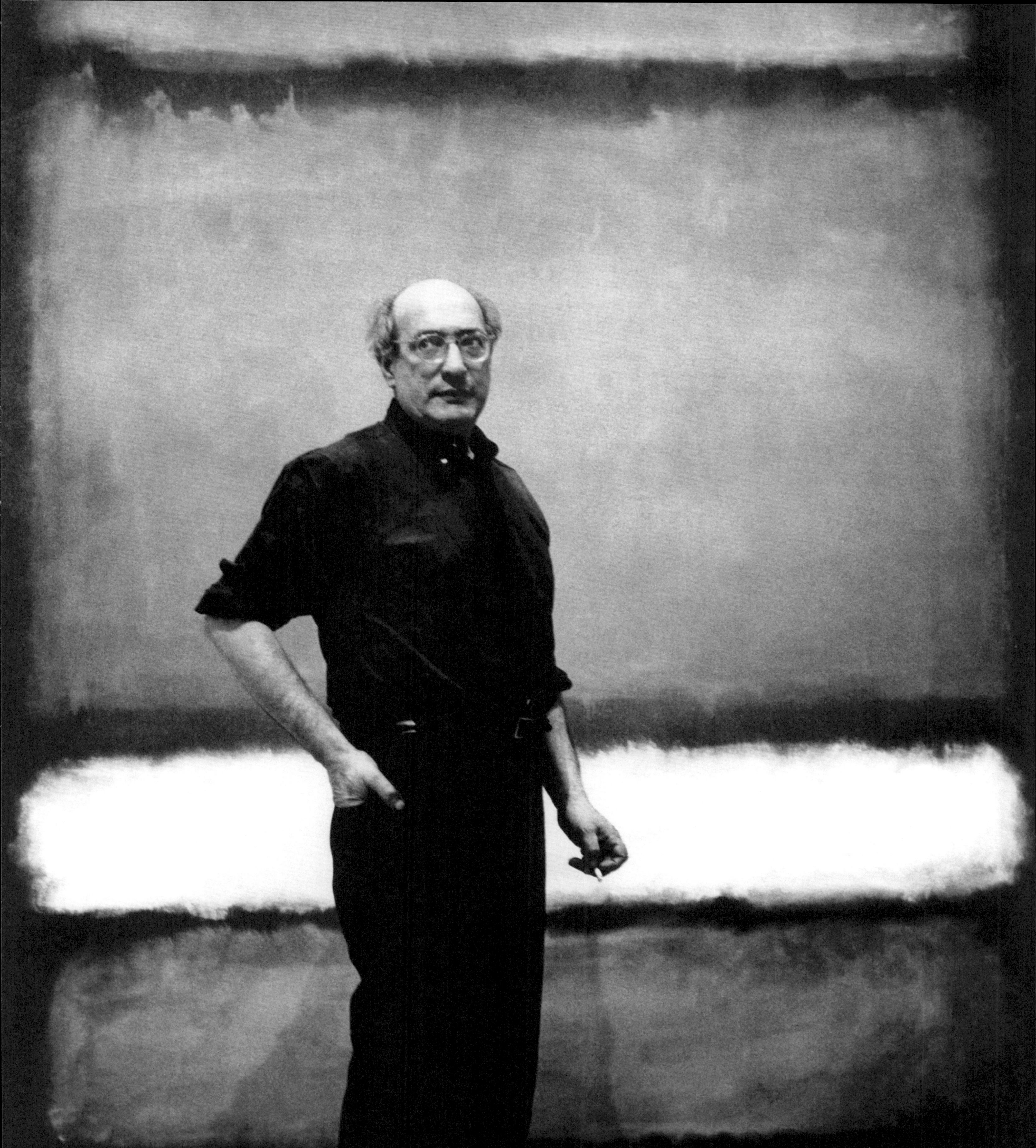

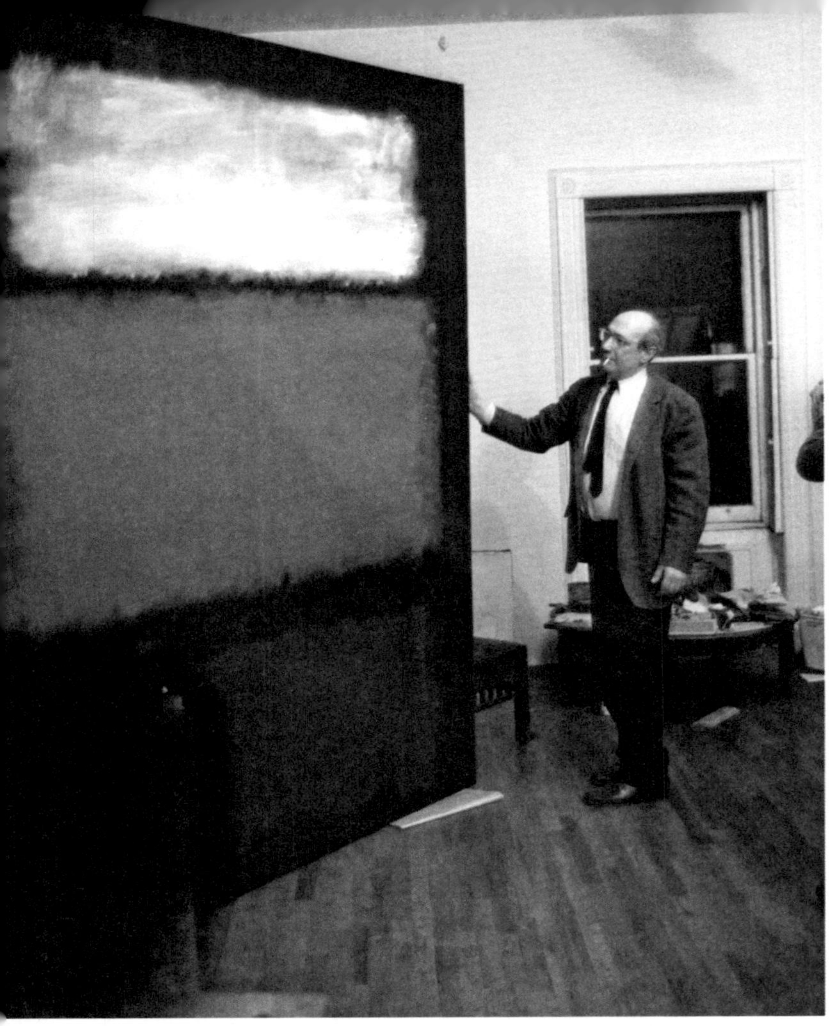
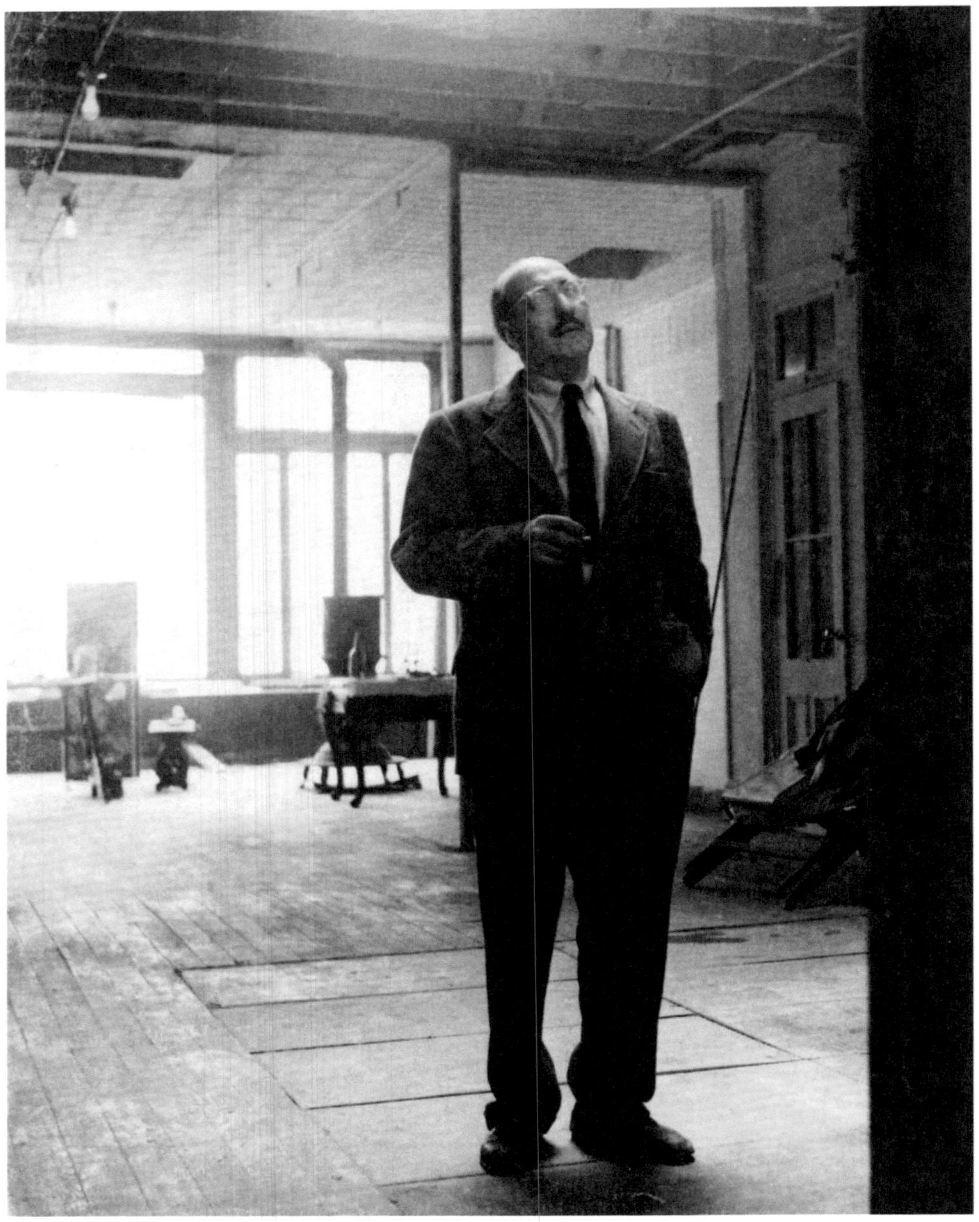
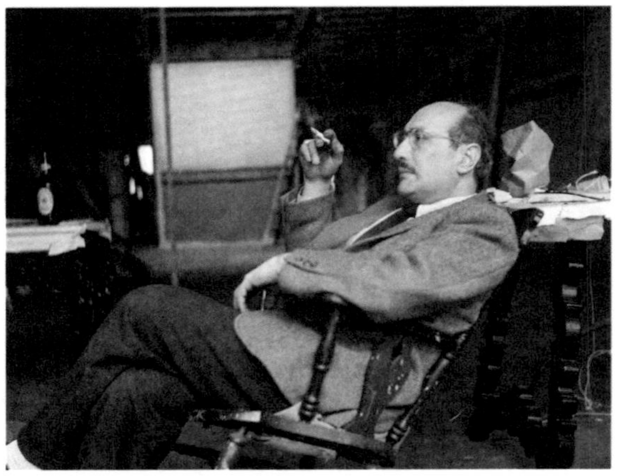
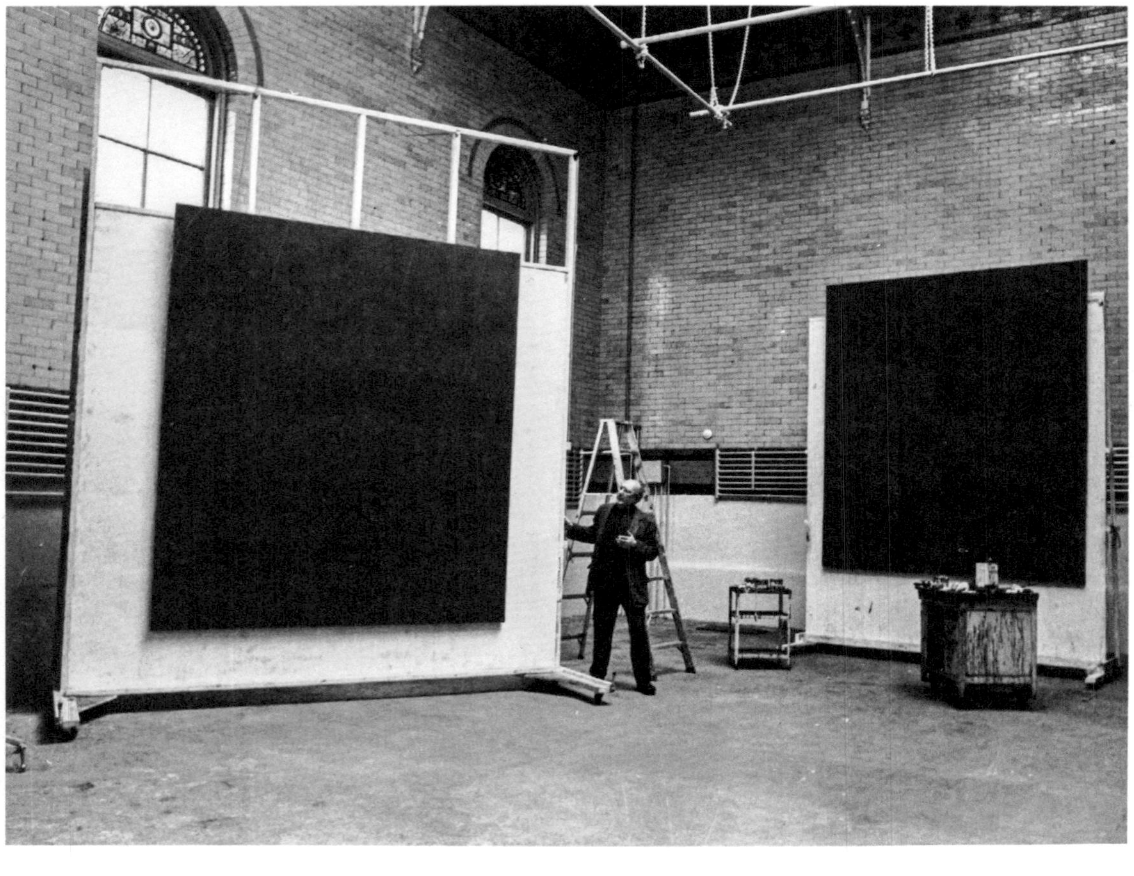
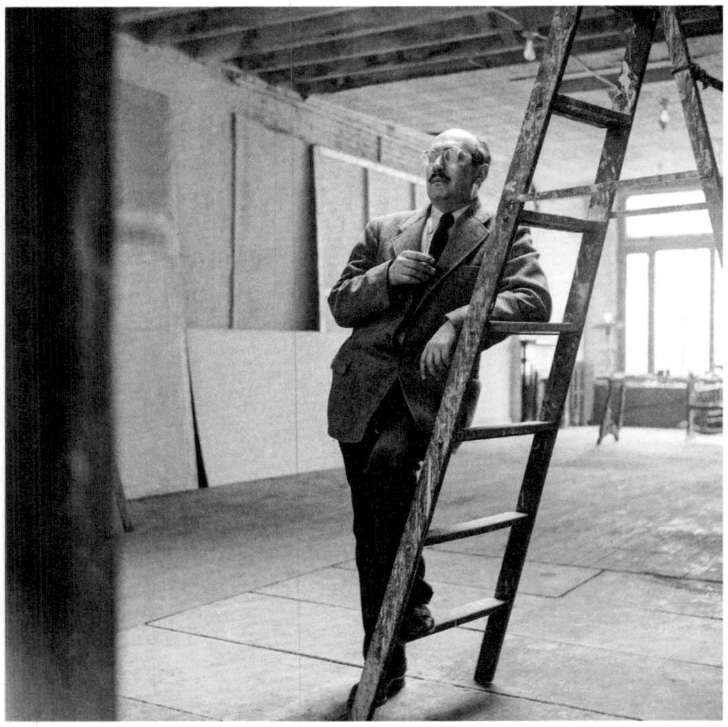

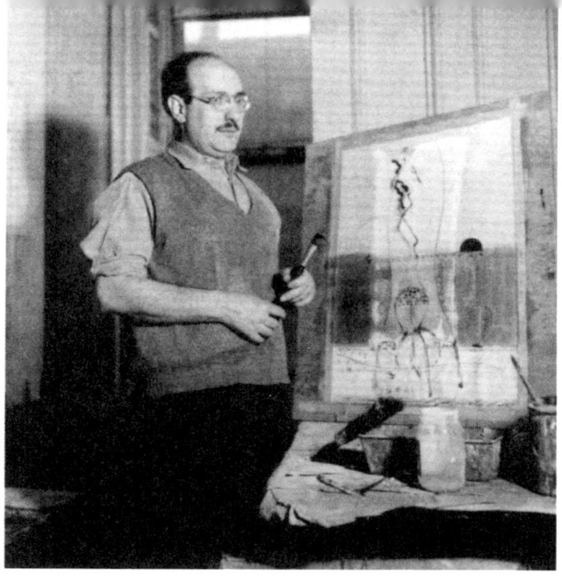

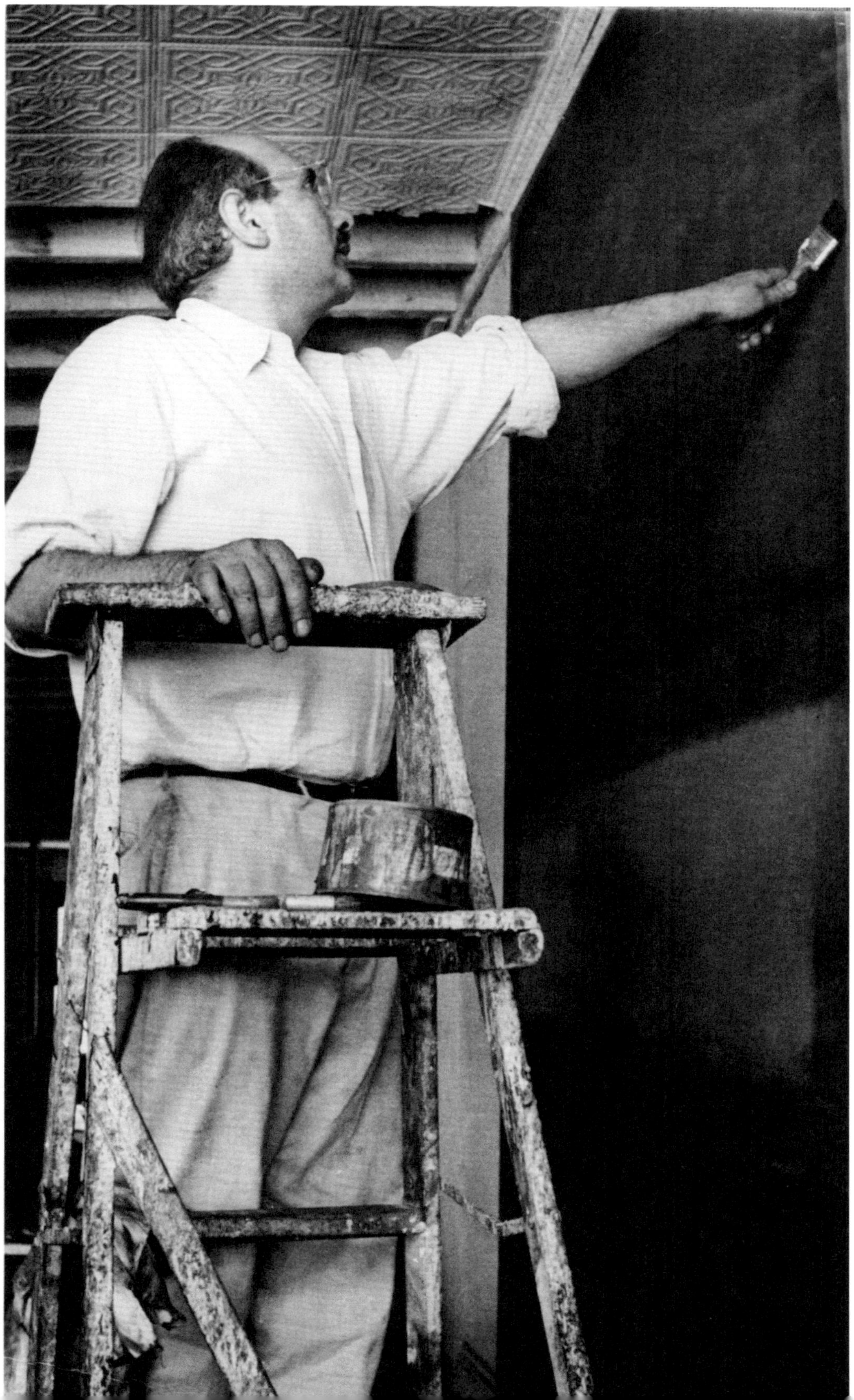

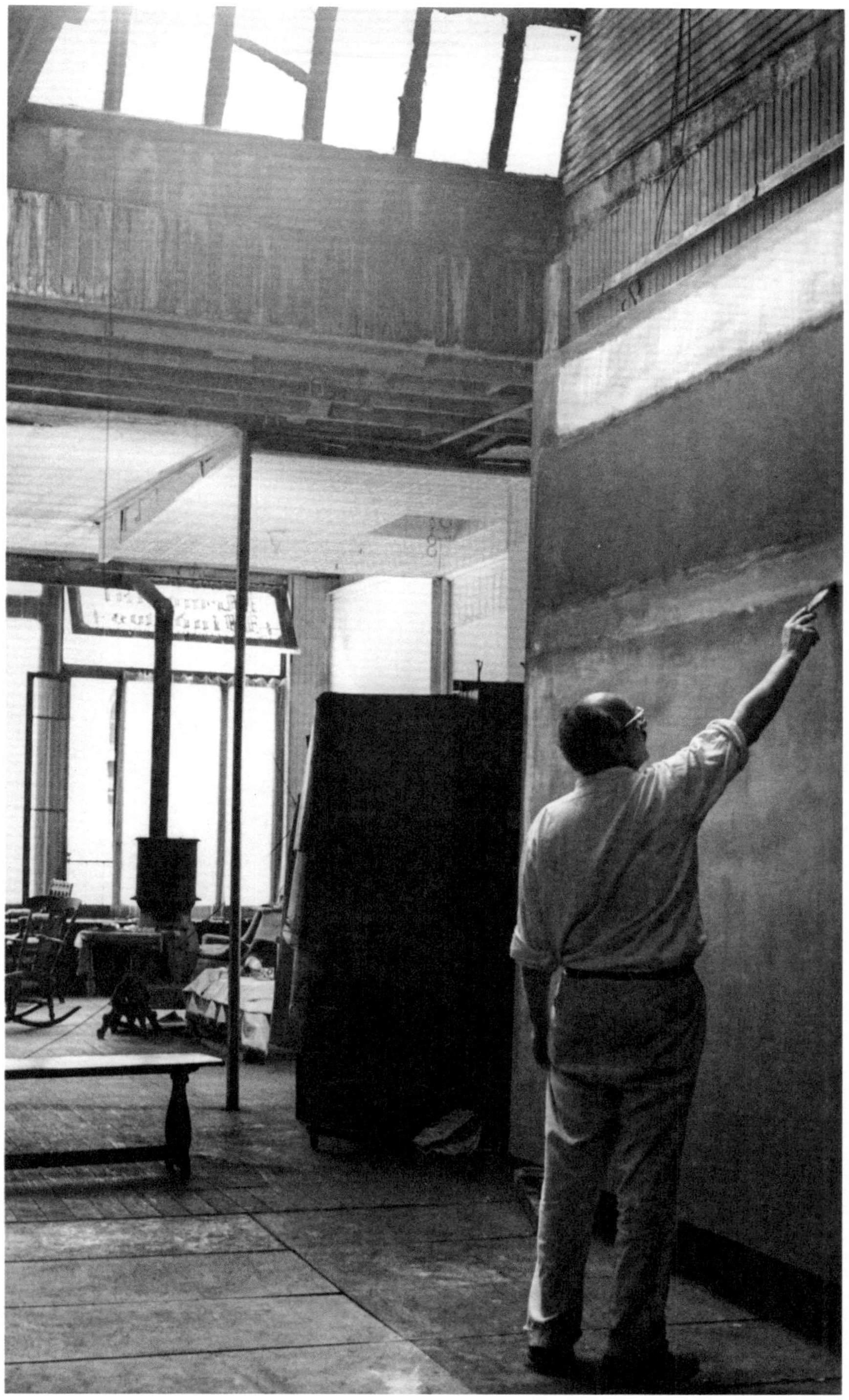

From top to bottom, left to right
Kurt Blum, Mark Rothko with *No. 1 (White and Red)*, 1962,
Fotostiftung Schweiz, Winterthur
Kay Bell Reynal, Mark Rothko in his studio, New York, 1952,
The Rothko Family Archive
Hans Namuth, Rothko in his studio, New York, 69th Street,
with unfinished murals for the entrance wall of the Rothko Chapel,
1964, Collection Center for Creative Photography, The University
of Arizona, Tucson
Kay Bell Reynal, Mark Rothko in his studio, 53rd Street, 1952,
The Rothko Family Archives
Kay Bell Reynal, Mark Rothko in his studio, 53rd Street, 1952,
The Rothko Family Archives
Mark Rothko about 1944–45, The Rothko Family Archives
Henry Elkan, Rothko in his West 53rd Street studio, painting
what may be a version of *Untitled*, 1952–53, c. 1953,
The Rothko Family Archives
Henry Elkan, Mark Rothko in his West 53rd Street studio, c. 1953,
The Rothko Family Archives

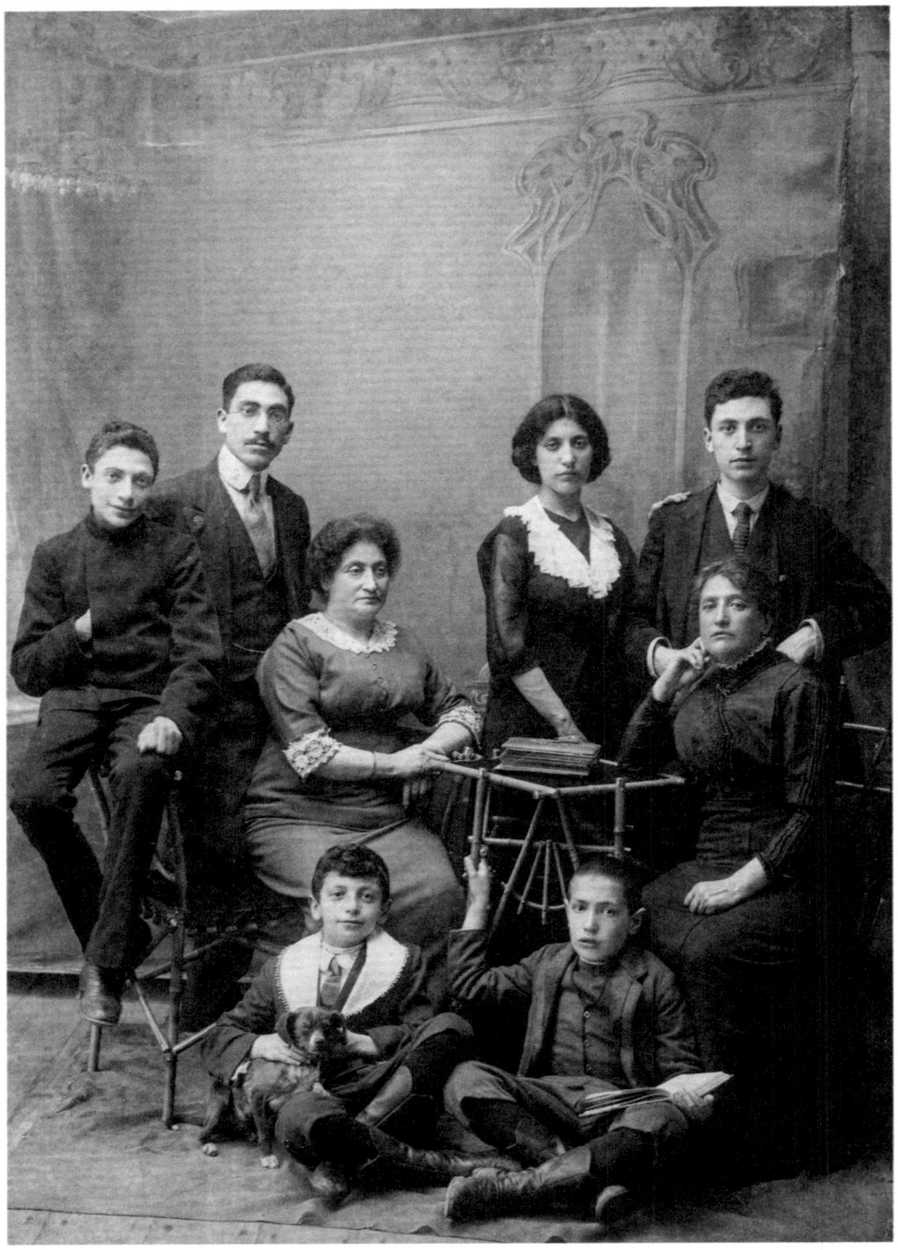

fig. 1 Marcus Rotkovitch aged ten years (seated right) with his family in Dvinsk, 1913. Behind him, seated on right, his mother, and standing with a white collar his sister Sonia, The Rothko Family Archive

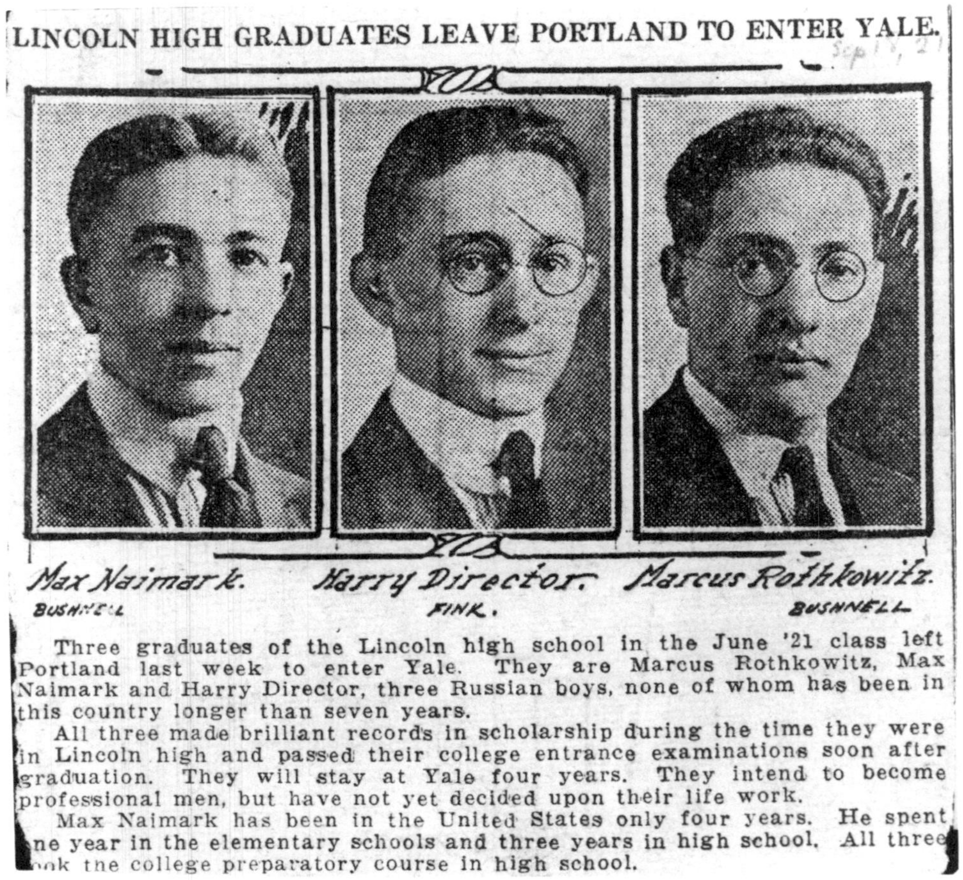

LINCOLN HIGH GRADUATES LEAVE PORTLAND TO ENTER YALE.

Three graduates of the Lincoln high school in the June '21 class left Portland last week to enter Yale. They are Marcus Rothkowitz, Max Naimark and Harry Director, three Russian boys, none of whom has been in this country longer than seven years.

All three made brilliant records in scholarship during the time they were in Lincoln high and passed their college entrance examinations soon after graduation. They will stay at Yale four years. They intend to become professional men, but have not yet decided upon their life work.

Max Naimark has been in the United States only four years. He spent ne year in the elementary schools and three years in high school. All three ook the college preparatory course in high school.

fig. 2 A Portland newspaper's announces the admission of Max Naimark, Harry Director and Marcus Rotkovitch at Yale University, September 18, 1921

*Chronology**

Claudia Buizza

1903–1909

Mark Rothko is born Marcus Rotkovitch on September 25, 1903, in Dvinsk, in the Russian empire (today Daugavpils, Latvia). He is the fourth child of Jacob Rotkovitch, a pharmacist, and Anna Goldin Rotkovitch, who came from an affluent family in St. Petersburg. He has a sister, Sonia, and two brothers, Moise and Albert. He attends the Talmudic school (*cheder*) for young children. He is the first member of his liberal Jewish family to receive a religious education.

1910–1913

Subsequent to financial difficulties and the increasing violence perpetrated against Jews, in 1910 Jacob Rotkovitch decides to emigrate to the United States to join his brother, Samuel Weinstein, in Portland, Oregon. Moise and Albert Rotkovitch join him two years later whereas Anna, Sonia, and Marcus Rotkovitch leave Russia on August 5, 1913. They travel second class on the SS *Czar* and arrive in New York on August 17. They cross the country by train to Portland, carrying small signs indicating that they do not speak English. In September, at the age of ten, Marcus is enrolled in a special class for immigrant children in the Failing Elementary School in Portland. His mother, Anna, changes her name to Kate.

1914–1920

On March 27, 1914, at the age of fifty-five, Jacob Rotkovitch dies of cancer; Sonia, Moise, and Albert work at the Weinstein family's textile clothing business, the New York Outfitting Company, while Marcus sells newspapers on the street. After attending Shattuck Elementary, he skips two grades and enteres Lincoln High School in the fall of 1918. He contributes to the student newspaper and participates in debates at the Jewish Community Center. As part of his preparation for college, he takes French classes and becomes interested in literature and drama. He does not take art classes, but he begins to draw.

* Sources: James E. B. Breslin, *Mark Rothko: A Biography* (Chicago and London: University of Chicago Press, 1993); Jessica Stewart, "Chronologie," in Suzanne Pagé et Jeffrey Weiss (eds.), *Mark Rothko,* exh. cat., Musée d'Art Moderne de la Ville de Paris, 1999.

1921–1923

Marcus Rotkovitch graduates in June 1921, after winning a scholarship to Yale University where he enrolls with two Russian friends from Portland, Aaron Director and Max Naimark (fig. 2). The subjects he studies include philosophy, French, European history, and introductory psychology. At the end of his first year, the scholarships for Rotkovitch and his friends are cut off due to new immigration policies, notably aimed at Jewish students. In order to finance college he begins working at the university laundry and as a messenger.

In February 1923, he and two classmates, Aaron Director and Simon Whitney, found a progressive newspaper called *The Yale Saturday Evening Pest*. In the fall of that year, disillusioned with the discriminatory atmosphere at the university, Rotkovitch leaves without graduating and moves to New York City.

1924–1926

After a friend invites him to attend life drawing classes at the Art Students League in New York, he enrolls in George Bridgman's art class in January 1924. In the early spring of the same year, he returns to Portland, where he studies acting in a theater company run by Josephine Dillon, Clark Gable's first wife. Early in 1925 he returns to New York in order to enroll in the American Laboratory Theater; he fails to get a scholarship, however, and thus falls back on the New School of Design. He returns to the Art Students League in October 1925, joining Max Weber's still-life class. Weber is a Jewish-Russian immigrant who had studied under Henri Matisse. Rotkovitch continues to study with Weber until May 1926, drawing and painting in a Cézannesque manner. From then on, he assiduously frequents New York galleries and museums, notably the Metropolitan Museum of Art, whose Rembrandt collection he particularly likes. In November 1926, Rotkovitch joins the Art Students League, which he leaves in 1930.

1927–1928

After some work in advertising, in 1927 he is commissioned to illustrate *The Graphic Bible: From Genesis to Revelation in Animated Maps and Charts* by Lewis Browne. The book is published in 1928 with no mention of his name. He sues Browne and the publisher, MacMillan. The case goes all the way to the Supreme Court, but the young man looses.

He runs into the violinist Louis Kaufman, whom he has known in elementary school in Portland, and who introduces him to painter Milton Avery and his wife Sally. They become great friends—Milton Avery will have a profound influence on his work. Bernard Karfiol, who teaches at the Art Students League, selects works by Avery and Rotkovitch for an exhibition at the Opportunity Gallery in New York. This is Rotkovitch's first exhibition, where he shows landscapes (CR 11; fig. 3).

1929–1932

Rotkovitch begins giving drawing lessons to children at the Center Academy of the Brooklyn Jewish Center. Becoming very interested in art education, he writes articles on the creative abilities of children.

He meets Adolph Gottlieb, and the two artists see each other regularly along with Milton Avery.

In July 1932, during a trip to Lake George, New York, Rotkovitch meets Edith Sachar, a saleswoman in a clothing store, whom he marries on November 12 (fig. 4). They move to 137 West 72nd Street, near the Averys.

Although he has never studied music, Rotkovitch spends his days playing the piano. He is deeply sensitive to music and nurtures a predilection for Mozart. The couple begins to frequent the Averys and the Gottliebs, with whom they spend several summer vacations in Massachusetts.

1933

Rotkovitch makes a large number of drawings and watercolors, mostly landscapes (fig. 6), some of which would be exhibited at the Portland Art Museum along with works by his students at the Center Academy in Brooklyn.

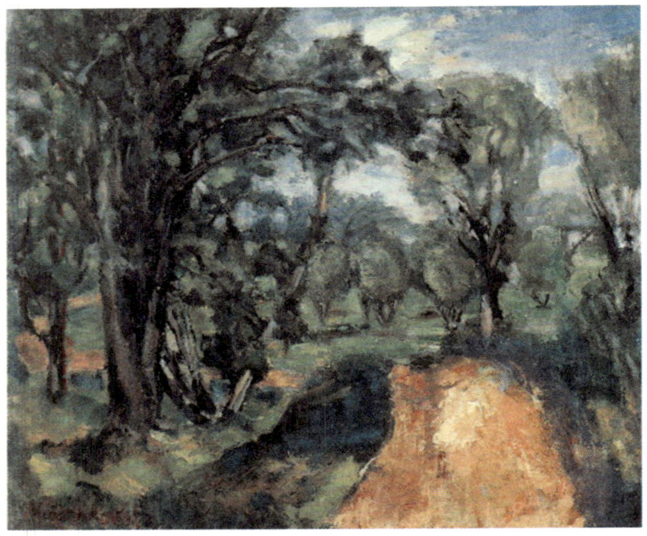

fig. 3 *Untitled (Landscape)*, c. 1928, oil on canvas, $25\frac{9}{10} \times 32$ in., Mobile Museum of Art, Alabama (CR 11)

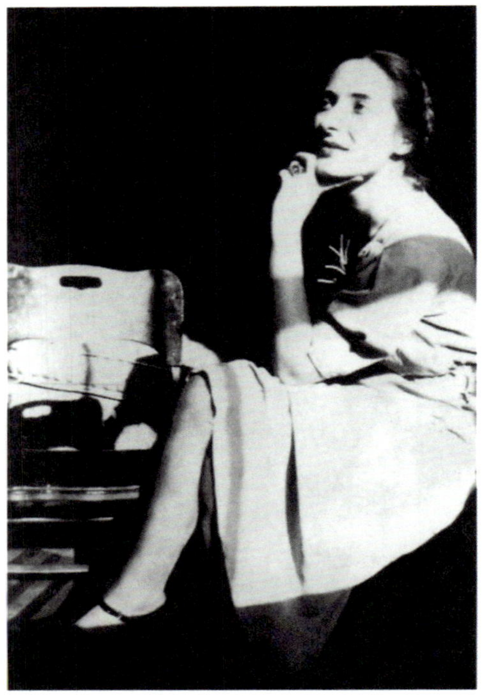

fig. 4 Edith Sachar, New York, 1935, in *George Carson Papers*, The Rothko Family Archive

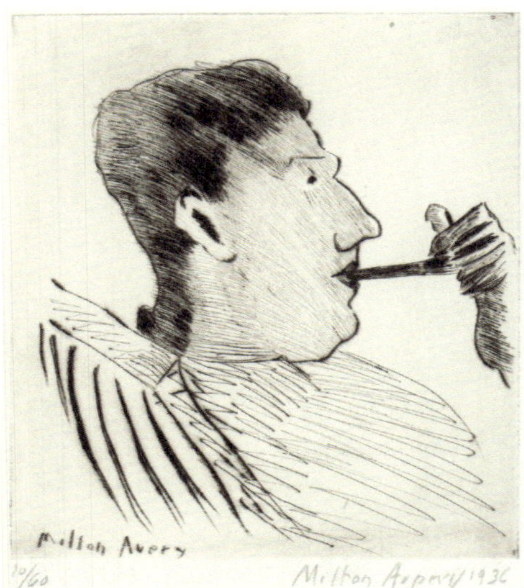

fig. 5 Milton Avery, *Rothko with pipe*, 1936, drypoint in brown-black on wove paper, $13\frac{7}{8} \times 11$ in. (sheet), National Gallery of Art, Washington, D.C.

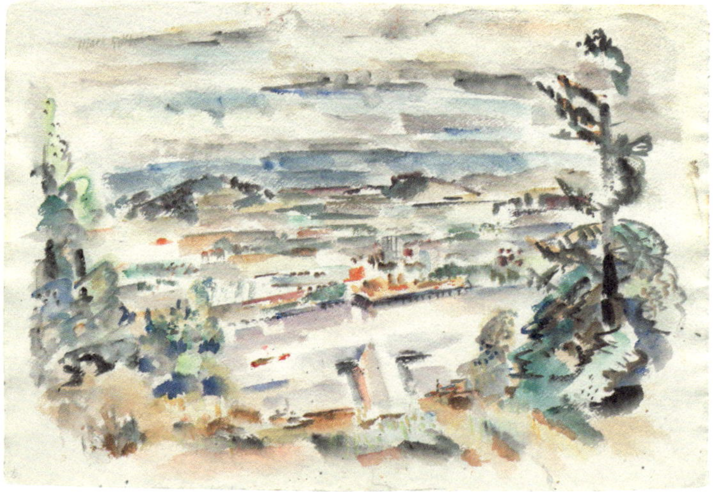

fig. 6 *Untitled (Portland, Oregon)*, 1933, watercolor on watercolor paper, 15 7/16 × 22 5/8 in., National Gallery of Art, Washington, D.C.

Rotkovitch and his wife Edith return to New York in the autumn and move to 1000 Park Place in Brooklyn. From November 21 to December 9, the Contemporary Arts Gallery in New York host Rotkovitch's first solo show, featuring fifteen paintings and ten works on paper, mostly portraits, plus *The Road*, 1932–1933 (pl. 2)

1934

After participating in a group exhibition at the Brooklyn Museum, Rotkovitch organizes an exhibition of 150 works by his students held at the same museum. The text he writes for the exhibition, "New Training for Future Artists and Art Lovers," is published in the February–March issue of the *Brooklyn Jewish Center Review* and reads: "... their paintings are so fresh, so vivid and varied. And it is these qualities, which, no matter how skilled an artist may be, he must obtain to make his work arresting and provoking of attention."

In February, Rotkovitch becomes one of the two hundred founding members of the Artists Union in New York. Along with Gottlieb and other artists, he participates in five group shows at the Uptown Gallery, run by Robert Godsoe. On December 15, Godsoe opens the Gallery Secession, where he shows Rotkovitch, Ben-Zion, Gottlieb, Harris, Kufeld, Schanker, and Solman. The exhibition is followed by a second group show.

1935

After brief periods of tension and separation, the Rotkovitches move to 3 Great Jones Street in Greenwich Village in the fall. During this period, Edith Sachar Rotkovitch studies metalwork and jewelry at the New York School of Arts and Trades, and is soon quite successful with her designs.

Not always happy with Godsoe's decisions, artists Ben-Zion, Ilya Bolotowsky, Gottlieb, Harris, Kufeld, Rotkovitch, Schanker, Solman, and Nahum Tschacbasov form a group called "The Ten", claiming that they are fed up with conservatism and that they want to experiment. The group meets monthly in the studio of one of its members; Rotkovitch serves as secretary. The Ten hold its first exhibition at the Montross Gallery in New York from December 16, 1935 to January 4, 1936. Rotkovitch shows three works painted around 1934, including *Subway* (CR 71) from 1935. The subway theme repeatedly appears in more than forty paintings up to 1939.

1936–1937

Rotkovitch paints his self-portrait (pl. 4). In January 1936, The Ten exhibit at the Municipal Art Galleries in New York. In February, he participates in the American Artists' Congress.

In June, Edith Sachar gets a job at the Works Progress Administration (WPA). Rotkovitch continues to teach at the Center Academy and at a school in Far Rockaway. In September he joins the Treasury Relief Art Project (TRAP), part of the WPA, and in May 1937 he moves to the easel painters' section. That fall he meets Barnett and Annalee Newman at a wedding breakfast hosted by Gottlieb. In November, The Ten exhibit at the Bonaparte Gallery in Paris.

The Museum of Modern Art in New York holds its *Fantastic Art, Dada, and Surrealism* show from December 2, 1936 to January 17, 1937. The show includes works by Giorgio de Chirico that will have a considerable impact on the artist's work.

The Ten have their second annual exhibition at the Montross Gallery in December 1936. Rotkovitch shows three works from 1936: *Interior* (CR 79), *Music* (CR 80), and *Portrait* (CR 81).

In late April 1937, The Ten exhibit at Georgette Passedoit's gallery. In December they show in Brooklyn, where an auction for child victims of the Spanish Civil War is held; Rotkovitch contributes four paintings, including *Street Scene,* c. 1937 (pl. 13).

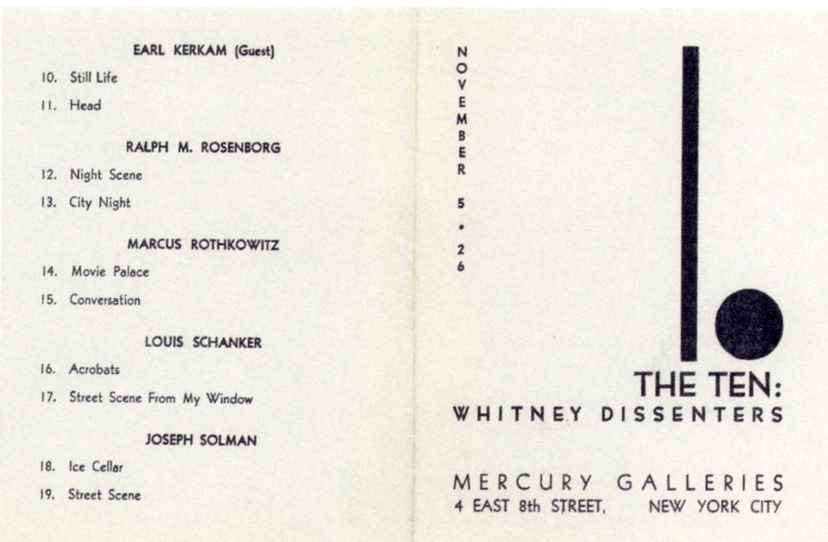

EARL KERKAM (Guest)
10. Still Life
11. Head
RALPH M. ROSENBORG
12. Night Scene
13. City Night
MARCUS ROTHKOWITZ
14. Movie Palace
15. Conversation
LOUIS SCHANKER
16. Acrobats
17. Street Scene From My Window
JOSEPH SOLMAN
18. Ice Cellar
19. Street Scene

NOVEMBER 5 • 26

THE TEN:
WHITNEY DISSENTERS

MERCURY GALLERIES
4 EAST 8th STREET, NEW YORK CITY

fig. 7 *The Ten: Whitney Dissenters, Mercury Galleries, New York*, invitation card, 1938, American Archives of Art, Smithsonian Institution, Washington, D.C.

1938–1939

On February 21, 1938, Rotkovitch is granted American citizenship. In the fall, the couple moves to 313 East 6th Street.

On November 5, *The Ten: Whitney Dissenters* opens at the Mercury Galleries (fig. 7). Rotkovitch shows *Movie Palace*, 1934–35 (pl. 1) and *Conversation*, c. 1937 (CR 102; fig. 8), which received considerable press attention. In the catalogue, Bernard Braddon and Rotkovitch criticize the policies adopted by the Whitney for its annual exhibition, running at the same time.

On August 17, 1939, Rotkovitch is fired from the WPA. In November, after an exhibition of The Ten at the Bonestell Gallery, the group breaks up. Rotkovitch and other members of The Ten attend the Museum of Modern Art's exhibition on *Picasso: Forty Years of His Art*, which opens on November 15.

1940

In January, the artist starts calling himself Mark Rothko, although the change does not become official until 1959.

The Neumann-Willard Gallery presents a selection of works by Solman, Rothko, and Marcel Gromaire. Rothko shows three paintings, including *Contemplation*, 1937–38 (pl. 16) and *Entrance to Subway*, 1938 (pl. 7). Rothko, Avery, Bolotowsky, Gottlieb, and Harris are among the artists who, on April 17, distance themselves from the American Artists' Congress; in June they found the Federation of Modern Painters and Sculptors, and they show their work at the New York World's Fair in the summer. During the course of the year, Rothko and Gottlieb begin new explorations of mythological themes, which entail anthropomorphic shapes, animal and plant forms, and legendary figures from Greek Antiquity. Rothko reads Aeschylus and Nietzsche. In October, he enters a competition to decorate a mural for the Social Security building in Washington, but his project is not selected.

He separates from Edith Sachar. He stops painting and devotes himself to reading and writing a manuscript on his vision of art. The manuscript, which remains unfinished, is found after the artist's death and published in 2004 as *The Artist's Reality*.

Due to poor eyesight, Rothko is not accepted for military service.

1941–1942

Around February 1941, Rothko moves back in with Edith Sachar at 29 East 28th Street.

In March, he takes part in the *First Annual Exhibition* of the Federation of Modern Painters and Sculptors at the Riverside Museum in New York, showing *Underground Fantasy*, c. 1940 (pl. 12), *Craftsman*, 1938–39, (CR 162), and *Subway*, 1939 (CR 166).

Samuel Kootz organizes an exhibition at Macy's department store in January. Rothko shows works with mythological subjects for the first time, including *Antigone*, 1939–40 (pl. 23) and *Oedipus*, 1940 (CR 189). The Federation of Modern Painters and Sculptors holds its second annual Salon at Wildenstein and Company in New York—Rothko contributes *Mother and Child*, c. 1940 (CR 176; fig. 9). At this time, Rothko is acting as the sales agent for Edith Sachar's jewelry design business.

1943

During the first annual exhibition of the Federation of Modern Painters and Sculptors, Rothko shows *Nude*, 1938–39 (pl. 18). At the third annual exhibition, in June, *New York Times* critic Edward Alden Jewell harshly criticizes Rothko's *Syrian Bull*, 1943 (CR 214; fig. 12) and Gottlieb's *Rape of Persephone*. The response by both artists (written with Newman's unacknowledged collaboration) is published in the June 13 issue (fig. 11).

Mark Rothko and Edith Sachar separate permanently in June (the divorce becomes final on February 1, 1944). Rothko has a breakdown and, after being examined at the hospital, decides to visit his family in Portland. On the west coast he meets artists Buffie Johnson and Clyfford Still, and also sees the Arensbergs' collection of modern European art for the first time.

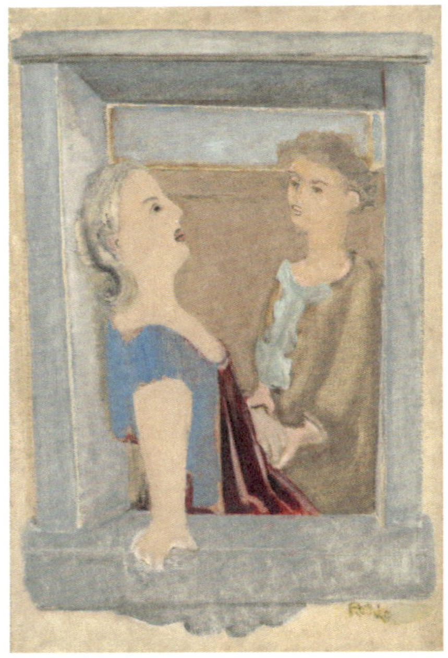

fig. 8 *Conversation (Untitled)* ou *Untitled (Two Woman at the Window)*, c. 1937, oil on canvas, 36 × 24 in., National Gallery of Art, Washington, D.C. (CR 102)

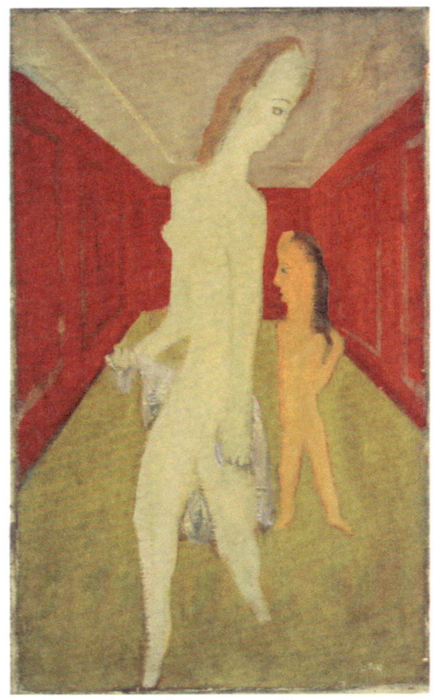

fig. 9 *Mother and Child*, c. 1940, oil on canvas, 36 × 22 in, Collection of Christopher Rothko (CR 176)

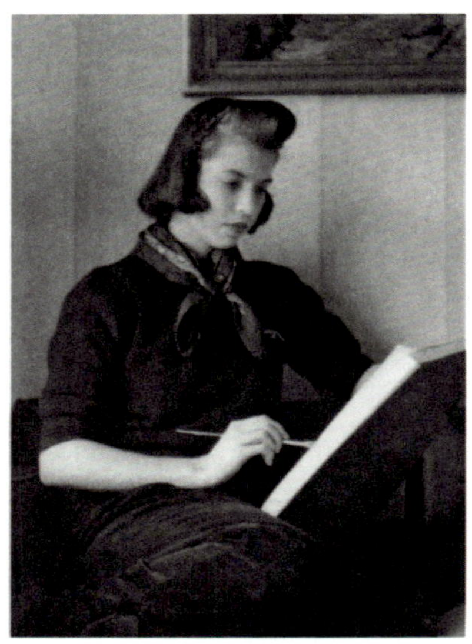

fig. 10 Mary Alice (Mell) Beistle, early 1940s, The Rothko Family Archive

"Consummated Experience"

Well, up to this point it seemed as if we might be going to get somewhere on a concrete basis. But—

these easy program notes can help only the simple-minded. No possible set of notes can explain our paintings. Their explanation must come out of a consummated experience between picture and onlooker. The point at issue, it seems to us, is not an "explanation" of the paintings, but whether the intrinsic ideas carried within the frames of these pictures have significance. We feel that our pictures demonstrate our esthetic beliefs, some of which we, therefore, list:

1. To us art is an adventure into an unknown world, which can be explored only by those willing to take the risks.

2. This world of the imagination is fancy-free and violently opposed to common sense.

3. It is our function as artists to make the spectator see the world our way—not his way.

4. We favor the simple expression of the complex thought. We are for the large shape because it has the impact of the unequivocal. We wish to re-assert the picture plane. We are for flat forms because they destroy illusion and reveal truth.

5. It is a widely accepted notion among painters that it does not matter what one paints as long as it is well painted. This is the essence of academism. There is no such thing as good painting about nothing. We assert that the subject is crucial and only that subject-matter is valid which is tragic and timeless. That is why we profess spiritual kinship with primitive and archaic art.

Period. But there is one paragraph more, which covers considerable ground and treads on enough toes to keep the chiropodists busy all Summer:

Consequently, if our work embodies these beliefs it must insult any one who is spiritually attuned to interior decoration; pictures for the home; pictures for over the mantel; pictures of the American scene; social pictures; purity in art; prize-winning potboilers; the National Academy, the Whitney Academy, the Corn Belt Academy; buckeyes; trite tripe, etc.

fig. 11 Adolph Gottlieb and Mark Rothko (with collaboration of Barnett Newman), excerpt of the reply to the Edward Alden Jewell's article, in *The New York Times*, June 13, 1943, The Archives of the Adolph and Esther Gottlieb Foundation, New York

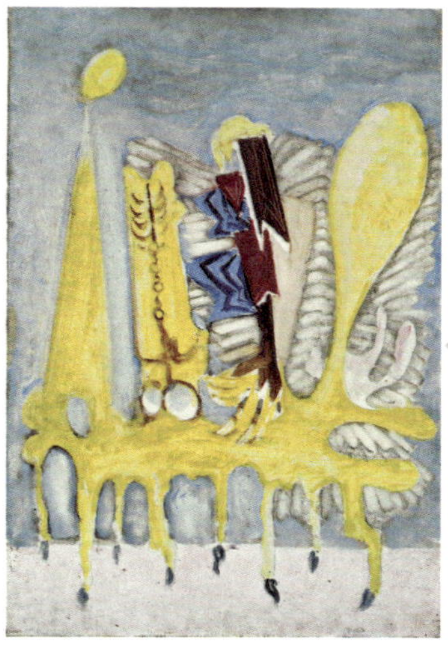

fig. 12 *The Syrian Bull*, beginning 1943, oil and graphite on canvas, 39 3/8 × 27 13/16 in., Oberlin College, the Allen Memorial Art Museum, Oberlin (CR 214)

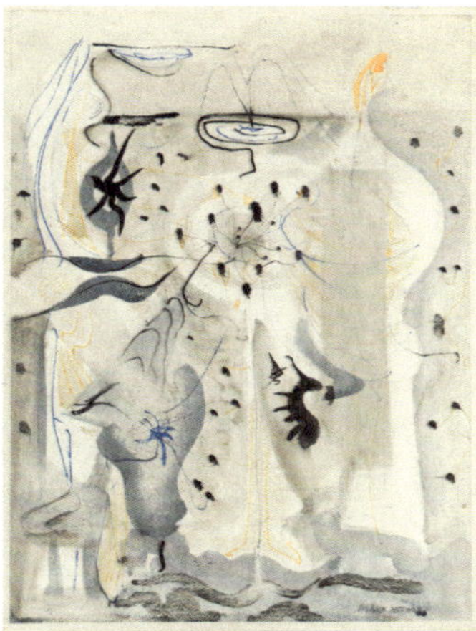

fig. 13 *Baptismal Scene*, 1945, watercolor and graphite pencil on paper, 20 1/2 × 14 1/2 in., Whitney Museum of American Art, New York

Once he returns to New York, Buffie Johnson introduces him to Peggy Guggenheim's advisor, Howard Putzel (Guggenheim has opened her Art of This Century gallery in October 1942, specializing in the European and American avant-gardes).

On October 13, on New York's WNYC radio station, Gottlieb and Rothko discuss "The Portrait and the Modern Artist." Rothko explains his interest in mythological subjects, which he considers timeless and universal, describing them as symbols of people's primitive fears and motivations, in all places and all ages, which may change in detail but never in substance.

Rothko, Gottlieb, Newman, and Johnson meet about once a week to discuss art and philosophy for several years. In early October, Rothko shares a studio at 22 West 52nd Street with Surrealist painter Boris Margo. The watercolors and oil paintings from this period clearly reflect Rothko's interest in Surrealism, especially the work of Miró, which he sees at the MoMA's in November 1942.

1944–1945

In the spring of 1944, Rothko participates in the *First Exhibition in America of Twenty Paintings* at the Art of This Century gallery, and Peggy Guggenheim begins representing him. Through the gallery, Rothko meets Hedda Stern and Max Ernst, as well as Betty Parsons, who will become his dealer in 1947.

In December, photographer Aaron Siskind introduces him to illustrator Mary Alice Beistle, known as Mell (fig. 10). Rothko paints *Slow Swirl at the Edge of the Sea*, 1944 (pl. 32), a key work in so far as it was associated with their encounter. He gives Mell a copy of Kafka's *The Trial* and immerses himself in Dostoyevsky and Kierkegaard.

From January 9 to February 4, 1945, a solo exhibition at the Art of This Century gallery feature fifteen paintings by Rothko, including *Slow Swirl at the Edge of the Sea,* 1944 (pl. 32), *Sacrifice of Iphigenia*, 1942 (pl. 27), *Tiresias*, 1944 (pl. 28), and *Hierarchical Birds*, 1944 (pl. 25).

On March 31, Rothko and Beistle get married in Linden, New Jersey. The newlyweds move to 1288 Sixth Avenue in New York and spend their vacation at Aaron Siskind's home. Rothko's *Primeval Landscape*, 1944 (CR 243) is selected for the *Annual Exhibition of Contemporary American Painting* at the Whitney Museum of American Art, New York.

1946

Rothko contributes his *Baptismal Scene* of 1945 (fig. 13) to the *Annual Exhibition of Contemporary American Sculpture, Watercolors, and Drawings* held at the Whitney Museum. He writes the foreword to the catalogue for Clyfford Still's solo show at the Art of This Century gallery. Rothko is described as a "mythomorphic abstractionist" in the April issue of *ArtNews* magazine.

He rents a summer villa in East Hampton, where he regularly meets with Baziotes, Motherwell, Pollock, and Harold Rosenberg. His style continues to evolve during this period, which he later views as a transitional phase. He produces the paintings called *Multiforms*.

1947

Rothko is invited to join a group show organized by Newman at the Betty Parsons Gallery, on the theme of "The Ideographic Painting," early in the year. He exhibits *Tiresias*, 1944 (pl. 28) and *Vernal Memory*, 1946 (CR 311). In March, he has his first solo show at the gallery, where he shows *Rites of Lilith*, 1945 (pl. 26), the largest of his paintings up to that point. Through Parsons, Rothko meets the artist Herbert Ferber, with whom he will become friends and swap works.

Between June 23 and August 1, Rothko teaches at the California School of Fine Arts (CSFA) summer school in San Francisco.

He decides not to submit a work to the seventh Salon of the Federation of Modern Painters and Sculptors, but he does sponsor Clyfford Still.

In September, the single issue of *Possibilities* magazine, edited by Robert Motherwell in conjunction with critic Harold Rosenberg, architect Pierre Chareau, and musician John Cage, publishes an article by Rothko titled "The Romantics were Prompted," in which he identifies his paintings as "dramas" and their shapes as "performers."

The October issue of *The Tiger's Eye* reproduces five works by Rothko and describes him as a painter of the "plasticity of inner life".

1948

His second solo exhibition at the Betty Parsons Gallery, *Mark Rothko: Recent Paintings*, include the first paintings to which Rothko, following Clyfford Still's example, gives a number as a title, such as *Aeolian Harp, No. 7*, 1946 (pl. 34). In the spring, Still resignes from the CSFA to move to New York and work on his plans for a school. Rothko, Still, Motherwell, and Baziotes are associated with this project. Even though Still ultimately abandons it at the end of the summer, the school—called Subjects of the Artist—nevertheless opens in the autumn, at 35 East 8th Street, with about fifteen students.

Rothko swaps works with Motherwell (fig. 16), who introduces him to Bernard Reis, Peggy Guggenheim's financial advisor for Art of This Century.

Rothko's mother dies on October 10, at the age of seventy-eight, after a long illness. Crushed by her death, he paints very little for a year.

1949

Early in the year, Rothko leaves the Subjects of the Artist school, which will close in the spring for financial reasons.

For his third solo exhibition at the Betty Parsons Gallery he assembles a suite of works numbered 1 to 10.

Once again invited to teach at the CSFA summer school, he leaves for San Francisco where he teaches courses in painting and the philosophy of art.

His painting *No. 19*, 1949 (pl. 42) is included in the Whitney's annual painting exhibition. His "Statement on his Attitude in Painting" is published in the October issue of *The Tiger's Eye*, where he states:

"The progression of a painter's work, as it travels in time from point to point, will be toward clarity, toward the elimination of all obstacles between the painter and the idea, and between the idea and the observer."

At this time, Rothko's *Multiforms* are characterized by large flat areas of thin, diluted color.

He sees Matisse's *Red Studio,* which MoMA has acquired that year.

1950

In January, he exhibits a series of paintings at the Betty Parsons Gallery, including *No. 14 (Golden Composition)* (pl. 41), *No. 5* (pl. 48), *No. 8* (pl. 49), *No. 11/No. 20* (pl. 43), and *No. 1* (pl. 45), all from 1949. The exhibition, photographed by Aaron Siskind (fig. 17), is reviewed by Thomas Hess in the February issue of *ArtNews*.

Having inherited money from Mell's mother, the Rothkos board the *Queen Elizabeth* on 29 March, which takes them to Europe for a five-month trip. When in Paris, Rothko found the city "alien and unapproachable."

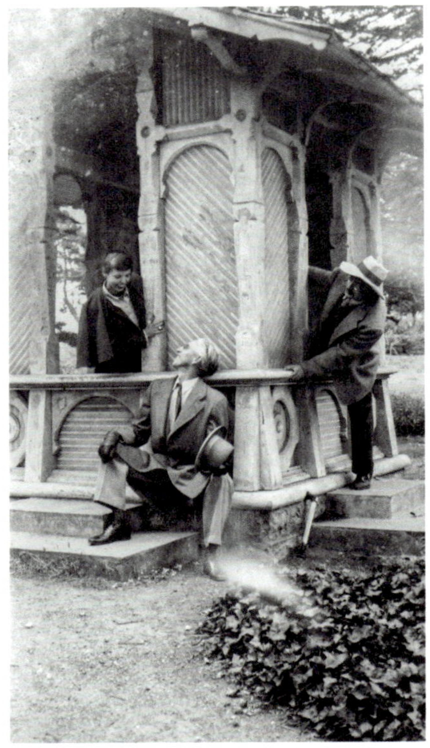

fig. 14 Mell and Mark Rothko and Clyfford Still, San Francisco, 1947, The Rothko Family Archive

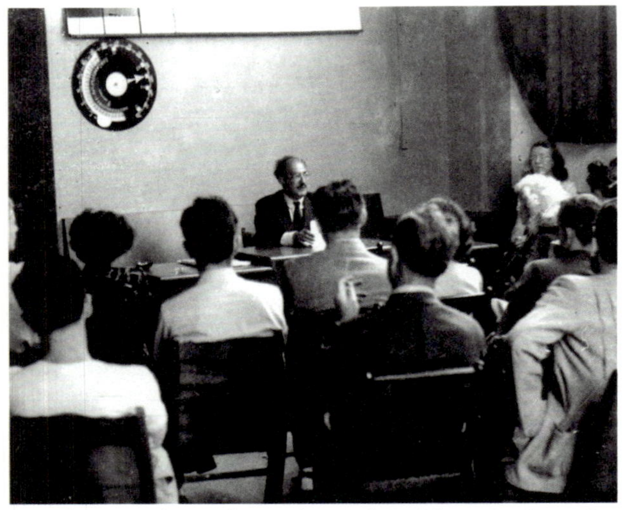

fig. 15 William Heick, Conference by Mark Rothko at Studio 18, San Francisco Art Institute, 1949, San Francisco Art Institute Archive

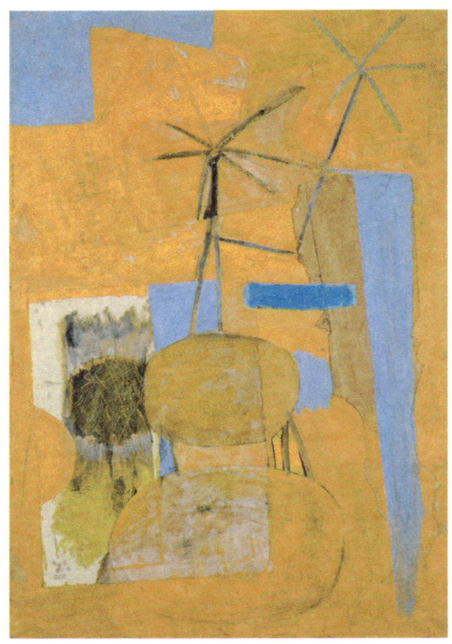

fig. 16 Robert Motherwell, *The Poet*, 1947, oil and glued paper on canvas, 55 25/64 × 39 9/64 in., former collection of Mark and Mell Rothko

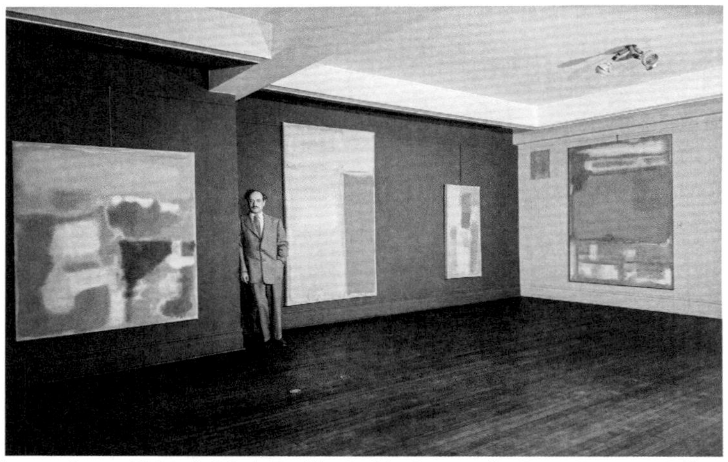

fig. 17 Aaron Siskind, Mark Rothko in his show at the Betty Parsons Gallery, New York, 1950

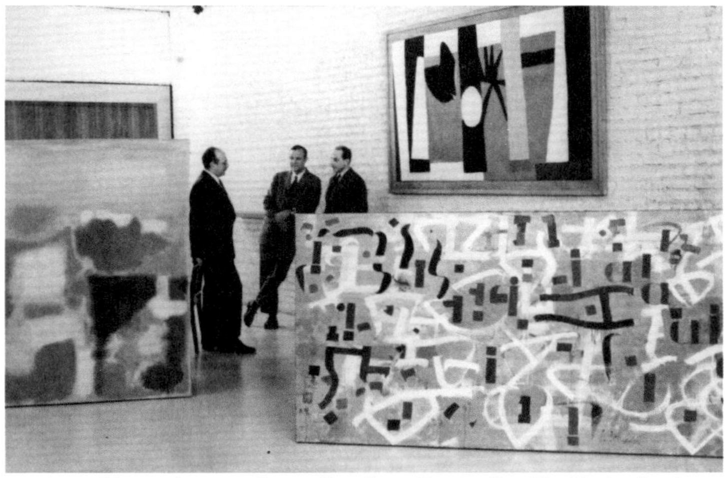

fig. 18 Mark Rothko, Robert Motherwell and Bradley Walker Tomlin in the Guest House of Mr. and Mrs. John D. Rockefeller 3rd, 1951. The paintings are Rothko's *Number 18*, (1948), Motherwell's *The Voyage* (1949) and Tomlin's *Number 9: in Praise of Gertrude Stein* (1950), MoMA Archives, New York

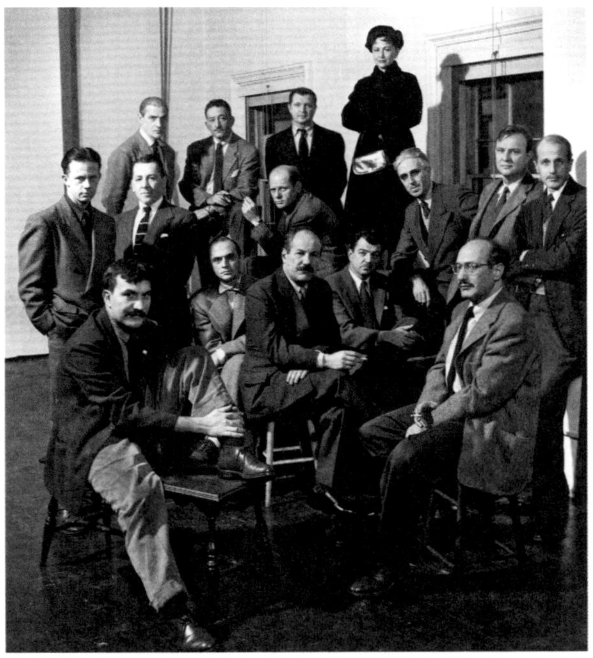

fig. 19 Nina Leen, *The Irascibles*, 1950, from left to right, from behind: Willem de Kooning, Adolph Gottlieb, Ad Reinhardt, Hedda Sterne; Richard Pousette-Dart, William Baziotes, Jackson Pollock, Clyfford Still, Robert Motherwell; Bradley Walker Tomlin; Theodoros Stamos, Jimmy Ernst, Barnett Newman, James Brooks and Mark Rothko, Museum of Modern Art, New York, acquired through the generosity of Donald B. Marro

They then go on to Cagnes-sur-Mer, Venice, Florence (where they admire Fra Angelico's frescoes in the monastery of San Marco), Arezzo, Siena, and Rome. Rothko later recounts that he has laid down on the floor of the Sistine Chapel to admire Michelangelo's ceiling. They return via Paris and London. On June 30, Rothko writes to Newman from Rome to tell him that Mell is pregnant. Katy Linn, known as Kate, is born on December 30 in New York.

1951

Rothko is among the eighteen artists who pose for the famous "The Irascibles" photograph in the January 15 issue of *Life* (fig. 19). The magazine cite their refusal to participate in the contemporary art exhibition at the Metropolitan Museum of Art.

Rothko has just been appointed assistant professor in the Department of Design at Brooklyn College, where Ad Reinhardt teaches. Clyfford Still will join them in 1952. On March 19, Rothko speaks on a panel discussion at MoMA on "How to Combine Architecture, Painting, and Sculpture." A statement published in the May 10, 1951, issue of *Interiors* magazine acknowledges his awareness that while "historically, the function of painting large pictures is something very grandiose and pompous. The reason I paint them however is precisely because I want to be intimate and human."

In April, Rothko shows paintings *No. 5/No. 22*, 1950 (pl. 50), *No. 7*, 1951 (pl. 51), and *No. 16*, 1951 (pl. 52) at his last solo exhibition at the Betty Parsons Gallery, where the public sees his first "Classic" paintings. Later that year, he meets Sally and William Scharf (who is to become his assistant), art historian Dore Ashton, and writer Stanley Kunitz.

1952–1953

In early 1952, Rothko takes a studio at 106 West 53rd Street. He declines an invitation to teach during the summer session at Black Mountain College in North Carolina, preferring to spend the summer in New York. In May, Jackson Pollock leaves the Betty Parsons Gallery and moves to Sidney Janis, triggering an exodus that Rothko will join in 1954.

From April 9 to July 27, Rothko is included in the *Fifteen Americans* show at the Museum of Modern Art in New York. He and Clyfford Still decide not to participate in a European tour of the exhibition because they can not supervise the hanging. Their withdrawal leads to the cancellation of the proposed tour. His relationships with Newman and Still become strained, and Rothko begins seeing more of artists Philip Guston and Robert Motherwell.

1954

In January, Rothko is included in the *Nine American Painters Today* show at the Sidney Janis Gallery, exhibiting *No. 14/No. 10 (Yellow Greens)*, 1953 (pl. 55). He leaves the Betty Parsons Gallery for Janis in the spring. On March 16, he looses his job at Brooklyn College. In April, the Rothkos move from their Sixth Avenue building to an apartment at 102 West 54th Street.

Katharine Kuh, a curator at the Art Institute of Chicago, invites Rothko to inaugurate a series of solo shows at her museum. This leads to a rich correspondence, excerpts of which they intend to publish. The publication never appeared, since Rothko prefers to let beholders discover his works without any commentary. For this, his first exhibition in a major American museum, Rothko shows recent works, including the *No. 6 (Yellow, White, Blue over Yellow on Gray)*, 1954 (pl. 59). He gives instructions on the hanging in a letter dated September 25 (fig. 21).

At the end of the year, he paints *Homage to Matisse* (CR 521; fig. 20) as a tribute to the late master, who has died on November 3.

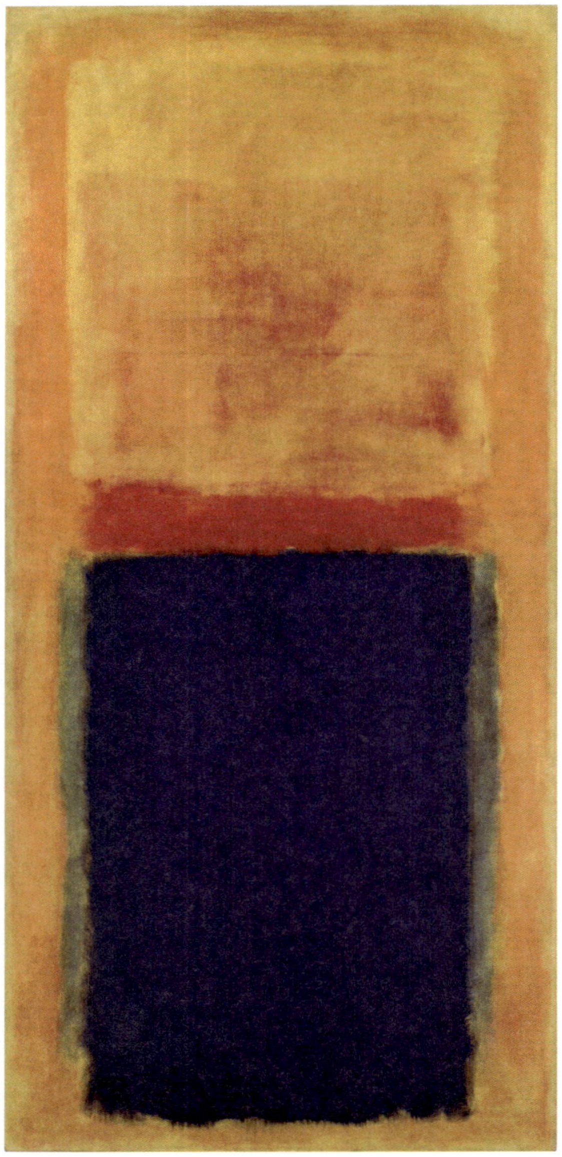

fig. 20 *Homage to Matisse*, 1954, oil on canvas, 105.6 × 51 in., private collection (CR 521)

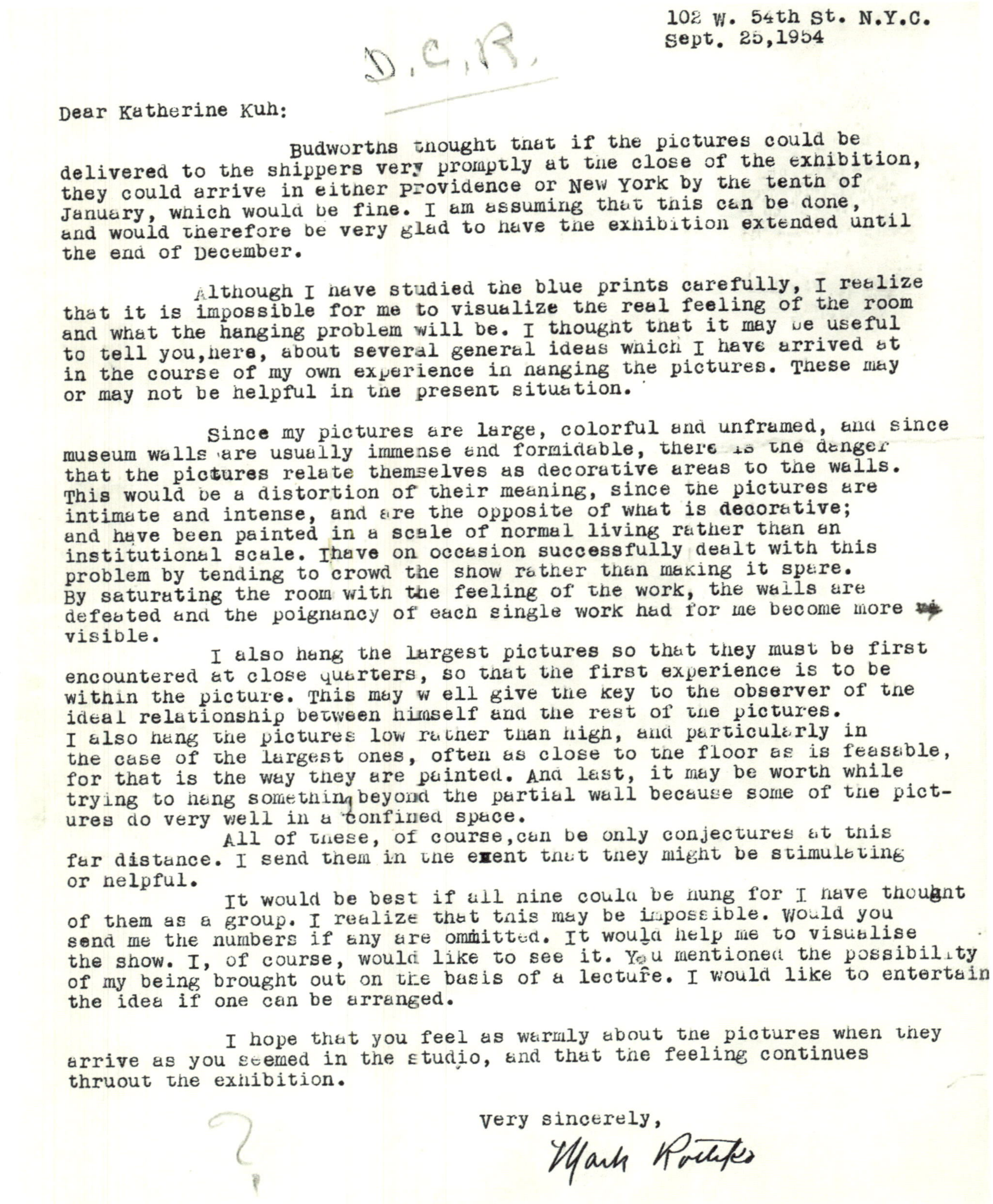

102 W. 54th St. N.Y.C.
Sept. 25,1954

D.C.R.

Dear Katherine Kuh:

Budworths thought that if the pictures could be delivered to the shippers very promptly at the close of the exhibition, they could arrive in either Providence or New York by the tenth of January, which would be fine. I am assuming that this can be done, and would therefore be very glad to have the exhibition extended until the end of December.

Although I have studied the blue prints carefully, I realize that it is impossible for me to visualize the real feeling of the room and what the hanging problem will be. I thought that it may be useful to tell you,here, about several general ideas which I have arrived at in the course of my own experience in hanging the pictures. These may or may not be helpful in the present situation.

Since my pictures are large, colorful and unframed, and since museum walls are usually immense and formidable, there is the danger that the pictures relate themselves as decorative areas to the walls. This would be a distortion of their meaning, since the pictures are intimate and intense, and are the opposite of what is decorative; and have been painted in a scale of normal living rather than an institutional scale. Ihave on occasion successfully dealt with this problem by tending to crowd the show rather than making it spare. By saturating the room with the feeling of the work, the walls are defeated and the poignancy of each single work had for me become more visible.

I also hang the largest pictures so that they must be first encountered at close quarters, so that the first experience is to be within the picture. This may w ell give the key to the observer of the ideal relationship between himself and the rest of the pictures. I also hang the pictures low rather than high, and particularly in the case of the largest ones, often as close to the floor as is feasable, for that is the way they are painted. And last, it may be worth while trying to hang somethin beyond the partial wall because some of the pictures do very well in a confined space.

All of these, of course,can be only conjectures at this far distance. I send them in the event that they might be stimulating or helpful.

It would be best if all nine could be hung for I have thought of them as a group. I realize that this may be impossible. Would you send me the numbers if any are ommitted. It would help me to visualise the show. I, of course, would like to see it. You mentioned the possibility of my being brought out on the basis of a lecture. I would like to entertain the idea if one can be arranged.

I hope that you feel as warmly about the pictures when they arrive as you seemed in the studio, and that the feeling continues thruout the exhibition.

Very sincerely,

Mark Rothko

fig. 21 Letter from Rothko to Katharine Kuh, September 25, 1954, The Art Institute of Chicago Archives

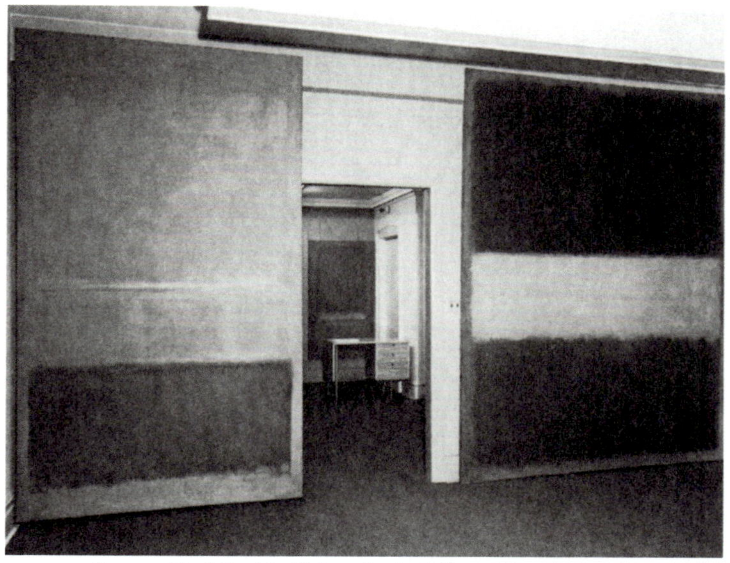

fig. 22 *Mark Rothko*, Sidney Janis Gallery, New York, 1955

fig. 23 *Orange and Yellow*, 1956, oil on canvas, 91 × 71 in., Albright-Knox Art Gallery, Buffalo, New York Gift of Seymour H. Knox (CR 548)

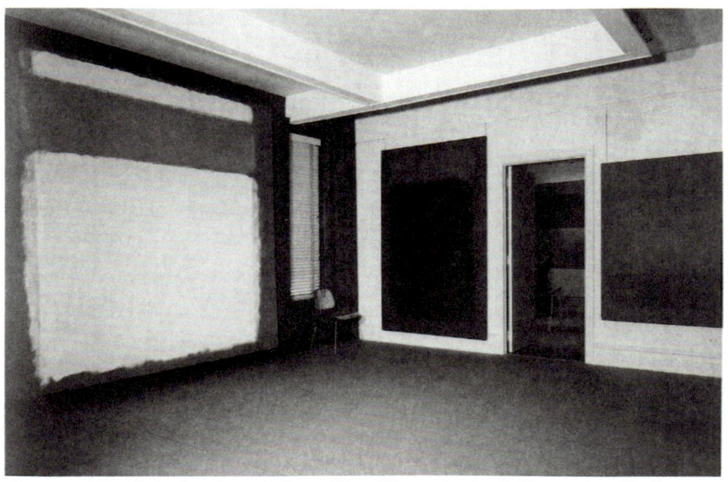

fig. 24 *New Paintings by Mark Rothko*, Sidney Janis Gallery, New York, 1958

1955

On March 30, 1955, an exhibition titled *Modern Art in the USA* opens in Paris, then travels to Zürich, Barcelona, Frankfurt, London, The Hague, and Vienna, ending in Belgrade in August 1956. The show includes, among other paintings, *No. 10*, 1950 (CR 449).

For his first solo show at the Sidney Janis Gallery from April 11 to May 14 (fig 22), Rothko hangs all his works himself, including *No. 9 (Dark over Light Earth/Violet and Yellow in Rose)*, 1954 (pl. 56) and *Ochre, Red on Red*, 1954 (pl. 72). Newman and Still both write to Sidney Janis criticizing Rothko as a "salon painter" and his work as "bourgeois." During the summer, Rothko is a visiting professor at the University of Colorado at Boulder. The December issue of *Fortune* magazine lists his work as a "speculative or 'growth'" investment. He reads Kierkegaard's *Fear and Trembling*.

1956–1957

Newman sues Ad Reinhardt and Rothko for libel following an article in the *College Art Journal*. The Supreme Court dismisses the suit.

Rothko spends two months in bed due to an attack of gout. He then takes a studio on West 61st Street, where he continues to work until the spring of 1958. He exhibits two paintings from 1956, *Orange and Yellow* (CR 548; fig. 23) and *Light over Gray* (CR 567), in the *Recent Paintings by Seven Americans* show at the Sidney Janis Gallery (September 24 to October 20, 1956).

He reads Sigmund Freud's letters to Dr. Fleiss.

In October, the collector Duncan Phillips expresses his desire to exhibit Rothko's work. On January 6, 1957, the exhibition *Paintings by Rothko, Bradley Walker Tomlin and Kenzo Okada* opens at the Phillips Collection in Washington, D.C. Phillips buys two of the paintings on show, *No. 16 / No. 12 [Mauve Intersection]*, 1949 (CR 400) and *No. 7 (Green and Maroon)*, 1953, (CR 491). In February-March 1957, Rothko is a guest resident at Tulane University in New Orleans.

His palette begins to darken at this time.

The Rothko family spends the summer in Provincetown. In the fall, the Contemporary Arts Museum in Houston, Texas, hosts a *Mark Rothko* exhibition that includes *No. 9/No. 5/No. 18*, 1952 (pl. 54), *No. 9 (Dark over Light Earth/Violet and Yellow in Rose)*, 1954 (pl. 56), *Green and Tangerine on Red*, 1956 (pl. 71), *No. 10*, 1957 (pl. 64), and *No. 15*, 1957 (pl. 73). Elaine de Kooning edits the catalog, but *ArtNews* publishes a letter from Rothko challenging de Kooning's article, which links his work to action painting.

1958

The Sidney Janis Gallery features *New Paintings by Mark Rothko* in January (fig. 24). The show reveales Rothko's new red-and-brown palette, as also seen at the 29th Venice Biennale from June 14 to October 19, where he represents the United States with David Smith, Mark Tobey, and Seymour Lipton (fig. 25). The Museum of Modern Art organizes a traveling *New American Painting* exhibition that includes five Rothko paintings, notably *No. 7*, 1951 (pl. 51) and *The Black and the White*, 1956 (pl. 75). The show opens in Basel, Switzerland, on April 19, then travels to Milan, Madrid, Berlin, Amsterdam, Brussels, Paris, and London, ending in New York in September 1959.

On May 18, Rothko, Robert Motherwell, Willem de Kooning, Philip Guston, and Franz Kline sign a contract with Bernard Reis, authorizing him to represent them in their dealings with Sidney Janis.

1958

On June 25, Seagram distilleries commissions Rothko to paint a series of murals for the Four Seasons Restaurant designed by Philip Johnson for Mies van der Rohe's Seagram Building (fig. 27). Rothko works on these paintings in his new studio, a former gym at 222 Bowery Street, where he sets up scaffolding the same size as the Four Seasons room (see pp. 277–79).

Unbeknownst to Rothko, Janis submits *No. 14 (White and Greens in Blue)*, 1957 (CR 588; fig. 26) to the Solomon R. Guggenheim Museum's international competition. In August, when the work wins the first prize—the United States National Award—Rothko refuses both the award and the $1,000 check.

Rothko discusses Kierkegaard's *Fear and Trembling* at a press conference on his work held at the Pratt Institute on October 27 (fig. 28), during which he lists the seven ingredients in his "recipe of a work of art":

> *1. There must be a clear preoccupation with death—intimations of mortality.... Tragic art, romantic art, etc., deals with the knowledge of death.*
> *2. Sensuality. Our basis of being concrete about the world. It is a lustful relationship to things that exist.*
> *3. Tension. Either conflict or curbed desire.*
> *4. Irony. This is a modern ingredient—the self-effacement and examination by which a man for an instant can go on to something else.*
> *5. Wit and Play ... for the human element.*
> *6. The ephemeral and chance ... for the human element.*
> *7. Hope. 10% to make the tragic concept more endurable.*
> *I measure these ingredients very carefully when I paint a picture. It is always the form that follows these elements, and the picture results from the proportions of these elements.*

1959

Art historian Werner Haftmann goes to see Rothko in the spring to suggest that he participates in the second *documenta* in Kassel. Rothko refuses because he does not want to send any works to Germany. But three paintings from private collections will be included, among them *Black in Deep Red,* 1957 (CR 592), *No. 18 (Brown and Black on Plum)*, 1958 (CR 627) and the one that wins the United States National Award, *No. 14 (White and Greens in Blue)*, 1957 (CR 588; fig. 26).

With Mell and Kate, Rothko boards the *Independence,* a liner bound for Naples, on June 15. His new passport, issued on May 16, makes his new name—Mark Rothko—official. In Italy, he visits Pompeii, where he senses a "deep affinity" between his work and the frescoes in the Villa of the Mysteries. The Rothkos also go to Paestum (fig. 29), Rome, and Tarquinia to see the murals of the Etruscan necropolis, as well as to Venice to meet Peggy Guggenheim, who takes them to the island of Torcello. The Rothkos leave Italy on July 15 for Paris. The family visits the Luxembourg Gardens, Notre-Dame Cathedral, and the Sainte-Chapelle. During their stay in Paris, they meet painter Pierre Soulages. They go to Chartres to admire the cathedral, and to the Bordeaux region and to the Dordogne to see the Lascaux cave paintings. Then they go to Brussels to visit Rothko's nephew, Kenneth Rabin, and his wife, as well as Anne-Marie and Morton Levine. They also go to Antwerp, Bruges, The Hague and Amsterdam, where they admire the Rembrandt collection at the Rijksmuseum. Heading on to London by train, they go to the Tate Gallery, which houses Turner's paintings and Rothko's *Light Red over Black,* 1957 (CR 601). In Cornwall, they visit the artistic community at St. Ives. On August 20, the Rothkos board the *Queen Elizabeth II.* After returning from the trip, Rothko dines at the Four Seasons with Mell: the place seems terribly pretentious to him. He immediately decides to abandon the commission and repay the advance he had received.

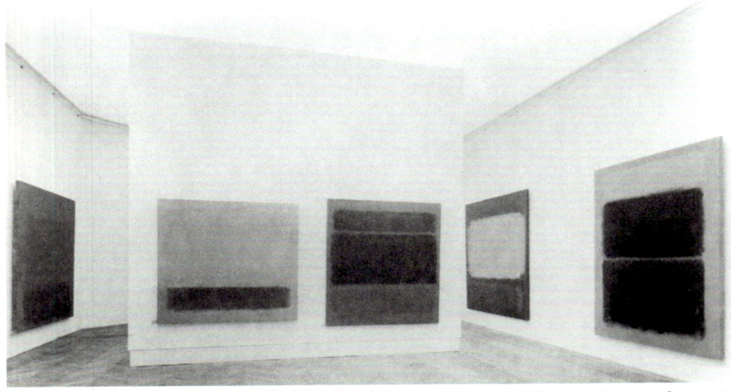

fig. 25 Rothko room in American Pavilion at the 29th Venice Biennale, 1958, with CR 609, CR 592, CR 593, CR 594, CR 601

fig. 26 *No. 14 (White and Greens in Blue)*, 1957, oil on canvas, 101 47/64 × 82 1/64 in., collection of Mr. Paul Mellon, Upperville (VA) (CR 588)

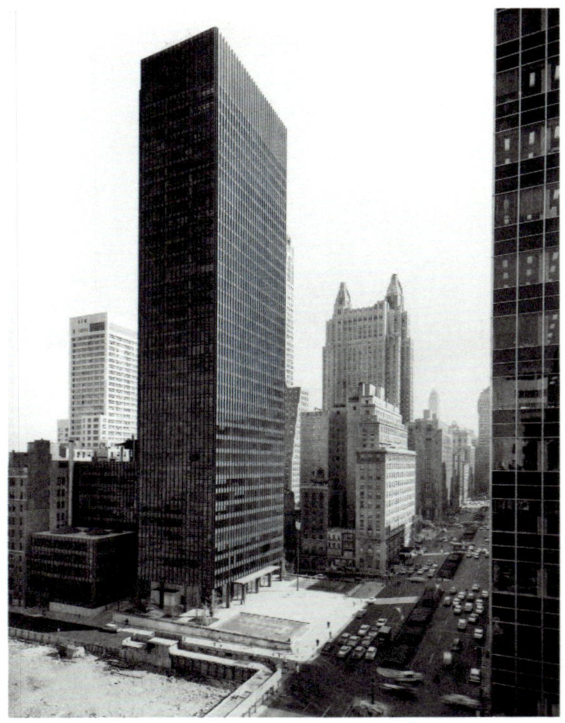

fig. 27 Ezra Stoller, Seagram Building, 375 Park Avenue, New York City, 1958, Canadian Center for Architecture, Montreal

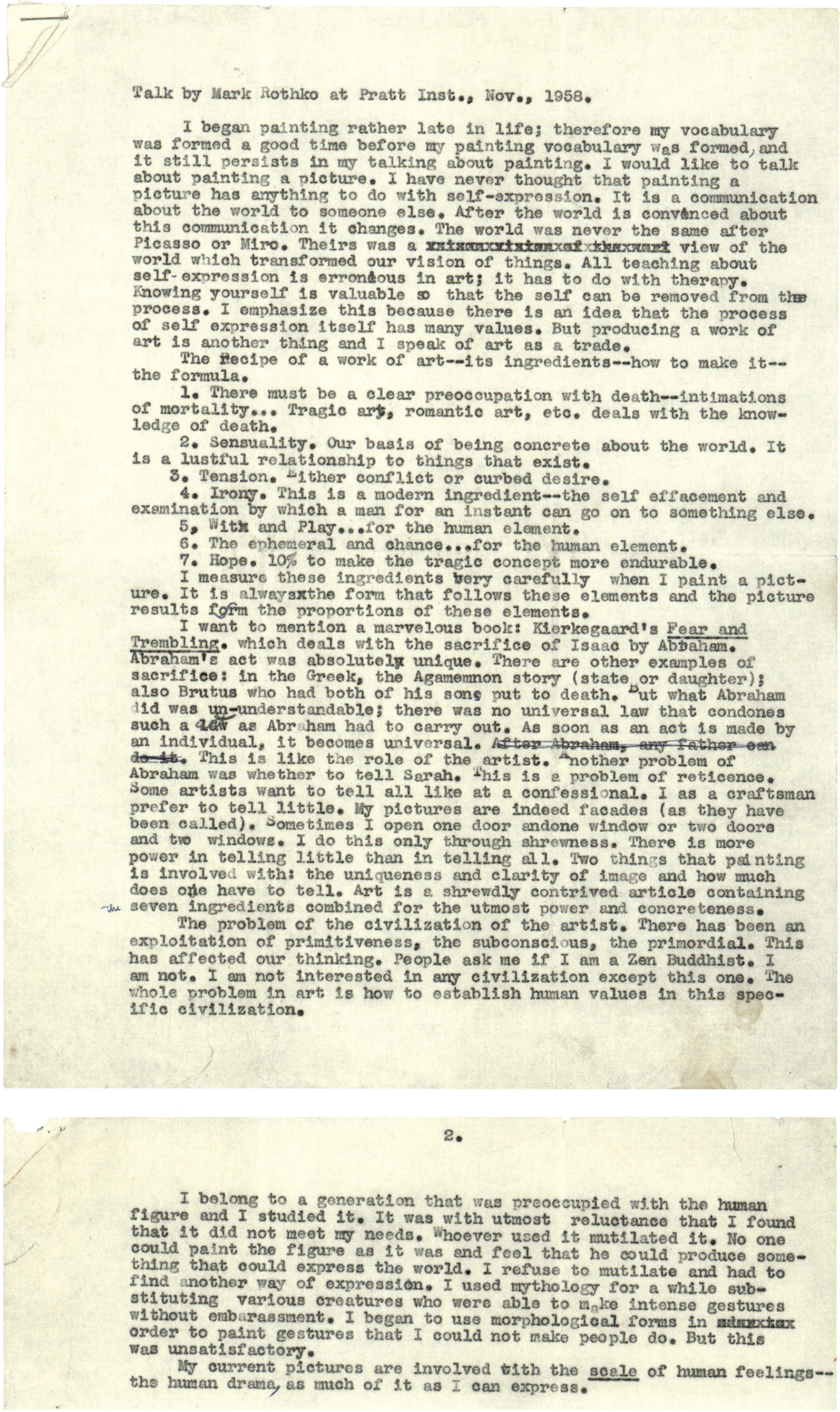
Talk by Mark Rothko at Pratt Inst., Nov., 1958.

I began painting rather late in life; therefore my vocabulary was formed a good time before my painting vocabulary was formed, and it still persists in my talking about painting. I would like to talk about painting a picture. I have never thought that painting a picture has anything to do with self-expression. It is a communication about the world to someone else. After the world is convinced about this communication it changes. The world was never the same after Picasso or Miro. Theirs was a ~~xxxxxxxxxxxxxxxxxxxxx~~ view of the world which transformed our vision of things. All teaching about self-expression is erroneous in art; it has to do with therapy. Knowing yourself is valuable so that the self can be removed from the process. I emphasize this because there is an idea that the process of self expression itself has many values. But producing a work of art is another thing and I speak of art as a trade.

The recipe of a work of art--its ingredients--how to make it--the formula.

1. There must be a clear preoccupation with death--intimations of mortality... Tragic art, romantic art, etc. deals with the knowledge of death.

2. Sensuality. Our basis of being concrete about the world. It is a lustful relationship to things that exist.

3. Tension. Either conflict or curbed desire.

4. Irony. This is a modern ingredient--the self effacement and examination by which a man for an instant can go on to something else.

5, Wit and Play...for the human element.

6. The ephemeral and chance...for the human element.

7. Hope. 10% to make the tragic concept more endurable.

I measure these ingredients very carefully when I paint a picture. It is always the form that follows these elements and the picture results form the proportions of these elements.

I want to mention a marvelous book: Kierkegaard's Fear and Trembling. which deals with the sacrifice of Isaac by Abraham. Abraham's act was absolutely unique. There are other examples of sacrifice: in the Greek, the Agamemnon story (state or daughter); also Brutus who had both of his sons put to death. But what Abraham did was un-understandable; there was no universal law that condones such a act as Abraham had to carry out. As soon as an act is made by an individual, it becomes universal. ~~After Abraham, any father can do it.~~ This is like the role of the artist. Another problem of Abraham was whether to tell Sarah. This is a problem of reticence. Some artists want to tell all like at a confessional. I as a craftsman prefer to tell little. My pictures are indeed facades (as they have been called). Sometimes I open one door andone window or two doors and two windows. I do this only through shrewness. There is more power in telling little than in telling all. Two things that painting is involved with: the uniqueness and clarity of image and how much does one have to tell. Art is a shrewdly contrived article containing seven ingredients combined for the utmost power and concreteness.

The problem of the civilization of the artist. There has been an exploitation of primitiveness, the subconscious, the primordial. This has affected our thinking. People ask me if I am a Zen Buddhist. I am not. I am not interested in any civilization except this one. The whole problem in art is how to establish human values in this specific civilization.

2.

I belong to a generation that was preoccupied with the human figure and I studied it. It was with utmost reluctance that I found that it did not meet my needs. Whoever used it mutilated it. No one could paint the figure as it was and feel that he could produce something that could express the world. I refuse to mutilate and had to find another way of expression. I used mythology for a while substituting various creatures who were able to make intense gestures without embarassment. I began to use morphological forms in ~~xxxxxx~~ order to paint gestures that I could not make people do. But this was unsatisfactory.

My current pictures are involved with the scale of human feelings--the human drama, as much of it as I can express.

fig. 28 Talk by Mark Rothko at Pratt Institute, November, 1958, The Rothko Family Archive

1960

The Rothkos buy a house at 118 East 95th Street.

The Phillips Collection in Washington, D.C., holds a small Rothko exhibition in May and acquires two works, *Green and Tangerine on Red*, 1956 (pl. 71) and *Orange and Red on Red*, 1957 (pl. 70). Shortly thereafter, the museum acquires *No. 7 (Green and Maroon)*, 1953 (CR 491). In November, the Phillips Collection becomes the first public institution to devote a room entirely to Rothko (see pp. 274–75).

Bernard Reis becomes the artist's tax adviser, accountant, and lawyer.

John and Dominique de Menil meet Rothko during a visit to his studio.

1961

In January, the Rothkos attend the inauguration of John F. Kennedy at the White House. While in Washington, the artist takes the opportunity to view his work at the Phillips Collection. He is pleased with the display, but demands slight changes to the hanging and asks that the chairs be replaced by a wooden bench.

Via the Sidney Janis Gallery, Count Giuseppe Panza buys three paintings chosen from the artist's studio early in the year: *No.* 301, 1959 (CR 665), *No. 61 (Rust and Blue)*, 1953 (CR 492), and *No. 7 (Dark over Light Earth / Violet and Yellow in Rose)*, 1954 (pl. 56).

On January 18, Rothko's first retrospective exhibition at the Museum of Modern Art opens with forty-eight works (fig. 31); the artist closely supervises installation of the show. Eager to see the public's reaction, he returns almost every day until the show closes. In addition to eleven canvases from the *Seagram series,* 1958–59, the show includes *No. 17 / No. 15*, 1949 (pl. 40), *No. 19*, 1949 (pl. 42), *No. 21*, 1949 (pl. 44), *No. 11 / No. 20*, 1949 (pl. 43), *No. 5 / No. 22* (1950 (pl. 3), *No. 9 / No. 5 / No. 18*, 1952 (pl. 54), *No. 14 / No. 10 (Yellow Greens)*, 1953 (pl. 55), *The Black and the White* (1956 (pl. 75), and *No. 14,* 1960 (pl. 88).

Well received by the critics, the retrospective travels to London (Whitechapel Art Gallery, fig. 32–33), where Rothko attends the opening on October 10, followed by Amsterdam (Stedelijk Museum), Brussels (Palais des Beaux-Arts), Basel (Kunsthalle Basel), and Rome (Galleria Nazionale d'Arte Moderna), ending in Paris (Musée d'Art Moderne de la Ville de Paris) on January 13, 1963. Before the first European show, Rothko sends Bryan Robertson, director of the Whitechapel Art Gallery in London, written instructions on how to hang and light the works (fig. 34).

At the request of Professor Wassily Leontief and John P. Coolidge, director of the Fogg Museum, Rothko accepts a commission to paint murals for the new premises of Harvard's Society of Fellows.

1962

In early spring, Rothko begins working in a studio at 1485 First Avenue. On October 24, he meets with the president of Harvard to discuss murals for a dining hall. Rothko, Gottlieb, Guston, and Motherwell leave the Janis Gallery in protest over a Pop Art show, *The New Realists*, which has opened on October 31.

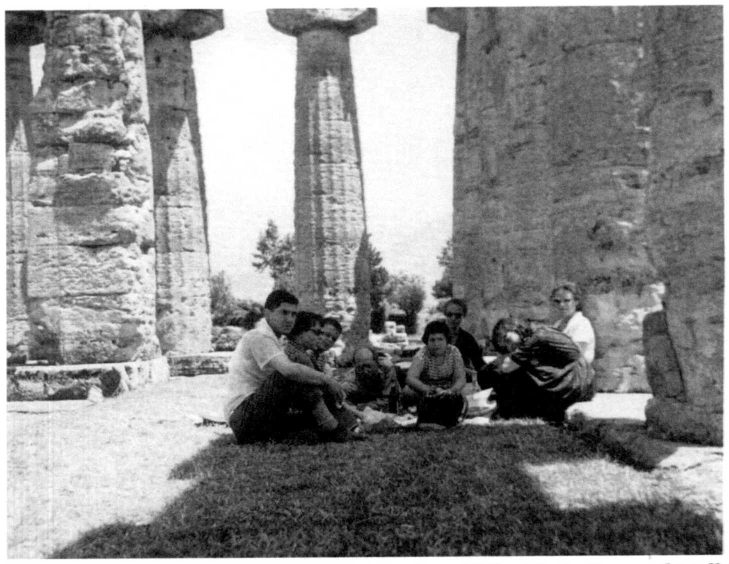

fig. 29 Temple of Hera, Paestum, June 26 1959. In the middle: Mark, Kate and Mell Rothko, with John and Elizabeth Fischer and their two daughters, The Rothko Family Archive

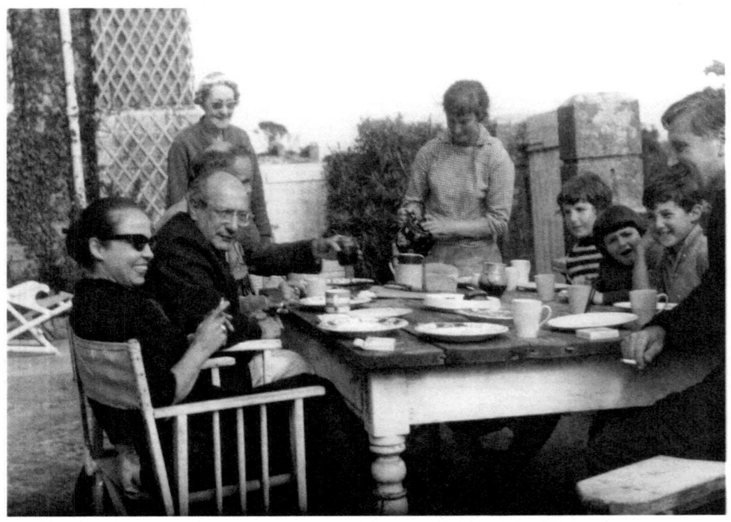

fig. 30 Paul Feiler, from left to right: Mell and Mark Rothko, Terry Frost, Mary Miles, June and Helen Feiler, Peter Layear, having lunch at the Chapel, Kerris, Cornwall, August, 1959, Courtesy Redfern Family Gallery, London

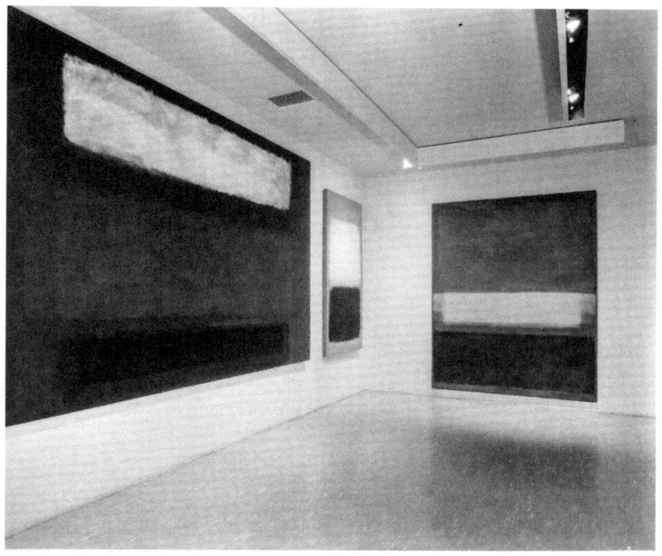

fig. 31 Mark Rothko's exhibition at the Museum of Modern Art, New York, January 18 – March 12, 1961, MoMA Archives, New York

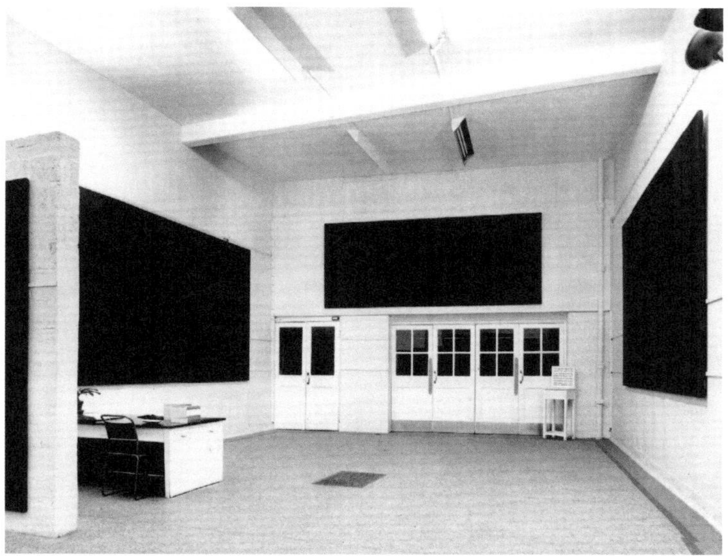

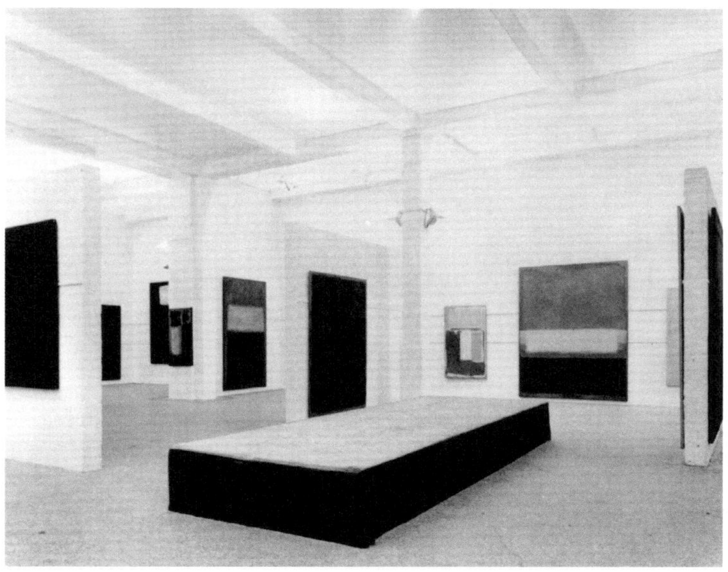

figs. 32–33 Mark Rothko's exhibition at Whitechapel Gallery, London, October 11–November 8, 1961, Whitechapel Gallery Archive, London

SUGGESTIONS FROM MR. MARK ROTHKO REGARDING INSTALLATION OF HIS PAINTINGS

Wall Color: Walls should be made considerably off-white with umber and warmed by a little red. If the walls are too white, they are always fighting against the pictures which turn greenish because of the predominance of red in the pictures.

Lighting: The light, whether natural or artificial, should not be too strong: the pictures have their own inner light and if there is too much light, the color in the picture is washed out and a distortion of their look occurs. The ideal situation would be to hang them in a normally lit room -- that is the way they were painted. They should not be over-lit or romanticized by spots; this results in a distortion of their meaning. They should either be lighted from a great distance or indirectly by casting lights at the ceiling or the floor. Above all, the entire picture should be evenly lighted and not strongly.

Hanging Height from the floor: The larger pictures should all be hung as close to the floor as possible, ideally not more than six inches above it. In the case of the small pictures, they should be somewhat raised but not "skyed" (never hung towards the ceiling). Again this is the way the pictures were painted. If this is not observed, the proportions of the rectangles become distorted and the picture changes.

The exceptions to this are the pictures which are enumerated below which were painted as murals actually to be hung at a greater height. These are:

1. Sketch for Mural, No. 1, 1958
2. Mural Sections 2,3,4,5, and 7, 1958-9
3. White and Black on Wine, 1958

The murals were painted at a height of 4'6" above the floor. If it is not possible to raise them to that extent, any raising above three feet would contribute to their advantage and original effect.

Grouping: In the Museum of Modern Art's exhibition all works from the earliest in the show of 1949 inclusive were hung as a unit, the watercolors separated from the others. The murals were hung as a second unit, all together. The only exception to this grouping of the murals is the picture owned by Mr. Rubin, White and Black on Wine 1958, which could take its place, but with a raised hanging among the other works since it is a transitional piece between the earlier pictures of that year and the mural series. In the remaining works, it is best not to follow a chronological order but to arrange them according to their

best effect upon each other. For instance, in the exhibition at the Museum the very light pictures were grouped together-- yellows, oranges, etc. -- and contributed greatly to the effect produced.

In considering your installation, it might be of interest that with three murals (Mural Section No. 3, 1959 in center, Mural Section No. 5, and Mural Section No. 7, each on flanking walls) were hung in a separate gallery in our Museum. The dimensions of this gallery were 16 1/2' x 20' which Rothko felt were very good proportions and gave an excellent indication of the way in which the murals were intended to function. If a similar room could be devised, it would be highly desirable.

fig. 34 Letter from Rothko to the Whitechapel Gallery, 1961, Whitechapel Gallery Archive, London

1963

In January, Rothko organizes the installation of five of his six murals at Harvard's Holyoke Center (fig. 35). Prior to their final installation, the works are exhibited at the Solomon R. Guggenheim Museum from April 9 to June 2. Rothko signs an exclusive contract with Frank Lloyd of the Marlborough Fine Arts Gallery, whom he meets through Bernard Reis. Rothko sells fifteen paintings to the gallery and gives it exclusive rights to sales in Europe and America for a period of one year.

On August 31, the couple's second child, Christopher Hall, was born.

In late November, Count Panza informs Rothko that financial difficulties mean he will not be able to acquire the five murals from the Seagram series, as originally planned.

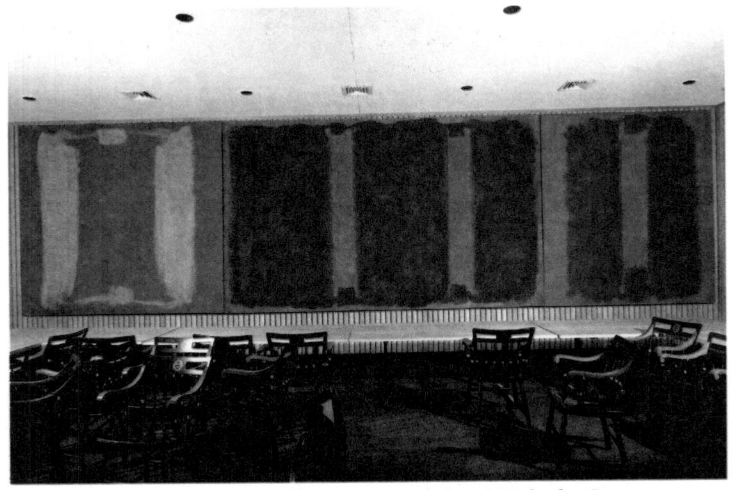

fig. 35 *Harvard Murals* (panel one, two and three) Holyoke Center, 1963, photo James K. Ufford and Michael Nedzweski, Havard University Archives, Cambridge (MA)

1964

Rothko goes to the Phillips Collection again. Duncan Phillips buys another painting, *Ochre, Red on Red*, 1954 (pl. 72), which is added to the Rothko Room.

Rothko's first solo show at the Marlborough Gallery in London takes place in February–March, and notably includes *Blue and Gray*, 1962 (pl. 91) and *Blue, Orange, Red*, 1961 (pl. 90).

On April 17, John and Dominique de Menil return to see Rothko and commission a group of paintings for the future chapel of the University of St. Thomas in Houston (see pp. 285–89).

In the autumn, Rothko rents a new studio at 157 East 69th Street, lit by a domed skylight. He hires William Scharf as his assistant. The two men equip the studio with a pulley system and a parachute-like mechanism to adjust the light; they also erect temporary walls of the same dimensions as the chapel. At that time, the artist has already begun his series called *Blackforms* (pl. 98–101).

1965

On January 7, Rothko delivers a eulogy at the funeral of Milton Avery, who has died four days earlier. He stresses Avery's artistic influence on his own career: "Avery had that inner power in which gentleness and silence proved audible and poignant. … Avery was a great poet-inventor who had invented sonorities never seen nor heard before. From these we have learned much and ill learn more for a long time to come."

Philip Johnson is approached about designing the chapel in Houston, but Rothko disapproves and the job goes to two other architects, Howard Barnstone and Eugene Aubry. In the certainty that this will be his most important work, Rothko entirely devotes himself to the chapel paintings for a year, during which he hires two assistants for the project, Ray Kelly and Roy Edwards.

On March 28, Rothko is awarded the Creative Arts Medal by Brandeis University in Massachusetts.

Norman Reid, director of the Tate Gallery in London, meets with Rothko in October to discuss the possible acquisition of paintings that he wishes to hang together in a specially designated room of the museum.

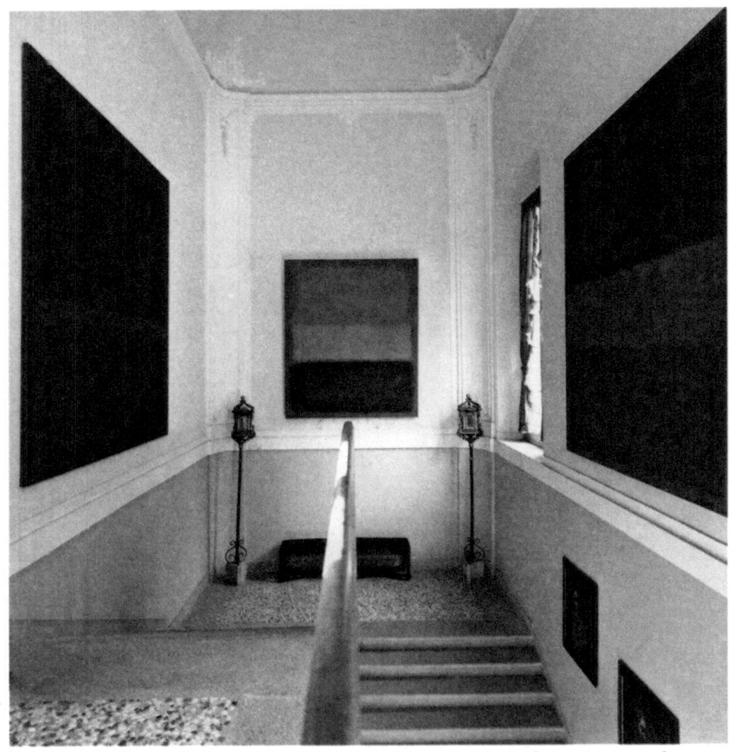

fig. 36 Panza Collection, Villa Litta, Varese, 1966, photo Ugo Mulas, Archivio Mulas, Milan

1966

The Rothkos travel to Europe for the third time, from June to August. They spend time in Lisbon, then in Majorca, before going to Rome, where they stay with Carla Panicalli, director of the Marlborough Gallery in Rome. Accompanied by Bernard and Becky Reis, they visit the Pantheon, the Forum, Hadrian's Villa, Santa Maria Maggiore, the Baths of Diocletian and Caracalla, and Piazza Navona. After Rome, they go to Spoleto to visit Gian Carlo Menotti. They also travel with curator Peter Selz to Assisi in order to admire the Giotto frescoes, and to Arezzo to see Piero della Francesca's cycle of frescoes. They continue their trip to Florence, still in the company of Selz, and Rothko again views the Fra Angelico frescoes in the San Marco monastery, and visit the Uffizi. While on the train to England, Rothko and his daughter decide to stop for a few days in Paris to admire Monet's *Water Lilies* at the Musée de l'Orangerie. They then go to the Netherlands, Belgium, and London, where they see the room in the Tate Gallery allocated to host his own work.

On August 11, the family boards the *Queen Elizabeth* to return to New York.
Rothko is very impressed with the *Turner: Imagination and Reality* show at the Museum of Modern Art.
Three more of his works, including *Green on Blue (Earth-Green and White)*, 1956 (pl. 66), are featured in the Museum of Modern Art's traveling exhibition *Two Decades of American Painting*, which tour Tokyo, Kyoto, New Delhi, Melbourne, and Sydney between October 15, 1966 and August 20, 1967.

1967–1968

In April 1967, Rothko finishes the fourteen paintings and four additional canvases for the Menil chapel.
During the summer, he is invited to teach for a month at the University of California at Berkeley.
Slow Swirl at the Edge of the Sea of 1944 (pl. 32) is included in the *Dada, Surrealism, and their Heritage* show at the Museum of Modern Art, March 27–June 9, 1968 (fig. 37). In the catalogue, curator William Rubin writes, "In *Slow Swirl at the Edge of the Sea* the biomorphism is attenuated by automatic drawing of an elegance comparable to the best of Surrealism at that time."
Following an aortic aneurysm, Rothko is taken to New York Hospital on April 20. After three weeks in the hospital, he returns home. His doctor advises him not to paint pictures more than three feet high.
On May 28, he becoms a member of the National Institute of Arts and Letters.
In July, the Rothkos rent a villa in Provincetown, near the Motherwells. This is a difficult period, marked by growing tension within the couple. Rothko paints works on paper in acrylic and expresses his desire to create works comparable to those he had done in the 1940s.
With the help of Bernard Reis, on September 13 he draws up a new will, which divides his estate between his family and the Mark Rothko Foundation. At the end of November, with the help of his assistants, he begins to make an inventory of his output: Rothko still has nearly eight hundred works in his possession. On the back of each work, the assistants write the dimensions, date, and inventory number. Morton Levine then systematically photographes them for the archives.

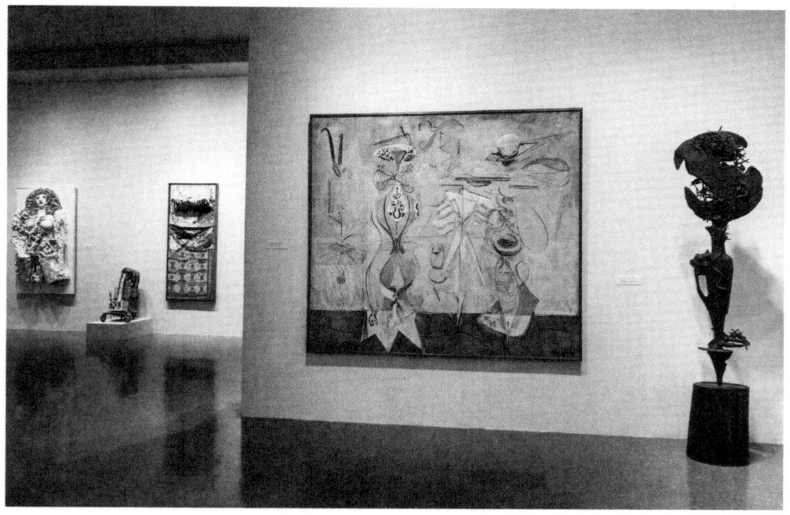

fig. 37 *Slow Swirl at the Edge of the Sea* shown at the exhibition *Dada, Surrealism and their Heritage*, March 27–June 19, 1968, photo James Mathews, MoMA Archives, New York

1969

Rothko leaves Mell on January 1 and moves to his studio on 69th Street.
Norman Reid comes to the studio to help choose the paintings to be donated to the Tate Gallery. In February, Rothko sells another twenty-six paintings and sixty-one works on paper to the Marlborough Gallery. He signs a contract making the gallery his exclusive agent for the next eight years.
In March he begins an affair with Ad Reinhardt's widow, Rita.
In the spring Rothko begins a series of large, dark paintings in shades of gray, black, and brown.
At the same time, he consideres a commission—which never came off—for UNESCO's Paris headquarters, where his paintings would be hung next to a sculpture by Giacometti (see pp. 282–83).
He travels to New Haven to receive an honorary doctorate from Yale University on June 9. Only his cousin Ed Weinstein attends the ceremony.
The Mark Rothko Foundation is incorporated on June 12. Rothko, Morton Feldman, Robert Goldwater, Morton Levine, Bernard Reis, Theodoros Stamos, and Clinton Wilder are named directors. The artist's death will nevertheless lead to a complex legal battle between his family and the executors of his will. The Rothko Foundation and the artist's son finally win the battle fifteen years later, in 1986, distributing over one thousand works to twenty-nine museums in America and abroad. The largest share—a selection of 295 paintings and works on paper, as well as 650 drawings—go to the National Gallery in Washington, D.C., which perpetuates the foundation's loan and exhibition activities.
Rothko still has serious health problems. On September 30, doctors diagnose him with bilateral emphysema. He is subsequently invited to teach at Hunter College, near his studio.

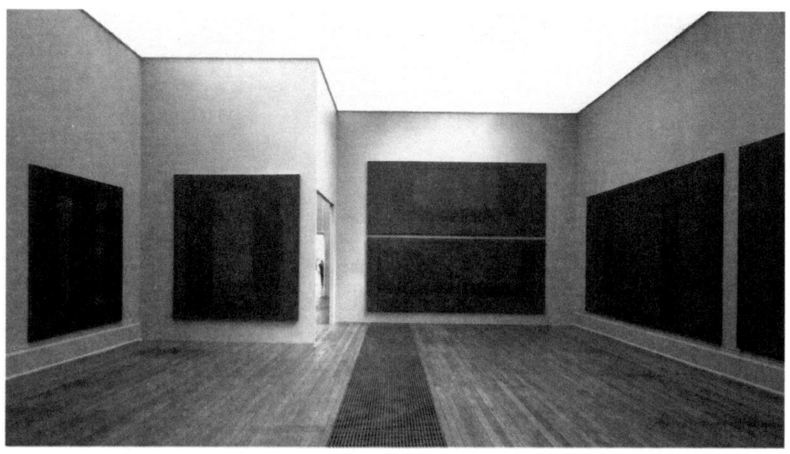

fig. 38 Photograph of Mark Rothko's *Seagram Murals* as first displayed in Tate Gallery, 1970, Tate Archives

In early November, Reid begins working with Rothko on a model of the proposed room in the Tate. Together they choose a set of murals from the second and third *Seagram series*. After the gift of his first mural in 1968, the artist donates eight more murals from this series to the Tate.

In December, Rothko held a reception in his studio to gather opinions on his new *Black and Grays* paintings from a small group of trusted professionals, including Brian O'Doherty and Bernard Reis.

1970

Rothko makes an appointment on February 25 with Donald McKinney, vice-president of the Marlborough Gallery, to discuss the terms of a new contract. In the early hours of the morning, he commits suicide. He is buried on February 28 at North Shore, Long Island.

On May 29, the Tate Gallery inaugurates its Rothko Room, hung according to the artist's instructions (fig. 38).

Over the summer, the Marlborough Gallery organizes a solo show at Ca' Pesaro in Venice as a tribute to the deceased artist.

1971

On February 27, the Rothko Chapel in Houston is consecrated as a place of interfaith worship.

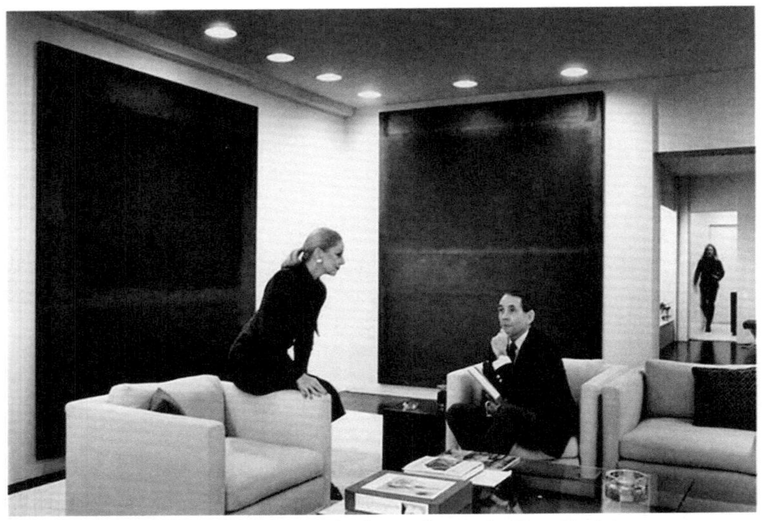

fig. 39 Donald and Vera Blinken at home in New York in 1978. The display was suggested and installed by Rothko

Facing page
Portrait of Mark Rothko, The Rothko Family Archive

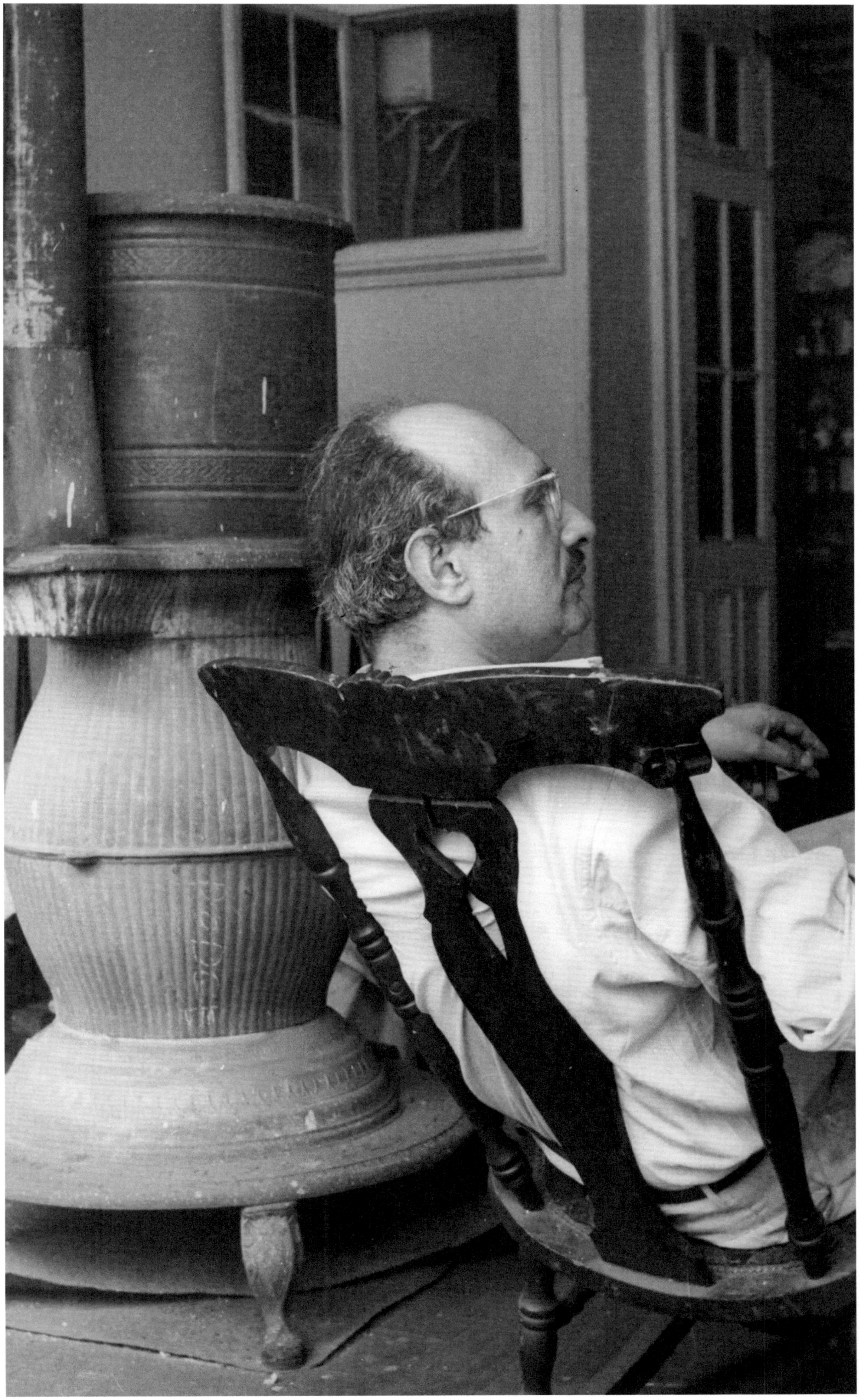

*The Rothko Room in the Phillips Collection**

Cordélia de Brosses

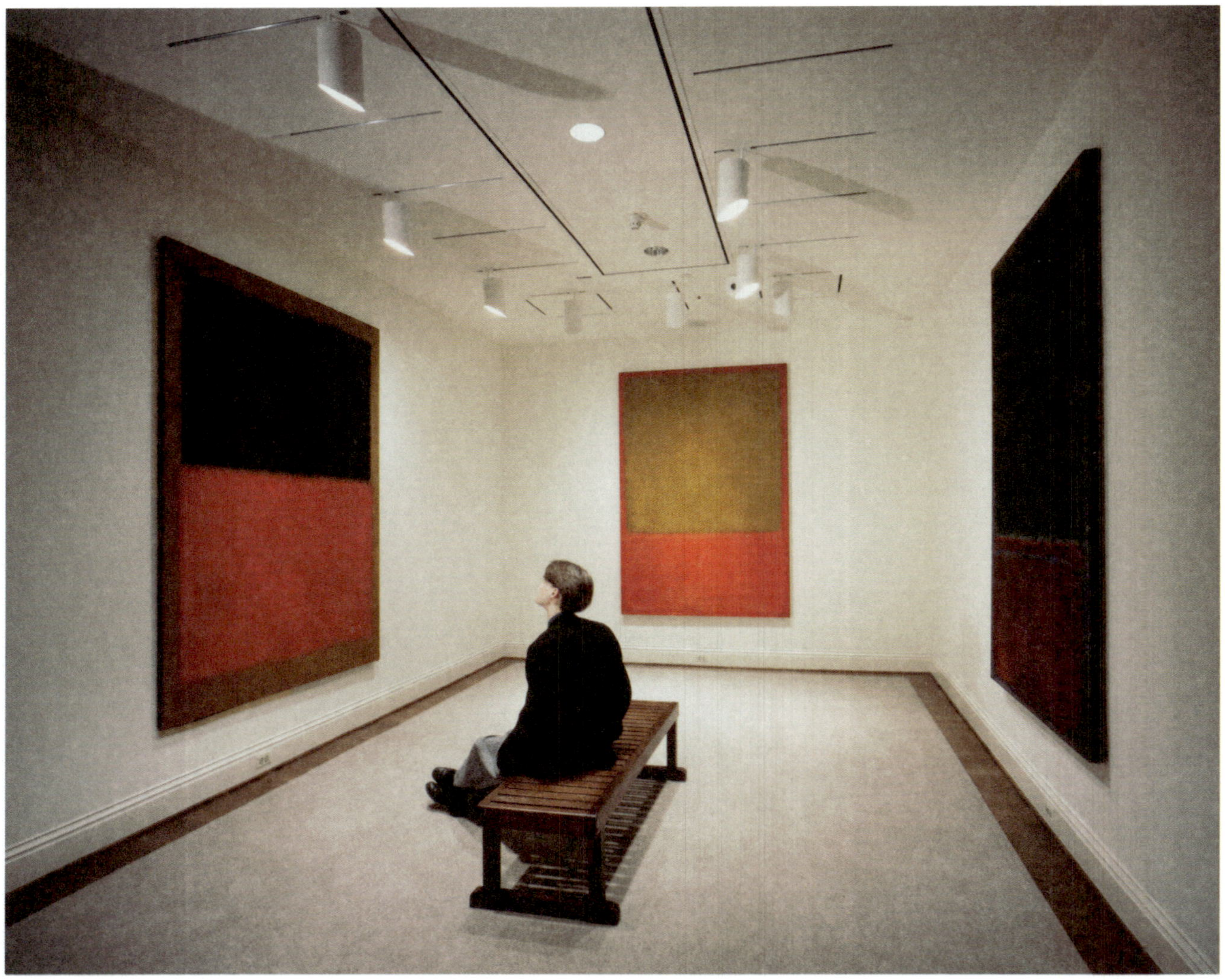

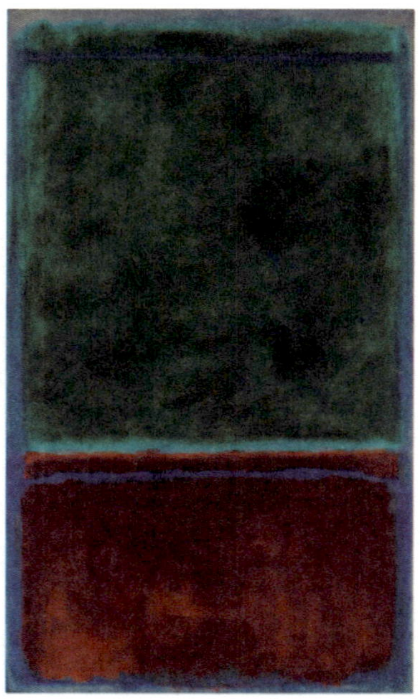

fig. 1 The Rothko Room in the new wing of the Phillips Collection, 1989, Lautman Photography, The Phillips Collection, Washington, D.C.
fig. 2 *Green and Maroon*, 1953, oil on canvas, 91 ⅛ × 54 ⅞ in., The Phillips Collection, Washington, D.C. (CR 491)

"I have been told that Mr. Rothko does not like to combine his work with any other painter."[1] Right from 1956 American collector Duncan Phillips noted the artist's wish to exhibit his paintings in a separate space. For a group show that same year, Phillips devoted an entire room to Rothko's work. In May 1960 he organized a solo exhibition of the artist's oeuvre and, six months later, inaugurated the "Rothko Room," the first one to be installed in a museum[2] and the only one open to the public during Rothko's lifetime.[3] This room was part of an extension to the American collector's growing collection in a new building in Washington, D.C. (fig. 1)[4] The narrow room, 13½ by 24 feet,[5] had gray walls and in 1960 held three large "intimate and intense"[6] paintings from the 1950s, the so-called Classic years, characterized by vibrant colors and a sfumato effect from which two distinct rectangles emerge. Each canvas, hung low, occupied one whole wall: *Orange and Red on Red* (1957; pl. 70) to the east, *Green and Tangerine on Red* (1956; pl. 71) to the south, and *Green and Maroon* (1953; fig. 2) to the north. The saturating effect of the works, in a space that Phillips compared to a chapel,[7] produced an impression of physical and spiritual immersion. Faced with a picture, the beholder experienced contrasting emotions: "What we recall are not memories but old emotions disturbed or resolved—some sense of well-being suddenly shadowed by a cloud—yellow ochres strangely suffused with a drift of gray prevailing over an ambience of rose."[8]

Rothko first saw this room on a trip to Washington for the inauguration of President John F. Kennedy in 1961. He suggested that the chairs be replaced by a wooden bench and that the lighting be dimmed in order to reinforce the immersive aspect of the whole. In 1966 another Rothko painting was added, *Ochre, Red on Red* (1954; pl. 72), placed on a wall opposite the west-facing window, in a configuration approved by Duncan Phillips.

According to the principles of hanging set out by Rothko in 1954, this room placed the beholder within the composition:

> *"Since my pictures are large, colorful and unframed, and since museum walls are usually immense and formidable, there is the danger that the pictures relate themselves as decorative areas to the walls. This would be a distortion of their meaning, since the pictures are intimate and intense, and are the opposite of what is decorative; and have been painted in a scale of normal living rather than an institutional scale....*[9] *By saturating the room with the feeling of the work, the walls are defeated and the poignancy of each single work had for me become more visible. I also hang the largest pictures ... so that the first experience is to be within the picture."*[10]

Opened in 1960, the Rothko Room would thereafter serve as a model, notably for the hanging of the major Rothko exhibition at MoMA in 1961[11] (fig. 3).

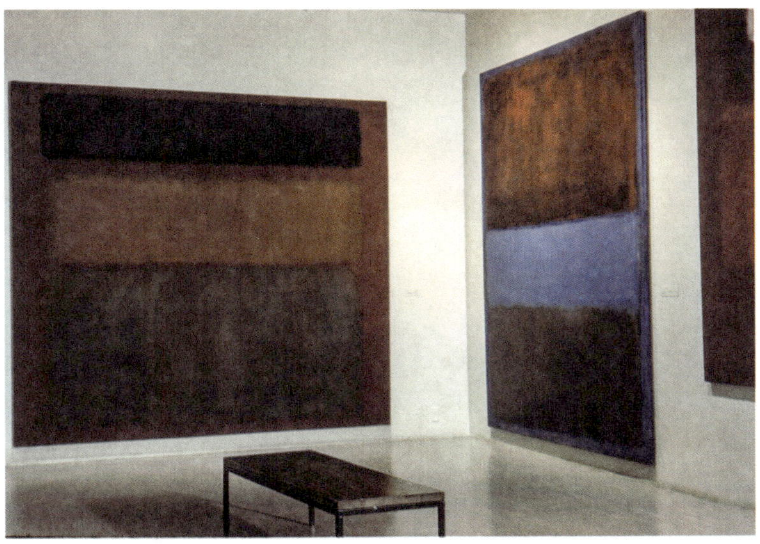

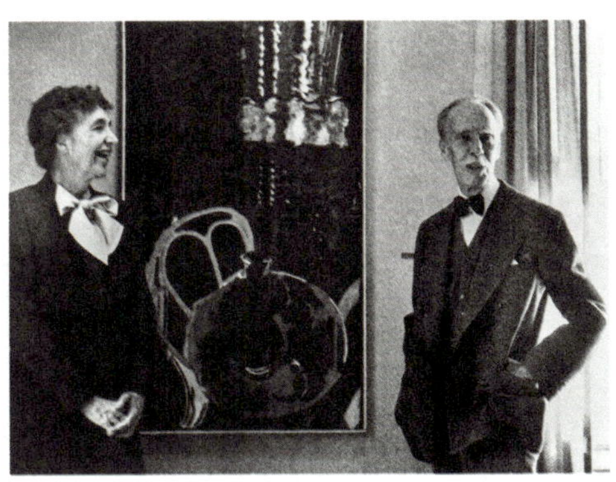

fig. 3 View of the MoMA show, 1961, following the example of the Rothko Room in the Phillips Collection, The MoMA Archive, New York
fig. 4 Marjorie and Duncan Phillips stand with Georges Braque's The *Philodendron*, 1954, photo Naomi Savage, The Phillips Collection Archives, Washington, D.C.

* The "Phillips Collection" in Washington, D.C., has changed names several time since it was founded in 1921. First called the "Phillips Memorial Art Gallery," and later the "Phillips Gallery" when it acquired its first paintings by Rothko, it took the name "Phillips Collection" in 1961, the year that Rothko saw his works installed in the museum in a permanent way. The commemorative nature of the original name is explained by the fact that Duncan Phillips founded the museum not long after the passing of his father in 1917 and the sudden death of his brother from Spanish flu in 1918.

1 Letter from Duncan Phillips to Sidney Janis, November 19, 1956. Phillips Collection archives.

2 For his show at the Sidney Janis Gallery in 1955, Rothko arranged a perfectly configured room, which probably served as inspiration for the Phillips Collection's Rothko Room, with its close hanging of large paintings the same size as the walls, under soft lighting.

3 Right from the founding of the museum, Phillips collected groups of works by artists he especially liked. He called these groups "Units." He therefore also referred to the Rothko Room as the "Rothko Unit."

4 Phillips also bought another work by Rothko, *Mauve Intersection* (1949), which was not included in the Rothko Room. It would be lent to the Museum of Modern Art in New York for the Rothko retrospective in 1961.

5 Phillip Kennicott, "Two Rooms, 14 Rothkos and a World of Difference," *The Washington Post*, January 20, 2017.

6 Letter from Mark Rothko to Katharine Kuh, September 25, 1954, courtesy the Art Institute of Chicago Archives, excerpted in a National Gallery of Art Press Release, January 2, 1998, https://www.nga.gov/content/dam/ngaweb/research/gallery-archives/PressReleases/1999-1990/1998/14A11_45099_19980102.pdf, accessed May 2023.

7 Arthur Hall Smith, personal communication to Susan Barnes, quoted in Susan E. Barnes, *The Rothko Chapel: An Act of Faith* (Houston and Austin: University of Texas Press, 1996), p. 37.

8 Duncan Phillips quoted on the Phillips Collection's page dedicated to "The Rothko Room": www.phillipscollection.org/curation/rothko-room.

9 The importance of scale, stressed by Rothko, also figured in Duncan Phillips's plan for a new approach to space. "We plan to try the effect of domestic architecture, of rooms small or at least livable." Quoted by Robert Hughes, "Art and Intimacy," in Erika D. Passatino (ed.), *The Eye of Duncan Phillips: A Collection in the Making* (New Haven and London: Yale University Press, 1999), p. 2.

10 Letter from Rothko to Kuh, September 25, 1954.

11 Peter Selz, November 1989, personal communication to Susan Barnes, quoted in Barnes, *The Rothko Chapel*, p. 38. In 2006 the paintings were moved to a new room on the second floor of the Sant Building, while retaining the same dimensions and same east–west orientation as originally devised in 1960.

The Seagram Murals

Magdalena Gemra

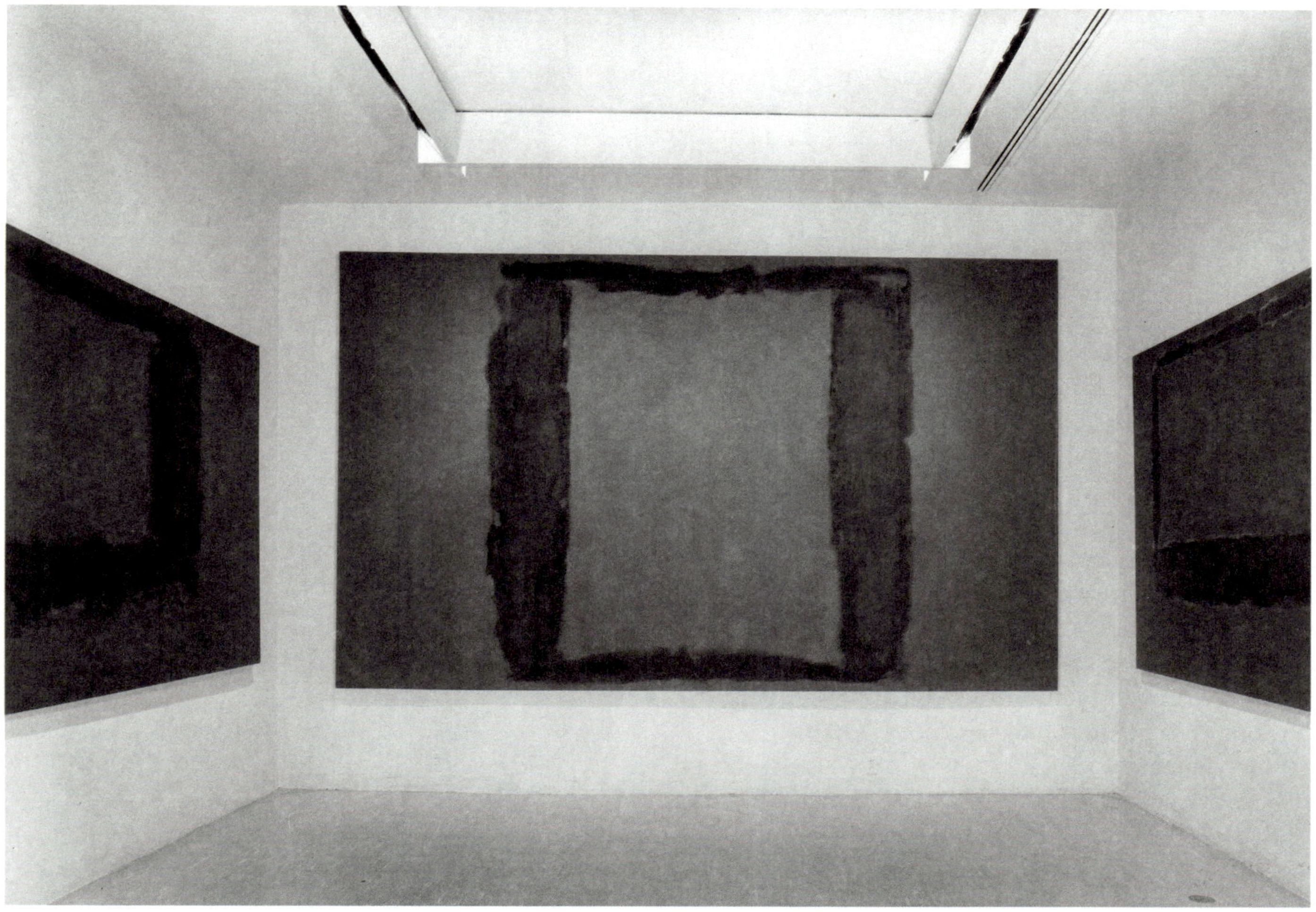

"They are not pictures."[1]

"The drive to be a public man—universal drive for a community
The solitude unmitigated by success, rather sharpened
The ideal situation of a commission
Neither the place nor the pictures yet exist.
The self-deception that drives the project to conclusion
in the hope of a miracle that the two can coincide."[2]

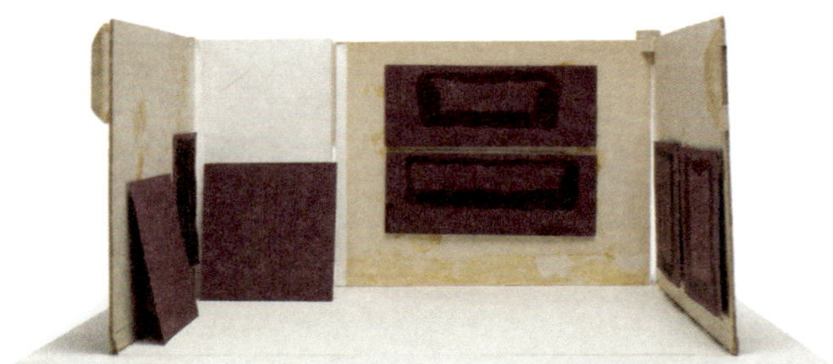

fig. 1 Exhibition view of the retrospective at MoMA, 1961.
fig. 2 Maquette for the first installation of Mark Rothko's *Seagram Murals* at the Tate Gallery, 1970. The cardboard model was sent by Tate to the artist, who prepared paintings that matched its scale.

In June 1958, Mark Rothko received a commission to paint a series of murals for the smaller of two dining rooms of the Four Seasons restaurant, on the ground floor of the Seagram Building, Mies van der Rohe's landmark skyscraper on Park Avenue in New York. The artist accepted the offer because it provided him with a permanent setting for a group of paintings. Although other *Seagram* panels exist, this set—now in Tate Modern in London—has a special authenticity because it was hand-picked by Rothko to create in a specific gallery of the museum a powerfully enveloping space conducive to meditation, one where he sought to attain what he called "the greatest eloquence and poignancy."[3]

The commission was a joint initiative by Philip Johnson, the architect responsible for the interior design of the building, and Phyllis Lambert, heiress to the Seagram & Sons, Inc. corporation.[4] The ambiguity of the historical record behind the commission—notably what Rothko knew of the future use of the room, and when he learned it—is further enhanced by the open quality of the ensemble. Whether Rothko understood that the room in which his works were to hang would be part of the Four Seasons restaurant, frequented by New York's high society, or whether he could reasonably have believed it was to be a meeting room open towards a staff cafeteria, he embarked on the task enthusiastically.[5] He rented a new, large studio—a former gym at 222 Bowery Street—where with help of an assistant he erected scaffolding approximately the size of the dining room, roughly 55 by 25 feet. In a matter of months, he produced three sets of large paintings, numbering some thirty canvases.[6] A final selection of paintings for the Four Seasons never seems to have been made, as witnessed by the varying sets exhibited in the subsequent decade.[7]

The upshot was an unified set where each painting contributes to the shared goal of a "darkly luminous frieze"[8] in which the bright high-keyed colors of Rothko's earlier works gave way to deep reds, crimsons, and maroons.[9] Obtained by layering many coats of translucent or opaque paint in overlapping sections, shiny reds seem to expand while mat reds recede into space in subtle spatial gradations. Although an impression of floating remained, it was henceforth the "frame", and not the background, that appeared to move. In addition, Rothko modified his compositional approach, going from a closed form to an open one that suggested a window or portal—a feature perhaps related to the architectural setting, since the paintings were to have been hung high enough to be seen behind seated people. This introduced a new requirement when seeking to connect with the beholder, for the paintings were now perceived as part of the architecture. Rothko acknowledged an artistic kinship with Michelangelo's Laurentian Library, as well as Fra Angelico's frescoes seen at the monastery of San Marco in Florence in 1950. He confessed his admiration for those spaces steeped in a cloistered atmosphere of silent meditation.[10]

In June 1959, the artist sailed to Europe with his family and visited Italy for the second time. On returning to New York, he famously dined with his wife at the Four Seasons. In December 1959, convinced that a restaurant was not the right setting for his work, Rothko withdrew from the commission, returned the money, and kept the paintings.[11] "The decision was easy and inevitable. What is depressing is the thought that there is really no real place for them. Where in this world are the edifices which share the motives from which our pictures are painted?"[12]

Shortly before he died, following many years of negotiations with Norman Reid, director of the Tate Gallery, Rothko donated nine of these panels to the Tate. He had been particularly impressed by the gallery's collection of works by J. M. W. Turner, having been marked by MoMA's 1966 exhibition.[13] Although only seven paintings would have fit into the restaurant, the number donated to the Tate was dictated by the size of the room chosen to host them.[14] The gift was accompanied by specific instructions: the paintings must be exhibited in the same room, must be shown together (even if some of them could be put aside), and must never be sold.[15] The works arrived at the Tate the day Rothko died, and are hung in the Rothko Room.

Although Rothko's concern for the display space was already evident in the way he had hung his shows since the early 1950s, the paintings known as the *Seagram Murals* constituted his very first pictorial environment and the first corpus of works conceived as a series. It was his first attempt to create an environment by merging painting with architecture, and in this respect these works represent a turning point in his career.[16]

1 Mark Rothko, quoted in Dore Ashton, *About Rothko* (Cambridge, MA: Da Capo Press, 2013), p. 155.

2 Untitled manuscript, The Rothko Family Archive. Published by Oliver Wick in the exhibition catalogue, *Mark Rothko* (Rome: Palazzo delle Esposizioni, 2007).

3 Letter from Mark Rothko to Norman Reid, September 4, 1966, Tate Archive. I am grateful to Katy Wan, assistant curator at Tate Modern, for providing access to their archives.

4 According to Phyllis Lambert, "Philip [Johnson] used powerful theatrical effects to interiorize the dramatic exterior substance of Mies's building." Phyllis Lambert, *Building Seagram* (New Haven and London: Yale University Press, 2013), p. 123. One effect involved placing the room in which Rothko's works were to hang above the main room—called the Pool Room—on a mezzanine framed by a screen that suggested a kind of proscenium, as Dore Ashton notably pointed out.

5 According to people close to him, Rothko thought that the smaller room would be a meeting room, and the larger one would be a cafeteria for employees. See Ashton, *About Rothko*, p. 154, and Dan Rice, interviewed by Arne Glimcher on September 22, 1978, in *Mark Rothko—The 1958–59 Murals: Second Series*, exh. cat. (New York: Pace Gallery, 1978). Yet according to Phyllis Lambert, Rothko "absolutely knew it was a restaurant" (letter from Phyllis Lambert to Philip Johnson, April 27, 1972, Tate Archive), as confirmed by Johnson in another letter (Philip Johnson to Ronald Alley, February 25, 1970, Tate Archive), which was annotated, "the news of Rothko's suicide arrived today! I really feel an enormous loss."

6 See David Anfam, *Mark Rothko: Works on Canvas, Catalogue Raisonné* (New Haven and London: Yale University Press, 1998), cats. 634–63. The fact that Rothko painted three successive series has been confirmed by many sources, including a letter from Norman Reid to Oliver Wick on August 20, 1988 (Tate Archive). It seems that the very first painting was *No. 9 (White and Black on Wine)*, 1958 (ref. 616). Other major groups from the series are now in the collections of the National Gallery of Art, Washington, D.C., and the Kawamura Memorial Museum of Art, Chiba-Ken, Japan.

7 Rothko exhibited a selection of five of these panels for the first time at this MoMA retrospective in 1961. A modified version of that show then traveled, notably to the Whitechapel Gallery in London, the Stedelijk Museum in Amsterdam, the Palais des Beaux-Arts in Brussels, the Kunsthalle in Basel, the Galleria Nazionale d'Arte Moderna in Rome, and the Musée d'Art Moderne de la Ville de Paris.

8 Werner Haftman, *Mark Rothko*, exh. cat. (Zürich: Kunsthaus, 1971), p. ix.

9 An important source of inspiration for these colors may have been frescoes from Pompeii seen at the Metropolitan Museum. Rothko's palette darkened from 1957 onwards through the introduction of blacks, deep reds, and dark greens, as confirmed by a letter Rothko wrote on February 1, 1960 to Ronald Alley at the Tate.

10 Rothko wrote, "The question of the dining room was always appealing to me for I immediately envisioned the refectory of the San Marco with the wall painting by Fra Angelico… When the project was achieved I realised that I had never forgotten M.A. [Michelangelo's] room which contained the stairway leading to the Lorenzo Library wherein the false bricked-in windows toward the top of the unrelieved brick walls made an interior world wholly pervasive and awesome." Quoted in Wick, *Mark Rothko.*

11 The day after the dinner, Rothko said to his assistant, "Anybody who will eat that kind of food for those kinds of prices will never look at a painting of mine." Dan Rice interviewed by Arne Glimcher, September 22, 1978, published in *Mark Rothko—The 1958–59 Murals: Second Series,* exh. cat. (New York: Pace Gallery, 1978).

12 Letter from Mark Rothko to William Scott, December 14, 1959. William Scott Archives.

13 During his second trip to Europe, Rothko considered buying a medieval chapel at Lelant, two miles from St. Ives in Cornwall, to turn it into his personal museum. See Annie Cohen-Solal, "Entre gratte-ciel de luxe et chapelle médiévale, premier ancrage britannique, 1958–1960," *Mark Rothko* (Arles: Actes Sud, 2013), pp. 203–04.

14 Letter from Norman Reid to Oliver Wick, in Wick, *Mark Rothko.*

15 Letter from Mark Rothko to the Tate, November 7, 1969. Tate Archive.

16 Rothko described space as follows in notes written between 1940 and 1941: "It constitutes the most comprehensive statement of faith, an *a priori* unity, to which all of the plastic elements are in a state of subservience." Mark Rothko, *The Artist's Reality: Philosophies of Art,* ed. Christopher Rothko (New Haven and London: Yale University Press, 2004), p. 59. Among the exhibitions of the 1950s, it is worth mentioning *Fifteen Americans* (New York: MoMA, 1952) and the 1954 show at the Art Institute of Chicago, as well as solo shows at the Sidney Janis Gallery, New York, in 1955 and 1957.

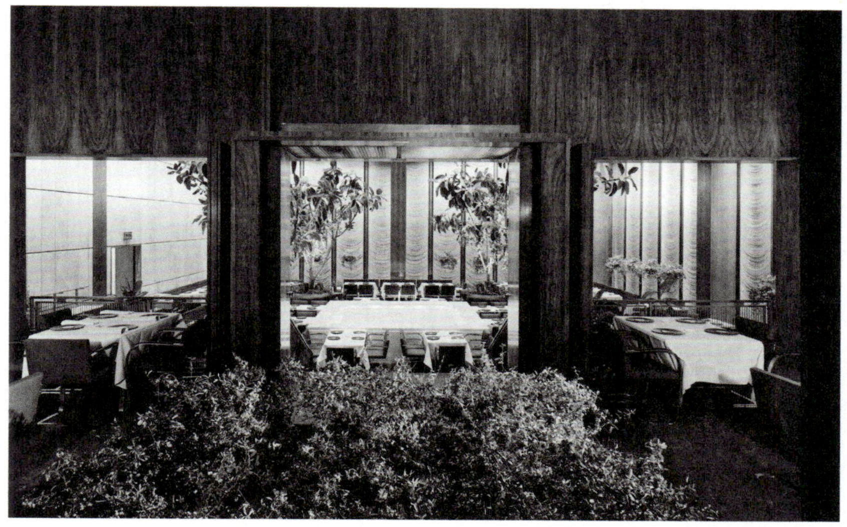

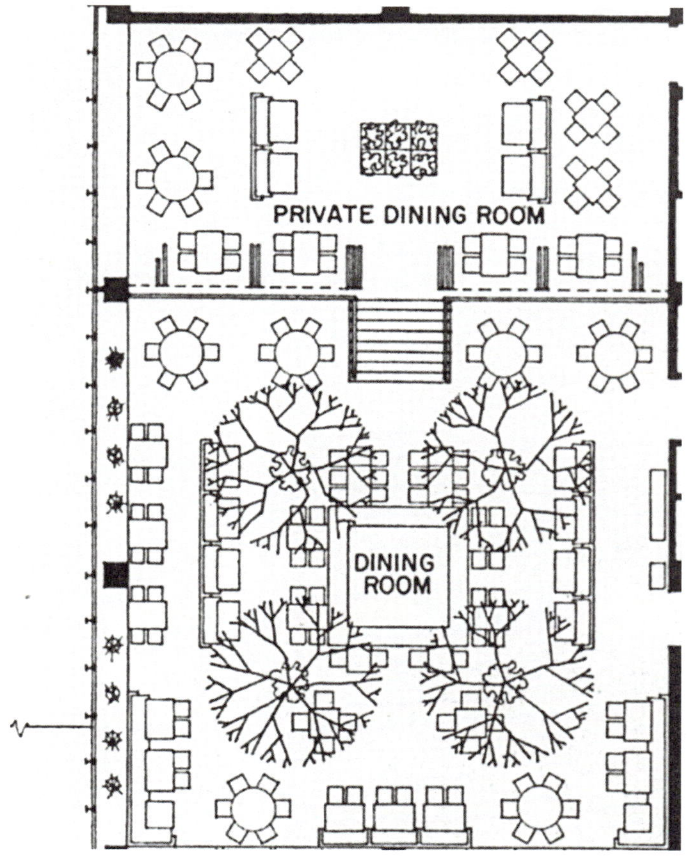

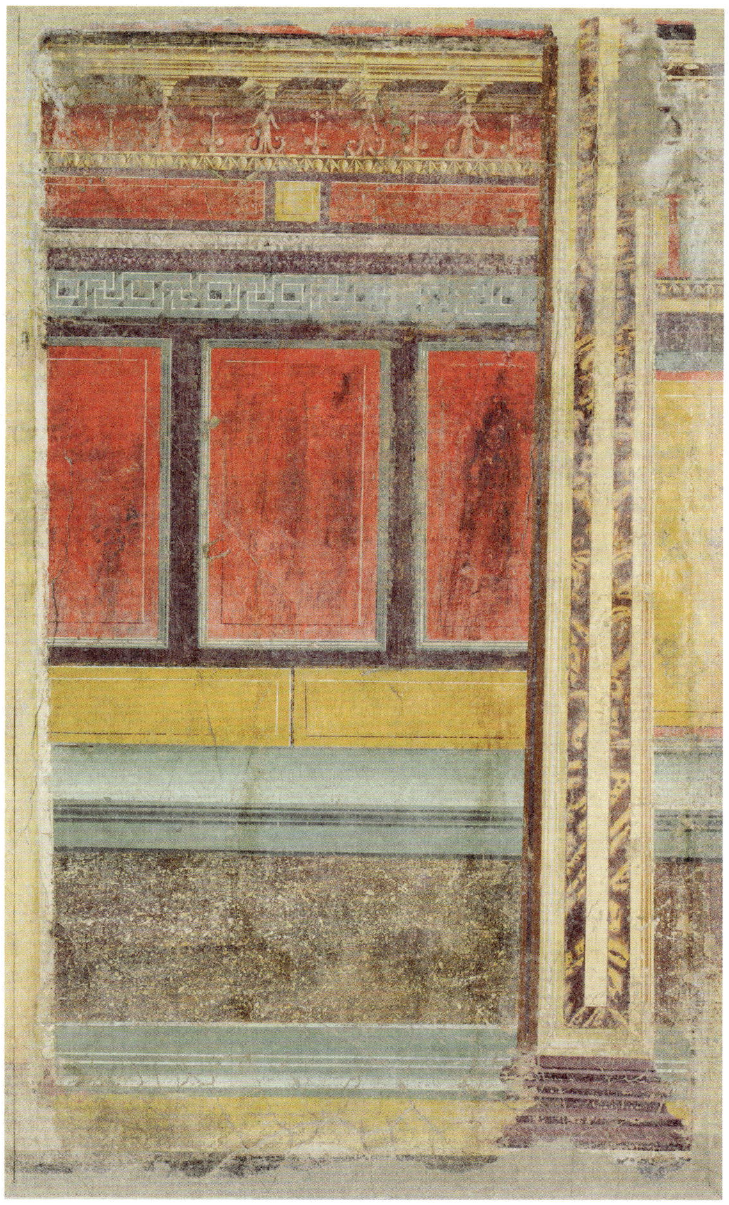

Following double-spread page
Rothko Room, Tate's *Seagram Murals* display, Tate Modern, c. 2008

fig. 3 An important source of inspiration for the colors may have been frescoes from Pompeii seen at the Metropolitan Museum, and then in situ in 1959. Wall painting from Room F of the Villa of P. Fannius Synistor at Boscoreale, c. 50–40 BC, 193.04 × 113.7 cm, The Metropolitan Museum, New York

fig. 4 View from the smaller dining room given to Rothko towards the Pool Room. Rothko's paintings were supposed to be hung above the doorways. The smaller room was placed on a mezzanine framed by a screen that suggested a kind of proscenium, one of the theatrical effects used by Philip Johnson to interiorize the dramatic exterior substance of Mies van der Rohe's building. Ezra Stoller, View of the Four Seasons Restaurant, 1958, Canadian Center For Architecture, Montreal

fig. 5 Philip Johnson, Plan of the Four Seasons Restaurant, Seagram Building, New York, published in *More Elegance at the House of Seagram*, Architectural Record 126, no. 5, November 1959, McGill University, Blackader-Lauterman Library of Art and Architecture, Montreal

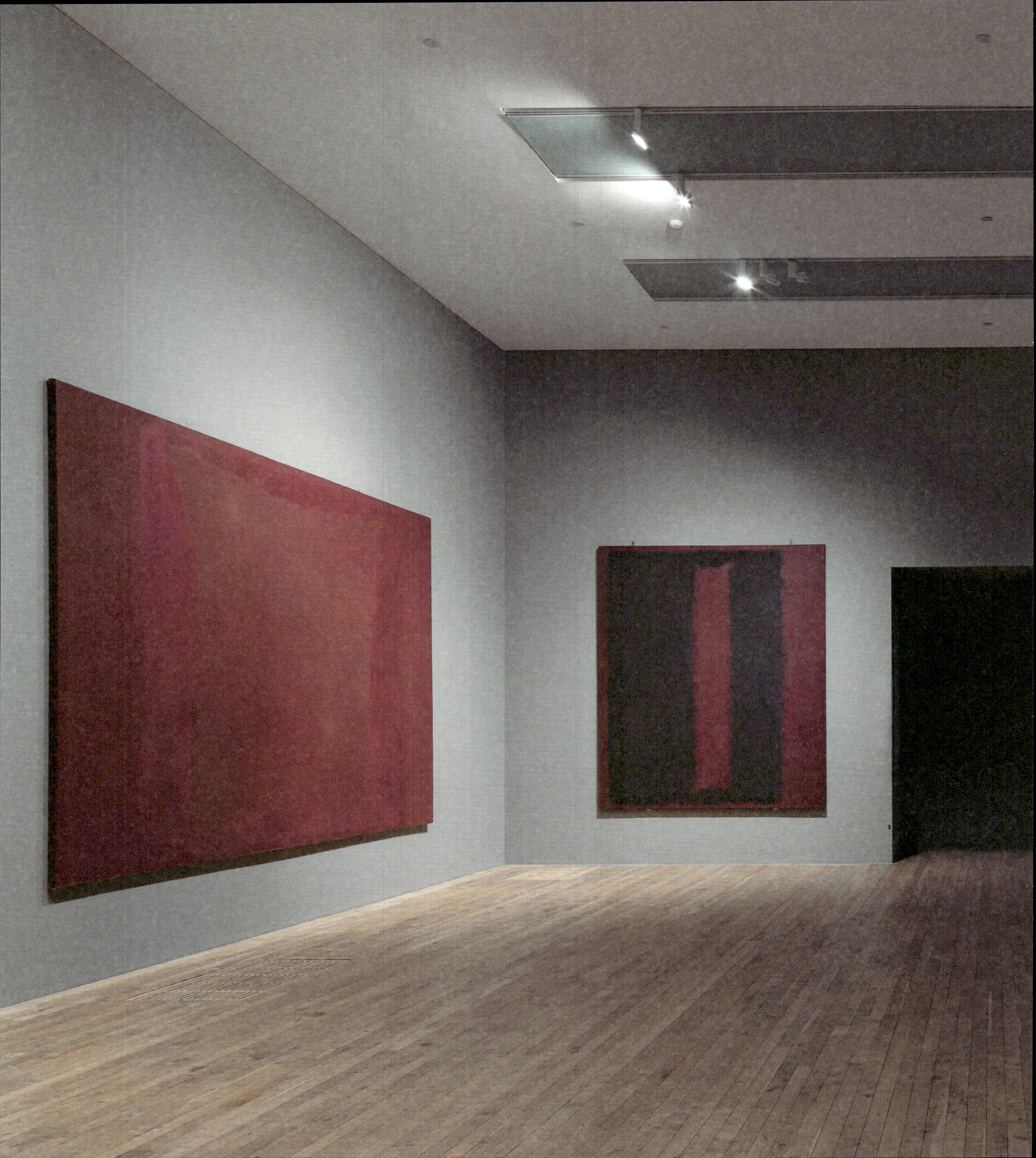

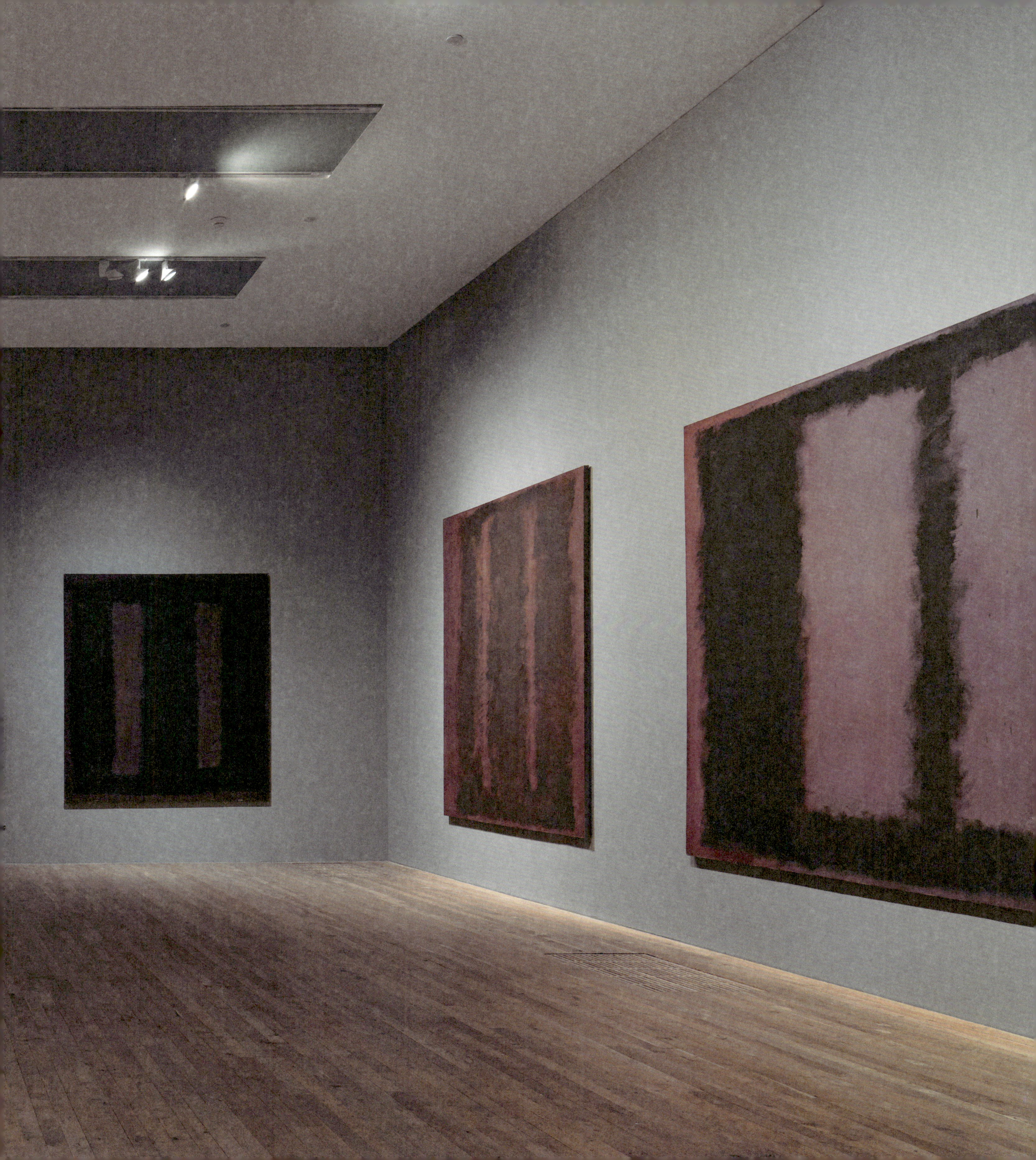

The UNESCO Commission's Project

Claudia Buizza

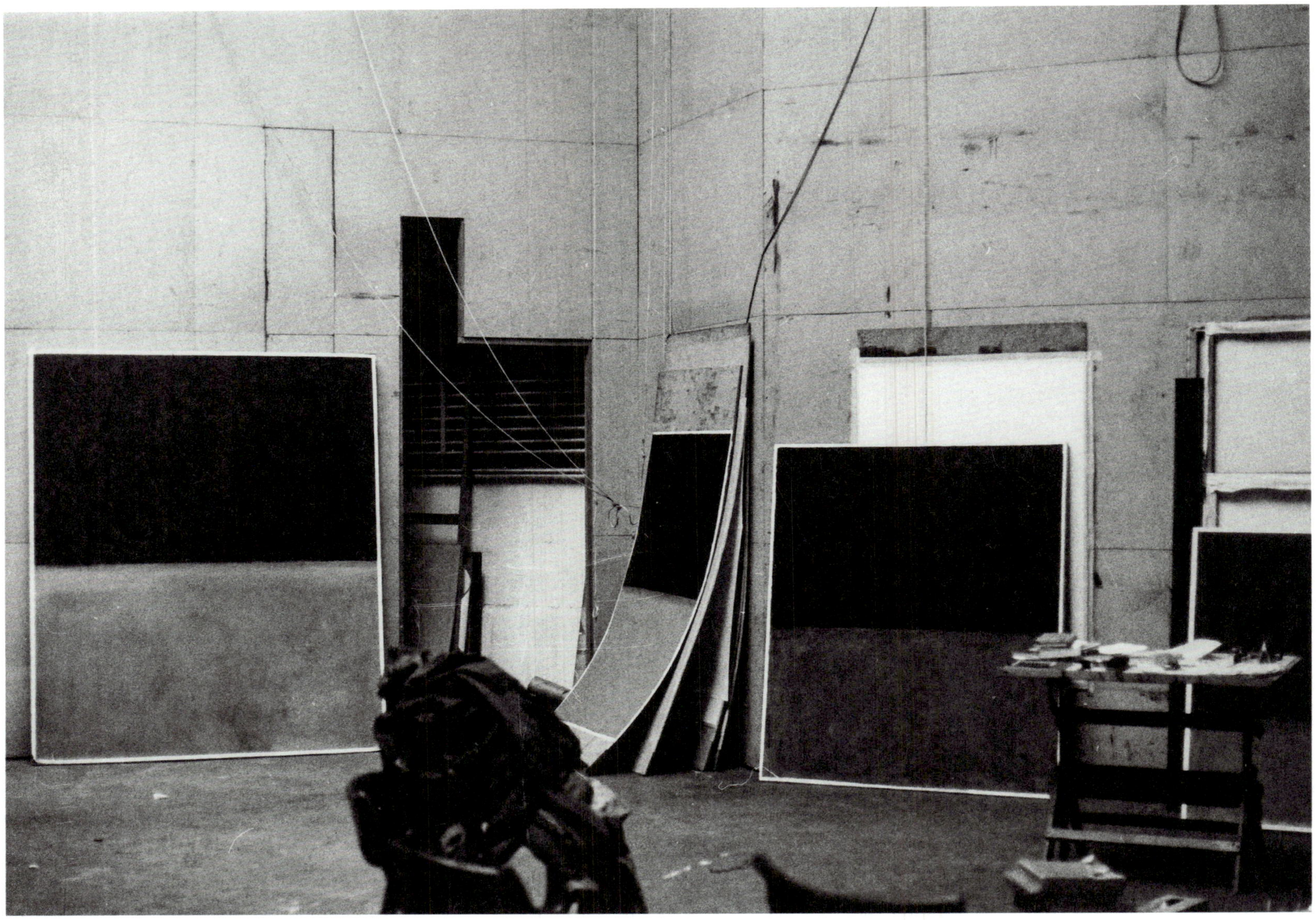

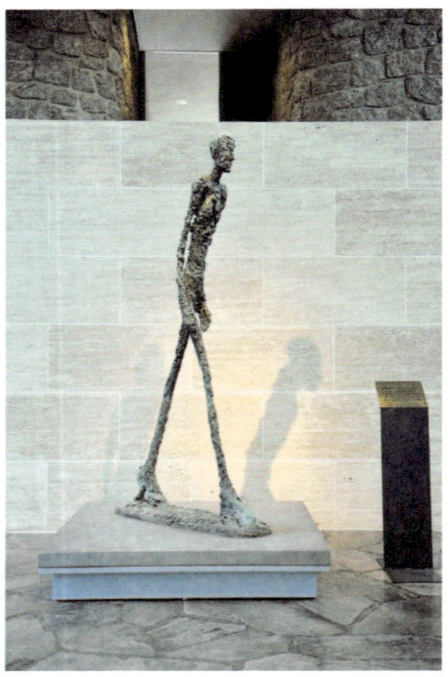

In late March 1969, Franz Meyer, the rapporteur for UNESCO's Committee of Art Advisers,[1] communicated an invitation to Mark Rothko to execute a work for a new building then being erected in Paris. The announcement was made over the telephone to Bernard Reis, Rothko's representative at the Marlborough Gallery in New York. There are few written traces of the proposal, which never came to fruition. The minutes of the meetings of the UNESCO committee and writings published by Robert Motherwell provide the only evidence on which the story of this never-executed commission can be based.

Following its meetings of March 25 and 26, 1967, the Committee of Art Advisors decided to commission "a large mural measuring roughly 30 sq. m. [to] cover the east wall of the bar. The work should be visible from three levels, including the large entrance hall... The Committee felt that work of this kind ought to be entrusted to one of the American artists who were used to handling large areas, and it recommended in order of preference; [Mark] Rothko, [Kenneth] Noland, [Robert] Indiana, [Ellsworth] Kelly."[2] The invitation to Rothko was ultimately issued two years later. Robert Motherwell reported Rothko's first reactions and ideas during a conversation on April 21, 1969:

> *"[W]hen I asked him about his present work, he told me that the UNESCO Headquarters in Paris were in touch with him about doing a room there which would also contain sculpture by Giacometti. When I asked him about how*

fig. 1 Morton Levine, Mark Rothko studio, 157 East 69th Street, New York, beginning March 1970, Dedalus Foundation, New York
fig. 2 Alberto Giacometti, *Walking Man I*, 1960, bronze, 70 ½ × 40 ¾ × 16 ⅜ in., UNESCO Archives, Paris

big the room was, he said it was not very large, maybe 28 by 20 feet, or something like that. Then he said that in any case, if he accepted the commission, it would be unlikely that he would make a single picture to cover the whole wall. . . . Then he mentioned, forgetting for the moment that he had shown them to me in his studio, that he had started a new series of paintings, "a different world from myself," that were partially inspired by the notion of having his paintings in a room with work by Giacometti, whom he obviously respects."[3]

At the time he spoke with Motherwell, Rothko had not yet received detailed documentation from architect Bernard Zehrfuss. He did not yet know that the configuration of the room entailed three different points of view that would prevent a global vision of the work, or that the lighting conditions were conflicting.[4] Nor was he informed that the entrance hall was expected to host two large wall installations by Jesus Rafael Soto, nor that Giacometti's sculpture would not be placed in the same room. It was nevertheless clear, according to the minutes of the meetings of March 20 and 21, 1969, that his mural would be visible through the window of the patio, "where the Giacometti sculpture might be set up." Rothko, who always paid close attention to the context of the display of his work, seems to have taken this information on board. According to Motherwell, Giacometti's presence might even have influenced the chromatic development of Rothko's recent series of *Black and Gray* paintings. "I was struck that they were grayish and brownish combined, rather than the extraordinarily personal hues that he usually used, indeed not unlike the colors that Giacometti himself uses in his own figure paintings."[5]

Nothing is known of subsequent discussions between Rothko, Reis, and UNESCO until the contacts made on June 23 and July 3, 1969, as reported in the minutes of those meetings. "As no reply had been forthcoming from Rothko, the Committee decided to make an immediate telephone call to the artist who was at that moment in New York. During this telephone conversation with Mr. F. Meyer, Rothko expressed regret at his inability, for health reasons, to execute this mural decoration."

Indeed, Rothko had been weakened by effects of an aneurysm diagnosed in the spring of 1968. On the advice of his doctor, in subsequent months he was restricted to painting watercolors less than three feet high. However, given the divergences between the conditions of the commission and Rothko's intentions as conveyed to Motherwell, it might be thought that, in addition to his health, other reasons were behind his withdrawal. Since the *sine qua non* of UNESCO's commission was the execution of a large painting on a single panel—rather than several, as Rothko wished—the artist's reversal of opinion may have been influenced by the inflexibility of that condition. Furthermore, Rothko probably knew which work by Giacometti was being solicited. The minutes for the meetings of March 20 and 21, 1969 record the committee's preference for a cast of a standing female figure some eight feet tall.[6] The impossibility of creating his own pictorial environment around a Giacometti sculpture might have influenced Rothko's decision. Following Rothko's withdrawal, the committee offered the commission to Ellsworth Kelly. In May 1970 the work made by Kelly, *Blue Green* (1969), was hung on the wall of the cafeteria, where it can still be seen today.[7]

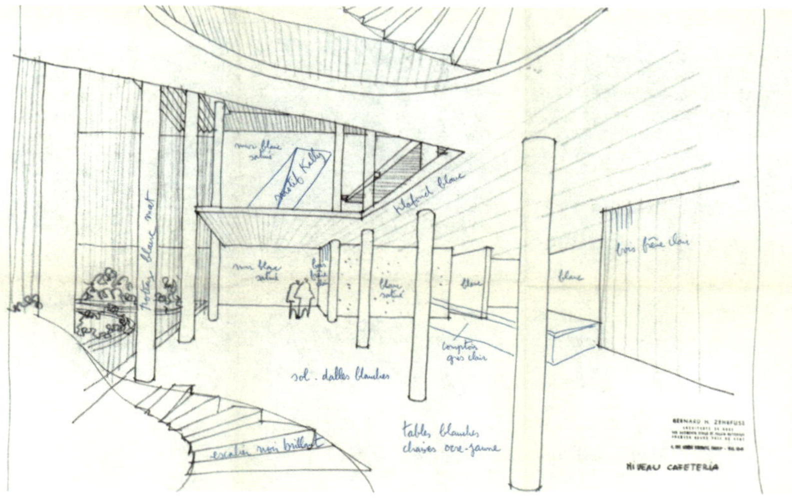

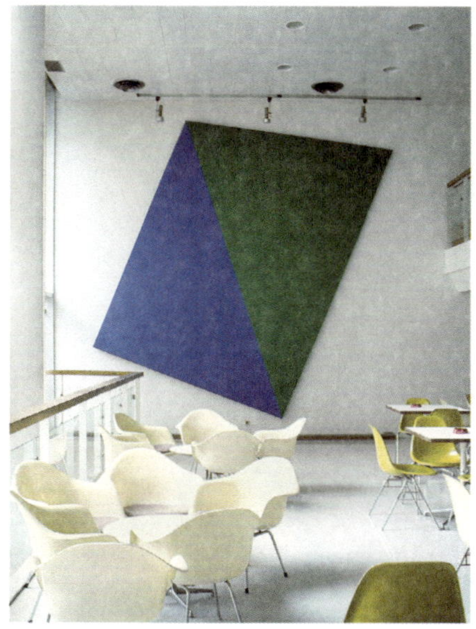

fig. 3 Drawing of Ellsworth Kelly's project for the UNESCO commission, Ellsworth Kelly Foundation, Courtesy Matthew Marks Gallery

fig. 4 Ellsworth Kelly, *Blue Green,* 1969, oil on canvas, 464.8 × 457.2 cm, Ellswoth Kelly Foundation, Courtesy Matthew Marks Gallery, Paris

1 The committee was chaired by Roland Penrose, with Jean Leymarie as vice-chair and Franz Meyer as rapporteur. Members included Bernard Zehrfuss (architect), Lourival Gomes Machado (head of the culture sector), and Yves Leguen (head of general services). The secretariat was handled by René Laheu (director-general), Ralph Skenazi (head of the procurement division), Michel Conil-Lacoste (director-general's office), and Brigitte Meynot (headquarters section).

2 Minutes of the meetings of March 25 and 26, 1967. DIR/GES/23, UNESCO Archives.

3 Robert Motherwell, "On Rothko," *The Collected Writings of Robert Motherwell*, ed. Stephanie Terenzio (Berkeley: University of California Press, 1999), pp. 196–97.

4 "People in the bottom-level cafeteria would glimpse the painting from below through a large opening in the ceiling. Those seated on the middle level would view the painting head-on, while those seated at the adjacent bar would have an oblique view of it from the right. . . . A wall of plate glass to the left of the painting would provide ample, if asymmetrical, illumination and give those assembled on the outdoor patio a slanted view through the window." *UNESCO Art Collection: Selected Works* (Paris: UNESCO Publishing, 2021), p. 35.

5 Motherwell, *The Collected Writings*, p. 197.

6 Following the major *Giacometti* exhibition at the Orangerie, Paris, in 1969, and with the approval of the artist's widow, Annette Giacometti, UNESCO ultimately selected *Walking Man I*, which arrived in time for the official opening of the building on March 17, 1970. Today this sculpture is found in the main UNESCO headquarters on Place de Fontenoy in Paris.

7 The author would like to thank Ms. Eng Sengsavang and Mr. Alexandre Coutelle for their assistance and permission to access the UNESCO archives. See also https://www.cnvill.net/cv-rothko-unesco.pdf, accessed May 2023.

The Rothko Chapel: Painting the Night

Cordélia de Brosses

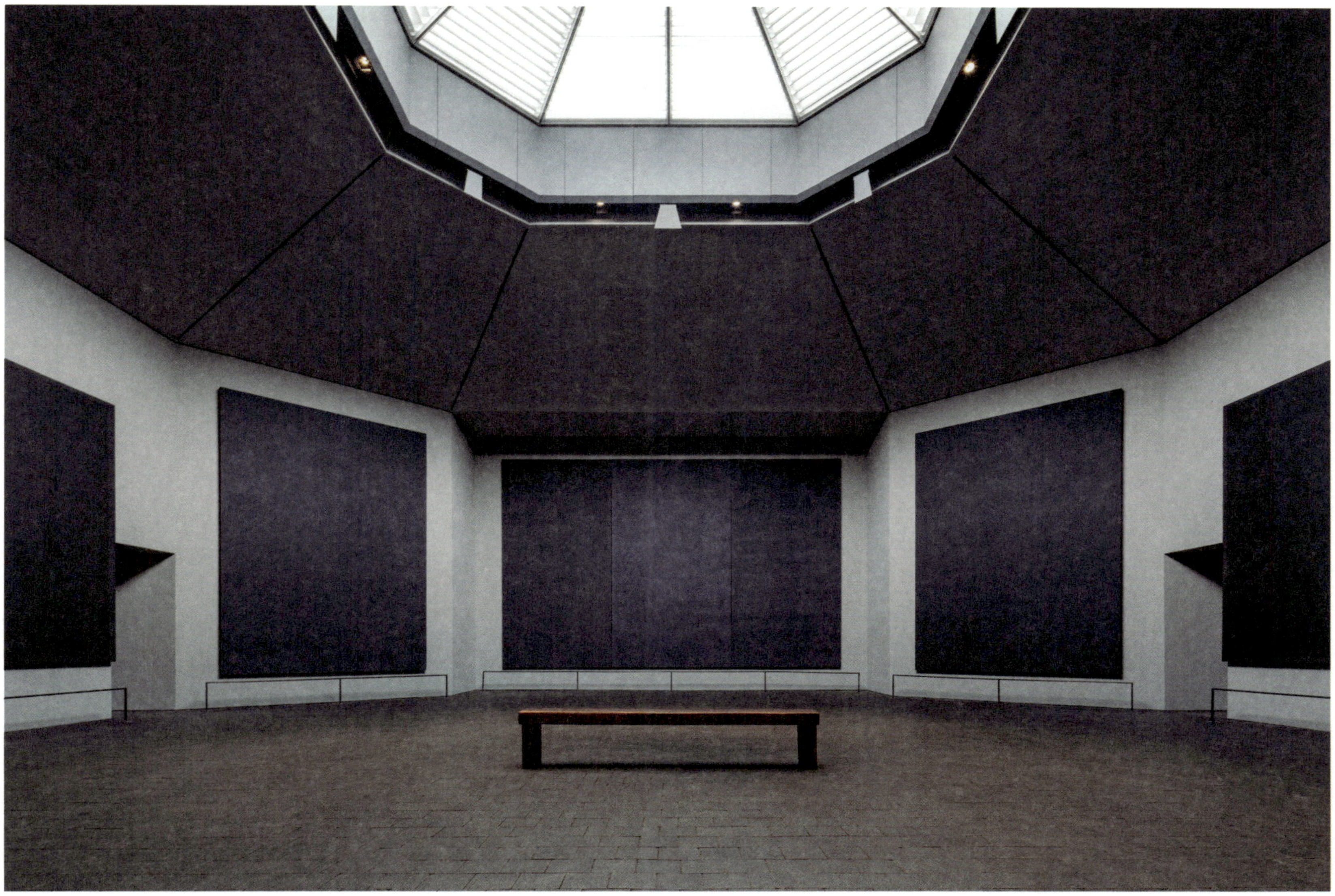

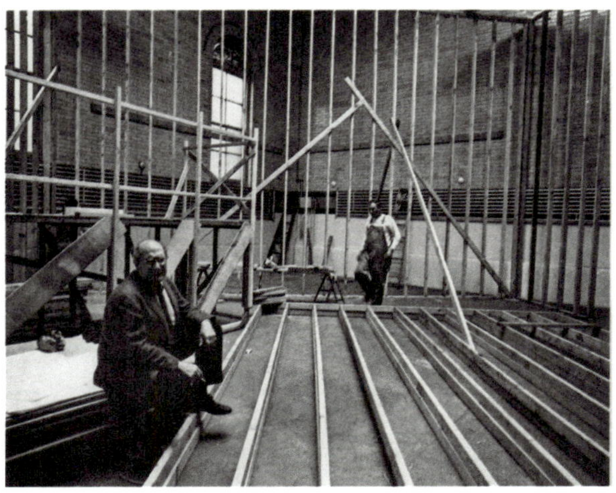

fig 1 Elizabeth Felicella, The Rothko Chapel, north side, 1964–67, Courtesy The Menil Collection, Houston
fig. 2 Hans Namuth, Rothko studio on 69th Street, New York, The Rothko Family Archive

Following double-spread page
Fig. 3 Thomas Struth, The Rothko Chapel, Houston, 2007, chromogenic print, 178 × 233.8 × 6 cm, Courtesy of the artist and Marian Goodman Gallery

"I felt instantly that not one muscle of my face should betray a surprise. I had expected bright colors! So I just looked. Oh miracle, peace invaded me. I felt held up, embraced, and free. Nothing was stopping my gaze. There was a beyond."[1] Thus Dominique de Menil lyrically described the impression of infinity generated by the dark paintings[2] in the Rothko Chapel, which she saw for the first time in 1967. Fourteen of those canvases, in a range of dark plums and dark burgundy reinforced by black fields,[3] now hang in the chapel[4] commissioned by Dominique and John (originally Jean) de Menil, a pair of French collectors who moved to Texas in 1941. The paintings comprise a triptych in the north apse (fig. 1 and 3), aligned with a vertical canvas to the south, two asymmetrical triptychs on the east and west sides,[5] (fig. 9) and four monochrome paintings on the intercardinal points.[6]

The project took shape in two stages. In 1960, struck by the spirituality of canvases from Rothko's *Seagram murals* series, the Menils offered to buy from the artist a group of these works to be hung in the Catholic chapel they planned to build in Houston. Rothko hesitated, because even though their proposal was attractive, the so-called Seagram paintings were conceived for a different space, namely the Four Seasons restaurant in the Seagram Building in New York.[7] He made a counter-proposal—to paint new works for the future chapel—which they initially rejected. However, four years later the sudden death of a friend of the Menils, Jermayne MacAgy, revived the plan for a religious site. In conjunction with MacAgy's friend, Louise Ferrari, Dominique de Menil reconsidered Rothko's suggestion. The artist accepted the commission and agreed to commit himself to the project full-time.[8]

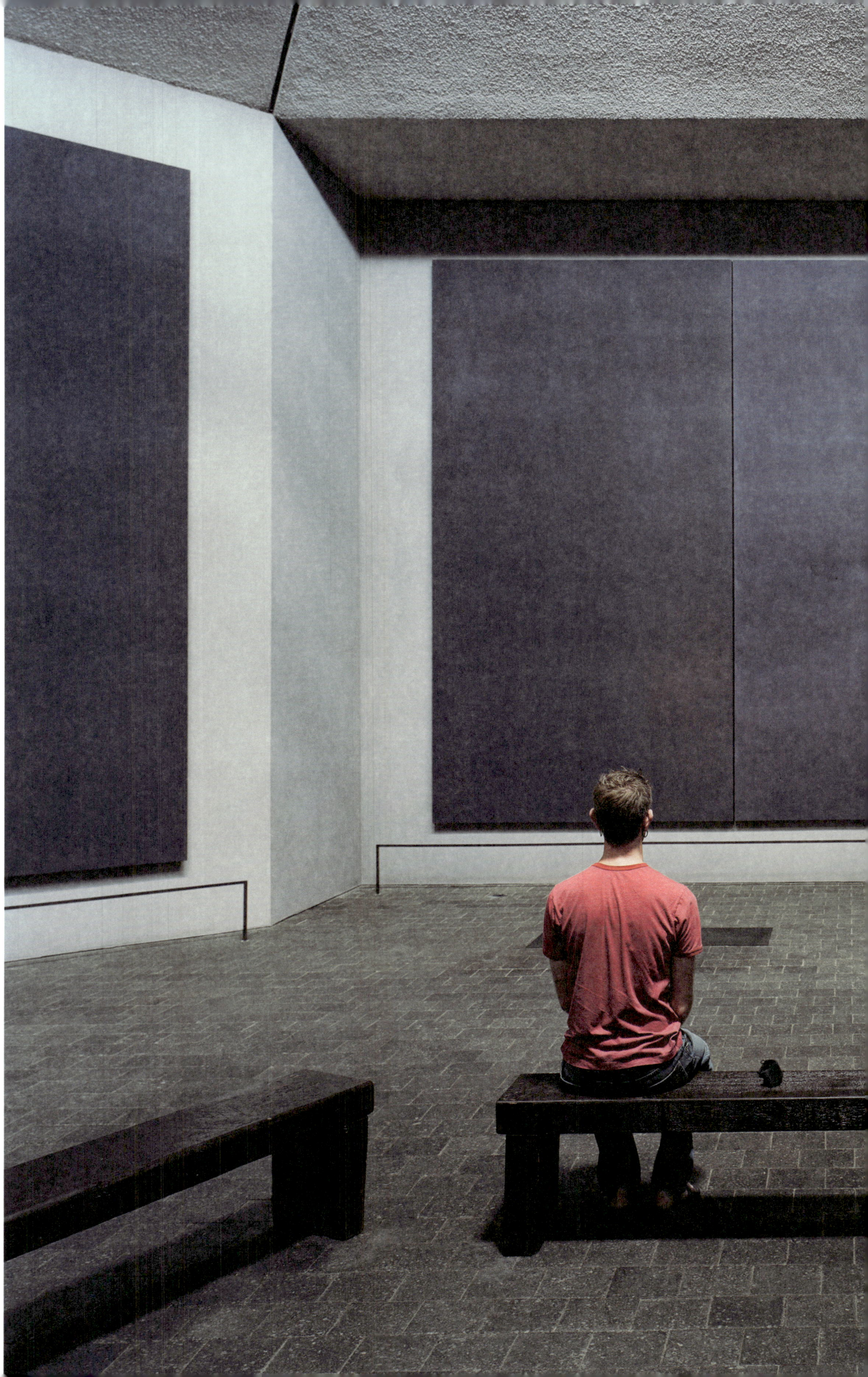

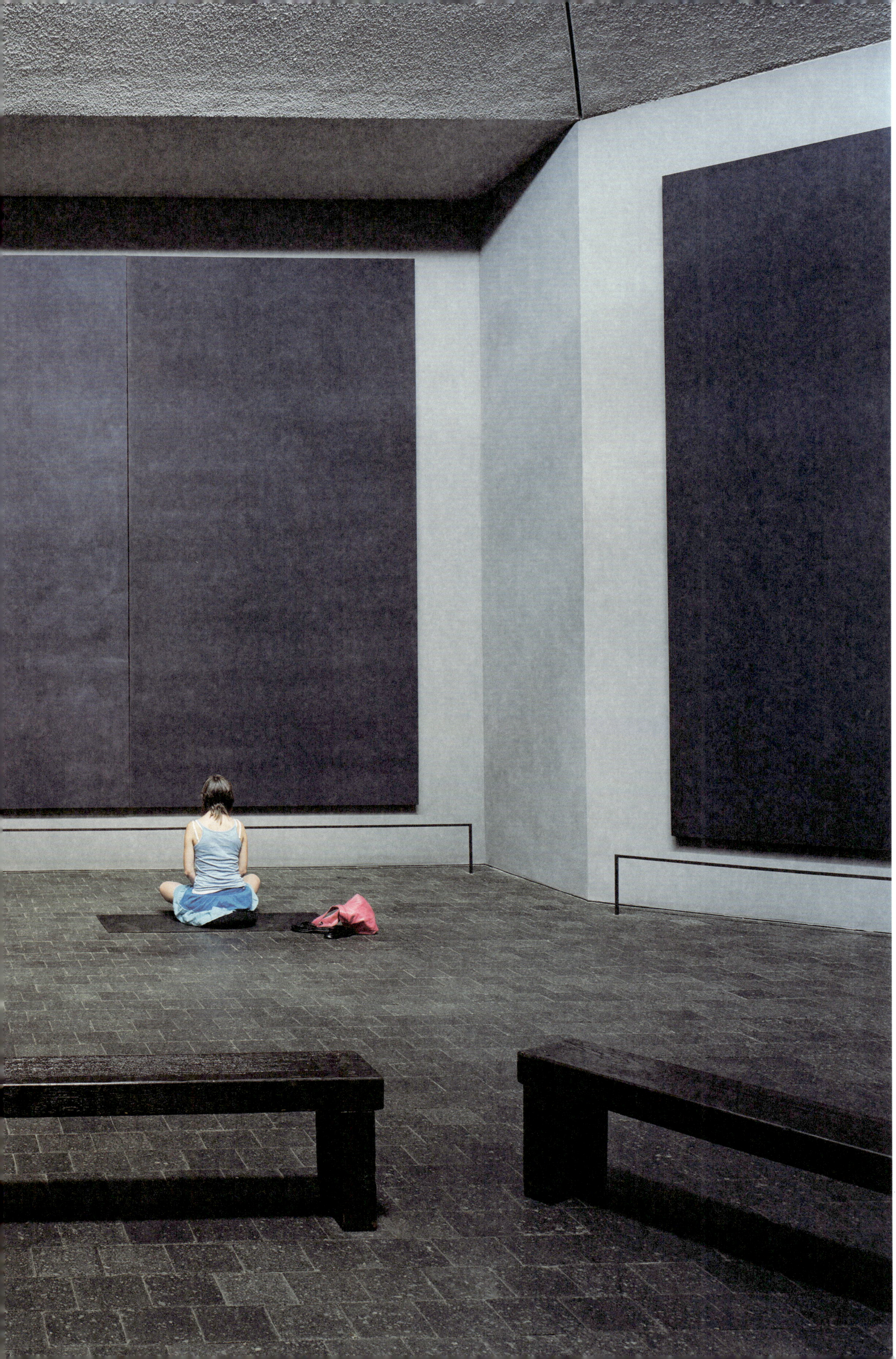

For the first time, Rothko actively participated in creating a building and spiritual environment to host his works, with the help of several architects. Right from the start (1964), he insisted on an octagonal plan and soon opposed architect Philip Johnson's idea for a pyramidal shape that would filter natural light. Johnson withdrew from the project in the fall of 1967, unable to come up with a solution acceptable to Rothko (who preferred sparer architecture) or to Dominique de Menil (who criticized Johnson's design by likening it to a crematorium).[9] Johnson was replaced by his two Houston associates, Howard Barnstone and Eugene Aubry.

In order to envisage the effect of paintings within the building, in December 1964 Rothko had a full-scale model of three of the chapel's eight walls built inside the vast New York studio rented for that purpose by the Menils (fig. 2, 5 and 12). His plans were the object of incessant study of proportions, as demonstrated by preparatory drawings[10] and comments by assistants[11] and friends. "Rothko had come to think of his chapel as a matter of finding the right proportions in an almost mystical way, like an alchemist."[12] Poet Stanley Kunitz, a friend of Rothko, evoked the feeling of communing with the works. "You would have to not only see the paintings, you would breathe them."[13] The chapel paintings are distinctive in their determination to simplify forms and their desire for clarity, as though seeking to eliminate what the artist called "all obstacles between the painter and the idea, and between the idea and the observer."[14] Furthermore, these pure, spiritual images might be associated with comments by a Dominican priest, Father Couturier (fig. 8), whose friendship with Dominique and John de Menil had predisposed them to commissioning work from a contemporary artist for the chapel.[15] "[M]odern art, strongly accused of materialism, will have been—in its principles and artistic essence, if not in its subject-matter—one of the most spiritual in history, and thereby one of the most stripped down, most detached of arts."[16]

The Menils enabled Rothko to produce an artistic ideal in unique conditions and perfect harmony with his patrons. Grateful, he thanked them in 1966 in the following terms: "The magnitude, on every level of experience and meaning, of the task in which you have involved me, exceeds all my preconceptions. And it is teaching me to extend myself beyond what I thought was possible for me. For this I thank you"[17] (fig. 11). While Rothko attended neither the hanging nor the opening of the chapel in 1971 (fig. 6), he was still discussing the plans with architect Aubry two weeks before his suicide in February 1970. He was aware of the 1969 change in the role of the chapel, which, in being transferred from the supervision of Saint Thomas University to that of the Institute of Religion and Human Development,[18] (fig. 11) was no longer designed solely for the Catholic religion but for all religions, thereby incarnating a humanist dimension congruent with Rothko's own universalism.

Rothko painted the darkness of night. "Often, towards nightfall, there's a feeling in the air of mystery, threat, frustration—all of these at once. I would like my painting to have the quality of such moments."[19] The apparent simplicity of the paintings in the chapel, their silence, and their profoundly dark hues spur beholders to confront themselves, their doubts, their fears, their own darkness, just as the Shakespearean character of King Lear who, in the midst of a storm, stripped of all his possessions, achieves—with a measure of violence—self-awareness.[20] Shakespeare had become one of Rothko's favorite writers. "As I have grown older, Shakespeare has come closer to me than Aeschylus, who meant so much to me in my youth. Shakespeare's tragic concept embodies the full range of life from which the artist draws all his tragic materials."[21]

1 Dominique de Menil, Foreword to Sheldon Nodelman, *The Rothko Chapel Paintings: Origins, Structure, Meaning* (Austin: University of Texas Press, 1997), p. 9.

2 The progressive darkening of the palette seen in this series was part of a permanent process that Rothko acknowledged but never explained. "I can only say that the dark pictures began in 1957 and have persisted almost compulsively to this day." Letter from Mark Rothko to the Tate Gallery, London, February 1, 1960, quoted in David Anfam, "Dark Illumination: The Context of the Rothko Chapel," in David Anfam and Carol Mancusi-Ungaro, *Mark Rothko: The Chapel Commission* (The Menil Collection, 1996), p. 6.

3 The paintings at the intercardinal points and to the north are plum-colored, while the panel on the south wall and the east and west triptychs are dark burgundy with black fields.

4 Rothko had painted four alternative canvases, which hang today in the museum housing the Menil Collection in Houston. A recent study by Sheldon Nodelman suggests that Rothko had included these alternative paintings in an earlier configuration. See the video "Rothko Chapel Revisited with Sheldon Nodelman & Christopher Rothko," June 9, 2021.

5 The central panels of these two triptychs are slightly raised with respect to the side panels.

6 It might be argued that the prelude to the "dark paintings" truly began one month before the Menil commission, when Rothko painted a series of dark canvases with distinct edges. For further information on the dark paintings, see Nancy Spector's essay in this volume, "Mark Rothko's Classic Paintings: Theaters of the Mind," p. 232–237.

7 Rothko had himself considered buying a medieval chapel at Lelant, in Cornwall, England, in order to hang his paintings there. See Annie Cohen-Solal, "Entre gratte-ciel de luxe et chapelle médiévale, premier ancrage britannique, 1958–1960," *Mark Rothko* (Arles: Actes Sud, 2013), pp. 203–204.

8 Dominique de Menil, Date Books, April 17, 1964, note dated June 2, 1975. De Menil Family Archives, Menil Collection, Houston. Quoted in William Middleton, *Double Vision: The Unerring Eye of Art World Avatars Dominique and John de Menil* (New York: Alfred A. Knopff, 2018), p. 476.

9 Light has remained one of the key issues for conserving the works in the chapel, which has been renovated several times only to return in 2020 to a solution similar to the one proposed by Rothko.

10 Carol Mancusi-Ungaro has shown that these drawings illustrate Rothko' methodical approach to adjusting his paintings. See "Nuances of Surface in the Rothko Chapel Paintings," in Anfam and Mancusi-Ungaro, *The Chapel Commission, op. cit.*, p. 26–27.

11 Rothko hired assistants not only to help build the model of the chapel but also to execute the large paintings for it.

12 Dore Ashton, *About Rothko* (Cambridge: Da Capo Press, 2013), p. 173.

13 Quoted by James E. B. Breslin, *Mark Rothko: A Biography* (Chicago and London: University of Chicago Press, 1998), p. 466.

14 Mark Rothko, "Statement on His Attitude in Painting," *Tiger's Eye* 9 (October 1949), p. 114, reprinted in Mark Rothko, *Writings on Art* ed. Miguel Lopez-Remiro (New Haven and London: Yale University Press, 2006), p. 65.

15 Father Marie-Alain Couturier sought to end the Catholic church's divorce from modern art, and had introduced the Menils to Léger's work on the exterior of the church at Assay, to Léger and Bazaine's work in the church of Audincourt and to Matisse's work for the chapel in Vence.

16 Marie-Alain Couturier, "Les moyens pauvres dans l'art moderne," *L'Évangile est à l'extrême: Disloquer les structures mentales dans l'Église* (Paris: Éditions du Cerf, 1970), p. 41. The above passage was taken from an article published in *L'Art Sacré* (July–August 1950).

17 Letter from Mark Rothko to Dominique and John de Menil, January 1, 1966. Rothko Chapel archives.

18 The affiliation lasted from 1969 to 1972, when the trustees of the Institute of Religion conferred autonomy upon the chapel. The chapel's ecumenical mission was based on principles elaborated by Father Yves Congar and quoted by Dominique de Menil in her opening-day address on February 27, 1971.

19 Quoted by David Sylvester, "The Ugly Duckling," in Michael Auping (ed.), *Abstract Expressionism: The Critical Developments*, exh. cat. (New York: Albright-Knox Gallery, 1987), p. 140. See also David Anfam, *Mark Rothko: The Works on Canvas, A Catalogue Raisonné* (Washington, D.C.: National Gallery of Art and New Haven: Yale University Press, 1998).

20 According to Rothko's daughter, Kate Rothko Prizel, *King Lear* was a very important play for her father. In an essay on the chapel, David Anfam refers to the cathartic effect of the blinding of Gloucester, a character in that play. See Anfam, "Dark Illumination," in Anfam and Mancusi-Ungaro, *The Chapel Commission.*

21 Rothko interview with Peter Selz, autumn 1960, quoted in *Mark Rothko*, exh. cat. (New York: MoMA, 1961), p. 12.

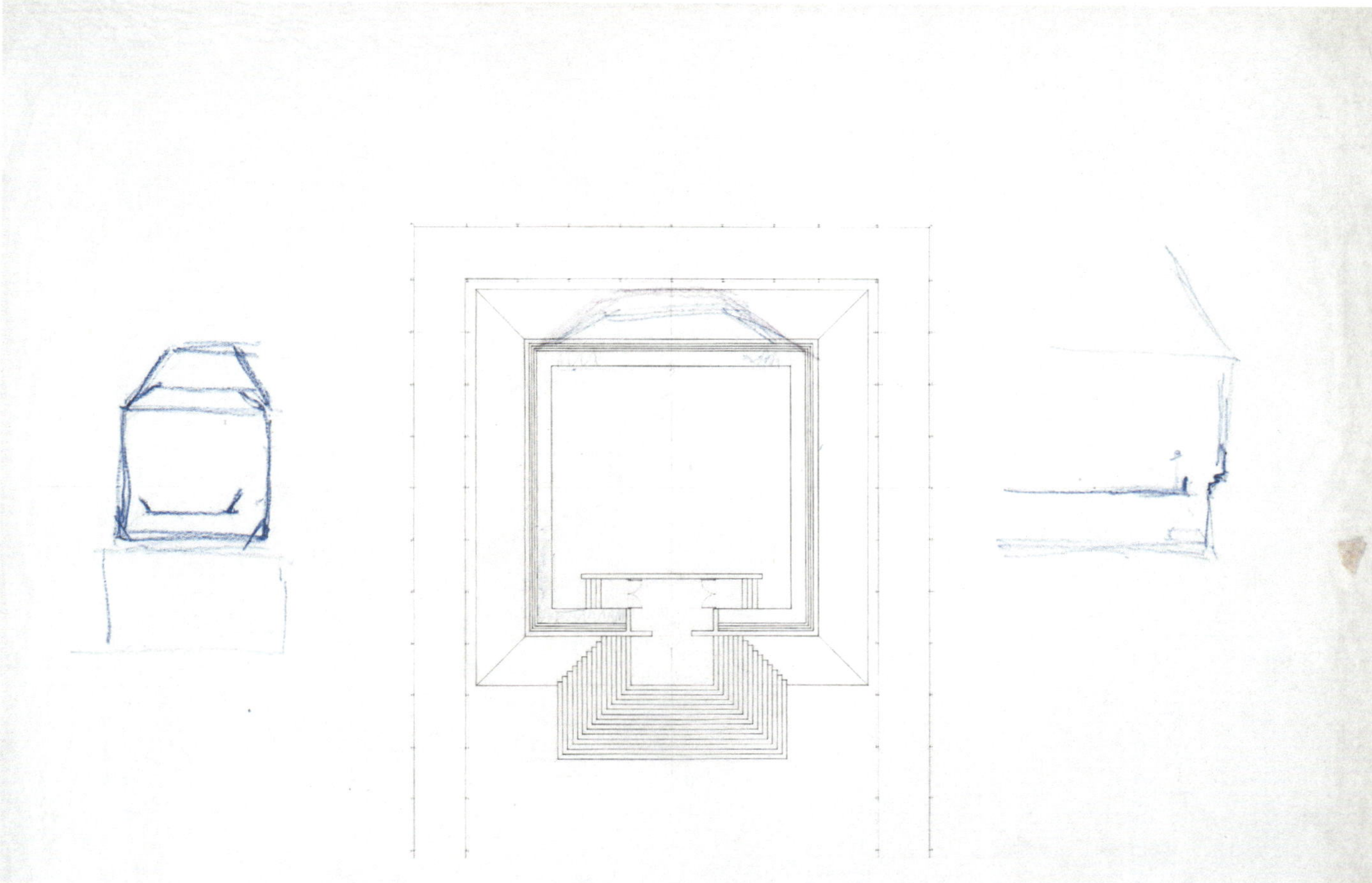

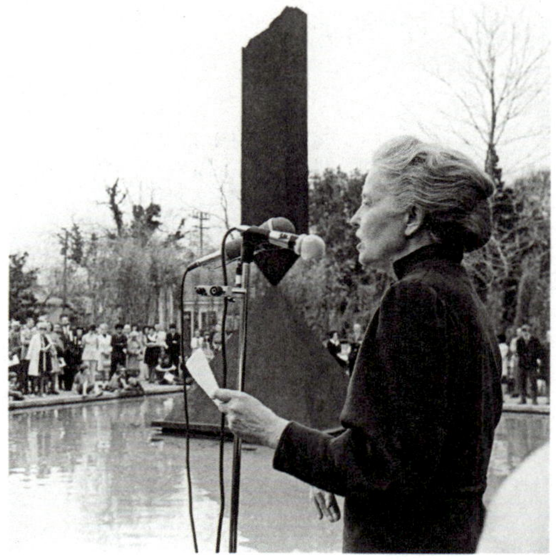

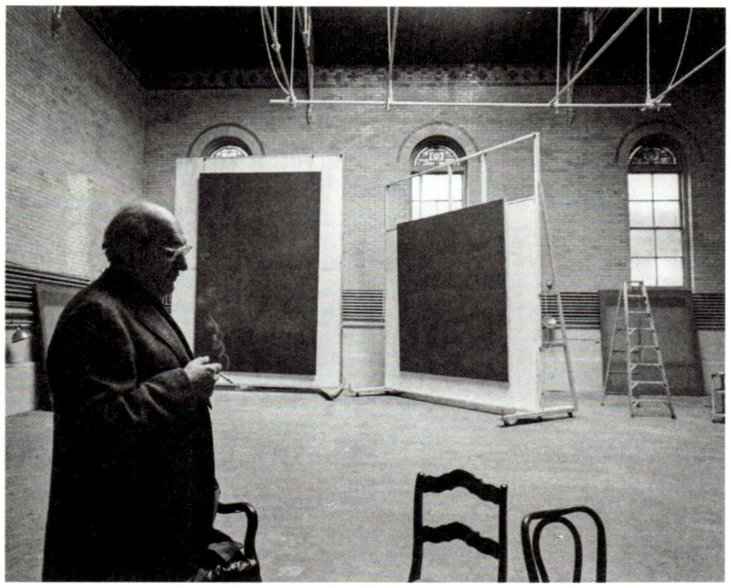

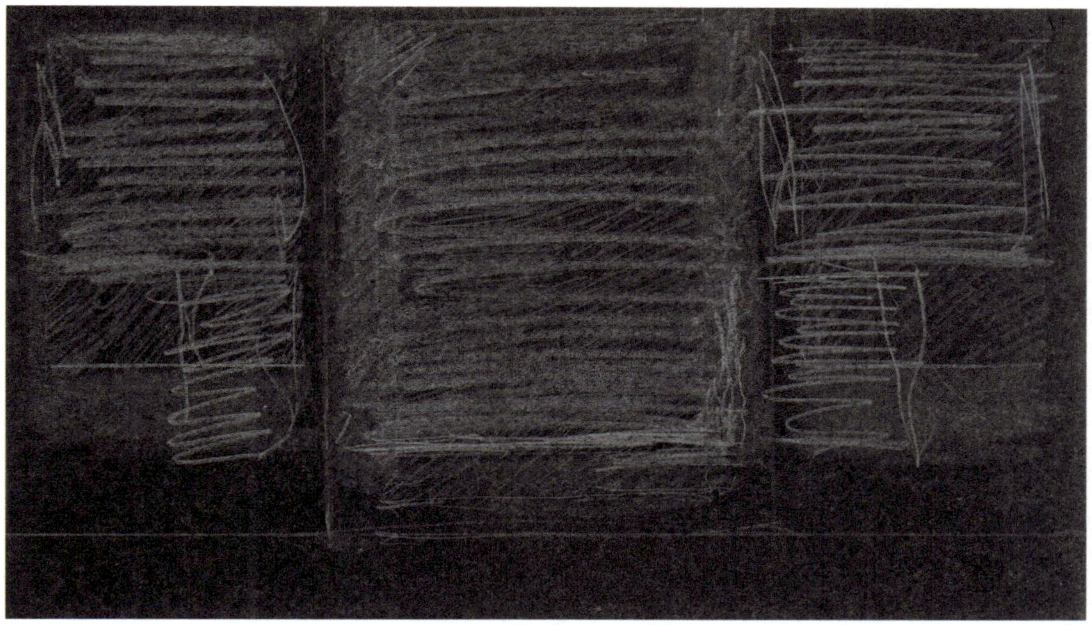

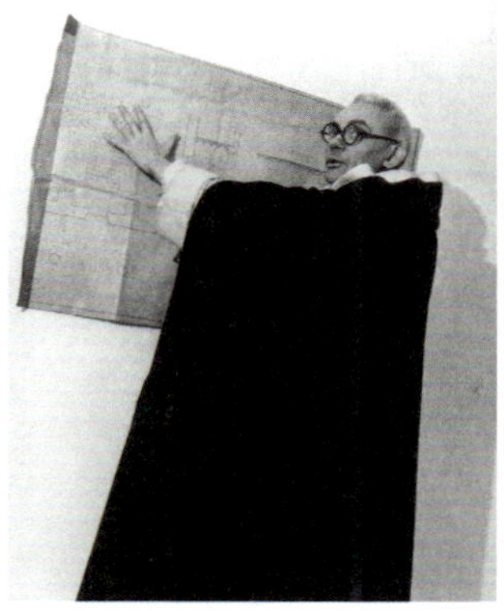

fig. 4 Philip Johnson, square plan, with the addition of the apse drawn by Rothko, 1964, The Menil Collection, Houston
fig. 5 Hans Namuth, Rothko in his studio with panel for the Rothko Chapel, 69th Street, New York, 1964, Collection Center for Creative Photography, The University of Arizona, Tucson
fig. 6 Hickey-Roberston, Dominique de Menil opening the Rothko Chapel, 1971, The Menil Archives, Houston
fig. 7 Mark Rothko *Study for Side-Wall Triptychs,* 1966, graphite and pencil on black paper, $6\frac{3}{4} \times 9\frac{3}{4}$ in., Menil Collection, Houston
fig. 8 Robert Doisneau, Father Marie-Alain Couturier, c. 1951, The Menil Archives, Houston

Following double pages
fig. 9 Paul Hester, The Rothko Chapel, west or east side, 1964–1967, Courtesy of The Menil Collection, Houston
fig. 10 Hickey-Robertson, Lowering of painting through chapel skylight, 1970, The Menil Collection, Archives
fig. 11 Letter from Rothko to John and Dominique de Menil, January 1, 1966, The Menil Archives
fig. 12 Hans Namuth, Rothko in his studio, 69th street, 1964, The Rothko Family Archive

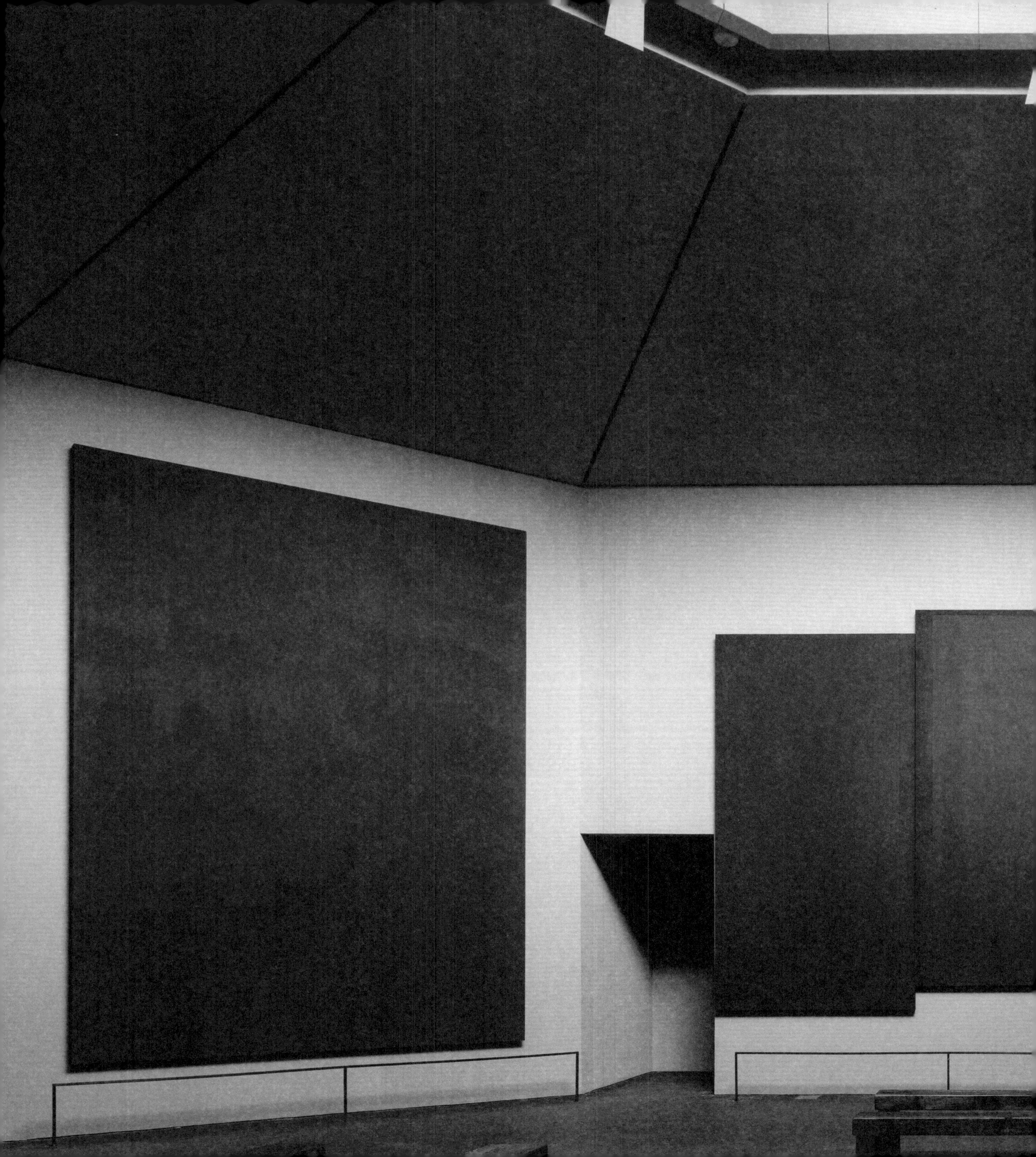

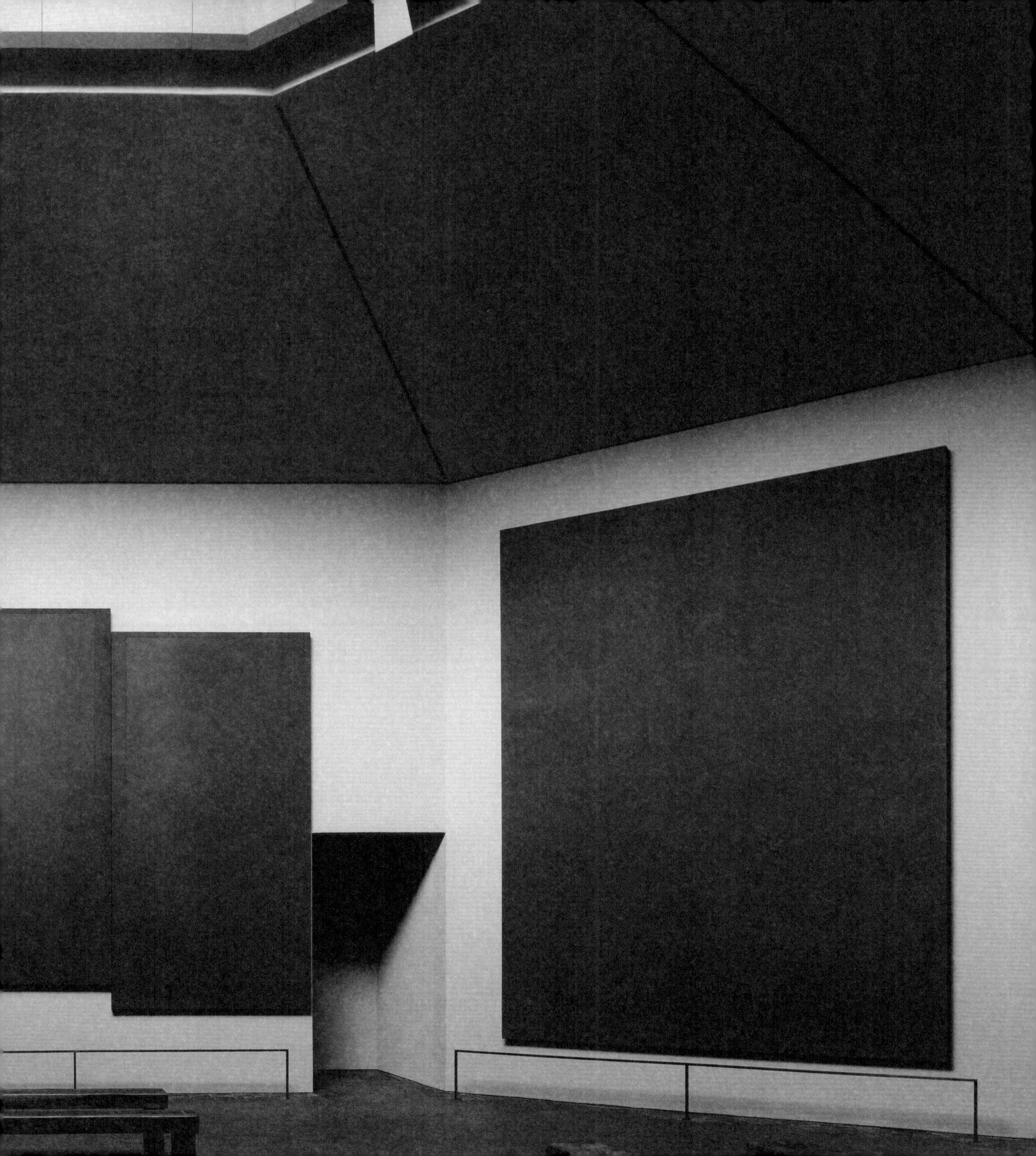

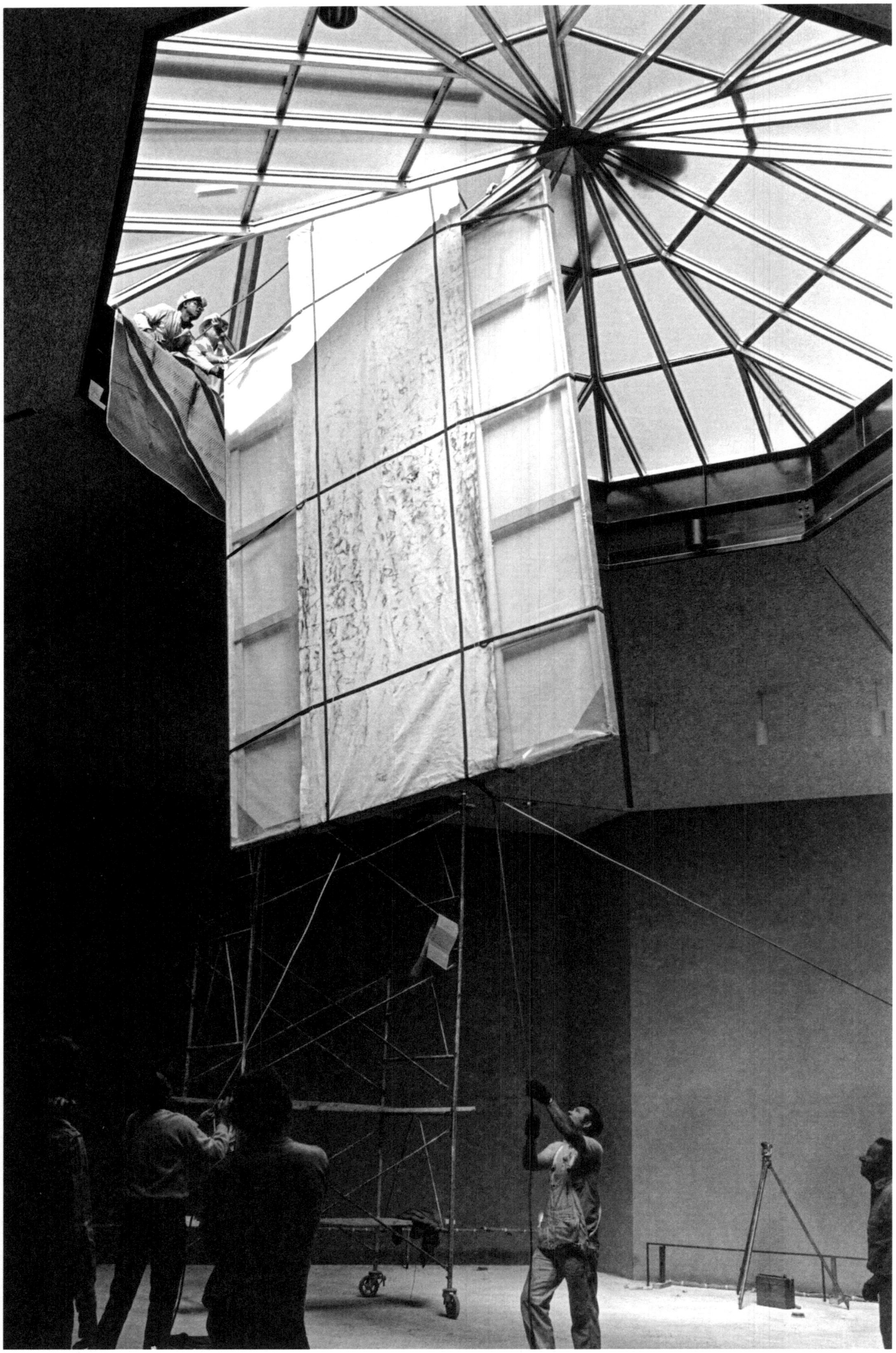

Jan 1, 1966

Dear John & Domenique DeMenil,

First, I would like to send the season's greetings to you and yours.

Secondly, I would like to say what a marvel that you exist, and that you move about in the world as you do. The magnitude, on every level of experience and meaning, of the task in which you have involved me, exceeds all my preconceptions. And it is teaching me to extend myself beyond what I thought was possible for me.

For this I thank you

Mark Rothko

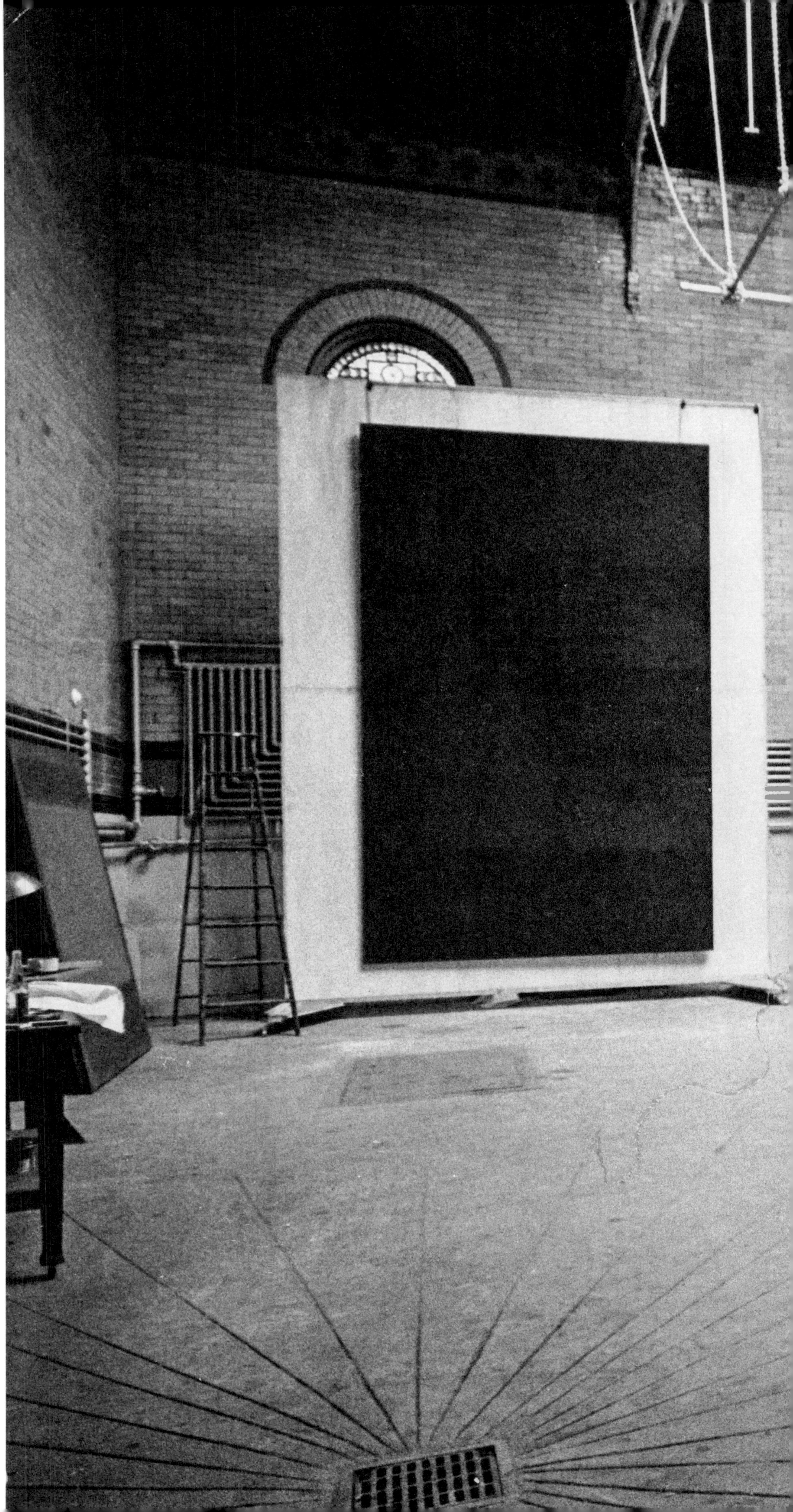

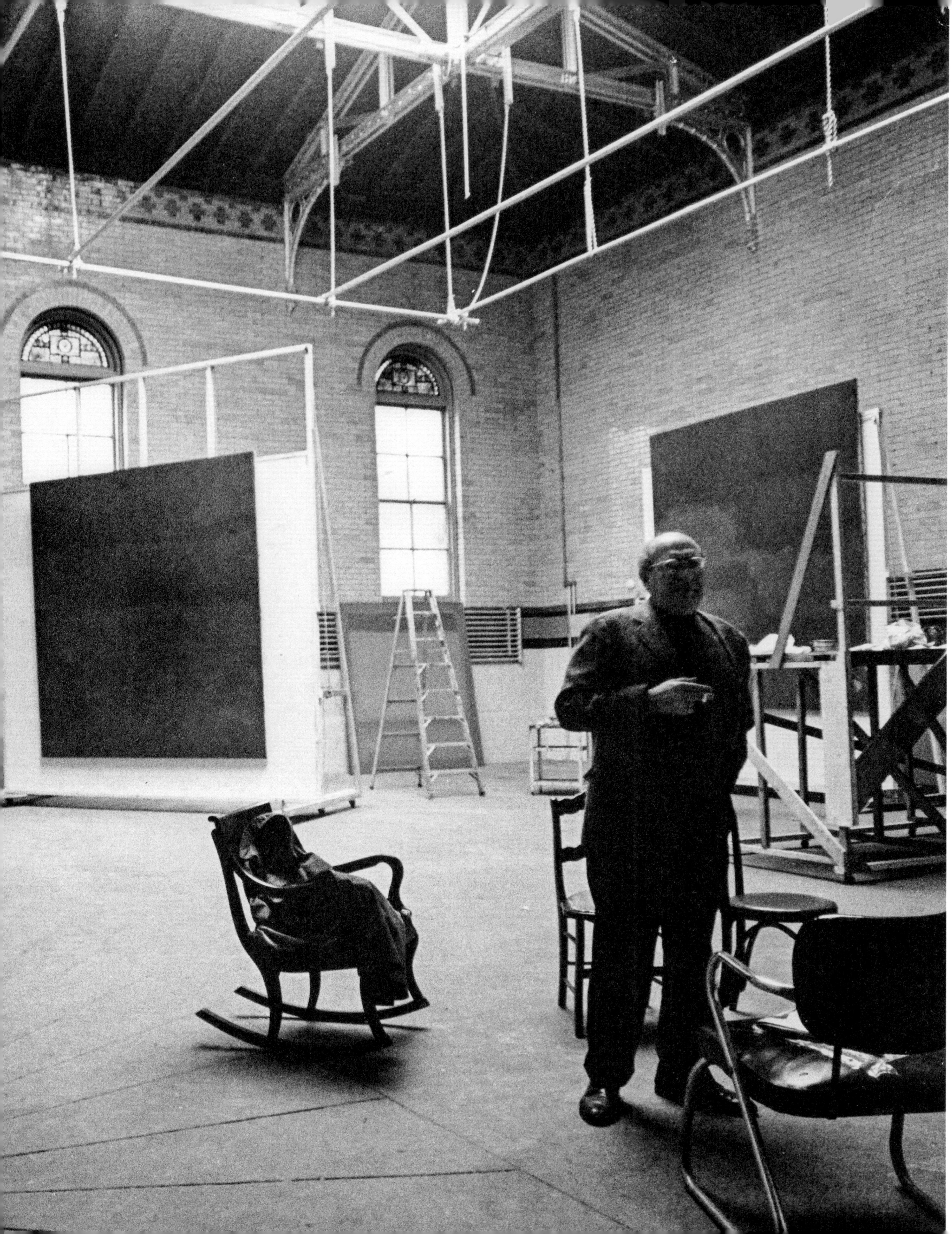

"Visitors
FLOAT THROUGH CLOUDS OF TINTED ATMOSPHERE
SEARCHING DISTANT HORIZONS
THROUGH PIGMENTED FIELDS
ALLOWING THE EYES TO PLUNGE INTO OCEANS OF COLOR
TRAVEL AIMLESSLY ALONG TINTED CURRENTS LEADING TO
ENCLOSURES OF PLEASURE
Hues, tones, and shadows float and disappear, then merge, cohabitate and rest peacefully."
Sheila Hicks

"Rothko was inspired by the Romantic tradition, and tormented by conflicts, by unrelieved anxiety. In his dim studios he used to have dozens of containers of powdered dry pigments, of every imaginable hue, which he mixed with his paint to intensify it—he loved Fra Angelico's bright tempera paintings, and often had used egg as a medium—like a chemist of the sort that in Europe used to have a of green and of red liquids in the window. Rothko's mixtures resulted in a series of glowing color structures that have no exact parallel in modern art, that, in the profoundest sense of Baudelaire's invocation to modern artists, are new. So new that if Rothko had not existed, we would not even know of certain emotional possibilities in modern art. . . . But Rothko's real genius was that out of color he had created a language of feeling. Thus with his death, a certain dimension left modern art, a certain contradiction that nevertheless glowed with an inner luminosity of color that is poignant—to employ one of his favored terms."
Robert Motherwell

The Collected Writtings of Robert Motherwell, 1993

"I had a print of a Rothko painting in my room when I was a teenager. I used to stare at it at night going to sleep. I think my mother bought it to give the room a splash of color. I didn't know the whole Rothko mythology then: the romantic/modernist tormented painter who committed suicide. I didn't know his role in the New York scene of the 1950s. And I wasn't seduced by the spirituality, what I later saw in the Rothko Chapel. But I remember looking at it and thinking I wanted to do that; I wanted to make surfaces. Later on, after reading about his work and Abstract Expressionism, I remember looking at the painting and feeling nullified by it—how much is not there, no women and no people of color. So it's perplexing. I don't buy the romanticism or the idea of channeling an inner life right onto the surface. But I am an abstract painter."
Mark Bradford

"Rothkoooo, I want to sing your name whose consonances I like. Beauty and spirituality only through color, colors, sometimes up to 20 layers of paint, which gives an endless depth... A mystical elevation close to ecstasy, 'We float!'" (Peter Gabriel sang that with his song "Us" in 1992)
Annette Messager

"En résonance"
Comments collected by Hans Ulrich Obrist

"Rothko more or less hovers over every American artist, and particularly anyone who works on flat surfaces. I feel more born of Rothko. For me, he's a kind of deity figure—more so than anyone else. It's almost as if he never walked the earth the way that he's discussed and the way that he's thought about, and the way that we understand and unpack his project—like a kind of a god figure. With Rothko, it's as if the work lives independently and we pray to it, in a sense. I really feel sustained by the inherent poetry in his project, and the way that it shines a light on the ethereal."
Rashid Johnson

"I think the reason why Rothko's work is so powerful and affects people in such a direct manner is because it absolutely is not abstract. But it feels, in a way, very close to the way music operates, in that it's representational, but it's representational of something that cannot be seen. It sits beyond the visual domain, and it also sits beyond language. It's what Wittgenstein says cannot be spoken of. It's that thing. And I think that comes through incredibly powerfully in Rothko's work. So I totally agree with him when he says it's not abstract, because if it were abstract, then it wouldn't have this effect. I think that's his connection to music."
Max Richter

On the occasion of this exhibition, the composer Max Richter was commissioned a piece on Rothko's work.

"Once Rothko said that 'The people who weep before my pictures, are having the same religious experiences I had when painting them.' This is exactly what happened to me. I find myself in the Rothko Chapel, uncontrollably crying, overwhelmed with the mixture between silence, melancholy, sensuality, tragedy."
Marina Abramović

"Rothko studied at Yale and accepted the prevalent theory that great art was tragic. Meanwhile, he developed a first class technique influenced by the surrealists. He was also influenced by Milton Avery and started painting vertical landscapes in the 1950s. In the late 1950s, from 1956 to 1962, he could do no wrong. The paintings had real substance and were very aggressive in styling. He wanted to paint tragedy—people, however, saw them as beautiful abstractions. Despite his pretentiousness, he painted some of the most beautiful paintings ever painted. Rothko was an inspiration and one of the most interesting artists on the planet."
Alex Katz

"Consciousness is like a lens—a lens that can project the external world into the mind. The external world is projected into a cave and rendered as a painting. And I believe that the light of the outside world, projected into the prehistoric cave, is the light of Rothko."
Hiroshi Sugimoto

"Coming first across Rothko's calming color fields as a high school kid in Cologne, observing the incredibly enchanted audience, wandering smilingly amongst his exhibition at the Musée d'Art Moderne in Paris, to the inescapable intensity of the Rothko Chapel paintings, one cannot help but feeling for this artistic surrender, its honesty, its tragedy, its beauty."
Thomas Struth

"Rothko's paintings give you the experience of looking at something and feeling you have to see it again to really make sure that you saw it. You can't really say what you see. It's neither a thoroughly conceptualized strategy that's visualized, nor is it just a phenomenon. It's a fascinating manifestation of single-mindedness that comes across as non-repetitive. And it makes him unique; it makes him stand out."
Katharina Grosse

"When I was a student at the Slade we would go and look at the Rothkos at the Tate with a hushed awe. Later I got to know early Rothko and works like Slow Swirl at the Edge of the Sea resonated deeply. The forms tremble on the edge of representation, like things coming to life. More than any artist (except perhaps Mondrian) there is in Rothko a progression that feels inevitable—you see the abstraction happen before your eyes as the slowly gyrating personages disintegrate and reassemble as nebulous clouds of color. They are dramas with an inner light that invites the spectator in with its extreme beauty and rewards slow looking, offering a kind of mirror for the unsayable."
Cecily Brown

List of exhibited works

1 *Movie Palace*, 1934 / 1935 (CR 64)
Oil on canvas, 24 × 31 ½ in. (64.8 × 82.2 cm)
Private collection
p. 58

2 *The Road*, 1932 / 1933 (CR 26)
Oil on canvas, 24 × 31 ½ in. (61 × 80 cm)
Private collection
p. 58

3 *Family*, c. 1936 (CR 89)
Oil on canvas, 20 ¼ × 30 ⅛ in. (51.4 × 76.5 cm)
National Gallery of Art, Washington, D.C.
Gift of the Mark Rothko Foundation, Inc.,
1986.43.97
p. 58

4 *Self-Portrait*, 1936 (CR 82)
Oil on canvas, 32 ¼ × 25 ¾ in. (81.9 × 65.4 cm)
Collection of Christopher Rothko
p. 59

5 *Untitled (The Subway)*, 1937 (CR 104)
Oil on canvas, 24 × 36 in. (61 × 91.4 cm)
Collection of Elie and Sarah Hirschfeld
p. 60

6 *Untitled*, 1935 (CR 70)
Oil on canvas, 32 ⅜ × 42 in. (81.3 × 106.7 cm)
Collection of Kate Rothko Prizel and Ilya Prizel
p. 60

7 *Entrance to Subway*, 1938 (CR 135)
Oil on canvas, 34 × 46 ¼ in. (86.4 × 117.5 cm)
Collection of Kate Rothko Prizel and Ilya Prizel
p. 61

8 *Untitled (subway)*, 1937 (CR 108)
Oil on canvas, 20 ⅛ × 30 in. (51.1 × 76.2 cm)
National Gallery of Art, Washington, D.C.
Gift of the Mark Rothko Foundation, Inc.,
1986.43.113
p. 62

9 *Interior*, 1936 (CR 79). Not exhibited
Oil on hardboard, 23 ⅞ × 18 ¼ in. (60.6 × 46.4 cm)
National Gallery of Art, Washington, D.C.
Gift of the Mark Rothko Foundation, Inc.,
1986.43.26
p. 62

10 *Untitled*, 1939 (CR 167)
Oil on canvas, 24 × 32 in. (61 × 81.3 cm)
Collection of Kate Rothko Prizel and Ilya Prizel
p. 62

11 *Street Scene*, 1936 / 1937 (CR 96)
Oil on canvas, 36 × 21 15/16 in. (91.5 × 55.8 cm)
National Gallery of Art, Washington, D.C.
Gift of the Mark Rothko Foundation, Inc.,
1986.43.45
p. 62

12 *Underground Fantasy*, c. 1940 (CR 174)
Oil on canvas, 34 ⅜ × 46 9/16 in. (87.3 × 118.2 cm)
National Gallery of Art, Washington, D.C.
Gift of the Mark Rothko Foundation, Inc.,
1986.43.130
p. 63

13 *Street Scene*, c. 1937 (CR 113)
Oil on canvas, 28 15/16 × 39 15/16 in. (73.5 × 101.4 cm)
National Gallery of Art, Washington, D.C.
Gift of the Mark Rothko Foundation, Inc.,
1986.43.21
p. 63

14 *Untitled*, 1938 / 1939 (CR 163)
Oil on canvas, 40 × 30 in. (101.6 × 76.2 cm)
Collection of Christopher Rothko
p. 64

15 *Portrait*, 1939 (CR 164)
Oil on canvas, 39 ⅞ × 30 ¼ in. (101.6 × 76.5 cm)
Collection of Christopher Rothko
p. 64

16 *Contemplation*, 1937 / 1938 (CR 116)
Oil on canvas, 24 ⅛ × 32 in. (61.4 × 81.3 cm)
National Gallery of Art, Washington, D.C.
Gift of the Mark Rothko Foundation, Inc.,
1986.43.38
p. 64

17 *Untitled*, 1938 (CR 144)
Oil on canvas, 50 × 37 in. (127 × 94 cm)
Private collection
p. 65

18 *Nude*, 1938–1939 (CR 161)
Oil on canvas, 36 × 24 in. (91.4 × 61 cm)
Private collection
p. 65

19 *Untitled*, 1939 (CR 171)
Oil on canvas, 23 ⅝ × 18 in. (60.6 × 46 cm)
Private collection
p. 65

20 *Untitled*, 1941–1942 (CR 192)
Oil on canvas, 35 13/16 × 23 ⅞ in. (91 × 60.6 cm)
National Gallery of Art, Washington, D.C.
Gift of the Mark Rothko Foundation, Inc.,
1986.43.35
p. 66

21 *Untitled*, 1940–1941 (CR 181)
Oil on canvas, 36 1/16 × 28 1/16 in (91.6 × 71.3 cm)
National Gallery of Art, Washington, D.C.
Gift of the Mark Rothko Foundation, Inc.,
1986.43.36
p. 66

22 *Untitled*, 1941–1942 (CR 189)
Oil on canvas, 24 × 31 ⅞ in. (61 × 81 cm)
National Gallery of Art, Washington, D.C.,
1986.43.33
p. 66

23 *Antigone*, 1939–1940 (CR 178)
Oil and charcoal on canvas, 34 × 45 ¾ in.
(86.4 × 116.2 cm)
National Gallery of Art, Washington, D.C.
Gift of the Mark Rothko Foundation, Inc.,
1986.43.119
p. 67

24 *The Omen of the Eagle*, 1942 (CR 206)
Oil and graphite on canvas, 25 ¾ × 17 ¾ in.
(65.4 × 45.1 cm)
National Gallery of Art, Washington, D.C.
Gift of the Mark Rothko Foundation, Inc.,
1986.43.107
p. 67

25 *Hierarchical Birds*, 1944 (CR 239)
Oil on canvas, 39 ⅝ × 31 11/16 in. (100.7 × 80.5 cm)
National Gallery of Art, Washington, D.C.
Gift of the Mark Rothko Foundation, Inc.,
1986.43.20
p. 67

26 *Rites of Lilith*, 1945 (CR 266)
Oil on canvas, 82 × 106 ⅝ in. (208.3 × 20.8 cm)
Private collection
p. 67

27 *Sacrifice of Iphigenia*, 1942 (CR 210)
Oil and graphite on canvas, 50 × 36 ⅞ in.
(127 × 93.7 cm)
Private collection p. 69

28 *Tiresias*, 1944 (CR 247)
Oil on canvas, 79⅞ × 39⅞ in. (202.6 × 101.3 cm)
Collection of Christopher Rothko
p. 69

29 *Gethsemane*, 1944 (CR 244)
Oil and charcoal on canvas, 54⅗ × 35½ in. (138.1 × 90.2 cm)
Collection of Kate Rothko Prizel and Ilya Prizel
p. 70

30 *Sea Fantasy*, 1946 (CR 298)
Oil on canvas, 44 × 36⅛ in. (111.8 × 91.8 cm)
National Gallery of Art, Washington, D.C.
Gift of the Mark Rothko Foundation, Inc., 1986.43.8
p. 70

31 *Agitation of the Archaic*, 1944 (CR 240)
Oil on canvas, 35 5/16 × 54¼ in. (89.9 × 137.8 cm)
Whitney Museum of Art, New York
Gift of the Mark Rothko Foundation, Inc.
p. 70

32 *Slow Swirl at the Edge of the Sea*, 1944 (CR 248)
Oil on canvas, 75¼ × 85 in. (191.1 × 215.9 cm)
Museum of Modern Art, New York
Bequest of Mrs. Mark Rothko through The Mark Rothko Foundation, Inc.
p. 71

33 *Untitled*, 1946 (CR 317)
Oil on canvas, 54⅛ × 27⅖ in. (137.5 × 69.5 cm)
Collection of Kate Rothko Prizel and Ilya Prizel
p. 72

34 *Aeolian Harp/No. 7*, 1946 (CR 308)
Oil on canvas, 38½ × 54⅜ in. (98.4 × 138.1 cm)
Collection of Christopher Rothko
p. 72

35 *Untitled*, 1946 (CR 323)
Oil on canvas, 89½ × 105⅞ in. (228 × 268.6 cm)
Private collection
p. 73

36 *Untitled: Abstraction Number 11*, 1947 (CR 334)
Oil on canvas, 39½ × 38½ in. (100.3 × 98.1 cm)
Munson Museum, Utica, NY
p. 74

37 *Untitled*, 1948 (CR 370)
Oil on canvas, 50¼ × 43¼ in. (127.6 × 109.9 cm)
Collection of Kate Rothko Prizel and Ilya Prizel
p. 74

38 *Untitled*, 1948 (CR 374)
Oil on canvas, 53⅞ × 30⅞ in. (136.8 × 78.4 cm)
Private collection
p. 74

39 *Untitled (Multiform)*, 1948 (CR 391)
Oil on canvas, 89 × 65 in. (226.1 × 165.1 cm)
Collection of Kate Rothko Prizel and Ilya Prizel
p. 75

40 *No. 17/No. 15*, 1949 (CR 401)
Oil on canvas, 51⅞ × 29⅛ in. (131.8 × 74 cm)
National Gallery of Art, Washington, D.C.
Gift of the Mark Rothko Foundation, Inc., 1986.43.142
p. 76

41 *No. 14 (Golden Composition)*, 1949 (CR 398)
Oil on canvas, 66 × 41⅛ in. (167.6 × 104.5 cm)
Private Collection, Torino
p. 76

42 *Number 19*, 1949 (CR 403)
Oil on canvas, 68 × 40⅛ in. (172.1 × 106.4 cm)
The Art Institute of Chicago
Anonymous gift, 1957.308
p. 77

43 *No. 11/No. 20*, 1949 (CR 419)
Oil on canvas, 93¾ × 53 in. (238.1 × 134.6 cm)
Collection of Christopher Rothko
p. 79

44 *No. 21 (Untitled)*, 1949 (CR 407)
Oil and mixed media on canvas, 94 × 53⅜ in. (238.8 × 135.6 cm)
The Menil Collection, Houston
Acquired in honor of Alice and George Brown with support from Nancy Wellin and Louisa Sarofim
p. 81

45 *No. 1*, 1949 (CR 408)
Oil on canvas, 78 × 38.7 in. (198.8 × 98.4 cm)
Private collection
p. 82

46 *Untitled*, 1949 (CR 425)
Pigmented hide glue and oil on canvas, 80⅜ × 66⅜ in. (206.7 × 168.6 cm)
National Gallery of Art, Washington, D.C.
Gift of the Mark Rothko Foundation, Inc., 1986.43.138
p. 83

47 *Untitled*, 1949 (CR 421)
Oil and acrylic with powder pigments on canvas, 56⅛ × 33 in. (142.6 × 83.8 cm)
The Metropolitan Museum of Art, New York
Gift of the Mark Rothko Foundation, Inc.
p. 84

48 *No. 5*, 1949 (CR 412)
Oil on canvas, 85 × 63 in. (215.9 × 160 cm)
Chrysler Museum of Art, Norfolk
Bequest of Walter P. Chrysler, Jr
p. 85

49 *No. 8*, 1949 (CR 415)
Oil and mixed media on canvas, 89⅞ × 65⅞ in. (228.3 × 167.3 cm)
National Gallery of Art, Washington, D.C.
Gift of the Mark Rothko Foundation, Inc., 1986.43.147
p. 87

50 *No. 5/No. 22*, 1950 (CR 442)
Oil on canvas, 117 × 107 in. (297.2 × 272.1 cm)
Museum of Modern Art, New York
Gift of the artist, 1969
p. 89

51 *No. 7*, 1951 (CR 455)
Oil on canvas, 94¾ × 54⅝ in. (240.7 × 138.7 cm)
Yageo Foundation, Taiwan
p. 91

52 *No. 16*, 1951 (CR 462)
Oil on canvas, 67⅝ × 44⅝ in. (171.8 × 113.4 cm)
Collection of Christopher Rothko
p. 92

53 *No. 7 (Dark over Light)*, 1954 (CR 506)
Oil on canvas, 90⅛ × 58⅝ in. (228.8 × 148.8 cm)
Nahmad Collection
p. 93

54 *No. 9/No. 5/No. 18*, 1952 (CR 477)
Oil on canvas, 116 × 91½ in. (294.6 × 232.4 cm)
Private collection
p. 95

55 *No. 14/No. 10 (Yellow Greens)*, 1953 (CR 499)
Oil on canvas, 77 × 67¾ in. (195 × 172.1 cm)
Frederick R. Weisman Art Foundation, Los Angeles
p. 97

56 *No. 9 (Dark over Light Earth/Violet and Yellow in Rose)*, 1954 (CR 508)
Oil on canvas, 83¼ × 68 in. (212.1 × 172.1 cm)
The Museum of Contemporary Art, Los Angeles, The Panza Collection
p. 99

57 *Untitled*, 1955 (CR 523)
Oil on canvas, 91⅗ × 69 in. (232.7 × 175.3 cm)
Yageo Foundation, Taiwan
p. 100

58 *No. 18*, 1951 (CR 464)
Oil on canvas, 81½ × 69⅞ in. (207 × 170.5 cm)
Munson Museum, Utica, NY
p. 101

59 *No. 6 (Yellow, White, Blue over Yellow On Gray)*, 1954 (CR 505)
Oil on canvas, 94½ × 59¾ in (240 × 151.8 cm)
Private collection
p. 103

60 *Untitled (Blue, Yellow, Green on Red)*, 1954 (CR 514)
Oil on canvas, 77¾ × 65½ in. (195.7 × 166.4 cm)
Whitney Museum of American Art, New York
Gift of The American Contemporary Art Foundation, Inc., Leonard A. Lauder, President
p. 105

61 *Untitled (Red, Black, White on Yellow)*, 1955 (CR 535)
Oil on canvas, 105 × 93 in. (266.7 × 236.2 cm)
National Gallery of Art, Washington, D.C.
Collection of Mrs. Paul Mellon, in Honor of the 50th Anniversary of the National Gallery of Art, 1992.51.14
p. 107

62 *Untitled*, 1955 (CR 542)
Oil on canvas, 81½ × 59⅝ in. (207 × 151.4 cm)
Private collection
p. 109

63 *Yellow Band*, 1956 (CR 555)
Oil on canvas, 86 × 79½ in. (218.8 × 201.9 cm)
Sheldon Museum of Art, University of Nebraska-Lincoln, Nebraska Art Association, Thomas C. Woods Memorial
p. 111

64 *No. 10*, 1957 (CR 585)
Oil and mixed media on canvas, 69¼ × 61½ in. (175.9 × 156.2 cm)
The Menil Collection, Houston
p. 113

65 *Light Cloud, Dark Cloud*, 1957 (CR 574)
Oil on canvas, 66 × 61¾ in. (167.64 × 156.85 cm)
Collection of the Modern Art Museum of Fort Worth
Museum purchase, The Benjamin J. Tillar Memorial Trust
p. 115

66 *Green on Blue (Earth-Green and White)*, 1956 (CR 543)
Oil on canvas, 91¼ × 64⅜ in. (228.6 × 161.3 cm)
The University of Arizona Museum of Art, Tucson
Gift of Edward Joseph Gallagher, Jr.
p. 116

67 *No. 3*, 1957 (CR 581)
Oil on canvas, 79½ × 69½ in. (201.9 × 176.5 cm)
Private collection
p. 117

68 *No. 15*, 1958 (CR 622)
Oil on canvas, 92¾ × 83⅜ in. (235.6 × 211.8 cm)
Private collection
p. 119

69 *No. 13 (White, Red on Yellow)*, 1958 (CR 620)
Oil and acrylic with powdered pigments on canvas, 95¼ × 81⅖ in. (241.9 × 206.7 cm)
The Metropolitan Museum of Art, New York
Gift of The Mark Rothko Foundation Inc., New York
p. 121

70 *Orange and Red on Red*, 1957 (CR 599)
Oil on canvas, 68⅞ × 66⅜ in. (172.4 × 168.5 cm)
The Phillips Collection, Washington, D.C.
Acquired 1960
p. 122

71 *Green and Tangerine on Red*, 1956 (CR 562)
Oil on canvas, 93⅝ × 69¼ in. (237.9 × 175.9 cm)
The Phillips Collection, Washington, D.C.
Acquired 1960
p. 125

72 *Ochre, Red on Red*, 1954 (CR 517)
Oil on canvas, 92⅝ × 63¾ in. (235.3 × 161.9 cm)
The Phillips Collection, Washington, D.C.
Acquired 1964
p. 127

73 *No. 15*, 1957 (CR 589)
Oil on canvas, 103 × 116½ in. (261.6 × 259.9 cm)
Private collection
p. 129

74 *Pink and White over Red*, 1957 (CR 577)
Oil on canvas, 105 × 116 in. (266.7 × 294.6 cm)
Anderson Collection at Stanford University, Gift of Harry W. and Mary Margaret Anderson, and Mary Patricia Anderson Pence, 2014.1.033
p. 131

75 *The Black and the White*, 1956 (CR 572)
Oil on canvas, 94 × 53¾ in. (238.8 × 136.5 cm)
Harvard Art Museums, Fogg Museum, Cambridge
Gift of Ruth and Frank Stanton
p. 133

76 *Brown and Black in Reds*, 1957 (CR 602)
Oil on canvas, 91 × 60 in. (231.1 × 152.4 cm)
Collection of Adriana and Robert Mnuchin
p. 135

77 *No. 9 (White and Black on Wine)*, 1958 (CR 616)
Oil on canvas, 105 × 168¾ in. (266.7 × 428.7 cm)
Glenstone Museum, Potomac, Maryland
pp. 136–37

78 *Black on Maroon*, 1959 (CR 647)
Oil and acrylic with powdered pigments on canvas, 105 × 90 in. (266.7 × 228.6 cm)
Tate: Presented by the artist through the American Federation of Arts 1969
p. 139

79 *Black on Maroon*, 1958 (CR 636)
Oil paint, acrylic paint, glue tempera and pigment on canvas, 90 × 81½ in. (228.6 × 207 cm)
Tate: Presented by the artist through the American Federation of Arts 1969
p. 141

80 *Black on Maroon*, 1958 (CR 644)
Oil paint, acrylic paint, glue tempera and pigment on canvas, 105 × 95 in. (266.7 × 241.3 cm)
Tate: Presented by the artist through the American Federation of Arts 1969
p. 143

81 *Black on Maroon*, 1958 (CR 642)
Oil paint, acrylic paint, glue tempera and pigment on canvas, 105 × 144 in. (266.7 × 381.2 cm)
Tate: Presented by the artist through the American Federation of Arts 1968
pp. 148–49

82 *Red on Maroon*, 1959 (CR 660)
Oil paint, acrylic paint, glue tempera and pigment on canvas, 105 × 94 in. (266.7 × 238.8 cm)
Tate: Presented by the artist through the American Federation of Arts 1969
p. 151

83 *Red on Maroon*, 1959 (CR 663)
Oil paint, acrylic paint, glue tempera and pigment on canvas, 72 × 180 in. (182.9 × 457.2 cm)
Tate: Presented by the artist through the American Federation of Arts 1969
pp. 152–53

84 *Red on Maroon*, 1959 (CR 661)
Oil paint, acrylic paint, glue tempera and pigment on canvas, 72 × 180 in. (182.9 × 457.2 cm)
Tate: Presented by the artist through the American Federation of Arts 1969
pp. 154–55

85 *Black on Maroon*, 1959 (CR 658)
Oil paint, acrylic paint, glue tempera and pigment on canvas, 105 × 180 in. (266.7 × 457.2 cm)
Tate: Presented by the artist through the American Federation of Arts 1969
pp. 156–57

86 *Red on Maroon*, 1959 (CR 657)
Oil on canvas, 105 × 180 in. (266.7 × 457.2 cm)
Tate: Presented by the artist through the American Federation of Arts 1969
pp. 158–59

87 *Untitled*, 1960 (CR 670)
Mixed media on canvas, 92⅞ × 81 in. (235.9 × 205.7 cm)
The Toledo Art Museum
Purchased with funds from the Libbey Endowment, Gift of Edward Drummond Libbey
p. 161

88 *No. 14*, 1960 (CR 679)
Oil on canvas, 114½ × 105⅝ in. (290.8 × 268.3 cm)
San Francisco Museum of Modern Art
Collection of Helen Crocker Russell Fund purchase
p. 163

89 *Number 207 (Red over Dark Blue on Dark Gray)*, 1961 (CR 707)
Oil on canvas, 92¾ × 81⅛ in. (235.6 × 206.1 cm)
University of California, Berkeley Art Museum and Pacific Film Archive; Museum purchase
p. 164

90 *Blue, Orange, Red*, 1961 (CR 700)
Oil on canvas, 90¼ × 81 1⁄16 in. (229.3 × 205.9 cm)
Hirshhorn Museum and Sculpture Garden, Smithsonian Institution, Washington, D.C.
Gift of the Joseph H. Hirshhorn Foundation, 1966
p. 165

91 *Blue and Gray*, 1962 (CR 723)
Oil on canvas, 79¼ × 69 in. (193 × 175 cm)
Beyeler Foundation, Riehen / Basel, Beyeler Collection
p. 167

92 *Untitled*, 1962 (CR 720)
Oil on canvas, 85¼ × 76 in. (206.5 × 193.5 cm)
Staatsgalerie Stuttgart
Erworben mit Lotto-Mitteln 1969
p. 169

93 *No. 1 (White and Red)*, 1962 (CR 717)
Oil on canvas, 102 × 90 in. (259.1 × 228.6 cm)
Art Gallery of Ontario, Toronto
Gift from Women's Committee Fund, 1962
p. 171

94 *No. 14*, 1961 (CR 701)
Oil on canvas, 92⅞ × 80 in. (235.9 × 203.2 cm)
Museum of Fine Arts, Houston
p. 173

95 *No. 5*, 1963 (CR 746)
Oil on canvas, 90 × 69 in. (228.6 × 175.3 cm)
Private collection
p. 174

96 *No. 2*, 1963 (CR 744)
Oil paint, acrylic and tempera on canvas, 80¼ × 69⅛ in. (203.8 × 175.6 cm)
Walker Art Center, Minneapolis
Gift of The Mark Rothko Foundation, Inc.
p. 175

97 *Untitled (Black, Red over Black on Red)*, 1964 (CR 764)
Oil on canvas, 80¾ × 76 in. (205 × 193 cm)
Centre Pompidou – Musée National d'Art Moderne, Paris
p. 177

98 *No. 8*, 1964 (CR 781)
Oil, acrylic and mixed media on canvas, 105¼ × 80¼ in. (266.7 × 203.2 cm)
National Gallery of Art, Washington, D.C.
Gift of The Mark Rothko Foundation, Inc., 1986.43.139
p. 179

99 *Untitled (Plum and Brown)*, 1964 (CR 769)
Oil on canvas, 81 × 69⅛ in. (205.7 × 175.6 cm)
Private collection
p. 181

100 *Untitled*, 1964 (CR 767)
Oil and acrylic paint on canvas, 69⅛ × 66⅗ in. (176 × 168.5 cm)
Louisiana Museum of Modern Art, Humlebaek
Donation: The Mark Rothko Foundation via the American Federation of Arts
p. 182

101 *No. 3*, 1967 (CR 807)
Oil on canvas, 66⅛ × 68⅛ in. (168 × 173 cm)
Private collection
p. 183

102 *Untitled*, 1967 (CR 806)
Oil on canvas, 80 × 69 in. (203.2 × 175.3 cm)
The Governor Nelson A. Rockefeller Empire State Plaza Art Collection, New York
p. 185

103 *Untitled*, 1969 (CR 814)
Acrylic on canvas, 92 × 78⅞ in. (233.7 × 200.3 cm)
Collection of Christopher Rothko
p. 187

104 *Untitled*, 1969 (CR 823)
Acrylic on canvas, 54¼ × 68¼ in. (137.8 × 173.4 cm)
National Gallery of Art, Washington, D.C.
Gift of The Mark Rothko Foundation, Inc., 1986.43.165
p. 189

105 *Untitled*, 1969 (CR 817)
Acrylic on canvas, 69⅝ × 62⅛ in. (176.8 × 157.8 cm)
National Gallery of Art, Washington, D.C.
Gift of The Mark Rothko Foundation, Inc., 1986.43.163
p. 191

106 *Untitled*, 1969 / 1970 (CR 831)
Acrylic on canvas, 68 × 64 in. (172.7 × 162.5 cm)
Private collection
p. 193

107 *Untitled*, 1969 (CR 816). Not exhibited
Acrylic on canvas, 100⅛ × 79⅘ in. (254.3 × 202.9 cm)
Private collection
p. 200

108 *Untitled*, 1969 (CR 820)
Acrylic on canvas, 81⅛ × 76¼ in. (206.1 × 193.7 cm)
National Gallery of Art, Washington, D.C.
Gift of The Mark Rothko Foundation, Inc., 1986.43.165
p. 197

109 *Untitled*, 1969 (CR 825)
Acrylic on canvas, 81¼ × 93¼ in. (206.4 × 236.2 cm)
Private collection
p. 195

110 *Untitled*, 1969 (CR 824)
Acrylic on canvas, 105 × 114 in. (266.1 × 289.6 cm)
Private collection
p. 201

111 *Untitled (Black and Gray)*, 1969 / 1970 (CR 829)
Acrylic on canvas, 68 × 60¼ in. (172.7 × 152.4 cm)
The Museum of Contemporary Art, Los Angeles
Gift of The Mark Rothko Foundation, Inc.
p. 203

112 *Untitled*, 1969 (CR 826)
Acrylic on canvas, 69¾ × 117 in. (177.2 × 297.2 cm)
Private collection
pp. 204–05

113 *Untitled (Black and Gray)*, 1969 (CR 822)
Acrylic on canvas, 93 × 76⅛ in. (236.2 × 193.4 cm)
Anderson Collection at Stanford University, Gift of Harry W. and Mary Margaret Anderson, and Mary Patricia Anderson Pence, 2014.1.023
p. 207

114 *Untitled*, 1967 (CR 808)
Oil on canvas, 68 × 60¼ in. (172.7 × 153 cm)
Private collection
p. 209

115 *No. 3 (Untitled / Orange)*, 1967 (CR 810)
Oil on canvas, 81 × 75 15⁄16 in. (205.7 × 196.6 cm)
Yale University Art Gallery, New Haven, Katharine Ordway Collection
p. 211

Works by Alberto Giacometti

Alberto Giacometti
L'Homme qui marche I [*Walking Man I*], 1960
Bronze, 183 x 26 x 96,5 cm
Fondation Marguerite et Aimé Maeght,
Saint-Paul-de-Vence, Inv. 0314

Alberto Giacometti
Grande Femme III [*Tall Woman III*], 1960
Bronze, ed. 6/6, 235,8 x 32,3 x 54 cm
Susse Fondeur Paris
Fondation Beyeler, Riehen/Basel,
Sammlung Beyeler, Inv.67.3

Alberto Giacometti
Grande Femme II [*Tall Woman II*], 1960
Bronze with dark brown patina, ed. 1/6,
277 x 29 x 57,2 cm
Susse Fondeur Paris, fonte de 1961
Fondation Louis Vuitton, Paris

Select bibliography

Exhibition catalogues

15 Americans (New York, Museum of Modern Art, April 9 – July 27, 1952), Miller, Dorothy C. (ed.), New York, Museum of Modern Art, 1952.

Lipton, Rothko, Smith, Tobey (Venice, XXIX[e] Biennale Internazionale d'Arte, Stati Uniti d'America, 1958), Hunter, Sam, Venice, Biennale, 1958.

Mark Rothko (New York, Museum of Modern Art, January 18 – March 12, 1961), Selz, Peter, New York, MoMA, 1961.

Mark Rothko: a Retrospective Exhibition Paintings 1945–1960 (London, Whitechapel Art Gallery, October – November 1961), Selz, Peter, Goldwater, Robert, London, Whitechapel Art Gallery, 1961.

Mark Rothko (Paris, Musée d'Art Moderne de la Ville de Paris, December 1962 – January 1963), Selz, Peter, Paris, Musée d'Art Moderne de la Ville de Paris, 1962.

Six Painters: Mondrian, Guston, Kline, De Kooning, Pollock, Rothko (Houston, University of St. Thomas Art Department, February – April 1967), University of St. Thomas Art Department, Houston, University of St. Thomas Art Department, 1968.

Mark Rothko (Venice, Museo d'Arte Moderna Ca'Pesaro, June 21 – October 15, 1970), Museo d'Arte Moderna Ca'Pesaro, New York, Marlborough Galleries, 1970.

Mark Rothko (Zürich, Kunsthaus Zürich, March 21 – May 9, 1971; Berlin, Staatliche Museen Preussischer Kulturbesitz, Neue Nationalgalerie, May 26 – July 19, 1971; Düsseldorf, Städtische Kunsthalle, August 24 – October 3, 1971; Rotterdam, Museum Boymans van Beuningen, November 20, 1971 – January 2, 1972; London, Hayward Gallery, February 2 – March 12, 1972; Paris, Musée National d'Art Moderne, March 23 – May 8, 1972), Baumann, Félix Andreas (ed.), Paris, Réunion des Musées Nationaux, 1972.

Mark Rothko, 1903–1970: A Retrospective (New York, Solomon R. Guggenheim Museum, October 27, 1978 – January 14, 1979), Waldman, Diane, New York, Harry N. Abrams, 1978.

Mark Rothko: The Surrealist Years (New York, The Pace Gallery, April 24 – May 3, 1981), Rosenblum, Robert, New York, The Pace Gallery, 1981.

Mark Rothko: Seven Paintings from the 1960's (Minneapolis, Walker Art Center, February 5 – March 27, 1983), Clearwater Bonnie, Minneapolis, Walker Art Center, 1983.

Mark Rothko: Paintings 1948–1969 (New York, The Pace Gallery, April 1–30, 1983), Sandler, Irving, New York, The Pace Gallery, 1983.

Mark Rothko. Works on Paper (New York, American Federation of Art and The Mark Rothko Foundation, May 6 – August 5, 1984; Pittsburgh, Carnegie Museum of Art, November 3, 1984 – January 6, 1985; New York, Solomon R. Guggenheim Museum, May 3 – June 16, 1985; Milwaukee Art Museum, November 22, 1985 – January 12, 1986; Portland Art Museum, February 11 – April 6, 1986; San Francisco Museum of Modern Art, May 8 – June 29, 1986; Saint Louis Art Museum, July 18 – September 1, 1986; Fort Worth Art Museum, September 21 – November 9, 1986), Clearwater, Bonnie, Ashton, Dore, New York, Hudson Hills Press, 1984.

Mark Rothko: The Dark Paintings 1969–1970 (New York, The Pace Gallery, March 29 – April 27, 1985), O'Doherty, Brian, New York, The Pace Gallery, 1985.

Mark Rothko, the Seagram Mural Project (Liverpool, Tate Gallery, May 28, 1988 – February 12, 1989), Compton, Michael, Liverpool, Tate Gallery, 1988.

Mark Rothko: Kaaba in New York (Basel, Kunsthalle Basel, February 19 – May 7, 1989), Kellein, Thomas, Basel, Kunsthalle Basel, 1989.

Mark Rothko: The Last Paintings (New York, The Pace Gallery, February 18 – March 19, 1994, O'Doherty, Brian, New York, The Pace Gallery, 1994.

Mark Rothko in Cornwall (St. Ives, Tate Gallery, May 4 – November 3, 1996), Stephens, Chris, St. Ives, Tate Gallery, 1996.

Mark Rothko, the Chapel Commission (Houston, The Menil Collection, December 13, 1996 – March 29, 1997), Anfam, David, Mancusi-Ungaro, Carol, Houston, Menil Collection, 1996.

Bonnard, Rothko: Color and Light (New York, PaceWildenstein, February 19 – March 22, 1997), Rose, Berenice, New York, PaceWildenstein, 1997.

Mark Rothko (Washington, D.C., National Gallery of Art, May 3 – August 16, 1998; New York, Whitney Museum of American Art, September 10 – November 29, 1998), Weiss, Jeffrey (ed.), Washington, D.C., National Gallery of Art / New Haven, Yale University Press, 1998.

Mark Rothko (Paris, Musée d'Art Moderne de la Ville de Paris, January 14 – April 18, 1999), Pagé, Suzanne, Weiss, Jeffrey, Paris, Paris-Musées, 1999.

Mark Rothko 1903–1970. Revised Edition (London, Tate Gallery, June 17 – September 1, 1987; Madrid, Fundacion Juan March, September 23, 1987 – January 3, 1988; Cologne, Museum Ludwig, January 30 – March 27, 1988), Compton, Mickael, London, Tate Gallery Publishing, 1999.

Mark Rothko (Riehen, Fondation Beyeler, February 18 – April 29, 2001), Wick, Oliver (ed.), Ostfildern-Ruit, Hatje Cantz, 2001.

Rothko. The Realist Years: Selected Works (New York, PaceWildenstein, October 31, 2001 – January 5, 2002), Kertess, Klaus, New York, PaceWildenstein, 2001.

Rothko: A Painter's Progress. The Year 1949 (New York, PaceWildenstein, January 23 – February 23, 2004), Rose, Berenice, New York, PaceWildenstein, 2004.

Black Paintings (Munich, Haus der Kunst, September 15, 2006 – January 14, 2007), Rosenthal, Stephanie, Ostfildern, Hatje Cantz, 2006.

Mark Rothko (Tel Aviv, Museum of Art, Sam and Ayala Zacks Pavilion, March 29 – June 30, 2007), Mordechai, Omer, Rothko, Christopher, Tel Aviv, Tel Aviv Museum of Art, 2007.

Mark Rothko and Barnett Newman: The Sublime Is Now! (Riehen, Fondation Beyeler, May 16 – August 5, 2007), cat. Anfam, David, Wick, Oliver, Riehen, Fondation Beyeler 2007.

Mark Rothko (Rome, Palazzo delle Esposizioni, October 6, 2007 – January 6, 2008), Wick, Oliver (ed.), Milan, Skira, 2008.

Rothko: The Late Series (London, Tate Modern, September 26, 2008 – February 1, 2009; Sakura, Kawamura Memorial Museum of Art, February 21 – June 14, 2009), Borchardt-Hume, Achim (ed.), London, Tate Publishing, 2008.

Rothko/Giotto (Berlin, SMB Gemäldegalerie Staatliche Museen, February 5 – May 3, 2000), Weppelmann, Stefan, Wolf, Gerhard (ed.), Munich, Hirmer Verlag, 2009.

Mark Rothko: the Decisive Decade, 1940–1950 (Columbia Museum of Art (SC), September 14, 2012 – January 6, 2013; Columbus Museum of Art (OH), February 1 – May 26, 2013; Denver Art Museum, June 16 – September 22, 2013; Little Rock, Arkansas Art Center, October 25, 2013 – February 9, 2014), Collins, Bradford R. (ed.), Anfam, David, Cooper, Harry, Fine, Ruth, Herman, Todd, Rothko, Christopher, New York, Rizzoli Electa, 2012.

Rothko/Sugimoto: Dark Paintings and Seascapes (London, The Pace Gallery, Oct. 4 – Nov. 17, 2012), Shiff, Richard, London, The Pace Gallery, 2012.

Rothko: Dark Palette (New York, Pace Gallery, November 4, 2016 – January 7, 2017), Glimcher, Arnold B., New York, Pace Gallery, 2016.

Mark Rothko (Vienna, Kunsthistorisches Museum, March 12 – June 30, 2019), Haag, Sabine, Sharp, Jasper (ed.), New Haven, London, Yale University Press, 2019.

Mark Rothko. 1968. Clearing Away (New York, The Pace Gallery, October 8 – November 13, 2021), Nairne, Eleanor, , New York, The Pace Gallery, 2021.

Monet Rothko (Giverny, Musée des impressionnismes Giverny, March 18 – July 3, 2022), Sciama, Cyrille (ed.), Paris, Flammarion, Giverny, Musée des impressionnismes Giverny, 2022.

Monographs

Anfam, David, *Mark Rothko: The Works on Canvas. Catalogue raisonné,* New Haven, London, Yale University Press / Washington, D.C., National Gallery of Art, 1998 (edition revised and corrected in 1999 then in 2001)

Ashton, Dore, *About Rothko*, New York, Oxford University Press, 1983. (2nd edition, New York, Da Capo Press, 1996 consulted)

Baal-Teshuva, Jacob, *Mark Rothko, 1903–1970: Pictures As Drama*, Cologne, Taschen, 2009. Barnes, Susan J., *The Rothko Chapel: An Act of Faith*, Houston, Rothko Chapel, 1989. (2nd edition in 1996)

Bishop, Janet, *Rothko: The Color Field Paintings,* San Francisco, Chronicle Books, 2017.

Breslin James E. B., *Mark Rothko. A Biography*, Chicago, University of Chicago Press, 1993. (2nd edition in 1998)

Chave, Anna C., *Mark Rothko: Subjects in Abstraction,* New Haven, Yale University Press, 1989.

Clearwater, Bonnie, *The Rothko Book*, London, Tate Publishing, 2007.

Cohen-Solal, Annie, *Mark Rothko: Towards the Light in the Chapel*, New Haven, Yale University Press, 2013.

Fer, Briony, "Picture", in *The Infinite Line: Re-making Art After Modernism*, New Haven, Yale University Press, 2004, pp. 5–25.

Glimcher, Marc (ed.), *The Art of Mark Rothko: Into an Unknown World*, New York, Clarkson N. Potter, 1991.

Grange, Susan, *Mark Rothko: Break into the Light*, London, Flame Tree Publishing, 2016.

Greenhalgh, Adam, Nasr, Laili, *Mark Rothko's Work on Paper. Catalogue raisonné,* Washington, D.C., National Gallery of Art, Online Resource Launched at rothko.nga.gov: https://www.nga.gov/press/2022/rothko-works-on-paper-catalog.html.

Janis, Sidney, *Abstract & Surrealist: Art in America,* New York, Arno. Press, 1944.

Jodidio, Philip (chief editor), La Batut, Virginie de (dir.), Ashton, Dore, Weiss, Jeffrey, Gibson, Michael, Pagé, Suzanne, Nodelman, Sheldon, *Connaissance des arts HS: Rothko*, no. 130, February 13, 1999.

Lambert, Phyllis, *Building Seagram*, New Haven, Yale University Press, 2013.

Menil, Dominique de, *The Rothko Chapel: Writings on Art and the Threshold of the Divine*, Houston, The Rothko Chapel, 2010.

Middleton, William, *Double Vision: The Unerring Eye of Art World Avatars Dominique and John de Menil*, 1st edition, New York, Alfred A. Knopf, 2018.

Motherwell, Robert, Ashton, Dore, Cotensin, Patrice, *Sur Mark Rothko*, Paris, L'Échoppe, 2005.

Nodelman, Sheldon, *The Rothko Chapel Paintings: Origins, Structure, Meaning*, Austin, University of Texas Press / Houston, The Menil Collection, 1997.

O'Doherty, Brian (ed.), *American Masters. The Voice and the Myth,* New York, Random House, 1973.

Phillips, Glenn, Crow, Thomas (ed.), *Seeing Rothko*, Los Angeles, Getty Research Institute, 2005.

Pleynet, Marcelin, *Rothko et la France*, Paris, Éditions de l'Épure, 1999.

Rodman, Selden, "Mark Rothko; Kenzo Okada; Herman Cherry; Ad Reinhardt," in *Conversations with Artists*, New York, Devin-Adair, 1957, pp. 92–99.

Rosenblum, Robert, *Modern Painting and the Northern Romantic Tradition. Friedrich to Rothko*, New York, Harper & Row, 1975.

Rothko, Christopher, *Mark Rothko: From the Inside Out*, New Haven and London, Yale University Press, 2015.

Rothko Prizel, Kate, Rothko, Christopher (ed.), *Mark Rothko*, New York, Rizzoli Electa, 2022.

Smart, Pamela, Fox, Stephen, Rothko, Christopher, Leslie, David, *Rothko Chapel: An Oasis for Reflection,* New York, Rizzoli Electa, 2021.

Vallier, Dora, Goldwater, Robert, *Mark Rothko reconnu et méconnu à Paris: suivi de Sur la peinture de M. Rothko*, Paris, L'Échoppe, 2019.

Venturi, Riccardo, *Mark Rothko: lo spazio e la sua disciplina*, Milan, Electa, 2007.

Waldman, Diane, *Mark Rothko in New York*, New York, Guggenheim Museum Publications, 1994.

Writings by Rothko (selection)

Rothko, Christopher (ed.), Rothko, Mark, *The Artist's Reality: Philosophies of Art*, New Haven and London, Yale University Press, 2004.

López-Remiro, Miguel (ed.), Rothko, Mark, *Writings on Art*, New Haven and London, Yale University Press, 2006.

Articles

Alloway, Lawrence, "The Biomorphic Forties," *Artforum*, vol. 4, no. 1, September 1965, pp. 18–22.

Alloway, Lawrence, "Notes on Rothko," *Art International*, vol. 6, no. 566, summer 1962, pp. 90–94

Andral, Jean-Louis, "Mark Rothko, peintre Classique," *Connaissance des Arts*, no. 557, January 1999, pp. 32–39.

Anfam, David, "A Note on Rothko's *The Syrian Bull*," *The Burlington Magazine*, 139, September 1997, pp. 629–31.

Arasse, Daniel, "La solitude de Rothko," *Art press*, no. 241, trans. Charles Penwarden, December 1998, pp. 27–35.

Ashton, Dore, "Mark Rothko," *Arts & Architecture Magazine*, vol. 74, no. 8, August 1957, pp. 8, 31.

Ashton, Dore, "Art: Lecture by Rothko: Painter Dissociates Himself From the 'Abstract Expressionist' Movement," *The New York Times*, October 31, 1958, p. 26.

Ashton, Dore, "Le pitture murali di Mark Rothko," *La Biennale di Venezia*, vol. XIV, no. 54, September 1964.

Ashton, Dore, "Rothko's Passion," *Art International*, vol. 22, no. 9, February 1979, pp. 6–13.

Ashton, Dore, "Painting Toward Nightfall," *Washington Post Book World*, December 13, 1998, p. 5.

Ashton, Dore, "Rothko's Mystery Remains", *Modern Painters,* 1, no. 4, winter 1998, p. 109.

Barnes, Rachel, "Leaving a Mark", *Art Review*, 48, May 1996, pp. 28–30.

Bétard, Daphné, "Mark Rothko: Le peintre qui voulait réparer le monde," *Beaux-arts magazine*, March 2014, pp. 36–37.

Bois, Yve-Alain, "The Big Pictures," *Artforum International*, 38, no. 2, October 1999, pp. 19–21.

Butor, Michel, "Les mosquées de New-York ou l'art de Mark Rothko," *Critique: revue générale des publications françaises et étrangères*, no. 173, October 1961, pp. 843–60.

Carion, Anne, "Mark Rothko," *FMR*, no. 96, February–March 1999, p. 10.

Cernuschi, Claude, "Mark Rothko from Alpha to Omega," *American Art Journal*, 38, no. 1–2, 1998, pp. 39–45.

Chave, Anna C., "Washington and New York: Mark Rothko," *The Burlington Magazine*, 140, October 1998, pp. 712–14.

Clark, Timothy J., "Défense de l'expressionisme abstrait," *Les Cahiers du Musée national d'art moderne*, 66, winter 1998, pp. 22–49.

Clearwater, Bonnie, "Shared Myths: Reconsideration of Rothko's and Gottlieb's Letter to *The New York Times*," *American Art*, vol. 24, no. 1, 1984, pp. 23–25.

Clearwater, Bonnie, "How Rothko Looked at Rothko," *ARTnews*, vol. 84, no. 9, November 1985, pp. 100–03.

Cohen, David, "Mark Rothko," *The New York Sun*, February 12, 2004, p. 18.

Coles, Richard, "The Rothko Chapel: Religious Art Without God," *Art Newspaper*, vol. 8, no. 72, July–August 1997, p. 45.

Colpitt, Frances, "Outtakes from the Chapel," *Art in America*, vol. 85, June 1997, p. 99.

Compton, Michael, "The Big Picture," *Tate: The Art Magazine*, no. 9, summer 1996, pp. 48–51.

Crow, Thomas, "In the tower: Mark Rothko," *Artforum international*, vol. 49, no. 4, December 2010, pp. 190–93.

Danto, Arthur C., "Rothko's Material Beauty," *The Nation 267*, no. 21, December 21, 1998, pp. 31–34.

Descargues, Pierre, "Mark Rothko," *Nouvelle Revue française*, no. 549, April 1999, p. 264.

Engelhard, Günther, "Abstraktion: Mark Rothko," *Art 7*, July 1996, pp. 14–27.

Feldman, Morton, "Crippled Symmetry," *RES: Anthropology and Aesthetics*, 2, 1981, pp. 91–103

Firestone, Evan, "Rothko's Androgny," *Word & Image*, vol. 22, no. 1, January–March 2006, pp. 39–53.

Fischer, John, "Mark Rothko: Portrait of the Artist as Angry Man," *Harper's Magazine*, no. 241, 1970, pp. 16–23.

França, José-Augusto, "Mark Rothko et l'espace continu," *Aujourd'hui: Art et Architecture*, no. 40, 1963, pp. 10–11.

Gibson, Ann Eden, "Regression and Color in Abstract Expressionism: Barnett Newman, Mark Rothko, and Clyfford Still," *Arts Magazine*, 55, no. 7, March 1981, pp. 144–53.

Gibson, Ann Eden, "New Myths for Old: Redefining Abstract Expressionism," *Art journal*, volume. 47, no. 7, autumn 1988, pp. 171–73.

Gibson, Ann Eden, "Abstract Expressionism's Evasion of Language," *Art Journal*, vol. 47, no. 3, autumn 1988, pp. 208–14.

Gintz, Claude, "La couleur tragique de Rothko," *L'Architecture d'Aujourd'hui*, no. 321, March 1999, p. 16.

Goldberg, Itzhak, "Rothko : La couleur métaphysique," *Beaux-Arts Magazine*, no. 176, January 1999, p. 62–69.

Goldwater, Robert, "Reflections on the Rothko Exhibition," *Arts magazine international*, vol. 35, no. 6, March 1961, pp. 42–45.

Goldwater, Robert, "Rothko's Black Paintings, *Art in America : an illustrated quarterly*, no. 2, March–April 1971, pp. 58–63.

Grant, Simon (interviewer), Rothko, Christopher (person interviewed), Rothko Prizel, Kate (person interviewed), "Rothko and Turner at Tate Britain: "This man Turner, he learnt a lot from me"," *Tate etc.*, no. 51, spring 2021, pp. 54–57.

Greenberg, Clement, "American-Type Painting," *Partisan Review*, XXII, no. 2, spring 1955, pp. 179–96.

Harris, Jonathan, "Mark Rothko and the Development of American Modernism 1938–1948," *Oxford Art Journal*, vol. 11, no. 1, 1988, pp. 40–50.

Jewell, Edward Alden, "Modern Painters Open Show Today," *The New York Times*, June 2, 1943, p. 28.

Kenedy, R. C., "Mark Rothko," *Art International*, vol. XIV, no. 8, October 20, 1970, pp. 45–49.

Kimmelman, Michael, "Art Review: Rothko's Gloomy Elegance in Retrospect," *The New York Times*, September 18. 1998, p. 31.

Kozloff, Max, "Mark Rothko's New Retrospective," *Art journal*, vol. XX, no. 3, spring 1961, pp. 148–49.

Lequeux, Emmanuelle, "Mark Rothko: La lumière noire," *Beaux-arts magazine*, no. 292, October 2008, pp. 120–27.

MacAgy, Douglas, "Mark Rothko," *Magazine of Art*, vol. 42, no. 1, January 1949, pp. 20–21.

Nodelman, Sheldon, "Rediscovering Rothko," *Art in America*, 87, no. 7, July 1999, pp. 58–65, 106.

Nodelman, Sheldon, "The Unknown Rothko," *Art in America*, vol. 96, February 2008, pp. 98–105.

O'Doherty, Brian, "Mark Rothko," *Art International magazine*, vol. 14, no. 8, October 1970, pp. 30–44.

Orton, Fred, Breyers, Gavin, "Feldman Interview," *Studio International*, 1970, pp. 244–48.

Pappas, Andrea, "Haunted Abstraction: Mark Rothko, Witnessing and the Holocaust in 1942," *Journal of Modern Jewish Studies*, vol. 6, no. 2, July 2007, pp. 167–83.

Piguet, Philippe, "Mark Rothko: A Celebration of the Sublime," *Cimaise*, 46, no. 257, January–February 1999, pp. 9–16.

Pleynet, Marcelin, "Exposition Mark Rothko," *Tel quel*, no. 12, winter 1963, pp. 39–41.

Polcari, Stephen, "The Intellectual Roots of Abstract Expressionism Mark Rothko," *Arts Magazine,* 54, September 1979, pp. 124–34.

Polcari, Stephen, "Mark Rothko", *Tate: The Art-Magazine*, no. 17, spring 1999, pp. 83, 85.

Polcari, Stephen, "Mark Rothko: Heritage, Environment, and Tradition," *American Art*, vol. 2, no. 2, spring 1988, pp. 32–63.

Ragon, Michel, "Un Américain tourné vers l'Orient," *Galerie des arts*, no. 3, 1963, p. 11.

Ragon, Michel, "Rothko," *Cimaise: revue de l'art actuel*, no. 62, November–December 1962, p. 84.

Roberts, Emma E., "St. Ives: Mark Rothko," *The Burlington Magazine*, 138, October 1996, p. 27.

Robertson, Bryan, "Bryan Robertson about Rothko," *Modern Painters: the International Art Magazine*, 11, no. 3, 1998, pp. 24–29.

Rosenberg, Harold, "The Art World: Rothko," *The New Yorker*, vol. 46, no. 6, March 28, 1970, pp. 90–95.

Rosenblum, Robert, "The Abstract Sublime," *ARTnews*, vol. 59, no. 10, February 1961, pp. 38–41.

Rosenblum, Robert, "Isn't It Romantic," *Artforum*, 36, no. 9, May 1998, pp. 116–19.

Schwabsky, Barry, "The Solitude of Mark Rothko," *New Art Examiner*, vol. 26, no. 5, February 1999, p. 47.

Seiberling, Dorothy, "Mark Rothko," *LIFE magazine*, November 16, 1959, p. 82.

Selz, Peter, "Mark Rothko," *L'Œil: revue d'art mensuelle*, no. 76, April 1961, pp. 36–43, 82.

Shaw-Eagle, Joanna, "Rothko's Art Colored by Emotion," *The Washington Times*, May 3, 1998, p. 4.

Sylvester, David, "Rothko," *New Statesman*, vol. 20, no. 6, October 1961, pp. 573–74.

Tuckman, Phyllis, "Rothko Rising," *Art Journal*, 58, no. 1, summer 1999, pp. 110–12.

Thomas, Morgan, "Nuancing the Pure. The Marks of Rothko," *Literature and Aesthetics*, vol. 9, October 1999, p. 31.

Vanel, Hervé, "Rothko, 'Artiste du Yo-Yo,'" *L'Œil*, no. 502, December 1998 – January 1999, pp. 34–41.

Venturi, Riccardo, "Le premier, non le sixième jour de la création : l'exposition de Mark Rothko au MoMA en 1961," *Bulletin de l'Association des historiens de l'art italien*, no. 12, 2007, pp. 119–25.

Venturi, Riccardo, "Plasticité et espace dans l'œuvre de Mark Rothko," *Ligeia: dossiers sur l'art*, nos. 73–76, 2007, pp. 160–88.

Weiss, Jeffey, "Science and Primitivism: A Fearful Symmetry in the Early New York School," *Arts Magazine*, 57, March 1983, pp. 81–87.

Rothko Archives

The Rothko Family Archive

James E. B. Breslin Research Archive on Mark Rothko, The Getty Research Institute, Los Angeles

American Art Archives, Smithsonian Institution
Menil Archives, The Menil Collection, Houston

Tate Library and Archive, London

The Phillips Collection Library and Archives, Washington, D.C.

Harvard University Archives, Cambridge

The Museum of Modern Art Archives, New York

Archives du Musée d'Art Moderne de Paris

Fonds Cardot-Joly, Bibliothèque Kandinsky, MNAM / CCI, Centre Pompidou, Paris

Select bibliography by Olivia Jacquinot

Following pages
Henry Elkan, Mark Rothko avec *Untitled, Red Black Orange and Pink on Yellow,* 1954, The Rothko Family Archive

Dan Budnik, Mark Rothko 1485 First Avenue Studio, New York, 1964, dye transfer print on paper, 20 × 24 in., Collection of the Kemper Museum of Contempoary Art, Kansas City, Missouri

Herbert Matter, Mark Rothko's studio, 222 Bowery, New York, 1960, The Rothko Family Archive

Hans Namuth, Rothko in his studio, 69th Street, 1964, The Rothko Family Archive

Alexander Liberman, Rothko in his studio, 69th Street, 1964, The Rothko Family Archive

Photo credits

Photographic credits
Courtesy of SFMOMA: front cover, pp. 18, 163. *National Portrait Gallery, Smithsonian Institution*: back cover, pp. 6–7 (this acquisition was made possible by a generous contribution from the James Smithson Society). © *Kay Bell Reynal*: pp. 1, 254 (middle, bottom right). *Courtesy The Rothko Family Archive*: pp. 2–3, 26–27, 226, 238, 252 (top left, top right, bottom right), 253, 254 (top right), 255 (bottom, right), 268 (bottom), 285, 309, 310–311, 314–315, 316; 14, 20 (top, bottom), 21 (top), 22 (top), 23 (middle, bottom), 28, 30 (top), 31, 32 (top), 34 (top), 35, 40 (top), 41 (bottom), 47, 53, 58, 59, 60 (bottom), 61, 62, 63, 64 (top right and left), 65 (top right and left), 66 (top right and left), 67, 68, 69, 70 (top), 71, 72, 73, 74 (bottom right and left), 75, 76 (right), 82, 83, 84, 85, 87, 89, 92, 93, 95, 99, 101, 103, 107, 109, 111, 113, 115, 116, 117, 121, 122, 125, 127, 129, 131, 133, 135, 161, 165, 173, 174, 175, 177, 183, 185, 187, 189, 191, 195, 200, 201, 203, 204–205, 207, 209, 211, 214, 216 (bottom), 217, 218, 220, 222 (bottom), 223, 230 (top), 232, 234, 236 (left, up right), 240 (up), 241 (bottom), 248, 256, 258 (top, middle), 260 (middle, bottom), 261 (right), 262 (top), 264 (left), 265 (middle), 266 (middle), 267, 268 (top), 273, 274 (bottom), 275 (top) (all rights reserved). © *J. Paul Getty Trust*: pp. 4–5. *Courtesy Center for Creative Photography*: pp. 8, 254 (bottom left), 263 (top), 289 (middle left), 294–95. © *Glenn Castellano, New York Historical Society*: pp. 20 (middle), 60 (top). *Courtesy The Menil Collection, Houston*: pp. 21 (middle), 81 (Hickey-Robertson, Houston); 52 (bottom), 289 (top right), 292 (Menil Archives, Hickey-Robertson, Houston); 40 (bottom) (Paul Hester); 289 (top left); 289 (middle right) (Gift of The Mark Rothko Foundation, Inc.). *Scala Archives, Florence*: pp. 21 (bottom), 70 (bottom), 105 (© Digital image Whitney Museum of American Art); 49, 74 (top) (© Munson Museum / Art Resource, NY); 236 (bottom), 252 (middle), 263 (middle), 266 (top), 269 (top left), 271 (top), 277 (top) (Digital Image © 2023, The Museum of Modern Art, New York). *The Phillips Collection Archives, Washington, D.C.*: pp. 12–124, 274 (top), 275 (bottom). © *Tate*: pp. 22 (middle), 38, 139, 141, 143, 144–46, 148–49, 151, 152–53, 154–55, 156–57, 158–59, 271 (bottom), 277 (bottom), 280–81. *Courtesy Fondation Beyeler, Basel*: p. 22 (bottom), 167. *Agence photographique de la Réunion des Musées Nationaux – Grand Palais, Paris*: pp. 23 (top), 169 (© BPK, Berlin/image Staatsgalerie Stuttgart); 52 (top), 279 (bottom) (The Metropolitan Museum of Art/image of the MMA); 77 (© Art Institute of Chicago/image The Art Institute of Chicago). *All rights reserved*: pp. 30 (bottom), 45, 65 (bottom), 76 (left), 79, 97, 119, 181, 193, 216 (top), 262 (middle), 264 (right), 265 (top, bottom), 267, 279 (middle). *Courtesy Adolph and Esther Gottlieb Foundation, New York*: p. 32 (bottom), 261 (left). *Courtesy Pace Gallery*: p. 33 (Bill Jacobson). *Bridgeman Images, Paris*: pp. 34 (bottom), 48 (bottom) (© Andrea Jemolo), 255 (top left) (PVDE). *Courtesy AGO*: pp. 36, 171. *IStock photo*: p. 41 (top) (Michele Rinaldi). *Courtesy NGA, Washington, D.C.*: pp. 42, 46, 48 (top), 50, 51, 64 (bottom), 66 (bottom), 70 (middle), 179, 197, 222 (top), 224 (top), 229, 230 (bottom), 240 (bottom), 243, 258 (bottom), 259 (top), 260 (top). *Courtesy Yageo Foundation Collection, Taiwan*: pp. 91, 100. © *Tim NighswanderImaging4Art.com*: p. 136–37. *Courtesy Berkeley Art Museum*: p. 164. *Courtesy Louisiana Museum of Modern Art, Humlebaek*: p. 182. © *Fondation Louis Vuitton / Ingélux*: pp. 198–99. *Philadelphia Museum of Art*: p. 224 (bottom) (Gift of Jacqueline, Paul, and Peter Matisse in memory of their mother, Alexina Duchamp, 1998, 1998-4-41). *Harvard Art Museums / Fogg Museum*: p. 228 (Gift of The Mark Rothko Foundation, Inc.). *Studio Richard Serra*: p. 241 (top). *Dedalus Foundation, New York*: pp. 244–45, 262 (bottom), 282 (top). *MUUS Collection*: p. 250. *Courtesy Peter Fetterman gallery*: p. 252 (bottom left). *Fotostiftung Schweiz, Winterthur*: p. 254 (top left). *American Archives of Art, Smithsonian Institution, Washington, D.C.*: p. 259 (bottom). *Shutterstock*: p. 263 (bottom) (© Nina Leen / The LIFE Picture Collection). © *Ezra Stoller / Esto*: pp. 266 (bottom), 279 (top). *Whitechapel Gallery Archive, London*: p. 269 (bottom left, right). *Harvard University Archives*: p. 270 (top) (UAV 605.295.18 Box 2, Folder: 1993-02-19). *Archivio Mulas, Milan*: p. 270 (bottom). *By kind permission of the Blinken family*: p. 272. © *UNESCO*: pp. 282 (bottom), 283 (top) (Works of art collection). *Courtesy Matthew Marks Gallery*: p. 283 (bottom). *Courtesy of the artist and Marian Goodman Gallery*: pp. 286–87. *Robert Doisneau / Gamma Rapho*: p. 289 (bottom). *Courtesy of Rothko Chapel*: pp. 290–91 (Paul Hester); 293. *Courtesy of The Estate of Dan Budnik*: pp. 312–13.

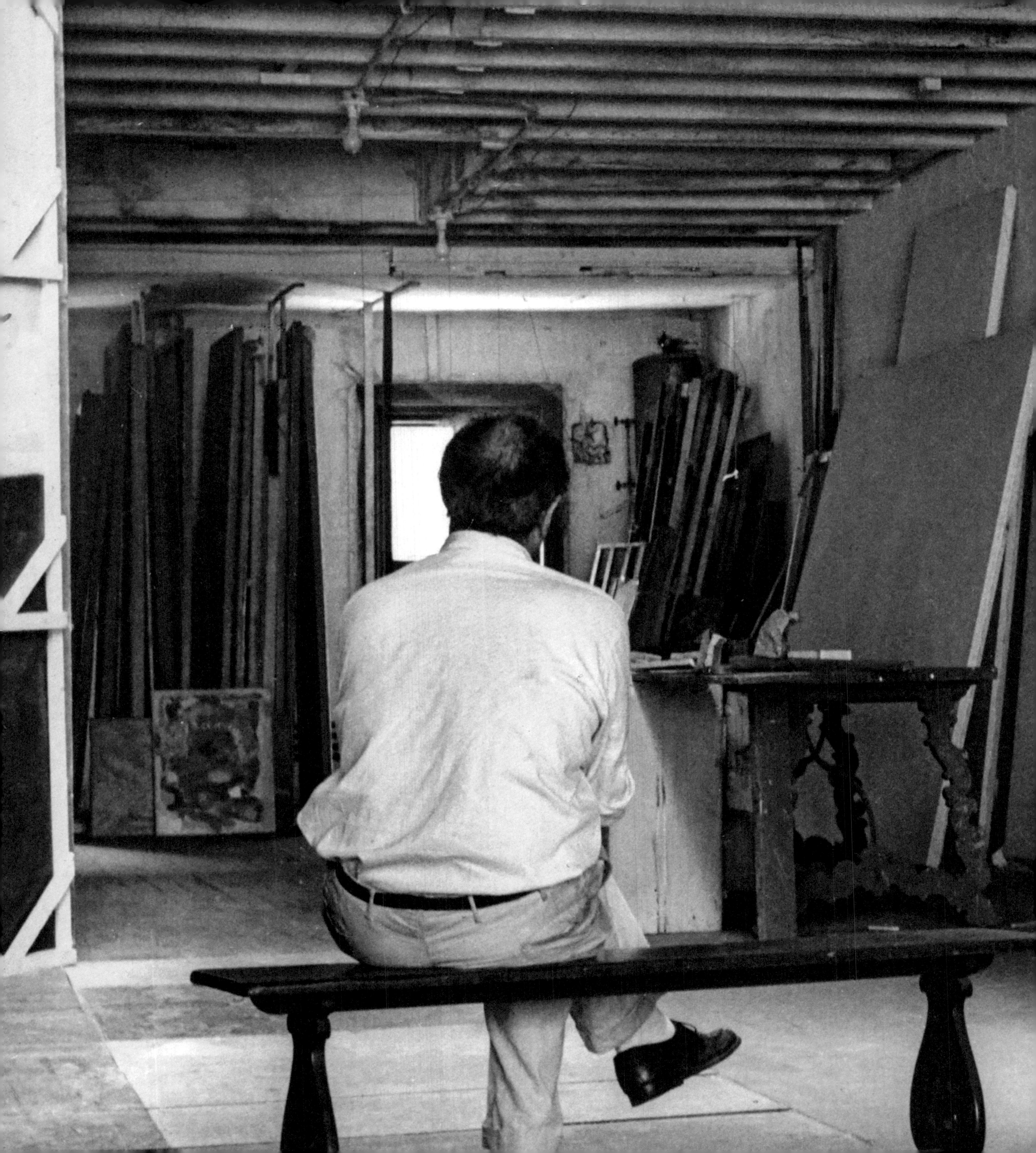

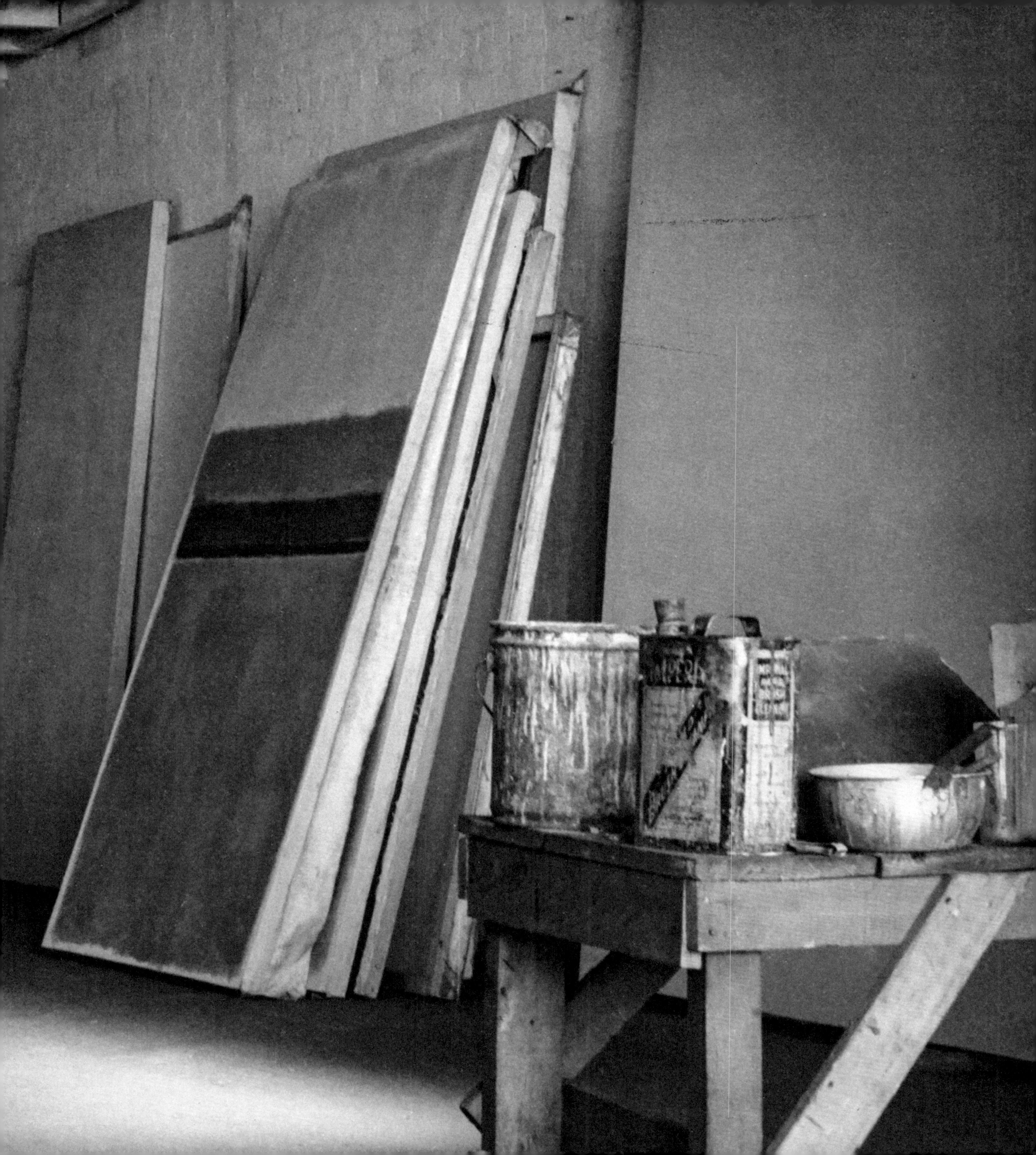

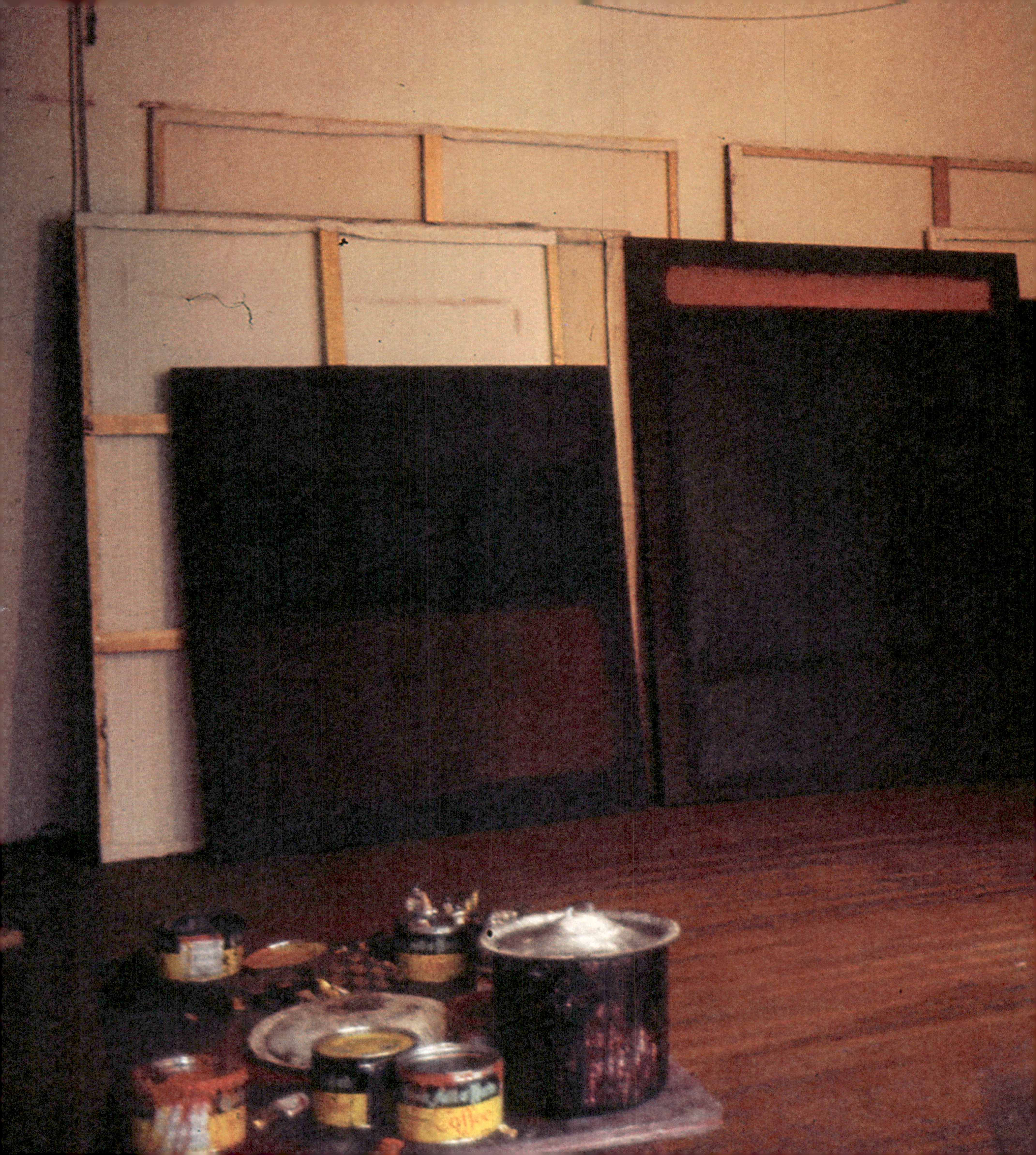

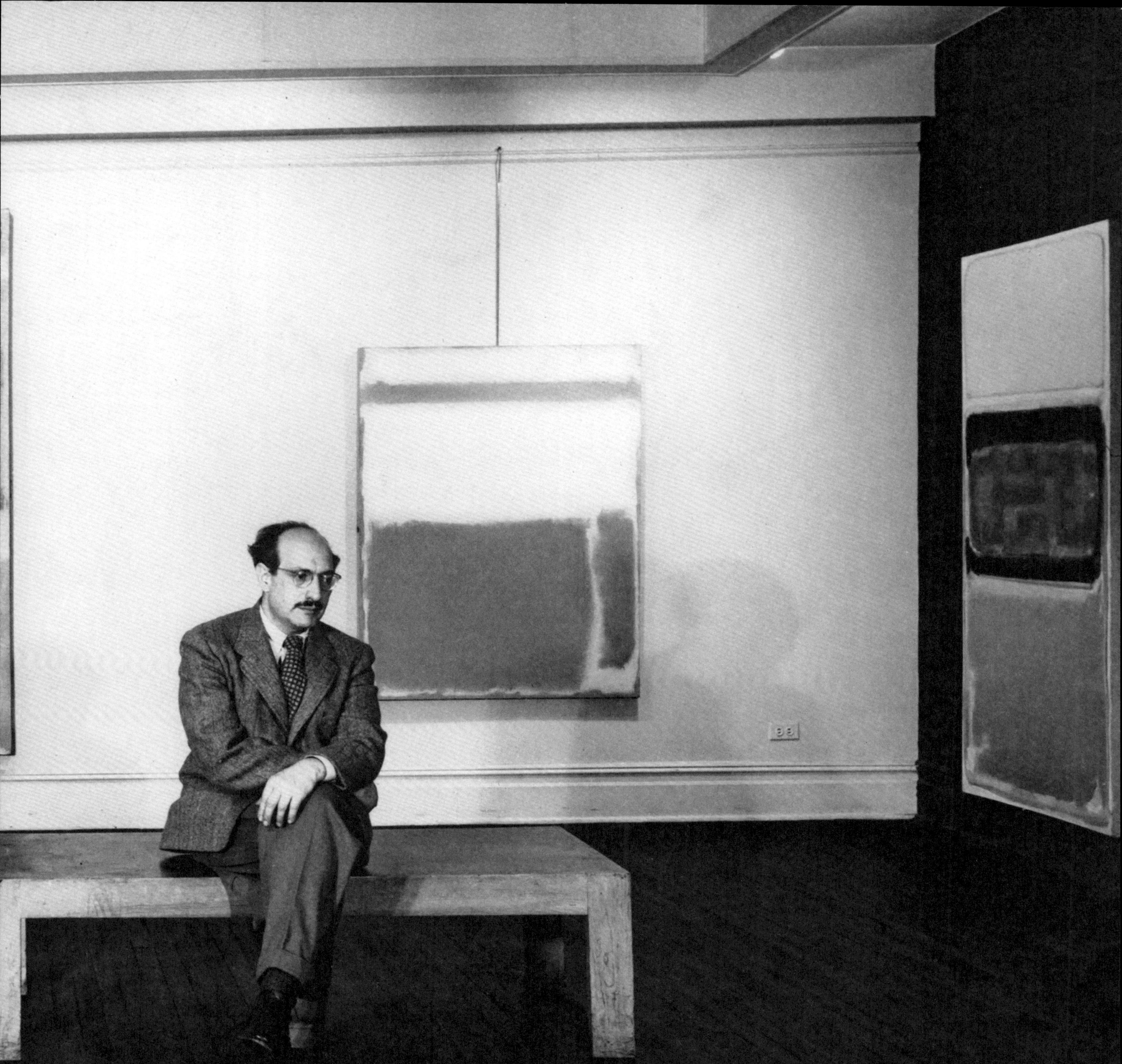

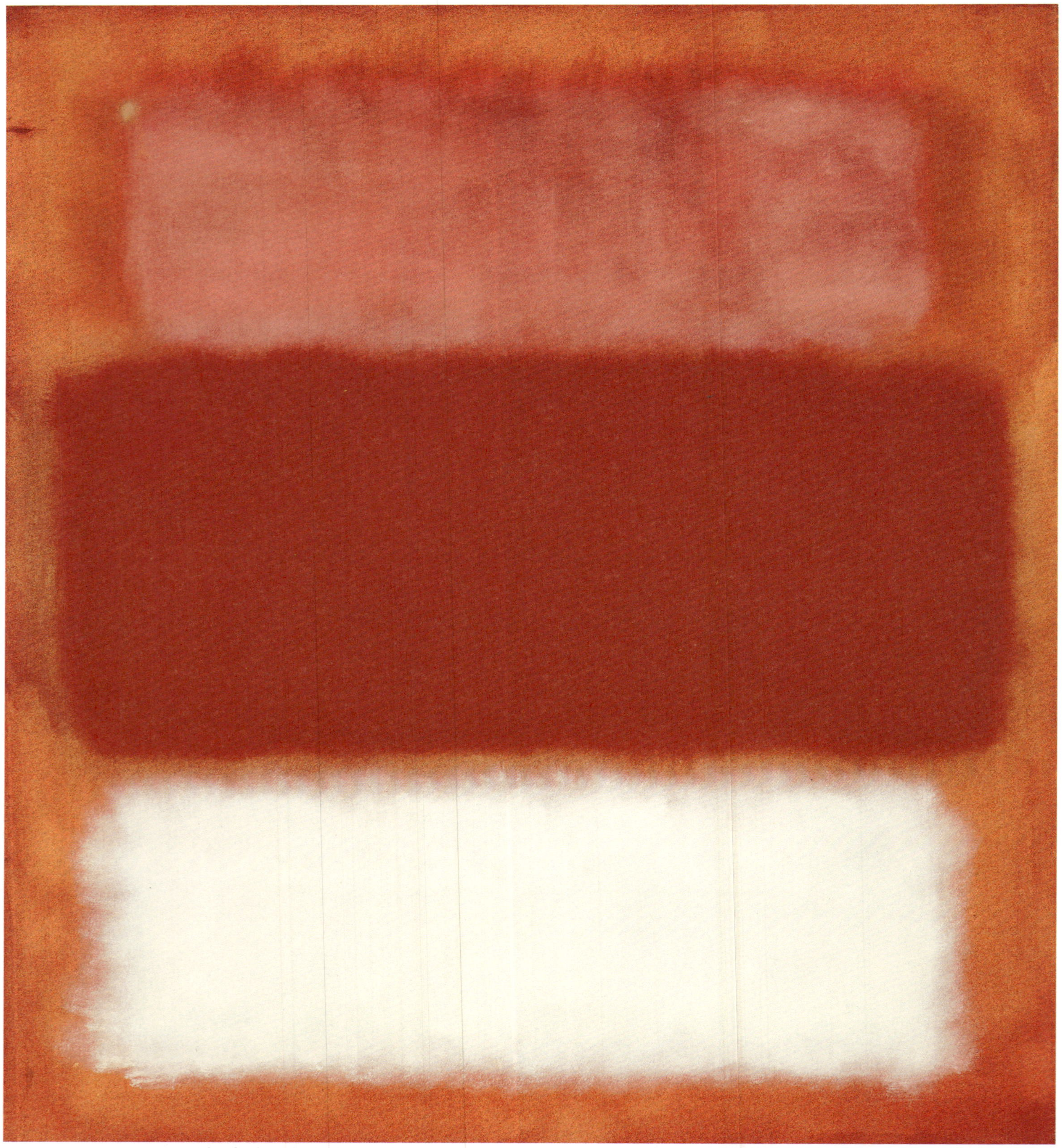

Light Cloud, Dark Cloud, 1957, oil on canvas, 66 × 61 ¾, Modern Art Museum of Fort Worth (CR 574; pl. 65)

Not Nothing
Christopher Rothko

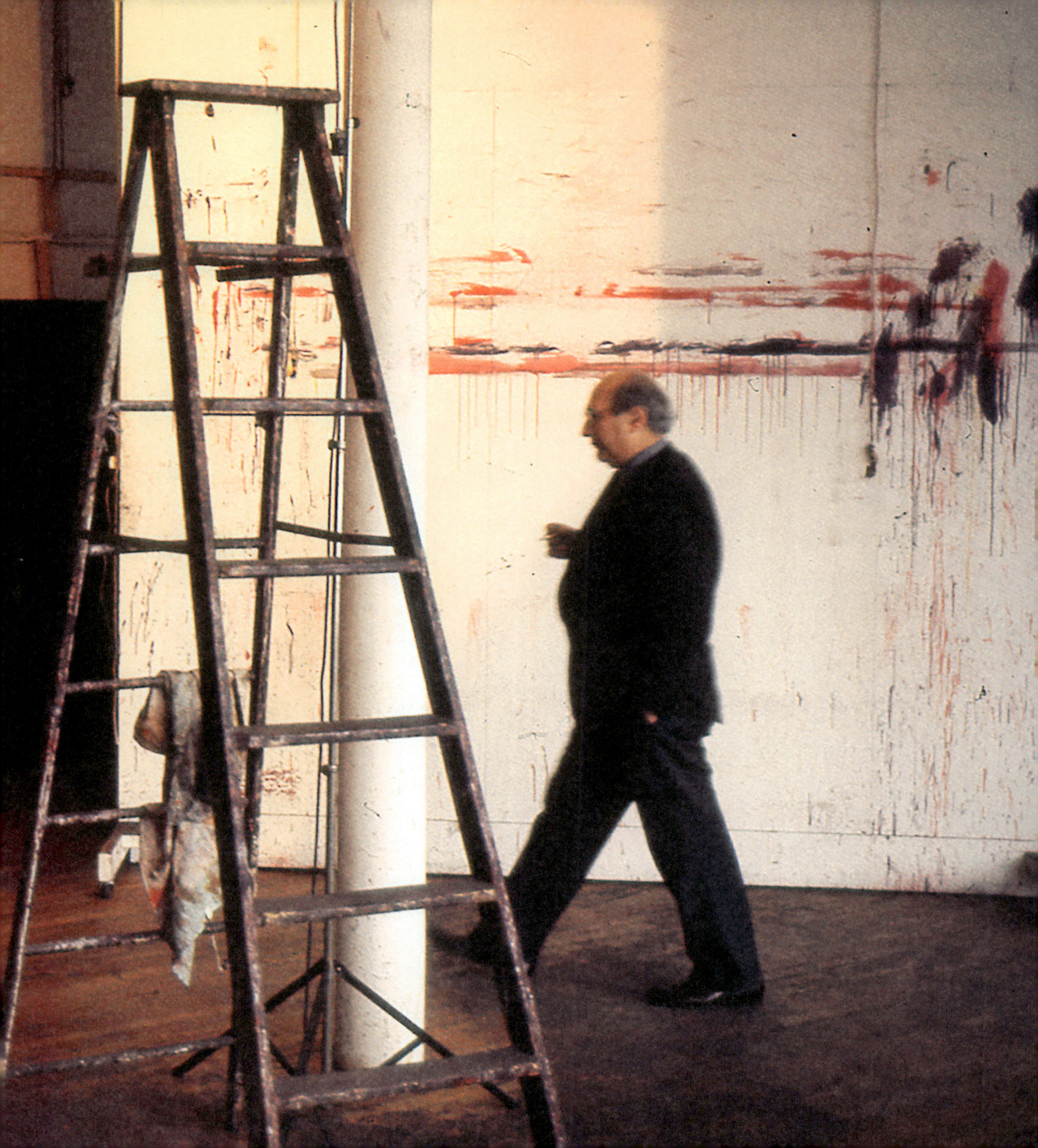

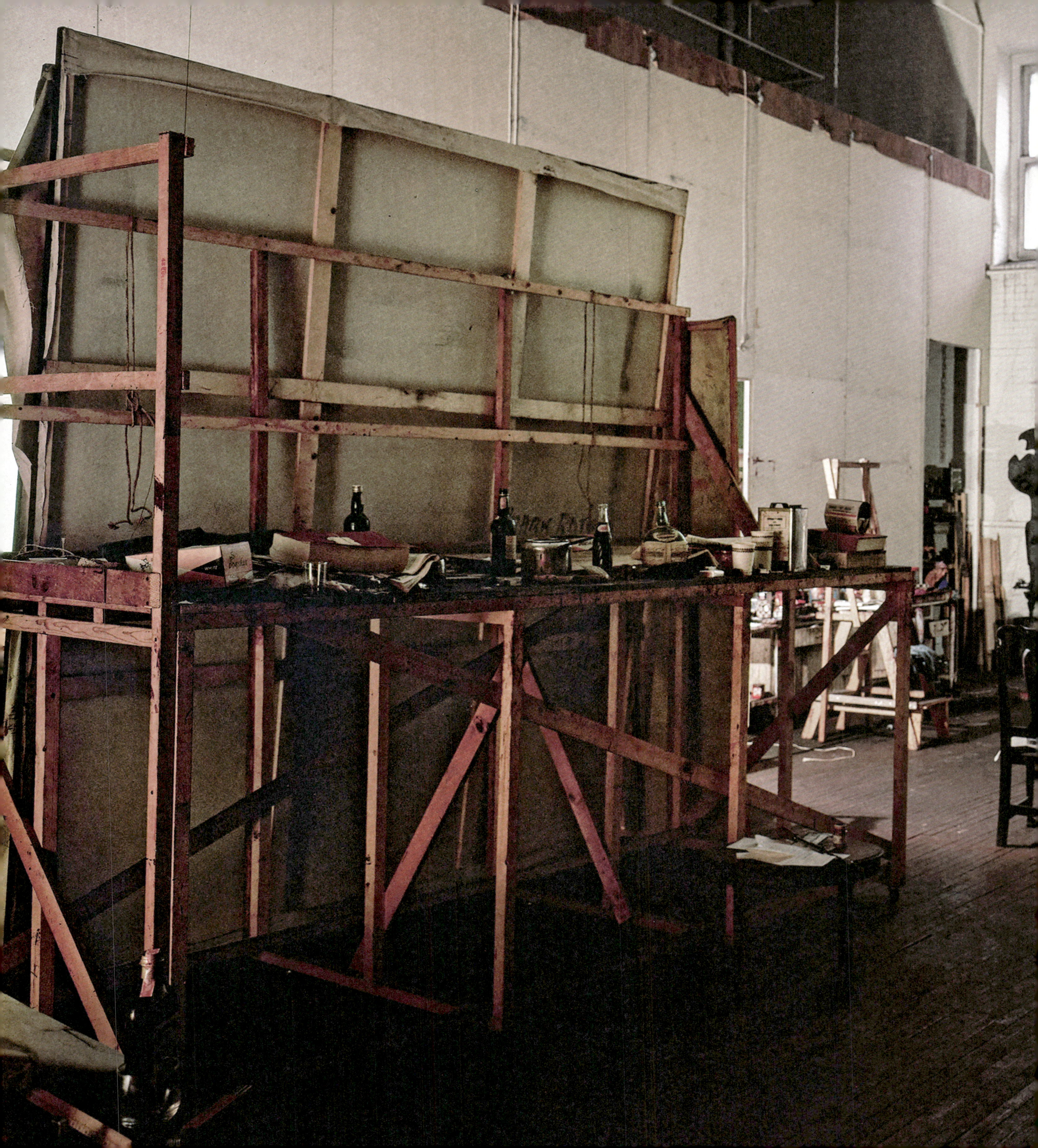

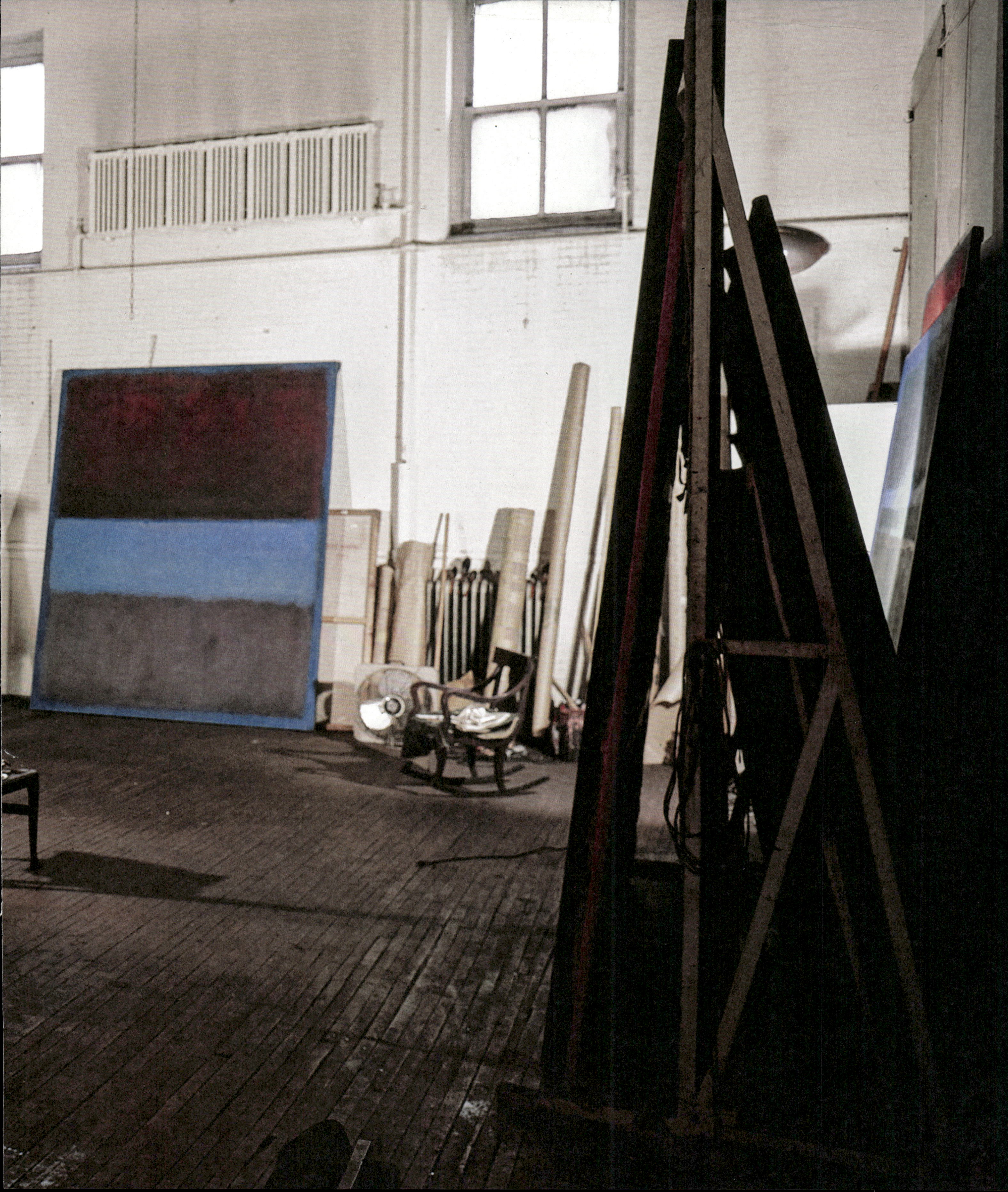

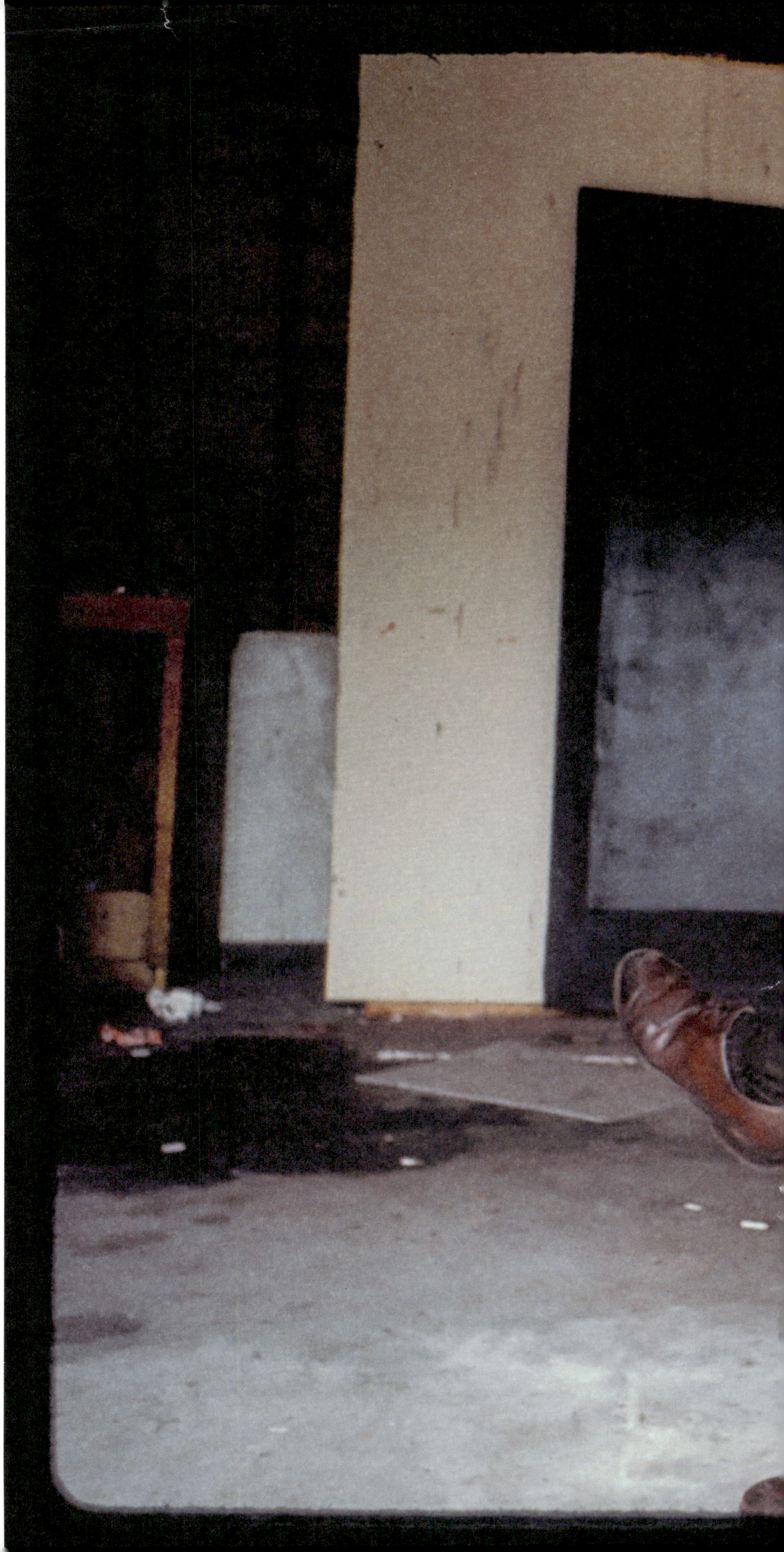

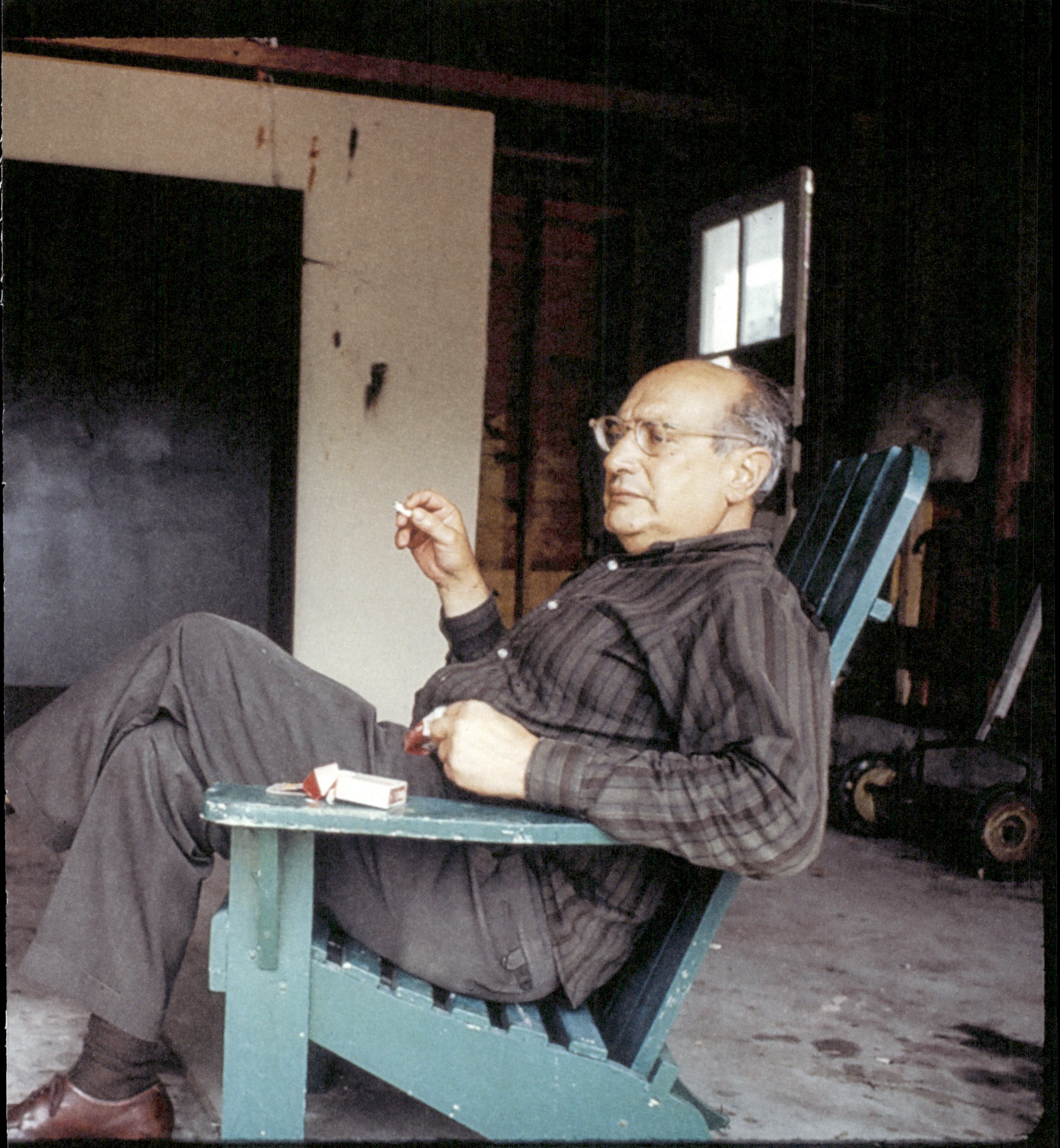

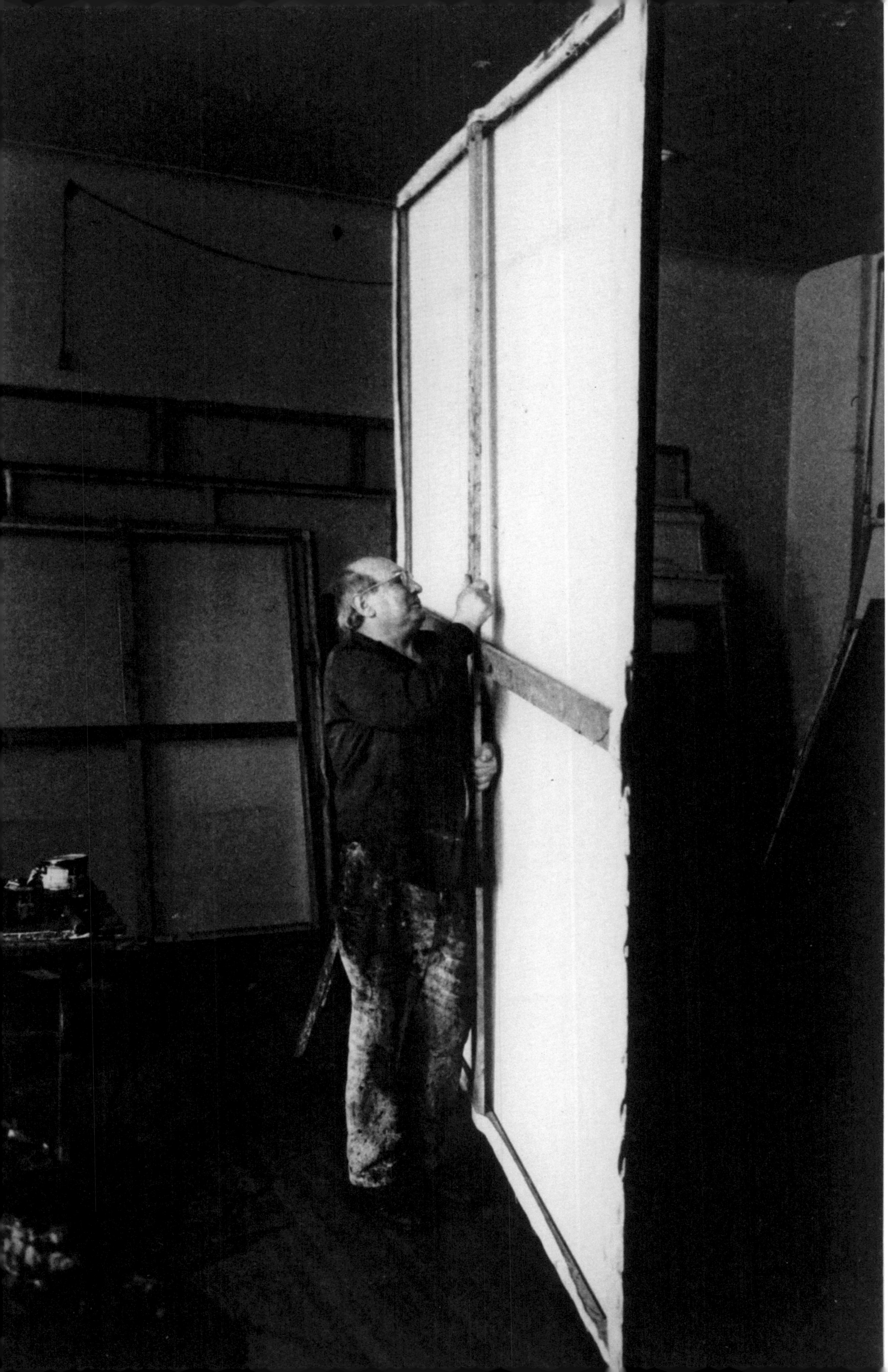